Adolescence

Sixth Edition

Adolescence

Continuity, Change, and Diversity

Nancy J. Cobb
California State University, Los Angeles

McGraw Hill

Boston Burr Ridge, IL Dubuque, IA Madison, WI New York San Francisco St. Louis
Bangkok Bogotá Caracas Kuala Lumpur Lisbon London Madrid Mexico City
Milan Montreal New Delhi Santiago Seoul Singapore Sydney Taipei Toronto

The McGraw-Hill Companies

Higher Education

ADOLESCENCE: CONTINUITY, CHANGE, AND DIVERSITY, SIXTH EDITION
Published by McGraw-Hill, an imprint of The McGraw-Hill Companies, Inc., 1221 Avenue of the Americas, New York, NY 10020.

This book is printed on acid-free paper.

1 2 3 4 5 6 7 8 9 0 DOW/DOW 0 9 8 7 6

ISBN-13: 978-0-07319472-1
ISBN-10: 0-07-319472-7

Editor in Chief: Emily Barrosse
Publisher: Beth Mejia
Executive Editor: Mike Sugarman
Senior Development Editor: Judith Kromm
Development Editor, Supplements: Meghan Campbell
Marketing Manager: Melissa Caughlin
Media Producer: Stephanie George
Production Editors: Melissa Williams and Melanie Field, Strawberry Field Publishing
Manuscript Editor: Margaret Moore
Interior and Cover Design: Violeta Diaz and Susan Breitbard
Senior Production Supervisor: Rich DeVitto
Photo Research: Alexandra Ambrose and Emily Tietz
Cover photos: (From Top): Couple, © Kirk Weddle/Getty Images; Group walking, © Comstock/PictureQuest; Group studying, © BananaStock / JupiterImages; Girl on bench, © Digital Vision

This book was set in 10/12 Minion by G & S Book Services, Inc. and printed on 45# Publishers Matte by RR Donnelley and Sons.

Photo and text credits can be found following the References on page C-1, a continuation of the copyright page.

Library of Congress Cataloging-in-Publication Data

Cobb, Nancy J.
Adolescence: continuity, change, and diversity / Nancy J Cobb. – 6th ed.
p. cm.
Includes bibliographical references and index.
ISBN-13: 978-0-07319472-1, ISBN-10: 0-07-319472-7
1. Adolescence. 2. Adolescent psychology 3. Teenagers—United States. I. Title

HQ796.C596 2007
305.235—dc21

2006058564

www.mhhe.com

For Michael,
as always

Brief Contents

Contents

CHAPTER 10 Work, Careers, and College: New Decisions, New Ways of Thinking 319

CHAPTER 11 Facing the Future: Values in Transition 357

CHAPTER 13 Positive Development in Adolescence: Meeting the Challenges and Making It Work 427

CHAPTER 14 Studying Adolescence: Research Methods and Issues 447

Research Focus Boxes in the Text

Research Focus Boxes on the Web Site (www.mhhe.com/cobb)

Preface

Writing the preface to the sixth edition of a text is something like making an entrance at your class reunion. You need to let old friends know that, despite some significant changes, you still retain the qualities that attracted them to you in the first place, all while introducing yourself to people you haven't met before. And so it is with the sixth edition of *Adolescence: Continuity, Change, and Diversity.* While this revision contains some significant changes, the essential characteristics that distinguish it from other texts remain the same. Let me call your attention first to these, and then move to what has changed in this edition.

Features of This Text

Clear and Engaging Writing Style

It continues to be a source of pride to me that since this text first appeared in 1992 students have found it enjoyable as well as informative. This is largely because the stories and vignettes chosen to illustrate concepts are "slices of life," drawn from the personal experiences of adolescents. These stories have the same narrative qualities that make all genuinely human stories engaging, in whatever the context, and draw on adolescents differing in ethnicity, gender, and life circumstances, enabling all readers to relate to what is being presented. I also believe the book is enjoyable to read because concepts are presented in sufficient depth that they become easily understandable.

Strong Research Base

Scientific rigor needn't be *rigor mortis.* That is, good science doesn't have to be difficult to understand. What makes scientific research rigorous has little to do with difficulty but, rather, with the validity of its theories and the strength of the evidence supporting these. For each of the topics covered in the text, I have presented the best evidence available. In several places, regarding such pressing social issues as sex education, the prevention of adolescent drug abuse, or improving high school graduation rates, I've contrasted programs that have been shown to be effective, based on scientifically rigorous research, with less effective, or even ineffective, programs and practices currently in place.

I have also chosen to present research methods in a way that differs from the approach taken in many other texts. Rather than imposing a full chapter about methods of psychological research at the beginning of the text, when students are least interested, I have adopted a different strategy. Every chapter contains a "Research Focus Box" which discusses a method or problem of research relevant to the topic of that chapter. Each box begins with a practical problem and illustrates how researchers have undertaken to solve it. Taken together, the boxes present a range of issues important for students' understanding of research methodology in developmental psychology. In this way, methodological issues are introduced gradually, and in a context in which they provide answers to meaningful questions. Additional research boxes are available on the companion Web site for the book.

At the conclusion of the book, a full chapter on research methods (Chapter 14), integrates the material presented in the individual research focus boxes. This arrangement places methodological solutions where they should be, following rather than preceding familiarity with the problem.

Unifying Themes: Gender, Ethnicity, Early Versus Late Adolescence, and Identity

Devoting an entire text to adolescence unavoidably suggests that somehow all adolescents are similar, in that what applies to one applies to all. Adolescents have many things in common, of course, or else they wouldn't constitute a category. But it's crucial that we not be captive to our categories; all adolescents are not the same, and there are systematic factors that make them different from each other. In this book, I focus on four important factors accounting for differences among adolescents: *gender, ethnicity, age,* and the *search for a stable identity.* These four themes run through all chapters.

Gender We are past assuming that the male experience is normative for both sexes, with just a few corrections to be made for females. There's no doubt now that females differ from males. And this difference plays an enormous role in the lives of adolescents. But we are still struggling to distinguish which of the acknowledged differences are "built in" and which are "socially constructed." In other words, which differences are simply "our biological nature and can't be changed" and which are "the way we make them and might be changed"? This uncertainty concerning the most fundamental of human distinctions makes gender potentially problematic for every adolescent and a natural topic for scientific investigation.

Ethnicity Like gender, ethnic differences play a crucial role in understanding adolescent development. But unlike gender, which still sorts the population into two roughly equal halves, the ethnic composition of the United States is rapidly changing, with minority adolescents promising to supplant those who now constitute the majority. Minority versus majority status in society carries implications for many aspects of development, and these statuses are changing faster than we, or our theories, can keep up. Theories of adolescent identity formation must address the tension between a changing self and an evolving society, yet most theories still presuppose a European American culture that no longer exists in much of the United States. While we still have no comprehensive account of the influence of ethnicity on adolescence, we do have a good deal of data and some "mini-theories" to account for them. I have incorporated these data and theories throughout the text so that even though we may not fully understand where we are, we are not deceived that we are still where we used to be.

Early and Late Adolescence Some differences are so obvious we don't take them seriously until we trip over them. At times, we forget all too easily that there are immense differences between a 12-year-old and a 17-year-old because they are both "adolescents." However, the 12-year-old is just one step beyond the comfortable routine of grade school, whereas the 17-year-old stands ready to exit high school and at the threshold of college or work. Similarly, the 12-year-old is just beginning to struggle with puberty and a new awareness of sexuality, while the 17-year-old is struggling to integrate sexuality into a meaningful relationship. In other words, the 12-year-old is in early adolescence and just leaving childhood, while the 17-year-old is a late adolescent and just entering adulthood. Throughout this text I have attempted to keep clear the unmistakable differences between these phases of adolescence.

The Search for a Stable Personal Identity You might not think of the search for a stable personal identity as a source of difference, but it is—and a powerful one too. A person's identity is stable to the extent that it reconciles all the various influences converging on it. But since each adolescent has a different mix of these influences, each adolescent is led to a different reconciliation, and thereby to uniqueness. To put it slightly differently, the search for a personal identity is a quest to do justice to the profusion of claims made on the individual. Each of the three factors that we have considered—gender, ethnicity and age—constitutes such a claim. An adolescent who finds it necessary to deny any one of these in coming to terms with the others is likely to have achieved only a tenuous and temporary adjustment that ultimately will require re-negotiation.

What's New in This Text

This new edition contains many changes. Some take the form of expanded and updated content and research, and some are primarily pedagogical changes that make it easier for students to master the material being presented. A number of the changes were suggested by instructors who teach the Adolescence course. First, I will highlight the expanded and updated content. Then I will describe the new pedagogical features and the changes recommended by reviewers.

Expanded and Updated Content and Research

Over a thousand research articles were reviewed for this edition from which current research studies were added. This research has been incorporated throughout the text, updating sections in every chapter.

A number of topics have received special attention in this edition. These topics are health and well-being; effective programs for adolescents, families, and communities; and social policy.

Health and Well-Being Chapter 1 presents research findings on adolescents' generally positive outlook on life, in contrast to the more common stereotype of adolescents as contrary and moody. Chapter 3 contains new sections on nutrition, physical activity, health care, and the current epidemic of overweight. Also in this chapter I have included research on adolescents' use of the Internet to find answers to embarrassing questions. Chapter 3 additionally describes the impact of poverty on adolescents' health with respect to poor-quality housing, increased exposure to air pollution and asthma-related allergens, inadequate health care, and unsafe neighborhoods. Chapter 7 discusses the impact of divorce on adolescents and the conditions that promote successful coping with divorce. Chapter 9 has a section on resources available through full-service schools. Chapter 12 includes a section on the health consequences of using various drugs. Chapter 13 covers the contributions of parental monitoring, community resources, teachers, and personal strengths, such as religious beliefs, to adolescents' health and well-being.

Effective Programs Chapter 3 describes an intergenerational mentoring program for adolescents living in low-income, high-crime neighborhoods that helped them resist drugs, reduced absenteeism, and led to more positive attitudes toward school and their own futures. This chapter also describes an innovative school lunch program that addresses the growing problem of obesity among adolescents. A critical interface where research on adolescence meets public policy relates to sex education programs. Chapter 6 reviews the most recent findings comparing the effectiveness of abstinence-only programs and comprehensive sex education programs in delaying sexual initiation and protecting against adolescent pregnancy. I have also included research on the effectiveness and potential consequences of virginity pledges.

Chapter 9 presents information on factors that contribute to the effectiveness of schools and describes a program for reducing school bullying. This chapter also discusses the effectiveness of early childhood intervention programs in improving academic achievement through adolescence and increasing graduation rates. A program for getting students who drop out back on track is spotlighted in this chapter as well. Chapter 12 documents the effectiveness of early childhood intervention programs for increasing parental involvement in their children's lives and for decreasing rates of delinquency. Chapter 13 includes a discussion of racial socialization, which explores the ways that minority parents prepare their children for life in the broader society, and a section on the conditions that foster positive youth development in all adolescents.

Social Policy Chapter 1 discusses the number of adolescents and their families living in poverty in the United States. The need to create jobs for inner-city youth and their families and to make health care more accessible is discussed in Chapter 3, as is the desirability of increasing the federal minimum wage to help families meet the basic costs of living. My presentation of issues concerning education and schools in Chapter 9 benefits from current research on the increasingly challenging tasks of making schools more effective and meeting the needs of all adolescents. The impact of poverty on academic achievement would be difficult to overestimate. Students in low-income neighborhoods attend schools that are poorly maintained and overcrowded and have larger classes, fewer resources, and teachers that frequently lack training for the subjects they are teaching. Chapter 9 also presents new information related to faulty formulas for determining high school completion rates, and the often wide disparities in these formulas as a function of race and ethnicity. In this chapter, too, I take a critical look at standards-based educational reform and examine the flawed formulas for assessing graduation rates that have caused us to turn a blind eye to the need for genuine educational reform.

Chapter 12 includes a section on delinquency, in which I review current statistics on disproportionate numbers of minority youth in the juvenile justice system. As we have learned from hurricane Katrina, money spent to prepare for a potential disaster can ultimately save the nation billions in repairs and restoration. What holds for levees in New Orleans also holds for adolescents in our inner cities. Solid research indicates what can be done to increase graduation rates and to decrease delinquency. As with natural disasters, the money we spend up front on such things as early intervention programs, teacher training, and improving community resources is much less than we might need to spend years later on damage control, and lives are enriched in the process. Chapter 12 also contains a new section on the importance of social policy for reducing the number of adolescents who smoke, and it outlines what is needed for effective school-based prevention programs.

The problems of adolescents cannot be neatly separated from problems facing our society as a whole. Consequently, many of the problems of adolescence cannot be addressed adequately until our nation confronts issues such as unemployment, poverty and crime in our inner cities, access to health care, and providing quality education for all. In the meantime, however, adolescents aren't waiting around for others to do something. In Chapter 13, I include a section on adolescents who volunteer at community agencies and charitable organizations or even start their own charitable programs.

Pedagogical Features

Chapter Overviews Information is easier to comprehend if you know what to expect. To help students anticipate what they will be reading, I have included chapter overviews at the beginning of each chapter that briefly summarize the main points of that chapter.

Marginal Glossary This is an improvement I should have made a long time ago. I have always been impatient with having to leave the page I'm reading to look up an unfamiliar term. I would have welcomed, as I believe students will in this edition, the definition of technical terms in the margin of the page on which they occur. Definitions for all glossary terms appear in the margins of the page where they are introduced.

Chapter Summaries and Chapter Objectives There's a useful adage common among journalists: Tell 'em what you're going to tell them, tell 'em the story, and then tell 'em what you've told them. The chapter objectives, chapter overviews, and chapter summaries for each chapter serve this purpose. The summaries in this edition are even easier to follow when reviewing the chapter because they include the chapter headings that identify each section as well as a summary of the material in that section.

Changes Suggested by Reviewers

It is immensely helpful to have suggestions and comments from colleagues within the discipline when preparing a textbook. I have been particularly fortunate to have received excellent recommendations for this revision. This section summarizes significant changes that I've made in response.

Chapter 1 has been reorganized to present more clearly the themes of the text and prepare students for what will follow. Also, I have taken pains to show how the various perspectives that inform an understanding of adolescence—historical, lifespan, contextual, and constructive—are not mutually exclusive. A number of reviewers commented that Bronfenbrenner's theory needed to be presented in more detail. I have done this and added more examples to make the model easier to understand. I have also included a diagram illustrating the similarities in the developmental tasks facing adolescents, their parents, and their grandparents so that the similarities stand out.

Chapter 2 includes a new opening to illustrate the usefulness of theories. In response to suggestions from several reviewers, I have included more real-life examples of theoretical concepts such as reciprocal determinism, apprenticeship, and guided participation.

In Chapter 3, the sex hormones are defined in more detail and a distinction is made between the two stages in puberty, adrenarche and gonadarche. A new section on health and well-being includes information on nutrition, physical activity, overweight, the accessibility of health care, and the impact of poverty. Additionally, the section on eating disorders has been moved to Chapter 12, along with other problematic behaviors, and the material on gender roles has been moved to Chapter 6, where it is included in a section on sexual identity. Finally, I have included new research showing that early maturation is not as advantageous for boys as previously believed.

Chapter 4 summarizes research on the relationship between brain maturation and impulsiveness that sheds light on why adolescents, who otherwise are charming and intelligent, will do things that, with even a moment's thought, they never otherwise would have attempted. Also in this chapter is a section on gender difference in intelligence. Controversy over gender differences seems never to subside for long. Casual remarks frequently reveal deep-seated beliefs that frequently surprise us. Chapter 4 summarizes current research on gender differences in intellectual functioning, as well as on difficulties in assessing these. I also have included recent research on potential gender bias in culture-fair tests of intelligence. Finally, I have moved material on classroom learning to the chapter on schools.

In Chapter 5, I have updated the extensive coverage of the contributions of gender and ethnicity to identity. A discussion of new research on bicultural identity rounds out the chapter.

The inclusion of gender roles, sexual identity, and sexual scripts at the beginning of Chapter 6 places the research on sexual decision making that follows in the broader contexts of self-definition and interpersonal relationships. Additionally, I have discussed the importance of parents in adolescents' sexual decision making. Material has been added on prejudice and discrimination in the discussion of homosexuality. Also, I have addressed misconceptions about the relative effectiveness of abstinence and comprehensive sex education programs, showing the latter to be effective in both delaying sexual initiation and promoting responsible behavior. Also new to this chapter is a section relating differences in attitudes toward adolescent sexuality held by those in the United States and European countries to higher rates of adolescent pregnancy and abortion in the United States.

Chapter 7 includes more examples drawn from adolescents' lives to illustrate patterns of interaction within the family, such as monitoring and ego development.

Added to the discussion of adolescent friendships in Chapter 8 is a new section on how attachment relationships with parents affect adolescents' well-being. I have added material on sociometric distinctions among popular, average, rejected, neglected, and controversial adolescents, and distinguished between different types of popularity. Also new is the inclusion of research on friendships among sexual-minority youth and material on youth cultures.

Chapter 9 opens with new material on structuring the learning environment that compares direct and differentiated instruction. Research on learning styles has also been included in this chapter, as has new research on the difficulties early adolescents experience in adjusting to secondary school. I have revised the discussion of academic tracking and added a section on what makes schools effective. A new section on the impact of poverty on academic achievement includes research describing effective intervention programs for low-income students. I also discuss ethnic differences in graduation rates and the use of faulty formulas that have masked the extent of these discrepancies, and include a description of alternative educational programs for students who drop out. A new section on current educational reforms examines reasons for the difficulty of improving the quality of education for inner-city students as this program presently exists.

Chapter 10 presents new statistics on part-time employment and spending patterns among adolescents, as well as new trends in employment opportunities and occupations with the largest job growth. I also have added material on the gender gap in pay and reorganized the chapter, removing or moving material on expertise, active and inert knowledge, and the discussion of thinking as problem solving.

I have added to the discussion of values in Chapter 11, including new data on the relationships between adolescents' values and those of their parents, and on the influence of gender, ethnicity, and religion on values. I have also expanded the coverage of religion in this chapter and throughout the text in response to reviewers' comments. Also in response to reviewers, I have included new research on cheating and streamlined the discussion of Freud.

The discussion of runaway adolescents in Chapter 12 adds useful information on shelters and help lines. Since relatively few adolescents experiment with drugs other than alcohol, cigarettes, and marijuana, I have streamlined the discussion of drugs and have added new material on drug prevention programs that are effective and those that are not.

Eating disorders are now included in this chapter. A number of reviewers suggested that I include helpful information when discussing these and other problem behaviors. Following this suggestion, I have made this edition more helpful as well as more current.

The discussion of stress in Chapter 13 has been streamlined and updated to reflect similarities and differences due to gender and ethnicity. The section on positive adolescent development includes more examples of community support and new material on the importance of teachers. I have also added material showing how an individual can make a difference. A new section describes successful programs organized by adolescents to improve the lives of others.

Incorporating new findings in the field of adolescence into the sixth edition of this text has been an exciting undertaking. It is my hope that this edition not only is informative and useful, but also communicates a sense of the immense richness of diversity in the lives of adolescents.

Supplements

The following supplements accompany the sixth edition of *Adolescence: Continuity, Change and Diversity.* Please contact your McGraw-Hill representative to learn more. To locate your representative, visit www.mhhe.com and click on "Rep Locator."

For the Instructor

The Instructor's Resource CD-ROM This CD-ROM includes the Instructor's Manual, PowerPoint presentation slides, Test Bank, and Computerized Test Bank. Valerie Hoffman at California State University, Los Angeles, and Kathleen Boyle at California State University, Northridge, extensively revised the Instructor's Manual and the Test Bank. The Instructor's Manual provides several helpful tools for organizing the adolescent development course. For each chapter, an outline, lecture organizers, and a selection of additional readings and related videos are provided. In addition, the Instructor's Manual includes in-class activities for the lifespan development course created by Patricia A. Jarvis and Gary L. Creasey at Illinois State University. Discussion questions encourage the incorporation of interesting and controversial topics into lectures. The Test Bank has been revised to include more conceptual multiple choice and true/false questions.

The Instructor's Manual is available only in electronic format on the Instructor's Resource CD-ROM and the book's Online Learning Center (www.mhhe.com /cobb6). The Test Bank and Computerized Test Bank are available only on the Instructor's Resource CD-ROM.

McGraw-Hill's Visual Assets Database (VAD) for Lifespan Development By Jasna Jovanovic, University of Illinois at Urbana-Champaign. McGraw-Hill's Visual Assets Database is a password-protected online database of hundreds of multimedia resources for use in classroom presentations, including original video clips, audio clips, photographs, and illustrations—all designed to bring to life concepts in developmental psychology. In addition to offering ready-made multimedia presentations for every stage of the lifespan, the VAD's search engine and unique "My Modules" program allows instructors to select from the database's resources to create their own customized presentations, or "modules." These customized presentations are saved in an instructor's folder on the McGraw-Hill site, and the presentation is then run directly from the VAD to the Internet-equipped classroom.

VAD's resources are available only to instructors using a McGraw-Hill text on human development. Contact your sales representative for more information.

PageOut Build your own course Web site in less than an hour. You don't have to be a computer whiz to create a Web site, especially with an exclusive McGraw-Hill product called PageOut. It requires no prior knowledge of HTML, no long hours of coding, and no design skills on your part. With PageOut, even the most inexperienced computer user can quickly and easily create a professional-looking course Web site. Simply fill in templates with your information and with content provided by McGraw-Hill, choose a design, and you've got a Web site tailored specifically to your course. Best of all, it's FREE! Visit us at www.pageout.net to find out more.

For the Student

Online Learning Center This extensive Web site, designed specifically for *Adolescence: Continuity, Change, and Diversity,* Sixth Edition, offers an array of resources for instructors and students. For students, the Web site includes a variety of interactive quizzes and exercises, key terms, chapter outlines, and summaries. This is a great way to hone critical thinking skills and stay up to date on current events in child development. Visit the Online Learning Center at www.mhhe.com /cobb6.

Acknowledgments

I am indebted to the many colleagues who reviewed the previous edition of this text for their insightful and helpful comments. It is easy to lose perspective when writing a text such as this, especially given the vast amount of research that has been published since the last edition. Incorporating their suggestions has substantially improved this edition. My thanks go to

Sandra K. Arntz, *Northern Illinois University*
Martha Bristor, *Michigan State University*
James I. Byrd, *University of Wisconsin-Stout*
Nancy DeFrates-Densch, *Northern Illinois University*
Jerome B. Dusek, *Syracuse University*
Richard L. Froman, *John Brown University*
Kathie E. Shiba, *Maryville College*
Ken Springer, *Southern Methodist University*
Ian E. Payton, *Bethune Cookman College*
Diana Walker, *Bladen Community College*

I am especially thankful for the opportunity to work with Maureen Spada, the developmental editor for this revision. Her fresh perspectives on each chapter, her ability to always find a better way to communicate the "big picture," as well as her attention to detail, have been immeasurably helpful.

I also wish to thank Executive Editor Mike Sugarman for his vision for this text; Senior Developmental Editor Judith Kromm, who managed the revision from afar; Manager of Publishing Services Melissa Williams and Production Manager Melanie Field, who shepherded it through production; Senior Designer Violeta Diaz; Marketing Manager Melissa Caughlin; and Editorial Coordinator Kate Russillo, who always seemed to have the right information just when it was needed.

Just as adolescents rely on the company of friends and family, I have as well. To all my friends at First Pres in Burbank, thank you for your prayers, and to Abba, Father God, thank you for the gracious ways You answered them. To Bill, thank you for the e-mails each day and the music to work by. To Michael—wise and witty beyond words—thank you for always being there and for simply being who you are. To Joshua and Jenny, who remain as amazing to me in adulthood as you did in adolescence—I celebrate your creativity and your courage.

Nancy J. Cobb
Burbank, California

Adolescence

CHAPTER OUTLINE

CHAPTER 1

Defining Adolescents: Who Are They?

CHAPTER OBJECTIVES

- To identify the four themes emphasized in this text: gender, ethnicity, age distinctions within adolescence, and identity
- To answer the question "Who are adolescents?" with a biological, a psychological, and a sociological definition
- To look at adolescence from an historical perspective, a lifespan perspective, a contextual perspective, and a constructive perspective
- To examine more closely the themes of gender, ethnicity, age distinctions, and identity

Each culture has its stories. They offer a way of understanding ourselves and our lives. Most of us accept the stories our culture tells us—stories we've heard since childhood. It is daring to live lives that are too different from these stories. But in adolescence, one may dream the daring. Listen to the story told by a Chinese American girl who dares to dream for herself the exploits reserved for boys—initiation into the rites of a warrior:

> *After I returned from my survival test, the two old people trained me in dragon ways. . . . Tigers are easy to find, but I needed adult wisdom to know dragons. "You have to infer the whole dragon from the parts you can see and touch," the old people would say. Unlike tigers, dragons are so immense, I would never see one in its entirety. (Kingston, 1977, p. 34)*

So Maxine Hong Kingston describes the fantasies of a Chinese American girl who dreamed of avenging her people as a fierce and beloved warrior.

Adolescents still dream of dragons. Fantastic? Of course. But in another sense, dragons are made of common stuff. They are what looms large when one feels small. So, too, with dreams. This girl's dreams were not that different from those of other adolescents. Dreams and dragons alike are personal. The dragon was spun from remarks surrounding her youth: "Better to raise geese than girls." "When you raise girls, you're raising children for strangers." The dream, of course, was to slay the dragon—and prove them wrong.

Each culture offers up its dragons. The Chinese are no different in this respect. The trick is to recognize a dragon when one finds it. As Maxine Hong Kingston tells us, they are too large ever to be seen. In studying the youth who pursue them, though, we will have occasion to examine some of their parts. These are rarely the same from one culture to the next, or even within the same culture when it is as diverse as ours. Nor are they the same early in adolescence as they are later in adolescence.

Studying Adolescents: Four Themes to Look for in This Text

All cultures have one part of the dragon in common. They hold up one set of stories for females and another for males, offering a different set of experiences to their youth depending on their sex. Adolescents of either sex, as a result, are likely to follow different developmental paths to maturity. Tracing the impact on adolescent development of these paths defined by **gender** will be a theme of this text.

Similarly, adolescents' lives reflect, in intimate ways, their cultural backgrounds. These cultures affect everything from which foods taste good to which language teenagers use when talking to their grandmothers. Cultures, like dragons, are too big to be seen by those who live within them, even though the very rituals, beliefs, and rhythms of one's culture provide the perspective from which one views the world. Members of a culture, because they share its rhythms and stories, share expectancies that give shape to the events they experience. Experience, you see, rather than being taken in raw, is interpreted; and culture, like a pair of eyeglasses, provides the interpretive lenses through which one looks. Just as with glasses, one sees *through* the lenses, missing the culture that makes that view of reality possible. The influence of **ethnicity** and culture on adolescents' development is a second theme of this text.

When looked at from a distance, adolescents may all appear to be facing similar challenges. If we step closer, however, we can see that, just as with childhood and adulthood, adolescence comprises several distinct periods. **Early adolescents** must contend with puberty, changing sex roles, developing more autonomous relationships with parents, and achieving more mature relationships with peers. **Late adolescents** face the need to pull all these changes together into a coherent sense of themselves, while looking ahead to roles that have traditionally defined adulthood: those of work, marriage, and parenthood. More adolescents today than in the past, however, are continuing education after high school, thus delaying commitment to work, and many are similarly postponing commitment to marriage and having children, thus creating a phase in life called **emerging adulthood.** Distinguishing early adolescence, late adolescence, and emerging adulthood is a third theme of this text.

Despite the many varying experiences of adolescents, all face the task of gaining a sense of themselves. Adolescents face a need to find out who they are, what distinguishes them from others, and what they have in common with others. Although early and late adolescents go about this in somewhat different ways, all address the central question of adolescence: "Who am I?" The task of achieving an **identity** is the fourth theme of this text.

gender The cultural and psychological contributions to being female or male.

ethnicity The cultural group to which an individual belongs.

early adolescence That period of adolescence between the ages of about 11 to 15, marked by the onset of puberty, changing gender roles, more autonomous relationships with parents, and more mature relationships with peers.

late adolescence That period of adolescence between the ages of about 16 to 19 that is organized around the central task of achieving an identity, in which adolescents integrate their sexuality into their relationships, prepare for a vocation, and fashion a personal set of beliefs.

emerging adulthood A period between adolescence and adulthood characterized by demographic unpredictability and increased opportunity for identity exploration.

identity The part of one's personality of which one is aware and is able to see as a meaningful and coherent whole.

adolescence The transitional and often ambiguous period of development between childhood and adulthood. The duration, characteristics, and even the existence of such a period depend very much on historical, social, cultural, and economic factors.

Chapter Overview

We begin our study of adolescents with some numbers, looking first at the percentages of individuals of different ages in the U.S. population and how these have changed over time, and then at some of the implications of these changes for adolescents today.

Next we turn to a definition of **adolescence.** Adolescence itself is not easy to define. Think for a moment of a 17-year-old boy who has just graduated from high school. He's as tall as his dad and can beat him in arm wrestling. He has a driver's license but isn't allowed to drink alcoholic beverages in his state. He's old enough to enlist in the army but can't vote for another year. It's clear that he is no longer a child, but is it just as clear that he is an adult? Even though he can drive a car and carry a gun, he is not old enough to vote or drink. Adolescence abounds with paradoxes such as these. To get a clearer picture of what adolescence is, we will look at a biological, psychological, and sociological definition of adolescence.

Following this, the chapter moves to a number of perspectives—historical, lifespan, contextual, and constructive—from which to view adolescence. From the **historical perspective** we will see that adolescence has not always existed as we know it today. Nor, for that matter, has childhood or adulthood. Two hundred years ago, most 16-year-olds worked alongside adults and saw little of the inside of a classroom. Today, 16-year-olds in industrialized countries such as our own spend most of the day in a classroom, an experience that clearly sets them apart from most adults and distinguishes them as a separate group within society.

The **lifespan perspective** draws from, and amplifies, the historical one. It enables us to see not only the historical forces that shape individual development, but also the ways in which adolescence, as one period in the lifespan, is related to other periods in life. For instance, the lives of an adolescent and a grandparent appear, and are, very different, yet beneath the surface each may be coping with similar issues. The adolescent, for example, may be trying to get the keys to the family car, whereas the grandparent may be facing the need to surrender them after a lifetime of use. The issue for both is the same—independence. If we were to study either of these ages apart from the other, we would miss important continuities to the experience of life.

Irrespective of historical time, or of timing within the life cycle, development takes place in real life contexts. "Development" may sound like an abstract concept, but it walks the corridors of schools and talks to parents over the dinner table. The **contextual perspective** examines the ways in which the course of development is influenced by these contexts—those of school, family, friends, community, and culture. This perspective underscores the importance of knowing, for instance, whether an adolescent girl's ethnicity confers majority or minority status in the day-to-day contexts of her school or neighborhood in order to understand the contribution of that ethnicity to her identity.

Lastly, the **constructive perspective** describes the active, constructive process by which individuals—irrespective of the historical period in which they live, or their age within the life cycle, or the particular contexts in which they find themselves—perceive their world. The constructive perspective assumes that we actively construct what we know of the world, interpreting our experiences, composing or making sense of the events to which we react. Thus an adolescent boy would be likely to hear a casual remark such as "Whatcha doin'?" as meaning one thing if said by a friend and as something entirely different if said by someone from a different crowd at his school—as a simple greeting in the first instance and a possible challenge in the second.

Who Are Adolescents?

Although youth all over the world enter their teens, not all become "teenagers." Much of what we consider typical of adolescents is, for the most part, characteristic only of those living in Western industrialized countries. In many **traditional cultures** in which traditions remain unchanged with the passage of time and recently industrialized **developing countries,** youth are not likely to spend their days in school, for instance, or hang out with friends, or go out on dates, or dress and speak in ways unique to their age (Larson & Wilson, 2004; Verma & Saraswathi, 2002). With this said, increasing trends toward **globalization** are beginning to change the experiences of youth in many non-Western

historical perspective An approach that considers the way patterns of individual development differ as a function of the historical context.

lifespan perspective The view that development is characterized by continuity as well as change throughout life.

contextual perspective The view that development is influenced by one's ethnicity and culture.

constructive perspective The view that perception is an active, constructive process in which individuals interpret and give meaning to their experiences.

traditional cultures Cultures that have maintained their values and practices over long periods. These cultures often find themselves in conflict with other traditional or more rapidly changing cultures or with internal pressures for change.

developing countries Countries that have only recently begun to adopt modern technology, social forms, and means of production. Such countries were previously termed "third world" countries.

globalization The process by which expanding international trade, communication, and travel erases national and geographical boundaries.

Adolescence spans the years from 11 to 19, a time of dramatic physical, emotional, and intellectual changes. Some of these junior high students still look like children, and others seem nearly adult.

cultures. Research comparing adolescents from various cultures differing in social and economic development, political systems, and regions of the world reveals considerable cross-cultural similarities (Dmitrieva, Chen, Greenberger, & Gil-Rivas, 2004; Vazsonyi, Hibbert, & Snyder, 2003). In this text, however, we will base our examination of adolescence primarily on research on adolescents in Western cultures, focusing primarily on those in the United States.

Adolescents in a Changing Society

Adolescents make up approximately 14.3% of the population (U.S. Bureau of the Census, 2001a). Nonetheless, they are a visible segment of society, perhaps because they highlight for us some of the ways in which society itself is changing. For one thing, we are living in an aging population. Adolescents today, in other words, are coming of age in a population that has a few more gray hairs about its ears than in the past. The population pyramids shown in Figure 1.1 illustrate this aging trend in our society.

The proportion of adolescents belonging to ethnic groups of color—including African Americans, Asian and Pacific Islander Americans, Hispanics, and Native Americans—has been steadily increasing (Figure 1.2). In 1950 ethnic minorities made up 10.7% of the population. By the turn of the century, this figure stood at 36%. By the year 2020, 45% of youth in the United States will belong to an ethnic minority, with Hispanics equaling 22% of all adolescents, African Americans 16%, and Asian and Pacific Islander Americans approximately 6% (U.S. Department of Health and Human Services, 2002a). Furthermore, many of these adolescents are multiracial, which means one or both of their parents have parents claiming different ethnic heritages.

Family characteristics are changing as well. More families are headed by single parents. Approximately 27% of all children under 18 live with one parent (U.S. Bureau of the Census, 2002). This figure is even higher for many minority children and adolescents, with 29% of Hispanic and 53% of African American children and adolescents living with a single parent. Over 84% of those living with a single parent live with their mother (U.S. Department of Health and Human Services, 2002a). These figures contain a hidden dimension for many adolescents—poverty (Figure 1.3). Among families with children under 18 that are maintained by single women, 42% qualify as poor (U.S. Department of Health and Human Services, 2002b). About 16% of children under 18 live below the poverty line (U.S. Department of Health and Human Services, 2002a). The difficulty of making it on one's own while maintaining a family is one factor contributing to other changes in family characteristics. Many single parents live with a relative, usually one or both of their parents, to make ends meet. About 4 million children—5.6% of all children under 18—live in the household of their grandparents, sometimes without either parent but more often with a parent as well. As we enter the twenty-first century, more families are likely to have a grandparent at the wheel and mom and the kids in the backseat.

Despite the challenges posed by social and personal change, adolescents by and large adopt a positive outlook on life. When asked who they look up to and admire, for instance, nearly twice as many mention someone they know rather than a media star or personality (Anderson & Cavallaro, 2002). And to the surprise of many parents, adolescents actually share their values. In other words, adolescents tend to view their world positively. This outlook is further reflected in the fact that a large proportion of youth

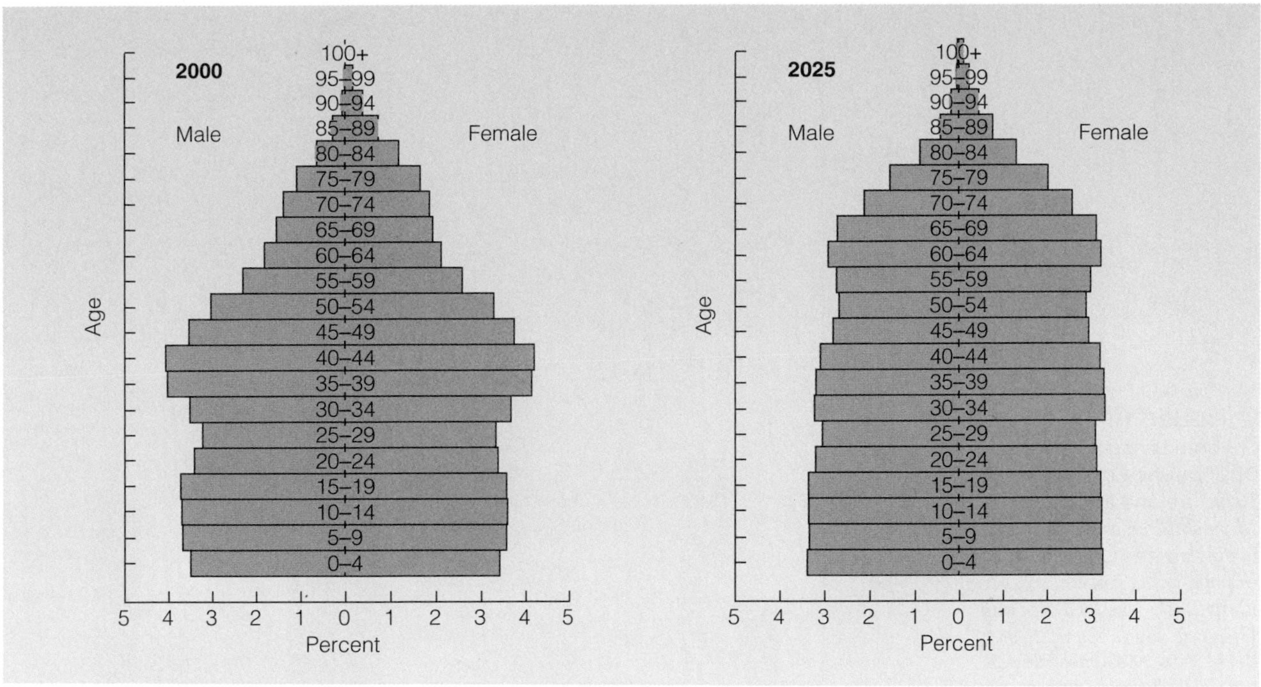

FIGURE 1.1
Population Pyramids for the Years 2000 and 2025. *The population pyramid for 2000 shows a "bulge" around the middle years as baby boomers reach middle age; the pyramid for 2025 shows how the population will age as boomers move into later adulthood.* Source: *National Population Projections*. U.S. Bureau of the Census, Population Division. (2002, August 2). Retrieved from http://www.census.gov/population/www/projections/natchart.html.

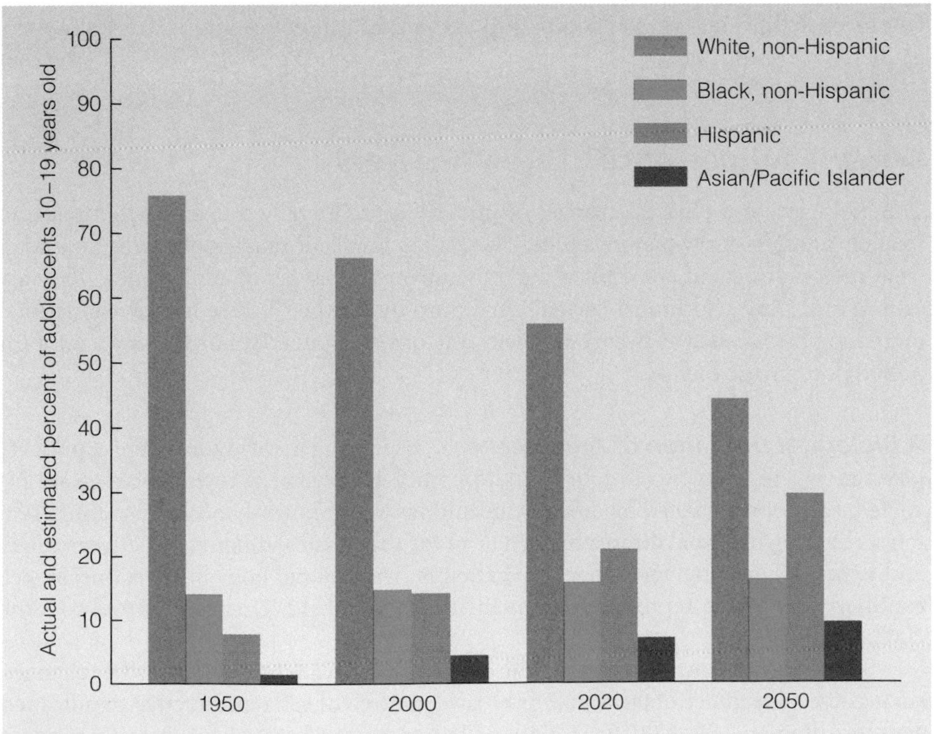

FIGURE 1.2
Increasing Ethnic Diversity. *Adolescents live in a society that is more diverse ethnically than the one in which their parents grew up.* Source: A. P. MacKay, L. A. Fingerhut, & C. R. Duran. (2000). *Adolescent health chartbook. Health, United States, 2000*. Hyattsville, MD: National Center for Health Statistics.

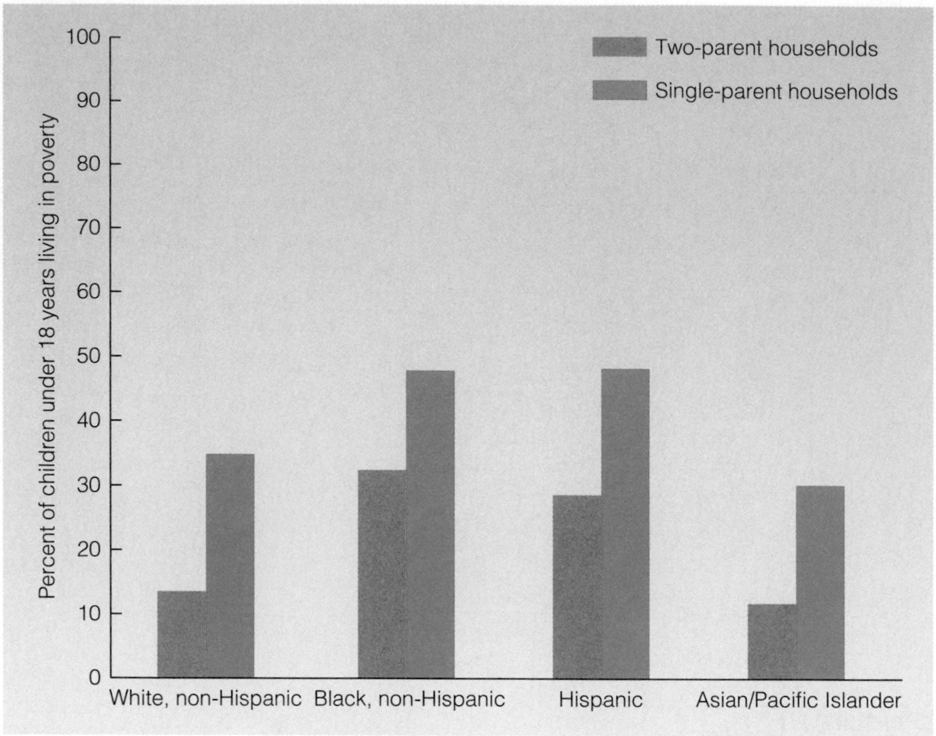

FIGURE 1.3
Children Living in Poverty, Distinguished by Family Structure and Ethnicity. *More children and adolescents in single-parent households live in poverty. As you can see, this is especially true for Black and Hispanic youth. Source: Health, United States, 2004 with chartbook on trends in the health of Americans.* Hyattsville, MD: National Center for Health Statistics.

volunteer for various types of community service, as can be seen in Figure 1.4 (Frisco, Muller, & Dodson, 2004).

What Is Adolescence? Three Answers

The biological and physical changes of puberty quite literally transform children into sexually and physically mature adults. These changes occur in all adolescents no matter what their culture and are, in fact, the only universal changes of adolescence. They are caused by a heady hormonal cocktail served up by Mother Nature herself. Sometimes increasing by as much as twenty-fold with the onset of puberty, hormones account for puberty's dramatic events.

A Biological Definition of Adolescence Beginning in early adolescence, **puberty** takes anywhere from two to four years to complete. Several growth processes are involved, each one regulated by different hormones and frequently occurring at different rates, resulting in **sexual dimorphism,** a term for the physical differences between males and females. These include differences in height, weight, and body proportions, as well as differences in the reproductive system itself (Archibald, Graber, & Brooks-Gunn, 2003; Ellis, 2004).

puberty Growth processes, including the skeletal growth spurt and maturation of the reproductive system, that begin in early adolescence and transform children into physically and sexually mature adults.

sexual dimorphism The physical differences that distinguish adult females and males.

Some changes, such as growth of the ovaries or uterus, go unnoticed. Other changes, such as the appearance of facial hair or breasts, though of less reproductive significance, are more dramatic. By age 10 or 11, nearly all preteens begin to look for signs of change in

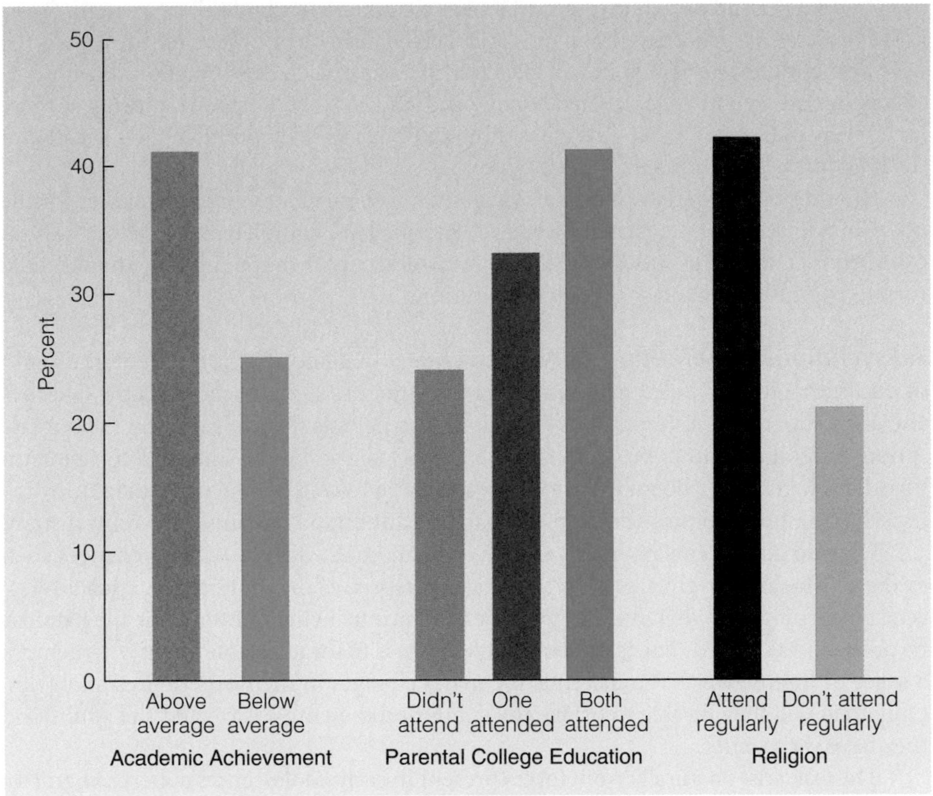

FIGURE 1.4
Characteristics Related to Volunteerism. *Many adolescents volunteer their time and services in charitable activities. Those who are most likely to volunteer are doing well in school, have parents who attended college, and attend religious services regularly.*
Source: M. L. Frisco, C. Muller, & K. Dodson. (2004). Participation in voluntary youth-serving associations and early adult voting behavior. *Social Science Quarterly, 85,* 660–676.

themselves. The events most closely associated with puberty—menstruation in girls and ejaculation in boys—actually occur fairly late in the process. Which changes will occur first and just when they will happen is hard to say for any one person. Wide variations exist in the timing and sequence of development from one individual to the next. Also, development is not necessarily even; some functions mature at a faster rate than others. However, some general statements can be made about the most likely course of events.

The physical growth spurt, one of the first noticeable changes for girls, is a period of accelerated growth beginning just after age 10 and peaking at about age 12. Boys begin to grow approximately two years later, peaking at about age 14. During this period girls grow approximately 3½ inches a year and boys slightly more. Growth in height is accompanied by a corresponding gain in weight and an increase in the rate of muscular development. Body proportions also begin to change, as girls' hips widen and boys' shoulders become broader (Graber & Brooks-Gunn, 2002).

Changes in the reproductive system and the appearance of secondary sex characteristics can also be charted. For boys, changes in the testes and scrotum and the appearance of pubic hair are among the first noticeable changes. For girls, the growth of breast buds and pubic hair typically coincides with growth of the uterus and vagina. Development of the external genitalia also typically occurs in the first year of puberty. Midway through puberty most girls begin to menstruate, usually coinciding with a peak in the growth spurt. Also midway through puberty boys first experience ejaculation, which may or may not be accompanied by orgasm. Most adult males usually experience orgasm at the same time as ejaculation; however, these are independent processes and may occur separately. Boys, in fact, typically experience erections and sometimes orgasm well before the time they first ejaculate (Hyde, 1991).

Toward the end of puberty, secondary sex characteristics find full expression. Some are long awaited, such as breasts in girls and facial hair in boys; others less so, such as the development of sweat glands and oil glands in the skin, which can be responsible for embarrassing odors and acne. Related to the production of the hormone androgen, these latter events affect boys and girls alike, although boys suffer more than girls because of the higher levels of androgen in their systems.

Even though puberty serves as a convenient, if somewhat imprecise, marker for the onset of adolescence, the changes we have described are completed well before adolescence ends. The task of specifying an end to adolescence is more difficult, and we must turn to psychological and sociological definitions.

A Psychological Definition of Adolescence Imagine, for the moment, the world of a 15-year-old boy. Video games, comics, and friends fill after-school hours. Old toys and a skateboard are scattered about his room; two pet rats sleep in a cage on the bureau. A notice about a summer program in math for the college-bound is pinned to a bulletin board. He hates math, doesn't know if he wants to go to college, and can't imagine working. His childhood seems to be slipping away, and adulthood remains impossibly distant.

How do adolescents maintain a sense of themselves when faced with changes such as these? The answer gives us a psychological perspective on adolescence. Each adolescent reaches a point when it is not possible to continue living out the same life patterns he or she did as a child. The task facing adolescents is to forge a stable identity, to achieve a sense of themselves that transcends the many changes in their experiences and roles. Only then will they be able to bridge the childhood they must leave and the adulthood they have yet to enter.

The task arises naturally from forces present in early adolescence: puberty, cognitive growth, and changing social expectations. The first force to make itself felt is usually puberty. In addition to visible changes in height, weight, and body proportions, puberty brings an inner world of sexual stirrings. These bodily changes are accompanied by cognitive ones, giving adolescents a new awareness of themselves and others' reactions to them. Social expectations subtly change as well. Parents and others expect a new maturity from adolescents. They expect adolescents to begin planning for their lives and thinking for themselves. In short, they expect them to be more responsible—to be more adult.

The convergence of physical maturation with changing personal and social expectations confronts adolescents with new developmental tasks (Havighurst, 1972). These tasks represent our culture's definition of normal development at different points in life (see Figure 1.5 on page 15). Because our sense of ourselves comes in part from our awareness of how others see us, cultural norms give shape to personal standards. Biological maturation contributes more heavily to some tasks, such as adjusting to an adult body, whereas cultural norms contribute more to others, such as developing social skills. In general, adolescents evaluate themselves more positively as they experience increasing mastery of these tasks (Pinquart, Silbereisen, & Wiesner, 2004).

Adolescents face eight developmental tasks in all. Each, however, can be thought of as a facet of one central task: achieving a continuing and stable sense of self as adolescents step into adulthood. Even teenagers who master these steps, however, find the gateway to adulthood locked and must wait for someone to come along with the key. The lock is sprung not by biological or even psychological maturity. The final tumbler is keyed to a sociological definition of adolescence.

A Sociological Definition of Adolescence Sociologists define individuals in terms of their status within society, reflected in large measure by their self-sufficiency. From a sociological perspective, adolescents emerge as individuals who are neither self-sufficient, and hence not adult, nor completely dependent, and thus not children. Adolescence becomes a transitional period whose end is marked by legislation specifying age limits for the legal protection of those not yet adult. David Bakan (1971) suggests that complex social conditions require the prolongation of childhood or, rather, the delay of entrance into adulthood. These conditions can be traced to the way this nation produced its goods.

The United States remained an agrarian and rural society well into the first half of the nineteenth century. With industrialization, both of these conditions changed. Mills and factories drew people like magnets to growing urban centers. Many were new immigrants drawn to the country by a recent labor shortage. Rising numbers of immigrants and unrest in new urban centers focused attention on the need for government to oversee the education and socialization of individuals into a new way of life. Three social movements surrounding industrialization contributed to the emergence of adolescence as a distinct new age group.

Compulsory education laws were introduced for children between ages 6 and 18 on a widespread basis in the United States in the late nineteenth century. Previously, children attended school, or did not, as their parents saw fit. Just as children had worked alongside their parents on farms and in fields when additional hands were needed, they now accompanied them to the factories. Their presence in the factories created certain problems. The hours were long and jobs were increasingly scarce, as the nation found that machines could indeed do the work of ten people. The cheap labor of children became an economic liability to the adults in the labor force. Compulsory education laws ensured basic skills among future workers—and also protected the jobs of adults in the workforce.

Similarly, **child labor laws** specifying minimum ages for different types of work restricted the numbers of children who could hold full-time jobs. In 1832, 40% of the factory workers in New England were children. These young factory workers became a liability to the nation rather than an asset, as industrialization solved the labor-shortage problem. Child labor laws ensured humane working conditions for children, but at the same time they protected the jobs of adults in the workforce (Bakan, 1971).

Finally, laws instituting separate legal proceedings for juveniles, giving us a separate system of **juvenile justice,** were introduced at about this time. These laws were intended to free the courts from punishing children as adults and to allow them to offer corrective measures instead. Bakan points out, however, that these laws also suspended important legal rights guaranteed to adults, such as due process and the presumption of innocence. This legislation, just as that governing child labor and education, specified an age group. Each social movement targeted the population to which it applied in terms of age. Adolescence emerged as a period in life bounded at one end by puberty and at the other by legal age requirements.

Each of the three definitions of adolescence that we have considered is incomplete by itself, but together they give us a fairly well-rounded picture of adolescence. Adolescence is a period in life that begins with biological maturation, during which individuals must accomplish certain developmental tasks, and that ends when they achieve a self-sufficient state of adulthood as defined by society.

compulsory education laws Legislation making school attendance mandatory for children and adolescents until they graduate or reach a minimum age.

child labor laws Laws that specify minimum ages for various types of work.

juvenile justice Legislation instituting separate legal proceedings for juveniles and adults.

Perspectives on Adolescence

Having a definition of adolescence in hand, we're now in a position to examine this period in life more closely. We will do so from four perspectives: the historical, lifespan, contextual, and constructive. Each of these offers a distinct way of understanding the developments that characterize adolescence, and, once again, by putting the pieces afforded by these perspectives together, our picture of adolescence will be more complete. The first of these perspectives informs us that conceptions of age have changed considerably over the centuries—in some historical periods, adolescence, as such, didn't exist.

The Historical Perspective

How many distinct ages are there in life? That was the riddle of the Sphinx: "What walks on four legs in the morning, on two at noon, and on three in the evening?" We all do, according to Homer. However, as with many questions, the answer one gets depends on who one asks. Homer divided the lifespan into three ages: infancy, youth, and old age. Shakespeare gave us six: "the infant mewling and puking . . . the whining schoolboy . . . the lover, sighing like a furnace . . . a soldier, full of strange oaths . . . the justice, in fair round belly . . . the sixth age shifts . . . with spectacles on nose . . . turning again toward . . . second childishness." Infancy, childhood, adolescence, young adulthood, middle age, and old age. Our conception of aging has expanded distinctly over the centuries, recently adding ages, such as early and late adolescence and emerging adulthood.

The pattern of growth may be the same for each generation, but people age in different ways depending on when they are born. Their year of birth defines their **cohort group.** Members of a cohort group undergo similar experiences in the course of their development, experiences they share and that frequently set them apart from other cohorts. One group may experience war, another economic depression, and another prosperity. Such societal changes in turn affect the availability of jobs or scholarships, the number of potential mates, the quality of schools and housing, and innumerable other life circumstances. Even more generally, history reveals that our conception of aging has expanded distinctly over the centuries.

A Time Before Childhood? Philippe Aries, a French historian, traces changes in attitudes toward various age groups by noting the words by which a group has, or has not, been identified. He notes that at certain points in history there were no words to refer to childhood. In the Middle Ages, a single word served for infancy, toddlerhood, childhood, and adolescence. Aries maintains that the absence of specific words for different ages implies that people did not feel it necessary to distinguish between them (Aries, 1962).

Neil Postman (1982) argues that childhood became a recognizably distinct stage in life only when conditions prompted a redefinition of adulthood. Postman suggests that childhood was born in the mid-1400s, to strange parents: a goldsmith named Gutenberg and a converted winepress. If the invention of the printing press created childhood, it did so by default. What it really created, maintains Postman, was adulthood. Adults came to be defined as those who could read the new documents, maps, charts, manuals, and books that were quickly becoming available. The concept of adulthood was based on reading competence, and childhood on reading *in*competence. Before this time, adulthood directly followed infancy, which was considered to end at about age 7, when children mastered spoken language. Postman adds:

> In a literate world to be an adult implies having access to cultural secrets codified in unnatural symbols. In a literate world children must *become* adults. But in a nonliterate world there is no need to distinguish sharply between the child and the adult, for there are few secrets, and the culture does not need to provide training in how to understand itself. (p. 13)

Printing brought about the concept of authorship and with it a new awareness of individuality. Postman (1982) believes this heightened sense of individual importance was

cohort group People born during the same historical period or undergoing the same historical influences.

critical in the development of childhood: "For as the idea of personal identity developed, it followed inexorably that it would be applied to the young as well" (p. 28). Prior to this point there was a striking lack of individuality, compellingly illustrated by the frequent practice of calling children within a family by the same name. Four sons might all be named John and distinguished only by order of birth.

The "knowledge gap" that developed with printing—something like 8 million books were printed in the first 50 years—created the need for schooling. Improving economic conditions made it possible for more families to send their children to school, and a new age group emerged in societies throughout Europe (Postman, 1982).

The Creation of Adolescence In a similar way, adolescence emerged from childhood in the middle of the nineteenth century. This time industrialization gave birth to the new age group. As we read earlier in the chapter, David Bakan (1971) suggests that adolescence emerged as a response to social conditions that required the prolongation of childhood. The machines of an industrialized society demanded skills as well as physical strength, and the entrance of young workers into the workforce was delayed until they had acquired those skills (Kett, 1977).

Other conditions sped the arrival of adolescence. Industrialization created a shift in the rural and urban population distribution. Large numbers of youths of the same age became concentrated in one place, a phenomenon unheard of in the days of the one-room schoolhouse. It became possible to have separate classes for youths of different ages. Finally, much as with the arrival of childhood, a growing middle class made it possible for parents to send their children to school in order to secure for them the better jobs that were becoming available. The first high schools were formed in these urban centers in the early 1900s, and the youths who attended them became a noticeable new age group.

Stepping into the twenty-first century, we find ourselves in a postindustrial, postmodern society that continues to change rapidly. As in the past, we can expect our concept of adolescence to change as a result of social forces such as globalization, technological innovations, and increased immigration (Larson, 2002). In fact, globalization and the introduction of new technologies into many non-Western developing nations have resulted in the emergence of a stage of adolescence where previously this had not existed. These non-Western experiences of adolescence bear their own cultural imprint and, in turn, can be expected to contribute to the "reconstruction" of adolescence in the United States as individuals immigrate from these cultures (Larson, 2002).

Media Contributions to Age Distinctions Postman (1982) suggests that just as the printing press created separate domains, a more recent invention has begun to merge them. The Gutenberg of our times is Samuel Morse, inventor of the telegraph (Postman, 1982). The telegraph ushered in the age of electronic communication and, with this, a parallel revolution from print to images. Images, unlike books, are readily available to those of any age; they require no interpretation and no years of preparation for their mastery. The "knowledge monopoly" that previously separated children and adults was broken. Postman (1982) writes:

> The essential point is that TV presents information in a form that is undifferentiated in its accessibility, and this means that television does not need to make distinctions between categories of "child" and "adult." . . . This happens not only because the symbolic form of television poses no cognitive mysteries but also because a television set cannot be hidden in a drawer or placed on a high shelf, out of the reach of children; its physical form, no less than its symbolic form, does not lend itself to exclusivity. (pp. 79, 80)

Television, movies, and home videos disclose secrets that were previously the domain of adults. For that matter, printed books did much the same thing 500 years ago when they broke the monopoly of the privileged few who could read and write. The difference is that literacy also established an obstacle that could be overcome only by years of preparation, as children learned to read and understand ever more complex forms of written expression. Television, however, tells all to anyone who may be watching; its images are self-explanatory. This point becomes important if one believes that groups are defined in significant ways by the exclusivity of the information available to their members. Lawyers are distinguished from doctors, students from teachers, or, in this case, children from adults by what they know. If the authority of adults derives, in part, from their ability to initiate children into their secrets, adult authority is diminished to the extent that there are no secrets (Postman, 1982).

The Lifespan Perspective

The lifespan offers a unique perspective from which to view adolescence. Developmental issues that arise in adolescence can be traced back to childhood and followed into adulthood. Issues of autonomy and competence, for example, are immensely important to adolescents. Both are also significant issues facing two other age groups: the elderly and toddlers. We can see continuities such as these and also note the more obvious changes that occur within the age category itself (Figure 1.5).

In the same way, similar developmental tasks are resolved and arise again at different periods in life. Just as early adolescents must come to terms with rapidly changing bodies and the resulting changes to their sense of themselves, so must their middle-age parents. An adolescent boy may notice a new "buffed" look; his father may be noticing a slight paunch around the middle and the tendency to become winded faster than he remembers.

Looking at the developmental tasks for different ages in Figure 1.5, we can see from the sheer number of tasks for adolescence and middle childhood that these ages are active times of change. A second look, however, shows middle age to be nearly as active as adolescence, just one task short. Parents may believe stress stalks in the form of adolescence, but it is just as likely to assume the form of middle age.

Interesting parallels exist between the tasks of both early and late adolescents and their parents. Early adolescents must revise their sense of self to accommodate the physical changes brought about by puberty, whereas their parents must come to accept and adjust to the physiological changes of middle age. Early adolescents also face the tasks of achieving emotional independence from parents and other adults; a parallel task for parents is assisting their teenage children to become responsible and happy adults, while simultaneously adjusting to the needs of their own aging parents. A task of late adolescence is to prepare for marriage and family life; that of middle age is to relate to one's spouse as a person. Just as late adolescents face the task of preparing for an economic career, their parents face the task of reaching and maintaining satisfactory performance in their occupations. Similarly, late adolescents must achieve socially responsible behavior, whereas their parents face the need to achieve civic responsibility.

No cause for surprise, then, that relationships between adolescents and parents are occasionally tense. But despite sources of potential tension, most adolescents report surprising levels of satisfaction with their parents. Most agree with the way they have been parented and report that they hold many of the same values as their parents (Pratt, Hunsberger, Pancer, & Alisat, 2003; White & Matawie, 2004).

Parallels exist for both early and late adolescents and grandparents as well. Just as early adolescents must come to terms with rapidly changing bodies and the resulting

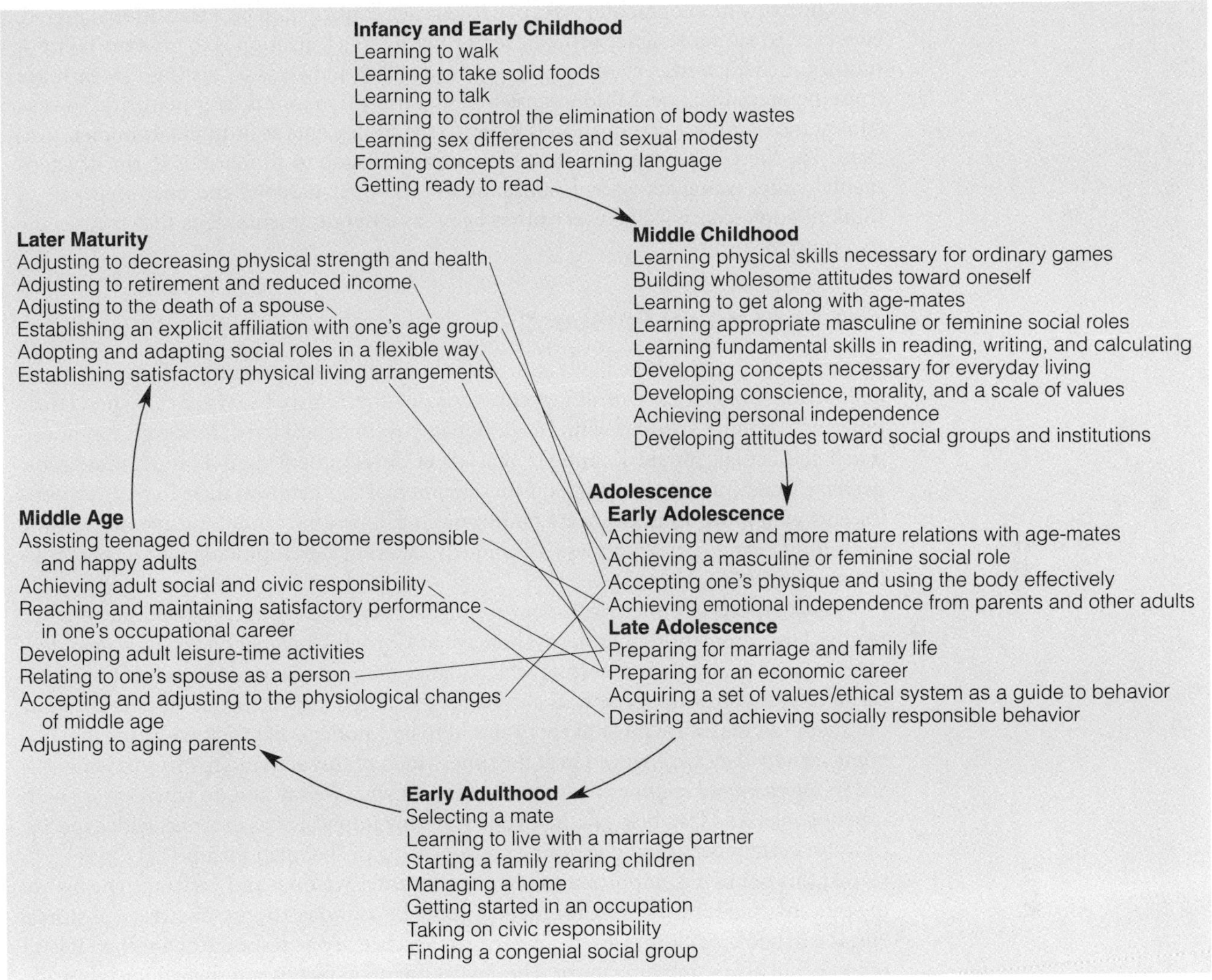

FIGURE 1.5
Developmental Tasks Throughout the Lifespan. *Note the similarities in the developmental tasks of adolescents and their middle-aged parents and their grandparents.*

changes to their sense of themselves, so must older adults. Similarly, late adolescents face the need to redefine the self in terms of an occupation, a task that requires commitment to a career. Conversely, grandparents face the need to maintain their sense of self once they have retired from a job that has been an important source of self-definition. The issue of economic independence also faces both of these age groups. Late adolescents may have to postpone work while they continue education; recently retired grandparents often face radically reduced incomes. In a similar fashion, most late adolescents are looking forward to marriage at a time when grandparents begin to worry about losing a spouse. Both face the task of adapting social roles to changing life circumstances. Finally, both face the need to establish satisfactory living arrangements, a problem for many late adolescents who continue to live at home while they pursue their education, as well as for grandparents who may not be able to maintain a separate residence of their own and face moving in with their children.

The many developmental tasks of adolescence confirm it to be a transitional period. However, to see adolescence just, or even primarily, as a transition is to miss the point—transition characterizes every age. It is, in fact, what allows us to distinguish each age from the preceding one. Middle age is no less a transition, nor is later maturity. To view adolescence simply as a transition is to fail to see adolescents as individuals in their own right. The lifespan perspective, then, draws our attention to similarities in the developmental issues facing adolescents and parents, and their parents, and encourages us to think of adolescence—like every other age—as a developmental lens that focuses the past onto the future.

The Contextual Perspective

The contextual perspective looks at the ways in which development is influenced by the daily settings, or contexts, of adolescents' lives, in other words, by where they spend their time and who they spend it with. In a uniquely psychological twist, however, it is not so much the actual, physical contexts that affect development as it is how adolescents perceive these contexts that leaves its developmental footprint on their lives. Even adolescents who grow up in the same family, or go to the same school, or live in the same community can experience these as uniquely different developmental contexts (Bronfenbrenner, 1979a, 1994).

What aspects of our environment are we likely to perceive and incorporate into our reality? Urie Bronfenbrenner, a psychologist at Cornell University, identifies three features of one's environment, each of which, rather than being a static aspect of the physical setting, involves the person in a dynamic exchange with it. Bronfenbrenner points out that individuals are most likely to attend to and notice what they are doing, the ongoing *activity* they are engaged in at the time. Much of this activity involves us with others, in *interpersonal relations* that take the form of what we say and do when we are with other people. And last, being with others invariably implicates us in a *role,* with expectations for certain behaviors depending on the setting or the relationship.

At this point, it is important to highlight the interpersonal and very intimate nature of one's environment. The environment is not to be found in rooms, or streets, or stores. Nor is it in books or clothes, or the presence or absence of one resource or another. It is all of these, but also something more. The environment, in fact, is not that which is outside the person or separate from the person. Rather than being something outside the self, the environment always *includes* the self, in the form of how we experience ourself in relation to something else, usually another person. Bronfenbrenner (1990) emphasizes this point when he stresses the importance of a young person developing a meaningful relationship with an adult who finds that young person "somehow special, especially wonderful, and especially precious" (p. 31). Such a relationship becomes a springboard from which adolescents can step into other contexts, determining how they will be perceived.

Bronfenbrenner adds that the environment does not exist as a simple, unified context, but takes the form of multiple, overlapping spheres of influence (Figure 1.6). At the most immediate level of environmental influence, that of the **microsystem,** are the various settings in which the adolescent moves throughout the day: at home, at school, with friends, at work. A characteristic of the microsystem is that the activities, interpersonal relations, and roles involve the adolescent in face-to-face interactions with others. It's relatively easy to imagine how such interactions might affect an adolescent, whether they take the form of a verbal exchange with a parent or teacher, or supportive eye contact from a friend.

microsystem One's immediate social contexts, involving firsthand experiences, such as interactions at home or in the classroom.

Bronfenbrenner maintains that adolescents are affected not only by face-to-face influences such as these, but also by various relations among the microsystems of daily

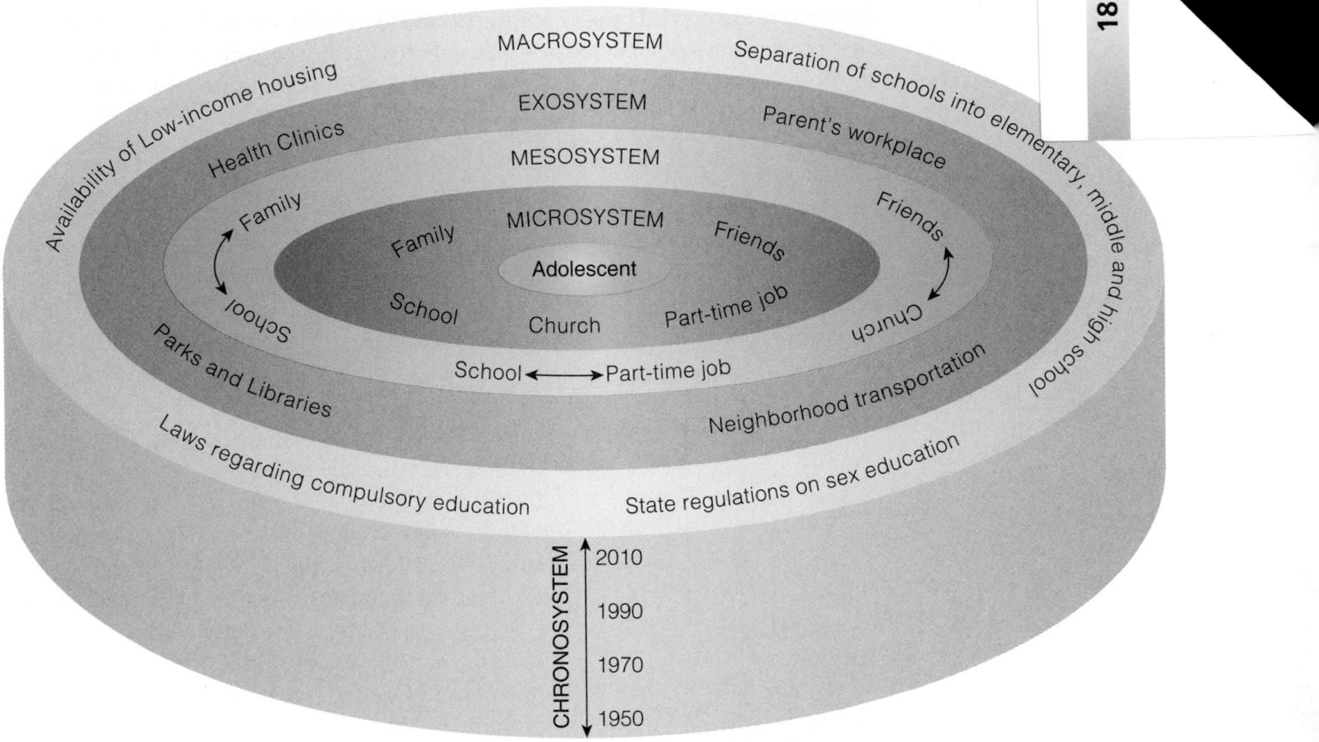

FIGURE 1.6
Bronfenbrenner's Contextual Theory. *Adolescents' daily lives are influenced by five overlapping systems, each of which can affect conditions in another sphere.*

life, influences at the level of the **mesosystem.** For example, a parent's involvement with school can significantly improve the adolescent's academic performance (Comer, Haynes, Joyner, & Ben-Avie, 1996). In addition to the microsystem and mesosystem, adolescents can be affected by environments in which they are not present but that affect their immediate surroundings. Bronfenbrenner refers to such influences as the **exosystem.** Conditions in a parent's workplace, for instance, can affect the amount of time the parent has to spend with the family or the amount of stress introduced into family life, thereby affecting the adolescent.

The **macrosystem,** which consists of the underlying social and political climate, is even further removed from adolescents' daily experiences, yet it impinges on their lives in very real ways. Laws concerning compulsory education, the mainstreaming of students with special needs, and the separation of grades into elementary school, middle school or junior high, and high school all illustrate the direct ways the macrosystem can affect the lives of adolescents. One way in which the macrosystem is affecting increasing numbers of adolescents is through geopolitical decisions that result in increased numbers of "triggers" for asthma, such as air pollution, exhaust fumes, and increased ozone levels. A national study of 9- to 17-year-olds found that 15.3% experienced recurrent attacks of asthma (Goodwin, Pine, & Hoven, 2003). In fact, asthma now affects approximately 6 million youth in the United States, making it the most common chronic illness.

Finally, development is affected by the **chronosystem,** which refers to the particular circumstances existing at any point in history within a culture that shape adolescents' experience of the various contexts of their lives. For instance, adolescents growing up in the United States prior to the industrial revolution were likely to attend schools in which

mesosystem Social contexts involving interactions of several microsystems, such as when parents meet teachers.

exosystem Contexts occurring at the level of the community, such as types of schools and housing.

macrosystem The underlying social and political climate at the level of society.

chronosystem The changing impact of the various environmental systems (micro-, meso-, exo-, macro) at different historical periods.

classes were not graded by age, simply because there weren't enough students of the same age to constitute a separate class. Consequently, the microcosm of school did not confer on adolescents the same sense of themselves as a distinct age group as it presently does.

The Constructive Perspective

The constructive perspective assumes that reality is not a given, that one person's reality is not necessarily shared by others. In a very real sense, we make it up. If you doubt that we actively "construct" the events to which we respond, take a moment to look at Figure 1.7. Notice that the very same lines that form the letter *B* in the top row also form the number *13* in the bottom row. What determines whether you will see these lines as a letter or as a number? The answer, obviously, is not in the physical arrangement of the lines themselves, because this arrangement is the same in either case. Rather, it is your, the reader's, expectancy to see one or the other figure that determines how the arrangement of lines will be read. This expectancy, in turn, is derived from the context in which the lines appear—that context being either a row of letters or a row of numbers.

FIGURE 1.7
What Do You See Here?
The same lines that form the letter B *are the very same lines that form the number* 13. *Nothing has been changed – except the way you see these!*

This same active, constructive process occurs at each of many levels of human functioning, from the microlevel of perceptual processing that has just been examined to the macrolevel of social interactions. An experiment by John Condry and David Ross (1985) illustrates that the same constructive process occurs in the perception of social behavior. These investigators showed college students a videotape of two children engaged in rough and tumble activity in the snow. The actual sex of the children couldn't be determined because of their bulky snowsuits; some viewers were told the children were boys and others that they were girls. Viewers who believed the children to be boys perceived the children's behavior to be playful. However, those who thought they were looking at girls saw the identical behavior (remember, they all viewed the same videotape) as aggressive. Boys' play, you see, is expected to be rough, and actions such as wrestling or pummeling each other with snowballs fit the viewers' expectations of how boys play. In other words, it was easy for them to "read" such actions as playful. Conversely, girls' play is expected to be quiet. Given that expectancy, wrestling and pummeling could only be perceived as aggressive.

What determined what each viewer saw? Just as in the previous example, the answer is not to be found in the videotape of the two children. The same videotape was seen by everyone. Rather, it is to be found in the expectancies of the viewers. What they saw is what they pieced together, guided by their expectancies, as these gave meaning to the activity they were viewing. The Research Focus "An Experiment" provides a further example of research into the ways that people give meaning to the behavior of others.

The Faces of Adolescents

We began this chapter by identifying four themes that will guide our study of adolescence throughout the chapters of this text: attention to issues of gender, ethnicity, early versus late adolescence, and identity. At this point, it pays to take a closer look at each of these.

RESEARCH FOCUS

An Experiment: "Who You Pushin', Buddy!" Perceptions of Aggressiveness

By Michael Wapner

People interpret experience by literally constructing or piecing together the events to which they respond. One of the most important manifestations of this interpretive construction occurs in determining the intentions of others. Even when an action is so obvious that it leaves little to interpretation, the motives behind the action still need to be understood, and this usually requires a good deal of cognitive construction. Observers may all agree that George bumped into Ira. But what the observers feel and do about it depends more on why they think George did it than the mere fact that he did. If George stumbled and could not keep from bumping Ira, that's one thing. But if George bumped Ira to get ahead of him in line, that's entirely different.

What is it that determines how observers interpret the intentions behind an act? Mary Lynne Courtney and Robert Cohen (1996) designed an experiment to investigate this question. In particular, they looked at the contribution of two variables to the interpretation of intention: (1) prior information and (2) the personality of the observer. These two variables, in addition to influencing an observer's interpretation of the intentions behind an action, illustrate, by their difference, something fundamental about the design of experiments in general.

Briefly, boys between 8 and 12 were shown a videotape of two boys playing tag on a playground. At a critical point in the middle of the tape, the boy being chased falls down after being tagged by the other boy. The fallen boy slowly gets up and resumes the game. The variables were introduced as follows:

(1) Prior Information: An Independent Variable

Previous research, and common sense, would suggest that observers' interpretation of the intention behind an act should depend on what else they know about the actors. Thus, one would guess that the subjects would more likely attribute hostile intent to the tag that caused the fall if they were told beforehand that the two boys were enemies and had just recently been fighting. Conversely, the likelihood of seeing the tag as accidental should increase if the observers believed the boys to be good friends. But what if the observers knew nothing about the boys? These three conditions—let us call them benign, hostile, and ambiguous—constitute the independent variable in the experiment.

In an *experiment,* each group of participants is treated differently than the others. In all other respects, the groups are equivalent. If the groups differ afterward, we can assume the difference is due to the way they were treated. In order to be confident about this assumption, however, we must be sure that the groups are the same at the outset. The simplest way to ensure this would be to start with identical groups. But because no two individuals are ever the same in all respects, such a tactic is impossible. An equally good approach is to make sure the groups don't differ in any *systematic* way. We can accomplish this by assigning individuals at random to each condition. If each person has the same chance of being assigned to each group, and if we assign enough people to each, the differences among the people would balance out among the groups. *Random assignment* will distribute any initial differences more or less evenly among the groups. Contrast this type of *independent variable* with a second variable these investigators studied.

(2) Aggressiveness of the Observer: A Classification Variable

Aggressive boys have been found to attribute hostile intentions to the actions of others more frequently than less aggressive boys. Courtney and Cohen incorporated the variable of aggressiveness by having classmates rate each boy for aggressiveness. Notice that unlike assignment to the prior-knowledge variable, aggressiveness scores could not be assigned randomly. Rather, participants were *classified* based on judgments of a preexisting characteristic—that is, aggressiveness. Thus, if we find a difference between aggressive and unaggressive boys, we cannot be sure that the difference is not due to something else that might be correlated with aggressiveness.

Now let's look at the results of the study. The participants (randomly assigned and classified as described above) were shown the videotape and asked to "segment" the action by pressing a button whenever one action stopped and another began. These points of segmentation are labeled "breakpoints." Of course, most natural behavior does not have discrete breakpoints. Rather, one activity flows into another. Thus, segmenting the flow of action is not simply marking what already objectively exists; rather, it is an act of cognitive construction and will vary from observer to observer.

(continued)

RESEARCH FOCUS *(continued)*

A dramatic example of segmentation as a cognitive construction lies in the fact that we hear our native language spoken in discrete word segments, although the sound issuing from the speaker's mouth is continuous, as can be demonstrated by visualizing normal speech on the screen of an oscilloscope. It is our knowledge of the rhythms and sounds of our native language, as well as familiarity with the vocabulary and current context, that allows us to segment accurately. You can test this proposition. Rent a film in an unfamiliar foreign language. Then gather a few friends who are equally ignorant of the language and all try to count the number of words spoken in two minutes of dialogue. You will be surprised at the wildly different counts.

Segmenting the action in Courtney and Cohen's videotape is roughly the same kind of cognitive task. But unlike speech, there is no cultural consensus as to where the breakpoints belong. Because the number of breakpoints should increase when an individual is seeking more information, it was expected that identifying breakpoints would be a function of how much information the boys had about the action. Recall, each boy got information from two sources: (1) from what he was told about the boys' friendship (the condition of prior information to which he had been assigned) and (2) from what he assumed (based on his level of aggressiveness). When participants were given information that the boys were enemies, aggressiveness did not predict the amount of segmentation. Everyone "knew," in other words, what was going on and didn't have to look for it. When participants were told the boys were friends, or were told nothing at all, participants who were more aggressive identified more breakpoints than less aggressive ones, suggesting that their perception of ongoing behavior differed from that of less aggressive boys. Aggressiveness relates not only to the motives one attributes to others, but also to the ways in which one organizes one's perception of ongoing events.

Source: M. L. Courtney & R. Cohen. (1996). Behavior segmentation by boys as a function of aggressiveness and prior information. *Child Development, 67,* 1034–1047.

One Face or Two? Sex and Gender

Few differences are more important to adolescents than those associated with being male or female. Yet few are as likely to be misunderstood. Misunderstandings arise from a basic confusion—that of sex with gender. Sex refers to whether one is biologically female or male and is determined at the moment of conception. **Sex differences** are biologically based. Examples include differences in the reproductive systems of males and females, or differences in the average height and body proportions of each sex. Gender refers to the distinctions a culture makes in what it considers masculine or feminine. **Gender differences** are socially determined. For example, most ethnic groups in our culture expect males to be strong and rational and females to be helpful and intuitive. One is *born* male or female, but one is *socialized* to be masculine or feminine.

A quick tour through a high school reveals many differences between students of either sex. It also reveals the difficulty we face in interpreting these differences. Walk into a math class, such as trigonometry or calculus, and you'll most likely see more males than females. Why? Is the male brain better suited to math than the female brain, or are males expected to be better in math and simply live up to that expectation? In other words, is this a sex difference or a gender difference? Continuing the tour, we'd probably find more females than males in an advanced-placement foreign language class. You might ask, "Is it in one's genes to be good at languages?" (a sex difference). Or "Are females encouraged to develop these skills in ways that males are not?" (a gender difference).

Gender stereotypes are the beliefs most people hold concerning what is typical for a male or female. These stereotypes encompass traits, roles, and occupations. For the most part, characteristics perceived as typically masculine are the opposites of those seen

sex differences Biological and physiological differences distinguishing the sexes.

gender differences Culturally determined differences in masculinity and femininity.

gender stereotypes The cultural expectations concerning behaviors that are appropriate for each sex.

Why are so few girls in advanced science and math classes? Are boys naturally better at these subjects, or are they simply behaving according to gender stereotypes?

as feminine (Constantinople, 1973). Males, for example, are thought to be independent, active, and rational. Females, on the other hand, are perceived as dependent, passive, and emotional. As a result of this either/or approach, gender stereotypes can be problematic for adolescents, when being different from the stereotype for their own sex brings them closer to the stereotype for the other. Consider a boy who approaches situations intuitively rather than rationally. Not only is he seen as less masculine than boys who adopt rational approaches; he is also seen as more feminine (Lips, 2005).

On a more positive note, gender roles are more flexible today than in the past, allowing adolescents to express both feminine and masculine qualities. Adolescents of either sex can be sensitive and assertive, gentle and self-reliant. These adolescents are called androgynous ("andro" for male and "gyno" for female). However, fashioning one's own gender role in this way usually occurs in late adolescence because it requires a degree of self-knowledge and confidence beyond the reach of most early adolescents.

Whether based on sex, race, or even age, stereotypes usually reflect differences due to status as well. In our society, males frequently have positions of higher status than females. Behaviors of females and males that are attributed to their gender can often be explained by differences in their status. The masculine stereotype, for instance, includes qualities such as independence, decision-making skill, and risk taking. The confusion of status differences and gender differences becomes clear when we think of reversing the roles typically held by females and males. When status roles are reversed, as in the case of a male secretary and a female boss, the differences attributed to their gender often disappear. Who is more likely to make decisions, and who to be helpful? Or who will likely take risks, and who will be more dependent? Differences between the sexes exist in a social context, and this context will affect our interpretation of them (Lips, 2005).

Social context gives rise to another difference facing adolescents: their cultural backgrounds. Increasing numbers of adolescents in the United States belong to ethnic minorities. All adolescents—those within the majority as well as those in minorities—are affected by increasing cultural diversity.

Faces of Many Colors: Ethnicity

Melissa Herman (2004), a sociologist at Northwestern University, captures the issues raised for many adolescents in our ethnically diverse culture:

> Carlos Petterson (not his real name) was in his ninth-grade English class when he filled out a survey that asked him, among other things, about his race: "Select the major ethnic group that best describes you." This request posed a problem because Carlos's mother is part Filipino and part Mexican, and his father is White. Carlos marked the box to indicate that he was White, thus raising a number of questions: What factors motivate a biracial adolescent's self-definition? How does Carlos differ from other White-Filipino-Mexicans? From "pure" Mexicans, Filipinos, and Whites? (p. 730)

Ethnicity can affect adolescents in many ways. Adolescents who belong to a minority are more aware of the racial or ethnic differences that distinguish them than are those who belong to the majority (Bracey, Bamaca, & Umana-Taylor, 2004). Majority adolescents may even be unaware that they, too, are members of a racial group. Thomas Kochman (1987) found that Whites distinguished each other in terms of ethnicity, but not race, referring to themselves, for example, as Irish or Polish, never as "White."

But what does it mean to belong to an ethnic group? Jean Phinney (1996), a psychologist at California State University, Los Angeles, points to the importance of examining ethnicity with respect to a number of *dimensions* that are critical in defining individuals' ethnicity: their cultural values and attitudes, their sense of belonging to the group, and their experience of being a member of a minority.

Although **culture,** the first dimension of ethnicity, is central to the identity of an ethnic group, there are such large differences in lifestyles and traditions within any group that culture alone is not enough to identify individuals as members of a group. The term *Hispanic,* for instance, includes not only Americans of Mexican descent but also people from more than a dozen South American countries, each with its own distinctive culture. Hispanic carries a different meaning for each of those cultures. What is important is that individuals belonging to the group are seen by others, and by themselves, as a separate group within society for whom their common heritage continues to be a significant part of their lives. Thus ethnicity is more than ancestry; it almost always involves culture, or the socially shared values, beliefs, and norms that determine one's way of life and that are passed on from one generation to the next (Betancourt & Lopez, 1993).

Individuals within an ethnic group differ as well in the degree to which they identify with their group, or in their **ethnic identity,** the second dimension of ethnicity. Ethnic identity itself is multifaceted, including how one labels or identifies oneself, as well as one's sense of belonging to a group and the degree to which one values and participates in one's group (Ashmore, Deaux, & McLaughlin-Volpe, 2004). Furthermore, one's ethnic identity can be seen to change developmentally, from an initial stage in which ethnicity is simply taken for granted, through a period of exploration into the significance of belonging to a group, to a secure sense of oneself as a member of that group (Phinney, 1989, 1993).

culture The values, beliefs, and customs that are shared by a group of people and passed from one generation to the next.

ethnic identity An awareness of belonging to an ethnic group that shapes one's thoughts, feelings, and behavior.

Being a member of an ethnic group typically brings with it the experience of minority status, the third dimension of ethnicity, although not always. For instance, in Can-

On school days, dual-culture adolescents blend in with the mainstream teenage culture of their friends, but with their family, they engage in traditional customs and may even speak a different language.

ada, English-speaking and French-speaking people are both members of dominant groups, yet each is a different ethnic group. At this point, the term *minority* deserves closer attention. It might seem, for example, that members of the majority would always outnumber those of a minority. Yet such is not always the case. Whites are actually in the minority throughout the world, though in the majority in the United States; however, White adolescents can experience minority status if they live in a community or attend a school in which some other ethnic or racial group predominates (Phinney, 1996). In certain areas of the United States, people of one race outnumber those of another yet are not considered part of the majority. In some counties of Mississippi, the ratio of African Americans to Whites is three to one, yet the latter are considered the majority. It could be argued that the majority status of the Whites is determined not by local ratios, but by those for the country as a whole. Yet a look at other countries suggests that qualifiers other than sheer numbers are involved in determining majority status. The British, for example, although vastly outnumbered in India, retained their majority status, as did Whites in South Africa (Simpson & Yinger, 1985).

Minority status has less to do with numbers per se than it does with the distribution of power within a society, being associated, at least for those of color, with lower status and less power, whether in positions of leadership or, even when education is equated, in annual income (Dovidio & Gaertner, 1986; Huston, McLoyd, & Garcia Coll, 1994). Stanley Sue (1991) argues that the very term *minority* connotes the unequal relationships that exist among various groups within a society, and that to fully understand the minority experience, one must understand the ways in which these relationships define patterns of exploitation.

Minority status also signifies, for one reason or another, a failure to be fully assimilated into the dominant culture. Louis Wirth (1945) defines a **minority** as

> a group of people who, because of their physical or cultural characteristics, are singled out from the others in the society in which they live for differential and unequal treatment, and who therefore regard themselves as objects of collective discrimination. The existence of a minority in a society implies the existence of a corresponding dominant group with higher social status and greater privileges. Minority status carries with it the exclusion from full participation in the life of the society. (p. 347)

Minorities can be set apart by ethnic background, religion, nationality, or other defining features. (The In More Depth box gives a personal account of minority socialization.) In fact, Wirth's definition of a minority could also include women, the elderly, those with disabilities, or adolescents themselves.

minority A social group, distinguished by physical or cultural characteristics, that often receives differential treatment.

IN MORE DEPTH

Socializing African American Children

When strangers stop me on the street or at airports, often it is to comment on the essays I write about my family. Those about life in our old home in Brooklyn provide the most response. "It is obvious," a nun in a brown habit said one day, "that yours was a house of joy." I loved the phrase, but it troubled me.

It was not, I started to say to her, always so joyful. In fact, there were times that were painful, as there might be in any family. Some of our dinner-table discussions touched sensitive subjects. For example, our parents often struggled to help us understand and battle racial rejection. It was not always easy for them, proud immigrants in a new land.

One of the heroes of our family in the late 1940s was Dr. Ralph J. Bunche. He was then this nation's highest-ranking Black diplomat. He was also a leading academic. His field at Harvard had been international organization, a subject of special interest to our family. It was at the time of the formation of the United Nations. There must have been a dozen pictures of Dr. Bunche around our home. We owned at least one copy of everything published under his name.

The difficult time came the night of Dr. Bunche's public humiliation. He was denied entry to the Forest Hills Tennis Club, then the scene of the most prestigious matches in the world of tennis. Dr. Bunche's rejection became our own. . . .

The idea that it would reject the hero of our family meant it had rejected each of us. . . .

As one of my three sisters, a tennis player, began to put her troubled thoughts into words, tears welled up in her eyes, and she stopped talking. My mother's eyes met my father's. I could tell they had been discussing this between themselves.

"I want you children to understand what you are seeing here." He pointed across to a side table where the *New York Daily News* lay. The story of Dr. Bunche's rejection was prominently displayed. "I know you feel sorry about Dr. Bunche, but I tell you my prayers tonight are for those men who have humiliated him. . . .

"People who create special rules of exclusiveness think they are showing the rest of us what great status they have achieved. In fact they are telling us the very opposite. . . ."

"The very opposite." My mother repeated my father's last phrase for special emphasis. They often reinforced each other's points by repeating a few of the exact words.

"In fact," my father continued, "when people need racial exclusiveness in their social lives, it is usually to prove to others they have 'arrived.' But that's not how I read such men. I read them as socially insecure. Have you ever noticed that truly confident people walk and work among all with ease? The strong do not need that sort of status; the wealthy but weak do."

"Dr. Bunche," my mother said with a wry smile, "is fortunate he will not have to associate with such people." At last we laughed.

Source: Adapted from R. C. Maynard. (1990, August 5). An example of how Afro-American parents socialize children. *Oakland Tribune.*

Peach Fuzz and Whiskers: From Early Adolescence to Emerging Adulthood

The developmental issues and experiences confronting early adolescents differ markedly from those of late adolescents. Similarly, those of late adolescence differ from the experiences defining emerging adulthood. Early adolescence is ushered in by the onset of puberty and the changes that transform the body of a child into that of an adult. Maturation of the reproductive system and a growth spurt put the adolescent eye to eye and nose to nose with his or her parents. Early adolescents must integrate their changing bodies and new feelings into a new sense of themselves.

By late adolescence, the changes of puberty no longer dominate experience; instead, late adolescents feel a need to discover themselves and achieve mutuality and intimacy in their relationships. The social worlds of early and late adolescents mirror this change. Instead of congregating in circles of same-sex friends, common in early adolescence, late adolescents pair off in intimate couples. In the intellectual realm as well, striking differences distinguish early from late adolescents. Early adolescents, for instance, are just beginning to think abstractly, whereas late adolescents use abstract thought to question not only their own values but also those of the society in which they live.

Finally, with respect to their daily routines, early adolescents are just one step beyond the comfortable routine of grade school, whereas late adolescents are on a path leading to the responsibilities of adult life. For early adolescents, a major psychosocial issue is achieving autonomy, primarily in their relationships with parents; in contrast, late adolescents are facing the need to consolidate the changes that accompany autonomy into a mature personality structure.

We interpret the behavior of others based on our own contextual perceptions. Some may perceive this teen as upset, while others may think he's concentrating.

Significant as these differences are, equally significant differences distinguish late adolescence from the years of emerging adulthood (Arnett, 2000; Roisman, Masten, Coatsworth, & Tellegen, 2004). Jeffrey Arnett (2000) focuses on the years of 18 to 25 as a distinct period in life which he terms emerging adulthood. He distinguishes emerging adults in three ways: by their demographic unpredictability, their opportunity for identity exploration, and their subjective experiences.

Arnett points first to demographic differences distinguishing emerging adulthood from either adolescence or adulthood. Major demographics for adolescents, such as whether they're in school (95%), where and with whom they live (95% with one or both parents), whether they're married (less than 2%) or have a child (less than 10%), are highly predictable. Nearly the same predictability exists for adults over the age of 30, though the trends are reversed, for example, less than 10% are in school and 75% have a child. For 18- to 25-year-olds, however, it's almost impossible to say whether they're in school, where or with whom they might be living, and so on.

The period of emerging adulthood also offers more opportunities for identity exploration than does adolescence, even though identity traditionally has been regarded as a crisis of adolescence. Nonetheless, emerging adults are able to more fully explore life options than are adolescents. Dating, for instance, can be recreational and fun, but "few adolescents expect to remain with their 'high school sweetheart' much beyond high school" (Arnett, 2000). Until the years of emerging adulthood, marriage, and considerations of what would make it work or fail, remains safely in the future. Arnett suggests that the demographic unpredictability of emerging adulthood reflects their opportunities for identity exploration, particularly with respect to intimate relationships, work, and beliefs and values. Support for this comes from findings that age-mates who do perceive themselves to be adult have a stronger sense of their identity than do emerging adults (Nelson & Barry, 2005).

A third way in which emerging adults can be distinguished is in terms of their subjective experience—they do not unambiguously see themselves as adults. In fact, when asked whether they think they're adult, they are likely to say "in some respects yes, in some respects no" (Arnett, 2001). They're clear that they are no longer adolescents, but they are not equally clear that they've reached adulthood. The criteria they use to mark this transition are relatively individualistic, such as being responsible for one's actions, making decisions independently, and being independent financially from their parents (Arnett, 2000; Nelson & Barry, 2005).

That's My Face: Identity

Children experience themselves in relation to their families. Ask them to tell you about themselves, and they will describe their families. They'll tell you what street they live on, who lives at home with them, how many sisters or brothers they have, and what they had for breakfast. Not so with adolescents. The once familiar answers no longer satisfy. They can tell you where they live, and who they live with, but this no longer informs them as to who they are.

Adolescents develop a stable identity by trying out new roles and relationships, such as volunteering in a local soup kitchen.

Erik Erikson identified the central and most pressing question of adolescence as a search for personal identity. Adolescents are aware that they are not the children they once were, but they are equally sure they are not the adults they see around them. So who are they? Answers become organized around the developmental tasks confronting them, tasks that arise as the physical changes of puberty and the changing expectations others hold for them determine the pace of their steps into adulthood.

Puberty gradually transforms the bodies of early adolescents into those of adults. Wide variations in physical development are typical, both within and between individuals, giving puberty a special mystery for the adolescent, who is "the fascinated, charmed, or horrified spectator that watches the developments, or lack of developments, of adolescence" (Tanner, 1972, p. 1). Nonetheless, *coming to terms with one's body* is an important developmental task of adolescence. *Achieving more mature relations with peers* is a second developmental task, and one very much affected by the rate at which adolescents are developing physically. Those who fail to develop at the same pace as their peers can find themselves dropped from their social group. These groups are important since they serve as social laboratories in which adolescents try out adult ways of interacting with others.

One of the obviously adult ways in which individuals interact is through relatively well-defined gender roles. These reflect our culture's view of characteristic male and female behavior. Most adolescents will conform in large measure to these expectations, *achieving a masculine or feminine social role.* Most, too, will tailor their gender roles, taking a tuck here or there, to achieve the best fit. Our culture expects males to be strong, active, assertive, and independent, and females to be weaker, passive, and dependent. Every Tarzan, in other words, needs a Jane. Fortunately for both Tarzan and Jane, as well as the rest of us, these roles have become more relaxed with time.

Adolescence is also the time when most of us redefine the sources of our personal strength; *achieving emotional independence from parents and other adults* is a developmental task confronting adolescents. As adolescents become responsible for more areas of their lives, they experience new personal strengths. Redefining responsibility, however, redefines their relationships with parents. Both parties are likely to greet these changes with mixed feelings. In return for self-reliance, adolescents must trade a comfortable dependence. Parents must in turn trade a final say in things for trust in adolescents' judgment. The process is painful for both; it is difficult to shed familiar roles when new roles are not well defined or fully understood. These four tasks are primarily the concern of early adolescents, just as the next four primarily concern late adolescents.

Adolescents typically are torn between the desire for emotional and financial independence from their parents and the reluctance to give up the comforts of dependence.

Preparing for marriage and family life is a developmental task of late adolescence. Individuals are marrying somewhat later than they did a generation ago, and they are less likely to view marriage as marking their entrance to adulthood, although having a child remains a defining event. Equally important is *being able to support oneself,* although achievement of this developmental task is also delayed for many adolescents because of the increased years of schooling needed to prepare for careers. Late adolescents also are expected to think for themselves, to *develop a set of values and an ethical system to guide their behavior,* another developmental task of late adolescence. Related to this is the developmental task of *achieving socially responsible behavior* as adolescents assume new social roles. Each of these developmental tasks confronts adolescents with the larger task of achieving a sense of themselves. Each is a necessary step into adulthood.

Summary

Who Are Adolescents?

- Although adolescents make up only 14% of the population, they are a visible group, perhaps because they highlight for us some of the ways in which our society is changing.
- Our society is aging. When the parents of today's adolescents were teenagers, the median age of the population was 30.6. The median age is expected to reach 38.5 by 2025.
- Our society is becoming more ethnically diverse. By the year 2020, 45% of youth in the United States will belong to an ethnic minority; many will be multiracial, with one or both of their parents having parents of different ethnic backgrounds.
- Family characteristics are changing; more youth are living in single-parent families and, with this, more are experiencing economic hardship. Approximately 16% live below the poverty line.
- Despite the challenges of change, adolescents tend to have a positive outlook on life; they share many of their parents' values and, as a group, are likely to serve as volunteers in community service projects.
- To be complete, a *definition of adolescence* must consider biological, psychological and sociological changes. All three of these definitions are needed to give a complete view of adolescence.
- The *biological definition* emphasizes the events of puberty that transform the bodies of children into those of sexually and physically mature adults.
- A *psychological definition* distinguishes adolescence in terms of the developmental tasks to be accomplished, each of which relates to the central task of achieving a personal identity.
- A *sociological definition* defines adolescents in terms of their status within society, specifically, as a transitional period between childhood and adulthood.

Perspectives on Adolescence

- The *historical perspective* reveals that our conception of age has changed distinctly over the centuries.

During the Middle Ages, childhood emerged as a distinct age with the development of widespread literacy and the need for schooling. Following the industrial revolution, three social movements contributed to the emergence of adolescence: compulsory education laws, child labor laws, and a separate system of juvenile justice.

- The *lifespan perspective* enables us to see continuities in the issues that arise at different points in life. Developmental issues that arise in adolescence can be traced back to childhood and followed into adulthood. Issues of autonomy and competence, for example, are immensely important to adolescents. Both are also significant issues facing two other age groups: the elderly and toddlers.
- From the *contextual perspective* we see that development is influenced by the daily settings, or contexts, of adolescents' lives—by where they spend their time and who they spend it with. Bronfenbrenner describes these contexts as multiple, overlapping spheres of influence. Activities at the level of the microsystem involve the adolescent in face-to-face interactions with others. Adolescents are affected not only by face-to-face influences, but also by various relations among the microsystems of daily life, or by the mesosystem. A third sphere of influence is the exosystem, or environments in which adolescents are not necessarily present but that can affect their surroundings. The macrosystem consists of the underlying social and political climate that impinges on adolescents' lives in very real ways. Finally, the chronosystem refers to the particular circumstances existing at any point in history within a culture that shape adolescents' experience of the various contexts of their lives.
- The *constructive perspective* assumes that reality is not a given, that one person's reality is not necessarily shared by others. According to the constructive perspective, we each construct our own reality, actively interpreting experiences and reacting to them on the basis of our interpretation.

The Faces of Adolescents

- This text focuses on the influence of *gender* on adolescent development. Few differences are more important to adolescents, from either their perspective or that of their society, than those associated with being male or female. Both sex differences, which are biologically based, and gender differences, which are socially determined, are examined in chapters throughout the text.
- *Ethnicity* is a second theme focusing our study of adolescent development. Today's adolescents are growing up in an ethnically diverse society. The strength of their identification as a member of a particular ethnic group depends on the extent to which they share the cultural values and attitudes of the group, feel they belong to the group, and experience being a member of a minority.
- A third theme is the need to distinguish *early adolescence, late adolescence, and emerging adulthood*. The developmental issues and experiences confronting early adolescents differ markedly from those of late adolescents. Similarly, those of late adolescence differ from the experiences defining emerging adulthood.
- A fourth theme of the text is that of *identity*. Erik Erikson identified the central and most pressing question of adolescence as a search for personal identity. Adolescents are aware that they are not the children they once were, but they are equally sure they are not the adults they see around them. So who are they? Answers become organized around the developmental tasks confronting them, tasks that arise as the physical changes of puberty and the changing expectations others hold for them determine the pace of their steps into adulthood.

Key Terms

gender
ethnicity
early adolescence
late adolescence
emerging adulthood
identity
adolescence
historical perspective
lifespan perspective
contextual perspective
constructive perspective
traditional cultures
developing countries
globalization
puberty
sexual dimorphism
compulsory education laws
child labor laws
juvenile justice
cohort group
microsystem
mesosystem
exosystem
macrosystem
chronosystem
sex differences
gender differences
gender stereotypes
culture
ethinic identity
minority

CHAPTER OUTLINE

CHAPTER 2

Theoretical Foundations of Adolescent Development

CHAPTER OBJECTIVES

- To understand how theories are related to the models that generate them
- To identify the assumptions of the environmental model and distinguish these from those of the organismic model
- To recognize the theoretical assumptions shared by the environmental theories of Havighurst, Skinner and Bandura
- To recognize the theoretical assumptions shared by the organismic theories of Piaget, Kegan, Freud, Horney, Erikson, Chodorow, and Gilligan
- To appreciate the contribution of the contexts in which development takes place

Sandra had to talk to someone, or she'd explode! She tried Janie's number again. Still no answer . . . she couldn't believe he'd done that! Whatever was he thinking? She dialed again. . . . Come on, Janie, pick up! The phone seemed to ring forever, and then her friend answered.

"Janie, listen to this. You know how Harrison and I were working on the lip-sync for the talent show? Yeah, that one. Well, you know how Elena was hanging around after rehearsal, all big eyes and smiles, and, like, talking to him? So you know what Harrison did? He said she could be in the act with us. How could he have done that! Doesn't he know . . . ? I mean, he's the one who told me all the things she'd said about me. I feel so betrayed. Why would he ever do that? He seemed so . . . so sensitive. How could he be so cold!"

"Sandy, slow down. He's a guy, and you know how guys are. They don't think about things like that, I mean, not until we say something, and then it's . . . oh, I'm so sorry. It's a guy thing, believe me. It wasn't cold, it's just that . . . well, they aren't sensitive . . . I mean, not like us. Trust me, he didn't mean anything by it!"

Not to offend any male readers, or support any unwarranted conclusions among female readers, but Janie has just stated a theory concerning gender differences in interpersonal understanding. The field of adolescent development abounds with theories. Some haven't been much better than Janie's. But when they are good, theories help to explain events and make sense of our observations; they also enable us to anticipate related events.

Chapter Overview

The first section of the chapter looks at the functions theories serve and at the models that generate them. Underlying every scientific theory are the beliefs we hold about the world we live in. Some individuals may believe, for instance, that although males and females frequently see things differently, these differences would disappear if children of either sex were raised more similarly. Others may believe that males and females *are* different—it's just in our natures—and that no child rearing will ever change that. These assumptions represent very different beliefs about reality. When beliefs such as these produce a complete model of behavior, they are given a name. As we shall see, the beliefs above illustrate two models of development: the environmental model and the organismic model.

The chapter begins with an examination of these models and then moves to the theories of adolescent development that each has generated. It is important to keep in mind that not every theory focuses on the same aspects of development. For instance, some theories stress the importance of feelings and personality development, whereas others emphasize thought and judgment. Thus a single theory may fail to cover all the things one might want to understand about adolescents. Almost no theory, for example, allows us to chart the development of females as well as males. And although many theories acknowledge the influence of culture on personality development, few have explored its implications for particular ethnic or racial minorities.

The first three theoretical approaches, those of Havighurst, Skinner, and Bandura, can be traced to the environmental model. Each of these approaches stresses the ways in which one's experiences, or the environment, structure development through the process of learning. Piaget and Kegan also treat intellectual development, but their theories derive from the organismic model in that they emphasize the way in which individuals actively structure the experiences to which they are responding.

Continuing on, the next organismic theorists to be considered, Freud, Horney, Erikson, Chodorow, and Gilligan, emphasize the motivational and social contributions to development. And finally, the contributions of the contexts in which development takes place are emphasized by Vygotsky, Rogoff, and Lerner.

Models and Theories

A Model Defined

Models represent the implicit beliefs we all hold about the world we live in. These assumptions can be so fundamental that they go unnoticed, yet they exert powerful influences on the theories they generate. For one thing, assumptions determine which questions appear reasonable and which seem foolish. If a scientist assumes that human behaviors are primarily reactions to events in the environment, then it makes sense to inquire how the events differ that immediately precede different behaviors. If another scientist assumes that behavior reflects goal-directed decisions, then it is reasonable to ask people about their goals and how they make their decisions. Notice that the first scientist—we can use the label "behaviorist"—is likely to observe *what* people do and what's going on around them when they do it. The second—a cognitive psychologist—is likely to ask people *why* they do what they do. In each case, the beliefs that direct scientific investigation are collectively called a **model**.

model A set of assumptions about reality in general and about human nature in particular from which theories proceed.

You might think that only scientists have models of human behavior. Actually, we all do. Do you think behavior is rational and goal-directed, or does it simply reflect past reinforcements? What motivates us? A succession of rewards and punishments? Inner goals? How much are we influenced by our biology? Do hormones and genes shape our interests and drives? Or do our interests and drives reflect acquired tastes and passions?

Not all of us share the same model. Models are easiest to see when the differences between them are extreme. Consider a teenager who is baby-sitting a young child. The child lost a tooth that day and insists on placing it under his pillow. The child's belief system (model) includes tooth fairies. The baby-sitter's does not. What would the baby-sitter think if the child were to run up to her later with money in his hand and explain that he found it under the pillow? The teenager would question her sanity before admitting to anything like the tooth fairy—and with good reason. Scientists and teenagers alike base their theories on assumptions about what is real and what is not, and most adolescents assume that fairies are not real. Although models are useful, they are too general and often too vague to test. Theories, on the other hand, are specific explanations of particular phenomena that can be confirmed or disconfirmed.

A Theory Defined

Mention the word *theory* and many people mentally close up shop and take a walk. The word sounds too abstract to suggest any help with day-to-day problems. Images of bespectacled academics come to mind. Yet each of us comes up with any number of "mini-theories" every day. In its simplest form, a theory offers an explanation by relating something that we don't understand to something else that we do.

How much do our personalities reflect inherited traits, and how much do they reflect environmental influences? Comparisons of the life course of twins have provided important information but no definitive answers about the relative influences of nature and nurture.

Theories reflect the models from which they derive. A look at our example shows us why. A **theory** consists of statements arranged from the very general to the very specific. The most general statements, the assumptions one doesn't question, derive directly from the model. Such an assumption in our example might be that inanimate objects (such as teeth) remain stationary unless moved by some external force. At the next level are **laws.** These state relationships that can be shown to be either true or false. Careful observations inform us of the validity of laws. Laws make it possible to predict specific events. We might predict that a tooth placed under a pillow would be there the next morning unless someone moved it.

All developmental theories have one thing in common: Each is an attempt to explain the constancies and changes in functioning that occur throughout the life course. Rather than embrace all aspects of functioning, developmental theories have limited themselves to particular aspects. Some, for instance, are concerned with personality development, others with social or intellectual development, still others with moral and ethical development. Whatever their focus, each theory looks at the similarities and differences that occur with age and attempts to explain them in terms of their sources or causes (Lerner, 2002).

theory A set of testable statements derived from the axioms of a model.

laws Relationships that are derived from axioms and can be proven to be true or false.

What has readied these athletes to compete in this race? The unfolding of genetically programmed stages of maturation and growth? Or a continuous process of development shaped by their environments?

Questions concerning the source of development have traditionally divided theorists into two camps. The division reflects their position on the **nature–nurture controversy:** Is nature—that is, heredity—primarily responsible for development, or is nurture—that is, the environment—responsible? Developmentalists who look to nurture for explanations emphasize conditions such as the home environment and learning. Those who view nature as organizing developmental variables emphasize the importance of factors such as genetic inheritance and maturation.

A second issue, following from the first, also distinguishes developmental theories. This issue concerns the laws themselves that relate behavior to either source: the **continuity–discontinuity issue.** Can one explain behavior at any, and every, point in the life cycle without formulating new sets of laws? Do the same laws apply to other species as well (continuity)? Or do lawful relationships change with age and across species (discontinuity)? Developmentalists who trace development to environmental sources are likely to see such forces as exerting the same influence independent of age or species. Conversely, those who stress the importance of genetic inheritance and maturation typically assume that different sets of laws are needed for species with different genetic endowments and, within a species, at different points in development due to maturation, with development occurring in discrete stages (Lerner, 2002).

Finally, developmentalists who believe that the same set of laws is sufficient to describe behavior at all points in the life cycle also assume that one can explain complex behavior by reducing it to its simpler components, or **reductionism.** Those who believe that new laws become necessary at different ages hold that new complexities in development emerge that cannot be predicted from earlier forms, or **epigenesis.** Thus, a reductionist explanation for differences in the way adolescents and schoolchildren think might emphasize adolescents' greater knowledge, which enables them to use more efficient strategies when solving problems. An epigenetic explanation would be likely to cite the biological maturation of neural structures that occurs in early adolescence.

Differences in these sets of assumptions characterize two models of behavior: the environmental model and the organismic model. The first considers the environment to be the primary source of behavior, assumes continuity to developmental laws, and

nature–nurture controversy The controversy concerning the primary source of development: nature (heredity) or nurture (environment).

continuity–discontinuity issue Disagreement as to whether the same set of laws is sufficient to explain behavior at all developmental levels and for all species (continuity assumption) or whether lawful relationships change with age and across species (discontinuity assumption).

reductionism Explaining complex behaviors by reducing them to their simpler components.

epigenesis The emergence of new complexities in development that cannot be predicted from, or reduced to, earlier forms.

is reductionist in nature. The second looks to genetic or maturational forces—that is, nature—to explain development, assumes a noncontinuity position, and views development as epigenetic. Each of the theories that derive from a model bear a strong "family resemblance." Even so, you will find in reading through this chapter that the degree to which they reflect the assumptions characterizing the model will vary: Some theories reflect the parent model's assumptions perfectly; others are only a good approximation.

The Environmental Model

The **environmental model** focuses on environmental forces in explaining development. These forces affect behavior in lawful ways; the laws are assumed to apply at all levels of development. The assumption of continuity to behavioral laws underlies a strong reductionist approach in environmental theories. Because everything from silicon chips to bones and brain tissue is made of atoms and molecules, the laws that describe their actions should describe the functioning of humans as well as the workings of a computer. To explain vision, an environmentalist would speak of the amount of light necessary to stimulate receptors in the retina, or of the exchange of sodium and potassium ions across the membrane of a neuron as the impulse is propagated along the neural fiber. Everything from a toddler taking her or his first steps to the virtuosity of a concert cellist playing a Bach fugue is understood as a sequence of simpler reactions, each prompted by the completion of the last and all traceable to an external force. In other words, "There is nothing special about the complex pattern of events we call psychological functioning. In the final analysis these events involve the functioning of the very same atoms and molecules that are involved in the workings of a liver, a kidney, or a shooting star" (Lerner, 2002).

This model reduces psychological phenomena to simpler components that operate, in principle, no differently than those in a machine. For example, in order to get a computer to work, you have to start it. A computer does not start on its own. You have to plug it in, push a button, or whatever. This sets off a chained sequence of events that takes the same form each time it unfolds. As long as the parts bear the same relationship to one another, tripping one will set the next in motion. A computer does only what it was programmed to do. But if you know what software you have, and just what point in the sequence is unfolding, you should be able to predict what it will do next.

Is human behavior as predictable? The environmental model assumes it is—ideally. In actuality, it is difficult, if not impossible, to specify the myriad parts that make up the human machine. Even if one could, must our actions be prompted by events external to ourselves, or is behavior self-initiated? The environmental and organismic models give us different answers (Reese & Overton, 1970).

If the model of the machine is correct, actions are primarily *re*actions to forces external to us. The environment becomes a primary source of our behavior. We, like computers, remain inactive until stimulated to act. The burden for explaining and changing behavior remains with the environment. Is an adolescent disruptive in class? Look for the events in the classroom that cause this behavior. Is this student likely to get the teacher's attention, or that of classmates, only when acting out? Is a teenager anxious in new situations? Have the adolescent make a list of situations, from the most to the least anxiety-producing, then tackle the easiest. Success will make the next situation more approachable. Although it is often difficult to trace behaviors to the events that occasion them, it would be infinitely more difficult if organisms could, at any moment, choose to alter what they were doing just because they felt like it. For those who hold to this model, however, human behavior is, at least in the abstract, predictable.

environmental model A set of assumptions in which the environment is taken to be the primary determinant of psychological development.

TABLE 2.1 Comparison of the Environmental and Organismic Models

Comparison Points	Environmental Model	Organismic Model
The human organism is:	Reactive	Active
Human activity is:	Structured by the environment	Internally organized
Development occurs through:	Behavioral conditioning	Environmental-genetic interactions
Developmental change is:	Continuous and quantitative	Discontinuous and qualitative
Developmental stages are:	Absent	Present
The focus is on:	Observable behaviors	Thoughts, perceptions and feelings

By looking at this table, you can see how the environmental and organismic models differ on each of six comparison points.

Before leaving this model, we will look at how it explains the way we perceive our world. The environmental model holds that knowledge is a direct copy of reality. Copy theory maintains that, rather than interpreting our sensations or in other ways trying to make sense of experience, our sensory systems do this for us. You recognize the letters in this sentence through receptors in the retina that fire in a pattern corresponding to the physical configuration of the letters. In a sense, the retina can be thought of as a film that retains the patterns of light to which it was exposed. Receptors carry the physical pattern of the letters through neural pathways to appropriate centers in the brain. All you need to do is simply keep your eyes open and make sure there's enough light to "expose the film."

For those of you who think you take a more active role in defining your world, read on. The organismic model differs sharply from the environmentalist position.

The Organismic Model: The Constructive Perspective

The **organismic model** provides the framework for the constructive perspective adopted in this text. This model takes the living, biological system as its metaphor for human behavior. It explains human development in terms of variables closely tied to the nature of the organism and governing its growth. Organismic theorists differ sharply from environmentalists, practically point by point, in their views of human nature (Table 2.1 shows these contrasts).

Three points summarize these differences. Organismic theorists view the human organism as active rather than passive. They believe this activity to be internally organized, rather than a reaction to external events. Finally, they understand behavior as the unfolding of genetically programmed processes, which produce discontinuous development, marked by qualitatively different stages. Let's look at each of these assumptions more closely.

organismic model A set of assumptions in which the unfolding of genetically organized processes is taken to be the primary determinant of psychological development.

The Active Organism Organismic theorists point out that environmental events become clear only when we respond to them. It takes an action from us to define the conditions that will then be perceived as events. Noam Chomsky (1957), a psycholinguist at MIT, has pressed this argument effectively (John Dewey made the same argument in 1896). Chomsky argued that many sentences appearing to have a single meaning actually have many. They appear clear because we have *already* assumed a context in which they are unambiguous. Consider the sentence "They are eating apples." Seems clear enough. What are they doing? They are eating apples. Yet, if the sentence is a response to the question "What kind of apples are those?" its meaning changes. There are different kinds of apples. Some are for cooking and others for eating. And what are those? They are eating apples.

Organized Activity Perhaps the description of a simple experiment will illustrate the point best. Individuals participating in the experiment heard a click every 20 seconds for several minutes. With the first click, heart rate, brain-wave activity, sensory receptivity, and electrical conductance of the skin changed. These changes make up the orienting response, a general reaction to novel events. With each recurrence of the click, the orienting response decreased until it barely occurred at all (Sokolov, 1963). When **habituation,** or decreased response, had been pretty well established, the click was stopped, and everyone reacted with a full-scale orienting response. What was the stimulus for their reaction? Could it have been the *absence* of sound? The same silence, however, did not produce a reaction before the procedure began.

The phenomenon of habituation tells us that organisms detect regularities in their surroundings and anticipate them. Events that match, or confirm, their anticipations provoke no further reaction. Those that do not match prompt a reaction. Notice that our definition of a stimulus has changed. The stimulus is no longer an external event. Nor is it simply an internal event. It is a product of both. The stimulus is the match, or mismatch, of input with what is anticipated. As such, the original meaning of stimulus, as a goad or prod to action, is lost (Miller, Galanter, & Pribram, 1960).

Developmental Stages Organismic theorists argue that as we age, we organize experience in different ways than we did during the preceding period of development. Each period is a separate **stage** with its own characteristics. For example, Jean Piaget, a Swiss developmentalist, described several stages in the development of thought, the last of which begins in adolescence. One of the most noticeable ways in which thinking in adolescence differs from that in school-age children is that it is abstract. If you were to ask a school child how an elephant and a snake were alike, for instance, the child would be likely to mention the similarity between an elephant's trunk and a snake's body, focusing on the physical characteristics of each. Adolescents, however, can think of both as members of a general class of things, that of animals, and enumerate all the properties of that class. But general classes such as this exist only in the mind!

A final point before leaving this model concerns the way we know our world. Recall that the environmental model views perception as a copy of reality. The organismic model maintains, predictably enough, just the opposite—that perception is an active, constructive process. In order to perceive the letters that make up this sentence, we scan them to see whether certain features are present. We look for angles or curves, vertical or horizontal lines. Detecting certain of these leads us to "see" one letter or another. Recall the example given in Chapter 1, in which the very same physical configuration of lines can be read as either a *B* or a *13* in one context or another, depending on what the reader expects.

Is perception simply the stimulation of sensory receptors, as copy theory asserts? If so, you should not be able to see the very same lines as either a *B* or a *13*. Organismic theorists argue that context—whether a succession of clicks or a series of numbers—establishes an expectancy that directs the extraction of information. Put a slightly different way, they are saying that we actively "construct" the events to which we respond (Neisser, 1967, 1976).

habituation Decreased responsiveness to a stimulus with repeated exposure to it.

stage A level of development that is assumed to be qualitatively different from the earlier level from which it evolves. Stages are assumed to occur in a fixed sequence and to occur universally within a species.

Is the organismic model better because it offers sophisticated approaches to cognition and perception? Or perhaps the environmental model is more "scientific," because it focuses on behaviors that can be observed and precisely manipulated? Comparisons all too frequently lead to evaluations, and someone usually ends up holding the short end of the theoretical stick. Comparisons can also be misleading. Each model addresses different aspects of human functioning. We need both to begin unraveling the knotty problems of adolescence. The organismic model helps us understand motives and feelings that otherwise would never see the light of day. The environmental model gives us objective and readily testable theories of behavior. Unless we are willing to settle for theories about adolescents who act but don't think and feel, or those who think and feel but can't act, we need the insights each model offers.

But what about the developmental theories generated by these models? Remember, a single model can parent many theories. We will look at several theories for each. Examining more than one theory should help distinguish the assumptions of the model from the particular form they take in a theory. We will consider environmental theories first, then turn to organismic, or constructive, ones. Among the latter, we will first look at theories focusing on intellectual development, then those addressing emotional and motivational aspects of development, and finally those focusing on the social or interpersonal aspects of development.

Environmental Theories

Focus on the Intellectual: Havighurst

Robert Havighurst, an educator from the University of Chicago, stressed the importance of learning in giving shape to development. "One learns to walk, talk, and throw a ball; to hold down a job, to raise children; to retire gracefully. . . . These are all learning tasks. To understand human development, one must understand learning" (Havighurst, 1952, p. 1).

Havighurst maintained that each of us masters a succession of such tasks throughout our lives. These tasks reflect social expectations for more mature behaviors as we age, with maturation frequently setting the pace for what is expected of us. Havighurst called these learning experiences **developmental tasks** and considered the successful mastery of each task to lay the foundation for the next (these tasks are listed in Figure 1.5 on page 15).

Despite the importance he gave to learning, Havighurst recognized that we can master a new skill only when we are physically ready to perform it. He spoke of "the teachable moment." Biological maturation prepares us for certain experiences that will have an optimal impact only if they occur when we are ripe to receive them. The same experiences will have practically no effect at all if they come too early or if the moment is lost by their coming too late.

A second environmental theorist, B. F. Skinner, considered every moment to be teachable.

Explaining the Motivational: Skinner

developmental tasks Age-related norms that reflect social expectations for normal development.

B. F. Skinner's ideas have influenced countless psychologists and educators and infuriated others, both for the same reason: Skinner reduced the nuances and complexities of human behavior to the events that follow it rather than to what might have preceded it.

Radical behaviorist B. F. Skinner (1904–1990) contended that behavior is determined by external forces and can be explained only in terms of what can be actually observed. The subconscious urges described by Sigmund Freud have no place in Skinner's theories.

His approach is a radical departure from the way most people understand their behavior. Most of us think that what we do is a response to inner states, to our feelings and thoughts. Skinner told us our behavior is under the control of external events. He called his approach **radical behaviorism.**

Skinner's first subjects were rats. He constructed a small box with a metal lever protruding from one wall and selected a simple behavior—pressing the lever—for study. Because there was little for an animal to do in such a small space, its explorations soon brought it near the lever. Skinner waited until the animal touched the lever, then dropped a food pellet into a chute that ended in a dish beneath the lever. Each time the rat pressed the lever, a pellet of food (**reinforcement**) dropped into the dish. In no time the rat began to steadily press the lever. Skinner had brought a voluntary behavior—putting a paw on a metal lever and depressing it—under the control of its consequences. By making food contingent on lever pressing, he controlled the frequency with which the rat pressed the lever (Skinner, 1938).

Critics reacted by saying that humans are different from animals or, at the very least, different from rats. Our behavior reflects motives and intentions, not contingencies. Skinner's reply to these objections was that our intentions reflect our reinforcement histories. We can analyze many social interactions in terms of their reinforcing consequences. Sometimes such an analysis seems especially appropriate for problem behaviors in the classroom. Let's look at one such exchange between an adolescent and his teacher. She has just told him, once again, to stop rapping his pencil against his desk while she is presenting material at the board. He responds, "Sure thing, teach'," with a slightly sarcastic edge to his voice. She reacts quickly and sharply, calling out his name so loudly that everyone looks over at him. He casually puts the pencil down on the desk. Has she effectively put an end to this problem behavior? Or has she unwittingly reinforced the very behavior she finds disturbing?

Let's take a closer look at what has just taken place. By calling out his name when she allowed herself to become engaged by his sarcasm, the teacher actually reinforced this student with her attention (he received additional reinforcement in the brief moment following her reaction, when all eyes in the classroom were on him). Attention is a powerful reinforcer, even when, as in this example, it is not what most of us might regard as positive.

Also notice that the student reinforced the teacher. By putting the pencil down when she called out his name (stopping the activity that displeased her), he reinforced her scolding, making it more likely she will scold in the future, thus providing the attention that maintains his irritating behavior! We can analyze many parent–adolescent interactions in the same way. For instance, have you ever noticed that adolescents frequently develop the very behaviors their parents find most objectionable? According to behaviorists such as Skinner, this is no accident. Those are the ones their parents are most likely to notice—and respond to.

Reinforcement is a powerful force in shaping and maintaining behavior. But must we actually do something or actually receive reinforcement in order to learn? Critics of radical behaviorism point out that we frequently know *what* to do before we ever do it. Many actions are novel, yet they unfold in smooth, successful sequences, not in the on-again, off-again manner one would expect if trial and error governed their performance. Language itself is perhaps the most intricate of all human activity, and the most difficult for Skinner to explain. We produce endless numbers of novel sentences each day. Has

radical behaviorism A form of behaviorism that reduces the causes of behavior to contingencies of reinforcement.

reinforcement Any event that when contingent on a behavior increases the probability of that behavior occurring again.

Young adolescents learn new skills by closely watching how other people behave and trying out those new behaviors themselves, either in fact or in their imagination. For social-cognitive theorists, the most important element of learning is observation; for behaviorists, it is actually performing the behavior.

each been shaped through reinforcement? How is radical behaviorism to account for each of these?

Albert Bandura, a psychologist at Stanford University, stresses the social nature of learning; his approach is called social-cognitive theory.

Focus on the Social-Interpersonal: Bandura

Bandura (1986, 2004) would agree that learning accounts for much of our behavior; however, his social-cognitive theory emphasizes the inner, cognitive processes by which individuals interpret their experiences as central to this learning. We needn't be directly reinforced for doing something in order to acquire new forms of behavior. We simply need to observe others engaging in these activities and note what happens to them. In other words, important elements of the learning process for adolescents, indeed for all of us, are the context in which this occurs and the sense we make of what is taking place.

These three elements of the learning situation—context, action, and cognition—exert bidirectional effects in a process known as **reciprocal determinism.** Consider an adolescent who is teased by a classmate for a mistake she's just made, but instead of shooting back a curt remark, she responds with humor, earning the grudging admiration of the other girl. The environmental context (teasing by a classmate) certainly prompted this adolescent's behavior, but by reacting as she did, she effectively changed the environment.

reciprocal determinism The two-way influence between person and environment; not only does the environment influence behavior but behavior changes the environment.

Social-cognitive theory has been put to effective use in the classroom by modifying adolescents' self-efficacy beliefs, in turn affecting their motivation to study and their resulting mastery of the material. Timothy Cleary and Barry Zimmerman (2004), at City University of New York, note that school-based programs are effective when they create self-motivating cycles of learning (Zimmerman, 2000). Students given training in the use of effective study skills can experience successes where previously they had failed, thereby changing their beliefs about their ability to master the material. Their beliefs, in turn, contribute to increased motivation and the ability to become more self-directed in their study habits.

Social-cognitive theorists share with other environmental theorists a belief in the importance of the environment in explaining behavior. For Havighurst, this environment took the form of the social expectations that subtly shape age-appropriate behavior. For Skinner, the environment exerted its effect through the events that immediately follow behavior, or reinforcement. Also shared is the belief that learning is primarily the mechanism of change. Although social-cognitive theorists recognize the importance of many of the same processes as organismic theorists—for example, thoughts and motives—they, just as other environmentalists, assume that developmental changes are continuous. They do not explain change as a succession of stages distinguished by qualitatively different features. Organismic theorists give us a very different view of things.

Organismic Theories: Adolescents Constructing Their Worlds

Focus on the Intellectual: Piaget and Kegan

Jean Piaget Perhaps because Piaget was first interested in biology, he approached human intelligence with questions a biologist might ask if discovering a new organism: How does a creature adapt to its surroundings? What does it do that allows it to survive? How is it changed by the processes that maintain it? For Piaget, intelligence was a means of adapting to one's environment, and only those forms of thought that promoted adaptation survived with increasing age.

Jean Piaget (1896–1980) developed his theory that we actively construct what we know of the world based on four stages of cognitive development.

By the time Piaget completed his doctorate, he had published extensively on mollusks (acquiring an international reputation in this field while still a teenager). After getting his degree in biology, he turned his interest to psychology, but instead of poking for life along the edges of waters, Piaget went to Paris to work with Alfred Binet, standardizing questions for Binet's scales of intelligence. His inquisitive mind guaranteed that he would still poke around for interesting new life forms, but in Paris these took the shape of children's ideas about their world.

Not surprisingly, Piaget viewed intelligence as biologically based. He assumed that the sequential nature of intellectual stages reflects an underlying maturation of the nervous system (Piaget, 1971). This emphasis did not prevent him from giving equal importance to environmental contributions. In fact, a singularly distinctive feature of his theory is the manner in which it accounts for intellectual development through the interaction of environmental and biological forces. Rather than viewing maturation as providing "readymade knowledge" or "preformed structures," Piaget (1971) viewed it as "open[ing] up new possibilities . . . which still have to be actualized by collaboration with the environment" (p. 21).

Piaget regarded intelligence as an adaptive process through which we maintain an equilibrium with our environment. This sequence of stages is presented in Table 2.2. Adaptation takes place through two related processes, assimilation and accommodation. **Assimilation** is the process by which individuals fit new information into their present ways of understanding, as when they act on a new object in a way that is similar to previous actions on other objects. Quite often—but not always—we can understand new experiences in terms of what we already know. And sometimes the actions by which we attempt to gain understanding are modified by the process of gaining it. **Accommodation** is the process by which cognitive structures are altered to fit new experiences.

assimilation Piaget's term for the process by which new events and experiences are adjusted to fit existing cognitive structures.

accommodation Piaget's term for the process by which cognitive structures are altered to fit new events or experiences.

TABLE 2.2 Piaget's Stages of Intellectual Development

Stage	Description
Sensorimotor (birth to 2 years)	Infants' awareness of their world is limited to their senses, and their reactions to general action patterns, such as sucking and grasping, through which they incorporate their experiences. This stage ends with the beginning of symbolic thought.
Preoperational (2 to 7 years)	Children can use symbols such as words and images to think about things, but confuse the way things appear with the way they must be (*intuition*), and may fail to realize that the way things appear to them is not the way they may appear to others (*egocentrism*). When solving problems, they tend to focus on a single aspect of the problem to the exclusion of others (*centration*).
Concrete operational (7 to 11 years)	Thinking becomes more flexible, allowing children to consider several dimensions of things simultaneously, realizing that though an object may look different, it has not necessarily changed (*conservation*). Piaget attributed this flexibility to *mental operations,* actions that children are able to carry out in their heads that can be reversed, or undone, enabling them to consider the same problem from several perspectives.
Formal operational (11 years and on)	Thinking becomes abstract, embracing thought itself. Adolescents can consider things that are only possible, as well as those that presently exist, enabling them to think of themselves in terms of future possibilities as well as the present. Their thinking is also more systematic and logical.

The processes of assimilation and accommodation must be complementary for us to remain in equilibrium with the environment. If assimilation predominates, the organism imposes its own order on the environment, and if accommodation predominates, the converse occurs. Neither one by itself represents the homeostatic state of balance between organism and environment that characterizes adaptation. Thus, with each assimilation, accommodation must occur. Piaget referred to the balance thus achieved as **equilibration:** the process responsible for the growth of thought.

Piaget studied many aspects of cognitive development by watching children and asking them questions about what they were doing. In the matter of moral development, Piaget watched children play marbles, a game common at the time. When he questioned them about the rules of the game, younger and older children answered his questions in different ways. The youngest boys (the players were rarely girls) regarded the rules as absolute and didn't think they could be changed. When asked where the rules came from, they assumed they had always existed in their present form. They didn't realize that rules are important only for the purpose they serve, making it possible to continue with the game when disagreements arise. Older boys knew that rules are a matter of convenience and are worked out by the players. They also knew rules can be changed if all agree (Piaget, 1965).

Piaget found that girls and boys approached rules differently. Girls were more lax, more practical, and willing to break the rules as the need arose. Piaget believed the girls' approach was not as well developed as that of the boys, who had a better sense of the legal function of rules. Because Piaget believed this sense to be critical for moral development, this difference has important implications for our view of the sexes, especially when held by one of the most influential theorists in child development (Piaget, 1965).

equilibration Piaget's term for the balance between assimilation and accommodation that is responsible for the growth of thought.

Piaget is not the only theorist to measure females against a yardstick developed with males (marbles was a boys' game) and find them lacking. Two other giants of personality theory, Freud and Erikson, have done the same. Carol Gilligan (1982), commenting on psychological theorists in general, writes:

> Implicitly adopting the male life as the norm, they have tried to fashion women out of a masculine cloth. It all goes back, of course, to Adam and Eve—a story which shows, among other things, that if you make a woman out of a man, you are bound to get into trouble. In the life cycle, as in the Garden of Eden, the woman has been the deviant. (p. 6)

Robert Kegan Building on the constructive process elaborated by Piaget, Robert Kegan (1982, 1994), a psychologist at Harvard University, argues that the most central human activity is that of "meaning making," of constructing from the moment a reality that makes sense given the balance one has already struck with the world. Such a balance, as represented in Piaget's stages, is the qualitatively different reality the individual achieves at different ages. This reality is shaped by mental structures that give form not only to our ways of thinking, as Piaget discovered, but also to our ways of feeling, our ways of relating to others, and our ways of relating to ourselves. These four dimensions—the cognitive, the affective, the interpersonal, and the intrapersonal—constitute the meaning-making arenas of the "self" (Kegan, personal communication).

Kegan suggests that, at all ages, individuals continuously "parse" experience into that which is "me" and that which is "not me," into "subject" and "object." Development occurs when aspects of the "me" become *differentiated* from the "not me," enabling us to perceive and relate to things that we had failed to see because they had been too much a part of us. Thus growth or development is a process by which those aspects of meaning making that we *cannot* see gradually move to a place where we *can* see them and be in charge of them.

Adolescents develop beyond the self-constructions of childhood when they become able to recognize, or actually see, their needs for what they are as opposed to seeing others through the perspective provided by these needs. With this, they are gradually able to relate more mutually, and less instrumentally. Consider a 12-year-old boy who has difficulty separating his growing need for independence from his perception of his father, whom he sees as domineering and controlling. Because of his inability to see his own struggle with issues of dependence, he sees his father as continually trying to micromanage his life. As a consequence, he finds it difficult to comply with any requests his father may make. As this boy becomes more confident in himself, and sees that he is able to make decisions and function independently, his perception of his father will most likely change as well. For him to relate to his father in a different way, however, he must first be able to see himself differently, to develop an ongoing sense of himself in which he can see his needs for what they are, rather than see himself and his father *through* his needs.

Sigmund Freud (1856–1939), the founder of psychoanalysis, defined five stages of psychosexual development. These particular stages have been subject to much debate, but many theorists have built on his general concept of developmental stages.

Focus on the Motivational: Freud and Horney

Sigmund Freud As a young physician with a private practice in neurology, Sigmund Freud might have been more surprised than anyone at the direction his career would take. Were it not for some of his patients who complained of mysterious ailments, he might have remained an obscure but successful Viennese doctor. The mysterious symptoms were no different from those he saw daily, such as numbness and paralysis from damaged nerves. But the nerves in these patients were unaffected; he found only healthy

TABLE 2.3 Freud's Psychosexual Stages

Stage	Description
Oral (birth to 1½ years)	Infants derive pleasure through activities that stimulate the mouth, e.g. nursing, sucking, biting. Conflict occurs over weaning.
Anal (1½ to 3½ years)	Toddlers derive pleasure through expelling and retaining feces. Conflict occurs over toilet training.
Phallic (3½ to 6 years)	Preschool-age children become interested in their genitals and derive pleasure from their stimulation. Oedipal conflict involves relationships with parents.
Latency (6 to puberty)	Sexual impulses are repressed in school-age children; there is little psychosexual conflict.
Genital (puberty through adulthood)	With the onset of puberty, sexual impulses reemerge; sexual gratification is sought with person(s) other than the parent. Conflict involves the competing demands of various aspects of the personality, e.g., id, ego, superego.

Distinct stages of development unfold as psychic energy (the libido) is expressed through different zones of the body.

neural tissue when he examined them. How could patients suffer neurological symptoms with no physical damage?

Freud eventually solved the mystery, but only by tossing aside current notions about the mind. He asserted that we have an active mental life of which we remain completely unaware, an unconscious that affects our actions in very direct ways. Thoughts, feelings, or problems that are too disturbing to face or that cannot be solved immediately are pushed out of the conscious mind, repressed to the unconscious realm of thought. Although repression momentarily reduces the distress, it does not get rid of the problem. The thoughts and feelings continue to exist and continue to push for expression, escaping in many ways—in dreams, actions, or even physical symptoms, as with Freud's patients. The only requirement limiting their expression is that the person remain unaware of their true meaning, thereby protected from the distress they occasion.

Freud formulated his theory of personality development while treating these unusual symptoms. He believed that they resulted from an inner war between conflicting aspects of the personality. Although Freud first noticed these aspects of the personality in his patients, he believed them to be present in all of us. For Freud, life is a battle, and we are all on the front lines. Two opposing forces, one within us and the other outside, fight for control. Because each is an integral aspect of our personalities, the victory of either one means a sure defeat to the individual. Instead, we must achieve a balance between internal biological instincts and external social constraints. We achieve this balance only with time and at some personal cost. As in any war, there are casualties. True spontaneity may be the first to go. The second loss takes the form of compromise: We learn to make do with lesser delights to avoid the anxiety provoked by indulging our first instincts. There are victories as well. We gain control over instinctual urges that otherwise, he believed, could destroy us and our civilization (Hall, 1999). Freud's stages of personality development are shown in Table 2.3.

Freud traced the source of the conflict to a human drama that he believed played itself out in the family. Freud believed that young boys fall in love with their mothers, the **Oedipal complex,** and girls with their fathers, the **Electra complex.** The resolution to this family triangle lays the foundation, according to Freud, for fundamental differences between the sexes. We shall look first at the Oedipal complex in boys, because Freud framed his theory around the male experience.

Oedipal complex A Freudian concept in which the young boy is sexually attracted to his mother, and the young girl to her father.

Electra complex A Freudian concept in which the young girl is sexually attracted to her father and regards her mother as her rival.

The young boy's feelings for his mother transform his father into a rival. Given the sexual nature of these feelings, the boy fears castration as a fitting punishment. Freud believed this fear (termed **castration anxiety**) motivated repression of the sexual nature of his feelings. In thus yielding to his father, the boy identifies with him and, in the process, takes on the father's values. The resulting personality structure, or **superego,** that emerges from this process is strong, because it reflects the power that the boy sees in his father.

Similarly, Freud assumed that the young girl falls in love with her father, with the mother becoming a sexual rival. The Electra complex, however, revolves around a different set of motives. Instead of anxiety, the girl experiences longing and inferiority because she does not have a penis. Of course these longings (which Freud calls **penis envy**) cannot be satisfied and are finally replaced by a compensatory wish: that her father give her a baby. Freud (1925a) writes, "Her Oedipus complex culminates in a desire, which is long retained, to receive a baby from her father as a gift—to bear him a child" (p. 124). Freud believed that the girl's longings for a penis and a child intermingle in the unconscious and prepare her for her future roles of wife and mother.

Notice that the girl never cleanly resolves the Electra complex; she retains a lingering longing in the unconscious that imbues her personality with its essential feminine features, one of which is a feeling of inferiority. Freud believed that the woman moves from feelings of personal inferiority to contempt for all women. Once she realizes that her lack of a penis is not a personal form of punishment for something she has done, but is shared by all women, "She begins to share the contempt felt by men for a sex which is the lesser in so important a respect" (Freud, 1925a, p. 253).

Freud was ahead of his time in many ways in his acceptance of women. He freely admitted women into his analytic circle and frequently referred patients to women analysts. However, his theory of the feminine personality is uniquely uncomplimentary (Chodorow, 2004). Freud believed females to be masochistic, vain, and jealous. The masochism (deriving pleasure from pain) stems from their frustrated longing for their fathers. The vanity and jealousy he attributed to penis envy. "If she cannot have a penis, she will turn her whole body into an erotic substitute; her feminine identity comes to depend on being sexy, attractive, and adored. Female jealousy is a displaced version of penis envy" (Tavris & Wade, 1984, p. 182).

Finally, Freud believed that the female superego is not as strong as that of males; the implication is that females are less moral. Two things account for their weaker superegos. Females are never as highly motivated as males to resolve Oedipal issues, because they literally do not have as much to lose, and they identify with a weaker figure than do males: The mother is more nurturant, and less threatening and powerful, than the father.

Anna Freud, Sigmund Freud's daughter, extended Freud's theory by focusing on the unique demands that adolescence places on the ego. She contended that the adult sexual drives that emerge with puberty strain the child's organization of the personality and require new and stronger defenses against the incestuous threats that these drives reintroduce. She noted that intellectual developments in adolescence make such defenses possible, namely in the form of *intellectualization,* or the ability to justify one's behavior in highly abstract terms. Even with new defenses, however, adolescents must create additional distance between themselves and their parents. In doing so, they establish social relations with age-mates, with whom expression of sexual drives becomes appropriate (Freud, 1969).

Karen Horney Karen Horney, a contemporary of Freud, objected to his interpretation of the feminine personality. She countered that he had not properly taken into consideration the male-dominated society in which his patients lived. Although women

castration anxiety In Freudian theory, a young boy's fear of being castrated by his father in punishment for the boy's sexual attraction to his mother.

superego The aspect of the personality in Freudian theory that represents the internalized standards and values of society.

penis envy In Freudian theory a girl's envy of, and desire for, a male sex organ.

Karen Horney (1885–1952) was a psychoanalyst who took issue with Freud's views on personality development in women. She believed that culture, as much as biological instincts, is responsible for many of the characteristics of the female personality.

Erik Erikson (1902–1994) built on Freud's theory of psychosexual development and formulated a psychosocial theory of development. According to his theory, people move from one stage to the next in response to social demands.

id The primitive aspect of the personality in Freudian theory, which seeks immediate gratification of biological impulses.

ego The executive aspect of the personality in Freudian theory, which seeks to satisfy impulses in socially acceptable ways.

might want the power and privileges that men have, this is a very different matter from Freud's penis envy. Further, women's economic dependence on men creates a psychological dependence and a need to have men validate their self-worth (Horney, 1967).

Although Karen Horney initially accepted Freud's ideas, she eventually came to question many of them. Most important, she asserted that our personalities take shape through adapting to life situations, not through dealing with primitive instincts. She also viewed the personality as a whole, rather than as compartmentalized into **id, ego,** and superego. She stressed the creative potential present in all of us, and at least the possibility for living lives that are in harmony with our surroundings, whereas Freud maintained that conflict between instinctual forces and societal inhibitions is inevitable (Munroe, 1955).

Horney also viewed the early influence of the family differently than Freud. She traced healthy personality development, which she viewed in terms of the ability to value oneself and to see that one is valued by others, to the child's first experiences of warmth and affection from parents. Conversely, she traced neurosis to the absence of true warmth and affection from parents. Although she considered early experiences to be important, she did not see them as having the determining effect on later personality that Freud did. Thus Horney placed less stress on biological instincts than Freud, giving more emphasis to the impact of culture. Nonetheless, she retained a firm belief that development reflects inner sources of growth (Horney, 1937).

Horney also questioned Freud's assertion that masochism is a central feature of the female personality. Freud maintained that because the Electra complex was never fully resolved in the girl, she retains a frustrated desire for her father, which becomes associated with later sexual pleasure. Horney pointed out that not all women obtain pleasure by sacrificing themselves to the needs of others, whereas some men do (Tavris & Wade, 1984). She further objected that Freud's analysis of the female personality not only ties their social condition to their biology, thereby making it unalterable, but it also suggests that they secretly desire to be in this state. She then reversed Freud's analysis of penis envy and asked why men would fear and envy women, pointing out that the very social conditions that suggest women's inferiority can also be seen as an active attempt by men to keep women in a one-down position (Tavris & Wade, 1984).

Horney mentioned that numbers of her male patients expressed envy and fear concerning pregnancy and childbirth. She suggested that men cope with these feelings by reacting with compensatory emotions. Rather than feeling inferior because they are not able to become pregnant, they feel contempt for women for not having a penis. Rather than fearing women's power to give birth, they feel contempt for their weakness.

Despite the force of Horney's arguments, hers remains a minority opinion. Although other female analysts made similar objections (Miller, 1973, 1976), the baton Freud carried was passed to a successor who also viewed development as unfolding in a single, universal sequence for females and males alike—a sequence that again takes a male perspective.

Focus on the Social: Erikson, Chodorow, and Gilligan

Erik Erikson Theories often reflect the personalities of their originators. Havighurst, who was an educator, saw development as a series of tasks to be learned. Piaget, who was intellectually precocious himself, developed a theory of intelligence. Horney stressed cultural contributions to development, as she reacted to the male bias in her society. Erikson as well developed a theory that reflected a personal issue. In his case the issue was a search for personal identity.

A growing body of research can describe the differences in identity development for these two adolescents due to their gender. Fewer researchers, however, have explored differences in identity development for various racial or ethnic groups.

Erik Erikson's parents separated before he was born. Rather than take the name of his biological father or his stepfather, Erikson named himself after his given name (Erik-son). As a young man, he traveled about Europe, earning a living as an artist and eventually teaching art in a school for young children. The position at the school proved to be a turning point in his life, for the school was established by the Freuds for the children of patients. Erikson studied with Freud's daughter Anna, who was herself a talented analyst. His theory takes off where Freud's ends, at adolescence with a search for oneself. It reflects his own awareness of the need to develop a sense of self.

Erikson built on Freud's analysis of the personality into id, ego, and superego and on his stages of psychosexual development. Yet he differed from Freud in several important respects. Perhaps the most significant is Erikson's emphasis on the healthy personality. Erikson stressed the social functions of the ego that allow individuals to cope successfully. These functions assume central importance in adolescence, as adolescents question who they are and where they are going.

Identity is a central aspect of the healthy personality, reflecting both an inner sense of continuity and sameness over time and an ability to identify with others and share in common goals, to participate in one's culture. Erikson (1963) believed that identity develops as adolescents assume commitments to future occupations, adult sex roles, and personal belief systems. It is no accident that identity assumes importance as individuals step from childhood into adulthood and, with this, into their culture. It is also no accident that identity emerged as a central concern to a young artist in search of himself. The Research Focus "Erikson's Psychohistorical Approach" offers a vivid look at group identity development.

identity The part of one's personality of which one is aware and is able to see as a meaningful and coherent whole.

epigenetic principle Erikson's assumption that an internal ground plan governs the timing or period of ascendence for each new development.

Psychosocial Stages of Development Erikson (1963) believed that new aspects of the person emerge through inner growth, making new types of social encounters possible. As with other stage theorists, he assumed that development occurs in the same set sequence for all, reflecting an internal ground plan in which each stage has its own period of ascendence, a time in which the individual is especially vulnerable to certain influences and insensitive to others. (This assumption is known as Erikson's **epigenetic**

TABLE 2.4 Erikson's Eight Stages: Development Through Life

Stage in Life	Psychosocial Crisis	Challenge to Be Met	Resulting Character Strength
BIRTH TO ADOLESCENCE			
Infancy	Trust versus mistrust	Trusting that others will take care of one	Hope
Toddlerhood	Autonomy versus shame and doubt	Becoming purposeful; doing things oneself	Will
Early childhood	Initiative versus guilt	Exploring and trying out new things	Purpose
Middle childhood	Industry versus inferiority	Mastering skills	Skill
ADOLESCENCE TO OLD AGE			
Adolescence	Identity versus identity confusion	Achieving a sense of oneself	Fidelity
Early adulthood	Intimacy versus isolation	Forming emotionally intimate relationships	Love
Middle adulthood	Generativity versus stagnation	Giving to the next generation	Care
Late adulthood	Integrity versus despair	Accepting one's life as having meaning	Wisdom

principle.) Society challenges us with new demands as we age. We experience these as crises. Each takes a slightly different form and gives each age its unique characteristics. Table 2.4 describes each of Erikson's life stages.

Each of the first four crises equips adolescents to meet the central challenge of achieving an ego identity. *Trust* establishes the confidence in themselves and in others that is needed to begin the task. *Autonomy* gives self-direction and purpose, the ability to follow goals that one sets for oneself rather than those set by others. *Initiative* allows adolescents to explore the options that open up with adolescence, and *industry* allows them to realistically evaluate these options and select the ones they will commit themselves to (Erikson, 1963, 1968).

The establishment of *identity* involves the individual in a succession of commitments to life goals that serve to define the self. The young adult faces the crisis of sharing that self with another—of *intimacy,* first with a mate and then, for most, with children. The crisis of *generativity* in middle adulthood extends the adult's concerns beyond this intimate group to others in the community. Older adults face a final crisis of reviewing their lives and accepting the decisions they have made. Erikson calls this last crisis one of personal *integrity.*

Just as with Freud, Erikson's theory reflects a male bias. Erikson considers the achievement of identity to be the central crisis of adolescence, even though he asserts that a different sequence exists for females. Most females resolve the crisis of intimacy, which Erikson places in early adulthood, *before* they complete identity issues. Their sense of themselves derives more from their relationships than from commitments to work and ideology. Although Erikson notes these differences, he does not change his sequence of life stages; that is, he equates the male experience with development in general (Gilligan, 1982, 2004).

RESEARCH FOCUS

Erikson's Psychohistorical Approach: A Clinician's Notebook from the Dakota Prairies

With Michael Wapner

> When we neared the simple, clean homestead, the little sons were playing the small Indian boy's favorite game, roping a tree stump, while a little girl was lazily sitting on her father's knees, playing with his patient hands. Jim's wife was working in the house. We had brought some additional supplies, knowing that with Indians nothing can be settled in a few hours; our conversation would have to proceed in the slow, thoughtful, shy manner of the hosts. Jim's wife had asked some women relatives to attend our session. From time to time she went to the door to look out over the prairie which rolled away on every side, merging in the distance with the white processions of slow-moving clouds. As we sat and said little, I had time to consider what Jim's place among the living generations of his people might be. (Erikson, 1963, pp. 120–121)

So begins Erikson's description of the conversations that contributed to his understanding of the Sioux's early childhood experiences and their difficulty as adults in finding meaning to life. More generally, these observations led to his understanding of the ways in which one's society influences the course of each person's development.

Erik Erikson developed a unique style of research that combined the tools of clinical analysis with those of fieldwork. His insights into human development reflected the same psychoanalytic training that Freud and others practiced in urban European offices. Erikson took these skills to the rolling plains of the Dakotas, and later to the forested dwellings of the Yurok in the Northwest, and in doing so, opened new vistas in our understanding of human development.

His observations made him keenly aware that human development takes place within a social community. Each community raises its children to participate in the world as adults—but there are as many worlds as there are communities. Children are indulged or controlled, taught to give away or to hoard, and so on, depending on the wisdom of their group—a wisdom that reflects the peace their group has made with the realities of geography and the historical moment. The area in which one lives determines the form life takes, whether in the specifics of what one eats or wears or in abstractions such as notions of goodness and propriety (Coles, 1970).

The Sioux, for instance, value generosity and regard the accumulation of wealth as tantamount to evil. Erikson traces these attitudes to a nomadic life in which they followed the buffalo across the plains. The buffalo existed in great numbers and the Sioux rarely experienced need. As nomads, the Sioux learned to live lightly, without the encumbrances of possessions. Generosity, because it reflected a more basic harmony with their surroundings, was a virtue. Conversely, the Yurok value thrift and a meticulous management of resources. They live in settlements along the Klamath River. Once a year, when the salmon return to breed, they experience the abundance that the Sioux lived with in every season. For the rest of the year, they must cautiously manage that brief harvest to avoid hunger and need.

These particular differences are less important than the common function served by the communal practices of either group. Ritual ways of living provided each with a group identity. It is from this group identity that members of the community derived a sense of their own identity. Erikson arrived at this observation after noting what he referred to as a "cultural pathology" among the present-day Sioux Indians. He traced this problem to their inability to find "fitting images to connect the past with the future" (Erikson, 1963, p. 117). The Sioux's lifestyle had been tied to the buffalo, the provider of meat for food; pelts for clothing and shelter; bones for needles, ornaments, and toys; and even dried droppings for fuel. The destruction of the buffalo herds by White settlers resulted in the destruction of the Sioux's way of life—and of the group identity from which new generations could derive a sense of themselves. Speaking of the present generation of Sioux, Erikson noted that "the majority of them have as little concept of the future as they are beginning to have of the past. This youngest generation, then, finds itself between the impressive dignity of its grandparents, who honestly refuse to believe that the white man is here to stay, and the white man himself, who feels that the Indian persists in being a rather impractical relic of a dead past" (1963, p. 121).

If Erikson's theory is correct, that without "fitting images to connect the past with the future" young people are lost, what are the images that performed this function for you? Is there any single or even small set of recurrent experiences that anchor you in your community and physical environment the way the buffalo anchored the Sioux? Is it possible that society in the United States at the beginning of the twenty-first century has no such single image? Perhaps these images

(continued)

RESEARCH FOCUS *(continued)*

belong to subgroups rather than the culture as a whole. For instance, is the gang for the East Los Angeles gang member in any way analogous to the buffalo for the Sioux? What functions would the gang have to fulfill for its members to qualify as an image? If it is an image in the Eriksonian sense, then what will it take to discourage gang membership in East Los Angeles and similar urban communities?

Sources: R. Coles. (1970). *Erik Erikson: The growth of his work.* Boston: Little, Brown. E. Erikson. (1963). *Childhood and society* (2nd ed.). New York: Norton.

Nancy Chodorow's research challenges Freud's and Erikson's assumptions of a universal developmental sequence. Because boys must define themselves outside their relationship with their mother but girls define themselves within that relationship, the course of identity development is fundamentally different for the two sexes.

Nancy Chodorow Another theorist, also influenced by Freud, gives us a very different view of development. Nancy Chodorow, at UC Berkeley, offers an alternative to the universal developmental sequence charted by Erikson. Chodorow (1978) attributes psychological differences in the makeup of women and men to the social fact that for most children the first intimate relationship is with a woman—their mother. This initial relationship has very different consequences for girls than it does for boys.

Chodorow asserts that infants experience themselves as continuous with the mother. They live within the boundless security of her presence, little caring which smile is theirs or whose hand reaches out to the other, all of it part of the same encircling awareness. Mothers, too, empathically relate to their infants and experience a continuity with them.

> In a society where mothers provide nearly exclusive care and certainly the most meaningful relationship to the infant, the infant develops its sense of self mainly in relation to her. Insofar as the relationship with its mother has continuity, the infant comes to define aspects of its self . . . in relation to internalized representations of aspects of its mother. (Chodorow, 1978, p. 78)

Important to Chodorow are the necessary differences in the way children of either sex develop beyond this point. Girls can continue to define themselves within the context of this first relationship. Mothers, as well, can see their daughters as extensions of themselves. Girls can experience a continuing attachment to the mother while still defining themselves as females. None of this is possible for boys. They must separate themselves from the mother much earlier than girls in order to develop as males. Mothers, too, experience their sons as separate and different from themselves, unlike the way they experience their daughters. Thus, boys embark on a developmental path marked not by attachment but by separation and increasing individuation.

Chodorow argues that because the primary caregiver is the same sex for girls, there is less need for the girl to differentiate herself in terms of ego boundaries. Chodorow brings us to a point made earlier by Freud: The personalities of women are frequently less differentiated than those of men and are more closely tied to their relationships. But she sees this difference as an asset, as a strength rather than a weakness. Girls can experience continuity with others and relate to their feelings. Chodorow points to the heavy costs males pay for their greater individuation. In curtailing their emotional attachment to the mother, they also limit their ability in general to relate empathically to others. Thus, differences in ego boundaries lay a foundation for a greater capacity for empathy in females than in males. In fact, Chodorow sees the capacity for empathy to be a core part of the feminine personality, giving them a sense of connectedness with others (Chodorow, 1978).

IN MORE DEPTH

Self-Descriptions of Two Adolescents

How would you describe yourself to yourself?

Jake: Perfect. That's my conceited side. What do you want—anyway that I choose to describe myself?

If you had to describe the person you are in a way that you yourself would know it was you, what would you say?

Jake: I'd start off with eleven years old. Jake [last name]. I'd have to add that I live in [town], because that is a big part of me, and also that my father is a doctor, because I think that does change me a little bit, and that I don't believe in crime, except for when your name is Heinz; that I think school is boring, because I think that kind of changes your character a little bit. I don't sort of know how to describe myself, because I don't know how to read my personality.

If you had to describe the way you actually would describe yourself, what would you say?

Jake: I like corny jokes. I don't really like to get down to work, but I can do all the stuff in school. Every single problem that I have seen in school I have been able to do, except for ones that take knowledge, and after I do the reading, I have been able to do them, but sometimes I don't want to waste my time on easy homework. And also I'm crazy about sports. I think, unlike a lot of people, that the world still has hope. . . . Most people that I know I like, and I have the good life, pretty much as good as any I have seen, and I am tall for my age.

Amy: You mean my character?

What do you think?

Amy: Well, I don't know. I'd describe myself as, well, what do you mean?

Amy: Well, I'd say that I was someone who likes school and studying, and that's what I want to do with my life. I want to be some kind of a scientist or something, and I want to do things, and I want to help people. And I think that's what kind of person I am, or what kind of person I try to be. And that's probably how I'd describe myself. And I want to do something to help other people.

Why is that?

Amy: Well, because I think that this world has a lot of problems, and I think that everybody should try to help somebody else in some way, and the way I'm choosing is through science.

Source: C. Gilligan. (1982). *In a different voice* (pp. 35–37). Cambridge, MA: Harvard University Press.

Carol Gilligan Carol Gilligan, a psychologist at New York University, notes striking differences in the ways males and females think of themselves. These differences extend to the ways they resolve issues involving others. Gilligan finds that males tend to see themselves as separate from others; females describe themselves in terms of their relationships with others. These themes of separation and connectedness appear over and over again in her writings and her research, whether she is studying morality and choice, descriptions of the self, or interpersonal dynamics (Gilligan, 1982, 2004).

Notice the way two of Gilligan's subjects, an 11-year-old boy and an 11-year-old girl, describe themselves, as shown in the In More Depth box on this page.

Jake describes himself at length. He first identifies himself by his age and name and then his status within his community. We never know what his mother does, but we know that doesn't contribute to his sense of position as does his father's occupation. He then identifies his abilities and interests. He ends with a description of an important

Carol Gilligan, a psychologist at New York University, has focused her research on female development and challenged the definition of developmental stages by Kohlberg and other developmentalists whose theories are based primarily on the experiences of male subjects.

physical characteristic. We get the impression of a distinct personality from this description. Gilligan agrees. Jake has described himself in terms of the things that distinguish him from others. His self-description emphasizes his uniqueness and separateness.

Amy's description of herself is brief. We know only that she enjoys school and wants to be a scientist. Otherwise, she describes herself in terms of her relationships with others. We know nothing about Amy apart from the qualities she believes will allow her to help others. Short, tall, freckled, funny, well-off, or disadvantaged—things that set her apart from others receive little attention. Gilligan stresses that this sense of responsibility for and connectedness to others frequently appears in girls' and women's descriptions of themselves. It is, she notes, a very real difference between most women and men.

We see this difference clearly when Jake and Amy are asked how one should choose when responsibility to oneself and responsibility to others conflict (In More Depth, page 53). Jake believes we are mostly responsible to ourselves. Being independent means taking care of ourselves and making sure that our actions don't hurt others. Jake starts with the assumption that individuals are separate and proceeds with the need for rules to protect each person's autonomy. Thus for Jake, responsibility is not doing certain things.

Amy's answer is much longer than the one she gave in describing herself. She puts her responsibility to others first. Not always, of course; but she differs in an important way from Jake in her view of responsibility. Amy sees responsibility as an action, as a positive response. She assumes a connectedness with others. She talks about people and caring, all on a very personal level, whereas Jake mentions the community and seems to imply a need for rules to regulate the actions of its members.

Amy and Jake have taken different paths through childhood. They are likely to follow different paths through adolescence and into adulthood. Amy experiences herself in terms of her connection with others, Jake through his separateness. Each is also developing different strengths: Amy in interpersonal relations, Jake in functioning autonomously. At this point, the strengths of one are the weaknesses of the other.

Gilligan suggests that because of the difference between females' and males' capacities for empathy, males should experience more problems with relationships and females with individuation. Because human development is charted, to date, in male terms—that is, in terms of increasing separation and individuation—when women have problems with individuation, these are seen as a sign of developmental immaturity. Men's problems with relationships, however, do not evoke a parallel interpretation. Gilligan pointedly notes that "women's failure to separate then becomes by definition a failure to develop" (Gilligan, 1982).

Gilligan points out that science has not been neutral. Our theories reflect "a consistent observational and evaluative bias." We tend to interpret "different" as either better or worse, because we have a tendency to work with a single scale. Because most scales are also standardized in terms of male development, male behavior is taken as the norm and female behavior as a departure from the norm. This approach is perpetuated by the fact that most research is done by males, with many important studies using only males as subjects (Yoder & Kahn, 1993).

Gilligan offers us a challenge: Can we see human behavior from other than this single perspective? She dares us to ask not only why women's feelings "get in the way" of their reasoning when thinking about others (a quality she does not regard as a weakness), but also why men's feelings do not.[1] Instead of asking why more women than men have

[1]Freud's (1925b) observation that females have a lesser sense of justice than males and are more influenced by their feelings received later support by Kohlberg and others in that females' moral judgments were more likely to reflect interpersonal concerns and males' to reflect abstract principles (Kohlberg & Kramer, 1969).

IN MORE DEPTH

Choosing Between Responsibility to Self and Responsibility to Others

When responsibility to oneself and responsibility to others conflict, how should one choose?

Jake: You go about one-fourth to the others and three-fourths to yourself.

Amy: Well, it really depends on the situation. If you have a responsibility with somebody else, then you should keep it to a certain extent, but to the extent that it is really going to hurt you or stop you from doing something that you really, really want, then I think maybe you should put yourself first. But if it is your responsibility to somebody really close to you, you've just got to decide in that situation which is more important, yourself or that person, and like I said, it really depends on what kind of person you are and how you feel about the other person or persons involved.

Why?

Jake: Because the most important thing in your decision should be yourself, don't let yourself be guided totally by other people, but you have to take them into consideration. So, if what you want to do is blow yourself up with an atom bomb, you should maybe blow yourself up with a hand grenade because you are thinking about your neighbors who would die also.

Amy: Well, like some people put themselves and things for themselves before they put other people, and some people really care about other people. Like, I don't think your job is as important as somebody that you really love, like your husband or your parents or a very close friend. Somebody that you really care for—or if it's just your responsibility to your job or somebody that you barely know, then maybe you go first—but if it's somebody that you really love and love as much or even more than you love yourself, you've got to decide what you really love more, that person, or that thing, or yourself.

And how do you do that?

Amy: Well, you've got to think about it, and you've got to think about both sides, and you've got to think which would be better for everybody or better for yourself, which is more important, and which will make everybody happier. Like if the other people can get somebody else to do it, whatever it is, or don't really need you specifically, maybe it's better to do what you want, because the other people will be just fine with somebody else so they'll still be happy, and then you'll be happy too because you'll do what you want.

What does responsibility mean?

Jake: It means pretty much thinking of others when I do something, and like if I want to throw a rock, not throwing it at a window, because I thought of the people who would have to pay for that window, not doing it just for yourself, because you have to live with other people

Amy: That other people are counting on you to do something, and you can't just decide, "Well, I'd rather do this or that."

(continued)

IN MORE DEPTH

Choosing Between Responsibility to Self and Responsibility to Others *(continued)*

and live with your community, and if you do something that hurts them all, a lot of people will end up suffering, and that is sort of the wrong thing to do.

Are there other kinds of responsibility?

Amy: Well, to yourself. If something looks really fun but you might hurt yourself doing it because you don't really know how to do it and your friends say, "Well come on, you can do it, don't worry," if you're really scared to do it, it's your responsibility to yourself that if you think you might hurt yourself, you shouldn't do it, because you have to take care of yourself.

Source: C. Gilligan. (1982). *In a different voice* (pp. 35–37). Cambridge, MA: Harvard University Press.

problems with individuation, we need also to ask why more men have problems with intimacy and relationships. Until we begin to ask and find answers to all of these questions, our psychology of human development will remain incomplete.

Gilligan brings a new awareness to the study of personality. She identifies two unique perspectives on human experience, each more dominant in one sex than the other. The first is individualistic, defining the self in terms of its uniqueness and separateness. Relationships with others are governed by a consideration of individual rights, rules, and the application of an impartial justice. Gilligan finds this approach more characteristic of males. The second perspective reflects a sensitivity to and connectedness with others. The self is defined through interpersonal relationships. Rather than rights and rules governing relationships, a sense of responsibility toward others arising out of one's connectedness with them shapes relationships. An ethic of care—rather than abstract justice—dictates personal responsibility in dealings with others. This second approach is more characteristic of females.

Gilligan's theory has generated considerable interest and debate. Its strength lies in giving us a more complete picture of the human condition, one that gives equal attention to the experiences of adolescent girls and to a characteristically female perspective (Brown & Gilligan, 1992; Spinazzola, Wilson, & Stocking, 2002).

Before leaving Gilligan's approach, let's go back to a point raised earlier when discussing Piaget: the differences he observed between girls' and boys' use of rules. Gilligan cites research by Janet Lever (1976, 1978), which found that boys' games occur in larger groups, are more competitive, and last considerably longer than girls' games. Of special interest is the fact that even if boys quarrel throughout the games, they never let the quarreling disrupt their play. They are always able to settle their disputes through the rules of the game. Girls play in smaller, more intimate groups, usually with a best friend. When disagreements occur among girls, they tend to stop the play.

On the face of it, these findings seem to support Piaget's contention that boys' moral (and social) development outpaces girls'. Gilligan interprets the data differently. She points to different priorities in the play of either sex. The game has first priority for boys, and rules enable them to continue it. With girls, the relationship comes first, and the need for rules to negotiate play signals danger. Girls will end the game in order to preserve the relationship. Is this a less-developed sense of morality? Surely not. But it *is* a very different dynamic, one that has been addressed by only a handful of developmental theorists to date.

The Worlds of Adolescents: A Contextual Perspective

In Chapter 1, we discussed the various overlapping contexts in which development takes place, from the moment-by-moment, face-to-face interactions that make up the "real stuff" of life, to the unseen, yet palpably present social and political climate, experienced in such things as the availability of part-time jobs, whether lawns in one's neighborhood are mown or go to seed, the condition of parks and libraries, and the number of computers at school. As Urie Bronfenbrenner has pointed out, each of these contexts affects us in numerous ways. For them to do so, however, they must be responded to and made sense of. In other words, the events to which adolescents respond do not have meaning until they are interpreted.

Internalizing the Context: Vygotsky and Rogoff

Lev Vygotsky Lev Vygotsky, a Russian psychologist living in the early part of the twentieth century, stressed the ways in which individuals internalize aspects of their surroundings. Vygotsky, like Piaget, believed that individuals acquire knowledge of their world simply in the course of doing whatever they happen to be doing, without having to be formally instructed. But Vygotsky differed from Piaget in an important respect. For Vygotsky (1978), this process is fundamentally social in nature, taking place under the tutelage of another, simply as a natural consequence of working alongside someone who has already discovered a better way of doing things. Vygotsky pointed out that for much of the time, as children and adolescents play or engage in their tasks, they frequently do so in the presence of someone who is older—and more skilled in the activity in which they are engaged. The discoveries of others, what Vygotsky refers to as cultural tools, get passed on to them in this social context, without breaking the flow of the activity or being labeled "learning." Through this process, individuals internalize the cultural wisdom of their society.

Take, as an example, a weekend project of painting a room. Everyone pitches in, the room finally gets painted, and the furniture is moved back into place. Mom, a veteran of many painted rooms, heads over to the window with a razor blade in her hand, handing one to her teenage son on the way. He watches her slide the blade under the dried paint on the pane and does the same, until they have cleaned paint off all the panes. The use of a tool—not the razor blade, but the wisdom that it is easier to scrape paint *off* than it is to put masking tape *on*—has been acquired in a social context, without the need for direct instruction.

Both Piaget and Vygotsky analyze, or view, the course of cognitive development in terms of progressive adaptations to one's environment. But they differ in what they take as the proper unit of analysis (Rogoff, 1990). Piaget takes as this unit the solitary individual, gaining a sense of his or her world through inspecting the objects that make it up. By observing what a person does and says, Piaget "enters" the mind of the individual and examines the processes by which that person grasps hold of her or his reality. Thinking, for Piaget, is a mental activity taking place in the mind of a person as that person adapts to her or his environment. As such, thinking is a *property* of the individual (Rogoff, 1990).

Vygotsky takes as his unit of analysis not the solitary individual, but a social person playing or working alongside others, engaging in activities that are characteristic of the group, whether these are learning the best way to remove paint from window panes or how to program the VCR. By observing people as they acquire the skills of those with whom they live—that is, of their culture—Vygotsky identifies thought in terms of the "tools" that enable the members of the culture to "grasp" things more easily. Thinking, for Vygotsky, develops as a person internalizes these tools through interacting with people who already use them. As such, thinking is a *process,* one that is fundamentally social in nature, and occurs as a result of living within a social group. The "mind" that Piaget observed within the individual (that is, the individual's grasp on reality) exists, for Vygotsky, in the society in which that person lives, in the form of the cultural wisdoms that the child internalizes through his or her interactions with those who are already skilled in their use. Thinking takes the form of the person's internalization of these cultural "tools." It is no accident that Vygotsky (1978) titled the book in which he set forth this theory "Mind *in* Society" (italics added).

Vygotsky believed that the mind of the apprentice learner grasps these cultural wisdoms, just as the hands would grasp tools. He believed, as did Piaget, that this acquired knowledge changes the way the mind apprehends reality, but unlike Piaget, Vygotsky did not regard cultural tools as being forged anew by the individual, through her or his own interaction with the physical world. Instead, he saw these tools as handed down from those who are more skilled to those who are less skilled in their use.

For something to be passed on in this manner, the person must be close enough to reach out for it. Vygotsky termed this closeness the **zone of proximal development.** This zone is the distance separating the person's current performance from what that optimally might be. *Proximal* means "near" or "close to." Thus, in order for people to profit from working alongside those who are more skilled, their own performance must come close to, or approximate, the behavior of others. The zone represents the range of skills that individuals must possess in order to profit from exposure to those who are more skilled. We see this zone illustrated in the example of removing paint from the windows. This boy was able to internalize the cultural wisdom that it's easier to scrape the paint off than to put something else on only because his own behavior was sufficiently close to the behavior he eventually acquired; that is, he was already skilled in using tools such as the one his mother handed him.

Barbara Rogoff Regarding the expertise of a culture as tools to be used by its members has implications for the way one thinks of intellectual development. Barbara Rogoff, a psychologist at Stanford University, speaks of this development as an "apprenticeship" in thinking.

The term **apprenticeship** suggests that development is fundamentally a social process and that thinking, rather than being a private event occurring within a person's head, is an activity that is shared with others. Thinking, in other words, is not so much a process by which we "produce thoughts" as one that guides "practical action" (Rogoff, 1990).

For Rogoff, as for Vygotsky, the unit of analysis is the activity in which the individual is engaged. For Vygotsky, however, this activity is initially only a social activity, taking place outside the person, and must be internalized in order to regulate behavior as thought. Rogoff does not make such a distinction. Rogoff's focus on the *shared* activity as the crucible of development avoids the age-old developmental question of what is on the outside and what is on the inside. Going back to the example of a mother and son painting a room, Rogoff does not regard the adolescent, the mother, or the social context (painting the room) as separable elements, but sees each as a part of the other. Instead of thinking of context as an influence *on* behavior, Rogoff sees behavior as embedded *in* context, taking its particular shape and direction from context. The shared activity (painting a room) is the unit of analysis—not the adolescent, not painting the room, and not the adolescent *and* painting the room.

zone of proximal development Vygotsky's term for the distance separating a novice's performance from what that performance might optimally be; for individuals to profit from working with those who are more skilled, their performance must already approximate that of the other person.

apprenticeship The process by which a child internalizes cultural concepts and skills through association with older members of a group.

These adolescents at basketball camp hope to improve their performance on the basketball court by following the behavior of the professionals.

Rogoff does not need to explain how this knowledge is internalized, that is, to explain how it moves from a social realm outside the individual to a realm of thought that is inside. Such a distinction would suggest a barrier of some kind across which the activity must pass, changing form in the process. Instead, Rogoff sees individuals as appropriating features of an activity in which they are already engaged with another. What they have practiced with the other is not on the outside, nor does it need to be brought inside, or internalized. Says Rogoff (1990), "The 'boundaries' between people who are in communication are already permeated; it is impossible to say . . . 'whose' a collaborative idea is" (p. 195).

The shared activities in which individuals engage are the setting for Rogoff's concept of **guided participation.** This concept extends Vygotsky's concept of the zone of proximal development in which it is the adult who is primarily responsible for structuring the process. In guided participation, both parties, the adolescent and adult alike, work to bridge the distance created by their separate perspectives, by mutually referencing (e.g., building on or referring to) what the other is doing. And they do this in order to further engage the other in the shared activity (Rogoff, 2003). Thus Rogoff focuses more than Vygotsky on the ways in which children and adolescents actively participate in their development. She says, "Children see, structure, and even demand the assistance of those around them in learning how to solve problems of all kinds" (Rogoff, 1990, p. 16). She also places greater emphasis than Vygotsky on the importance of tacit or unspoken forms of communication.

Rogoff points out that an adolescent's strategies for learning his or her culture are the same that one would recommend to any visitor to a foreign culture: Stay close to your guide, watch what the guide does, get involved whenever you can, and pay attention to what the guide may tell or show you. The "guide" complements the individual's activity by adjusting the difficulty of the activity to match the person's abilities, modeling the behavior that is sought while the person is watching, and accommodating his or her own behavior to what the person can grasp.

guided participation Rogoff's term for the shared activity of a novice and one who is more skilled in which both participate to decrease the distance between their respective contributions to the activity.

Rogoff views development as multidirectional. Unlike Piaget, for instance, she does not see development as moving toward a single endpoint, toward a universal set of achievements, such as Piaget's formal thought. Instead, the course of development can take any of a number of forms, depending on the types of skills that are valued in one's culture. These skills, whether they be literacy or goat herding, establish the developmental goals that are local to each culture. Thus, Piaget's developmental endpoint of logical, abstract thought reflects our society's value of scientific reasoning. Formal thought, in other words, represents the "local" goals of Western societies.

The Significance of Context: Protective Versus Risk Factors

Richard Lerner (2003), a psychologist at Tufts University, and his associates point out that development, to be understood, must be studied in the many contexts of daily life, contexts that not only influence individual development, but are themselves changed by that individual's presence. Lerner asserts, in other words, that developmental influences are bidirectional, or reciprocal. Individuals are both influenced by their families, friends, and teachers *and* exert an influence on these very same contexts. Additionally, Lerner, just as Bronfenbrenner, analyzes the many features of one's environment in terms of overlapping spheres of influence, simultaneously operating at the biological and physical, psychological, and sociocultural levels. Lerner suggests that in order to know what research questions to ask, or even to fully understand the implications of our findings, we must study children and adolescents in real life settings, in their families, neighborhoods, and classrooms. This approach, known as **developmental contextualism,** makes it possible to integrate developmental research with policies and programs designed to meet the practical needs of youth and their families.

Lerner raises a warning call to our society, pointing out that increasing numbers of children and adolescents, currently more than 20%, are growing up in poverty. Although poverty in itself does not necessarily place adolescents at risk for developmental problems, it is associated with other **risk factors** that do, such as deteriorating neighborhoods, inadequately funded schools, neighborhood gangs, unemployment, lack of health insurance, and crime, to mention a few. The list goes on, of course (Crockett, 2003).

The focus of much of the research in the past has been on risk factors such as these and on the problems that attend them. Recently, more research has studied positive youth development and **protective factors** that protect adolescents from potential missteps (see Chapter 13). These can include factors at the level of the individual, family, and community (Lerner, Anderson, Balsano, Dowling, & Bobek, 2003).

Emily Werner (1989) and her colleagues conducted a 30-year longitudinal study of all infants born in a single year on the island of Kauai, some 698 infants in all. The majority of these children grew up in stable homes with supportive relationships; 10%, however, were identified as "high risk" children because of the presence of multiple risk factors, such as congenital problems, poverty, uneducated parents, family strife, alcoholism, or mental illness. Despite the many strikes against them, fully a third of these high-risk children grew up to become competent adults who "loved well, worked well and played well."

One of the protective factors consistently noted in the lives of these individuals, illustrating the influence of context at the psychological level, was the establishment of a close emotional bond with at least one other person who took care of them, someone who regarded them as special and wonderful. Resilient individuals also received considerable emotional support from outside their families. This support could come from teachers, classmates, or a church group, or it might take the form of extracurricular activities such as working on the school newspaper or playing in the school band (Werner, 1989).

developmental contextualism The position that development must be studied in real life settings, thereby facilitating the integration of research with applied policies and programs.

risk factors Conditions present in individuals, families, communities, or society that place adolescents at risk for developmental problems.

protective factors Conditions present in individuals, families, communities, or society that promote healthy development.

Constitutional factors such as **temperament,** the underlying predispositions contributing to an individual's activity level, emotionality, and sociability, illustrate the influence of context at the biological level (Goldsmith et al., 1987; Stams, Juffer, & van Jzendoorn, 2002). Such constitutional differences can be assumed to serve as protective factors. Individuals who are easygoing, affectionate, active, and even-tempered are likely to prompt positive responses from others. These individuals, in a sense, establish their own supportive contexts, making friends at school and in the neighborhood, frequently making school a home away from home, a retreat from an otherwise chaotic life.

Supportive contexts, whether given or created, give the sense that life is manageable and meaningful. The ability to effectively cope, with the help of one's friends, provides a sense of mastery as well as feelings of hopefulness. As adults, Werner (1989) found these resilient individuals' lives to be characterized by determination, competence, a supportive relationship with at least one other person, and a strong religious faith.

Development Within a Personal Context: The Lifespan

A final context in which development must be understood is the context of one's own life. The accomplishments of one stage in life, in other words, become the unfinished business of the next. For instance, adolescents who achieve a sense of themselves, by resolving identity issues central to adolescence, find themselves in a position to share that self with others, bringing them face-to-face with the issues of intimacy that are considered central to early adulthood. Similarly, adolescents who have successfully redefined their relationships with parents, so that they no longer are taken simply "as kids" but are appreciated as adults, must then find their place *as* adults within the communities they enter.

Daniel Levinson (1978) has proposed, based on data collected through interviews with adult men, that development progresses through a series of partially overlapping stages, separated by transitional periods, during which the tasks of the earlier era are completed and those of the new one are initiated. Stages are distinguished from transition periods in terms of fundamental differences in the work to be accomplished in each. At bottom, the tasks to be accomplished in any stage are to make the choices that will reshape one's life and to then live in such a way as to maximize the quality of that life. The tasks of transitional periods, by contrast, are to question and reevaluate the structure one has created. As we might expect, given the interlocking nature of the developmental tasks that define adjacent ages, considerable continuity exists from one stage to the next, despite differences in the issues faced in each.

temperament The underlying predispositions contributing to an individual's activity level, emotionality, and sociability.

Summary

Models and Theories

- *Models* reflect basic assumptions about the nature of reality. Models, although too general to test, are useful because they generate theories.
- *Theories* consist of statements arranged from very general ones, derived from the assumptions of the model on which they are based, to specific, testable statements. The latter are specific explanations of phenomena that can be confirmed or disconfirmed.
- Developmental theories differ in the emphasis they give to *heredity (nature)* and the *environment (nurture)* in influencing the course of development.

Two Models of Human Behavior

- The *environmental model* views behavior as a *re*action to events in the environment. Behavior becomes linked to these events through respondent and operant conditioning. These laws of learning describe development in terms of quantitative changes.

- The *organismic model* assumes that the behavior is internally organized rather than structured by environmental events. Behavior is seen as an unfolding of developmental stages, each of which is qualitatively different from the last.

Environmental Theories

- *Robert Havighurst* stressed the importance of learning in giving shape to development. He traced development across a succession of developmental tasks that reflect social expectations for more mature behavior with age.
- *B. F. Skinner* assumed that most behavior is learned, coming under the control of the events that follow it (*reinforcers*), rather than being controlled by preceding motives or intentions.
- *Albert Bandura's* social-cognitive theory emphasizes the importance of inner processes such as attention and memory for learning. Bandura assumes that most human learning occurs through observing others rather than through direct conditioning.

Organismic Theories

- *Jean Piaget* viewed intelligence as biologically based. He assumed that knowledge, rather than being a simple copy of reality, is an active construction of what we know of the world. He also assumed that our experiences are organized in qualitatively different stages with age.
- *Robert Kegan* assumes that the most central human activity is meaning making, or constructing a reality that corresponds to our sense of self in relation to events and other people. Development is the cumulative process of differentiating our sense of "me" from "not me."
- *Sigmund Freud* formulated his theory of personality development around the tensions developing when children fall in love with their opposite-sex parent, thus creating a rival of the same-sex parent. Anna Freud focused on the demands placed on the ego by the adult sexual drives that emerge in adolescence.
- *Karen Horney* placed less stress on biological instincts than Freud; she assumed that our personalities take shape through adapting to life situations, not through dealing with primitive instincts. In particular, Horney reinterpreted Freud's analysis of the feminine personality as a reflection of living in a male-dominated society and of women's economic dependence on men.
- *Erik Erikson* assumed that society challenges us with new demands as we age and that we experience these as psychosocial crises. Each crisis takes a slightly different form and gives each stage its unique characteristics. Achievement of a personal identity is the central crisis of adolescence; this involves adolescents in a set of commitments to life goals that give definition to the self.
- *Nancy Chodorow* attributes gender differences to the social fact that for almost all children the first intimate relationship is with a female—the mother. Girls can continue to define themselves within the context of this first relationship, but boys must separate themselves in order to develop as males. As a consequence, girls' development is characterized by attachment, and boys' by separation and individuation.
- *Carol Gilligan* notes how differences in the ways individuals of either sex define themselves extend to the ways they resolve issues involving others.

Contextual Theories

- *Lev Vygotsky* assumed that intellectual development is fundamentally social in nature, taking place under the tutelage of others, occurring as a natural consequence of working alongside someone who has already discovered a better way of doing things. Learning is thought to occur within a zone of proximal development, which refers to the distance separating the person's current performance from what that optimally might be.
- *Barbara Rogoff* views intellectual development as occurring through a process of guided participation, in which the learner shares with an adult an activity in which both participate to decrease the distance between their respective contributions to the activity. Rogoff also sees development as multidirectional, depending on the goals and values of the particular culture.
- *Richard Lerner's* developmental contextualism emphasizes the bidirectional nature of the contexts influencing development. These contexts not only influence an individual's development but also are changed by that individual's presence.
- *Daniel Levinson's* lifespan approach to development suggests a number of distinct developmental stages in adulthood, separated by transitional periods during which the tasks of the earlier era are completed and those of the new one are initiated.

Key Terms

- behaviorist
- cognitive psychologist
- model
- theory
- laws
- nature–nurture controversy
- continuity–discontinuity issue
- reductionism
- epigenesis
- environmental model
- organismic model
- habituation
- stage
- developmental tasks
- radical behaviorism
- reinforcement
- reciprocal determinism
- assimilation
- accommodation
- equilibration
- Oedipal complex
- Electra complex
- castration anxiety
- superego
- penis envy
- id
- ego
- identity
- epigenetic principle
- zone of proximal development
- apprenticeship
- guided participation
- developmental contextualism
- risk factors
- protective factors
- temperament

CHAPTER OUTLINE

CHAPTER 3

The Biological and Physical Changes of Adolescence

Puberty, Health, and Well-Being

CHAPTER OBJECTIVES

- To understand the role of hormones in initiating the stages of puberty and the feedback system regulating these
- To look at the biological and physical changes that take place during puberty
- To consider the psychological changes that accompany puberty and the social implications of pubertal changes
- To know what factors contribute to health in adolescents and what might be done to improve the well-being of all adolescents

She checked herself in the mirror again. Maybe she'd wear the new shirt. Or maybe she'd put the bag it came in over her head, and go to school that way. Glasses . . . braces . . . and two more pimples! Wonder what Helen of Troy had looked like at 13? She had probably been cute—and short. This face wouldn't get a rowboat off the beach. And she was taller than everyone in her class—including the teacher. Being different was lonely at times. Sometimes she felt left out altogether.

Feeling left out and being rushed into changes too quickly are common for adolescents. Although both of these things happen to all teenagers, the process of change is faster for some than for others. In the space of a few years, adolescents exchange the bodies of children for those of adults—complete with a full set of emotions and fancy accessories. But none of the equipment is road-tested as yet. And for most adolescents, it seems someone else must have the owner's manual.

Chapter Overview

This chapter maps the journey into maturity. The first stop takes us deep within the body, to the headquarters of an elaborate communications network, the endocrine system. This network of glands and hormones plays a significant role in regulating the changes of puberty. A finely tuned feedback system triggers the onset of puberty and then shuts it down, much as a thermostat signals a furnace to click on and off once the temperature reaches a preset level. This biological thermostat regulates delicate changes within the body that transform immature sexual organs into those capable of sexual reproduction. The endocrine system is also responsible for everything from a remarkable growth in height to the nose becoming disproportionately large for one's face. (Although it stays this way only briefly, it can leave a lasting dread of what surprises the body might bring next.)

The second stop checks out the remarkable *physical* changes that take place in height, weight, and body contours. Puberty involves a surge of growth that brings adolescents eye to eye and nose to nose with their parents. Adolescents add inches in a single year at the peak of their growth. Sex differences become noticeable with changing body proportions and gains in weight; girls add more subcutaneous fat than boys do, and boys add more muscle mass than girls. Not all adolescents grow the same amount, or at the same rate. Nor do they start at the same age; some will begin years ahead of others. And to the confusion of all, different parts of the body mature at different rates. Yet trends exist, and we will review them.

Many factors affect the rate at which growth proceeds. Conditions as diverse as diet, amount of exercise, psychological stress, and even altitude can affect the rate of growth during puberty. And of course one's particular genetic inheritance plays a part as well. The growth spurt ends in sexual dimorphism, the characteristic physical differences between sexually mature females and males. We will explore these differences before moving to a discussion of the secular trend, a trend toward earlier and faster development that has occurred over the past several centuries.

Changes as significant as those of puberty can have far-reaching psychological and social effects, and these effects are discussed in the third part of the chapter. Puberty brings with it a heightened emotionality, along with changes not only in adolescents' experience of themselves, but also in their relationships with their parents. As one might expect, these relationships are among the first to be affected.

Pubertal changes themselves may not be as important as when they take place for a particular individual. Staying the same when all one's friends are changing can be every bit as stressful as experiencing the changes oneself. The timing of puberty is important, along with its end results. Early and late maturers face different advantages and different challenges.

The physical changes of puberty prompt adolescents to take a new look at themselves. Some like what they see and others are not so sure. We will examine changes in body image during adolescence before moving to a consideration of adolescents' health and well-being. Adolescents stride into adulthood at the peak of fitness and health. Most give little thought to health issues or concerns, yet all are developing habits that shortly will begin to affect their health as adults as well. We will look at issues vital to the well-being of all adolescents: nutrition, exercise, maintaining proper weight, and obtaining health care, and will consider what could be done to improve the well-being of all adolescents.

Throughout the chapter we will pay particular attention to gender differences as we look at the ways in which puberty transforms the bodies of girls and boys into those of physically mature females and males. We will also note ethnic differences in the timing of pubertal changes or their implications. Puberty ushers in identity issues, as will be apparent as we move from one section to the next of this chapter. However, since pubertal changes typically take place in early adolescence, little mention will be made of late adolescence or early adulthood.

The Endocrine System

Not all of the changes of puberty, such as those of the endocrine system, can be seen. But it is important to understand these in order to better understand the physical changes they bring about—and adolescents' reactions to these. And so, we'll start from the inside out, with the endocrine system.

The **endocrine system** consists of glands within the body that produce hormones and structures in the central nervous system that regulate their activity. It is part of a larger feedback system that controls the timing of puberty. The production of **hormones,** chemical messengers that travel through the bloodstream, first increases during middle childhood. A dramatic rise in sex hormones (androgens in males and estrogens in females) and in the hormones that govern their release occurs in early adolescence. The action of these hormones is part of a complex chain of events that triggers the onset of puberty (Fechner, 2003). Figure 3.1 shows the major glands of the endocrine system and the hormones each one secretes.

Hormonal Activity

Because of the complexity of the hormones themselves and the changes that accompany their production, hormonal action is difficult to study. As hormone production increases, for instance, the sensitivity of the tissues they stimulate also changes. These changes differ for different types of tissues. Tissues that form the male reproductive organs are most sensitive to **androgens,** the general class of male sex hormones. Important among these is **testosterone,** which is associated with numerous changes in males such as development of the genitals, skeletal growth, and the appearance of facial hair. Similarly, tissues forming female organs are most sensitive to **estrogens,** the female sex hormones. Among these, **estradiol** contributes to changes such as breast development, the distribution of body fat, and, in conjunction with **progesterone,** regulation of the menstrual cycle.

The chemical composition of male and female sex hormones is similar, allowing the body to convert one hormone into another as needed. Thus progesterone, which plays an important role in the female menstrual cycle, forms the basis for androgen, which in turn can be converted into estrogen. Individual differences from one adolescent to the next also complicate the study of hormonal action. Adding to the complexity, the production of hormones changes with the time of day and day of the month, as well as with stress, diet, weight, altitude, exercise, and medications (Ellis, 2004; Snowden & Ziegler, 2000).

The effectiveness of hormones depends on many things besides the sensitivity of different tissues to their action. Also important are the levels at which hormones circulate through the blood and whether they exist in bound or unbound form. Hormones are molecules that act by attaching themselves to receptor sites on target tissues. Bound hormones have other molecules attached to them and are not free to act on their targets. Levels of concentration in the blood of molecules that might normally attach to the sex hormones have been found to decrease at puberty. At puberty, these molecules also change in ways that affect their ability to bond, thereby freeing the sex hormones (Bedecarras et al., 1998).

Puberty: A Two-Step Process

Although puberty is commonly thought of in terms of the physical changes that occur in adolescence, in reality puberty occurs in several steps, the first of which actually begins in childhood. This initial phase of puberty, or **adrenarche,** begins quite early, at

endrocrine system The system of the body that includes the glands that produce hormones and those parts of the nervous system that activate, inhibit, and control hormone production.

hormones Chemical messengers that are secreted directly into the bloodstream and are regulated by the endocrine system.

androgens Male sex hormones.

testosterone A sex hormone, present in higher levels in males than in females.

estrogens Female sex hormones.

estradiol A sex hormone that is present in higher levels in females than males and contributes to breast development, distribution of body fat, and regulation of the menstrual cycle.

progesterone A sex hormone that is present in higher levels in females than in males and contributes to regulation of the menstrual cycle.

adrenarche The initial phase of puberty that involves activity of the adrenal androgens.

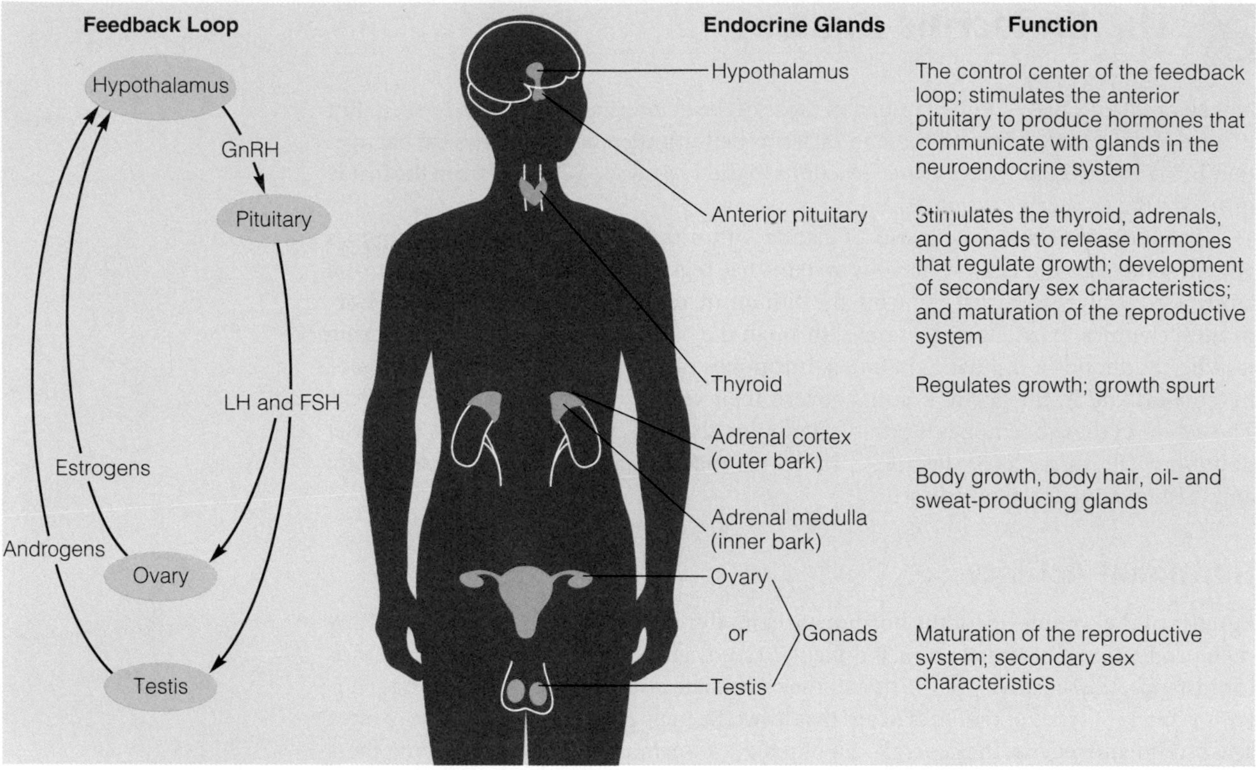

FIGURE 3.1
The Major Endocrine Glands Involved in Puberty and Their Functions. *The feedback loop shows the path taken by hormones that regulate pubertal change; the glands producing these hormones appear within the body, together with a description of their general functions.*

6 to 8 years of age. The second phase, **gonadarche,** which ushers in adolescence, begins at about 9 or 10 in girls and approximately a year later in boys. We'll look first at adrenarche.

Pre-puberty: Adrenarche The adrenal glands, which are located right above the kidneys, increase their production of androgens starting at ages 6 to 8 in children of both sexes. Levels of **adrenal androgens** continue to rise through adolescence until they peak at about 20. The adrenal androgens are involved in a number of pubertal changes, such as skeletal growth, the growth of pubic and underarm hair, oil and sweat glands, and the external genitals in males. They have also been found to affect daily moods in preadolescent girls (Archibald, Graber, & Brooks-Gunn, 2003). However, relatively little research has examined these early hormonal influences on behavior (Susman, Dorn, & Schiefelbein, 2003).

Puberty: Gonadarche The timing of the second phase of puberty, gonadarche, is intimately connected to centers within the brain tucked beneath the cortex (the "gray matter"), a few inches behind the bridge of the nose. The most important of these centers is the hypothalamus. The **hypothalamus** has sometimes been called the body's master clock, because it serves as a control center for biological rhythms, including the ones of puberty. The pituitary, an endocrine gland, hangs from the hypothalamus by a slender stalk (the infundibulum). The pituitary has two lobes, or sections. The one closer to the nose is the anterior (front) lobe. The one farther is the posterior (back) lobe.

gonadarche The second stage of puberty that is regulated by the neuroendocrine system.

adrenal androgens Hormones produced by the adrenal glands and that initiate the initial stage of puberty.

hypothalamus A center within the brain that regulates hormonal activity and regulatory activities such as eating, drinking, and body temperature.

The hypothalamus is actually very small, just one three-hundredths of the brain's total size. Yet it is involved in many aspects of bodily functioning and plays a central role in regulating the events of puberty. Most of what we know about the hypothalamus comes from experiments with laboratory rats. For example, if the blood supply from the hypothalamus to the pituitary is cut off, a rat's reproductive organs soon begin to wither and the animal becomes sterile (Restak, 1984). But what is this important substance carried in the blood?

Research has shown that the hypothalamus secretes a hormone called **gonadotropin-releasing hormone (GnRH),** which tells the **anterior pituitary** to manufacture gonadotropic hormones, which act directly on the gonads. The **gonads** are the sex glands—the ovaries in females and the testes in males. Two gonadotropic hormones—**luteinizing hormone (LH)** and **follicle-stimulating hormone (FSH)**—stimulate the gonads to produce their own sex hormones, estrogens in females and androgens in males. The whole system acts sort of like a row of dominoes. Knocking the first one over trips the second, which affects the third, and so on. In the laboratory rats, when the blood supply from the hypothalamus failed to reach the anterior pituitary, the anterior pituitary stopped producing the hormones that stimulate the gonads. When the gonads were no longer stimulated, they shut down and withered, reverting to an earlier state (Restak, 1984).

The hypothalamus functions like a clock by measuring out its signals in rhythmic pulses. A single pulse of GnRH normally reaches the anterior pituitary each hour. The timing of these pulses is critical. If the pulses decrease to one every several hours or even increase, the mechanism breaks down and the anterior pituitary fails to release its gonadotropins into the bloodstream; the gonads will not develop (Frohman, Cameron, & Wise, 1999).

Both LH and FSH circulate through the bloodstream in low levels during childhood. Levels of each increase prior to puberty, starting at about age 8 or 9 in girls. By the beginning of puberty, pulses occur more frequently during sleeping than waking hours, especially for LH. Figure 3.2 illustrates the marked difference in pre-pubertal and pubertal LH release, with the sleep-associated release occurring only during puberty. By the end of puberty and throughout adulthood, LH is again released evenly over waking and sleep cycles (Archibald, Graber, & Brooks-Gunn, 2003).

A Feedback System The level at which hormones circulate in the bloodstream is controlled by a delicate feedback system involving the hypothalamus, the anterior pituitary, and the gonads, as shown in Figure 3.1. A feedback system sends information from one point in a sequence back to an earlier point, thereby regulating later activity. A **gonadostat,** much like the thermostat controlling the heat in your home, is located in the hypothalamus. Instead of sensing temperature, it senses the presence of circulating hormones. When the levels drop too low, the hypothalamus signals the anterior pituitary to increase production of gonadotropic hormones, which in turn stimulate the gonads to produce more sex hormones. As levels of sex hormones increase, the hypothalamus decreases its signals to the anterior pituitary.

During childhood, the gonadostat is set at a low level. This makes the feedback system especially sensitive to circulating hormones. Even small amounts prompt the hypothalamus to cut back its signals to the pituitary. This low set-point keeps the pre-pubertal level of circulating hormones low. Late in the pre-pubertal period, the hypothalamic gonadostat is reset, allowing the levels of circulating hormones to increase (Fechner, 2003). Genetic factors have been found to contribute significantly to the activation of this feedback system (Eaves et al., 2004). This feedback system is sensitive to more than circulating hormones. Alcohol has been found to interfere with the secretion

gonadotropin-releasing hormone (GnRH) A hormone released by the hypothalamus and involved in regulating the timing of pubertal events.

anterior pituitary A center within the brain that produces hormones that act on the gonads.

gonads The sex glands; the ovaries in females and the testes in males.

luteinizing hormone (LH) A gonadotropic hormone produced by the anterior pituitary that acts on the gonads.

follicle-stimulating hormone (FSH) A gonadotropic hormone produced by the anterior pituitary that acts on the gonads.

gonadostat Cells within the hypothalamus that are sensitive to the level of circulating hormones and are part of the feedback system regulating the timing of puberty.

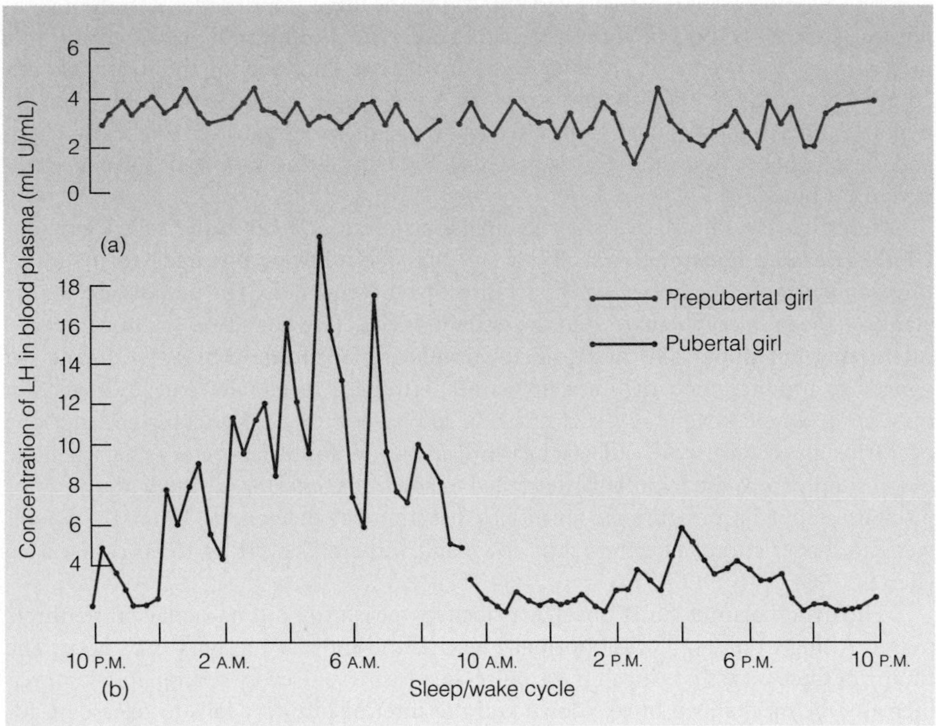

FIGURE 3.2 Release of LH During Waking and Sleep Cycles in (a) a Pre-pubertal Girl and (b) a Pubertal Girl. *Sleep is important in adolescence, especially for the activity of many hormones. This graph shows that LH, a hormone that stimulates the sex glands to produce hormones that are responsible for many of the changes of puberty, is released primarily during sleep in adolescent girls; during waking hours, only small amounts of LH are released, no greater than in childhood (blue line).*
Source: Adapted from M. P. Warren (1983). Physical and biological aspects of puberty. In J. Brooks-Gunn & A. C. Petersen (Eds.), *Girls at puberty: Biological and psychosocial perspectives.* New York: Plenum Press.

of reproductive hormones (Dees, Dissen, Hiney, Lara, & Ojeda, 2000; Hiller-Sturmhofel & Bartke, 1998). Even moderate drinking in early adolescence, if engaged in on a regular basis, has the potential to affect pubertal development in girls. Alcohol not only can affect the secretion of hypothalamic and pituitary hormones but also can interfere with control mechanisms within the ovaries that help to regulate reproductive functioning (Dees, Srivastava, & Hiney, 2001). These findings are especially important in the light of research showing that early maturing girls are more likely to have friends who drink and to engage in drinking themselves than are late maturing girls (Dick, Rose, Pulkkinen, & Kaprio, 2001).

The Physical Changes of Puberty

Puberty brings about the physical differences that distinguish females and males. Differences in the reproductive system itself, such as growth of the ovaries in females and the testes in males, constitute **primary sex characteristics.** Other changes, such as the growth of pubic hair, the development of breasts in females and facial hair in males, represent **secondary sex characteristics.** Not all of these changes occur at once, of course, and not all are viewed as equally important by adolescents. The changes that occasion most fascination, such as menstruation in girls or facial hair in boys, are not usually the first to occur, although the timing of these changes varies considerably (Archibald, Graber, & Brooks-Gunn, 2003).

The sequence of changes varies less than their timing. One adolescent can be almost fully matured before another has begun to develop, yet each will experience the events of puberty in roughly the same order.

primary sex characteristics Sex differences in the reproductive system that develop during puberty.

secondary sex characteristics Differences between females and males in body structure and appearance, other than differences in the reproductive system; include differences in skeletal structure, hair distribution, and skin texture.

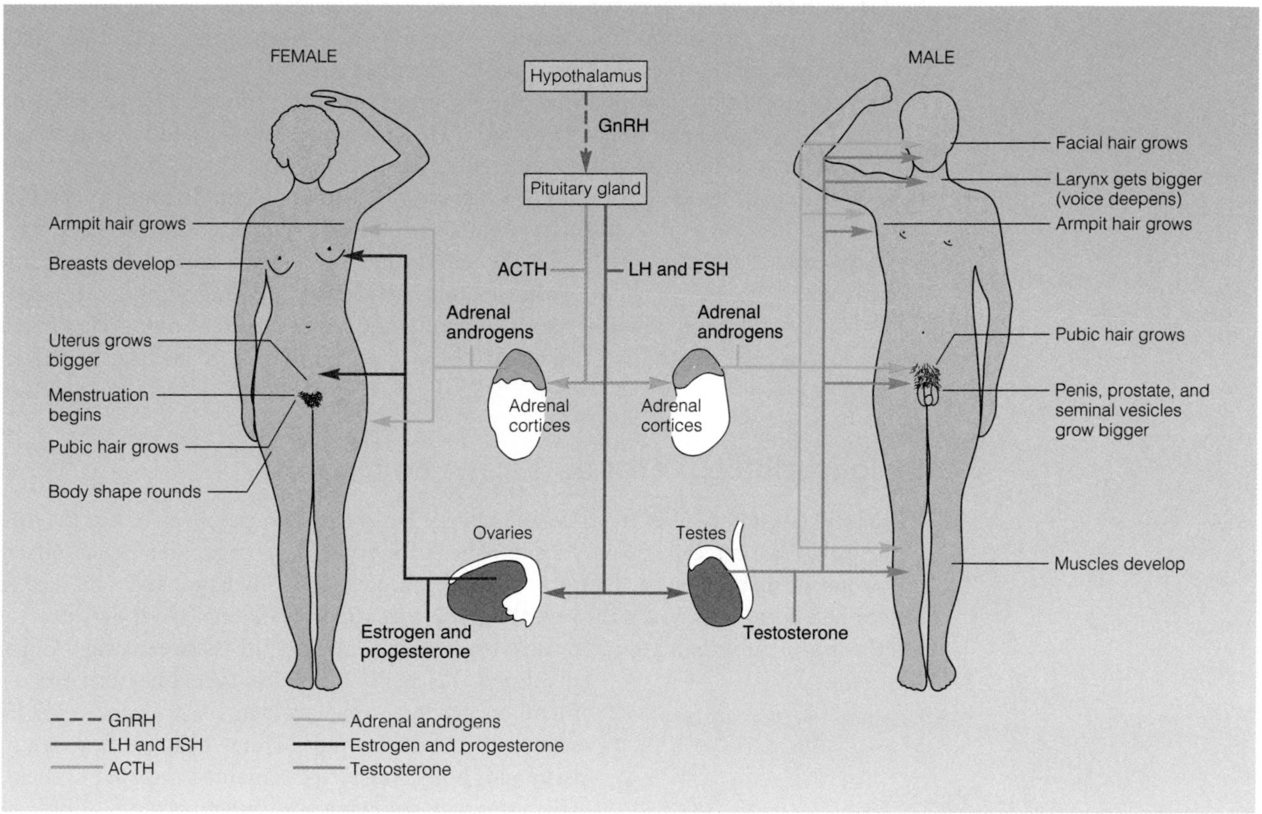

FIGURE 3.3
Effects of Hormones on Physical Development and Sexual Maturation at Puberty.

The changes of puberty are easiest to follow if we chart them separately for each sex (Figure 3.3). Girls are generally a year or two ahead of boys (Archibald, Graber, & Brooks-Gunn, 2003). We will start with them first, as nature has done. An adolescent named Ana will serve as our model.

Recollections of an Adolescent Girl

Ana reports that the first change she noticed was in her breasts. She was in the fifth grade at the time, not quite 11 years old. It was such a small change that she almost didn't notice it at first. A slight mound had appeared just below each nipple. Sometime later the skin around the nipple darkened slightly. She couldn't see any difference when she was dressed, but by the time school let out for the summer, she felt a bit self-conscious in a bathing suit.

Ana remembers the day she discovered a few wisps of pubic hair. It seemed as if they had appeared overnight. Actually, they had been growing for quite some time, but she hadn't noticed because they were unpigmented and very soft. Other changes were occurring within Ana that she would never see. Her uterus and ovaries were enlarging and developing as the level of hormones circulating through her bloodstream increased.

She didn't notice anything else until the sixth grade. By then it became obvious how much faster she was growing, compared to before. By winter vacation, most of her fall back-to-school clothes were too short, and she was taller than most of the boys in her class. She spent a lot of time that vacation shopping for clothes. By the end of the sixth grade, she had grown several inches since the previous year.

Just before spring vacation, when she was in the seventh grade and 12 years old, Ana had her first menstrual period. She had known for a while that it could happen at any time. A number of her classmates had begun menstruating this year, as had one or two the year before. She knew girls in the ninth grade who had not begun to menstruate. Her mother told her that a girl could start as early as 10 or as late as 16.

She stopped growing as quickly as she had started—a relief, because she'd started to identify with the giants in children's stories. She had also begun using an underarm deodorant and was shaving under her arms. Actually, she remembered thinking she looked pretty mature. Her figure had begun to fill out, and no one asked her age at PG-13 movies.

Recollections of an Adolescent Boy

Victor will talk about his experiences of puberty. He, too, is just as typical for boys as Ana is for girls. Victor recalls being very impatient for something to happen. With mixed emotions, he first noticed a change in his scrotum. It was slightly larger and a bit darker than it had been. This was in the seventh grade, just after he had turned 12. Very shortly after, wisps of pubic hair appeared at the base of his penis. Despite these early signs of his manhood, his penis remained the same size. He remembers having some problems with acne once he started the seventh grade. Other changes had begun within his body, but Victor remained unaware of them. His testes were growing and secreting more androgen than before, and his seminal vesicles and prostate were developing. Maturation of the testes would be necessary for the ejaculation of seminal fluid, the wet dreams he had heard so much about.

Hormones contribute to more than the physical changes of puberty. Exuberant, inexperienced, and self-centered thinking can lead to risk-taking behavior. This boy knows his behavior is risky, but he does not seem to understand that he could be seriously hurt.

By the end of the seventh grade, he had started to grow. It had begun slowly at first, but during the eighth grade, he grew 3 inches in a single year. His parents complained they couldn't keep him in clothes: As soon as they bought new ones, he outgrew them. During the eighth grade he noticed, too, that his penis had started to grow longer. What a relief. He remembers dreading gym class; he couldn't face the showers. A few of the guys in there looked as mature as his father. Of course, others still looked like kids.

Victor recalls continuing to grow a lot in the ninth grade. By then he was 14 and his voice was starting to change. He experienced his first ejaculation at about this time, too. He had the sexiest dream with it. His pubic hair was now thick and curly, and he had started to get some axillary (underarm) hair. He was still growing but says he started to slow down a bit after the ninth grade. He still didn't have any hair on his face. He was 15 before he noticed a few hairs growing in over his upper lip. His mom called it peach fuzz. He didn't have a real beard until he was 16. By then he also had a fair amount of hair on his body. Victor says he didn't actually stop growing until his early twenties. He also developed more hair on his chest, back, and stomach all through his late teens.

The typical sequence of these events appears in Figure 3.4, along with their age ranges. Ana and Victor are typical adolescents. However, other adolescents can pass through these changes at different ages, or even in different sequences, and still be just as normal. You can see that for some events, such as menstruation in girls or body growth in boys, some adolescents can be as much as six years ahead of others and each will be within a range considered normal for development. With differences like these, the exception is almost the norm.

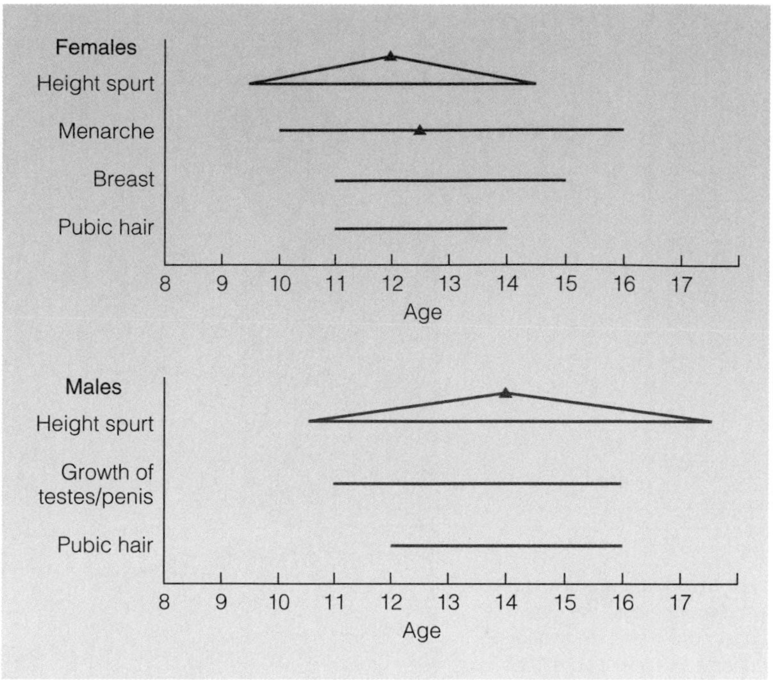

FIGURE 3.4
Sequence of Pubertal Changes in Females and Males. *Pubertal changes in females start with breast budding and pubic hair, followed by the height spurt, then menarche (average ages marked with triangles); changes in males start with growth of the testes, followed by pubic hair, then growth of the penis and the height spurt.*
Source: Adapted from A. B. Archibald, J. A. Graber, & J. Brooks-Gunn. (2003). Pubertal processes and physiological growth in adolescence. In G. R. Adams & M. D. Berzonsky (Eds.), *Blackwell handbook of adolescence* (pp. 24–47). Malden, MA: Blackwell.

The Growth Spurt

Females Growth is regulated by the growth hormone (secreted by the anterior pituitary) and the sex hormones (secreted by the gonads). The growth hormone affects the timing and amount of growth mostly by serving as a "gate crasher" for amino acids, the body's building blocks, helping them cross cell membranes and promoting cell multiplication. This results in a dramatic spurt of growth. The growth hormone also affects changes in the bones during puberty. Early in adolescence, bones begin to grow rapidly in size; this growth is followed, in mid-adolescence, by an increase in the mineralization, or hardening, of the bones. Approximately a third of the minerals eventually deposited in bones accumulates in a relatively brief period (3 to 4 years) following the onset of puberty, a fact which can only underscore the importance of nutrition and exercise in early and mid-adolescence (Susman, Dorn, & Schiefelbein, 2003).

Girls experience a period of rapid growth in height starting at about age 11. The **growth spurt** usually lasts a little over two and a half years. For some girls it can be as brief as one and a half years, and for others it can last up to four years. Girls gain about 8 to 10 inches in height from the start of the growth spurt until they have finished growing. The most rapid growth occurs in the year before and the year after menarche, the beginning of the menstrual cycle (Susman, Dorn, & Schiefelbein, 2003).

Body proportions begin to change even earlier. About one and a half years before the growth spurt, girls' legs start to grow faster than their bodies, giving them a long, leggy look. Most of the early gain in height is due to a lengthening of the legs. The shoulders also widen before the actual growth spurt. Somewhat later, during puberty itself, the hips widen. These growth patterns give young adolescent girls a characteristic look: relatively long legs, slender bodies, wide shoulders, and narrow hips—our present standard of beauty.

Males The growth spurt can begin anywhere from age 10½ to age 16 in boys. Boys grow for a longer time than girls, reaching their peak rate in growth two years later than girls reach theirs (Susman, Dorn, & Schiefelbein, 2003). The average height of boys prior to the height spurt is 58 inches. They add another 12 or 13 inches during the growth spurt. Most of this increase is due to a lengthening of the trunk, because the legs began to grow earlier. Again, it's important to note that adequate diet and exercise need to

growth spurt A period of rapid growth that often occurs during puberty.

Even though these adolescents are the same age, the girls appear older since they begin puberty a year or two earlier than boys.

be present before puberty begins in order for these to optimally affect growth (Cheng et al., 1999).

Striking sex differences begin to appear in muscle mass and body fat. By the time males reach adulthood, they will have one and a half times more muscle mass than females, and females will have twice as much body fat, as can be seen in Figure 3.5 (Fechner, 2003). In addition to obvious differences in muscle mass, males also develop larger hearts and lungs; they have higher systolic blood pressure, can carry more oxygen in their blood, and can dispose of the chemical by-products of exercise more efficiently than females. They also have more red blood cells. These differences, though genuine sex differences, can reflect differences as well in activity levels between females and males that become more pronounced during adolescence. The most obvious change, however, is in the shape of the body itself: In males, the shoulders widen relative to the hips, whereas the opposite is true for females (Susman, Dorn, & Schiefelbein, 2003).

The Reproductive System

ovaries Structures within the female reproductive system flanking the uterus that house the immature eggs and produce female sex hormones.

ovum (plural **ova**) The female sex cell, also called the egg; the male equivalent is sperm.

uterus A muscular enclosure at the top of the vagina that holds the fetus during pregnancy.

vagina The muscular tube in females leading from the labia at its opening to the uterus.

Females Beginning at about the age of 9 to 10 in European American girls, and a year earlier in African American girls, the **ovaries,** which flank either side of the uterus, grow in size and increase their production of female sex hormones (Susman, Dorn, & Schiefelbein, 2003). These hormones, in conjunction with FSH and LH, stimulate the development and release of a mature **ovum,** or egg, in a monthly cycle. The uterus, ovaries, and vagina also increase in size. The length of the **uterus** doubles, and the **vagina** grows to its adult length of 4 to 6 inches, becoming more flexible and developing a thick lining. Many girls mistakenly think of the vagina as a hollow tube leading to an even larger space inside. This misunderstanding can cause some teenage girls to be fearful of losing tampons in some vast, unknown space within. Figure 3.6 shows that the walls of

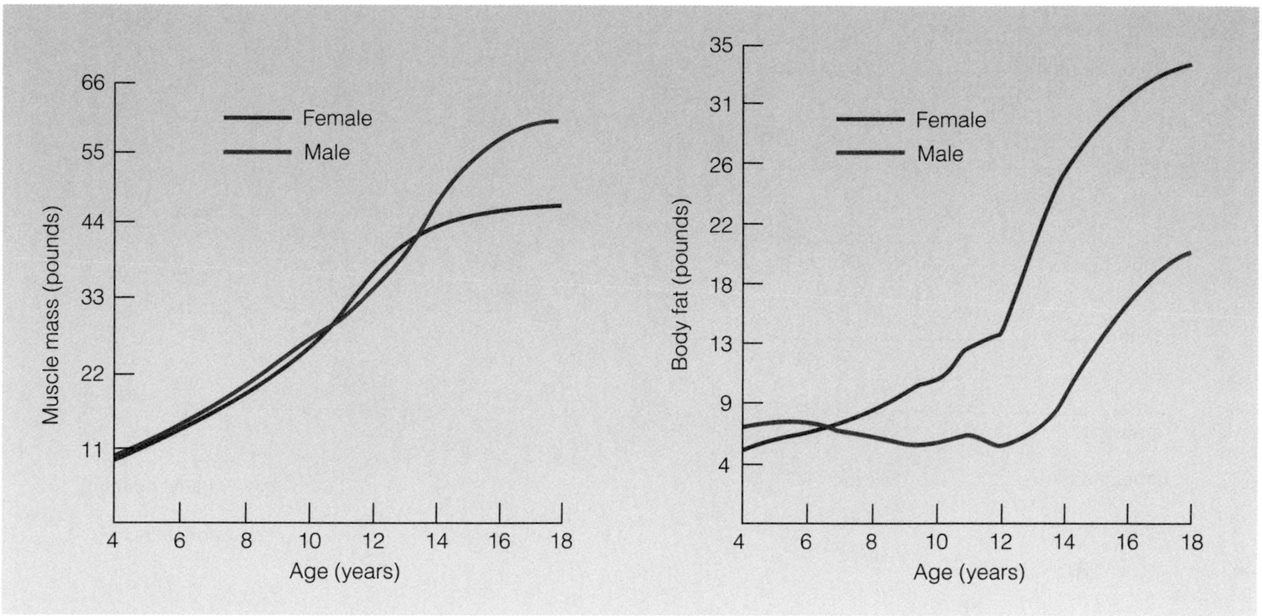

FIGURE 3.5
Development of Muscle Mass and Body Fat for Females and Males. *A dramatic increase in muscle mass accompanies the height spurt in males, starting at age 14 (graph on left). An increase in body fat begins in late childhood in females, prior to the height spurt (graph on right).*
Source: Adapted from D. B. Cheek. (1974). Body composition, hormones, nutrition, and adolescent growth. In M. M. Grumbach, G. D. Grave, & F. E. Mayer (Eds.), *Control of the onset of puberty*. New York: Wiley.

the uterus lie against each other and that the vagina is closed off at the inner end by a tight, muscular gate, the **cervix.**

The opening to the vagina is partially covered by a fold of skin called the **hymen,** sometimes referred to as the "cherry." This delicate membrane is frequently torn or stretched during childhood. Activities ranging from bicycle riding to using tampons can stretch the hymen. Folklore holds that first intercourse ruptures the hymen and that an intact hymen is a sign of virginity. However, relatively few females today survive their active childhoods with the hymen intact.

The **clitoris,** not the vagina, is the primary source of sexual stimulation. The clitoris is similar to the penis, in that both have a glans, a shaft, and a prepuce. The **glans** is supplied by an extensive network of nerve endings, making it the most sensitive part of the clitoris. Hidden beneath the skin and connected to the glans is the **shaft.** Numerous blood vessels, which develop during puberty, feed into the shaft. During arousal, these become engorged with blood, causing the clitoris to become erect. A thin covering of skin, the **prepuce,** covers the glans.

Males The **testes** begin to develop at around 11 years of age (Figure 3.7). The same hormones that stimulate the ovaries to develop and produce female sex hormones stimulate the testes to develop and produce male sex hormones. These, in combination with FSH, stimulate the testes to produce **sperm,** which can be found in the urine of boys by about the age of 14 (Fechner, 2003; Kulin, 1991b).

The testes themselves are about the same size, but the left testis frequently appears larger, perhaps because it hangs a bit lower than the right. The scrotal sac protects the testes from harm. One might argue that they would be even safer if tucked securely

cervix The opening to the uterus.

hymen A fold of skin partially covering the opening to the vagina.

clitoris That part of the external genitals in females that is the primary source of sexual stimulation.

glans The part of the clitoris or penis that is most sensitive to stimulation.

shaft The part of the clitoris or penis that becomes erect during sexual stimulation.

prepuce A thin skin covering the glans of the clitoris or penis.

testes Structures within the male reproductive system contained in the scrotum that produce sperm and male sex hormones.

sperm The male sex cell; the female equivalent is the ovum.

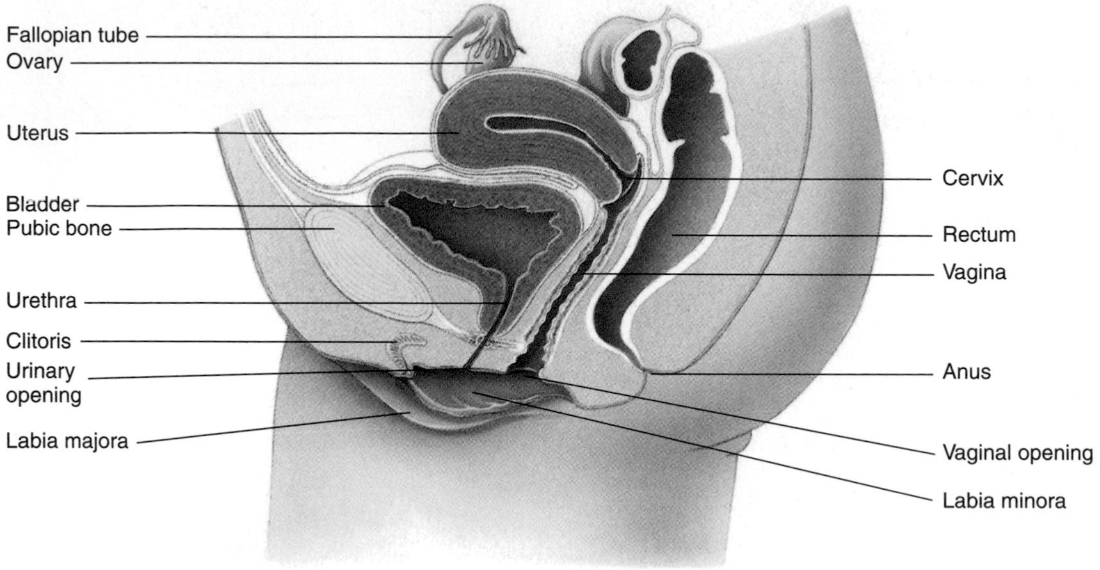

FIGURE 3.6

Female Reproductive System. *Source:* P. M. Insel & W. T. Roth. (2000). *Core concepts in health* (8th ed., 2000 Update). Mountain View, CA: Mayfield. Reproduced with permission of The McGraw-Hill Companies.

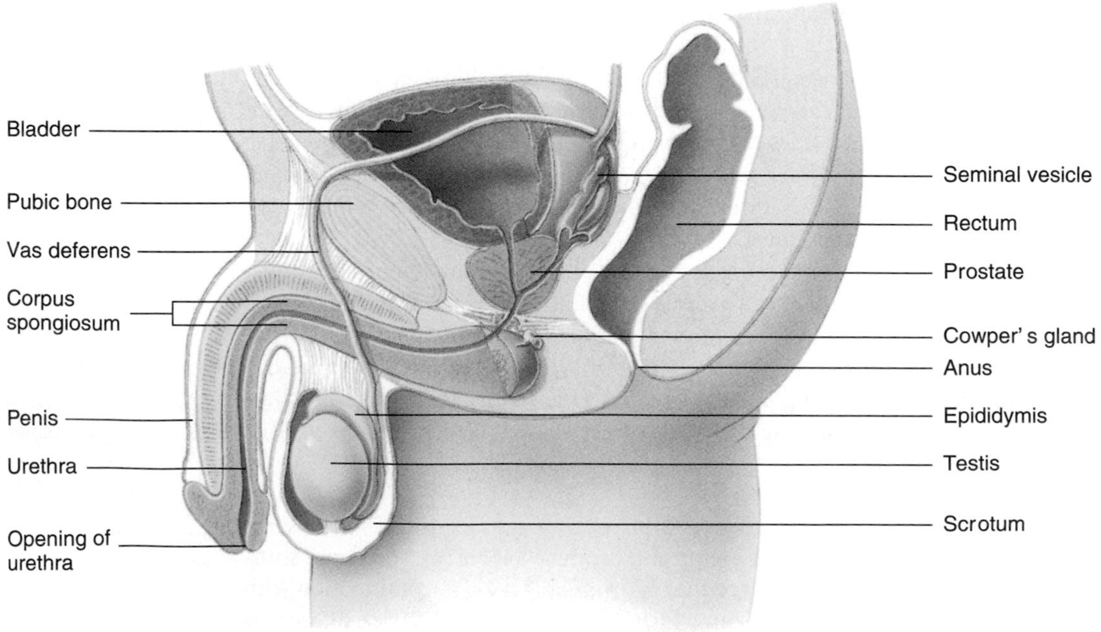

FIGURE 3.7

Male Reproductive System. *Source:* P. M. Insel & W. T. Roth. (2000). *Core concepts in health* (8th ed., 2000 Update). Mountain View, CA: Mayfield. Reproduced with permission of The McGraw-Hill Companies.

inside the body, as indeed they would. However, the temperature within the body is a few degrees too high for the optimal production of sperm. The range of temperatures ideal for the breeding of sperm is relatively narrow. The scrotal sac accommodates to temperature fluctuations by contracting or relaxing, adjusting the distance of the testes from the warmth of the body cavity. Adolescent males may notice that the scrotum contracts in the cold, drawing the testes closer to the body. In hot weather, or after a hot shower, it hangs lower, keeping the testes farther from the body.

The penis doubles in length and thickness during puberty, growing to about 3 to 4 inches. Adolescent boys frequently express concerns about the size of their penis. These concerns almost surely reflect the considerable variability in size that exists from one boy to the next and the mistaken belief that the size of the penis is related to masculinity and sexual prowess.

Some girls may feel ambivalent about menarche, whereas others accept it as a natural part of maturing. The difference is due in large part to how parents prepare their daughters for the physical changes of puberty.

The prepuce, sometimes called the foreskin, is a thin fold of skin that covers the glans of the penis. The prepuce is frequently removed surgically, usually right after birth, in a procedure known as **circumcision.** Circumcision is widely practiced in the United States, for both hygienic and religious reasons. Although female circumcision bears the same name, the procedure is in no way comparable and is more accurately termed **female genital mutilation.** Instead of removing the prepuce, the clitoris of the female is cut out; frequently the **outer labia** are sewn together, leaving only a small opening for the passage of urine (Jones, Ehiri, & Anyanwu, 2004; Toubia, 1994). The procedure is comparable to cutting off the penis! It robs the female of the source of sexual pleasure and makes even simple acts, such as walking, sitting, or urinating, difficult. This procedure is practiced on millions of girls in non-Western nations today and has recently entered the United States and other Western countries with those emigrating from these nations (Whitehorn, Ayonrinde, & Maingay, 2002).

Menarche

The term for a girl's first menstrual period is **menarche.** The average age for reaching menarche is presently about 12½ in the United States (Fechner, 2003). The menstrual cycle is regulated by the feedback loop between the ovaries, the anterior pituitary, and the hypothalamus. At the beginning of the cycle (counting from the first day of the menstrual period), the level of circulating estrogen is low, prompting the release of FSH by the anterior pituitary. A second hormone, LH, is released by the anterior pituitary by the second week of the cycle, which, together with estrogen, prepares the follicle to release an egg.

Once empty, the follicle produces progesterone, which inhibits the release of LH. If the ovum is not fertilized, the follicle decreases its production of hormones, and the uterus, sensitive to the low levels of progesterone and estrogen, contracts, shaking loose the lining that has formed to receive a fertilized egg. The shedding of this lining by the uterus is the menstrual flow. The hypothalamus also reacts to low hormonal levels by

circumcision Surgical removal of the prepuce covering the glans of the penis.

female genital mutilation Cutting out the entire clitoris, the primary source of sexual stimulation in females, along with removing the inner labia and sewing shut most of the outer labia.

outer labia The outer folds of skin surrounding the opening of the vagina and the clitoris.

menarche The occurrence of a girl's first menstrual period.

signaling the anterior pituitary to release FSH, thus initiating the next monthly cycle (Insel & Roth, 2000).

Menstrual cycles sometimes occur without the release of an egg; such cycles are called **anovulatory.** They feel no different from those in which an egg is released and occur only because the hormonal feedback cycle is not sufficiently developed to release an egg each time. Up to half of a girl's cycles can be anovulatory for the first several years, but only about one-fifth are by the end of her teens.

It is impossible to say with any certainty when a girl will ovulate. Ovulation usually occurs 14 days before the next period starts. If a girl's menstrual periods occur regularly every 28 days, she would ovulate on the 14th day of the cycle. Most adolescents do not have regular cycles, at least at first, and some evidence even suggests that a girl may occasionally ovulate several times during a cycle. Variability in the timing and frequency of ovulation has at least one practical implication: It is not possible for the adolescent to identify a time during her cycle when she *cannot* become pregnant.

Reaching a certain proportion of body fat has been thought to be critical for menarche to occur (Frisch, 1984). We know, for instance, that athletes with proportionately less fat for their total weight tend to have delayed menarche and irregular periods (Weimann, 2002). Body fat plays a role in converting androgens into estrogens, important to monthly cycles, and provides a supply of easily converted energy that the body could use, if necessary, to support a pregnancy. What remains to be explained is how the presence of these fat stores could be communicated to the feedback system that regulates the changes of puberty.

The hormone **leptin** may play a significant role. It seems that fat cells secrete this hormone, which may serve as a messenger indicating when necessary levels of fat stores have been reached (Susman, Dorn, & Schiefelbein, 2003). If leptin serves as a metabolic signal, one would expect to find a correspondence between body fat and levels of leptin in the blood. In a longitudinal study in which pre-menarcheal girls were followed over a period of four years, precisely this relationship was found. Furthermore, the higher the concentration of leptin in the blood, the lower the age at menarche (Matkovic et al., 1997). However, research showing that age, independent of body fat, influences levels of leptin (Clayton et al., 1997) suggests that leptin, though necessary for menarche, is not sufficient to trigger it (Cheung, Thornton, Nurani, Clifton, & Steiner, 2001; Clayton & Trueman, 2000; Graber, 2003).

Girls' reactions to menarche vary considerably, with some reporting positive feelings, others negative ones, and still others a mixture of both (Beausang & Razor, 2000; Ruble & Brooks-Gunn, 1982; Teitelman, 2004). Overall, however, differences such as these tend to be slight. For instance, one girl who was interviewed said, "I was happy that I finally got it, but I wasn't too ecstatic" (Teitelman, 2004).

Generally, girls are more likely to have positive experiences when they have been prepared for menarche and know what to do (Rembeck & Gunnarsson, 2004; Teitelman, 2004; Yeung, Tang, & Lee, 2005). Similarly, those who view menarche as a natural and healthy bodily function have more positive reactions (Hoerster, Chrisler, & Rose, 2003; Teitelman, 2004; Yeung, Tang, & Lee, 2005), as do those who have positive self-concepts themselves (Yeung, Tang, & Lee, 2005).

Not only the attitudes of girls but also those of their families affect their reactions to menarche. Anne Teitelman (2004) interviewed 14- to 18-year olds and found that family scripts played an important role in defining menarche for girls. As one girl said, "It was really celebrated in our family. Actually, I'm really glad I had that. A lot of people don't. Either it's just like, 'whatever,' or they're kind of happy, or some of them are upset about it. But, for me, it was really a rite of passage." Another said, "I was really happy

anovulatory Menstrual cycles that do not include the release of an egg.

leptin A hormone secreted by fat cells that may play a role in menarche.

about it . . . but we were so rushed that I didn't even get a chance to tell my mom. . . . Then we went over to my grandparents' house to have dinner that night, so I told my mom and my grandmother at the same time, and they were both really happy for me. My grandpa made me my favorite thing. He made his macaroni and cheese, which is my favorite food" (Teitelman, 2004).

Finally, to the extent that the reactions of families reflect ethnic or cultural differences, we might expect to see such differences in girls' reactions. A review of research examining ethnic differences notes that African American girls report more positive reactions from their mothers than do European American girls when informing them of their first period. Also, when asked what they might tell a younger sister about menarche, African American girls' remarks are more positive and reassuring. Finally, girls' depressive symptoms were related to pubertal status only in European American and not African American or Hispanic adolescents (Michael & Eccles, 2003).

Despite differences in their reactions to menarche, most girls tell their mothers right away, and most soon discuss their experiences with friends (Archibald, Graber, & Brooks-Gunn, 2003; Brooks-Gunn & Ruble, 1982). Mothers also are the most frequent source of information (Costos, Ackerman, & Paradis, 2002). However, older sisters, teachers, and friends are also important. Fathers play a small role (Koff & Rierdan, 1995). It may be that girls are less willing than are their fathers to discuss menstruation. More than three-quarters say they would not report their menstrual status to their fathers, whereas a small sample of fathers who were interviewed said they would be comfortable talking with their daughters. It is interesting that girls who tell their fathers, or who know their mothers have told them, report fewer menstrual symptoms such as cramps or other discomfort. This inclusion of the father may reflect a more open, relaxed attitude about menstruation.

Spermarche

A boy's first ejaculation of seminal fluid, or **spermarche,** usually occurs early in his teens, by about 13 to 14 (Archibald, Graber, & Brooks-Gunn, 2003; Halpern, Udry, Suchindran, & Campbell, 2000). For some boys, it will occur spontaneously in a **nocturnal emission** (also known as a wet dream); for others, through masturbation or intercourse. Relatively few boys are likely to have anyone explain any of this to them. Peers and books or magazines are the most likely sources of information; in fact, boys learn more about menarche than about ejaculation in their health classes. Despite the relative lack of preparation, most boys are not alarmed, although most do admit to being surprised. Generally, reactions are positive, boys reporting feeling excited, grown up, and glad (Gaddis & Brooks-Gunn, 1985; Stein & Reiser, 1994).

Boys are not likely to discuss their experience with friends or with their fathers. This reaction to spermarche contrasts sharply with that of girls to menarche, most of whom tell their mothers immediately and share their new status with friends. The difference may reflect the closer association of first ejaculation with masturbation for boys. Among all experiences related to sex, boys are least willing to discuss masturbation (Halpern et al., 2000). For girls, the lack of any association of menarche with masturbation may account for their greater willingness to discuss it. Or it may be that they have had discussion modeled for them by their mothers, because most are prepared for menarche, whereas most boys have not been prepared for first ejaculation by their fathers (Gaddis & Brooks-Gunn, 1985). In general, adolescent boys receive considerably less information than girls about pubertal changes. Few fathers explain nocturnal emissions to their sons, and neither parent is likely to explain menstruation to them.

spermarche A boy's first ejaculation of seminal fluid.

nocturnal emission A spontaneous ejaculation of seminal fluid during sleep; sometimes called a wet dream.

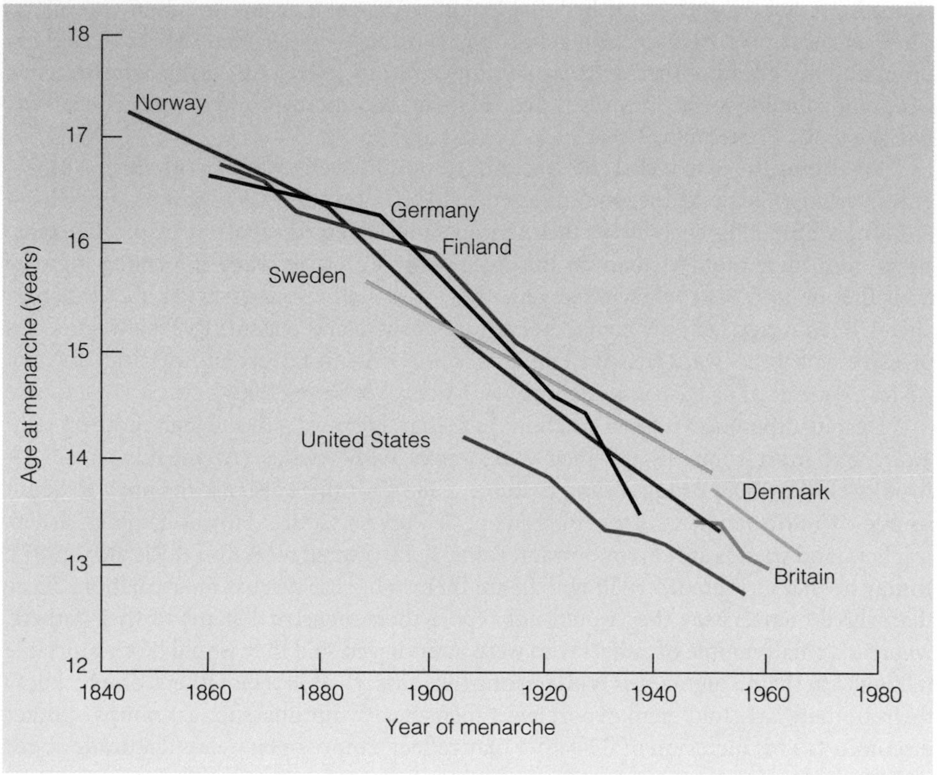

■ **FIGURE 3.8**
Trends in the Age of Menarche. *Puberty begins earlier than it has in previous years. This graph shows how the age of menarche has been steadily dropping. Source:* Adapted from J. M. Tanner. (1968). Earlier maturation in man. *Scientific American, 218,* 26.

The Secular Trend

Quite a bit of evidence indicates that puberty begins earlier today than it did in the past. This downward shift in age is called the **secular trend** (Susman, Dorn, & Schiefelbein, 2003). Figure 3.8 shows a striking drop in age at menarche over a period of 130 years for a number of countries. The greatest changes occurred from the mid-1800s to the mid-1900s. Age at menarche dropped by about three to four months every ten years (Tanner, 1991).

Not only do adolescents begin puberty earlier than in previous generations, but they also grow faster. Although we have only scanty records from earlier centuries, the pieces fit a predictable pattern. In the nineteenth century in Britain, females reached their adult height at about 21. Adolescent girls stop growing today by 16 to 18. British men in the nineteenth century continued growing well into their mid-twenties, reaching their adult height at 23 to 25. Adolescent boys today reach their adult height by 20 to 21. Even after skeletal growth is completed, adolescents' bones continue to develop, increasing in density and in bone mineral content (Magarey et al., 1999).

Adolescents also grow to be larger than they once did, girls growing half an inch to an inch taller than their mothers and weighing about 2 pounds more. For boys these differences can be even greater. Generational differences are startling when we make comparisons across centuries. The decks of the USS *Constitution* were only 5 feet 6 inches high. Similar evidence from medieval armor, old clothing, and antique furniture all point to a dramatic increase in stature over the centuries. The seats of La Scala opera house in Milan, for example, built in 1776, were 18 inches wide. Most seats today are 24 inches wide (Muuss, 1975; Tanner, 1991).

secular trend The earlier onset of puberty, faster growth, and larger size reached by adolescents today than in the past.

A number of conditions have contributed to the secular trend. Improved nutrition is almost surely an important cause of the accelerated growth patterns. One can reasonably ask, however, when this trend will level off. Some researchers suggest that it already has done so. They note that not all measures of puberty have continued to drop with age, and point out that those that have are ones associated with increased body fat. Since obesity also is more common among adolescents today, there simply may be the appearance of a continuing trend where in actuality there is none (Fechner, 2003; Shalitin & Phillip, 2003). Puberty sets in motion a number of changes, not all of which are physical. Some of these changes affect adolescents' emotions and their relationships with their parents.

The Psychological and Social Implications of Puberty

Even experiences as close to a biological ground zero as those of puberty do not necessarily have the same significance from one adolescent to the next. Adolescents continually interpret the biological frontiers they are crossing, reading the reactions of friends and family for the meaning of the changes they are going through. Nor are they alone in doing so. Their parents, siblings, friends, and teachers also read significance into the biological script unfolding before them. Not surprisingly, puberty affects adolescents' closest relationships in intimate ways.

Reed Larson and Maryse Richards (1994) were able to document the details of adolescents' lives by having them wear beepers and paging them at random intervals throughout the day and evening, when they would report on their activities and feelings. These investigators remind us of what we too easily forget about our own lives—that even the simplest activities that make up a day, things such as having breakfast or hassling over kitchen responsibilities, are often suffused with emotion. They also remind us that such activities, when they involve more than one member of the family, are rarely experienced in the same way by each of them, that there are as many realities to be experienced as individuals to experience them. This reminder should strike a familiar note at this point, illustrating one of the central assumptions of the constructive approach taken in this text: namely, that we continually interpret our experiences, putting events together in ways that make sense to us, constructing the reality to which we eventually respond.

Heightened Emotionality

Larson and Richards point out that tensions are greatest in early adolescence, when puberty tips the psychosocial balance established throughout childhood. As adolescents' bodies assume more adult proportions, those around them, particularly parents and teachers, expect them to behave in more adult ways as well. Crowding in on the heels of puberty are additional stressors such as starting middle school or junior high, navigating problematic relationships with peers, redefining relationships with parents, and, for many, facing increasing pressures to experiment with sex and drugs. Because of the secular trend, adolescents as young as 10 or 11 begin to face these pressures of puberty, often before either they or their parents are ready for them (Larson & Richards, 1994).

How do early adolescents react to these changes? A common stereotype is that, with puberty, adolescents become moody, their emotions swinging from one extreme to

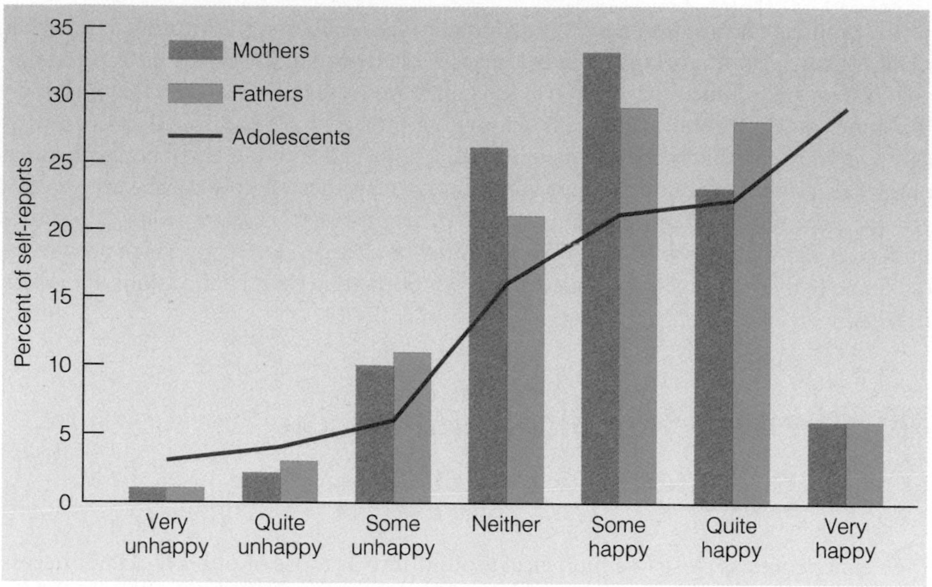

FIGURE 3.9
Frequency with Which Family Members Feel Gradations of Happiness and Unhappiness.
Follow the red line with your eyes to see how adolescents' emotions differ from those of their parents; although adolescents are frequently characterized as being more moody, they differ mostly in how very happy they feel.
Source: Adapted from R. Larson & M. H. Richards. (1994). *Divergent realities.* New York: Basic Books.

another with little predictability. Larson and Richards indeed found some support for heightened emotionality in adolescence. Figure 3.9 shows that adolescents more frequently report experiencing extreme states than do their parents. They also report a wider range of emotions. In addition to simply feeling happy, for instance, adolescents report feeling great, free, cheerful, proud, accepted, in love, friendly, and kindly. They also report a wider gamut of negative feelings, describing themselves as unsure, lonely, awkward, ignored, and nervous, or as Larson and Richards (1994) put it, "a whole array of painful feelings that remind us adults why we never want to be adolescents again" (p. 83). Even though they feel self-conscious and embarrassed two to three times as often as their parents, they are also bored more, perhaps because they feel less in control and less invested in the moment, often saying they would rather be doing something else. Furthermore, despite the advantage of youth, adolescents are more likely to say they feel tired, weak, and have little energy. These differing inner realities, as well as the more visible differences of their exterior lives, virtually ensure that misunderstandings with parents will arise.

Relationships with Parents

Good relationships with parents can provide a powerful buffer against the stresses of adolescence. Adolescents who see their parents as warm and loving, for instance, experience fewer emotional or behavioral problems (Wagner, Cohen, & Brook, 1996). For most adolescents, however, closeness with parents temporarily decreases and the intensity of conflict increases with the onset of puberty (Laursen, Coy, & Collins, 1998). Adolescents begin to demand a greater role in family decision making and more freedom in areas that their parents still believe require parental oversight, such as the adolescents' well-being (see Chapter 5). For their part, parents may see that the ways they have always parented are no longer appropriate, yet they have no ready substitutes for outmoded forms of discipline and guidance. The resulting scuffles, though often uncomfortable, lay the groundwork for renegotiated relationships. With few exceptions, however, studies of these changes have involved European American middle-class families.

Brooke Molina and Laurie Chassin (1996) compared parent–adolescent relationships in Hispanic and non-Hispanic families. These investigators found increased con-

Adolescents' emotions are often more extreme than they were when children, or will be as adults.

flict and decreased closeness with pubertal onset only in European American adolescent boys. For Hispanic boys, just the opposite occurred, with puberty actually bringing parents and sons closer together. Hispanic boys reported less conflict and greater emotional support from their parents once they began puberty. This increased closeness may reflect the value Hispanic families place on the traditional male role. Supporting this interpretation, Hispanic girls did not experience a comparable improvement in their relationships with parents.

The Timing of Change: Early and Late Maturers

Differences in the timing of pubertal change from one adolescent to the next, or within any adolescent, are collectively known as **asynchrony.** Asynchrony simply means that all changes do not occur at the same time. For adolescents who believe changes should occur together, the fact that they haven't, or that they occurred together but at the wrong time, can have enormous implications. Many changes receive cultural as well as personal interpretation. These interpretations affect the way adolescents feel and think about themselves. Change can be difficult enough when all goes according to schedule, but when adolescents develop faster or slower than their friends and classmates, or at obviously uneven rates within their own lives, differences can be hard to ignore.

It is common for adolescents to experience asynchrony. In fact, our society seems to foster adolescent asynchrony. Most adolescents are biologically and intellectually mature by their mid- to late teens, yet many remain emotionally and socially dependent on parents while they obtain the education they need to succeed in increasingly technological jobs. Relatively little information exists on the possible effects of these asynchronies on personality development. Certainly, we need more research on this important topic and the ways in which it can affect the lives of adolescents and their parents.

asynchrony Differences in the timing of pubertal changes within an adolescent or from one adolescent to the next.

Early maturing boys often show off their strength at the expense of smaller, later maturing boys. Will their different rates of maturation affect the development of self-image in these two boys?

Early and Late Maturing Boys

Initial studies comparing early and late maturers found that **early maturation** conferred distinct advantages for boys. Boys who matured earlier than their peers were more self-confident, more popular, and achieved more recognition in activities ranging from captain of the football team to class president than did their **late maturing** peers (Jones, 1965; Jones & Bayley, 1950).

Subsequent research, however, suggests that these advantages may come at a price. Early maturing boys have also been found to be more likely to engage in behaviors posing health risks, such as smoking or drinking (Susman, Dorn, & Schiefelbein, 2003), as well as in delinquent activities (Alsaker, 1995; Cota-Robles, Neiss, & Rowe, 2002). Questions as to why they may do so are not that easily answered. It may simply be that early maturing boys take advantage of their physical maturation to associate with older boys. Their pubertal status, in other words, affords them access to an older crowd, and this increases the likelihood they will engage in behaviors more characteristic of older adolescents. Data from a four-year longitudinal study of Finnish adolescents support this interpretation (Dick, Rose, Pulkkinen, & Kaprio, 2001).

Other research, however, suggests that early maturing boys may experience more adjustment problems independent of who they associate with (Alsaker, 1995; Ge, Conger, & Elder 2001a; Lam, Stewart, Leung, Lee, Wong, & Ho, 2004). Xiaojia Ge, Rand Conger, and Glen Elder (2001b) found that early maturing boys experienced more distress, such as feelings of sadness or anxiety, than other boys their age, as well as more hostility toward others. They also had more difficulty coping with other stressful events going on in their lives than did age-mates who had not yet entered puberty.

The boys studied by Ge, Conger, and Elder were all Anglo Americans and all were from rural areas or small towns in the Midwest. However, a national sample comparing European American, Hispanic, and African American boys similarly revealed more problem behaviors among early maturing boys from each of the three ethnic groups (Cota-Robles, Neiss, & Rowe, 2002). It is rare, however, when the findings of research are entirely consistent, and findings related to pubertal timing offer no exception, with some studies showing more adjustment problems associated with late maturation in boys (Graber, Lewinsohn, Seeley, & Brooks-Gunn, 1997; Graber, Seeley, Brooks-Gunn, & Lewinsohn, 2004).

early maturation Pubertal maturation occurring earlier in adolescents than the norm for their sex.

late maturation Pubertal maturation occurring later in adolescents than the norm for their sex.

Early and Late Maturing Girls

The picture for girls is clearer. Early maturation confers few, if any, initial advantages and a number of problems. Recall that girls begin to develop approximately two years ahead of boys, which means that early maturing girls are not only ahead of all the other girls, but also ahead of all the boys their age as well. Many are self-conscious about their adult bodies, have lower **self-esteem,** and lack the poise of late maturing girls (Dusek & McIntyre, 2003; Susman, Dorn, & Schiefelbein, 2003). Their height, menarcheal status, and developing breasts can be sources of embarrassment among classmates who still have the bodies of children (Summers-Effler, 2004). The picture brightens with junior high, where early maturing girls are no longer set apart by their adult bodies and can enjoy a new prestige and, with this, frequent popularity.

Even so, a number of problems have been found to be associated with early maturation in girls. They, like early maturing boys, are more likely to associate with peers who are somewhat older and to engage in behaviors that pose health risks, such as drinking, smoking, or disordered eating (Susman, Dorn, & Schiefelbein, 2003). They also are more likely to experience negative moods and depression than late maturing girls (Ge, Conger, & Elder, 2001a). When such problems occur, these tend to be more pronounced in girls than in boys.

Research by Eccles and her associates, however, finds that African American girls are not likely to experience distress due to early maturation. They appear to be less vulnerable than European American girls, protected by a more positive sense of self and a greater openness to their feelings (Michael & Eccles, 2003).

Perhaps not unexpectedly, early maturers of either sex are more likely to engage in early sexual behavior (Cavanagh, 2004; Susman, Dorn, & Schiefelbein, 2003). However, Shannon Cavanagh (2004), studying a nationally representative sample of adolescents, found earlier sexual activity to be associated with pubertal timing only for European American and Hispanic girls, not for African American girls.

Why might being off-time in development affect adolescents? Most of us know from our own experiences how difficult it can be, at any point in life, to be out of step with those around us. This difficulty is compounded for adolescents who go through so many changes so quickly, and who draw much of their support from peers. Being off-time sets adolescents apart from their age-mates and, with this, from the social supports to which they customarily turn. This explanation, known as the **maturational deviance hypothesis,** suggests that timing is important because it changes adolescents' status relative to their peers. Since girls generally mature several years ahead of boys, early maturing girls are the most deviant and should experience more disruption.

A second explanation, the **stage termination hypothesis,** suggests that early maturers simply don't have as much time to complete the developmental tasks of middle childhood. That is, they must cope with the experiences, expectations, and feelings attending puberty when they have not yet completely resolved the issues of middle childhood. Again, most difficulty would be expected for those facing the demands of adolescence first, that is, for early maturing girls. A positive note for these adolescents is that they have more time to complete the tasks of adolescence.

A third explanation, the **adult status hypothesis,** suggests that the advantages or disadvantages of early and late maturation depend on the status that awaits adolescents when they become adults (Block, 1978). Adult males generally enjoy a higher status in society than females. They are frequently the decision makers within the family and have positions of greater power and influence in society. Movement toward adulthood for girls does not carry the clear advantages it does for boys, supporting the finding that when problems related to maturational timing occur, they tend to be greater for girls than boys.

In summary, then, research suggests that adolescents who develop off-time from their peers, either earlier or later, may experience more difficulty coping with the changes of puberty than their on-time age-mates. It is also the case that early maturation appears to be more of a problem for girls than for boys. It should be noted, however, that

self-esteem The individual's overall positive or negative evaluation of herself or himself.

maturational deviance hypothesis An explanation for the effects of asynchronous development that attributes the effects of timing to changing adolescents' status relative to their peers.

stage termination hypothesis An explanation for the effects of early maturation to not having as much time as needed to complete the developmental tasks of middle childhood.

adult status hypotheses An explanation for the effects of asynchronous development that attributes the effects of timing to the status that awaits adolescents of either sex when they become adults.

not all research finds a relationship between maturational timing and subsequent adjustment, and even when these are found to be related, research has not always found timing to offer either consistent advantages or consistent disadvantages. Finally, although reported differences may be statistically significant, they may not be sufficiently large to account for much of the variability that actually exists from one adolescent to the next.

What does all this mean for individual adolescents and their families? Most adolescents can expect to travel the road to maturity with few, if any, missteps. This is also true for those who develop either earlier or later than their peers. Of course, this is not to say that pubertal changes do not present new challenges, or that there won't be problems that take time before yielding to adolescents' attempted solutions. But needing to cope with challenges in new ways is not unique to adolescent development, and most adolescents cope effectively.

With this said, adolescents frequently have questions to which they need answers, often simply to know if what they are experiencing is normal. They also need to be able to talk to someone who is a good listener about what they are experiencing and feeling. Ideally, these needs would be met by discussions with a parent, or perhaps their physician. A national survey, however, found that 58% of adolescents had personal concerns they would not want to discuss with their parents, and 69% indicated concerns they would not want to discuss with friends (Cheng, Savageau, Sattler, & DeWitt, 1993). Furthermore, confidentiality was an issue for 82% of youths in another national survey (Rideout, 2001). Frequently, the concerns early adolescents are embarrassed to talk about are seen as relatively commonplace by older adolescents and adults (e.g., menstruation, penis size), but they can be momentous to a young adolescent.

Problems related to embarrassment, confidentiality, and finding a good listener at 2 A.M. are addressed by increasing numbers of adolescents who turn to the Internet. Approximately 20% of adolescents report having used the Internet, going to such sources as Web pages, chat rooms, and bulletin boards (Pew Internet and American Life Project, 2001). The most frequent questions adolescents ask on the Internet clearly reflect the new issues they face resulting from maturational changes, and are presumably the ones they are reluctant to discuss with parents, a doctor, or even their friends (Subrahmanyam & Greenfield, 2004; Suzuki & Calzo, 2004).

Lalita Suzuki and Jerel Calzo (2004) looked at questions posted on two bulletin boards, one on teen issues and one on teen sexual health (Table 3.1). Despite the potentially embarrassing nature of many of these questions, teens frequently responded by giving their personal opinions and by talking about their own experiences. Adolescents most likely feel less awkward due to the anonymity afforded by the Internet, something which is not possible in face-to-face conversations, yet they still are able to feel a sense of connection to others (Gray, Klein, Noyce, Sesselberg, & Cantrill, 2005; Suzuki & Calzo, 2004). Of course, use of the Internet in this way raises concerns about the accuracy of information adolescents are getting and whether teenagers who need medical attention are as likely to receive it. As Suzuki and Calzo suggest, participation by health professionals on sites such as these is one way of providing more accurate information.

Body Image and Self-Esteem

How satisfied adolescents are with their bodies depends a lot on how others react to them. Adolescents' self-images include the attitudes of others, or their perceptions of these attitudes, as well as their own evaluations of how attractive a particular trait may be. Body images are reflected by social mirrors and always capture comparisons with others.

TABLE 3.1 Most Frequently Asked Types of Questions and Replies on General Teen Issues Bulletin Boards

Type of Question	%	Example
Romantic relationships	36.9	"How do I ask a girl out, or at least talk to her?"
		"I feel awkward hugging and kissing my girlfriend with everyone around."
Physical health	14.6	"Will I get skin cancer if I go tanning for only two weeks?"
		"I have a problem with a lot of sweat coming from my underarms."
		"I have a hooked penis, do you know how to fix this?!?! PLEASE HELP ME!!!"
Body image/Exercise	10.7	"I would really like to drop 10 pounds in the next 2 months."
		"I feel so fat compared to some of my friends who wear such small sizes."
Type of Reply	**%**	**Example**
Personal opinion	63	"I don't think zits would turn me off. Lousy personality would."
		"I don't think weight matters just as long as you're a healthy person."
Advice	44	"You can put an anti-itch lotion very lightly there and see how that helps."
		"Just be yourself and express how u feel to him and u never know he might like u too."
Concrete information	37	"If your penis is truly bent, then there is no home remedy for it. You will have to see a doctor."
		"A cold sore is Herpes, and the only thing that will help it go away is a cream."
Personal experience	33	"I know what you mean. . . . I didn't start wearing tampons until a couple of years after my period. But I realized how much more comfortable they are!"

Source: L. K. Suzuki & J. P. Calzo (2004). The search for peer advice in cyberspace: An examination of online teen bulletin boards about health and sexuality. *Applied Developmental Psychology, 25,* 685–698.

These images can get pretty distorted at times, especially in adolescence, when bodies change in so many ways. In early adolescence, physical changes contribute heavily to adolescents' senses of themselves. Adolescents' self-images are strongly tied to their body images; this is true for both sexes. Furthermore, just how satisfied adolescents are with their bodies roughly predicts their levels of self-esteem, especially for girls. Superficial or not, this relationship reflects something of a social reality.

Mainstream cultural messages on the importance of being thin are clear: To be considered attractive, females need to be thin (Field, Cheung, Wolf, Herzog, Gortmaker, & Colditz, 1999; Stice, 2002). For instance, nearly three-quarters of the female characters on television are actually underweight; most of the males, however, are of average

Adolescents' self-images are tied to their body images, which always involve comparisons with others.

weight (Fouts & Burggraf, 1999; Silverstein, Perdue, Peterson, & Kelly, 1986). Television is not unique in communicating to females the importance of being thin. Silverstein and colleagues (1986) sampled advertisements in popular women's and men's magazines for messages about body shape. Ads for diet products in women's magazines outnumbered those in men's magazines 60 to 1. Despite the clear message to stay thin, women's magazines contained over 1,000 advertisements for food; 10 appeared in all the men's magazines.

Perhaps not surprisingly, boys have more positive **body images** than girls (Field et al., 1999; Rosenblum & Lewis, 1999). Girls tend to be critical of the way they look, believing themselves to be heavier than they are and wanting to be thinner (Lowry, Galuska, Fulton, Burgeson, & Kann, 2005). Boys, on the other hand, are more content with their appearance. Girls' tendency to overestimate their weight declines after mid-adolescence; however, their dissatisfaction with their bodies continues to increase through late adolescence (Phelps et al., 1993).

Important differences exist among adolescent girls in terms of body image—African American girls view their bodies quite differently than European American girls do (Michael & Eccles, 2003; Thompson, Corwin, Rogan, & Sargent, 1999). A team of researchers at the University of Arizona, studying junior high and high school students, found that although nine out of ten European American girls are dissatisfied with their body weight, seven out of ten African American girls are satisfied. Additionally, whereas 62% of European American girls said they had been on a diet within the past year, a comparable percentage of African American girls, many of whom also had dieted, nonetheless believed it is better to be somewhat overweight than underweight (Parker et al., 1995). Table 3.2 summarizes the results of this body satisfaction survey. Among preadolescent girls and boys, however, a comparison of those who were Hispanic versus European American revealed no differences (Markey, Tinsley, Ericksen, Ozer, & Markey, 2002).

body image Individuals' satisfaction or dissatisfaction with their image of their bodies.

TABLE 3.2 Body Satisfaction Among African American and European American Adolescent Girls

African American Girls	European American Girls
70% express satisfaction with their bodies.	90% express dissatisfaction with their bodies.
64% believe it is better to be somewhat overweight than somewhat underweight.	62% report dieting within the past year.

Source: S. Parker, M. Nichter, M. Nichter, N. Vuckovic, C. Sims, & C. Ritenbaugh (1995). Body image and weight concern among Afro American and White adolescent females. Differences that make a difference. *Human Organization, S4*, 103–115.

Health and Well-Being

It is typically the case that bad news gets more press than good news, and this is true for news about adolescents' health. We hear alarming statistics about adolescent health problems, yet few reports concerning their well-being. Yet the good news is that adolescents are at the peak of fitness and health. Muscles have increased in size and strength from childhood, fourteenfold in boys and tenfold in girls, bringing obvious increases in strength and agility, and the cardiovascular and respiratory systems reach their adult levels of efficiency. Chronic diseases are relatively rare, and those that eventually occur following years of "wear and tear" have not yet had a chance to get a foothold. In short, adolescents are stronger, better coordinated, and healthier than ever before.

Yet concerns about adolescents' health are legitimate for several reasons. For one thing, by far most of the causes of disease and death that occur among adolescents can be traced to their own behavior. For another, their behavior becomes progressively more under their control, and less under their parents', with age (Connell & Janevic, 2003). Lastly, many of their behaviors reflect lifestyle choices that eventually become habits. For some, these habits will give years of youthful energy; for others, they will prematurely impair the good health they presently enjoy.

Nutrition

Among the first health choices that adolescents make each day are what they will eat. Despite the increased nutritional needs introduced by rapid growth, many adolescents eat erratically. They are not alone. Poor eating habits are fast becoming part of the national character. Fast foods, frozen dinners, snacking, missed meals, and fad diets are common to all age groups. Nearly half of all the meals eaten in the United States are eaten in restaurants, most of which are fast-food chains. The nation is being fed by the Colonel, McDonald's, and assorted take-out stands.

Even though salads, milk, and juices are not at the top of the menu for most fast-food restaurants, adolescents can still eat at such places and meet nutritional needs. The biggest problem is not that they fail to get necessary nutrients, but that they get too many other things along with them. Fast foods taste good because of the excess fats, sugars, and salt in them; but these ingredients add calories—and with these, increased risk of overweight. Healthy meals can still be selected from these menus with a few simple substitutions. A 10-ounce carton of low-fat milk, for example, provides twice the recommended daily allowance of calcium of a milkshake and less than half the calories. By adding a piece of fruit or a salad, burgers, wraps, and pizzas can add up to a nutritious meal.

Physical Activity

How much exercise adolescents get can profoundly affect their health and well-being. Regular physical activity not only contributes to adolescents' health through building and maintaining bones and muscles and controlling weight, but also is related to lower blood pressure and cholesterol levels. Being physically active also contributes to psychological well-being by reducing stress and anxiety and improving adolescents' self-esteem (CDC, 2005a).

Just how active are adolescents? Approximately two-thirds of high school students say they engage in some form of vigorous physical activity, for at least 20 minutes, 3 or more days a week (CDC, 2005a). However, they are less likely to do so as they get older; although 72% of 9th graders indicate being this active, only 56% of 12th graders do (Towey & Fleming, 2005). Adolescents also differ in their physical activity depending on their sex and ethnicity. Boys are more active than girls, with 70% of boys reporting vigorous physical activity in comparison to 55% of girls, and European American adolescents are somewhat more active (65.2%) than either African American (54.8%) or Hispanic adolescents (59.3%) (CDC, 2005a; Lowry et al., 2005). These differences assume added significance, as we will see, when considered in light of increasing trends for being overweight.

One might wonder why these figures for physical activity are not higher, since most schools require PE classes and many adolescents participate in team sports (a topic we will look at in Chapter 13). Many schools, however, exempt students from PE for any of a number of reasons, such as participation in school or community sports or even in community service activities. Additionally, relatively few schools offer daily PE classes for all students throughout the year (CDC, 2005a). A recent national survey found that by 9th grade only 38% of students attended PE classes on a daily basis and that by 12th grade this figure dropped to 18%. It is also the case that, although most students in a PE class spend at least 20 minutes exercising or playing some sport, this does not always involve vigorous activity (CDC, 2005a).

Another factor that limits the extent of physical activity for some adolescents is their physical environment, namely, living in a low-income—and for many, higher crime—neighborhood (Connell & Janevic, 2003; Krieger & Fee, 1994; Romero, 2005). In such neighborhoods, factors such as traffic, poor air quality, inadequate public transportation, or the presence of gangs can make it difficult getting to or being safe in recreational areas. Adolescents in such neighborhoods are likely to be more physically active when they can spend time in after-school programs where they feel themselves to be safe around the adults present there (Romero, 2005). Although a majority of schools nationwide (71.6%) open their facilities for use before or after-school hours and on weekends (CDC, 2005a), responsible adults may need to be present at these in order for adolescents to feel safe using them. Given the lifelong health benefits of physical activity, federal and state funding to ensure safe recreational centers in all communities, as well as to provide daily physical education classes in middle and high schools, needs to be reexamined as a national priority.

Physical activity assumes added importance when we consider another aspect of adolescents' health and well-being, that of maintaining healthy weight.

Overweight

overweight Individuals are considered to be overweight when their weight is at or above the 95th percentile for their body mass index.

The number of adolescents who are **overweight** has tripled since the 1970s, with an estimated 16% of 12- to 19-year-olds currently overweight and another 15% who are at risk of becoming overweight (CDC, 2005b). Adolescents who are overweight are more likely to be so as adults as well, thereby increasing their lifetime risk of a number of dis-

Being active during adolescence promotes physical health and contributes to psychological well-being.

eases such as hypertension, heart disease, diabetes, and certain forms of cancer (Towey & Fleming, 2005). The frequency of being overweight differs with ethnicity, being more common among Mexican American (23%) and African American (21%) adolescents than among European American adolescents (14%) (CDC, 2004a). For a creative approach to this problem, see the In More Depth Box on The Edible Schoolyard.

Adolescents are considered to be overweight if their weight is at or above the 95th percentile for their BMI-for-age (**body mass index**), and at risk of being overweight if they are between the 85th and 95th percentiles (CDC, 2005b). One's BMI is easy to compute; the formula for this is {weight in pounds/(height in inches) × (height in inches)} × 703, and BMI-for-age charts can be found on the Internet at www.cdc.gov/growthcharts/.

Overweight adolescents tend to have somewhat different eating patterns. They are more likely to eat irregularly, miss meals, and snack, habits that make it difficult to maintain a balance between hunger and satiation. Overweight adolescents are also more likely to eat rapidly, to eat somewhat larger portions, and to eat food that is denser in calories (Lucas, 1988; Wadden, Brownell, and Foster, 2002). But perhaps the biggest difference is in how active they are, not how much they eat. Overweight adolescents are considerably less active than their peers of average weight and thus are less likely to burn off the excess calories they are taking in.

The relationship between overweight and inactivity highlights the importance of exercise in weight reduction programs. Exercise increases the body's metabolism, allowing the body to burn excess calories more rapidly; in moderate amounts, exercise also depresses appetite. Dieting alone can have paradoxical effects, frequently causing a preoccupation with food, which in turn can prompt reactive overeating. Ellen Satter (1988) recommends programs that incorporate procedures that foster a reliance on internal cues rather than on external constraints, such as counting calories and diets. The latter force one to continually think about food and ways of avoiding it—which can be just about as hard as trying *not* to think of a pink elephant.

Adolescents attempting to lose weight often have unrealistic expectations. Many view their weight as central to all of their problems and expect that once they lose weight,

body mass index (BMI) One's weight in kilograms divided by the square of one's height in meters (kg/m^2); since body fatness varies with age and sex, percentiles for BMI are specific to age and gender.

IN MORE DEPTH

The Edible Schoolyard

Two generations ago, when a presidential commission revealed that U.S. schoolchildren were physically unfit, schools and educators responded by building gymnasiums, adding courses in physical education to the curriculum, and hiring teachers trained to teach them (Waters, 2005a). Forty years later, the health of schoolchildren is again compromised. Nearly one-third of 12- to 19-year-olds are seriously overweight, placing them at risk for diseases such as hypertension, heart disease, and diabetes (CDC, 2005b; Hedley, Ogden, Johnson, Carroll, Curtin, & Flegal, 2004; Irwin, 2004; Muntner, He, Cutler, Wildman, & Whelton, 2004). Yet despite the seriousness of this problem, we have done little in our schools to address the situation.

The Edible Schoolyard, an innovative program located on the campus of Martin Luther King Junior Middle School in Berkeley, California, may be a first step in changing that. The Edible Schoolyard is a nonprofit program that grew out of a conversation between chef and author Alice Waters and Neil Smith, former principal of Martin Luther King Junior Middle School. The student body at King Middle School had grown too large for the school cafeteria to accommodate them all, and the cafeteria had been closed. For lunch, students bought packaged food sold at the other end of a parking lot adjacent to the school. Rather than viewing this situation as just one more problem to be solved in the same old way, Waters and Smith saw it as an opportunity for a bold experiment—they turned the parking lot into a garden.

In The Edible Schoolyard, students learn how to plant, cultivate, harvest, and prepare their own food. Learning doesn't stop there, however. These experiences are integrated into the academic curriculum, transforming what otherwise might remain as bookish facts, such as the nitrogen cycle, into meaningful knowledge. Similarly, concepts taught in class provide information they will need in maintaining the garden. The Edible Schoolyard program is supported not only by students and teachers, but also by parents, volunteers, local farmers, and neighbors who are committed to the success of this project. An additional benefit to this support is that as students come into contact with others who share their interest in this project, they learn the importance of community and of their mutual dependence on each other and their environment.

So, what is lunch at King Middle School? It's not processed. It's not eaten alone. And it's not consumed mindlessly. In fact, at this middle school, lunch starts well before students ever sit down to eat. It's homegrown, in soil that's been mulched, cultivated until it's soft enough to hold the seeds students tuck beneath the surface. It's food that adolescents, working together, have planted and grown. And it's adolescents, sitting and talking together at tables, savoring their food — and their accomplishments.

As Alice Waters is ready to point out, "A school lunch curriculum is not a quick fix for the obesity epidemic. But by bringing kids into another kind of relationship with their food, we can bring about a deep and lasting change in the way they feel about themselves" (Waters, 2005b).

Information on The Edible Schoolyard is available at http://www.edibleschoolyard.org

their problems will be solved—they will become popular, make the team, and so forth. When their problems do not roll away with the pounds, adolescents can become frustrated and fall off their diets. The most successful programs are multifaceted. Finally, the success of a weight control program for adolescents almost always depends on successfully integrating the family into the program (Epstein, 1994; McVey, Pepler, Davis, Flett, & Abdolell, 2002).

Health Care

How likely are adolescents to receive health care when they need it? A number of factors are important.

As an age group, adolescents and young adults experience poorer access to health care than young children or older adults. Perceived access may be problematic in a number of ways. Adolescents report such things as difficulty knowing where to go, finding transportation, anxiety as to what might be done, not wanting their parents to know, and not having insurance coverage.

Although these middle school students may all be the same age, they're not necessarily all adolescents yet. The start of adolescence is signaled by puberty rather than by a particular chronological age.

Most of these problems are intensified for adolescents living in rural communities or non-urban settings. Barbara Elliott and Jean Larson (2004) found higher rates of foregone care for these adolescents than for those living in urban settings. The 10th graders in their study reported reasons similar to those given by other adolescents, but for small-town and rural adolescents, costs of medical care and not having insurance can be more serious barriers, since adolescents in rural areas are less likely to be insured (Health Access Survey, 2003). Confidentiality is also a larger concern. In small towns, everyone's a neighbor—including the person scheduling your doctor's appointment or the pharmacist filling the prescription.

Another significant factor influencing the accessibility of health care is health care coverage. Presently, over 9 million children and adolescents in the United States do not have health insurance even though 5.8 million of these could receive free health insurance through either Medicaid or the Children's Health Insurance Program (CHIP). CHIP provides health insurance to children in families whose annual incomes disqualify them from receiving Medicaid, yet which are not high enough to purchase health insurance. In order for youth to be covered under Medicaid or CHIP, however, parents must apply for this coverage, and many parents are unaware that their children are eligible (Children's Defense Fund [CDF], 2005).

The Children's Defense Fund, established by Marion Edelman, has developed an outreach project, called SHOUT (**S**tudent **H**ealth **Out**reach), in which high school and college student volunteers help low-income families enroll children for free health care coverage (CDF, 2005). The Student Health Outreach Project is active in a number of states, and individuals interested in starting a local Project or joining one can get information on the Children's Defense Fund Web site.

Poverty

Perhaps the single most important factor affecting the health and well-being of adolescents in the United States is the presence of poverty—in their families and in their neighborhoods. These adolescents live with conditions over which they have no control, yet which constitute significant risks to their well-being. For a look at a program designed to increase the well-being of adolescents in low-income neighborhoods, read the Research Focus "Randomized Versus Quasi-Experimental Designs." Approximately 20% of U.S.

RESEARCH FOCUS

Randomized Versus Quasi-Experimental Designs: What's in a Name? Communication Across the Ages

Joey was beginning to like his name. He liked the soft way it sounded when Mrs. Thomas spoke to him, even though this was usually when they were talking about his homework. Funny, a year ago he would never have thought of doing homework, or going to a museum with his class or even to school basketball games. But he did now, and his mom did too, every now and then, when Mrs. Thomas called her. For that matter, a year ago he would never have thought he'd even know anyone as old as Mrs. Thomas. She must be at least 60, he thought, as he watched her coming into the room with a pencil and another piece of pie.

Joey lives in a low-income, high-crime neighborhood in Philadelphia. His sixth-grade class is part of an intergenerational mentoring program in which older members of the community, such as Mrs. Thomas, volunteer time with students, doing things such as helping with homework or school projects, going to games or cultural events, and taking part in community service activities. The purpose of the program is to increase the protective factors in the lives of high-risk children. By working with these students, mentors serve as friends and role models, as well as advocates and challengers, helping to build the self-esteem, confidence, and skills they need to stay drug-free.

In addition to *mentoring*, this unique program involves students in *community service*, offers classroom-based instruction in life skills, and includes a workshop for parents. The *community service* aspect of the program enables these students to see how they can help others, giving them a sense of personal and social responsibility and contributing to their self-esteem. In contrast, the *classroom instruction* teaches skills applicable to students' real life problems within their families and with their friends and with peer pressure. Finally, the *workshop for parents* helps the students' parents develop more effective parenting skills and more positive ways of interacting within the family. Essential to the success of the program are the teachers and school personnel who have been trained in its implementation and evaluation.

Programs like this are expensive — not only in money, but also in a community's investment of its limited reserves of passion and hope. How might one determine whether an intergenerational mentoring program such as this one effective? Leonard LoSciuto, Amy Rajala, Tara Townsend, and Andrea Taylor (1996), at Temple University, employed a *randomized pretest-posttest control group design*. Three sixth-grade classes per school were randomly selected from all of the sixth-grade classes in schools that were willing to participate in the study (almost all of them). Within each school, each class was randomly assigned to one of three conditions:

1. Students received the complete program of mentoring, community service, instruction in life skills, and parent workshops.
2. Students received everything but mentoring.
3. Students received no intervention at all. They were the control condition.

At the beginning of the academic year, prior to starting the intervention program, all the students were pretested on a variety of measures assessing their knowledge, attitudes, and behavior related to the program goals. All students were tested again with a series of posttests at the end of the academic year. This type of experimental design, because it randomly assigns subjects to conditions and uses a separate control comparison (see the Research Focus "An Experiment" in Chapter 1), in addition to the comparison between pretest and posttest performance, has high internal validity (see the Research Focus "Internal and External Validity" on the Web site). This internal validity enables the investigators to conclude that the changes they observe are actually due to the program and not to some other factor.

Because the students are randomly assigned to conditions and each student has the same chance as any other of being assigned to each group, one can be reasonably certain that the three groups do not differ in any systematic way at the outset of the program. Additionally, pretesting students before they begin the intervention program makes it possible to determine whether equivalence has, in fact, been achieved.

Pretesting offers other advantages as well. Pretests allow investigators to assess the extent to which individuals *change* over time. Thus, if some students are responsive to the treatment whereas others are not, pretesting may suggest clues, which can be followed up in subsequent research, as to why some are more responsive than others. Pretesting is also useful when subjects drop out of the program, as is common for lengthy programs. Loss of subjects in this manner is known as *subject mortality* and is a potential source of bias if it is systematically related to the experimental conditions. For instance, poorer students might be least responsive to the demands of mentoring and community service and most likely to drop out, leaving proportionately more of the better students in the intervention group. In this way, even interventions that have no effect may appear to result in improved performance. By inspecting the pretests of students who drop out, however, one can determine whether they differ from the students who remain in the program. Pretesting also has a disadvantage. It can sensitize subjects to the purpose of the investigation, making it possible for them to figure out what is expected of them and potentially affecting the way they respond to the experimental treatment.

Many intervention programs are not able to randomly assign subjects to experimental and control conditions. Research about such programs is termed *quasi-experimental* because it relies only on comparisons of pretest and posttest performance. A number of problems exist with quasi-experimental designs. Because there is no control condition, we don't know how to interpret the findings. Suppose, for instance, posttest scores are no better than pretest scores. Can we conclude that the program is ineffective? Not necessarily. It's always possible that performance could have declined during that time and that only because of the program did scores remain the same. Similarly, increases in performance on the posttest do not lend themselves to a simple interpretation. Several potential *confounds* exist. These can be due to maturation, testing, history, instrument decay, or statistical regression.

Maturation reflects any systematic changes that occur over time. These can be long-term, such as the developmental changes in intelligence discussed in Chapters 4 and 10, or short-term, such as changes due to fatigue, boredom, or practice. *Testing effect* reflects any changes that occur due to familiarity with the tests. Because pretests usually involve the same type of questions as posttests and frequently measure knowledge about the same subject matter, testing effects are likely. *History* refers to events that occur between testings that can affect the behavior being measured. For example, at the same time as the intervention program, television might run a series of public service spots featuring famous athletes who warn kids against the use of drugs. *Instrument decay* reflects changes in the measures used; these are especially likely when people are the "instruments"; for example, counselors or teachers can become more practiced over time, or they may change their standards in other ways. *Statistical regression* can occur when students are selected for a program because they are atypical, that is, because their scores are either especially low or high. Because no two tests can ever be perfectly correlated, most scores will change somewhat. Students who are selected because of especially low scores will look like they have improved due to the program, but because they were at the bottom of the distribution, their scores could *only* go up. By the same token, students with especially high scores on a pretest would show a drop in performance on the posttest. In each case scores "drift," or regress, toward the mean of the distribution, because that is where most scores are to be found.

None of these confounds, however, threaten the validity of the research of LoSciuto and his colleagues about the intergenerational mentoring program. These investigators found that students who received all four components of the program were likely to do best. They were more likely to react appropriately when offered drugs, were absent from school less, and had more positive attitudes toward school, community service, and their own futures. There is also some indication that mentoring resulted in increased feelings of self-worth and well-being and reduced sadness and loneliness.

Source: L. LoSciuto, A. K. Rajala, T. N. Townsend, & A. S. Taylor. (1996). An outcome evaluation of Across Ages: An intergenerational mentoring approach to drug prevention. *Journal of Adolescent Research, 11*, 116–129.

adolescents live in **poor families,** with incomes below the federal poverty level (U.S. Bureau of the Census, 2005), and another 12% in **low-income families** with incomes no greater than twice that (National Center for Children in Poverty [NCCP], 2003).

Whether poor or low-income, these adolescents face many of the same health concerns. They experience greater exposure to toxins, more air pollution, inferior drinking water, more noise pollution, poorer housing, greater exposure to asthma-related allergens both inside and outside their homes, and they live in more hazardous neighborhoods (Evans, 2004). Understandably, the conditions of poverty are strongly related to stress (Chen, Langer, Raphaelson, & Matthews, 2004) and to elevated levels of risk-related injuries (Evans, 2004).

Solutions to the health concerns of these adolescents will require the nation's creative attention since the conditions contributing to their poverty do not necessarily reside within their families, but instead result from broader societal conditions (Ozawa, 2004). For instance, it is simply not the case that poverty can be explained away by suggesting that parents are unwilling to work. In most poor or low-income families, either one parent, or frequently both parents, work a full-time job! It's also the case that most parents who are not employed full-time indicate this is because they are unable to find a job (NCCP, 2003).

A number of obvious policy implications arise from these data. As the Department of Health and Human Services points out, support for low-income families will necessitate institutional changes at the broadest levels of society (CDC, 2004b). One of the first of these changes would be to create more jobs. As William Wilson (1996), a sociologist at Harvard, notes, there is a new inner-city urban poverty. It is a jobless poverty. That is, poverty has always existed in poor inner-city neighborhoods—by definition. But in the past, a majority of the adults in these neighborhoods held jobs. This is no longer true. In Wilson's words, "The United States is hemorrhaging jobs." He suggests the establishment of a federal jobs program similar to the federal program that got our nation back on its feet following the Depression (Wilson, 1996).

A second obvious policy implication would be to raise the minimum wage (Douglas-Hall & Koball, 2003). The current **federal minimum wage** of $5.15/hour clearly is not adequate to support a family. Consider this: If both parents in a family of four each work a full-time job paying the minimum wage, their total earnings will be $19,776 per year, $224 below the federal poverty threshold for a family this size (U.S. Department of Health and Human Services, 2006)! This income barely covers food and housing, let alone costs of health care, child care, and transportation.

Since social policy affects the lives of adolescents in many significant ways, we will consider social issues throughout the chapters of this text.

poor families Families with incomes below the federal poverty level.

low-income families Families with incomes no greater than twice the federal poverty level.

federal minimum wage Federal policy determining the minimum wage to be paid workers.

Summary

The Endocrine System

- The *endocrine system* consists of glands within the body that produce hormones and of structures within the central nervous system that regulate their activity, and is part of a feedback system that controls the timing of puberty.
- Puberty occurs over two distinct phases: adrenarche and gonadarche. *Adrenarche* begins at 6 to 8 years of age and involves increased production of adrenal androgens that contribute to a number of pubertal changes such as skeletal growth. *Gonadarche* begins several years later and involves increased produc-

tion of hormones governing physical and sexual maturation.

- The *production of hormones* governing pubertal changes is regulated by a feedback system in which hormones secreted by cells in the hypothalamus stimulate the anterior pituitary to produce hormones that act directly on the gonads. These, in turn, increase their production of the sex hormones — estrogens in females and androgens in males — until the hypothalamus, which is sensitive to levels of circulating hormones, adjusts its signals to the anterior pituitary when these get either too high or too low.

The Physical Changes of Puberty

- Puberty ushers in a *growth spurt* and maturation of the reproductive system. Primary sex characteristics involve changes in the *reproductive system* itself; other changes, such as the appearance of pubic hair and the growth of breasts in females and of facial hair in males, represent secondary sex characteristics.
- Considerable variability exists from one adolescent to the next in the timing and, to a lesser degree, the sequence of these changes. In girls, the appearance of pubic hair is one of the first visible signs of change. Breasts begin to develop at about the same time. The uterus, vagina, and ovaries all develop simultaneously with the breasts. In boys, who begin puberty an average of two years later than girls, the first sign of change is an enlargement of the scrotum, due to the developing testes, followed by the appearance of pubic hair. The penis starts to grow a year later. The height spurt precedes a change in voice and the appearance of facial and underarm hair.
- The *growth spurt* is regulated by the growth hormone and the sex hormones and results in a period of rapid growth in height. In girls, the most rapid growth occurs in the year immediately preceding and the one following menarche; girls typically gain 8 to 10 inches. Boys reach their peak growth rate two years later than girls and grow for a longer period of time; they typically gain 12 to 13 inches.
- *Menarche,* the onset of menstrual periods, occurs midway through puberty. Most girls reach menarche in their 12th year. The menstrual cycle is regulated by a feedback loop involving the ovaries, the anterior pituitary, and the hypothalamus. When levels of estrogen reach a peak at midcycle, ovulation occurs. Most adolescent girls have irregular cycles at first, many of which do not involve the release of an ovum. Reactions to menarche reflect how well prepared they are for this event, as well as the attitudes of their families and cultures.
- In boys, the presence of testosterone and other hormones stimulates the testes to produce sperm. Most boys experience *spermarche,* the first ejaculation of seminal fluid, by mid-adolescence. Despite the relative lack of preparation, most boys are not alarmed, though most admit to being surprised.
- Puberty begins earlier today than in past generations. Adolescents also grow faster and grow to be taller than in the past, a trend known as the *secular trend*. Improved nutrition is a likely cause of the secular trend.

The Psychological and Social Implications of Puberty

- Adolescence is a time of *heightened emotionality*. Adolescents experience more intense emotions than their parents and report a wider range of emotions.
- *Good relationships with parents* can provide a powerful buffer against the stresses of adolescence. Adolescents who experience their parents as warm and loving experience fewer emotional or behavioral problems. For most adolescents, however, closeness with parents temporarily decreases and conflict increases. Ethnic differences suggest that puberty may involve less conflict for Hispanic than European American males.

The Timing of Change: Early and Late Maturers

- Differences in the timing of pubertal change are referred to as asynchrony. Comparisons of *early and late maturing* boys find initial social advantages for early maturing boys, but also more adjustment problems. In contrast to boys, early maturation in girls carries few initial advantages. Like boys, however, early maturing girls experience more problems of adjustment, although ethnic differences suggest these are less likely among African Americans than European Americans.
- Three explanations have been offered for the more disruptive effects of early timing, particularly with respect to girls.

  (1) The *maturational deviance hypothesis* assumes that timing is important because it changes adolescents' status relative to their peers, setting them apart from peers and from the social supports to which they customarily turn.

(2) The *stage termination hypothesis* assumes that early maturers do not have as much time to complete the developmental tasks of middle childhood and must cope with the challenges of puberty when they have not yet completely resolved those of middle childhood.

(3) The *adult status hypothesis* assumes that movement toward adulthood does not carry the same advantages for girls as it does for boys since most adult males enjoy a higher status in society than females.

- Pubertal changes bring about changes in adolescents' body images. How satisfied adolescents are with their bodies also is influenced by their perceptions of how they are evaluated by others. Females generally have less positive *body images* than males.

Health and Well-Being

- *Nutritional requirements* increase with growth. Nearly half of all meals eaten in the United States are eaten in restaurants, most of which are fast-food chains. However, adolescents can eat nutritious meals at these places by including more fresh fruits and vegetables and substituting low-caloric items for those high in calories.
- Regular *physical activity* contributes to adolescents' health through building and maintaining bones and muscles and controlling weight, and by reducing stress and activity, and by improving their self-esteem. Even so, older adolescents are less active than younger ones.
- The number of adolescents who are *overweight* has tripled since the 1970s, with an estimated 16% of 12- to 19-year-olds currently overweight and another 15% at risk of becoming overweight. Overweight adolescents have somewhat different eating patterns, but one of the most important differences is that they are less active than adolescents who are not overweight. The relationship between overweight and inactivity highlights the importance of exercise in weight reduction programs. The success of a weight control program for adolescents almost always depends on successfully integrating the family into the program.
- As an age group, adolescents and young adults experience poorer access to *health care* than young children or older adults. Adolescents report difficulty knowing where to go, finding transportation, anxiety as to what might be done, not wanting their parents to know, and not having insurance coverage. These problems are magnified for adolescents living in rural communities or non-urban settings who are less likely to have health insurance.
- A significant factor influencing the accessibility of health care is health care coverage. Presently, over 9 million children and adolescents in the United States do not have health insurance. Yet 5.8 million of these could receive free health insurance through either Medicaid or the Children's Health Insurance Program (CHIP). The Children's Defense Fund has developed an outreach project, SHOUT (**S**tudent **H**ealth **Out**reach), in which high school and college student volunteers help low-income families enroll children for free health care coverage.
- Perhaps the single most important factor affecting the health and well-being of adolescents in the United States is the presence of *poverty*. Approximately 20% of U.S. adolescents live in poor families, with incomes below the federal poverty level, and another 12% in low-income families with incomes no greater than twice that. These adolescents experience greater exposure to toxins, more air pollution, inferior drinking water, more noise pollution, poorer housing, and greater exposure to asthma-related allergens both inside and outside their homes, and they live in more hazardous neighborhoods. The conditions of poverty are strongly related to stress and to elevated levels of risk-related injuries.
- Solutions to the health needs of low-income adolescents will require the nation's creative attention since the conditions contributing to their poverty do not necessarily reside within their families, but instead result from broader societal conditions. Two of the most important of these are the decreasing numbers of jobs in the United States and the low wages they pay.
- Support for low-income families will necessarily involve institutional changes at the broadest levels of society, with attention to those that create more and better-paying jobs.

Key Terms

- endocrine system
- hormones
- androgens
- testosterone
- estrogens
- estradiol
- progesterone
- adrenarche
- gonadarche
- adrenal androgens
- hypothalamus
- gonadotropin-releasing hormone (GnRH)
- anterior pituitary
- gonads
- luteinizing hormone (LH)
- follicle-stimulating hormone (FSH)
- gonadostat
- primary sex characteristics
- secondary sex characteristics
- growth spurt
- ovaries
- ovum
- uterus
- vagina
- cervix
- hymen
- clitoris
- glans
- shaft
- prepuce
- testes
- sperm
- circumcision
- female genital mutilation
- outer labia
- menarche
- anovulatory
- leptin
- spermarche
- nocturnal emission
- secular trend
- asynchrony
- early maturation
- late maturation
- self-esteem
- maturational deviance hypothesis
- stage termination hypothesis
- adult status hypothesis
- body image
- overweight
- body mass index (BMI)
- poor families
- low-income families
- federal minimum wage

CHAPTER OUTLINE

CHAPTER 4

The Cognitive and Intellectual Changes of Adolescence

CHAPTER OBJECTIVES

- To identify three distinguishing features of adolescent thought: thinking abstractly, hypothetically, and logically
- To understand how brain maturation enables adolescents to think in new ways
- To examine the intellectual changes that take place in adolescence from the constructive perspective of Piaget and Kegan
- To look at current measures of intelligence, and to consider whether these accurately represent differences due to culture and gender
- To examine the approaches to intelligence offered by Sternberg and Gardner
- To look at the ways in which cognitive development affects adolescents' daily lives, and how it affects their ability to understand themselves and others and to experience new emotions
- To see how cognitive development enables adolescents to function more effectively and solve new types of problems in the classroom

Yuan-Pin — Pete, to his friends — read alternatives "b" and "c" again. He knew this material. He had distinguished his family with good marks in this very subject before coming to this country. Yet he couldn't understand the question. The two choices seemed the same to him. He could feel the heat rising in his face as the words danced and mocked him. Blindly, he marked "c" and moved on. The bell would ring soon. So much depended on him. He would have to study his English again tonight after he and his father closed the shop. No time for hanging out, for video games or the sitcoms his friends watched each night. No wonder they thought he was a loner. Sometimes he thought he was crazy. How could he explain one world to the other? Or to himself?

Sehti's mind wandered as she stared at the quiz. She was still angry that she hadn't been able to study more last night. She'd had to help her mother with dinner. Why had her uncle and aunt picked that night to visit? And why couldn't her brothers have helped? They didn't have half the homework she had, and they never had to help. Her mother said it was women's work, that she should leave her brothers alone. The bell — oh, no! She quickly marked alternative "b." Why couldn't she concentrate?

Joe looked at the quiz: 15 questions. He knew the answers to all of them — all but number 11. Actually, it was the way the question was worded. He could make an argument for either "b" or "c." Joe loved junior high. Math, social studies, drama, English lit — each left him more excited than the last. By the end of the day, he was filled with ideas, ideas he framed easily in words that he spoke with quiet confidence. The bell! He chose "b" and wondered how successful he'd be in convincing Mr. Allen of his reasoning if his teacher had keyed "c" as correct.

Chapter Overview

You have just met three students, each competent, each standing on the threshold of a new world of thought and experience. All adolescents embark on the journey these three are beginning. Not all travel the same distance. Yuan-Pin, Sehti, and Joe probably will not either. They aren't likely to get the same grade on this quiz or to do equally well in junior high. Is this unfair? Differences in their grades will not necessarily reflect their capabilities. Yuan-Pin is still learning English; he doesn't have a chance to show what he knows. Sehti's concentration is scattered by conflicting demands at home and at school. Intellectual performance almost always reflects more than what one knows. Motives, interests, and even expectations held by others can affect performance.

Early adolescents face intellectual changes that are every bit as profound as the biological changes discussed in the previous chapter. These changes usher in adult forms of thought, just as the latter usher in adult bodies. Adolescents can plan for the future, imagine the impossible, catch multiple meanings to words and situations, understand nuance, follow a philosophical discussion, and respond to a simple question with an answer that would make the captain of a debating team proud. We will look at the nature of these changes and at explanations that have been offered for them. We will also consider conditions that affect intellectual performance in adolescents such as Yuan-Pin, Sehti, and Joe.

Piaget and Kegan view intellectual development from a constructive perspective. For Piaget, the ability to imagine the possible, rather than thinking only of the actual, is the most important quality of mature thought. With this step, thought becomes abstract. It also becomes logical and systematic. Adolescents can think of problems in terms of the variables that define them, isolating first one and then the other, until they come up with all possible combinations.

Some developmentalists believe that what stage theorists identify as new forms of thought may only reflect continuous growth in abilities already present. Because these abilities are known to increase with age, one could explain Piaget's formal thought in terms of age changes in general intelligence. This approach, known as a psychometric approach, focuses on the abilities that underlie general intelligence and on how these are measured.

We will look at how intelligence tests are constructed, what they measure, and some of the problems they introduce when not interpreted correctly. The greatest strength of intelligence tests is in predicting academic success. This strength is also a weakness. The paradox arises from our inability to distinguish what success reflects: the general abilities presumed to be tapped by the tests, or the degree of familiarity with the culture required to understand the questions? Just as Yuan-Pin experienced difficulty on his math quiz, he would have difficulty with many of the items on the intelligence test.

A final approach to cognitive and intellectual development focuses on age-related changes in the strategies people use to catalogue and process information. Robert Sternberg analyzes intellectual functioning into three components: one that organizes strategies for thinking, another that does the actual work, and a third that gathers new information when needed. Howard Gardner suggests there are seven or more different forms of intelligence. He divides intelligence into areas as diverse as bodily-kinesthetic intelligence and logical-mathematical intelligence.

Throughout the chapter, we will look at the implications of intellectual development for everyday life: Adolescents can think about themselves in new ways, as well as imagine the thoughts of others, understand social nuance, experience new emotions, and argue more effectively.

Adolescents can solve problems that younger children can't because they can think abstractly.

How Adolescents Think

Thought takes interesting turns in early adolescence and carries teenagers places children don't easily go. Adolescents can think about things that don't exist and may never exist. They can think about what is possible as well as what actually is. Thinking becomes highly systematic and logical. This is not to say that adolescents are always logical and that children never are, or that children never consider possibilities as well as realities, or that adolescents always reason in the abstract. It is, rather, that adolescents do so more often and with greater ease. Each of these characteristics of adolescent thought—thinking abstractly, thinking hypothetically, and thinking logically—is discussed in the sections that follow.

Thinking Abstractly

"How is a horse like a goldfish?" If you ask adolescents this question, they are likely to come up with any number of answers. They might say, "Well, a horse and a fish are both animals," or "Both have to eat to live," or "Both take in oxygen and give off carbon dioxide." Children are more likely to stare you down. You can almost hear them think, "That was a stupid question!" In any event, they are not likely to think of any similarities. Why is their response so different from that of adolescents?

Children tend to think of things in terms of their physical properties. With horses and goldfish, this approach doesn't take them very far. If you had asked how a horse was like a dog, they would have had no problem: Both have four legs. They could tell you how a horse is like a cow: Both are large and eat grass. But as long as their thoughts are bound by the physical characteristics of things, fish remain worlds removed from horses. Adolescents can think of things as members of classes and can even think of ways to classify those classes (Drumm & Jackson, 1996). An adolescent can say, for example, "Both are animals, and animals can be either aquatic or terrestrial."

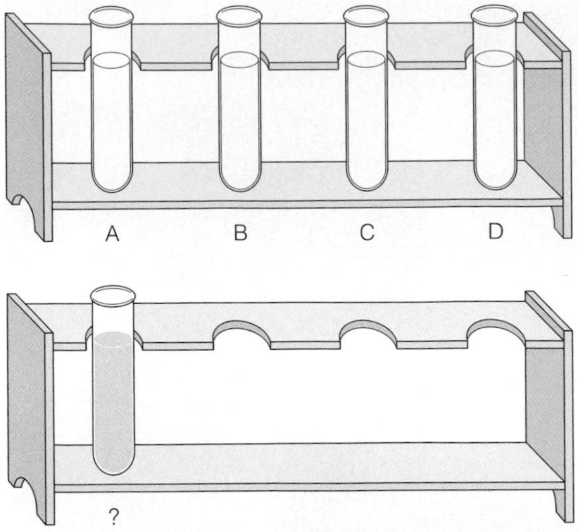

■ **FIGURE 4.1**
A Problem Involving Chemical Solutions That Requires Hypothetical Thinking to Solve. *When asked which combination of these four solutions produces a yellow liquid, adolescents think of all the possible combinations and systematically test each one, whereas children combine the solutions in a haphazard way.* *Source:* Adapted from B. Inhelder & J. Piaget. (1958). *The growth of logical thinking from childhood to adolescence.* New York: Basic Books.

Thinking Hypothetically

Thinking abstractly is related to another characteristic of adolescent thought: hypothetical thinking. Adolescents can turn a problem around in their minds and come up with possible variations it might take (Figure 4.1). Only then do they start to work, testing each possibility to find the one that applies in that situation. Being able to imagine what is possible, instead of thinking only of what is real, allows adolescents to think hypothetically.

Children, in contrast, focus on the actual, perceptible elements of a situation and rarely speculate about possibilities they cannot generate by actually doing something. They are more likely to jump in and do something with no plan of attack. Even if they succeed in solving the problem, they are not likely to have kept a record of what they did. John Flavell, a psychologist at Stanford University who has written widely on cognitive development, remarks that the school child's "speculations about other possibilities—that is, about other potential, as yet undetected realities—occur only with difficulty and as a last resort. An ivory-tower theorist the elementary school child is not" (Flavell, Miller, & Miller, 1993).

Thinking Logically

As thought becomes abstract, adolescents are able to test different ideas against one another to establish their truth. They become aware of the logical relations that exist among ideas and can use logical consistency to determine whether a statement is true or false. Children check their ideas against hard facts; so do adolescents, but logical consistency is equally compelling for them.

This difference is dramatically illustrated in a simple experiment. Adolescents and children are shown poker chips and asked to judge whether statements about the chips are true or false. Sometimes the chips are hidden in the experimenter's hand; at other times they are clearly visible. The experimenter has just picked up a green chip and holds it in clear view. He says, "The chip in my hand is either green or not green." Both the adolescent and the child agree that the statement is true. Next the experimenter holds up a chip that is hidden in his hand and says, "The chip in my hand is either red or not red." The adolescent knows the statement must be true and agrees. The child says, "I can't tell," and asks to see the chip! Children evaluate statements such as these by comparing them to what they can see, not realizing that they could still evaluate their truth based on logical properties. Adolescents know that thoughts can be checked against themselves for logical consistency (Osherson & Markman, 1975).

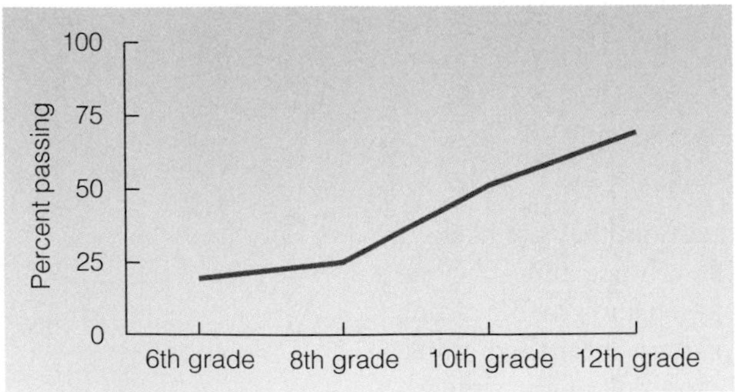

■ **FIGURE 4.2**
Adolescents Passing Piaget's Measures of Formal Thought. *Reasoning improves with age throughout adolescence; late adolescents can solve more of Piaget's tasks than early adolescents.* *Source:* S. C. Martorano. (1977). A developmental analysis of performance on Piaget's formal operations tasks. *Developmental Psychology, 13,* 666–672.

One might assume, at this point, that all adolescents think and solve problems alike. But thinking, like every other aspect of development, is highly individual. Tremendous differences exist among early adolescents in the rate at which they acquire new reasoning abilities, and many adolescents do not reason in these ways even by the end of middle school or junior high (Figure 4.2). Instead, thinking improves with age throughout adolescence (Arnett & Taber, 1994).

Models of atomic structures and other abstract concepts are meaningful only to students who have reached a level of cognitive development that enables them to use symbolic representations to evaluate the logical consistency of ideas.

Biological Bases to Intellectual Development

It's common knowledge that most 14-year-olds know more, reason faster, and remember better than most 10-year-olds. They can solve harder problems, think through abstract dilemmas, understand complex social situations, and even spell better. What interests developmentalists is not *if* there is a difference between the way adolescents and children think, but what to make of that difference. Is it only that each additional year adds a bit more to what one knows? Or does a more fundamental change occur somewhere between childhood and adolescence to account for this difference? Considerable data suggest that biological maturation of neural structures contributes substantially to intellectual development (Mukherjee et al., 2002).

Brain development continues well into adulthood, with different regions developing at different rates at different points in life. This development takes a number of forms. One of these is the continued **myelination** of neural fibers, as shown in Figure 4.3. Myelin is a fatty substance that coats the length of the neural fiber, thereby insulating it from the activity of neighboring neurons and enabling it to conduct impulses more rapidly (Hof, Trapp, deVellis, Claudio, & Colman, 1999). The sequence in which fibers in different areas of the brain are myelinated correlates with the timing of anticipated use of the pathways involved. Myelination of most neural fibers is largely completed by about age 7, an age at which children show decided shifts in intellectual performance (this shift corresponds to Piaget's transition to concrete operational thought; see Table 2.2, page 42).

myelination The formation of a fatty sheath surrounding a nerve fiber (axon), which increases speed of neural conduction.

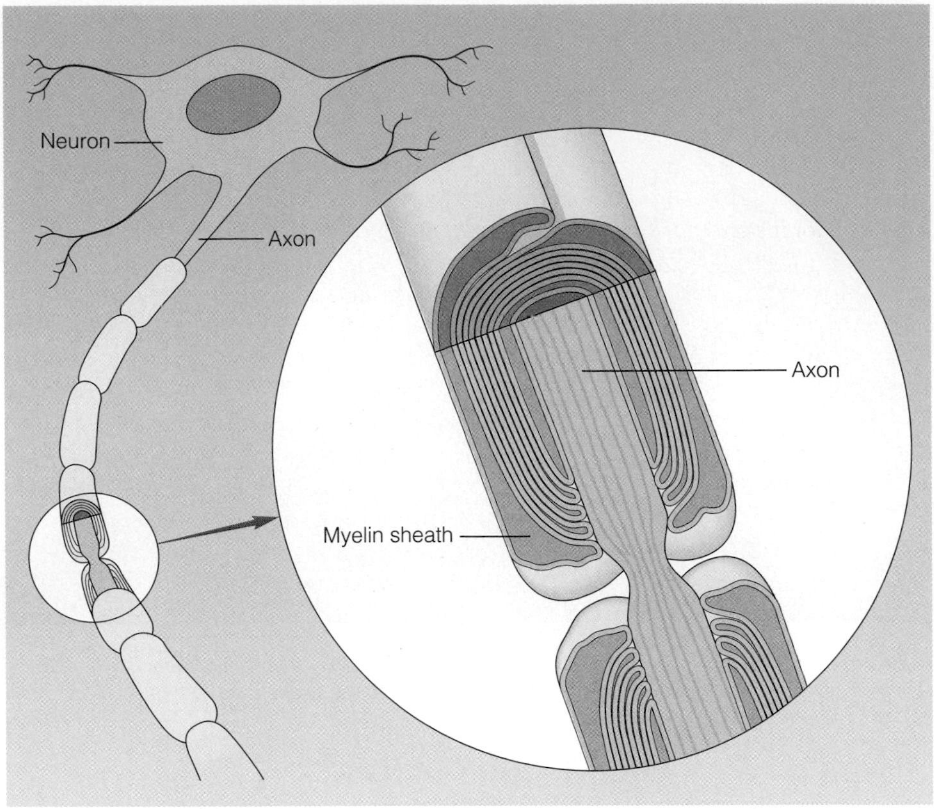

■ **FIGURE 4.3**
Myelin Sheath Coating Axon. *The formation of a myelin sheath around neural fibers enables them to conduct impulses more rapidly. Myelination continues in adolescence in regions of the brain involved in abstract thought.*

Myelination continues to occur, however, well into adolescence in regions of the brain that play a role, in one way or another, in abstract thought, by integrating neural input from various areas (Sowell, Thompson, Tessner, & Toga, 2001). Finally, and perhaps not surprisingly to most parents, neural pathways involved in speech show continued myelination into late adolescence (Paus et al., 1999).

Additionally, the **prefrontal cortex,** the "gray matter" located right behind one's forehead, shows continued development during adolescence (Bunge, Dudovic, Thomason, Vaidya, & Gabrieli, 2002; Hooper, Luciana, Conklin, & Yarger, 2004). This area of the brain is primarily responsible for abstract thought, enabling one to hold on to information long enough to relate it to something else. For this reason, the prefrontal cortex is involved in planning—either on a short-term basis, such as choosing from among several things in front of one (e.g., the cupcake or the apple), or long-term, such as envisioning the consequences of one's actions or planning for one's future.

Thus, changes in the ways in which the brain continues to grow can be observed at about the age at which adolescents begin to show characteristic changes in thinking, lending strong support to a biological basis for their occurrence.

Cognitive Development: A Constructive Perspective

prefrontal cortex Region of the cortex located behind the forehead involved in abstract thought.

A number of years ago, there was a particularly scary horror movie, *A Nightmare on Elm Street,* in which the villain, Freddy Krueger, reached his victims through their minds, appearing to them in their dreams. Unlike other dreams, these took on a chilling reality because they didn't end when the person woke up. The villain was able to step into one's waking life, making the villain as close as a heartbeat and only a thought away. Children across the country didn't sleep for nights after watching this movie. Freddy Krueger had a power to terrorize that other villains lacked: Other monsters could be more easily separated from one's self.

The idea that thought gives substance to reality is a powerful one, taking different forms depending on one's age and even at different times in history. The ancient Hebrew alphabet, for instance, lacked symbols for vowels. These had to be supplied by the reader. Unlike consonants, which are formed as the tongue or teeth stop the flow of air, vowels are unstopped breaths. In Hebrew, the word for breath is the same as the word for spirit, *ruach.* In reading, one had to breathe life into the message, fleshing it out with the thoughts that made one vowel more probable than another. Similarly, ancient texts, even up to medieval times, lacked punctuation, making it necessary for a reader to interpret the text in order to decipher it. Because reading was such an active, even creative, process, a person would often initial a text after reading it.

As you may recall from Chapter 1, the constructive perspective that informs this text assumes that individuals must continually interpret, or make sense of, all experience—whether deciphering printed words on a page, recognizing a familiar face, or listening to a conversation. In fact, this perspective argues that events remain ambiguous *until* we respond to them. Only by responding does the meaning of an event become explicit. Noam Chomsky (1957), a psycholinguist at MIT, illustrated this point by asking the meaning of the sentence "Flying planes can be dangerous." Does this mean that it is dangerous to fly a plane *or* that it is dangerous to be around planes that are flying? We rarely notice such ambiguities because we, just as the readers of ancient texts, breathe life into our experiences on a moment-by-moment basis. Pilots will hear Chomsky's sentence one way, and those living near airports will hear it another, the expectancies of each giving shape to their experience. Only when one is new to a task do expectancies fail, making it necessary to assemble understanding piece by piece. As any 5-year-old would tell you, reading is hardly automatic, even today.

Piaget and Kegan

Piaget adds a developmental twist to the constructive perspective. He assumed not only that we actively construct what we know of the world, but also that this understanding is organized in qualitatively different ways with age. Cognitive development, for Piaget, is a gradual freeing of thought from experience. This progression begins with infants, for whom thought is literally embedded in the physical actions they perform on things, and culminates with adolescents, who are able to think of things they have never touched or seen and to consider possibilities that do not exist and perhaps never will.

Sensorimotor Thought (Birth to 2 Years) In infancy, thought is limited to what is experienced through one's sense and actions: It is *sensorimotor.* To know something is to know how it feels, tastes, or smells, or to anticipate what will happen when one does something to it. It is to know, for instance, that candy is sweet, or that something held in one's hand will drop if released. Piaget maintains that, at first, infants cannot represent these experiences in their minds. As a consequence, he assumes infants do not realize that objects continue to exist when they no longer see them; that is, they do not have a concept of **object permanence.** Infants expand their world through countless daily experiments, such as dropping, sucking, or banging, which allow them to discover what things do. Piaget calls actions such as these **schemes.** A scheme is a class of actions that infants can apply to any number of objects; the precise form of the action varies slightly from one object to the next. After all, it's not as easy to wrap one's mouth around a

object permanence Piaget's term for the infant's recognition that objects exist even when they cannot be seen.

schemes Piaget's term for the precursors of concepts; ways of representing experience through one's actions.

rubber ball as it is a rattle or a cookie. But in each case, the baby explores an object by bringing it to the mouth.

Preoperational Thought (2 Years to 7 Years) In the preschool years, children are able to represent their experiences through symbols; these are richly evidenced in their language, drawings, and fantasy play. Despite this progression, there is a "stuck" quality to preoperational thought, an apparent inability to move something around in one's mind and catch it from another angle. As a result, thought is often dominated by how things look.

Concrete Operational Thought (7 Years to 11 Years) School-age children are able to imagine actions that can be carried out in their heads and then reversed or undone. These **mental operations** allow children to take a mental step off the spot from which they have viewed a problem and gain a new perspective on it. Being able to relate one aspect of a problem to another allows them to impose a new order on experience instead of taking it as a given. Thought becomes more integrated and logical.

In one of Piaget's most dramatic tests of **conservation,** which he used to demonstrate whether children knew that things remained unchanged even when they appeared to be different, he poured liquid from a short, wide glass into a tall, narrow one, causing the level of the liquid to rise, and asked if the liquid was still the same. Younger children are unable to distinguish how the liquid *looks* from how it *is* and say there is more in the taller glass. Older children, however, agree that the amount of liquid in either container must be the same. They say things such as, "I could pour the liquid back and it would look the same," a mental operation that Piaget referred to as "negation," or "This glass may be taller, but it's also narrower, and the one makes up for the other," which Piaget called "reciprocity." It is this ability to move from one perspective to another, and back again, using either of these operations, that enables older children to understand that the liquid is unchanged, giving their world stability, "concreteness."

The dawning of operations burns through the mists of childhood thought like the morning sun. New skills follow as the day follows night. Mathematical concepts such as multiplication emerge from addition, concepts such as one's home state can be understood as larger than one's hometown and smaller than one's nation, and stamp albums, baseball cards, and doll collections reflect a new ability to mentally order one's world.

Formal Operational Thought (11 Years and Older) Despite the flexibility of school-age children's thought, it is still limited. Children do not think easily about things they cannot see, and they think of things that are absent only through simple extensions of their thoughts about those that are present. Operations may organize experience and at times even extend it, but they do not create for the child, as they do for the adolescent, another world in which "the real becomes a special case of the possible" (Flavell, 1963).

Formal operational thought begins at about age 11. In a sense it is simply an extension of the concrete operations children have used all along in sorting and classifying the objects around them. In another sense it is an extension that quite literally opens up new worlds of possibilities for adolescents. The extension is a simple one: Adolescents can extend their earlier operations on classes of *objects* to classes of *classes.* The adolescent mind can include itself in the things it considers.

Thought evolves through the complementary processes of assimilation and accommodation. Through assimilation, one is able to interpret new experiences in familiar ways, ways that are already a part of the self, fitting the new into what one already knows. Through accommodation, in order to understand something new, one must change the way one views things; one must work at understanding, sounding out the experience as a new reader does with a word, a process that also changes

conservation The realization that something remains the same despite changes in its appearance.

one ever so slightly, making the other familiar only by changing the self.

Building on the constructive process elaborated by Piaget, Robert Kegan (1982, 1994) argues that intellectual growth takes place through a process of **differentiation** of self from other, a process that has the effect of simultaneously defining new aspects of one's surroundings and of one's self. In a manner similar to Isaac Newton's second law of motion, in which every action has an opposite and equal reaction, when one gives meaning to events out there, one's sense of self in relation to these events also changes.

Kegan gives the example of two young boys, 5 and 9 years old, surveying a street scene from the observation deck of a skyscraper. They exclaim their wonderment in different ways. The younger one says, "Look at the people. They're tiny ants." The older one says, "Look at the people. They look like tiny ants." There is a complexity to the older boy's remark that is lacking in the younger boy's. We hear in his remark a comment that has to do as much with *how* he is perceiving as with *what* he has perceived. His awareness of people looking *like* ants, rather than simply being the size of ants, adds a reflective quality in which he is aware both of the percept and of the evaluating self—both of what he is seeing and of himself seeing it.

The ability to separate himself from his perceptions enabled him to see them for what they were—as ways of seeing or perspectives. When perspectives emerge for the child's inspection, the child can move from one perspective to another and back again, seeing that the object has not changed even though its appearance may. This understanding gives the child a new grasp on things. Things that previously expanded and shrank when seen from different vantage points, like reflections in a fun house mirror, now hold still and become concrete (Kegan, 1982).

Because most middle school and junior high students are in transition from concrete operational thought to formal operational thought, they need a lot of hands-on activities in the classroom.

Just as older children become aware of their perspectives, adolescents become aware of how these can be coordinated. They can see that the liquid in Piaget's test of conservation remains the same either because one could always pour it back or because the width of the second glass compensates for its height. They can also see that not only is the amount of liquid similar in the two glasses, but so are the *ways* by which they arrive at this understanding similar—that is, that negation and reciprocity are comparable. Note, however, that each of these operations is a way of thinking, a point which illustrates a central characteristic of adolescent thought, namely, that they are able to *think* about their thinking.

What enables adolescents to view the world differently than school children? Differentiation occurs when adolescents become aware of their part in creating this stability. When they distinguish what they do in coordinating different perspectives from the perspectives themselves, the concrete world of stable objects can be seen for what it is, as one of the many ways they might see their world.

The ability to think about thought allows adolescents to arrive at possibilities they could never reach otherwise. We can see this quality of thought at work in one of Piaget's tasks, a game in which balls are shot onto a gameboard with a spring launcher. The balls differ in size and in the smoothness of their surfaces. Eventually each stops rolling, the larger and rougher ones first. Piaget asks adolescents to explain why they stop. At first, adolescents identify wind resistance and friction as important. But they soon realize something else: that the balls would roll forever if neither of these were present. This

differentiation A process by which one distinguishes or perceives differences not previously recognized.

These adolescents contradict Piaget's assumption that once formal thought emerges, individuals think logically all the time. Even though these young women are certainly aware of the health risks of smoking, their behavior does not reflect their ability to reason logically or to envision the long-term consequences of their actions.

conclusion can be reached only through thought, because the conditions under which this would occur are never actually present (Flavell, Miller, & Miller, 1993).

How does all of this relate to Freddy Krueger's power to terrorize? For 5-year-olds, who have difficulty separating how things appear from how they are, people are tiny ants—and Freddy Krueger is in the room with them. Schoolchildren become aware not only of what they are seeing but of themselves seeing it, of watching a monster in a horror movie; Freddy Krueger is still scary for them, but at heart they know they are reacting to a character in a movie. Adolescents' awareness that the villain in the movie is simply one of any number of monsters that could be imagined, that Freddy Krueger is the product of someone's imagination, makes it possible, and even fun, for them to think of ways to make him scarier.

Contextual Effects and Formal Thinking

Does development progress at the same rate and take the same form independent of the particular context in which adolescents find themselves? Quite a lot of evidence suggests that it does not. Perhaps the first place in which to look for contextual influences on cognitive development is school.

Piaget believed that the changes he chronicled were not simply due to learning, but became possible only with the biological maturation of underlying mental structures. Yet Lavee Artman and Sorel Cahan (1993), working with large numbers of fourth-, fifth-, and sixth-graders, found that schooling contributed more to their success on certain Piagetian-type problems than did age.

The assumptions we bring to a problem, irrespective of how it may be presented to us, also affect the type of logic we bring to bear in solving a problem. These assumptions are formed through daily experiences with everyday objects. Take a look at the problem illustrated in Figure 4.4. People were told to pretend they were postal workers sorting letters, whose job was to determine whether all letters that were sealed had a 39-cent stamp (i.e., if P, then Q), and to handle as few letters as possible when sorting. But even adults find problems like this difficult—the most frequent mistake is to turn over Q as well as

Test Your Logic: Thinking About a Concrete Problem

Imagine that you are a postal worker sorting letters. You know that sealed letters must have a 37-cent stamp. Among the letters below, select just those you would need to turn over to determine whether they break this rule.

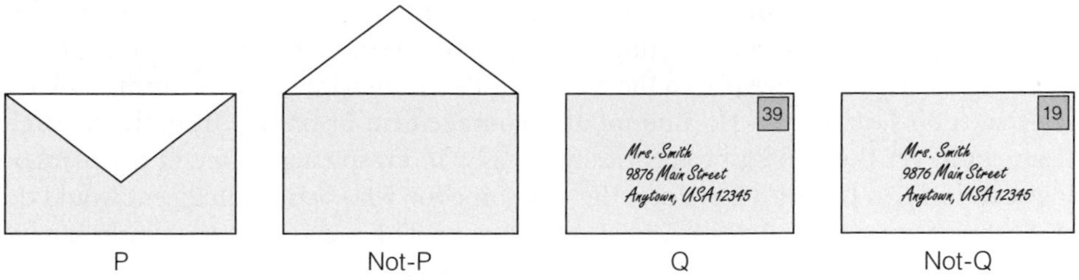

Now read on and see what others did when given this problem.

FIGURE 4.4 Logical Thinking About a Concrete Problem. *Source:* Adapted from P. C. Wason & P. N. Johnson-Laird. (1972). *Psychology of reasoning: Structure and content.* Cambridge, MA: Harvard University Press.

P, even though there's no need to check Q since it already bears the full postage. So why turn it over? It's hard to break a habit, and we've had years of experience checking letters to see if they're sealed (by turning them over) before dropping them in the mail. Even so, it's still easier to think logically about problems such as this when the alternatives are envelopes than when they're symbols such as P, Not-P, Q and Not-Q (Wason & Johnson-Laird, 1972).

Not only our habits but also our preferences can affect the way we think. Tschirgi (1980) gave individuals a story to read about baking a cake in which substitutions were made for several of the ingredients in the recipe. Some of the stories ended with the cake turning out just fine, but in others it turned out badly. In each case, individuals were asked to evaluate why the cake might have turned out as it did. Only when it turned out badly, however, did they think logically, considering each of the alternatives one at a time while holding other conditions constant. Of course, they may have felt that only then would they need to know what went wrong, but this also suggests that we treat positive information differently than negative information. When asked to evaluate personality characteristics, for instance, we tend to view positive traits as more enduring and stable than negative ones, and to place greater weight on individuals' successes than their failures when judging competence (Heyman & Giles, 2004).

Although research indicates that thinking changes dramatically with adolescence, it is equally clear that individual differences are large and that even adolescents who use formal logic do not apply it in all situations. Critics of Piaget's constructive developmental approach have suggested that measures of formal reasoning actually reflect the more general abilities that contribute to intelligence at all ages. This argument brings us to a second approach to intellectual development, one that comes out of the intellectual testing movement.

A Psychometric Approach to Intelligence

The **psychometric approach** focuses on individual differences in the general abilities that contribute to intelligence. Even though intelligence tests have been widely used to predict performance in a variety of settings, how they do this isn't clear. Furthermore, explanations of *how* quickly reduce to questions of *what* when items included in standard measures of intelligence are used to test individuals from other cultures. Robert Sternberg, a psychologist at Yale University, tells an amusing story that illustrates

psychometric approach An approach that focuses on the measurement of individual differences in abilities contributing to intelligence.

Does practicing the guitar develop intelligence? The answer depends on whether intelligence is a single innate capacity or one of several specific abilities, such as musicality or numerical ability.

some of the difficulties in measuring whatever it is we call intelligence, let alone in understanding what that is.

A team of psychologists had administered a number of tasks to people from a village in a traditional culture. One of the tasks involved sorting pictures. In our culture the best, or most intelligent, approach to this task is to sort categorically, to put a picture of a robin under that of a bird, and so on. The people of this village did not adopt this "intelligent" approach. Instead of sorting the pictures categorically, they sorted them functionally. For instance, they placed the picture of the robin with that of a worm, explaining that robins eat worms. No amount of encouragement or hinting from the research team could get them to sort categorically. Finally, in exasperation, one of the psychologists told them to sort the pictures the way someone who *wasn't* intelligent would do it. Each person executed a perfect categorical sort! These people were clearly intelligent enough to sort categorically. They just thought that it wasn't a smart way to do it (Baron & Sternberg, 1987).

Intelligence: What Is It?

Intelligence is a term that most of us use almost daily. Out of sheer familiarity, one might think it would be easy to define. But it is not. In fact, even experts in the field have come up with widely differing views of what it is. Yet most agree that intelligence allows us to profit from our experiences and adapt to our surroundings and that it frequently involves abstract reasoning.

Differences among the experts as to the nature of intelligence are primarily between the "lumpers" and the "splitters," those who view intelligence as a single, general capacity versus those who view it as numerous specific abilities (Garlick, 2002; Juan-Espinosa, Garcia, Colom, & Abad, 2000; Mayr, 1982).

The measures that we have—intelligence tests—are simply collections of questions that reflect the information and abilities of the average person in our society. Depending on which questions are included, people with different experiences will do either better or worse on the tests.

One's score on an intelligence test, or one's IQ, reflects how one performs relative to others the same age. Comparisons with age-mates are important not only because they share similar cultural experiences, but also because, as noted earlier in the chapter, the brain continues to develop in adolescence, leading to changes in performance with age (Figure 4.5). Intelligence tests are constructed so that the average person at any age will score 100.

A Closer Look: The WAIS-R

One way of understanding intelligence is to take a look at what is measured by an intelligence test. We will use the Wechsler Adult Intelligence Scale (**WAIS-R**) as our example, because it is one of the most commonly used measures of intelligence. The WAIS-R includes 11 subtests, grouped into Verbal and Performance Scales. Despite these different scales, David Wechsler was a "lumper." Each scale contributes to an overall IQ score.

Rather than ask questions that reflect academic knowledge, such as "What is the distance between the earth and the sun?" Wechsler asked questions that reflect general information. Questions on the Information subtest, for instance, tap the type of information average people are expected to acquire on their own. Examples of such questions are "What is the distance between London and San Francisco?" and "How tall is the average American man?"

intelligence The ability to profit from experience and adapt to one's surroundings; measured by intelligence tests.

WAIS-R An intelligence scale for adults that is individually administered.

Notice that what can be considered general information in one culture is not necessarily so in another. Sehti, one of the adolescents in the introduction to this chapter, might be more familiar with the height of men in India than in the United States, for example. And Yuan-Pin might be able to estimate the distance between Beijing and Bombay more accurately than the distance between London and San Francisco.

Intelligence itself appears to be increasing over time, with mean scores on various intelligence tests showing gains of several IQ points per decade (Flynn, 1984). Among the most likely explanations for this increase are better nutrition and the need to adapt to an increasingly complex and stimulating environment (Colom, Lluis-Font, & Andres-Pueyo, 2005; Wicherts et al., 2004). As with the secular trend in physical development, however, there is some evidence that this trend may be leveling off (Sundet, Barlaug, & Torjussen, 2004). The Research Focus "Cross-Sectional and Sequential Designs" examines the issue of changes in intelligence with age.

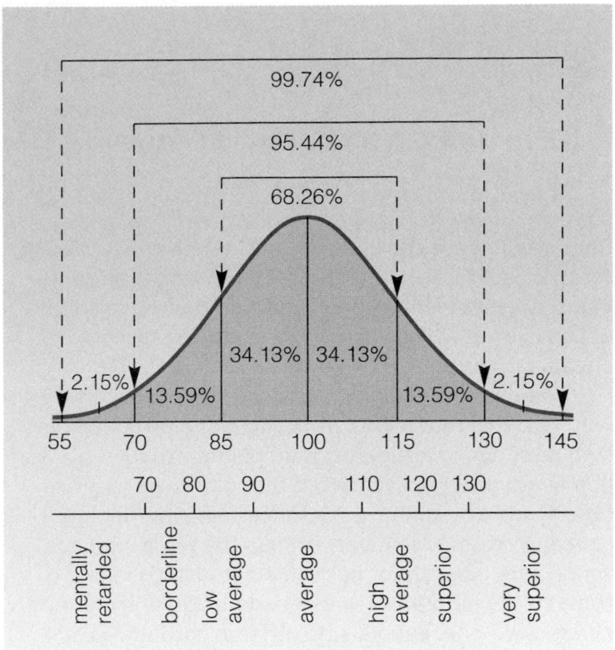

■ **FIGURE 4.5**
Percentage of Individuals and Intelligence Classifications at Different Points From the Mean IQ of 100. *Source:* From Ronald J. Cohen & Mark E. Swerdlik. (1999). *Psychological testing and assessment* (4th ed.). Mountain View, CA: Mayfield.

We began our discussion of intelligence with a warning that intelligence tests have an arbitrary quality to them. The questions they contain don't only tap the capacities with which one is born; they also tap a general knowledge gained by living in a culture. People from another culture, though theoretically just as intelligent, will not do quite as well as those from our own. If different questions were included, ones that reflected their particular cultural experiences, their performance would improve, whereas that of the average North American would drop slightly. These differences do not reflect ability so much as the nature of the questions themselves, as can be seen when adolescents from different cultures are tested in their own countries on equivalent tests of primary abilities (Li, Sano, & Merwin, 1996). Adolescents' cultural backgrounds, then, can be expected to affect their perspective on and approach to problems.

Intelligence Tests and Culture

Imagine the following scene of a teenager taking the Picture Arrangement subtest of the WAIS-R. She is a first-generation Japanese American. The examiner places a set of four cartoon drawings on the table in front of her and tells her to arrange them so that they

■ **FIGURE 4.6**
Example of a Type of Item in the Picture Arrangement Subtest of the WAIS-R. *A series of pictures is shown out of sequence to an individual, who is asked to place them in their proper order to tell an appropriate story. The order of arrangement may vary based on the individual's culture.*

RESEARCH FOCUS

Cross-Sectional and Sequential Designs: Does Intelligence Slip with Age?

With Michael Wapner

Does intelligence decline with age? When can adolescents expect to peak intellectually? Putting it more bluntly, just how many good years do they have ahead of them? And why can't we give them any straight answers to questions such as these?

Straight, unambiguous answers are possible only with research that allows us to rule out alternatives. In such research, investigators manipulate variables by randomly assigning individuals to the conditions they are observing. Why can't we say for certain whether intelligence increases, decreases, or stays the same with age? Simply put, age cannot be manipulated. Individuals come to the laboratory with a certain age; they cannot be assigned one. People who differ in chronological age—that is, are of different cohort groups—also differ in other ways, namely, in their social and historical backgrounds. These differences don't always have to affect the way they respond to the measures we are taking, but they might. Cohorts are more likely to have similar cultural experiences than people of different ages. Adolescents today live in relatively plentiful times, and most grow up in urban or suburban settings. Adolescents born in 1930 grew up in the shadow of the Depression and were more likely to live in rural areas. Differences such as these appear in all sorts of attitudes and behaviors and can easily be confused with age changes. They are known as **cohort differences.**

Most of the studies finding that intelligence declines with age are cross-sectional. **Cross-sectional research** tests groups of individuals of different ages all at the same time. An obvious advantage to this approach is that one need not wait around while individuals grow older. A disadvantage is that differences between the groups can reflect either age changes or cohort differences. In contrast to longitudinal research, in which age is confounded with times of measurement, cross-sectional research confounds age with cohort differences.

Is there any way around the difficulties inherent in cross-sectional and longitudinal designs? **Sequential designs** provide a solution. These designs combine cross-sectional and longitudinal approaches. They test several cohort groups at several times of measurement. In a way, the sequential design can be thought of as a number of longitudinal studies, each starting with a different age group.

You might ask, "Won't *both* cohort and time of measurement effects be present?" Yes. But because they are, we can measure them and estimate their contribution. By substracting these estimates from our estimates of age differences, we can statistically isolate these confounds from genuine age changes. The resulting design appears in the figure.

By looking at the cells that form the diagonals, we can compare 10-year-olds with 15-year-olds and 20-year-olds. Cells 1, 7, and 13 are groups of 10-year-olds. Cells 2, 8, and 14 are 15-year-olds. And cells 3, 9, and 15 are 20-year-olds. "That's our age effect," you note. Not so fast. Even though the means of the diagonals reflect the performance of different ages, they can also contain cohort effects (e.g., any differences that might exist between 10-year-olds who were born in 1980 versus 1985 versus 1990) as well as differences due to time of measurement (depending on whether they were tested in 1990,1995, or 2000). If all we had were

cohort differences Experiential differences between groups of people born at different periods in time; these differences can be confounded with age changes.

cross-sectional research A research design in which several age cohorts are compared at a single time of measurement.

sequential designs A research design in which several age cohort groups are compared at several times of measurement; essentially, a number of longitudinal studies, each starting with a different age group.

tell a story. The first drawing shows a man baiting a hook with a worm as he fishes by a river. A second shows a woman exasperatedly pointing to a garden patch while the man looks on. The third shows the man digging in the garden and discovering a worm, and the fourth shows him getting gardening tools out of a shed. The girl tries first one arrangement, then another. None seems right to her. Finally the time runs out. You are puzzled. Why was this difficult for her? You quickly arrange the pictures mentally to tell a story. The story? The man has been told by his wife to garden, gets out the tools, discovers a worm as he works, and, reminded of more pleasant pursuits, goes off fishing. It's easy for most North Americans—unless they happen to be of Japanese descent. In Japan, wives don't give chores to their husbands. The girl knew that, and the pictures made no sense to her. To see how you would do on this type of subtest, try arranging the pictures in Figure 4.6.

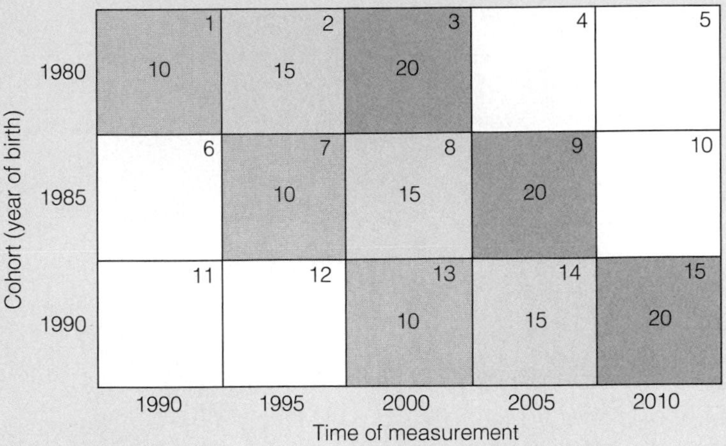

A Sequential Design
The cells are numbered in the upper right-hand corner. The numbers in the centers of the cells are ages.

the diagonals, we couldn't say anything about the relationship of intelligence to age.

But sequential designs give us more. We have vertical and horizontal means as well. The first of these, the column means, allow us to estimate differences due to time of measurement, and the second, the row means, the effect for cohorts. Comparing performance measured in 1995 (cells 2 and 7), with performance measured in 2000 (cells 3, 8, and 13), with that in 2000 (cells 9 and 14) provides an estimate of the amount of variability in intellectual functioning that is contributed by time of measurement. Differences among row means allow us to estimate the size of a cohort effect. By subtracting each of these estimates from the diagonals, we end up with an estimate of age effects.

Does intelligence slip with age? Sequential designs find that age effects are minimal. Simply put, adolescents can expect to hold on to their smarts as they enter adulthood. But what shall we make of the cross-sectional data indicating (erroneously as it turns out) that intelligence declines in adulthood? Obviously, some measures of intelligence confound the period in which one lives, the historical context, with attributes of the individual. The result of that confusion is to stigmatize older people. Sound familiar? This problem is reminiscent of similar complaints that intelligence tests penalize ethnic and racial minorities because they confound cultural and economic conditions with attributes of the individual.

Source: A. Anastasi. (1988). *Psychological testing* (6th ed.). New York: Macmillan.

Performance on measures such as the preceding one reflect not only a person's ability but also the extent to which that person's background is similar to that of the dominant culture. If one belongs to certain minorities, one is not as likely to do as well as someone from the dominant culture. Differences exist even among individuals within the same culture but from different social classes. Adolescents from lower-income homes can score as much as 15 to 20 points below their age-mates from the middle class. Ethnic and racial differences can be equally as large, and the latter have prompted considerable debate (Neisser et al., 1996).

Thomas Sowell, a behavioral scientist at Stanford University, has pointed out that the performance of minorities today closely resembles that of other minorities in the

Will standardized performance tests fully reveal this young woman's abilities? Many researchers believe that such tests may be weighted with questions based on experiences of the dominant culture and that the scores from such tests may not accurately represent the capabilities of adolescents from nondominant cultures.

early 1900s, whether of European or non-European descent, before they assimilated into the culture (Sowell, 1978). Sowell suggests that degree of assimilation, not racial or ethnic differences, best predicts a group's level of functioning on measures of intelligence. Those groups that are upwardly mobile—one of our best indices of assimilation—show marked increases in intelligence from one generation to the next. Groups for whom assimilation is blocked do not show an equivalent increase with time.

One last set of differences deserves our attention before we leave this approach to intelligence. These differences concern the sexes. It is only natural to ask whether males and females differ in their intellectual functioning.

Are There Gender Differences in Intellectual Functioning?

Stereotypes abound in this area as in so many others. Before we go any further, however, keep in mind that there is no gender difference in overall intelligence. Even so, several distinct patterns to performance can be noted. Females do somewhat better on measures of verbal reasoning and fluency, comprehending written passages, and understanding logical relations (Hedges & Nowell, 1995; Li, Sano, & Merwin, 1996). Additionally, with respect to disabilities, females are less likely than males to stutter, be dyslexic, or have other reading disabilities (Neisser et al., 1996).

Gender differences in spatial ability also exist. Males do better on tests that require one to mentally manipulate things or remember a visual figure in order to find it in a more complex figure. Whenever gender differences emerge, it is natural to ask whether these might be biologically based. Research exploring this question has found support for a relationship between spatial abilities and levels of circulating hormones, performance improving with higher levels of testosterone and, conversely, with lower

Are males more logical and females more intuitive? Are males better at numbers and females better at language? Does any difference matter between males and females, or between any two adolescents, regardless of sex, when it comes to mastering the computer?

levels of estradiol (Davison & Susman, 2001; Hausmann, Slabbekoorn, Van Goozen, Cohen-Kettenis, & Guentuerkuen, 2000). However, not all research has confirmed these findings (Liben et al., 2002). Certainly, the relationship between spatial ability and hormonal influences is complex and, given the influence of hormones, is likely to reflect earlier organizational patterning as well as their subsequent effects (Sanders, Sjodin, & de Chastelaine, 2002).

Gender differences in spatial ability assumes added importance because of their potential contribution to a commonly used test of intelligence, the Raven Progressive Matrices Test. This measures was developed as a **culture-fair test,** eliminating cultural biases by asking individuals to match arrangements of symbols rather than to answer questions verbally. Through mid-adolescence, females and males perform the same on the Raven; however, from about 16 years on, males perform appreciably better than females (Lynn & Irwing, 2004a, 2004b). When differences in spatial ability are statistically controlled for, this advantage disappears (Colom, Escorial, & Rebollo, 2004). However, if individuals' performance on the Raven is not evaluated in light of this difference, assessments of their intelligence may eliminate one type of bias, that due to culture, only to add another that due to gender.

Gender differences are also evident in standardized achievement tests such as the SAT, the most widely used of the college entrance exams. Each year college-bound high school males outscore females by a wide margin on the math portion of this exam. Given the importance of the SAT for students who plan to go to college, there's a pressing need to ensure that the questions comprising it are free from gender bias (Hyde & Kling, 2001). This need is even more compelling given the absence of commensurate differences in other measures (Braswell et al., 2001).

The psychometric approach to intelligence has done much to further our understanding of intelligence. A more recent approach, to which we turn next, has contributed

culture-fair test A measure of intelligence that minimizes cultural bias by using materials or requiring skills not likely to be more familiar to one segment of the population than to another.

As adolescents grow older, they can retrieve items from memory more quickly, use memory strategies more effectively, and because of greater content knowledge, assimilate new information more readily.

considerably to our understanding of the processes that underlie intellectual functioning in all individuals, regardless of sex or culture.

Beyond IQ: An Information Processing Approach

Have you ever missed part of an ongoing conversation after hearing someone else mention your name? Have you ever caught yourself repeating a phone number until you can write it down? Some things are so second nature to us that we hardly pay them any mind, yet these two examples illustrate two fundamental characteristics of cognition. Simply put, we are limited in just how much we can attend to at any point in time, and we are very good at adapting the way we think to the demands of the task or the moment.

Those who adopt an **information processing** approach to cognitive development focus on the specific processes involved in developmental change, rather than on the characteristics of any stage of thought, or on individual differences in measured intelligence. A number of such processes show progressive changes with age; these include automaticity, speed of processing, encoding, the use of strategies, and metamemory.

information processing An approach to cognition that focuses on the processes by which information is encoded, retrieved, and utilized.

automaticity The ability to perform highly practiced cognitive operations without conscious attention.

speed of processing The rate at which a cognitive operation (e.g., encoding, decoding, retrieval) or a combination of these can be performed.

working memory A brief memory that holds information for less than a minute while further processing occurs.

Automaticity refers to the increased efficiency with which individuals process information that occurs with age. For instance, adolescents can easily scan instructions for taking a test rather than have these read to them by a teacher, or effortlessly pronounce unfamiliar words that younger children would have to sound out letter by letter. As a consequence, these activities require less immediate attention, thereby freeing adolescents to focus on the next level, such as formulating the best strategy for taking the test or understanding the meaning of the passage they are reading (Siegler & Alibali, 2004).

Speed of processing also continues to develop into adolescence, reaching adult levels by mid-adolescence (Luna, Garver, Urban, Lazar, & Sweeney, 2004). How quickly information can be processed potentially affects a number of cognitive processes and is closely related to the efficiency of our **working memory,** the brief memory, lasting less than a minute, that we use to hold on to information while working with it. An example of working memory would be remembering what one has just read in order to make sense of what one is presently reading, or knowing where one is within the sequence of steps in a long-division problem, or simply remembering a phone number without writing it down. Working memory continues to improve in adolescence (Gathercole, Pickering, Ambridge, & Wearing, 2004).

Encoding refers to the form in which experience is mentally represented. The features that one notices, or encodes, predictably change with age, with adolescents being better than younger children at recognizing which features of a problem are most important, as well as at processing these more efficiently. Related to this, adolescents are also able to attend to more features of a problem at once, and to organize information more systematically, thus giving them greater flexibility of thought, enabling them to shift their attention from one aspect of a problem to another, rather than perseverating in outworn strategies (Keselman, 2003).

Another process contributing to developmental change concerns the use of strategies. **Strategies** are the activities that we consciously engage in to improve our performance, such as categorizing things in order to remember them, writing things down, or putting something needed for the next day in a place where it will be seen. Adolescents are more likely to recognize the need for strategies and to use strategies that are more efficient. One of the reasons they do so is that they are more aware of their thinking. This awareness is termed **metacognition.** Adolescents use their knowledge to monitor what they do. They know, for example, just how long a passage can be before they must reread it in order to remember it, or whether they are familiar with a name and hence likely to need more information about it. They know what strategies work best for them, are aware of using them, and realize how much they help (Siegler & Alibali, 2004).

Automaticity enables this adolescent to easily scan the instructions for assembling this project, freeing him up to focus on precisely aligning and attaching the parts.

In addition to developmental changes in these basic processes, knowledge also changes with age. Adolescents simply know more than younger children. This knowledge provides a context for assimilating new information, increasing the likelihood that relevant features will be processed and encoded. Because information can be related more easily to what one already knows, it has more meaning and is more easily used and remembered.

encoding The process by which information is transferred from one form to another in memory.

strategies Activities that organize cognition so as to improve performance, such as repeating a phone number or categorizing a list of things to be remembered.

metacognition Awareness of one's thinking, cognitive abilities, and style.

metacomponents Higher-order cognitive functions that select and monitor lower-order cognitive functions, for example, metacomponents are employed to determine which performance components are required to perform a task.

Sternberg's Componential Intelligence

Compared to younger children, adolescents process information faster and use more intelligent and efficient strategies. They also know more about the limitations of their memories and adapt their strategies to compensate for anticipated failings. Robert Sternberg, a psychologist at Yale University, accounts for these differences, as well as others, by analyzing intellectual functioning in terms of the processes, or components, that operate on information. Sternberg (1984, 1985) identifies three kinds of components: metacomponents, performance components, and knowledge-acquisition components.

Metacomponents decide when more information is needed and whether a particular strategy should be used or another one constructed, and monitor and keep track of one's progress. **Performance components** carry out the actual procedures selected by the metacomponents. If metacomponents are the supervisors, performance components are the actual workers. Performance components might decipher information in sensory memory, encoding this as names of letters. They might compare elements, inferring similarities or differences, or apply a procedure completed in one domain to another aspect of the problem. **Knowledge-acquisition components** acquire new information as it is needed. They sift through information, picking out that which is relevant to the problem and integrating it with what one already knows, giving it new meaning.

We can apply this analysis to the way people solve problems. Sternberg studied analogies because they reveal interesting age differences. An example of an analogy is the following: "Swift is to *Gulliver's Travels* as Pope is to: (a) the *Baedeker,* (b) 'The Rape of the Lock,' (c) the Vatican." To construct an analogy, one must choose the term that completes the second pair so that the two terms bear the same relationship to each other as the terms in the first pair.

To begin, one must encode each item: Does "Swift" refer to speed, or is it someone's name? (Encoding is a performance component.) The word *Travels* suggests the first alternative, and you know that the *Baedeker* is a travel guide. But then what is Pope? You may decide at this point that you need more information (a metacomponent) and search your memory for anything related to travel. You remember that *Gulliver's Travels* is the name of a book; then Swift could be the name of its author. Notice that one uses inference (another performance component) to determine the relationship between the first two terms. Encoding Swift as an author's name would mean that Pope is the name of an author. This last step has involved another performance component, mapping, or using the relationship between the first two terms to establish a relationship between the last two. Thus the fourth term must refer to something that Pope wrote. This extension rules out the Vatican, and because the *Baedeker* travel guide bears the name of its author, you are left with "The Rape of the Lock." You justify your selection by noting that the terms are all capitalized, as they would be in a title, and respond with alternative (b).

People of all ages use the same components to construct analogies, but spend different amounts of time on each (Sternberg & Rifkin, 1979). Adolescents and adults spend proportionately more time encoding the items than doing any of the other steps, whereas children spend relatively little time encoding. How does this fact relate to the characteristics of adolescent thought we reviewed earlier? Recall that adolescents tend to think of all the possible forms something might assume before they begin to work with any of them. They generate a world of possibilities, whereas children latch on to the first thing that comes to mind, their time for encoding being relatively brief. Sternberg (1981, 1984) also finds that with age, people spend much more time planning how to solve a problem than actually carrying out the steps. Once again, this difference reflects the tendency of adolescents to generate a strategy, and contrasts with the tendency of children to jump right in and move things about.

Notice, too, that analogies might be difficult for children because they require one to find the appropriate class for each term and then map the relationship between the classes of one set to those of the other. This higher-order, or abstract, form of thought awaits adolescence. Most children have as much success with analogies as they do in relating horses to goldfish (Sternberg, 1984).

Sternberg's componential analysis gives us an expanded view of intelligence. Rather than ranking one person relative to another in terms of a single number, such as IQ, we get a picture of intelligence at work: setting priorities, allocating resources, encoding information, monitoring feedback, and so on. But is it a single intelligence that works for us, or does intelligence take more than one form?

performance components Cognitive mechanisms, selected by metacomponents, that operate directly on the information to be processed.

knowledge-acquisition components Cognitive mechanisms—e.g., perception, memory retrieval—that, under the direction of metacomponents, acquire new information as needed.

Gardner's Multiple Intelligences

Howard Gardner, a psychologist who has written extensively on the development of intellect and creativity, proposes not one but **multiple intelligences,** such as musical, bodily-kinesthetic, logical-mathematical, linguistic, spatial, interpersonal, and intrapersonal intelligence. Gardner (1983, 1999), like others, defines intelligence in terms of one's ability to solve problems as they arise, but the range of problems that he accepts as legitimate for the study of intelligence is much broader than it is for others.

Gardner points out that most measures of intelligence tap a limited range of abilities, which he identifies as logical-mathematical. Because these measures are also good at predicting success at school, they continue to be used. But what about problems that don't call for logical-mathematical analysis, such as finding our way back to a parking lot in a new area of town or recognizing the composer of a piece of music? Do these tasks call upon intelligence? Do musicians, athletes, or surgeons have more of some talent in common than the rest of us? Gardner would answer yes to both.

Of course, one could list endless problems or talents and claim a separate intelligence for each one. Gardner uses several criteria to isolate legitimate intellectual domains. He points out that a domain must be universal to all humans and should show development with age. Each intelligence should be capable of being expressed in its own symbol system, for example, words for language, equations for mathematics, or notes for music (Walters & Gardner, 1986).

These ballerinas illustrate Howard Gardner's bodily-kinesthetic intelligence.

Evidence for separate intellectual domains also comes from child prodigies, idiot savants, and people who have suffered brain damage. In each case we can see an uneven profile of abilities. Prodigies such as Mozart or Yehudi Menuhin showed musical genius at an early age, yet remained quite ordinary in other domains. Cases have been reported of autistic children who could perform rapid mental calculations yet not be able to carry on a conversation or dress themselves. Similarly, people who have suffered brain trauma may have some areas of functioning spared (Gardner, 1983, 1999). Table 4.1 shows seven of Gardner's forms of intelligence, with corresponding potential professions.

Gardner anticipates objections to labeling these domains as intelligence. But he replies that nothing is sacred about the word *intelligence.* His choice of the term over other equally suitable ones, in fact, is deliberate. It emphasizes his point that present measures of intelligence are limited because they place logical-mathematical and linguistic abilities on a pedestal above other abilities, such as musical and interpersonal ones. In doing so, our measures of intelligence reflect our culture's bias in favor of logical and verbal abilities over abilities such as kinesthetic or artistic ones. Gardner (1983, 1999) argues that to call one type of ability "intelligence" and another "talent" reflects this bias. He challenges us to consider them all talents or to consider them all intelligence.

multiple intelligence The view that intelligence is comprised of a number of different capacities each relevant to a different domain—e.g., music, linguistics, mathematics, interpersonal relations. One's ability in each domain is not necessarily highly correlated with ability in others.

TABLE 4.1 Garder's Seven Forms of Intelligence and Corresponding Potential Professions

From of Intelligence	Potential Professions
Musical	Musician Music teacher
Bodily-kinesthetic	Dancer Athlete
Logical-mathematical	Scientist Mathematician Teacher
Linguistic	Interpreter
Spatial	Artist Architect Landscape designer
Interpersonal (understanding others)	Psychologist Counselor
Intrapersonal (understanding the self)	Poet Writer

Source: H. Gardner. (1983). *Frames of mind.* New York: Basic Books.

Practical Intelligence

Gardner is not alone in viewing present measures of intelligence as overly narrow and related more to academic than real life experiences. Some psychologists speak of a **practical intelligence,** which they distinguish from the academic intelligence tapped by intelligence tests. Neisser (1976) defines this type of intelligence as "responding appropriately in terms of one's long-range and short-range goals, given the actual facts of the situation as one discovers them" (p. 137). He points out that the problems one must solve on tests that tap academic intelligence share a number of features: They are designed by someone else, are usually not very interesting, and have nothing to do with daily experience. Also, most test problems are well defined; they have a single answer and only one way of arriving at it (Wagner & Sternberg, 1986). In contrast, practical intelligence applies when one must discover the problem, instead of having it defined by someone else. Another difference is that finding the solution is frequently pleasurable. Finally, usually a number of approaches will work, each leading to a slightly different solution.

practical intelligence To be distinguished from "academic intelligence" or intelligence measured by IQ tests, practical intelligence requires the individual, rather than a teacher or an examiner, to define the problem to be solved and decide what constitutes a solution.

How much has our view of intelligence been influenced by the tests we use to measure it? Probably too much. Even though these tests can predict academic success, they often have little or no connection to other areas of life. Nothing illustrates this last point better than adolescents themselves, who may reach a pinnacle of intellectual achievement as measured by tests of intelligence, only to be pulled up short by the simplest of life's situations. Despite arriving at the cutting edge of thought, adolescents frequently nick themselves in the process.

Implications for Everyday Life

Pseudostupidity

Many of the intellectual advances of early adolescent thought have their downside. The ability to hold a problem in mind and consider it from all possible perspectives occasionally leads teenagers to make things more complicated than they actually are. David Elkind (1978), a psychologist who writes extensively on thinking in childhood and adolescence, suggests that frequently teenagers fail to see the obvious not because the task is too hard for them, but because they have made a simple task more complicated than it actually is. He refers to this tendency as **pseudostupidity.** While a teenager is mentally ticking off all the oddball but nonetheless possible alternatives, someone else usually comes up with the obvious. Teenagers can feel stupid, asking themselves, "Why didn't I think of that?"

Early adolescents also frequently read complex motives into situations where none exist. A simple request such as "Would you hand me the paper on your way out?" can be viewed with skeptical eyes. The teenager may wonder, "Is this just another attempt to control?" To avoid being controlled, the adolescent may consider refusing but may also suspect that the need to refuse is merely another response to control. Neither able to comply nor to refuse, the teenager shoots back an angry remark to the effect that the news isn't worth the ink it takes to print it and storms out, leaving the parent to wonder what would have been done with something as loaded as "How was your day?"

An Imaginary Audience

One of the hallmarks of adolescent thought is the ability to think in the abstract, and nothing is more abstract than thought itself. Adolescents can think about thinking, not only their own thoughts but those of others as well. This ability can bring its own problems. Elkind (1967, 1985) assumes that this ability underlies a new form of egocentrism in early adolescence. Early adolescents frequently lose perspective as to what concerns them and what concerns others as well. Because so many of their concerns focus on themselves, they can have the feeling that others, too, are thinking about them. Elkind refers to this loss of perspective as the **imaginary audience.** Adolescents can have the feeling that every eye is on them and every thought is about them. The imaginary audience may explain adolescents' exaggerated feelings of self-consciousness, as well as their intense need for privacy.

The imaginary audience goes hand in hand with a second construction, known as the **personal fable,** which confers a feeling of being special (Elkind, 1967). Adolescents believe themselves to be unique, invulnerable, and omnipotent. The personal fable can have some very personal consequences for adolescents. One is a confusion over what they have in common with others and what is genuinely unique to themselves. Confusions such as this lead to the belief that no one else can understand their feelings, because they are the only ones to have ever felt this way. It's not unusual, for example, for early adolescents to tell their parents that they couldn't possibly understand how it feels to be in love! Another consequence is the mistaken assumption that they won't be harmed by what they see happening to others, and that there is no limit to what they can do once they set their mind to something. Elkind (1978) suggests that the personal fable explains many of the tragic cases of adolescents who appear to be self-destructive. Their behavior may not be motivated as much by a desire to destroy themselves as by their belief that what they see happening to others won't happen to them—that because they are unique, they are invulnerable to the events that touch others' lives.

pseudostupidity The inability to see the obvious by making a simple task more complicated than it is.

imaginary audience The experience of being the focus of attention that emerges with adolescents' ability to think about thinking in others and their confusion of the concerns of others with their own preoccupation with themselves.

personal fable The feeling of being special; thought to derive from the imaginary audience.

Adolescents assume that everyone is as preoccupied with them as they are with themselves. This self-focused perception often leads to extreme self-consciousness and an intense need for privacy as well as a feeling of being unique and special.

The capacity of adolescents to catch glimpses of themselves in the eyes of others may be important to gaining a sense of themselves. Erikson (1968) speaks of identity formation as a process by which adolescents come to see themselves as individuals and, at the same time, as members of a social group. Even while assessing their individual worth, adolescents use the standards and norms shared by members of their social group. How they see themselves will reflect the way they measure up in the eyes of others. The ability of adolescents to examine their thoughts and to imagine the thoughts of others underlies a new awareness of their own separateness from others and of what they have in common with others through shared values and behaviors.

Understanding Others

Adolescents' awareness of others' thoughts contributes as well to **social understanding,** which develops as adolescents become better at assuming another's perspective and coordinating this with their own. Although preadolescents can put themselves in another's place and understand how that person might be feeling, they have difficulty relating this understanding to their own point of view and thus considering the situation from both perspectives. The ability to attend to multiple aspects of a problem at once, which develops in adolescence (discussed earlier in the chapter under "Thinking Hypothetically"), enables adolescents to move from one perspective to another. This, in turn, enables them to anticipate the outcome of adopting one course of action or another. Adolescents can infer how another might be thinking *and* anticipate how that person will react to their reactions to them. An adolescent, for example, might get angry with her friend upon hearing that the friend once again drank too much after swearing he wouldn't, but may keep her anger to herself, guessing that her friend is also afraid, and angry with himself, and will not confide in her in the future if she loses her temper. Compare this type of understanding with that of a preadolescent, who might blurt out either her own feelings or those she suspects of her friend, with no ability to anticipate the consequences of doing either.

Despite significant developments in social understanding, adolescents often fail to consider the impact their remarks can have on others. Joan Newman (1985) describes a family conversation about where the Russian satellite *Cosmos* might fall. Neither parent had any idea where this might be, but the teenage son knew that it had already fallen, landing ENE of the tiniest island southwest of Madagascar. So impressed was he with his superior knowledge that he ridiculed the rest of the family saying, "You don't know anything, do you?" Yet this same teenager couldn't find his math homework or remember where he left his sneakers that morning.

New Emotions

social understanding The ability to assume another's perspective and coordinate this with one's own.

How one feels depends on the interpretations one gives to experience. "Did that person just brush me off, or simply fail to notice that I was going to say something?" Depending on which interpretation one gives, the encounter can occasion either feelings of irritation or no feelings in particular. Intellectual development in adolescence makes it possible for teenagers to react emotionally in new ways. Children focus on the immediate elements of the situation: To a compliment they react with pleasure; to a present, with happiness. Adolescents do all of this and more.

These girls may have been friends for years, but with early adolescence, they begin to relate to each other in new ways.

Adolescents can consider what a situation might mean as well as the way it appears. By being able to turn something around in their minds, they can assign more than the obvious meaning to social encounters. Adolescents do not always complicate life in this way, but they do so more than children and also more than most adults. A compliment can be the occasion for anger if seen as an attempt to win a favor. Or a present can cause depression if seen as an emotional bribe. Adolescents also experience emotions that are relatively foreign to children; they get high on themselves, moody, depressed, or elated (Larson & Richards, 1994). Unlike children, adolescents relate their feelings to their experience of themselves as well as to the events that may prompt the feelings, adding an extra level of magnification to their view of the world.

Arguing

The ability of adolescents to consider the possibilities in any situation affects more than their emotions. An immediate consequence is that adolescents can argue better than children can. To carry out an argument, whether in a debating class at school or with a parent in the kitchen, one must come up with ideas for or against something. Adolescents are not limited, as are children, to testing their ideas against facts; they can test them against other ideas. (Remember the experiment with the green and red poker chips?) This new ability makes it possible for adolescents to argue for or against an idea regardless of whether they actually believe in it. The test of the argument is whether it has an inner logic. Children are limited to arguing either for things they believe in or against those they do not. The only test they can apply is to compare what they say with how things really are for them—how they feel or what they believe.

Because of their literal approach, children cannot consider that a statement could mean something other than it says it does: It's simply taken at face value. A father's complaint, "If we had no dandelions, this would be a fine lawn," will bring a response of "But we have lots of dandelions, Dad," or "I like our lawn." Adolescents can consider statements about things that are contrary to the way they presently are or about things that don't exist. They can imagine a lawn that is free of dandelions or even a lawn of *nothing but* dandelions. Perhaps this ability to divorce thought from fact, to think in ideals, even when these are counter to fact, provides the basis for adolescents' increasing ability to plan and to gain new perspectives on themselves, their families, and their friends.

During some discussion, this father may realize that his son's arguments are better constructed and more difficult to refute. This adolescent's improved ability at argumentation may at times be frustrating, but it is also a sign of increasing maturity.

Doubt and Skepticism

Prior to the development of formal thought, children believe that knowledge comes simply with exposure to the facts, never considering that factual information can be interpreted in more than one way. As a consequence, differences of opinion are treated as one person being wrong and the other one right. With formal thought, adolescents realize that what they have regarded as truth is simply one fix on reality and that other, equally compelling interpretations are possible. The result can be a profound skepticism in which they come to doubt the possibility of ever knowing anything in this "newly created world of wholesale uncertainty" (Boyes & Chandler, 1992).

Implications for the Classroom

The intellectual developments we have talked about so far prepare adolescents for new challenges in the classroom. Courses in mathematics, science, and literature require increasingly abstract and logical thought. In algebra, for instance, when solving a problem in which x equals 5, they must know better than to assume that x really *is* 5 (Bjorklund, 1989). Literature courses ask them to discuss the nuances of motives and meaning in characters that live only in the pages of their books. In physical science, they must make observations, generate explanations for these, then systematically test each one out, controlling for extraneous conditions as they do.

Reasoning

inductive reasoning Reasoning from the particular to the general.

Both inductive and deductive reasoning improve during adolescence (Muller, Overton, & Reene, 2001). **Inductive reasoning** takes one from the particular to the general, from specific events to the class to which these belong, that is, to an explanation. For instance, to find that water in a closed container boils at several degrees below the point at which it boils in an uncovered container is a single observation resulting in a single fact—interesting, perhaps, but of limited value to science or the student. The logical thought process that enables a student to extrapolate from this single fact to a general rule (that there is an inverse relationship between the pressure exerted on a liquid and its boiling point) is an example of inductive reasoning.

Similarly, the adolescent who must write an essay analyzing why Hamlet was so slow to avenge his father's murder is also confronted with a task of induction. Shakespeare describes specific events in the life of Hamlet—conversations, thoughts, actions. To explain Hamlet's motives, the student must use induction to arrive at his character, that is, the source (class) of likely actions and the rules of their occurrence. The events Shakespeare actually shows us are analogous to the individual observations of a chemistry experiment such as the one above, and the step from these particulars to a general personality is as much an act of induction as formulating the rule relating pressure on a liquid to its boiling point.

Deductive reasoning works the other way, going from the general to the particular, that is, checking a hypothesis by seeing what happens when conditions change. Thus, starting with the rule that the boiling point of water drops by a certain amount with every increase of pressure, one can deduce (predict) any particular boiling point for any given pressure. Likewise, given the diagnosis of Hamlet as indecisive but impulsive (the general personality or rule from which spring all of his actions), one can predict (deduce) that left to himself Hamlet will have difficulty formulating a plan of action but, once provoked, will act quickly and rashly.

The ability to think logically, abstractly, and hypothetically increases with age throughout adolescence. Even so, adolescents find it easier to reason about propositions that make sense ("If you are caught running in the halls, then you will be punished") than those that don't ("If you are caught running in the halls, then you are wearing sneakers") (Ward & Overton, 1990). (See Figure 4.7.) At times, adolescents experience more difficulty than children simply because they are able to think about aspects of problems not immediately relevant to their solution (Spiel, Glück, & Gössler, 2001).

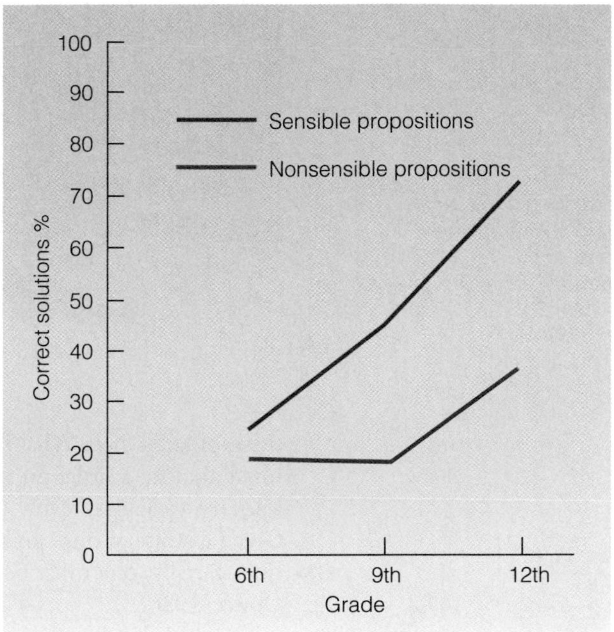

FIGURE 4.7
Deductive Reasoning for Sensible and Nonsensible Propositions. *Adolescents, just as children and adults, find it easier to think about problems that make sense to them.*
Source: S. L. Ward & W. F. Overton. (1990). Semantic familiarity, relevance, and the development of deductive reasoning. *Developmental Psychology, 26*, 488–493.

Can Adolescents Think Like Scientists?

Adolescents can marshal facts to support or oppose principles, generate a realm of possible alternatives for any situation, think in abstractions, and test their thoughts against an inner logic. These abilities set them apart from children. They also make new forms of learning possible in the classroom. Adolescents' systematic approach to problems, for one thing, lends itself especially well to science.

Much of the excitement of science involves discovery. Often the first discovery is the nature of the problem itself. Alexander Fleming, for example, documents the discovery of penicillin by telling of a mold that had formed in one of his petri dishes. He noticed that the bacteria surrounding the mold had died. Instead of cleaning out the dish and starting a new culture, Fleming was puzzled (that is, he had discovered a problem). Why had only the bacteria around the mold died?

One could identify other, less interesting, problems, such as "What did I do wrong?" Perhaps Fleming did, too, but he chose to move on to why the bacteria surrounding

deductive reasoning Reasoning from the general to the particular.

Science requires adolescents to put what they learn in class to the test, reasoning through complex processes and anticipating results.

the mold had died. What Fleming saw illustrates the first step in solving a problem. One must analyze a situation to discover its salient features (what a scientist would call the relevant variables). Only when these have been isolated can a strategy be formulated. Given a strategy, one can begin to test each of the features to see which produce a solution. Finally, one must be able to reach conclusions based on these tests (Ginsburg & Opper, 1988).

Notice that the success of the whole endeavor rests on the ability to think the situation through before starting to work on it. Adolescents can do this. They can identify each of the possible variables, then generate combinations. Remember that a characteristic of adolescent thought is to think in terms of possibilities. In doing so, they are also generating a strategy, because each possibility must be tested.

A strategy makes for a systematic approach to problems. Adolescents know, for instance, that they must hold all the conditions constant except the one they are testing. Only then can they be sure their test reflects the possibility they have in mind instead of some other. They know, too, that frequently an effect can result from more than one combination of conditions. Even though they may discover that the bacteria die under one particular combination of conditions, they will continue with their tests, exhausting all the possibilities.

Study Skills and Knowing What You Don't Know

One of the factors contributing to better learning is that adolescents, more so than children, are aware of what they don't know and adjust the way they study to accommodate for the gaps in their knowledge. Children, on the other hand, often fail to realize when they have not learned what they have been studying. Campione and Brown (1978) observed fifth-graders through college students as they studied material in a textbook. Younger students focused on the same information each time they reviewed the material, whereas older students, realizing what they had missed, directed their attention to that material on subsequent readings. The development with age of metacognitive skills, and the consequent use of strategies, underlies this improvement.

Students who fail to monitor their performance can be taught to do so. Poor readers who were shown how to assess their reading comprehension by noting what they have missed climbed from the 20th percentile to the 56th percentile (Palinscar & Brown, 1984). Similarly, students taught to attend to cues such as chapter headings or to focus on cues embedded in the passages (such as "in comparison to" or "on the other hand") improved in their comprehension (Spires, Gallini, & Riggsbee, 1992).

Adolescents, more so than children, are aware of what they don't know, so they are better able to focus on filling the gaps in their knowledge and skimming over what they've already learned.

Metaphors and Meaning: When Is a Ship a State?

Children interpret remarks literally; adolescents can understand multiple levels of meaning. When asked to interpret an expression such as "His bark is louder than his bite," for example, children might answer that "you can't hear a dog bite" or that "some dogs bark loudly." Adolescents can understand the expression to mean that some individuals bluff their way through situations. Their ability to understand figurative uses of language makes many types of literature accessible that previously were not.

Adolescents can also appreciate *metaphor;* a metaphor makes an implicit comparison between ideas or objects to show some hidden similarity. They understand that when politicians refer to a government as a "ship of state," they are communicating that the fate of all citizens is bound together, just like the fate of passengers and crew on a ship at sea. Similarly, the phrase "evening of life" communicates that life is drawing to an end, just like the day at the approach of evening. Adolescents easily understand expressions such as these; children do not.

Adolescents also begin to understand irony, sarcasm, and satire. Their ability to think in terms of hypothetical situations as distinct from actual ones makes an understanding of these concepts possible. Being able to consider the perspective of another and anticipate the other's intended effects by his or her remarks almost surely contributes to this new appreciation. Adolescents can appreciate the irony in passages from works such as *Pilgrim at Tinker Creek,* in which Annie Dillard (1974) writes the following:

> Somewhere, and I can't find where, I read about an Eskimo hunter who asked the local missionary priest, "If I did not know about God and sin, would I go to hell?" "No," said the priest, "not if you did not know." "Then why," asked the Eskimo earnestly, "did you tell me?"

The ability of adolescents to appreciate the irony in this story may be especially acute. They, like the Eskimo, face a challenge to change because of what they know. In the chapter that follows, we will examine the way changing perceptions of themselves and others affect adolescents' family relationships.

Summary

How Adolescents Think

- Thinking becomes more abstract in adolescence; adolescents can think of things in terms of class membership and can classify the classes. They can even think about thinking itself.
- Thinking becomes hypothetical in adolescence; adolescents can think of thinks that are only possible but not necessarily real.
- Thinking becomes more logical in adolescence; adolescents are able to test different ideas against one another to establish their truth.

Biological Bases to Intellectual Development

- Brain development continues throughout adolescence, with different regions developing at different rates.
- The *myelination* of neural fibers, in which a fatty insulating sheath develops along the length of the neural fiber, enables them to conduct impulses more rapidly. Myelination continues to occur in adolescence in regions of the brain that play a role in abstract thought, by integrating neural input from various areas.
- The *prefrontal cortex* continues to develop during adolescence. This area of the brain is responsible for abstract thought, planning, and anticipating the consequences of one's actions.

Cognitive Development: A Constructive Perspective

- According to the constructive perspective, we continually interpret experience. Piaget applies this constructive perspective to development by suggesting that we organize how we understand the world in qualitatively different ways as we grow older. Sensorimotor thought is limited to what the infant experiences through its senses and actions. Preoperational thought, though symbolic, is dominated by the appearance of things. Concrete operational thought is more flexible and allows children to move beyond how things look to how they must be. Only with formal operational thought can adolescents think of abstract ideas and consider hypothetical situations.
- Kegan suggests that intellectual growth takes place through a process of differentiation of self from other. Differentiation progresses at different rates in each individual because of different contextual influences and daily experiences.

A Psychometric Approach to Intelligence

- Although difficult to define, most agree that *intelligence* allows us to profit from our experiences and adapt to our surroundings and that it typically involves abstract reasoning.
- Common measures of intelligence, such as the *WAIS-R,* reflect the knowledge and abilities of the average person in our society.
- Most intelligence tests reflect one's familiarity with the culture. Racial and ethnic differences in intelligence exist and may reflect different rates of assimilation into the dominant culture.
- There is no gender difference in overall intelligence; however, several specific differences can be noted.
  - Females do somewhat better on measures of verbal reasoning and fluency, comprehending written passages, and understanding logical relations.
  - Males do better on measures of spatial ability such as those that require one to mentally manipulate objects. This gender difference may contribute a source of bias to *culture-fair tests* that rely heavily on spatial ability.
  - On standardized achievement tests such as the SAT, males score higher than females on the math portion of the exam.

Beyond IQ: An Information Processing Approach

- The *information processing* approach to cognitive development focuses on the specific processes involved in developmental change, rather than on the characteristics of any stage or thought, or on individual differences in measured intelligence.
- A number of processes show progressive changes with age:
  - *Automaticity,* the increased efficiency with which individuals process information, increases with age.
  - *Speed of processing* continues to develop up to mid-adolescence and contributes to the efficiency of working memory, the brief memory we use to hold on to information while working with it.
  - *Encoding* refers to the form in which experience is mentally represented. Adolescents are better at encoding the most important features of a problem and process these more efficiently. They are also able to attend to more features of a problem at once, giving them more flexibility of thought.

- Adolescents are more likely to use strategies and to use more-efficient strategies. They also are more aware of their thinking and use their knowledge to monitor what they do.

Sternberg's Componential Intelligence

- Sternberg analyzes intellectual functioning in terms of components, or processes that operate on information. He distinguishes among three types of components: (1) metacomponents allocate processing resources, (2) performance components carry out the actual procedures, and (3) knowledge-acquisition components require new information as it is needed.

Gardner's Multiple Intelligences

- Gardner defines intelligence as one's ability to solve problems as they arise, but includes problems from a much broader domain than most experts in the field. His multiple forms of intelligence include musical, bodily-kinesthetic, logical-mathematical, linguistic, spatial, interpersonal, and intrapersonal intelligence.

Implications for Everyday Life

- *Pseudostupidity:* Adolescents frequently make problems more complex than they are and feel stupid when someone else comes up with the obvious solution.
- *Imaginary audience:* The ability of adolescents to think about thinking leads them to create an imaginary audience in which they feel themselves to be the center of everyone's attention. The personal fable is the complement of the imaginary audience; adolescents believe they are unique and invulnerable.
- *Understanding others:* Adolescents' awareness of others' thoughts contributes to social understanding which is reflected in adolescents' ability to assume another's perspective and coordinate this with their own. Adolescents can infer how another might be thinking and anticipate how that person will react to their reactions to them.
- *New emotions and arguing:* Gaining new perspectives on themselves and their families affects adolescents' emotions and their abilities to argue for what they believe in.

Implications for the Classroom

- Adolescents' ability to think hypothetically makes it possible for them to study science, and their ability to appreciate multiple levels of meaning broadens their understanding of literature. They can understand irony, sarcasm, satire, and metaphor.

Key Terms

myelination
prefrontal cortex
object permanance
schemes
mental operations
conservation
differentiation
psychometric approach
intelligence
WAIS-R
cohort differences
cross-sectional research
sequential designs
culture-fair test
information processing
automaticity
speed of processing
working memory
encoding
strategies
metacognition
metacomponents
performance components
knowledge-acquisition components
multiple intelligences
practical intelligence
pseudostupidity
imaginary audience
personal fable
social understanding
inductive reasoning
deductive reasoning

CHAPTER OUTLINE

CHAPTER 5

Defining the Self

Identity and Intimacy

CHAPTER OBJECTIVES

- To examine the ways adolescents define themselves within the context of their relationships with parents
- To consider the nature of gender differences with respect to identity development
- To examine the contributions of ethnicity to identity development
- To look at the developing self-concept and at self-esteem in adolescents
- To explore the relationship between intimacy and identity

Annie is 15 and standing in the dark on her aunt's doorstep. It's 2:30 in the morning. Only blocks away, Annie's frantic mother has called the police to say that her daughter has run away. That morning Annie's mother, looking for the medical card she had given Annie to use, found two joints in Annie's purse. When she confronted Annie about them, Annie screamed that her mother was spying on her, grabbed the purse, and said that she was leaving for good. Annie's mother stood in the doorway and said they had to talk, but Annie pushed past her and nearly knocked her over. Later, when the police, Annie's mother, and Annie all converge in her aunt's living room, Annie tells them she ran away because her mother is cold, selfish, demanding, and doesn't love her. Annie's mother describes Annie as bright and sweet, but immature, irresponsible, and thoughtless. Each has nothing to say that will reach the other.

If asked to describe herself, Annie's mother would never use words such as *cold* or *selfish*, nor would she say that she didn't love her daughter. Nor would Annie describe herself as immature or thoughtless. How can the two of them see things so differently? What has gone wrong? How much of their difficulty is because of Annie? How much is because of her mother? And how much is because Annie is 15?

Eddie, 13, is sitting in his room waiting for his father to open the door. His little sister went running to get him after she saw all the hair in the bathroom and found her mother crying in the kitchen. It hadn't been all that good around the house lately. Things came to a head, literally, when Eddie shaved both sides of his head, leaving a swath down the middle, which he dyed green and spiked with hair gel. His mother said she had never seen anything like that. Who knows what his father will say. Or do. Eddie tells himself he doesn't care. He has never felt so alone in all his life.

How is it possible for Eddie to feel alone with his family all around him? And what possessed him to give himself a green Mohawk?

Chapter Overview

It's time to take a look at where we have been and where we are going. The preceding two chapters set the stage for what we will be discussing in this chapter. The biological changes discussed in Chapter 3 have important implications for the way adolescents and their parents interact. Among European American adolescents in our culture, puberty ushers in increased conflict and decreased closeness with parents. As adolescents develop the bodies and feelings of mature adults, their and their parents' expectations change. Adolescents, for their part, expect to be treated in more adult ways, to be given more autonomy and a greater say in family decision making. Parents, in turn, expect adolescents to be more responsible and to act in more adult ways. Conflict frequently results.

Achieving an identity is not an easy process, and outward changes in dress or hairstyle enable adolescents to see themselves in fresh ways while they work on differentiating new aspects of themselves.

These trends are not universal, and the importance of the way a culture interprets, or constructs, biological events such as puberty cannot be overemphasized. Puberty, for instance, is associated with very different changes among Hispanic adolescents, at least for boys, for whom relationships with parents actually improve, perhaps reflecting the value their families place on the traditional male role (Molina & Chassin, 1996).

A second factor contributing to a renegotiation of relationships in early adolescence is the way adolescents begin to think. The intellectual changes discussed in the preceding chapter give adolescents a new perspective from which to view themselves and their relationships with others. The ability to attend to multiple dimensions of a problem, for instance, enables adolescents to consider any situation not only from their own point of view but also from that of someone else. Of course, emotions can get in the way of logic, as we have also seen in the preceding chapter.

Going back to Annie and Eddie, despite other differences between them, both have one thing in common: Both have organized the way they have constructed the self, or the way they perceive themselves, in terms of their relationships with their parents. If asked to talk about herself, Annie would likely say something such as "The problem's not me so much as it is my mother. She doesn't really care about me and wants to control me." Annie has a hard time separating her feelings from how she sees her mother, her *self* from the *other*. One could say that she simply is not being honest. But the truth is, she is being honest. This is the way things are for her. In order for her to relate differently to her mother, she must be able to see *herself* differently, to differentiate the needs and feelings she has at the moment from her larger sense of who she is, from her sense of self (Kegan, 1982).

And what about Eddie? How are we to understand his feelings of loneliness? The differentiation that eventually leads to greater mutuality in relationships with parents takes years to achieve. Eddie didn't have years to spend on differentiation that afternoon. He knew he wasn't a child, like his sister, but he was not sure what it was that made him different from children her age or, for that matter, different from adults such as his parents. He didn't want to be seen as a kid anymore, nor did he want to be like his parents. At 13, scissors and paint, cutting and pasting, promised a quick fix to an identity. Why, then, was he feeling so lonely? Eddie had lost something. He had lost the self he had known himself to be, and he had not put together a way of being to step into when he stepped out of the other.

In life, one frequently finds oneself in the middle of something without knowing exactly what it is one is doing, or precisely what one wants to get out of it—not at all a new experience for adolescents as they attempt to understand themselves in new ways. Change at any age doesn't come easily, and the more people who are involved, the more difficult it is, for as adolescents define themselves in new ways, so, too, must those around them, most notably their parents. The first section of this chapter examines the way adolescents put together their experiences within the family to gain a new sense of self.

The next section of the chapter looks at the psychosocial crisis of identity. Adolescents' search for the truth about themselves begins when the separate worlds in which they live begin to pull apart. Adolescents begin to see themselves as more than their parents' children, to question where the skills they are acquiring in school will take them, to ask who they will be living with in the future. Erik Erikson (1968) suggests that the search ultimately leads to a sense of "sameness and continuity" that allows adolescents to transcend the differences they experience in their many roles—full-time student, part-time employee, daughter, son, friend, neighbor, and so on.

Gaining a sense of themselves almost seems to require the tools of a magician or an actor: mirrors, sleight of hand, impressive costumes. Adolescents frequently find themselves playing out roles that are just a bit too big for them or not quite right. They try on these roles because the comfortable ones of childhood no longer fit. Adolescents find themselves looking inward and outward all at once, one eye on the inner self and another on those around them. They are well aware others may be judging them in terms of the cultural images they share, but also in terms of how well the others have achieved precisely what they themselves are attempting to do (Erikson, 1968). The images adolescents hold up to themselves may fit some better than others, a point we will consider in sections on gender differences in identity formation and on the contributions of ethnicity to identity.

The chapter moves next to an examination of changes in the self-concept in adolescence and in self-esteem before closing with a look at adolescents' capacity for intimacy as a measure of maturity.

Autonomy and Individuation

The drama of gaining a sense of themselves unfolds on a well-known stage: at home as adolescents interact with parents, pressing for greater autonomy. In winning new responsibilities, they discover strengths that are uniquely theirs and that distinguish them from their parents, a process known as individuation.

Autonomy

One of the major issues confronting early adolescents is to become more autonomous, to be more independent and responsible for their actions. **Autonomy** takes a number of forms. Perhaps the most basic of these is simply choosing to be part of the

autonomy Being independent and responsible for one's actions.

Keeping secrets from parents can contribute to adolescents' feelings of independence and their experience of autonomy.

decision-making process, asking to be treated as more adult. As adolescents take part in this process, they come to feel more confident about the choices they make and their ability to do things on their own (Noom, Dekovic, & Meeus, 2001). As you might expect, the number of decisions adolescents make by themselves increases with age, and those they share with parents or that are made by parents alone decrease with age.

One of the decisions adolescents appear to make early on is just how much of what they think and feel they will keep secret from their parents. Secrecy is often thought of negatively, but with adolescents it appears to have a positive side to it as well. To keep a secret means that one *chooses* what to reveal, and has sufficient self-control to follow through with that. Even more fundamentally, secrecy separates adolescents, the ones in the know, from their parents, who are left in the dark. Catrin Finkenauer at Free University, the Netherlands, and Ruger Engels and Wim Meeus (2002) at Utrecht University, also in the Netherlands, found that secrecy contributed to adolescents' experience of autonomy. These investigators reasoned that secrets define a type of boundary between adolescents and their parents that, when controlled through what they reveal or conceal, contributes to adolescents' sense of independence (Finkenauer, Engels, & Meeus, 2002).

Another way in which adolescents attempt to maintain autonomy over what they think and do is by lying to their parents. Of course adults lie as well, often citing altruistic motives such as protecting the feelings of others. Although adolescents also mention these, they are most likely to justify lying to parents when they believe that the decision in question is one that is rightfully theirs to make (Jensen, Arnett, Feldman, & Cauffman, 2004).

Bids for greater autonomy might be expected to occasion some conflict with parents, and they do. Most conflicts are over everyday events, such as what clothes they can wear or how late they can stay out. Interestingly, conflicts occur not so much because adolescents contest their parents' right to set standards and make decisions as they do because of disagreements with parents over which areas of their lives they can do this in. Issues that parents believe require supervision are often those which adolescents see as personal issues that should be left to them (Smetana, Campione-Barr, & Daddis, 2004).

Autonomy is a much larger issue for early adolescents than for older ones. Arehart and Smith (1990) found that concern with questions of autonomy accounted for nearly half of the variability among early adolescents' answers to a measure of psychosocial maturity. For boys, age is the single most important determinant of increasing independence, whereas for girls, parenting style, especially that of mothers, is particularly important (Bumpus, Crouter, & McHale, 2001). For both, however, reliance on parental support becomes progressively less important for adolescents' emotional adjustment (Meeus, Iedema, Maassen, & Engles, 2005). By the end of high school, issues concerning autonomy are largely resolved.

Parents can either facilitate or hinder the growth of autonomy. As adolescents vie for a say in and eventual control over the decisions that affect them, some conflict with parents may be inevitable. Not all parents react the same to these demands. Some are able to turn over increasing responsibility to their children. These parents tend to be firm yet warm when interacting with their children, and to focus positively on how their children are developing rather than negatively on how to control them. As one would expect, adolescents thrive under these conditions and develop the competencies their parents expect of them (Kenny & Gallagher, 2002; Pratt, Norris, van de Hoef, & Arnold, 2001; Steinberg, 2001). However, some research suggests that adolescents growing up in high-risk families may actually fare better with less autonomy (McElhaney & Allen, 2001).

We look next at adolescents themselves and a developmental process known as individuation.

Individuation

In order for adolescents to grow into themselves and discover their own strengths, they must disassemble the psychological structure they have lived in through childhood, the protective shelter of parents who seemed bigger than life. Adolescents do this by critically examining the attitudes, beliefs, and values they acquired from their parents. This process of growth is termed **individuation** (Josselson, 1980, 1988).

Adolescents accomplish this growth in ordinary ways—by making decisions for themselves and by living with the consequences of these decisions. The major decision all adolescents face is who is going to make the decisions, but because decisions take many different forms, this point is easily missed. Adolescents find themselves arguing about who they can go out with, how baggy is too baggy for pants, how late they can stay up, when they do their homework, or who gets to say what courses they can take in school. Much of the process is repetitive. Decisions made one day must be renegotiated the next, as the same issues continue to come up in different forms.

Perhaps the process is repetitive because it involves learning in a real life situation instead of in a classroom. In the classroom, principles are stated explicitly, frequently apart from any context, and adolescents must relate these principles to real life situations. Just the opposite occurs when learning outside the classroom. Outside their classes, adolescents learn by doing and by experiencing the consequences. No one is there to help identify which principles operate in that situation. As a result, it is often difficult to separate the elements that remain constant across situations from the situations themselves. Are adolescents really arguing about how loud their music can be, or about who gets to decide how loud is too loud?

There is another reason why adolescents tend to repeat the decision-making process: Frequently, what they learn from their decisions has very personal consequences, which they may not be ready to accept. Discovering how to solve an algebraic equation has little bearing on life outside math class; algebra is "safe" knowledge. But discovering that you are the only one who can make decisions for yourself, and that there is no one to blame or praise but yourself, is something else again. Understanding is rarely just an intellectual matter; it also reflects one's emotions and beliefs, and some things can be understood only when one is prepared to let go of old beliefs. Sometimes adolescents, or adults for that matter, cannot allow themselves to understand until they can live with the consequences of that understanding. They may prefer to live with isolated actions, not seeing how one fits with another to form a larger picture (Wapner, 1980).

Even though the daily decisions adolescents make often seem trivial, the process itself never is; it is a way of separating themselves as individuals. The process is also frequently lonely. Rejecting parental attitudes and values can often leave adolescents with an

individuation The process of distinguishing one's attitudes and beliefs from those of one's parents.

IN MORE DEPTH

The Joys of Parenting Early Adolescents

"He is a talented athlete, and his soccer team got to a championship game. He scored the winning goal, and when he took off with the ball down the field, I was very proud of him. It was a unique feeling of being proud that someone I had helped to create was doing that. He had felt a lot of pressure in the game, so to see how incredibly pleased he was gave me great joy."—*Father*

"It's nice to see her being able to analyze situations with friends or with her teachers and come to conclusions. She said about one of her teachers, 'Well, she gets excited and she never follows through with what she says, so you know you don't have to take her seriously.'"—*Mother*

"I was so impressed and pleased that after the earthquake, he and a friend decided to go door to door and offer to sell drawings they made of Teenage Mutant Ninja Turtles. He raised $150 that he gave for earthquake relief. I was very proud that he thought this up all by himself."—*Father*

"I was very happy one day when I found this note she left on my desk. It said, 'Hello!!! Have a happy day! Don't worry about home, everyone's fine! Do your work the very best you can. But most important, have a fruitful life!!' I saved that note because it made me feel so good." —*Mother*

"He's very sensitive, and his cousins two years older than he ask his advice about boys. They may not take it, but they ask him even though he's younger." —*Father*

Source: J. Brooks. (1999). *The process of parenting* (5th ed.). Mountain View, CA: Mayfield.

empty feeling; they've discarded old ways before developing new ones of their own. Ruthellen Josselson (1980) suggests that emotions help adolescents with this transition. The very intensity of their emotions lets them know there is still someone inside. This function may account for some of the emotional intensity of early adolescence. Older adolescents have become surer of their decisions, and much of the earlier emotional overkill drops out. By late adolescence most have disentangled their needs and ideas from those of their parents and have a sense of being in charge of their lives. They no longer need emotion to fill a psychic void or to convince themselves, or others, that they are in control.

Throughout the individuation process, adolescents attempt to preserve a sense of sameness of their inner selves and of what they mean to others. The identities that emerge must be continuous with their past and also allow them to project themselves into the future. Adolescents who successfully sort through their own and their parents' attitudes and beliefs can maintain a comfortable closeness with their parents, without fearing a loss of their own individuality. (In More Depth describes some of the benefits of parenting early adolescents.) This closeness is an important source of continuity in their lives. Adolescents do not need to discard old relationships or adopt completely new lifestyles in order to be their own person (Mazor & Enright, 1988). Individuation involves both a growing independence from parents, such as in managing daily events or needing less support, and positive feelings about one's independence.

The very conditions that foster healthy development at one age within the lifespan should be similar to those promoting development at other ages as well. This appears to be true with respect to the conditions that promote individuation. Adolescents whose parents are emotionally open and supportive are those who feel free to explore life possibilities. Similarly, Ainsworth (1973, 1993) found that infants whose caregivers are sensitive and responsive are more curious and more likely to explore their surroundings. Individuation, like attachment, reflects a healthy balance between a growing independence and continued closeness with parents. To the extent this balance is maintained, adolescents are able to assume increasing responsibility for their own individuality without fearing that doing so will distance them from their parents (Allen, McElhaney, Kuperminc, & Jodl, 2004; MacKinnon & Marcia, 2002).

When adolescents' own need for emotional closeness threatens their independence, or when their need for autonomy hampers emotional closeness with parents, healthy development can be affected. Ernest Hodges, Regina Finnegan, and David Perry (1999) found that early adolescents' relationships with parents that reflected both connectedness and independence predicted healthier patterns of adjustment over time than those in which these relationships were skewed.

Family Interaction and Adolescents' Individuation

The family has a critical role in the personality development of adolescents. But how do families exert their effect? Are parents models for the behaviors adolescents acquire, or do these behaviors develop in the context of interactions among family members?

Individuality and Connectedness in the Family Harold Grotevant and Catherine Cooper (1986), developmentalists at the University of Minnesota and the University of California, Santa Cruz, identified dimensions of family interaction that contribute to the development of individuation. They used a deceptively simple approach to study family interactions: They asked families to make plans for an imaginary vacation and analyzed the communication patterns that developed within the family. They looked for patterns that evidenced two qualities they believed to be critical for the development of individuation: individuality and connectedness. **Individuality** is the ability to have and express one's own ideas (*self-assertion*) and to say how one differs from others (*separateness*). **Connectedness** reflects one's openness to others' opinions (*permeability*) and one's respect for their ideas (*mutuality*). The In More Depth "Communication Patterns That Foster Individuation" illustrates their approach. These investigators looked for statements that illustrate each of these four factors.

Adolescents in an individuated relationship have a clear sense of themselves as distinct from other people yet feel emotionally connected with them. They have their own ideas, which they can express, and are open to the ideas of the person they are with. In a sense, individuation allows them to respect each person as an individual—including themselves. Equally important, individuated relationships allow adolescents to experience their connectedness with another person and still see how they are different. Research on individuation suggests that adolescents who achieve high levels of individuation can remain close to their parents without feeling a loss of their own distinctiveness. The research also supports the view that parent–adolescent relationships continue to be close as they move toward greater mutuality (Pinquart & Silbereisen, 2002; White, Speisman, & Costos, 1983).

Adolescents do not have to have an individuated relationship with both parents. A single relationship in which there are moderate to high degrees of separateness and permeability makes individuation possible. Adolescents who achieve the highest levels of individuation, however, are likely to come from families in which members delight in examining their differences yet experience connectedness with each other.

Adolescents low in individuation typically have families who avoid disagreeing with each other and are so responsive to others' opinions that they cannot form a differing opinion of their own. Families with few disagreements communicate one important message to their members: that it is important to agree. Adolescents from these families must express the family point of view in order to voice anything at all. Doing so reassures others that they agree with them. As an extreme example, when the mother in one

individuality A quality of family interactions thought to be important for individuation, reflecting the ability to express one's ideas and say how one differs from others.

connectedness A quality of family interactions thought to be important for individuation, reflecting openness to and respect for others' opinions.

IN MORE DEPTH

Communication Patterns That Foster Individuation

Tanya: Why don't we visit Grandma and then go someplace exotic like the Everglades?

Willie: Do you know how hot it is in Florida in August? I vote to skip the family visit this year and go to Acapulco. That's a real vacation.

Dad: I could sure use some time on a beach.

Willie: Right, Dad, but you don't want to share it with a crocodile, do you?

Tanya: They're alligators, not crocodiles, Surfer Joe.

Mom: I'd like to see the pyramids in Mexico. We could stop off at Acapulco on the way.

Tanya: Hmm.

Dad: How far inland are they?

Mom: I don't know, but I could call a travel agent.

Willie: Get real, Mom. Do you think you can get us to sweat a path through the jungle once we've seen the sands of Acapulco?

Tanya: Willie'd die in the heat there, too.

Dad: Maybe we should think of a winter vacation.

Tanya: All right, let's vote on this.

Willie: Okay, let's vote.

INDIVIDUALITY

Self-Assertion—The ability to have one's own ideas and express them. "I'd like to see the pyramids in Mexico."

Separateness—The ability to say how one differs from others.

1. Requests action
   "All right, let's vote on this."
2. Directly disagrees
   "Get real, Mom. Do you think you can get us to sweat a path through the jungle once we've seen the sands of Acapulco?"
3. Indirectly disagrees
   "Do you know how hot it is in Florida in August?"
4. Irrelevant comment
   "They're alligators, not crocodiles, Surfer Joe."

CONNECTEDNESS

Permeability— Openness and responsiveness to the opinions of others.

1. Acknowledges
   "Hmm."
2. Requests information or validation
   "How far inland are they?"
3. Agrees with another's ideas
   "I could sure use some time on a beach."
4. Relevant comment
   "Maybe we should think of a winter vacation."
5. Complies with a request
   "Okay, let's vote."

Mutuality— Sensitivity and respect for others' ideas.

1. Indirect suggestion of action
   "Why don't we visit Grandma and then go someplace exotic like the Everglades?"
2. Compromise
   "I'd like to see the pyramids in Mexico. We could stop off at Acapulco on the way."
3. States another's feelings
   "Willie'd die in the heat there, too."
4. Answers request for information/validation
   "I don't know, but I could call a travel agent."

Source: Adapted from C. R. Cooper, H. D. Grotevant, & S. M. Condon. (1983). Individuality and connectedness in the family as a context for adolescent identity formation and role-taking skill. In H. D. Grotevant & C. R. Cooper (Eds.), *Adolescent development in the family.* San Francisco: Jossey-Bass.

family asked where they should go on their vacation, each member responded by repeating the father's suggestion of going back to Spain. When asked for more suggestions by her father, the adolescent daughter could not elaborate and fumbled an "I don't know," indicating her father should offer more suggestions. It was hard for this adolescent to explore issues outside her family's belief system, even when they only involved choices for an imaginary family vacation (Grotevant & Cooper, 1986). Adolescents who can experience their separateness from other members of the family are freer to develop their own point of view. Even so, their explorations take place in an emotional context of connectedness, which provides the security that allows them to examine ideas.

IN MORE DEPTH

Parents' Reflections About Late Adolescence

"I wish that I had got my children involved in more family activities. When they were mostly through adolescence, I heard a talk by a child psychiatrist who said that often when teenagers say they don't want to do something with the family, at times you have to insist because they do go along and enjoy the event. I wish I had known sooner, because I accepted their first 'No,' when I perhaps should have pushed more."—*Mother*

". . . When you read about independence, it sounds like it's carefully planned out. When it actually happens, all of a sudden they want to do something that they have never done before and which you firmly believe they have no idea how to do. It can be driving for the first time or suddenly announcing they want to go somewhere with friends. I knew it was going to happen, but exactly how to handle it myself and handle it with them so they got a chance to do something new without it being dangerous has been a challenge to me."—*Father*

"I wish I had known to be more attentive, to really listen, because kids have a lot of worthwhile things to say and you come to find out they hold a lot of your viewpoints."—*Father*

"I wish I had known it was important to spend time with children individually. We did things as a family, but the children are so different, and I think I would have understood them better if I had spent time with them alone."—*Mother*

Source: J. Brooks. (1999). *The process of parenting* (5th ed.). Mountain View, CA: Mayfield.

To develop a point of view, adolescents must be able to see how their ideas differ from those of others. Interactions that focus on differences and similarities provide important developmental experiences; they can also involve conflict. Conflict itself isn't necessarily bad. In the context of clarifying a position, it can help adolescents gain a sense of what they believe. For adolescents to have their ideas challenged without experiencing this as criticism, a supportive family atmosphere is important. See In More Depth "Parents' Reflections About Late Adolescence" for parents' insights on this process.

Individuation gives adolescents a set of attitudes and ways of acting that are genuinely their own; however, they must still put these together into a working whole that reflects an inner sense of self. Although the process begins in early adolescence, adolescents do not consolidate these changes until late adolescence or even early adulthood when choices about jobs, college, and relationships force identity issues to a head. We turn to a consideration of identity next.

Identity: The Normative Crisis of Adolescence

"Normative crisis" sounds like an oxymoron, a combination of contradictory terms like "thunderous silence." Doesn't "normative" refer to a standard, a pattern, something that is predictable and regular? And doesn't "crisis" mean something *out* of the ordinary, something that violates the pattern, that *doesn't* happen every day?

In discussing the concept of "identity crisis," Erik Erikson (1968) noted that, although the phrase later acquired a distinctive meaning, at the time he first coined it, he considered himself to be naming something so familiar as to be taken for granted. He illustrated this point with a story about an old man who vomited each morning but refused to see a doctor. Finally, his family convinced him to get a checkup. After examining him, the doctor asked how he was feeling. "Fine, just fine" the old man replied. The

Successfully resolving an identity crisis means finding an adult course that fits one's talents and inclinations and that is fulfilling. These adolescents are learning about adult roles by assuming responsibility for animals as members of the 4-H Club.

doctor, impatient with what appeared to be denial of a serious problem, responded, "But your family tells me you vomit every morning!" The old man looked at the doctor in surprise. "Of course I do, doesn't everybody?" he asked.

Erikson's point to this story is that "identity crisis" describes something that all of us have experienced, and have taken for granted, but would have no difficulty recognizing once it is labeled, something that is, despite the upset, quite normative (Erikson, 1968).

Similarly, Erikson used the word *crisis* to refer not to some imminent catastrophe but, rather, to a developmental turning point in which the individual must choose one course or another simply because it is no longer possible to continue as before (Erikson, 1968).

Perhaps no term is more closely associated with the writing and thinking of Erik Erikson than *identity* (see Chapter 2). Erikson was, above all else, a clinician whose concepts reflected real life experiences. In writing about the personality, Erikson noted that "old troubles" return when we are tired or otherwise defenseless, simply because we are what we *were* as well as what we might want to become or presently may be (Coles, 1970; Erikson, 1954).

Erikson believed that, like his patients, adolescents have to confront "old troubles" in arriving at an identity. Consider Erikson's (1968) description of Jill, a young woman he knew:

> I had known Jill before her puberty, when she was rather obese and showed many "oral" traits of voracity and dependency while she also was a tomboy and bitterly envious of her brothers and in rivalry with them. But she was intelligent and always had an air about her (as did her mother) which seemed to promise that things would turn out all right. And, indeed, she straightened out and up, became very attractive, an easy leader in any group, and, to many, a model of young girlhood. As a clinician, I watched and wondered what she would do with that voraciousness and with the rivalry which she had displayed earlier. Could it be that such things are simply absorbed in fortuitous growth?
>
> Then one autumn in her late teens, Jill did not return to college from the ranch out West where she had spent the summer. She had asked her parents to let her stay.

> Simply out of liberality and confidence, they granted her this moratorium and returned East.
>
> That winter Jill specialized in taking care of newborn colts, and would get up at any time during a winter night to bottle-feed the most needy animals. Having apparently acquired a certain satisfaction within herself, as well as astonished recognition from the cowboys, she returned home and reassumed her place. I felt that she had found and hung on to an opportunity to do actively and for others what she had once demonstrated by overeating: she had learned to feed needy young mouths. But she did so in a context which, in turning passive into active, also turned a former symptom into a social act.
>
> One might say that she turned "maternal" but it was a maternalism such as cowboys must and do display; and, of course, she did it all in jeans. This brought recognition "from man to man" as well as from man to woman, and beyond that the confirmation of her optimism, that is, her feeling that something could be done that felt like her, was useful and worthwhile, and was in line with an ideological trend where it still made immediate practical sense. (pp. 130–131)

Jill fashioned her identity, as Erikson said we all do, out of old cloth, but she tailored it to the needs of the present. She translated what she *was*—an energetic, intelligent, but envious and dependent child—into a mature personality, capable of responding to her own and others' needs.

Identity, as Erikson used the term, refers to the sense of self that we achieve through examining and committing ourselves to the roles and pursuits that define an adult in our society (see Chapter 2). Identity gives us a sense of who we are, of knowing what is "me" and what is "not me." As Jill's story demonstrated, the "me" includes more than the present. Identity allows us to experience a continuity of self over time. We can relate what we have done in the past to what we hope to do in the future, to our ambitions and dreams. Finally, our perception of self includes how others see us, the importance they attach to our values and accomplishments.

Jill's story illustrates these aspects of identity. Her new maturity grew out of familiar issues, her "old troubles," that she approached in new ways. Because the "me" that she had been as a child was still recognizable in her more adult concerns, there was a continuity to her experience over time. Lastly, her perception of herself, her confidence and self-esteem, resulted not only from becoming skilled in something she valued, but also from receiving the recognition of the society in which she achieved this, the cowboys she had worked with.

As Erikson illustrated in this case study, Jill experimented with a way of being, one of many possible ones, that incorporated much of what she already recognized in herself but enabled her to realize new strengths. Erikson (1959) suggested that adolescents imagine a number of **possible selves,** mentally trying them on to get a sense of who they might become, of what their lives might be like. Some of these versions of the self are positive, or hoped-for selves, whereas others represent feared outcomes that adolescents nonetheless believe could be possible as well. High school students, when asked to generate all the possible selves they can think of, think of quite a few, averaging about 13. The majority of these are positive, and also are seen as more likely than feared possible selves (Knox, Funk, Elliott, & Bush, 2000).

In defining identity, Erikson considered three domains to be of paramount importance: sexuality as expressed in an adult gender role; occupation; and ideology, or religious and political beliefs. Each of these domains will be more closely examined in the chapters that follow. Chapter 6 will consider sexuality and gender roles; Chapter 10 will

identity The part of one's personality of which one is aware and is able to see as a meaningful and coherent whole.

possible selves Life options that adolescents imagine for themselves; some are positive, or hoped-for, and others are feared, or negative, possibilities.

One signal of an adolescent's developing sense of self is involvement in a cause—whether against drugs in the neighborhood or for the preservation of an endangered species. Ideology, or commitment to principle, is the name Erik Erikson gave to this domain of identity formation.

examine careers and college; and Chapter 11, values and moral development. But, for now, we will examine the process of identity formation itself.

Variations on a Theme of Identity

Although Erikson was the first to describe and elaborate the concept of identity as a normative crisis in adolescence, James Marcia has been largely responsible for generating research on identity formation, primarily by constructing a measure of ego identity, which has made it possible to empirically test many implications of Erikson's writings.

Identity Statuses

Most of the work we do on our identity takes place in adolescence; however, as Marcia notes with a touch of humor, if identity formation were necessary by the end of adolescence, many of us would never become adults. His point is that achieving a personal identity is not an easy process. Adolescents must be willing to take risks and live with uncertainty.

Some of the uncertainty comes from exploring possibilities and options in life that differ from those chosen by one's parents. Most adolescents expect this exploration to be risky. Few adolescents, however, expect the risks that occur when they must make commitments based on their exploration. Adolescents form their identities both by taking on new ways of being *and* by excluding others. It is every bit as important to let go of their fantasies and commit themselves to a definite course of action as it is to challenge the familiar by exploring possibilities never even considered by their parents or families. Marcia (1966; Marcia, Waterman, Matteson, Archer, & Orlofsky, 1993) refers to these two dimensions of the identity process as exploration and commitment.

James Marcia's theory of identity statuses suggests that some of these young men are considering a military career because of a family military tradition, that others are motivated by a personal commitment to serve their country, and that still others see military service as a way to postpone deciding what they ultimately want to do with their lives.

Marcia distinguishes four ways by which adolescents arrive at the roles and values that define their identities. Each of these ways, or identity statuses, is defined in terms of the dimensions of commitment and exploration. Adolescents who are committed to life options arrive at them either by exploring and searching for what fits them best or by forgoing exploration and letting themselves be guided by their parents' values. The first alternative results in the ego reorganization that Erikson characterized as identity formation; the second leaves parental identifications unchallenged and unchanged. Adolescents who have searched for life options that fit them best are termed **identity achieved;** those who adopt their parents' values without question are termed **identity foreclosed** (Marcia, 1980, 2002).

Similarly, two paths lead to noncommitment. Some adolescents begin to evaluate life options but don't close off certain possibilities because the decisions are too momentous to risk making a mistake; as a result, they remain uncommitted to any path. These adolescents are in **moratorium.** Others remain uncommitted for the opposite reason: failure to see the importance of choosing one option over any other. They are termed **identity diffused.** Even though adolescents in moratorium begin to question parental ways, like foreclosed adolescents they ultimately do not challenge parental identifications for fear their choices may be wrong. Identity-diffused adolescents fail to challenge earlier identifications because they lack the sense of urgency that would prompt them to make decisions that would distinguish them as individuals.

The process of reorganizing earlier identifications continues into late adolescence—and beyond. Self-definition in areas of occupational choice, religious and political beliefs, and gender roles continues into early adulthood (Archer, 1989a; Kroger, 2003). Jane Kroger (2003) notes that even among late adolescents, about half remain in the foreclosed or diffused status with respect to at least one of the domains of self-definition.

Given that we expect individuals to become more mature with age, to think things through for themselves and commit themselves to life tasks that reflect their values, there is an implicit developmental trend in these statuses. Identity-achieved adolescents, in whom development is characterized by both exploration and commitment, should be

identity achievement The resolution of the psychosocial crisis of identity through the formulation of personal goals and personally defined religious and political commitments.

identity foreclosure The resolution of the psychosocial crisis of identity through the assumption of traditional, conventional, or parentally chosen goals and values without the experience of crisis or conflict over identity issues.

moratorium The experience of conflict over the issues of identity formation prior to the establishment of firm goals or long-term commitments.

identity diffusion The resolution of the psychosocial crisis of identity without the experience of crisis or commitment over identity issues.

Most, if not all, of these football players probably dream of sports scholarships or even going pro. But as they go through the process of identity formation, they will gradually let go of such fantasies and commit themselves to more realistic futures.

the most mature. Conversely, identity-diffused adolescents, in whom neither of these measures of maturity is evident, should be the least mature. Support for this ordering comes from longitudinal studies that have found the achieved status to become more frequent with age, and the diffusion status less frequent (Cramer, 1998; Kroger, 1995). Theoretical support comes as well from attachment theory research, in which secure attachment to a caregiver in childhood has been found to be associated with a number of markers of maturity, such as increased resilience and social competence, later in development (Sroufe, 1989). Adolescents who are classified as securely attached are more likely to be identity achieved, whereas those classified as insecurely attached are more likely to be identity diffused (Zimmermann & Becker-Stoll, 2002).

But what of the moratorium and foreclosed statuses? Do exploration and commitment, as developmental virtues, contribute equally to maturity? Given the high value our culture places on thinking for oneself and being independent, individuals who think through a course of action *before* committing themselves to anything are regarded as more mature than those who commit themselves to something they have not thought about. By this standard, adolescents in the moratorium status should be more mature. Again, longitudinal research supports this ordering for college students, finding that a transition from foreclosure into moratorium is more frequent than the reverse (Kroger, 2000).

Do adolescents simultaneously address identity issues in each of the different domains? That is, do they consider occupational, ideological, and sexual alternatives at the same point in time? Or do different domains become salient at different points in an adolescent's life? Can a 17-year-old male be identity achieved in his occupational plans ("I'll work in construction with my uncle") but foreclosed in his gender role ("I want my wife to stay home with the kids the way Mom did"), diffused in his political beliefs ("I don't see the point in getting too worked up over political issues; after all, what can one person do?"), and in moratorium about his religious beliefs ("I don't think of God the way I did as a kid, but I can't dismiss the idea that God is interested in me personally")?

In a two-year follow-up study of late adolescents, Jane Kroger (1988) found that only half the adolescents she studied had a common status in any two domains; another 9% had no domains in common. These data suggest that identity is not "a unitary structure, but . . . a sequence of distinct psychosocial resolutions involved in the definition of self" (1988, p. 60). Kroger's findings are comparable to those of other investigators in suggesting that adolescents do not work simultaneously on all identity domains (Archer, 1989a; Goossens, 2001; Kroger, 2003).

Lea Pulkkinen and Katja Kokko (2000), at the University of Jyvaskyla, in Finland, followed individuals into their mid-thirties, assessing their identity status at the age of 27 and again at 36. These investigators found significant changes in the distribution of identity statuses across nearly all domains for both women and men. In general, the number of individuals in the diffusion and moratorium statuses decreased with age and those in foreclosure and achievement increased with age. In other words, as individuals aged, more of them moved into the achievement *and* foreclosure statuses.

These patterns of change in mid-adulthood stand in contrast to those found for college students. If we assume, however, as did these investigators, that identity development in adulthood should reflect an increasing commitment to the values one holds in life, this progression makes sense. The individuals in this study were no longer in college, a setting designed to maximize students' exploration of options but, when last interviewed, were in their mid-thirties. Movement into foreclosure, as opposed to moratorium, would reflect these adults' growing commitment to the life tasks of adulthood. Thus the relative maturity of an identity status must be considered within the larger context of the developmental tasks facing individuals at different points in their lives. What constitutes the most adaptive response to the developmental tasks of adolescence is not necessarily the most adaptive in adulthood.

For some young people, travel is a way to learn more about themselves and the world. For others, however, it is a way to put off making life decisions.

Moratorium and Possible Selves

Pulkkinen and Kokko are not alone in finding that individuals are not likely to remain in the moratorium status. In fact, Curt Dunkel (2000), at Illinois Central College, has suggested that moratorium is less an identity outcome than it is a transitory state. Dunkel points out that longitudinal studies may have shown us the *path* adolescents follow, but they have not identified the developmental *mechanisms* responsible for change (Josselson, 1987; Kroger, 1988; Marcia, 1976). Dunkel suggests that one such mechanism is at work during moratorium, and it takes the form of generating possible selves. That is, if identity formation involves the construction of a self, individuals need to explore the form this self might take, and they do so during moratorium. In support of this, Dunkel found that, when asked to think about all the selves they might be, college students who were in the moratorium status endorsed more possible selves than did those in any other status (see Figure 5.1; Dunkel, 2000; Dunkel & Anthis, 2001).

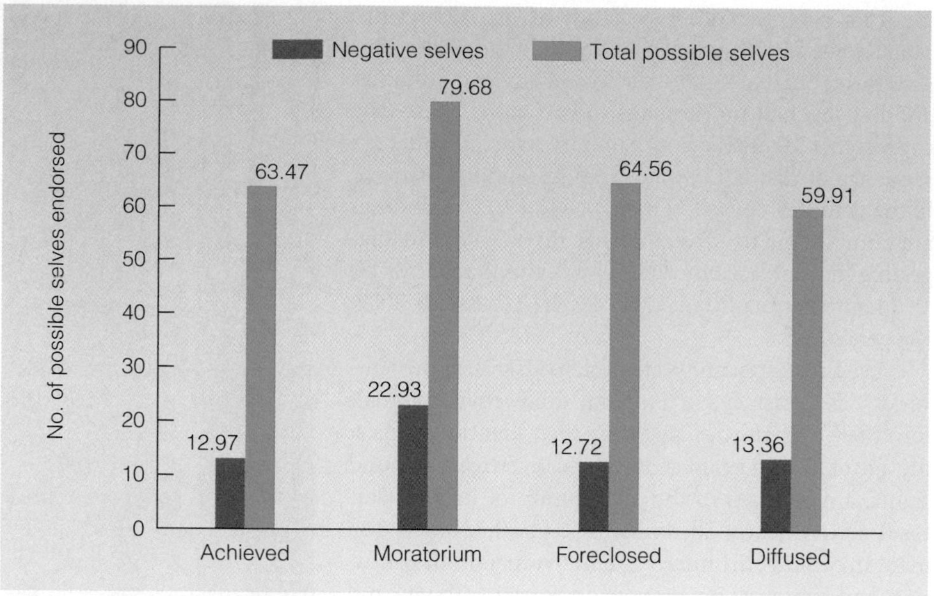

■ **FIGURE 5.1**
Identity Status and Possible Selves. *When asked to think about all the possible selves, or alternatives in life, youth in the moratorium status are the most undecided; they also envision more negative possibilities than do youth in the other identity statuses. Source:* Adapted from C. S. Dunkel (2000). Possible selves as a mechanism for identity exploration. *Journal of Adolescence, 23,* 519–529.

Identity Styles

Michael Berzonsky (1992; Berzonsky, 2004) has proposed an alternative way of thinking about identity statuses. To use Jane Kroger's (1992) distinction, Berzonsky envisions identity statuses as "organizers" of experience, not as "organizations" of experience. In other words, Berzonsky views identity statuses as an input variable rather than an outcome variable, as a process rather than a structure.

Berzonsky suggests that individuals differ in the way they process information relevant to the self; these differences underlie Marcia's statuses. Some individuals, for instance, actively search for any information that might be relevant to the problems they face; then they carefully evaluate this information before making their decisions. This **information oriented** style characterizes identity-achieved and moratorium individuals. Others appear to do just the opposite, putting off decisions and avoiding problems by procrastinating. Berzonsky calls this style, which characterizes identity-diffused persons, **diffuse/avoidant.** Finally, some individuals, when faced with problems, use as information social norms, or the expectations of significant others such as parents. Berzonsky identifies this processing style as **normative oriented** and notes that it characterizes those who are foreclosed (Berzonsky, 2004). The Research Focus "Operationalizing Concepts" illustrates the relationships among identity styles and identity statuses.

information orientation A style of information processing characterized by actively searching for and evaluating information.

diffuse/avoidant orientation A style of information processing characterized by procrastinating and avoiding decisions.

normative orientation A style of information processing characterized by reliance on social norms and the expectations of relatives and friends.

Identity: Gender and Ethnicity

Gender Differences in Identity Formation

Adolescents look for answers to questions concerning their identity by examining the societal roles they see around them, roles they will soon assume. Erikson considered the most central of these roles to be that of a future occupation. Following close on the heels of this decision come decisions about political and religious beliefs and the expression of an adult gender role (Erikson, 1968). Occupation, political stance, and ideology—all of these characterized males more than females at the time Erikson formulated this concept. Ruthellen Josselson (1987) writes:

> At this point in his writing, it becomes more apparent that Erikson, like Freud and most other important psychological theorists, is writing about men. Indeed, all Erikson's psychobiographies analyze identity as it develops in men, and most of his case examples are from male patients. All Erikson had to say about women was that much of a woman's identity resides in her choice of the men she wants to be sought by. (p. 22)

Erikson on Gender Differences *Was* Erikson writing primarily about males? If so, how did he think females formulated an identity? Was it, as Josselson summarizes, through the men in their lives?

Erikson did, in fact, believe that the process of identity formulation differs for males and females—in content, timing, and sequence. With respect to the content of identity, he considered interpersonal issues, rather than vocational and ideological ones, to be central for females. He also thought the timing of identity resolution to be different for males and females, with females keeping their identity options partially open, rather than resolving them as males do, so that they might better complement a potential mate. Erikson also believed that females resolve identity and intimacy issues more or less concurrently, whereas males resolve these issues sequentially (Patterson, Sochting, & Marcia, 1992).

Why would male and female adolescents go about so fundamental a process in different ways? In partial answer, Erikson referred to a "profound difference . . . between the sexes in the experience of the ground plan of the human body" that "predisposes" adolescent males and females to work out their identities in different ways. He believed that women find "their identities in the care suggested in their bodies and in the needs of their issue, and seem to have taken it for granted that the outer world space belongs to the men" (1968, p. 274). According to Erickson, males achieve their identities by exploring this outer world and finding pursuits and beliefs to which they can commit themselves—an occupation and an ideology.

Was Erikson right? Do sex differences such as the "ground plan of the human body" primarily shape the process by which one achieves an identity? Do we see the same pattern of concerns and commitments among adolescents today as Erikson believed to hold true? A number of studies supply us with answers to these questions.

Research on Gender Differences Research has found few differences among male and female adolescents in identity development with respect to the numbers of males and females in each of the identity statuses (Cramer, 2000; Dunkel & Anthis, 2001; Goosens, 2001; Kroger, 2003; Pulkkinen & Kokko, 2000; Schwartz & Montgomery, 2002). When gender differences emerge, these most frequently show interpersonal concerns to figure more centrally in females' than males' identities (Archer, 1989a; Cramer, 2000; Pulkkinen & Kokko, 2000; Schwartz & Montgomery, 2002). Even then, research that finds interpersonal issues to be more salient for females than males does *not* find occupational concerns to be of less importance than they are for males (Archer, 1989a; Goosens, 2001; Pulkkinen & Kokko, 2000). Additionally, interpersonal issues have been found to be more important for males than earlier assumed (Kroger, 2000). With respect to the timing of identity formation, however, issues of identity and intimacy are more apt to be resolved concurrently in females than males (Patterson et al., 1992).

RESEARCH FOCUS

Operationalizing Concepts: What Kind of Decision Maker Are You?

By Michael Wapner

Lucky for Henry there was a category for undeclared majors. It had let him postpone that decision for a year and a half. But here it was the end of the first semester of his sophomore year and he was still "undeclared." He had just about finished his general education requirements, and he had taken intro psych, intro soc, intro anthro, and intro poli sci. No way to keep going much longer without choosing a major. But how was a guy to know what he'd want to do three years from now? He'd pretty much narrowed it down to a social science. Or, really, it had been narrowed down for him. He wasn't much good at math or music. He didn't like chemistry or physics. And he couldn't paint or dance. So social science was about all that was left—but which one?

Really, to tell the truth, it wasn't just choosing a major. Henry hated choices in general. He never ate in the cafeteria. Barbara chose the movies they would see and even went shopping with him to pick out his clothes. (Come to think of it, he didn't really *choose* Barbara. They had been fixed up for a blind date and just kept going together.) In fact, he was even at this college because he had delayed so long in deciding that all the other colleges had withdrawn their acceptances.

Although Henry may be an extreme example, he is not unique. His style of dealing with decisions makes him a good candidate for what Michael Berzonsky, at the State University of New York, Cortland, calls a diffuse/avoidant identity orientation.

Berzonsky's social-cognitive model identifies three types of *identity orientation,* or ways an individual approaches (or avoids) the task of constructing and revising a self-identity. These three types are informational, normative, and diffuse/avoidant. The *informational orientation* is characteristic of individuals who are in an identity-achieved or moratorium identity status, and it is marked by deliberate self-exploration, a personally defined identity, an internal locus of control, problem-focused coping, and an openness to novel ideas, values, and actions. The *normative orientation* is associated with a foreclosed identity status, and it is distinguished by a tendency to be closed to information that would cause one to evaluate central aspects of the self and by conformity to the expectations of others. A *diffuse/avoidant orientation* is associated with a diffuse identity status, a greater likelihood of depression and neurosis, a less particular and pleasant interaction style than that of the other two categories, and a reluctance to deal with problems and decisions.

Berzonsky contends that each identity orientation is characterized by a different strategy of decision making. Information-oriented individuals are most likely to gather as much information as possible, by such means as talking to others or reading up on a subject, before they make a decision. Individuals with diffuse/avoidant orientations, such as Henry, are most likely to procrastinate and engage in defensive avoidance and other self-defeating approaches that are designed to escape decisions more than to make them. (In the research we are currently considering, Berzonsky made no particular predictions regarding the decisional strategies of normatively oriented individuals.)

Having hypothesized these relationships between identity orientation and decisional strategy, Berzonsky and his colleagues undertook extensive research to demonstrate them. However, before data on the question could be gathered, an essential step had to be taken. The concepts under consideration (identity orientation and decisional strategy) had to be *operationally defined.* Because concepts are, by definition, abstract, there are

Serena Patterson, Ingrid Sochting, and James Marcia (1992) have suggested that, in addition to exploration and commitment, a third dimension, relatedness, is important in defining identity statuses for females. Is this suggestion contrary to research finding that the process of identity formation is more similar than different between adolescents of either sex? Sally Archer (1992) offers a tentative resolution to this apparent contradiction. She points to a remarkable tunnel vision that she noticed in her interviews with adolescents when it came to seeing the implications that commitments in one domain have for another domain. For instance, an adolescent boy might describe his vocational plans in detail as well as his plans for marriage and children, and yet not connect the two.

usually a number of different ways of interpreting them. Operationally defining a concept pins it down by expressing it in terms of the methods used to measure it. Operationalizing is a very fundamental process employed in all empirical science. Even a seemingly simple concept like "friendliness," in order to be studied, might be operationally defined in terms of a score on a friendliness scale or a questionnaire filled out by an individual's acquaintances. By operationalizing a concept, investigators define it in a way that others can use and follow and be sure they are studying the same concept.

But not all operational definitions are equally adequate. Suppose, in studying friendliness, we operationally defined a "friendly" person as "anyone who is smiling the first time that person is observed." Although that does fulfill the minimum requirement for an operational definition—that is, it specifies what operation to perform to determine if someone is friendly (observe the person and see if that person is smiling)—it is not likely to be a satisfactory definition. It is likely to be deficient with respect to the two most important criteria for any measure—*reliability* and *validity*—that is, its consistency and the degree to which it measures what we assume it is measuring.

To assess, or operationally define, identity orientation, Michael Berzonsky and Joseph Ferrari employed a questionnaire—the Identity Style Inventory (ISI)—constructed and revised just for this purpose (Berzonsky, 1992). The ISI contains a 10-item informational-style scale with items such as "I've spent a great deal of time thinking seriously about what I should do with my life"; a 10-item diffuse/avoidant scale with items such as "I'm not really thinking about my future now; it's still a long way off"; and a 9-item normative-style scale with items such as "I prefer to deal with situations where I can rely on social norms and standards." Subjects were asked to rate the degree to which statements applied to them.

To assess decisional strategies, Berzonsky and Ferrari used a decision-making questionnaire, in which subjects were asked to rate the extent to which they engage in various decision-making practices. The subscales include vigilance ("When making decisions I like to collect lots of information"); panic ("I feel as if I'm under tremendous time pressure when making decisions"); and decisional avoidance ("I avoid making decisions").

Were these measures reliable? One way of determining reliability is to give the measure to the same individuals on two separate occasions. The *test–retest reliability,* or consistency in responding to questions from one time to the next, was relatively high. Of equal, if not greater, interest is whether the measure is a valid one. One way to determine a measure's validity is to see how well the measure relates to other measures of the construct. This assessment of validity is known as *construct validity.* In originally constructing the Identity Style Inventory, Berzonsky (1989) selected a number of measures that were known to distinguish individuals in each of the identity statuses themselves, and administered these to another group of individuals, together with his measure of decision styles. Would the decision-making scores correspond in a meaningful way with those on the other measures? Berzonsky found that they did.

Berzonsky and Ferrari administered the Identity Style Inventory and the decision-making questionnaire to college students. They also administered two scales of procrastination. Are different identity orientations characterized by different strategies of decision making? As expected, students who could be classified as information oriented were likely to use decisional practices in which they gather information, and individuals who could be classified as diffuse/avoidant oriented were more likely to procrastinate and engage in avoidance, excuse making, and other maladaptive behaviors.

Sources: M. D. Berzonsky. (1989). Identity style: Conceptualization and measurement. *Journal of Adolescent Research, 4,* 268–282. M. D. Berzonsky & J. R. Ferrari. (1996). Identity orientation and decisional strategies. *Personality and Individual Differences, 20,* 597–606.

Thus, potential conflicts, such as who would care for the children if his wife also chose a career or whose career would determine where they would live, simply are not anticipated. Those interviewed by Archer who were most likely to make connections between domains were late adolescent females. A sense of relatedness for females, an awareness of themselves in relation to others, may prompt them to integrate identity domains.

Taken together, the research on gender differences reveals more similarities than differences. Adolescents of either sex who allow themselves to question, explore, and experience the uncertainty of not knowing—to experience a period of crisis—mature in this process.

Identity-achieved females appear to focus on achieving a balance between self-assertion and relatedness. They use strengths drawn from their relationships to fuel their solo efforts.

Because our sense of self reflects an awareness of how others see us, cultural values as well as individual experiences contribute to the development of identity. We turn to a consideration of ethnicity and identity next.

Contributions of Ethnicity to Identity Development

As adolescents look to the culture in which they live to gain a glimpse of themselves, some will find a clearer image reflected back than will others. Adolescents who are members of the White majority will see themselves more easily in the faces of those around them than will adolescents who are members of an ethnic minority. For the later, the process of identity formation includes an additional step, on of resolving issues related to an ethnic identity.

Ethnic identity consists in seeing oneself as a member of an ethnic group, and in the way one values and participates in that group. Simply put, it is a way of understanding oneself in terms of one's ethnicity (Phinney, 1996, 2005). The boundaries that define one's group provide members with a feeling of belonging. When boundaries are clear, they allow adolescents to distinguish between their own and other groups, and result in stronger ethnic identity. Some boundaries are maintained from within by the group, others are imposed on the group by the dominant culture. Internal boundaries come about through identifying with others in one's group. Adolescents adopt the values, attitudes, and perspectives of their group. Interactions with those outside the group provide a second type of boundary, through which minority adolescents experience the social opportunities and constraints that exist for members of their group—the relative status and value given them by others. The status of one's group within society is an important component of ethnic identity (Phinney, 1996).

As might be expected, adolescents' consciousness of their ethnic identity varies with the situations they are in (Harris & Sim, 2002; Herman, 2004). Rosenthal and Hrynevich (1985) found that adolescents experience a strong ethnic identity when they are with their family or speaking their parents' native language, but feel part of the dominant culture when with others from that culture, such as when they are at school. They also found that the strength of the inner boundary of the ethnic group relates to adolescents' pride in their ethnic identity. This strength is reflected in the institutional completeness of the community, the extent to which it provides its own schools, markets, churches, and other institutions.

ethnic identity An awareness of belonging to an ethnic group that shapes one's thoughts, feelings, and behavior.

acculturation A socialization process by which members of a minority adopt the customs of the dominant group, while maintaining a separate cultural identity.

In the process of **acculturation,** the outward behaviors of minority adolescents frequently become less distinct from those of the majority culture; however, attitudes and values are more likely to remain unchanged because they are more central to their sense of belonging to their group. Thus, minority adolescents whose behavior closely resembles that of peers from the dominant culture may still have strong ethnic identities in other respects. Doreen Rosenthal and Shirley Feldman (1992), comparing ethnic identity in first- and second-generation Chinese American and Chinese Australian adolescents, found that despite differences in knowledge about their culture and in observable behavior between first- and second-generation minorities, the core aspects to their ethnic identities differed little; both first- and second-generation adolescents ascribed the same importance to their ethnic group membership and evaluated their ethnicity equally positively.

William Cross, at City University of New York, distinguishes several steps to the process of forming an ethnic identity. In the *pre-encounter* stage, individuals identify with the dominant culture. They notice differences between themselves and the dominant culture but do not consider them important. The second stage of identity formation, which happens only for minority adolescents, is the *encounter.* Cross traces the emergence of this stage to one or more vivid incidents in which adolescents experience discrimination. These experiences precipitate an awareness that they are not seen as part of the dominant culture. This stage is a turning point in the development of an ethnic identity in which minority adolescents turn from the dominant culture and begin to explore the traditions and values of their ethnic group (Cross, 1980, 2005).

In the stage that follows, which Cross called the *immersion* stage, adolescents immerse themselves in the ways of their ethnic group, developing a high degree of awareness and valuation of those ways, along with a devaluation of those of the dominant culture. This stage is frequently characterized by social activism or even militancy. Finally, in the *internalization* stage, adolescents become able to appreciate themselves and others as individuals and to recognize differences that don't always correspond to group membership. Attitudes toward others reflect personal characteristics rather than group membership, as in the previous stage. Ethnic identity is less strident, and attitudes toward the dominant culture are less negative (Miville, Koonce, Darlington, & Whitlock, 2000; Umaña-Taylor, Diversi, & Fine, 2002).

This progression parallels a number of other developmental progressions in which development moves from a focus on the self to a focus on the group, to respect for the individual.

Stages of Ethnic Identity Development Jean Phinney, a psychologist at California State University, Los Angeles, points out that the progression toward an ethnic identity parallels differences among Marcia's identity statuses. Although Marcia did not initially think of the statuses developmentally, most research suggests that identity achievement is the most mature resolution and diffusion the least, with foreclosure and moratorium as intermediate steps (Josselson, 1982; Orlofsky & Frank, 1986). Phinney (1989, 1993) has proposed a stage model of ethnic identity development that parallels Marcia's analysis of identity.

Three distinct stages to ethnic identity development emerge. Just as with Marcia's identity statuses, it is possible for minority adolescents to avoid exploring the implications of their ethnicity and to remain committed to the values of the dominant culture. Adolescents with an **unexamined ethnic identity** have simply internalized the values and attitudes of the dominant culture, in a way similar to that of foreclosed adolescents, and have little understanding of issues related to their ethnicity. Those in an **ethnic identity search,** or moratorium stage, are involved in exploring the meaning of their ethnicity and may experience a growing conflict between the values of the dominant culture and those of their ethnic group. Adolescents with an **achieved ethnic identity** have a clear sense of their ethnicity that reflects feelings of belonging and emotional identification. They have little defensiveness and show confidence in their ethnicity (Phinney,

unexamined ethnic identity An initial stage in ethnic identity formation that involves a lack of awareness of the issues related to one's ethnicity and a simple internalization of the values of the dominant culture.

ethnic identity search An intermediate stage in ethnic identity formation involving exploration of the meaning of one's ethnicity.

achieved ethnic identity A stage in ethnic identity formation in which one has a clear sense of one's ethnicity that reflects feelings of belonging and emotional identification.

Adolescents with an achieved ethnic identity have a clear sense of their ethnicity that reflects feelings of belonging and emotional identification.

1989; Phinney & Rosenthal, 1992). Although different procedures and the use of somewhat different definitions make it difficult to compare findings from one study of ethnic identity development to those of the next, research suggests that psychosocial adjustment is associated with an achieved, or internalized, ethnic identity (Bracey, Bámaca, & Umaña-Taylor, 2004; Newman, 2005; Phinney & Kohatsu, 1997; Yasui, Dorham, & Dishion, 2004).

Phinney (1989) interviewed tenth-graders from different ethnic backgrounds regarding ethnic identity issues. These adolescents were Asian Americans, Blacks, Hispanics, and Whites. The interviews contained questions that tapped their exploration of and commitment to their ethnicity. An exploratory question was "Do you ever talk with your parents or other adults about your ethnic background or what it means to be _____?" Commitment was tapped by questions such as "Some people find these questions about their background pretty confusing and are not sure what they really think about it, but others are pretty clear about their culture and what it means to them. Which is true of you?" Adolescents also completed measures of ego identity, self-evaluation, sense of mastery, social and peer relations, and family relations.

As Phinney expected, stages of ethnic identity development correlated positively with the measure of ego identity. Similar correlations existed for measures of a sense of mastery and peer and family interactions. These findings suggest that the stages are indeed developmental, although we can't say that they increase with age. Slightly less than 50% of the minority adolescents had explored the implications of their minority status by the tenth grade. Even though a direct comparison is not possible because different samples are involved, this percentage is still higher than that for eighth-graders found in a previous study (Phinney & Tarver, 1988).

The stages themselves were independent of any particular minority. As shown in Table 5.1, just about the same percentage of adolescents from the three minority groups was in each of the three stages of ethnic identity formation. This latter finding suggests that adolescents from different minority groups have the same need to come to terms with the personal implications of minority membership. The important element appears not to be the particular minority group the adolescent is from, but the adolescent's stage

TABLE 5.1 Percentage of Minority Adolescents in Stages of Ethnic Identity Formation

	Unexamined	Search (Moratorium)	Achieved
Asian Americans	57.1%	21.4%	21.4%
Blacks	56.5	21.7	21.7
Hispanics	52.1	26.9	21.7
Total	55.7%	22.9%	21.3%

Source: Adapted from J. Phinney. (1989). Stages of ethnic identity development in minority group adolescents. *Journal of Early Adolescence, 9,* 34–49.

Stages of ethnic identity formation are comparable across the different minority groups, suggesting that adolescents from all minorities have the same need to resolve the personal implications of minority membership.

of development of an ethnic identity. The one exception to this finding comes from White adolescents, who had no sense of their own ethnicity and saw themselves only as "American." Phinney notes that this ethnocentric attitude is out of touch with our increasingly pluralistic society in which minorities constitute about one-third of those between the ages of 15 and 25.

Somewhat different issues are important for different ethnic groups. Asian American adolescents were more likely to express concerns related to academic achievement, for example, quotas for universities that might exclude them. Black males expressed concern about job discrimination and negative images of Black adolescents, and Black females mentioned standards of beauty that did not include them, for example, long, flowing hair and "creamy" skin. Hispanic adolescents reported most concern with prejudice (Phinney, 1989). Despite these concerns, relatively few minority adolescents appear to have internalized negative attitudes toward their group. Only 20% mentioned negative attitudes during the interview, and these were distributed evenly across identity statuses (Phinney, 1989).

Achieving a Bicultural Identity

How do minority adolescents identify themselves with respect to the several cultures to which they belong? Do they arrive at a **bicultural identity** by keeping the two cultures separate? By combining them? Or do they deemphasize the whole issue of ethnicity and culture? Jean Phinney and Mona Devich-Navarro (1997) interviewed African American and Mexican American tenth- and eleventh-graders, asking them questions similar to those just mentioned.

Approximately 90% of those who were interviewed thought of themselves as bicultural. However, there were differences in the ways in which they integrated the two cultures. Some considered themselves to be equally members of their ethnic group and of the wider culture, expressing a strong sense of being American without denying their ethnicity and resolving issues raised by culture either by combining elements of both cultures or by deemphasizing differences. Others indicated that their ethnicity was more central to their sense of themselves. These adolescents often reported thinking of themselves differently depending on where they were or who they were with, such as feeling more American at school and more ethnic at home. These two groups of biculturals differed not so much in the importance of their ethnicity but, rather, in their identification with the U.S. culture. The former were more likely to see the U.S. culture as inclusive,

bicultural identity The process by which minority adolescents identify themselves with respect to the two cultures to which they belong.

and also as diverse, thus making it possible to see themselves as fitting in. Those whose identity was more situational had less of a sense of connection with being American. A much smaller group of adolescents saw themselves primarily in terms of their ethnicity in all situations. When cultural issues arose, they dealt with them by keeping the two cultures distinct.

Perhaps nothing better reflects the difficulties involved in achieving a bicultural identity than differences in the ways multiracial adolescents label, or identify, themselves when in different situations. Even though the 2000 U.S. Census places the number of adolescents who are multiracial at 13.6%, only 6.8% of adolescents in a large national sample identified themselves this way when interviewed at school, and even fewer, 3.6%, did so when interviewed at home (Harris & Sim, 2002).

As you might expect, a number of factors are related to how closely adolescents identify with one cultural group or another. Melissa Herman (2004) found that experiencing discrimination and having a positive ethnic identity were associated with identifying oneself in terms of one's ethnic background. In contrast, adolescents were more likely to identify themselves as White if they believed others perceived them that way and if ethnic identity was less important (Herman, 2004).

The Self

The search for identity is a central task facing all adolescents. Adolescents are brought face-to-face with this task by two forces, one from within and the other from without. The first force—puberty—radically alters bodies that have become as comfortable as an old shoe. The shoe begins to pinch when adolescents develop the physiques, feelings, and cognitive capacities of adults. The second force, in the form of psychosocial expectations, confirms these inner changes. Adolescents are expected to be more adult—to start making decisions for themselves, to be responsible, to plan for their futures. But despite this alliance of culture with nature, someone within still asks, "Who am I?"

Self-Concept: Who Am I?

Each of us has a theory about ourself; it helps explain the way we feel, what we like or do not like, what we are good at, and why. Developmentalists call this theory the **self-concept.** Just as with any theory, the self-concept is a way of explaining and interpreting the facts one experiences in daily life, a way of constructing the self.

Adolescents' ability to relate isolated events in terms of more general principles allows them to pull different experiences together into general assumptions about themselves. A girl who backpacks and bikes, plays ball well, and is on the swim team can think of herself as athletic. A friend who belongs to the drama club, is starring in the class play, and gets As in his theater classes can think of himself as talented. Both adolescents are making generalizations about themselves from specific experiences.

The capacity for self-reflection that comes with adolescence brings with it a concern about personality in general and thoughts about oneself in particular. Adolescents' observations about themselves begin with specific events (for example, being on the swim team or swimming the 100-meter faster than anyone else). These soon take the form of more general beliefs ("I am a good swimmer"). At an even more general level, the adolescent who can say of himself that he is a good swimmer, a strong runner, and a good ball player can integrate these into a sense of himself as athletic. If this adolescent also is

self-concept The individual's awareness of the self as a person; a theory about the self that explains personal experience.

Adolescents' sense of self includes who they have been as well as who they hope to be. Formulating their self-identity requires them to discover what they like, what they are good at, and what they believe in.

a good student and holds down a part-time job, he can formulate even more general self-statements, such as "I'm competent" and "I'm responsible."

The beliefs adolescents have about themselves determine many of their emotional reactions. Which of these beliefs are central to their sense of self? Adolescents can easily know which are most central by the way they react when these ideas are challenged. An adolescent who values her independence, for example, will find herself in frequent arguments whenever someone tells her that she cannot do something. One who values his competence will resent having anyone tell him he is not able to manage a task.

Because so many of the beliefs about the self in adolescence are recently formulated, they lack experiential support. As a consequence, adolescents' new self-concepts are particularly vulnerable to disconfirming evidence. Perhaps because of this, adolescents spend a lot of time and energy gathering evidence in support of their theories of the self. Events that otherwise might be commonplace take on significance if they support adolescents' beliefs about themselves. Getting a driver's license and going out on a first date are examples of experiences that assume this kind of significance, because they validate important beliefs, such as "I'm adult" or "I'm attractive" (Okun & Sasfy, 1977). Many of the self-statements adolescents include in their self-concepts reflect potential more than actual accomplishments. These discrepancies also explain why the theory of self is at first so vulnerable to disconfirming evidence.

To be healthy, self-concepts need to be self-correcting. When they are, adolescents can face new information about themselves openly. When teenagers feel threatened, they tend to close themselves off to defend their beliefs, incapable of seeing the ways in which their experiences fail to confirm these beliefs. But adolescents who feel secure about themselves are able to revise their beliefs in light of their experiences. Remaining open to

Self-esteem is the overall positive or negative evaluation of oneself. Opportunities for responsible work help to build positive self-esteem.

new views of the self is especially difficult in adolescence because so much changes, and the need to explain these changes is so great.

The self-concept becomes more abstract, more differentiated, and more adaptive during adolescence. Children derive their sense of themselves from concrete, physical characteristics. Adolescents think of themselves in terms of psychological characteristics such as being impulsive, shy, loud, or witty. Children draw their characters in bold strokes—as either good or bad, right or wrong, strong or weak. Adolescents make finer distinctions; they see subtleties and nuance. They understand how a characteristic can be both a strength and a weakness. A 15-year-old might pride himself on his reflectiveness in social situations and his sensitivity with his friends, yet realize that these very same qualities can be his downfall when faced with a taunting classmate, knowing that a less-reflective friend would simply swing a punch at the offender. Self-concepts also become more adaptive as adolescents accumulate more years of decision making. These decisions provide a history of successes and failures. Most have learned that they usually make good decisions and that, even when they make mistakes, these are not devastating.

Self-Esteem: Do I Like Myself?

If the self-concept is a set of beliefs about the self, then **self-esteem** is a measure of how good one feels about these beliefs. A girl who describes herself as athletic, a social leader, witty, short, and friendly does not stop there. She evaluates each of these qualities. "Is it really okay to be as athletic as I am? So I'm witty, but is that as good as being a brain? Am I too short or just tall enough?" The answers she comes up with contribute to her feelings of adequacy and self-worth. Self-esteem is the adolescents' overall positive or negative evaluation of herself or himself (Simmons & Blyth, 1987).

Foundations of Self-Esteem Relationships with parents provide the foundation for self-esteem. When parents are loving, children feel lovable and develop feelings of self-worth. These feelings become established early in life. Infants quickly learn whether the world in which they live will meet their needs; when those around them are responsive, they develop a sense of trust. The establishment of trust in these first, basic relationships permeates all later ones. Self-esteem among adolescents still reflects their interactions with parents (Bolognini, Plancherel, Bettschart, & Halfon, 1996; Turnage, 2004). Adolescents with authoritative parents, who stress self-reliance, shared decision making, and willingness to listen, have higher feelings of self-worth (Bartle, Anderson, & Sabatelli, 1989; Garber, Robinson, & Valentiner, 1997).

Two especially important sources of self-esteem in adolescence come from interactions with peers and from satisfaction with one's body (DuBois, Felner, Brand, Phillips, & Lease, 1996; Klomsten, Skaalvik, & Espries, 2004; Williams & Currie, 2002).

self-esteem The individual's overall positive or negative evaluation of herself or himself.

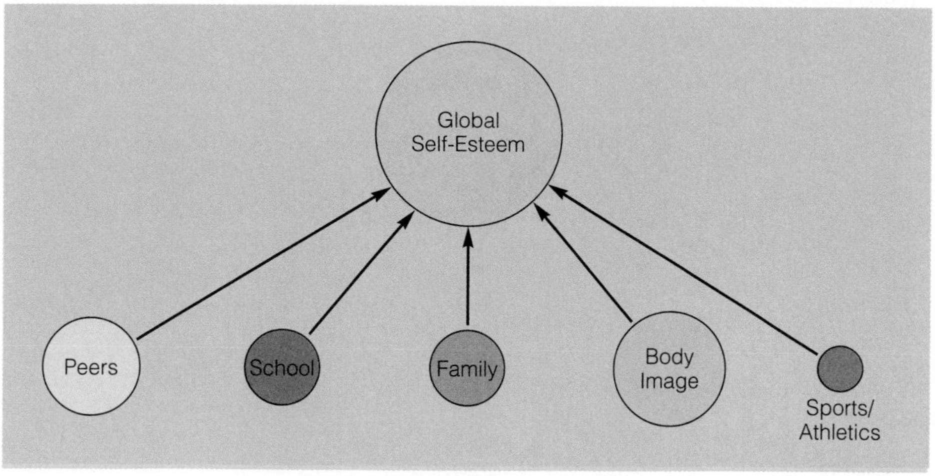

FIGURE 5.2
Sources of Global Self-Esteem, Indicated by Their Relative Importance. *Many things contribute to adolescents' feelings of self-esteem; two of the most important are friends and having a positive body image.* Source: D. L. DuBois, R. D. Felner, S. Brand, R. S. C. Phillips, & A. M. Lease. (1996). Early adolescent self-esteem: A developmental-ecological framework and assessment strategy. *Journal of Research on Adolescence, 6,* 543–579.

David DuBois, at the University of Missouri, and his associates (1996) assessed the contribution of five domains of experience to self-esteem in early adolescents: family, peers, school, body image, and sports/athletics. As can be seen in Figure 5.2, peers and body image are the two largest contributors to global self-esteem. In general, males tend to have somewhat higher self-esteem than females (Baldwin & Hoffmann, 2002; Kling, Hyde, Showers, & Buswell, 1999).

Ethnicity and Self-Esteem In general, Black adolescents have significantly higher self-esteem than any other group of adolescents, including Whites (Herman, 2004; Twenge & Crocker, 2002). Minority membership, however, does not confer the same advantage for other ethnic groups. In the same meta-analysis, White adolescents were found to have significantly higher self-esteem than Asian Americans, Hispanics, or Native Americans (Twenge & Crocker, 2002). The advantage enjoyed by Blacks relative to Whites may be due to a more positive racial identity (Phinney, Cantu, & Kurtz, 1997).

The ways in which minority adolescents resolve their relationship with the majority culture, confronting and coping with issues such as racism and discrimination, have been found to be associated with differences in self-esteem. Different ways of resolving this relationship, recall, are represented by the various stages of ethnic identity, discussed earlier in the chapter. Thus, pre-encounter adolescents, who have a White cultural orientation, have been found to have lower self-concept scores and generally show poorer psychological adjustment than bicultural or internalized adolescents who have a strong sense of their ethnicity as well as a sense of belonging to the larger culture (Phinney & Kohatsu, 1997).

Gender is an important variable mediating self-esteem in minorities. The difference in self-esteem between Black and White adolescents, for instance, is even greater among females than it is among males. For Asian Americans and Hispanics also, self-esteem relative to that in Whites is lower for males than for females (Twenge & Crocker, 2002).

Gender and Self-Esteem Self-esteem tends to be higher in boys than it is in girls (Baldwin & Hoffman, 2002; Khanlou, 2004). As can be seen in Figure 5.3, this difference increases dramatically with age. Roberta Simmons and Dale Blyth (1987) noticed that girls are more likely to negatively evaluate the characteristics about themselves they consider to be most important. In mid-adolescence, for example, nearly one-third of all girls

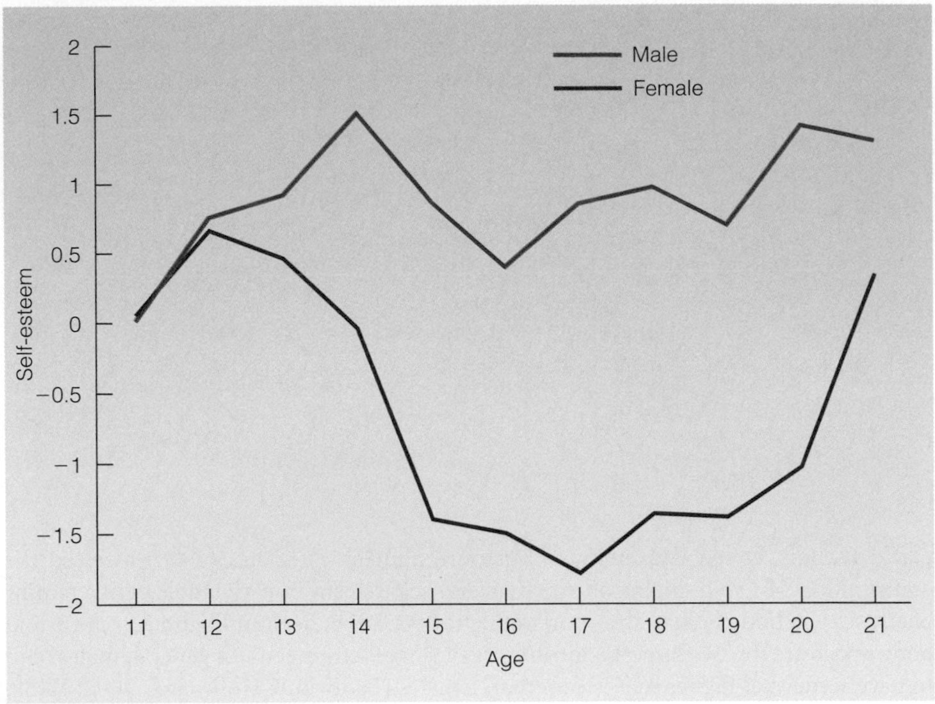

FIGURE 5.3
Changes in Boys' and Girls' Self-Esteem with Age. *Self-esteem is higher in boys than it is in girls throughout adolescence. Source:* Adapted from S. A. Baldwin & J. P. Hoffmann. (2002). The dynamics of self-esteem: A growth-curve analysis. *Journal of Youth and Adolescence, 31,* 101–113.

who care either "a great deal" or "pretty much" about their appearance are not satisfied with the way they look. Similarly, more than 50% of all ninth-grade girls who are not satisfied with their weight still care about it very much. Also, when asked to list all the possible selves they can think of, both positive and feared, girls have been found to rate feared possible selves as somewhat more likely to occur than boys (Knox et al., 2000). Self-esteem has nowhere to go but down under conditions such as these.

The greater resilience of boys' self-esteem during adolescence shows up in another respect as well. Their self-esteem is less vulnerable in the face of change than is that of girls. All adolescents face some transitions in common: puberty, a change in schools, and, with dating, a reordering of their social world. Some adolescents must also cope with geographic relocations and with family disruption, when parents change jobs or divorce. Having time to gradually get used to one change before having to cope with another makes it easier to adjust to such transitions.

The more changes adolescents must cope with simultaneously, the more likely they are to show the effects of related stress. As the number of changes increases, self-esteem also drops, especially in girls (Baldwin & Hoffmann, 2002; Simmons & Blyth, 1987). However, the more stability adolescents have in any one area, the better they can cope with changes in others.

Consider a hypothetical 14-year-old girl who is midway through puberty and just beginning to date. Her parents are recently divorced, and she lives in a new neighborhood. She has so many things to talk about with her friends, but she never gets to see them. She doesn't know which of the physical changes she's experiencing are normal and which are weird. She feels angry all the time—except when she's depressed. When she tells her counselor at school, he tells her it's because of her hormones. The last person she can talk to is her mother, who feels even worse than she does. Her grades have fallen, and she's lost interest in doing things at school. When asked how she feels about herself, she has a hard time thinking of any qualities that she likes.

This adolescent's experiences are extreme, yet the situation she faces is increasingly common for many. Under conditions such as these, self-esteem understandably suffers in adolescence.

How do adolescents come up with a sense of themselves that they can live with and like? Puberty forces the issue, but it also sets the stage for new answers. Because of pubertal changes, adolescents find it difficult to think of themselves as they did as children. But they also develop ways of thinking that give them the means to combine aspects of the old self with newly developing ones. Some of these aspects involve others; we turn to intimate relationships next.

Intimacy: Discovering the Self Through Relationships

Intimacy is often misunderstood. Like many adults, most adolescents associate it with romance, passion, being together, or being so close one can finish the other's sentences. Yet arguments, like romance, can provide the ground for intimate encounters, passion can involve little sharing of feelings, and always being together may signal a relationship that provides little room for being oneself. As for being able to finish another's sentences, this may mean the other has said nothing new for some time. What is **intimacy,** then? It is a sharing of one's feelings and thoughts in an atmosphere of caring, trust, and acceptance. Intimacy begins with oneself and only then can it be extended to others.

Knowing Oneself

In order to develop intimate relationships with others, adolescents need to be in touch with their own feelings and needs. That is, adolescents' capacity for intimacy should develop under the conditions that make it safe for them to know themselves. We discussed some of these conditions in the context of individuation. Families that allow members to express their ideas, even when they differ from those of others, communicate that it is safe to disagree. Once adolescents have this safety, they are able to examine how they really feel (Grotevant & Cooper, 1986).

Self-acceptance is also important for intimacy. Adolescents who like themselves are free to be themselves without trying to change anything. Self-acceptance and self-awareness go hand in hand. Those who have accepted themselves can be aware of desires and feelings that they otherwise might feel a need to deny or distort. Because a common way of distorting needs is to attribute them to others (that is, projection), self-awareness makes it possible for adolescents to perceive others more accurately as well. In appreciating the complexity of their own feelings, they can realize that the feelings of others are similarly complex and can validate those emotions. Self-acceptance creates a self-perpetuating cycle; having been validated, others are able to hear what these adolescents are saying and, in turn, validate them (Bell & Bell, 1983).

An important ingredient to self-acceptance is liking oneself. Adolescents who like themselves can let others get close enough to see them as they really are. People who don't like themselves frequently feel ashamed and are unwilling to let others get close. Often

Intimacy The ability to share oneself with another; characterized by self-disclosure and mutuality.

Adolescents have to learn to accept themselves before they are ready for an intimate relationship, which requires having the self-confidence to let someone else know them as they really are.

they feel it necessary to put up a front to look better or to use their relationships to prove to themselves that they are acceptable (Masters, Johnson, & Kolodny, 1988). These approaches block intimacy, either by not being open with the other person or by using that person for one's own needs. Adolescents who feel negative about themselves are likely to handle their feelings of depression and anxiety in ways that block self-knowledge, by escaping into alcoholism or drug abuse, seeking distractions such as television, or finding substitutes such as eating. None of these behaviors lends itself to intimacy. Of course, adolescents need not be happy with themselves all the time. As William Masters, Virginia Johnson, and Robert Kolodny (1988) note:

> Generally, we separate what we like from what we don't like and use this process to try to change. If we are honest in our self-appraisals, the intimate knowledge we develop helps us relate to others. At the same time, a person who *never* looks inward (whether out of fear, laziness, or self-hatred) has such distorted self-perceptions that it is unlikely he or she can contribute fully to a relationship with someone else. (p. 318)

Intimacy with Others

Self-disclosure is important to intimacy. Adolescents who are intimates share their thoughts and feelings with each other (Orlofsky, Marcia, & Lesser, 1973; Schiedel & Marcia, 1985). Not everything they share is personal (often it's just gossip), but much of it is. Intimacy takes time to develop, as adolescents learn to trust one another with increasingly personal aspects of themselves. Self-disclosure has to be mutual to be comfortable; one adolescent cannot tell all and the other tell nothing. We tend to shy away from people who tell us everything about themselves the moment we meet them. Choosing to disclose things about oneself is a bit like taking off one's clothes. How undressed one appears depends on how much others are wearing. Someone in a bathing suit has enough on when lounging poolside, but at a dance would look nearly naked.

Adolescents are willing to share their personal experiences when they can trust that others will respect their confidence. Trust takes time to develop and usually requires some testing of the waters. An adolescent may start by sharing things she would not be devastated to hear repeated, such as what she thinks of a particular teacher, and work her way up to her most private thoughts and feelings, for example, what she really thinks of her stepfather or the details of her relationship with her boyfriend. This kind of trust requires a commitment to a relationship (Montgomery, 2005).

Intimacy and Identity: Different Paths to Maturity?

To what extent are intimacy and identity related? Can adolescents be close to others without knowing themselves well? Can they develop a sense of themselves apart from their intimate relationships with others? Erikson believed that identity is a necessary precursor to intimacy. He wrote that "true engagement with others is the result and the test of firm self-delineation" (1968, p. 167). Intimacy assumes developmental significance for Erikson only after identity has been achieved.

This developmental progression, however, is not typical of females. Josselson (1988) writes that development in females takes place on an "interpersonal track" that is not represented in Erikson's scheme. Erikson wrote, for example, about industry (the crisis preceding that of identity) as the development of competence by learning how things are made and how they work. Competence for females is more likely to take the form of increasingly complex interpersonal skills (Marcia, 1980). These two types of skills set a different stage for the drama that unfolds during adolescence than that envisioned by Erikson. Prior developments prepare females to define themselves *interpersonally* through skills that bring them into relationships with others, whereas the same developments prepare males to define themselves *impersonally* through skills that result in products. As girls move into adolescence, their social networks relate to their self-esteem and to their perceived self-competence across a variety of areas, in ways that boys' relationships do not (DuBois et al., 1996; Feiring & Lewis, 1991). In early adulthood, relationships continue to contribute more heavily to identity than does school or occupation (Meeus & Dekovic, 1995).

Erikson viewed intimacy as a characteristic of relationships with others. For females, it is also a process by which they define themselves. Rather than postponing identity consolidation until they find a mate, as Erikson suggested, female adolescents *achieve* self-definition through intimacy, through their relationships with others (Gilligan, 1982; Josselson, 1988; Marcia, 1980). Josselson (1988) states:

> Intimacy, or interpersonal development, among women *is* identity and resides not in the choice of a heterosexual partner, but in the development, differentiation, and mastery of ways of being with others (not just men) that meet her standards for taking care, that connect her meaningfully to others, and that locate her in an interpersonal network. (p. 99)

If relationships assume a different developmental significance for females, we should expect to see gender differences in levels of intimacy during adolescence, and we do (Montgomery, 2005). Don Schiedel and James Marcia (1985), both at Simon Fraser University, classified late adolescents into intimacy statuses that reflected commitment to and depth of relationships, as shown in Table 5.2. They found significantly more females in the higher intimacy statuses than males. In fact, females were nearly twice as likely as males to be in the highest two statuses. Perhaps because the individuals they studied were in late adolescence or early adulthood, the proportion of females high in intimacy did not increase with age. This proportion did increase for males, however, suggesting that males, as Josselson and Gilligan imply, are not as prepared for relationships

TABLE 5.2 Intimacy Statuses in Late Adolescence

ISOLATE	Relationships consist only of casual acquaintances.
STEREOTYPED	Relationships are shallow and conventional.
PSEUDOINTIMATE	Relationships are similar to those of Stereotyped but have commitment to long-term sexual relationship; these defined through conventional roles rather than self-disclosure.
PREINTIMATE	Close, open relationships characterized by mutuality; ambivalence regarding commitment to long-term sexual relationship.
INTIMATE	Relationships are similar to those of Preintimate but also have commitment to long-term sexual relationship.

Source: D. G. Schiedel & J. E. Marcia. (1985). Ego identity, intimacy, sex role orientation, and gender. *Developmental Psychology, 21,* 149–160.

as are females. This pattern may be changing, however. When 15- to 18-year-old high school students were asked to respond to dilemmas involving identity and intimacy choices, females as well as males assigned greater importance to identity choices, and males were as likely as females to mention intimacy considerations, either by themselves or fused with identity issues (Lacombe & Gay, 1998).

But what about the relationship between intimacy and identity mentioned earlier? A number of studies support Erikson's suggestion that intimacy is contingent on achieving identity but find this relationship to be more characteristic of males than females (Dyk & Adams, 1990; Schiedel & Marcia, 1985). These findings support Josselson's contention that for females intimacy *is* a means by which identity is resolved.

Does development take the form of increasing autonomy and separation? Most personality theorists have answered yes. Every now and again a few voices raise alternatives, and some of these have been incorporated into mainstream developmental theory (Gilligan, 1982; Gilligan, Lyons, & Hanmer, 1989; Josselson, 1987, 1988).

David Bakan (1966) distinguishes two aspects of mature functioning. **Agency** captures qualities of assertiveness, mastery, and distinctiveness, and **communion** reflects qualities of cooperation and union. Bakan considers these two facets of personal functioning to be balanced in the mature person. Developmentalists have traditionally translated these aspects of maturity into a developmental progression moving *from* communion *to* agency, thereby assigning greater maturity to agency. An alternative interpretation of Bakan's view of maturity, but one that equally distorts it, has assigned agency to the masculine personality and communion to the feminine. This approach easily reduces to the first because development in females often falls short of that in males when comparisons use measures that have been standardized with males (for example, Kohlberg's measure of moral development or the use of rules in games). Most Western cultures implicitly confirm either of these translations through the greater value they place on agentic over communional behaviors. Our society, for example, defines success in terms of individual accomplishment and achievements rather than the quality of a person's relationships.

agency An aspect of mature functioning characterized by assertiveness, mastery, and distinctiveness; the complement of communion.

communion An aspect of mature functioning characterized by cooperation and union; the complement of agency.

But is development most accurately thought of as increasing separation and individuation? Josselson (1988) notes that research in two areas within psychology—adolescent development and the psychology of women—reveals difficulties in viewing development this way.

Some theorists believe that females define themselves primarily in the course of their relationships but that males must define themselves before they are capable of close relationships. If they hope to build a lasting relationship, young couples need to be willing to accept changes in their partner's self-definition.

Developmental Issues in Adolescence

Development during adolescence does not require an end to, but rather a modification of, significant relationships with parents. Adolescents achieve a sense of themselves *within* their relationships, not in spite of them (Josselson, 1988). Research with adolescents and their parents such as that of Harold Grotevant and Catherine Cooper (1986) finds that attachment and separation are not opposites but are different aspects of the same process. If the task of adolescence is to break ties with parents, then either adolescents accomplish this task or they don't—they either separate *or* remain attached. If the task is for adolescents to renegotiate relationships with parents to achieve greater mutuality and equality, they can separate as persons *and* remain emotionally connected or attached (Josselson, 1988). Any theory that emphasizes separation as developmentally more advanced gives a distorted view of development in which an autonomous self is accepted as the pinnacle of maturity (Josselson, 1988).

A second challenge to the prevailing view of development as progressive separation and individuation comes from attempts to chart female development. These attempts bring a new awareness of the male bias in much developmental theory. Developmentalists have assumed their theories to be universal, that is, to cover issues fundamental to the whole of human experience. Yet theories are not totally objective representations of human nature; they are interpretations that often reflect the personal experiences of the theorists. And most personality theorists have been males. There is a growing recognition that theories address experiences that are more common among, or even unique to, males (Adelson & Doehrman, 1980; Bettelheim, 1961; Gilligan, 1982, 1986; Josselson, 1988).

Erikson, for instance, thought of identity as an exploration of issues related to vocation, political views, and religion. When females are interviewed about their identity concerns, one hears about their relationships—not about industry, autonomy, or ideology. Autonomy may well serve the function of a developmental organizer for most males in our society, but relationships serve this function for most females. Josselson (1988) adds, "Because women define themselves in a context of relationship, a developmental orientation that equates growth with autonomy will automatically relegate women to lower rungs of development" (p. 99). She notes in support of this point that the cultural myths that exist in our society make it difficult to view the "achievement of adult commitment, fidelity, intimacy, and care [as] meaningful and heroic" (p. 99).

Gilligan (1986) comments that the adolescent girl especially faces a problem in that, as she affirms her connection with her mother, she sees how disconnected they both are from a society in which the male experience defines reality. Gilligan (1986) writes:

> The ability to establish connection with others hinges on the ability to render one's story coherent. Given the failure of interpretive schemes to reflect female experience and given the distortion of this experience in common understandings of care and attachment, development for girls in adolescence hinges . . . on the courage to challenge two equations: the equation of human with male and the equation of care with self-sacrifice. Together these equations create a self-perpetuating system that sustains a limited conception of human development and a problematic representation of human relationships. (p. 296)

Dimensions of Relatedness

Josselson points out that social scientists have developed a rich vocabulary for talking about the self, distinguishing among terms such as *self-consciousness, self-awareness, self-control, self-concept,* and *self-esteem,* yet have few words to describe the self in relation to others. A single term, *relationship,* serves to describe the many, varied ways we have of interrelating. The paucity of our language has, in turn, contributed to a cultural blindness in which "when we wish to know people, we are therefore more likely to ask about what they do than about how they love. But in fact we would know them better if we knew how they are with others and what they want from them" (Josselson, 1992, p. 2).

Josselson (1992) gives us a multifaceted theory of human connection, describing eight dimensions of relatedness. Each of these follows a developmental course, being expressed initially in concrete and literal ways, and only with time symbolically. The dimensions themselves are independent of one another, one not being reducible to the other, and develop more or less simultaneously rather than as stepwise stages. Also, either the relative absence of each form of relatedness in a person's life or the excessive indulgence of it is unhealthy. Table 5.3 shows the dimensions and these two poles. The first four dimensions—holding, attachment, passionate experience, and eye-to-eye validation—are present either from birth or shortly thereafter. The second four do not develop until later. Idealization and embeddedness require that one experience the self apart from others as well as see that self in relation to those others, both of which require a certain cognitive maturity. Similarly, mutuality and tending require the capacity to be responsive to others, which can develop only when the child moves beyond egocentrism.

Gender Differences in Relatedness

Josselson (1992) cautions against overstating gender differences in relatedness, pointing out that considerable variability exists among individuals of the same sex in their expressions of relatedness, but she notes several important differences as well.

Females describe greater complexity to their relationships, catching more nuance to experience and being able to incorporate contradictory elements, whereas males approach their relationships in more straightforward and simpler terms. Females tend

TABLE 5.3 Josselson's Eight Dimensions of Relatedness

Insufficient Presence	Healthy Expression of Relatedness	Excessive Dependence
Falling	*Holding:* Gives a sense of being contained and bounded; provides sense of security. Later takes the form of feeling "supported" by others, of having others who are "there" for us.	Suffocation
Aloneness, loss	*Attachment:* The need to be close to those who are important to us, which the infant expresses by crying in protest when its mother leaves; an essential ingredient of human connection.	Fearful clinging
Inhibition, emotional deadening	*Passionate Experience:* Others become the objects of our desires; ranges from the need to suck in infancy to sexual desire in adolescence and adulthood.	Obsessive love
Annihilation, rejection	*Eye-to-Eye Validation:* Lets us see ourselves through the eyes of others and gives us a sense of ourselves in relation to them.	Transparency
Disillusionment, purposelessness	*Idealization and Identification:* Expansion of our sense of ourself by reaching out to and embracing those who are bigger, stronger, grander.	Slavish devotion
Loneliness	*Mutuality and Reasonance:* By sharing our experiences with another, we arrive at something jointly created; an expression of our social nature.	Merging
Alienation	*Embeddedness:* A sense of belonging, having a place in the group, experiencing communality.	Overconformity
Indifference	*Tending and Care:* Nurturance that is intentional and deliberate; our capacity to care for others reflects our own need to be needed.	Compulsive caregiving

Source: Adapted from R. Josselson. (1992). *The space between us.* San Francisco: Jossey-Bass.

Individuals have many ways of interrelating with each other. Notice that healthy expressions of relatedness are balanced and that either too little or too much reliance on a way of relating to others is unhealthy.

to view relationships as evolving over time. In contrast, males see them as more static than dynamic, more as products that, once arrived at, will remain that way. And, finally, individuals of either sex emphasize different dimensions of relatedness.

Josselson traces these differences to several underlying factors. First, males tend to fit their relationships into an abstract conceptual system, whereas for females relationships are more immediate and experiential. For instance, in their interviews, males would frequently mention being influenced and moved by the works of men whom they had never met, such as artists and philosophers, yet with whom they had carried on passionate inner dialogues. These intellectual exchanges *felt* relational to them. Females, in contrast, needed some measure of "affective coloring" before they experienced an exchange as relational.

Josselson locates this abstractness in males within a second factor, one concerning gender definition. If, as Nancy Chodorow points out, a boy needs to separate himself from his mother in order to develop as a male, he achieves masculinity at the *expense* of emotional closeness (see Chapter 2). This distancing has implications for all future relationships, in which "he learns to relate to others across a gulf that both separates him and guards his masculinity" (Josselson, 1992, p. 225). In contrast to the boy, the little girl

Although differences among individuals of the same sex can be greater than those between the sexes, men and women do characteristically differ in the way they relate to other people. Females pay more attention to relationships and expect them to change over time.

need not distance herself from the mother but instead learns what it is to be herself within the context of relatedness, comfortable with "the paradox that she is both merged and distinct, both connected and separate" (p. 225).

Having to define oneself as a male this way requires action on the boy's part, that is, separating from the mother, whereas defining oneself as a female does not. A third factor, then, is that males gain a sense of themselves through their actions, through doing, and females through their relationships, through being. Males evaluate themselves in terms of what they can do, their skills and accomplishments, how far they can kick a soccer ball or how many space aliens they can knock out in a video game. Conversely, observes Josselson (1992),

> girls are not liked for being smart or good at soccer, as boys are, but for ill-defined qualities, such as responsiveness to others, self-confidence, playfulness, and charm. And the girl understands, quickly and deeply, that she, too, will be labeled and located in this slippery interpersonal universe. She will be responded to for how she is deemed to be, not for what she wills or for her skills. (pp. 226–227)

Because of these factors, gender differences in relatedness are to be expected. For instance, females are more comfortable experiencing mutuality than are males. "For women," says Josselson (1992), "the regulation of closeness and distance, and the shared experience of emotion is the essence of relating" (p. 232). Eye-to-eye validation is also a more significant dimension of relatedness for females, because their sense of self is rooted more deeply in others' responses to them. Passionate experience that is expressly sexual, on the other hand, is more of a driving force in males' relationships. Also, because

Males, on the other hand, tend to define relationships according to fixed categories and to assume that they'll always remain the same. The difference in the genders' view of relationships may be partly due to differences in identity formation: Males are defined more in terms of what they can do, and females are defined more in terms of how they relate to others.

the way males know themselves is more closely tied to action and doing, identification and idealization are more salient to their relationships than to those of females. Males' ambitions are personalized through identification with figures who are bigger than life, heroes to be idealized and modeled. Females are more apt to draw their strength from those who are close at hand (Josselson, 1992).

A New Definition of Maturity

Josselson (1988) asserts that gender differences in individuals' sense of self are sufficiently great that we need to redefine identity to include the concept of self in relation to others. Presently, our definition of identity views separation as contributing to the mature individual's experience of self; Josselson argues that our approach to identity must give equivalent weight to a person's relatedness to others. Maturity involves movement toward a greater capacity for relationships. Contributing to this capacity are assertion and autonomy. Josselson turns the tables and makes self-in-relationship the more embracing concept of which autonomy and separateness are components.

Does development move from dependence to autonomy, as traditional theory asserts? Does it involve increasingly articulated ways of relating to others? Adolescents of both genders work out their identities in the context of continuing significant relationships with others, and males as well as females face intimacy as a central issue leading to adulthood. Josselson maintains that each person has a need for separateness *and* attachment, for inclusion *and* exclusion. Each of these creates tensions, but to give in to one and not strive for balance is to forfeit some degree of maturity (Josselson, 1988).

Summary

Autonomy and Individuation

- The process of defining the self leads to a renegotiation of the parent–child relationship during adolescence. This renegotiation initially is prompted by the biological changes of puberty and changes in the way adolescents think.
- Adolescents become more autonomous as they choose to be part of the decision-making process, asking to be treated as more adult. The number of decisions they make by themselves increases with age. One of their early decisions is how much they will keep secret from their parents; controlling what they will reveal contributes to adolescents' sense of independence.
- Frequently, adolescents' bids for *autonomy* bring conflict with parents over household routines, especially with mothers. Parenting style, especially of mothers, is related to girls' autonomy. Age is the best predictor of increased autonomy for boys.
- Increased *individuation* accompanies autonomy as adolescents sort through values and views to discover which ones reflect the way they think. This discovery involves making decisions for themselves and living with the consequences of these. Individuation gives adolescents a set of attitudes and ways of acting that are genuinely their own.
- Family characteristics of individuality and connectedness facilitate the process of identity achievement.
- *Individuality* refers to having and expressing ideas of one's own and being able to say how one differs from others.
- *Connectedness* reflects one's openness to others' opinions and respect for their ideas.
- These qualities of family life help adolescents explore options while feeling emotionally supported even when family disagreements arise.

Identity: The Normative Crisis of Adolescence

- Achieving an *identity* is a central task facing adolescents.
- Resolving the psychosocial crisis of identity gives one a coherent, purposeful sense of self.
- Erikson used the word *crisis* to refer to a developmental turning point in which adolescents must choose one course or another simply because it is no longer possible for them to continue as before.
- In the course of developing their identity, adolescents imagine a number of *possible selves,* some negative but most positive.

Variations on a Theme of Identity

- Four identity statuses can be distinguished based on the presence or absence of exploration of life options and commitment to self-chosen alternatives.
- Adolescents in the *identity-achieved* status have explored life options and values and committed themselves to self-chosen alternatives.
- Adolescents in the *identity-foreclosed* status remain committed to parental ways and values without exploring alternatives.
- Adolescents in the *moratorium* status have begun to explore life options but remain uncommitted to any alternatives.
- Adolescents in the *identity-diffused* status have neither explored life options nor committed to alternatives.
- Adolescents may move from one status to another, depending on their willingness to accept new challenges and to experience anxiety.
- As adolescents move into adulthood, they are likely to change identity statuses again, with more moving to foreclosure and achievement statuses as they increase their commitment to the life tasks of adulthood.

Identity: Gender and Ethnicity

- Even though Erikson believed the search for identity to be a central task facing all adolescents, he assumed that females and males approach this differently. The task for males involves making choices and commitments about an occupation, a set of beliefs, and their sex role. Erikson believed females arrive at their identity primarily by committing themselves to a future mate.
- Research shows that gender differences in identity development are minimal. The process and timing of development suggest more similarities than differences. Interpersonal concerns may be somewhat more important to women's than to men's identities, but occupational concerns are equally important to men and women.
- *Ethnic identity* development progresses through several stages. Adolescents with an *unexamined ethnic identity* internalize the values and attitudes of the dominant culture. Those in an *ethnic identity search* are exploring the meaning of their ethnicity, and those with an *achieved ethnic identity* have a clear sense of their ethnicity and emotionally identify

with their ethnic group. These stages correlate with ego identity statuses.

- Some bicultural adolescents see themselves as equally members of their ethnic group and the dominant culture; for others, however, one identity or the other predominates according to the situation.

The Self

- The *self-concept* becomes more abstract, differentiated, and adaptive during adolescence. The capacity for self-reflection allows adolescents to think of themselves in terms of psychological characteristics; they appreciate subtlety and nuance. Increased experience in making decisions contributes to more adaptive self-concepts.
- *Self-esteem* reflects the overall positive or negative attitude adolescents have about the self. Relationships with parents and peers and satisfaction with one's body provide the foundations for self-esteem.
- Self-esteem varies somewhat with ethnicity and gender. Some aspects of self-esteem are higher among minority adolescents than majority ones; others are not. In general, males have higher self-esteem than females during adolescence.

Intimacy: Discovering the Self Through Relationships

- *Intimacy* is the sharing of innermost feelings and thoughts in an atmosphere of caring, trust, and acceptance. To be intimate with others, adolescents must first know and accept themselves.
- Self-disclosure may provide a vehicle for intimacy with others. Intimacy is often contingent on achieving identity, at least for males. For females, intimacy is often the means by which identity is resolved.

Intimacy and Identity: Different Paths to Maturity?

- Development has traditionally been viewed in terms of increasing autonomy and separation from others. Research on adolescent–parent relationships and on female development questions this view.
- Relationships between adolescents and parents show that continuing emotional attachment and increasing autonomy coexist and are different aspects of the same process.
- For females, relationships with others contribute importantly to their sense of self.
- New definitions of maturity will need to include movement toward a greater capacity to relate to others, as well as increasing autonomy and separateness.

Key Terms

autonomy
individuation
individuality
connectedness
identity
possible selves
identity achieved
identity foreclosed
moratorium
identity diffused
information oriented
diffuse/avoidant
normative oriented
ethnic identity
acculturation
unexamined ethnic identity
ethnic identity search
achieved ethnic identity
bicultural identity
self-concept
self-esteem
intimacy
agency
communion

CHAPTER OUTLINE

CHAPTER 6

The Sexual Self

Close Relationships in Adolescence

CHAPTER OBJECTIVES

- To look at the ways in which adolescents construct a sexual identity by examining sexuality within the more general context of identity formation
- To examine the ways in which gender roles and sexual scripts contribute to adolescents' sexual identity
- To look at factors contributing to the ways adolescents make sexual decisions, and at the sexual behaviors in which they engage
- To explore the nature of sexual orientation and the contribution of biological and psychosocial factors to this
- To examine the risks and responsibilities that contribute to adolescents' sexual health, paying particular attention to contraception for sexually active adolescents, the prevalence of STDs, and what information is most helpful in sex education classes

"Hey, Raffie," Arnie grinned over the locker door. "You a lucky man this morning, or not?"

"Or not," thought Raffie, as he grabbed his books and gave the door a slam. But he grinned back, "You think you're the only one around here gets lucky?"

"All right!" exclaimed Arnie, giving his friend a "deadarm" and heading for his first class on the run.

Raffie glared at Arnie's back as he disappeared down the hall. What was it with his friends? Did they really have all the sexual adventures they said they had? Was he the only one who was different?

Raffie was 16, and he was worried. Raffie was a virgin.

Now imagine the same scenario between two female adolescents.

"Hey, Rachel," Annie grinned at her friend. "Make anything happen last night, or what?"

"Or what," thought Rachel, but she grabbed her books and grinned back. "You think you're the only 'happening' one around?"

"All right," said Annie, giving her friend an affectionate squeeze. She promised to catch all the details over lunch, then ran off to class.

Rachel stared at her friend as she rushed off. "Am I really that different?" she wondered.

Chapter Overview

Is the second scene harder to imagine than the first? What does the phrase "getting lucky" communicate about a sexual encounter? Are females and males equally likely to think of sex this way? Would Raffie's father have been as embarrassed in his day by sexual inexperience? Is Rachel likely to be? What are the sexual attitudes and practices of adolescents today, and how do these contribute to teenagers' sense of self?

The topic of sexuality raises questions at any age, but especially during adolescence. Sexuality looms large in adolescence, in part because it takes exciting new turns and in part because it contributes so heavily to adolescents' developing sense of themselves. We begin the chapter by considering cultural stereotypes of masculinity and femininity, along with a third alternative of androgyny. We then examine the identity implications of adolescents' sexuality, and look at how adolescents see themselves as sexual beings and at the sexual scripts that guide their behavior.

Sexual decision making brings adolescents several steps closer to adulthood. Some adolescents will limit their experiences to necking, others will go further. Each decision involves others. We examine adolescents' sexual attitudes and practices next.

For most adolescents, sexual attraction involves someone of the opposite sex. A small percentage discover they are attracted to those of their own sex. The biological and psychosocial bases of sexual attraction is another topic that receives attention in this chapter.

The sexual response cycle is strikingly similar for all individuals, despite differences in gender or sexual orientation. Research reveals four phases of response: excitement, plateau, orgasm, and resolution. We examine similarities in sexual response before discussing myths and misconceptions about sexual functioning that are common among adolescents.

Sex means different things to different people. To a lover, it is the stuff of dreams. To a biologist, it is a means of reproduction. Adolescents are better lovers than biologists, and relatively few consistently take care not to reproduce. The chapter moves to a consideration of contraception use before examining some consequences of adolescent sexuality: sexually transmitted diseases and unintended pregnancies. The chapter ends with a discussion of programs aimed at helping adolescents make informed sexual decisions.

Sexual Identity

As we have seen in the last three chapters, adolescents are poised to see themselves in new ways. And one of the most significant of these is in terms of their sexuality. Before going any further, we should be clear that "sexuality" is not equivalent to "sexual behavior." Sexuality refers, in the most general sense, to one's sexual character and embraces general aspects of one's sense of self, such as expressions of one's masculinity or femininity, the social roles one has within a family, and how one is seen in society. In constructing a sexual identity, then, adolescents are integrating sexuality into their sense of self.

Erik Erikson (1968) considered sexuality in this general sense to be one of the domains in which an adult identity is established, the other domains being those in which occupational and ideological preferences and commitments are established. As such, constructing a sexual identity is a healthy developmental process, a normal step taken by adolescents on the path to adulthood. Certainly, it's true that aspects of this sexuality include sexual thoughts and feelings, but as any adolescent might tell us, "It's not just about sex, it's about who I am."

As such, let's take a look at how adolescents see themselves with respect to this domain of identity.

Gender Stereotypes: The Meaning of Masculine and Feminine

The process of constructing a sexual identity introduces questions of what it means to be masculine or feminine. Adult sex roles, in the form of gender stereotypes, provide cultural answers. **Gender stereotypes** are the cultural expectations concerning which behaviors are appropriate for each sex. These stereotypes play an important role in self-definition as adolescents integrate questions posed by their sexuality into their developing sense of themselves.

The Masculine Gender Role Attitudes concerning what it is to be masculine and feminine in our society are surprisingly resistant to change despite significant changes in the roles of men and women both at home and in the workplace. When these attitudes are assessed with a well-known measures of sex-role stereotyping, the Bem Sex-Role Inventory (Bem, 1974), or BSRI, we find that males are expected to be self-reliant, self-sufficient, and able to defend their beliefs, make decisions, take a stand, and be leaders. With respect to sexual decision making, a topic we will consider later in the chapter, the masculine gender stereotype portrays males as the sexual risk takers, the ones to make the moves, to be aggressive, dominant, assertive, and forceful. The Research Focus "Between-Subjects Design" examines an alarming distortion of this gender stereotype.

The Feminine Gender Role Components of gender stereotypes are often polar opposites of each other. Consequently, females face quite a different set of cultural expectations. The feminine gender stereotype portrays females as sensitive to the feelings of others, in touch with their own emotions, understanding, affectionate, warm, and tender. Despite the implicit maturity in such an interpersonal stance, in other respects the cultural stereotype of femininity portrays females as dependent, passive, and childlike. These latter qualities become especially problematic when considered in light of the fact that adolescent females typically assume responsibility for contraception.

Androgyny Happily, these stereotypes communicate as much myth as truth. Adolescents have more latitude in fashioning their gender roles today than they have had in previous generations, and many score high on both masculine and feminine characteristics on the BSRI. These adolescents are **androgynous**. Adolescents of either sex can be assertive and sensitive to the needs of others, self-reliant and understanding. Androgyny allows adolescents to tailor-make a gender role instead of having to select one off the rack.

But freedom has its price. The very same loosening of gender-role definition, which allows increasing choice and individuality, may bring with it new ambiguities and conflicts. When role definition is rigid and conformity unanimous, everyone knows what to expect from the other and what the other expects. Although that may sound unexciting, it certainly simplifies a relationship, especially in its early stages. On the other hand, the greater the freedom and flexibility in the social definition of roles, the more that is left to be decided by the individual or negotiated in the heat of a relationship.

gender stereotypes The cultural expectations concerning behaviors that are appropriate for each sex.

androgynous A personality in which there are both masculine and feminine attributes.

RESEARCH FOCUS

Between-Subjects Design: Date Rape

It was well past midnight when Carol Ann slipped into the darkened house.

"Is that you, honey?" her mom called out in a sleepy voice.

"Yeah, Mom," she whispered hoarsely as she hurried to the bathroom.

Safe behind the closed door, she tore off her crumpled clothes, turned on the shower, and let the steaming water scald her skin pink.

She felt so dirty. She still didn't know how she had gotten away. She remembered struggling, punching, fighting back. Ugly bruises reddened on her arms and body as she choked back sobs of rage and humiliation. He had tried to rape her!

It had been their third date. He had been so polite and attentive each time before, never out of line. She hadn't been concerned when he suggested a party at a friend's house and turned down a dark road. What could she have said or done to make him think . . . ? And why did *she* feel so responsible? So terribly ashamed?

Carol Ann's experience is not that unusual. Judith Vicary, Linda Klingaman, and William Harkness (1995), looking at assault and date rape in high school females, found that 15% had experienced date rape over the 4-year period of the study; 60% of acquaintance rapes among college students occur in a dating situation (Koss, Dinero, Seibel, & Cox, 1988). What kind of male violates the consent of his date? Is it one whose sex drive is so strong that once aroused, he cannot stop himself? Or does date rape first start in the mind—with an attitude?

Rape myths are stereotyped perceptions of rapists and victims that minimize rape as a crime by shifting blame to the victim. As the term implies, they represent myth, not fact. Are males who endorse such statements more accepting of violations of consent on a date? Would they be more likely to answer yes than no? Several of these myths appear below:

- If a girl engages in necking or petting and she lets things get out of hand, it is her fault if her partner forces sex on her.
- Any healthy woman can successfully resist a rapist if she really wants to.
- In the majority of rapes, the victim is promiscuous or has a bad reputation.
- A woman who is stuck up and thinks she is too good to talk to guys on the street deserves to be taught a lesson.
- When women go around braless, or wearing short skirts and tight tops, they are just asking for trouble.
- Many women have an unconscious desire to be raped and may then unconsciously set up a situation in which they are likely to be attacked.
- If a woman gets drunk at a party and has intercourse with a man she's just met there, she should be

As adolescents begin to integrate sexuality into their identities, one could expect either an increase or a decrease in the flexibility with which they approach gender stereotypes. On the one hand, a decrease in flexibility might occur as they experience the cultural constraints of gender-role expectations at a time when a heightened concern about their sexuality could polarize their attitudes. On the other hand, they are also in a better position to realistically evaluate these gender norms, due to continued intellectual development, making it possible to more flexibly adapt cultural roles to their own needs. Of course, none of these changes occur in a vacuum, and real life contexts in which adolescents work out their sexuality must also be considered.

Gender Roles in Context One of these contexts is the transition in school settings that brings younger adolescents in daily contact with older ones, the transition that occurs as they move from elementary school into middle school or junior high and then into high school.

considered fair game to other males at the party who want to have sex with her too, whether she wants to or not.

Are beliefs such as these more likely to be held by certain people than by others? What other attitudes are they related to? Do they predict attitudes toward other intimate behaviors such as kissing, necking, petting, or even holding hands? Do attitudes about violations of consent depend on the level of assumed intimacy in the relationship? How could we find out?

Leslie Margolin, Melody Miller, and Patricia Moran (1989) found answers to these and similar questions by having male and female students read a description of a dating situation in which a male tried to kiss a female while they were at a movie together; when she refused, he kissed her anyway. Some of the students read that John and Mary were on a first date, others that they had been going together for 2 years, and others that they were married. Can you identify the independent variable in this experiment? If you said something like "level of intimacy," you were right. The other variable—gender—is a classification variable. (See Chapter 1, Research Focus "Who You Pushin' Buddy!" for definitions of terms.)

These investigators used a *between-subjects design*. In this type of experiment, each subject experiences only one level of the independent variable. Remember that some of the students read that John and Mary were on a first date, others that they were going together, and still others that they were married. When subjects are randomly assigned to one and only one level of an independent variable, it is a between-subjects design. Why might this matter? Why might we care whether they experienced more than one experimental condition?

A major advantage to this type of design is that investigators need not worry that subjects' responses will reflect the effects of another condition that may still be present. In other words, what if subjects assigned to the "first date" condition had just previously read of a similar incident involving a couple who was married? Could we safely assume that these subjects would be able to separate their reactions to each situation? In a between-subjects design, one need not worry about such matters. Also, because subjects can be assigned at random to conditions, investigators can be reasonably confident that groups do not initially differ until they impose different treatments. Both assumptions involve the issue of internal validity. To the extent that guarantees exist in experimental research, between-subjects designs offer high guarantees of internal validity.

What did these investigators discover about attitudes toward violations of consent? They found that acceptance of rape myths *is* related to acceptance of violations of consent, regardless of level of intimacy. They also found that males are more accepting of rape myths than are females. Consequently, they were not surprised to find that males also were more supportive of John's right to violate Mary's consent to be kissed.

Sources: Adapted from M. P. Koss, T. E. Dinero, C. A. Seibel, & S. L. Cox. (1988). Stranger and acquaintance rape: Are there differences in the victim's experience? *Psychology of Women Quarterly, 12,* 1–24. L. Margolin, M. Miller, & P. B. Moran. (1989). When a kiss is not just a kiss: Relating violations of consent in kissing to rape myth acceptance. *Sex Roles, 20,* 231–243. J. R. Vicary, L. R. Klingaman, & W. L. Harkness. (1995). Risk factors associated with date rape and sexual assault of adolescent girls. *Journal of Adolescence, 18,* 289–306.

Thomas Alfieri, Diane Ruble, and E. Tory Higgins (1996) asked fourth- through ninth-graders to indicate whether each of a number of gender-stereotypic adjectives was associated with males, females, or both. A tally of "both" responses was used as their measure of flexibility in gender stereotypes. Some of the early adolescents they studied made the transition to junior high in the seventh grade and some in the eighth grade. As can be seen in Figure 6.1, flexibility increases up through the first year of junior high, whether this occurred in the seventh grade or the eighth, but, as these cohort samples were followed over the next two years, flexibility could be seen to decrease dramatically.

Why might gender roles be more flexible early in adolescence than later? These investigators remind us that as early adolescents enter junior high, their status changes from that of being the oldest and wisest to that of being the youngest and most ignorant. Furthermore, their older schoolmates present them with a broader range of gendered behaviors than they have previously encountered. Faced with new challenges to what they have held to be true, it makes sense for early adolescents to put their beliefs on hold as they survey their new surroundings in order to learn more about gender. Decreases in

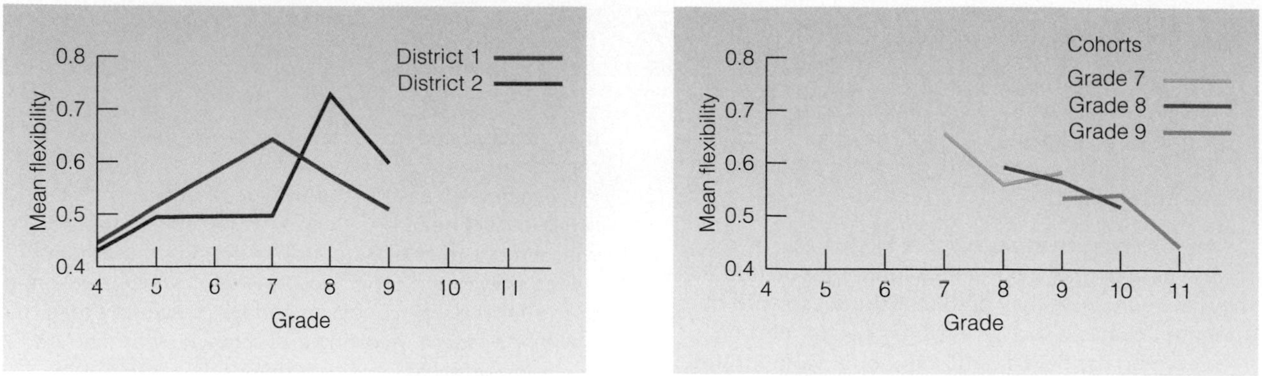

FIGURE 6.1
Gender-Role Flexibility by Grade. *The figure on the left shows increases in gender-role flexibility until adolescents reach junior high, in either the seventh grade (blue line) or the eighth grade (red line) and then a decrease. The figure on the right shows a continuing decrease in flexibility in gender roles through junior and senior high.* Source: Adapted from T. Alfieri, D. N. Ruble, & E. T. Higgins. (1996). Gender stereotypes during adolescence: Developmental changes and the transition to junior high school. *Developmental Psychology, 32,* 1129–1137.

flexibility are to be expected as they consolidate new beliefs and attitudes, in the face of increasing pressures to adopt more adult gender roles. The irony to these developments is that adolescents' flexibility is prompted by entering an environment in which the individuals who populate it hold relatively *in*flexible beliefs about gender. Gender stereotypes persists to varying degrees into young adulthood and across the lifespan.

Constructing a Sexual Identity

Most research on sexuality has not examined its identity implications but has focused instead on relatively narrow aspects of adolescents' behavior, such as their attitudes regarding sexual practices. But how do adolescents think of themselves as sexual beings? That is, how do they conceptualize their *sexual selves*? And how does this sense of themselves then relate to their sexual behavior?

Simone Buzwell and Doreen Rosenthal (1996) distinguish several aspects of the sexual self, each of which is thought to contribute to the ways in which adolescents construct a sense of themselves as sexual beings. The constructive perspective, recall, assumes that we actively put together the events to which we respond and, in the process, give meaning to experience. This activity of imposing an order on, and thereby gaining a sense of, our world is not limited to what we take to be external to us, but applies equally to our perception of ourselves. With respect to the sexual self, adolescents are likely to construct self-perceptions along at least three dimensions: their perception of their worth as sexual beings (*sexual self-esteem*), the control they perceive themselves to have over their sexual experiences (*sexual self-efficacy*), and their beliefs about their sexual needs (*sexual self-image*). These dimensions are presented in Table 6.1.

Sexual Styles These investigators identified five sexual styles, or approaches, taken by adolescents in the construction of their sexual selves. Each style represents a different combination of these dimensions of the sexual self.

Sexually naive adolescents had little confidence in their sexual attractiveness and, with the exception of being able to say no to unwanted sex, felt themselves to have little control over a sexual situation. Perhaps not surprisingly, sexual situations occasioned more anxiety than desire and were attractive only in the context of a committed

TABLE 6.1 Dimensions of the Sexual Self

SEXUAL SELF-ESTEEM: PERCEPTION OF ONE'S WORTH AS A SEXUAL BEING
Perceptions of one's sexual appeal: "I am confident that males/females find me sexually attractive."
Feelings concerning one's sexual adequacy: "I know how to behave in a sexual situation."
SEXUAL SELF-EFFICACY: CONFIDENCE IN ONE'S MASTERY CONCERNING SEXUAL ACTIVITIES
Ability to say no to unwanted sex: "I am confident that I could tell my partner that I do not want to have sex."
Ability to purchase and use condoms: "I am confident that I could put a condom on an erect penis."
SEXUAL SELF-IMAGE: PERCEPTION OF ONE'S SEXUALITY AND BELIEFS ABOUT ONE'S SEXUAL NEEDS
Perception of openness to sexual experimentation: "I would like to experiment when it comes to sex."
Commitment to a single sexual partner: "There needs to be commitment before I have sex with someone."

Source: Adapted from S. Buzwell & D. Rosenthal. (1996). Constructing a sexual self: Adolescents' sexual self-perceptions and sexual risk-taking. *Journal of Research on Adolescence, 6,* 489–513.

relationship. These adolescents were the youngest in the sample, and most of them were girls; most also were virgins.

A second group of adolescents, the *sexually unassured,* also had low self-esteem and little sense of control in sexual encounters but were somewhat more interested in exploring their sexuality. They, too, were anxious in sexual situations and most were young. Most of them tended to be boys, and, as with the first group, most were sexually inexperienced.

A third group, the *sexually competent,* were confident of themselves, both in terms of their sexual appeal and in their ability to control a sexual situation. These adolescents were less anxious and more interested in exploring their sexuality, though they did so with moderate levels of relationship commitment. The adolescents in this group, made up of both girls and boys, were for the most part in the twelfth grade, and most were sexually experienced.

Adolescents in the two remaining groups were highly confident of their sexual attractiveness and of their ability to take charge of their sexual encounters. The *sexually adventurous* were distinguished by high levels of sexual arousal and interest in sexual exploration, in combination with little anxiety and little relationship commitment. Most of these adolescents were older and were sexually experienced, and a majority were boys.

The *sexually driven* were similar to the sexually adventurous with the exception of being unable to say no to sex, whether they considered the partner desirable or not. Most of these adolescents also were sexually active boys.

Differences in sexual style are associated not only with sexual experience but also with different patterns of sexual behavior. For instance, adolescents with greater confidence in their sexual attractiveness and in their control over sexual encounters take greater risks and have more sexual partners and more one-night stands. Buzwell and Rosenthal emphasize that sexual behavior is closely tied to adolescents' personal constructions of their sexuality. In other words, adolescents' beliefs about themselves as sexual beings, apart from demographic factors such as ethnicity or social class, are associated with differences in their behavior. In fact, these investigators observed striking differences in sexual behaviors among adolescents who, in other respects, had very similar backgrounds.

Sexual Scripts

Adolescents are not left to themselves to map this sexual terrain; blueprints exist, in the form of sexual scripts, for them to follow. **Sexual scripts** are learned expectations organized around cultural roles and gender stereotypes. They provide a set of guidelines concerning expected patterns of behavior in a sexual situation, informing adolescents not only of what they should do and feel, but also of what the person they are with is likely to do and feel.

These scripts reflect the behaviors that comprise the masculine and feminine gender stereotypes. Stereotypically feminine characteristics, such as tenderness and sensitivity, translate into a sexual script in which females are motivated by a desire for emotional intimacy and love. Conversely, stereotypically masculine characteristics, such as dominance and risk taking, provide a script in which males are motivated by a desire for physical, rather than emotional, satisfaction. Not surprisingly, adolescent females are more likely than males to report being in love as a reason for being sexually active, and males to say they find sex itself exciting. For instance, when asked how they had felt after first having intercourse, many more males (72%) than females (26%) said they felt "thrilled," and many more males (75%) than females (18%) felt "sexually satisfied" (Woody, Russel, D'Souza, & Woody, 2000).

With respect to beliefs concerning the causes of sexual desire in others, there is remarkable agreement among adolescents and emerging adults, among females and males alike. Most believe that for males, erotic factors, such as how sexy a woman looks, cause sexual desire, whereas for females, thoughts of love or romance are important. Simply being male, it seems, is reason in itself for causing sexual desire, whereas this is not assumed to be the case if one is female (Crawford & Popp, 2003; Regan & Berscheid, 1995; Woody et al., 2000).

Making Sexual Decisions

Puberty brings new sexual feelings and emotions, and the natural need to integrate these into a sense of oneself. Rather than simply adding new sexual feelings to an old self, adolescents must revise that self so that what they add fits. In other words, adolescents cannot continue to see themselves as children and merely add sexual feelings and behaviors to this self-image. "Sexy children" is a contradiction in terms in most societies—to be sexual is to be adult. To integrate sexuality into their sense of themselves, adolescents must take a big step toward adulthood—and away from childhood. For many, this step is a hard one not so much for what they are stepping into as for what they are leaving behind.

Not surprisingly, adolescents frequently experience conflict when contemplating their own sexuality. Conflict, in itself, isn't necessarily bad; but it can interfere with responsible sexual decision making, often leading to avoidance and denial. Translated into the terminology of making sexual decisions, adolescents who experience conflict may deny that they are assuming a stance that is any different from that which they have always taken. Rather than consciously thinking through the consequences of becoming actively sexual, these adolescents are likely to engage in sex without planning to do so—and without doing so responsibly.

sexual scripts Learned expectations derived from cultural roles and gender stereotypes that guide behavior in sexual situations.

Talking with Parents

Unlike many attitudes, those surrounding sexuality are not likely to be openly discussed, especially with parents (Rosenthal & Feldman, 1999; Troth & Peterson, 2000). In itself, that may not be surprising, but adolescents also find it hard to talk openly about sex with friends and even with sexual partners (Troth & Peterson, 2000). Those who do talk with their parents are not as likely to begin their sexual experiences early or to engage in high-risk behavior once they have begun (Karofsky, Zeng, & Kosorok, 2001; Lehr, DiIorio, Dudley, & Lipana, 2000; Sionean et al., 2002). Similarly, those who can talk openly with their sexual partners engage in sex more responsibly (Darling & Hicks, 1982; Leland & Barth, 1993).

It's difficult to interpret findings such as these, that is, to know just what it is that contributes to delaying sexual initiation or avoiding risky behaviors. Perhaps it's what gets said in the course of a conversation, but it's also possible that adolescents who can talk with their parents have closer relationships with them, and it is the quality of the relationship that contributes to responsible decision making. Or it may be characteristics of the adolescents themselves, in that those who are able to talk about sex also are able to say "no" to a partner.

When adolescents do talk with their parents, they report talking more with their mothers, perhaps because they regard their mothers as somewhat better at communicating about sexuality than fathers (Feldman & Rosenthal, 2000; Rosenthal, Senserrick, & Feldman, 2001). Mothers also are more likely than fathers to talk with their children, and both parents talk more with daughters than with sons (Nolin & Petersen, 1992). As a result, sons have less opportunity than daughters to discuss sexual matters with the same-sex parent. When discussions occur between parents and sons, they are less likely to touch on issues of morality or values than are discussions with daughters. Of course, values can be communicated in many ways, not necessarily through talking. One important way is by teaching adolescents to be responsible for their actions and to have respect for others. Parents also influence their teenagers' sexual practices by maintaining strong bonds with them, thereby lessening their need for peer approval (DiBlasio & Benda, 1992; Miller & Fox, 1987).

Sexual Attitudes and Behaviors

With age, adolescents are increasingly likely to engage in various forms of sexual activity. Most will follow a predictable progression that starts with necking, moves to touching breasts, first over and then under clothing, to touching genitals, again over then under clothing, to oral sex and intercourse (Gowen, Feldman, Diaz, & Yisrael, 2004; Halpern, Joyner, Udry, & Suchindran, 2000). By the end of high school, just under half of all adolescents have engaged in sexual intercourse. The average age for first intercourse is 17 (Centers for Disease Control and Prevention, 2004; Else-Quest, Hyde, & DeLamater, 2005).

But what do we know about the other half? What sexual experiences are they likely to have had? Data from large, representative samples are not available. However, Jane Woody and her associates (2000) at the University of Nebraska at Omaha obtained information from several hundred young adults, ages 18 to 21, about their sexual activities as adolescents. In addition to asking about intercourse, these investigators asked about a number of noncoital activities, and about occasions when adolescents had come close to having intercourse but had decided not to.

Approximately half of their respondents had remained virgins as adolescents, and of these, 48% had abstained from all forms of sexual activity. The remaining virgins,

Starting with a kiss, adolescents follow a predictable progression of sexual behavior as they grow older, although the progression varies somewhat among ethnic and racial groups.

however, had engaged in a wide variety of noncoital sexual behaviors, as had those who had engaged in intercourse as adolescents.

It's difficult to say how representative these findings are of adolescents nationwide since the participants in the above study were all from the same region of the country. However, regional differences in national samples are not large for the percentages of adolescents engaging in sexual intercourse, and this average is similar to that reported by the participants in the above study (Centers for Disease Control and Prevention; 2004).

With respect to other sexual behaviors, such as touching a partner's genitals, males are likely to be the ones to first touch their partners, perhaps because males experience more permission to be sexually active than females. In fact, adolescent girls need more commitment in a relationship in order to touch their partners than they do to allow their partners to touch them. This suggests that it still may be difficult for most girls to assume an active role in sexual encounters even when most hold positive attitudes about the behaviors in question.

The percentage of adolescents indicating they have had sexual intercourse increases with age, as can be seen in Figure 6.2. Over the past 15 years, however, the percentage of adolescents who are sexually active has decreased substantially. In 1991, for instance, 54.1% said they had sexual intercourse by the end of high school, whereas by 2003 this figure had dropped to 46.7% (Centers for Disease Control and Prevention, 2004).

A second trend is apparent in Figure 6.2. Looking at ninth-graders, one sees that more boys than girls are sexually active. By the tenth grade, however, this difference all but disappears. Thus, although boys are likely to initiate sexual activity earlier than girls, once adolescents reach the tenth grade, there is little difference in the percentages of either sex who are sexually active. To appreciate the significance of this trend, we need only consider their parents' generation where, by the age of 17, the percentage of boys who were sexually active was still nearly twice that of girls (Hayes, 1987).

Attitudes toward oral sex are more positive than they have been in previous generations; this activity also has increased in frequency among adolescents (Woody et al., 2000). Among adolescents who were asked to recall a typical occasion in which they had stopped short of having intercourse, approximately 40% mentioned engaging in oral sex, as did even more of those who went on to have intercourse (Woody et al., 2000).

Self-Stimulation

A sexual practice that evokes considerable concern among adolescents is **self-stimulation,** more commonly referred to as masturbation. Even though most adolescents engage in this, most regard the practice with mixed feelings (Halpern, Udry, Suchindran, & Campbell, 2000).

self-stimulation Self-stimulation of the genitals.

Novelist Philip Roth (1969) depicts these concerns in a boy:

> It was at the end of my freshman year of high school—and freshman year of masturbating—that I discovered on the underside of my penis, just where the

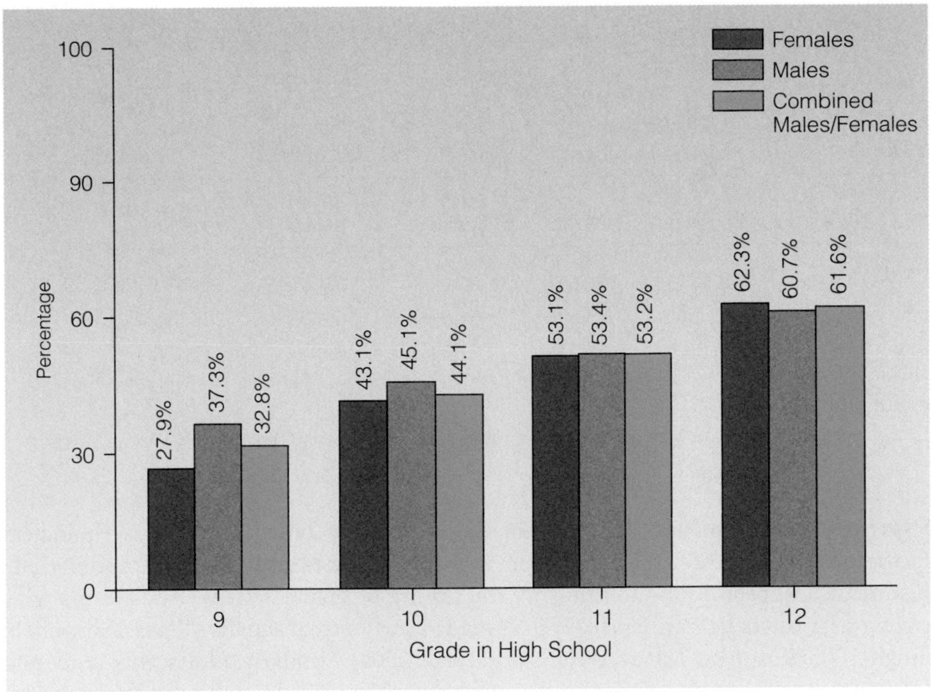

FIGURE 6.2 Percentage of High School Students Who Indicate They Have Had Sexual Intercourse, United States, 2003. *Source:* Centers for Disease Control and Prevention. (2004, May 21). Youth risk behavior surveillance—United States, 2003. *Morbidity and Mortality Weekly Reports, 53.*

> shaft met the head, a little discolored dot that has since been diagnosed as a freckle. Cancer. I had given myself cancer. All that pulling and tugging at my own flesh, all that friction, had given me an incurable disease. And not yet fourteen! In bed at night the tears rolled from my eyes. "No!" I sobbed. "I don't want to die. Please—no." But then, because I would shortly be a corpse anyway, I went ahead as usual and jerked off.

Attitudes toward self-stimulation have changed radically. Past generations were taught that masturbation was morally wrong and were warned that excessive masturbation could result in physical deformities or disease. Adolescents today learn that self-stimulation is a normal sexual outlet. Self-stimulation even can help females and males alike learn how their bodies respond sexually. Although most adolescents no longer believe that masturbation is abnormal or dangerous, most still view it with some embarrassment (Strong & DeVault, 2001).

The age at which adolescents become sexually active differs considerably for adolescents from different ethnic backgrounds. As Table 6.2 shows, among African American and Hispanic adolescents, males are more likely to be sexually active than females; however, the reverse is true among Caucasian adolescents. Within each sex, as well, differences due to ethnicity are relatively large.

Protective Factors

Biologically Based Factors As one might expect, adolescents who mature later are less likely to become sexually active at an earlier age (Meschke, Zweig, Barber, & Eccles, 2000). Gender is also related to the age at which adolescents become sexually active, with girls becoming sexually active later than boys (Centers for Disease Control and Prevention, 2004). Perhaps less expectedly, intelligence is also related to the timing of sexual activity, with adolescents of higher intelligence being more likely to delay sexual activity (Halpern et al., 2000).

TABLE 6.2 Sexual Activity Among African American, Caucasian, and Hispanic High School Students

	Ever Had Sexual Intercourse		Currently Sexually Active		Condom Use During Last Sexual Intercourse		Birth Control Pill Use Before Last Sexual Intercourse	
Ethnicity[1]	Females	Males	Females	Males	Females	Males	Females	Males
African American	60.9%	73.8%	44.2%	54.0%	63.6%	81.2%	11.7%	4.4%
Caucasian	43.0%	40.5%	33.1%	28.5%	56.5%	69.0%	26.5%	17.3%
Hispanic	46.4%	56.8%	35.8%	38.5%	52.3%	62.5%	12.1%	10.3%

[1] Percentages for Asian American adolescents were not available.

Source: Adapted from Centers for Disease Control and Prevention (2004). Youth risk behavior surveillance—United States, 2003. *Morbidity and Mortality Weekly Reports, 53,* No. SS-2.

Psychological Factors In addition to biologically based factors, psychological factors, such as adolescents' religious beliefs, their values and attitudes, and emotional adjustment have been found to influence the timing of sexual activity. Adolescents with strong religious beliefs are less likely to engage in early sexual activity (Jones, Darroch, & Singh, 2005; Rostosky, Wilcox, Wright, & Randall, 2004). Similarly, adolescents' academic interests, as reflected in their day-to-day involvement in school activities and their aspirations for college, are related to postponing sexual activity (Whitbeck et al., 1999). Conversely, permissive attitudes toward sex and, for boys, placing importance on being popular have been found to be associated with earlier sexual activity (Meschke et al., 2000).

Social Factors A third domain of influence consists of social factors, such as parents and peers. Families remain a significant influence in adolescents' lives, and adolescents' sexual behavior is no exception. Adolescents who have stable family environments are more likely to delay sexual activity, as are those whose parents provide more supervision, hold higher expectations, and remain emotionally connected to their children (Klein, 2005). Parental monitoring, such as knowing where adolescents are and who they are with, is also effective in delaying sexual activity, at least for younger adolescents (Capaldi, Stoolmiller, Clark, & Owen, 2002). Adolescents whose mothers have strong religious beliefs are more likely to delay sexual intercourse (Whitbeck et al., 1999). With respect to peers, steady dating has been found to increase the likelihood of early sexual activity especially for girls with older boyfriends (Gowen, Feldman, Diaz, & Yisrael, 2004; Meschke et al., 2000), as has the use of alcohol and associating with delinquent peers (Blinn-Pike, Berger, & Hewett, 2004; Whitbeck et al., 1999).

Despite the fact that many teenagers are likely to be sexually active today, many of them engage in intercourse infrequently. Some adolescents appear to have had their first sexual experiences for reasons not necessarily sexual but, instead, as a rite of passage or to satisfy their curiosity. Once they have proven themselves or discovered what they wanted to know, they abstain until they become involved in a relationship. Adolescents who decide not to become sexually active mention a number of reasons for remaining abstinent. The most common of these are their fears of becoming pregnant and of contracting a sexually transmitted disease. Waiting for the right person and waiting until they're older, as well as values and religion, are also reasons frequently given by early adolescents (Blinn-Pike et al., 2004).

The most immediate context in which sexual behavior can be studied is the very private world of the human sexual response. Like much else related to adolescent sexual functioning, our understanding has been late to develop.

IN MORE DEPTH

Descriptions of the Experience of Orgasm

Research finds that trained judges can't tell which written descriptions of orgasm are given by females and which by males. Can you? (See answers below.)

1. "Like a mild explosion, it left me warm and relaxed after a searing heat that started in my genitals and raced to my toes and head."
2. "Throbbing is the best word to say what it is like. The throbbing starts as a faint vibration, then builds up in wave after wave where time seems to stand still."
3. "When I come it's either like an avalanche of pleasure, tumbling through me, or like a refreshing snack—momentarily satisfying, but then I'm ready for more."
4. "My orgasms feel like pulsating bursts of energy starting in my pelvic area and then engulfing my whole body. Sometimes I feel like I'm in freefall, and sometimes I feel like my body's an entire orchestra playing a grand crescendo."
5. "Some orgasms feel incredibly intense and earth-shattering, but other times orgasms feel like small, compact, self-contained moments."
6. "There is a warm rush from my toes to my head, with a strong, pulsing rhythm. Then everything settles down like a pink sunset."

1.M 2.M 3.F 4.F 5.M 6.M

Source: Adapted from W. H. Masters, V. E. Johnson, & R. C. Kolodny. (1988). *Human sexuality* (3rd ed.). Boston: Little, Brown.

The Sexual Response Cycle

Sputnik had orbited the earth and Neil Armstrong had one foot on the moon before scientists began to unravel the complexities of the human sexual response. William Masters and Virginia Johnson studied actual sexual encounters between men and women, which revealed a sexual response cycle consisting of four phases: excitement, plateau, orgasm, and resolution. Two processes underlie each phase. **Vasocongestion** is an accumulation of blood in the vessels serving the erogenous zones (areas of the body that are particularly sensitive to sexual arousal), and **myotonia** is an increase in muscular tension. The tension is more like a building up of energy in the muscles rather than a state of feeling tense. At each phase of the cycle, striking similarities exist in the response of females and males.

Excitement Vasocongestion is responsible for the first signs of *excitement,* or sexual arousal, in both males and females. In males it causes blood to pour into the spongy tissues in the shaft of the penis, making it erect. Masters, Johnson, and Kolodny (1988) note that because an erection is caused by an increase in fluid pressure, it is essentially a "hydraulic event." Vaginal lubrication, one of the first signs of sexual arousal in females, occurs when blood vessels in the pelvic area swell with blood, pressing fluids into the tissues surrounding the vagina. In both sexes, the nipples harden and muscular tension increases throughout the body (myotonia).

Plateau Continued vasocongestion during the *plateau* phase causes the erection in males to become harder. Drops of lubricating fluid appear at the opening of the glans. Because this fluid frequently contains live sperm, withdrawal prior to ejaculation, a birth control practice common among teenagers, is not an effective means of preventing pregnancy. In females, continued vasocongestion causes the walls of the vagina to swell, constricting the size of the vagina and making penis size relatively unimportant for stimulation. Because females require more pelvic congestion than males to reach orgasm, the plateau stage lasts longer in females.

Orgasm The sensations of *orgasm* result from rhythmic muscular contractions and discharge of tensions resulting from vasocongestion and myotonia. Despite similarities

vasocongestion An accumulation of blood in the vessels serving the erogenous zones.

myotonia An increase in muscular tension.

Interviews with adolescents reveal that many are surprisingly ignorant about even the basics of sexual intimacy and its consequences.

in its physiological bases for both sexes, orgasm tends to be a more consistently uniform phenomenon in males than in females; however, individuals of both sexes describe their experience of orgasm in similar ways. In More Depth presents some of these descriptions.

Resolution In the *resolution* phase, following ejaculation, the penis becomes flaccid, and males experience a *refractory period,* lasting anywhere from several minutes to several hours, during which stimulation will not produce an erection. Resolution lasts much longer in females, because vasocongestion in the pelvic area dissipates slowly, and they can experience *multiple orgasms.*

Sexual Functioning: Myths and Misconceptions

Despite today's relatively open attitudes toward sex, considerable ignorance and myth surround sexual functioning. Interviews with adolescents found that many are surprisingly uninformed about even the basics. A 16-year-old girl remarked, "I wasn't ready for it being so *real.* Because in movies they don't get sweaty and—you know—all this awkward stuff." One boy commented, "I wish sex came with instructions. All the time I was thinking about doing it, I was worrying, *How* do you do it?" Ignorance concerning sexual functioning is by no means limited to adolescents. Countless adults cannot accurately name the parts of their own genitals or those of the opposite sex.

Bigger Is Better For adolescent boys, concern about the size of their penis is at the top of the list. Many boys don't know what size is normal and are sure theirs is too small. This concern is fueled by large variations from one boy to the next in the timing and rate of growth. Comparisons are inevitable, and a boy's penis almost always looks shorter to him than someone else's simply because his visual perspective (in looking down) foreshortens it (Masters, Johnson, & Kolodny, 1988).

Size assumes added importance as a result of the common misconception that penis size is related to sexual adequacy—which is simply untrue. Vaginal constriction corrects for differences in circumference of the penis, and because there are few nerve endings in the upper vagina, length is unimportant. Although one penis can differ noticeably from another in size when flaccid, this difference all but disappears when erect. Masters, Johnson, and Kolodny (1988), in fact, refer to an erection as "the great equalizer."

A common concern among adolescent girls concerns their breasts. Many notice that one breast is slightly larger than the other. Girls may wonder if it's normal for one breast to be smaller than the other (it is) and what they can do about it (nothing short of cosmetic surgery). Boys face a similar concern when they notice that one testicle is higher than the other, which is also quite normal.

Capacity for Sexual Pleasure Perhaps the most pervasive cultural myth among adolescents is that males experience more sexual pleasure than females. The fact that females take longer to reach orgasm may contribute to this myth. Once they reach orgasm, however, their capacity to achieve additional orgasms exceeds that of males. Similarities in the phases of the sexual response cycle in either sex, and in the way individuals describe orgasm, suggest similarities in the pleasure each experiences.

Need for Orgasm A related misconception is that only males need to reach orgasm. Considerable discomfort can result from reaching the plateau phase and not experiencing orgasm. Both males and females experience this discomfort, the result of blood vessels remaining engorged in the pelvic and genital areas. This vasocongestion underlies orgasm in both sexes, and failure to release the accumulated blood and the muscular tension produces discomfort in both males and females.

Intercourse During Menstruation Numerous cultural taboos exist regarding intercourse during menstruation. Some cultures even isolate menstruating females, fearing that they might contaminate the things with which they come into contact. What dangers might befall a male? Misconceptions range from fears of infection to impotence and loss of virility. There is no factual basis for any of these fears.

Current attitudes concerning menstruation are less negative than in previous generations, but reference to it as "the curse" is still common. Cultural messages—for example, advertisements and commercials for pads and tampons—communicate in subtle ways that menstruation is an untidy and unsanitary condition, to be cleaned up by using "sanitary napkins." Similarly, advertisements for tampons communicate that if a female handles things properly, she can go about her business almost as if she were "normal" (Lips, 2005).

Intact Hymen and Virginity Another common misconception is that the presence of a hymen indicates virginity. The hymen is actually likely to tear in most girls during childhood with active play or curious exploration (see Chapter 3). Some girls are not even born with a hymen, and in others intercourse only stretches the hymen and does not rupture it.

Sexual Orientation

One of the central tasks of adolescence, particularly late adolescence, involves achieving a personal identity, and a major component of this is one's sexual identity. Although children label themselves as being one sex or the other from the earliest years on, sexual

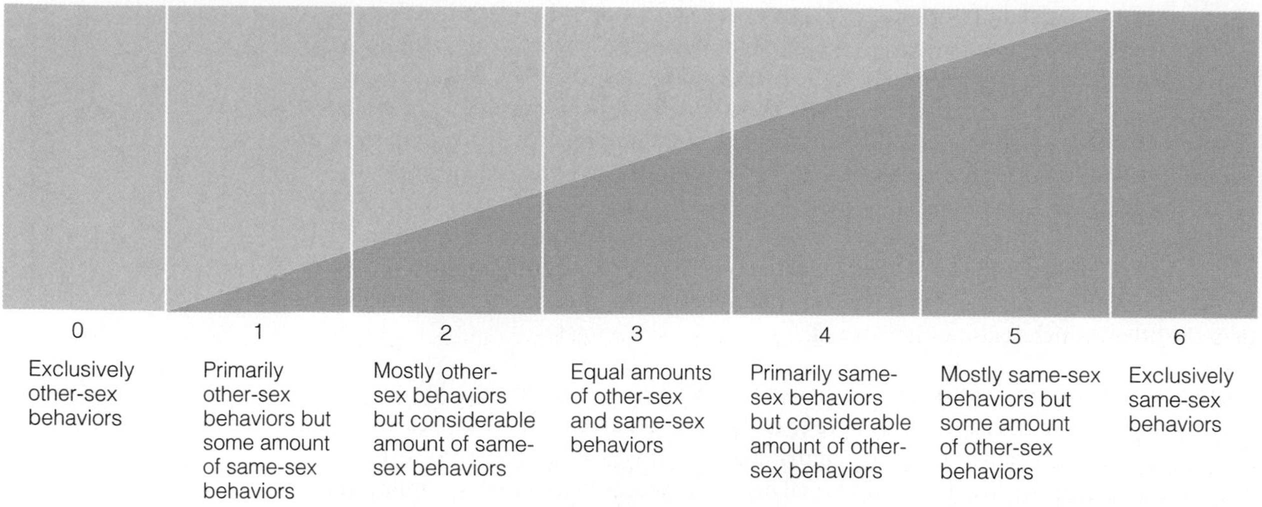

FIGURE 6.3

Kinsey's Continuum of Sexual Orientation. *With respect to sexual orientation, individuals can't be neatly sorted into categories; there are gradations of complexity. Source:* Adapted from A. C. Kinsey, W. B. Pomeroy, & C. E. Martin. (1948). *Sexual behavior in the human male.* Philadelphia: Saunders.

orientation does not become firmly established until adolescence. It is then that sexual experimentation embellishes and confirms, or disconfirms, these earlier labels. Late adolescence brings the additional task of infusing relationships with emotional intimacy.

Sexual orientation refers to the attraction individuals feel for members of the same or the other sex. Those with a **heterosexual** orientation are attracted to people of the opposite sex, those with a **homosexual** orientation are attracted to members of their own sex, and **bisexually** oriented people are attracted to individuals of both sexes. Heterosexuals are often referred to as *straight,* homosexual men as *gay,* and homosexual women as *lesbian.*

How many adolescents share each of these orientations? Simple answers are not forthcoming, for a number of reasons. Rather than discrete categories into which individuals neatly sort themselves, sexual orientations are more like segments along a continuum, as shown in Figure 6.3. It is not always clear where one orientation leaves off and another begins. For instance, although many adolescents, particularly males, report having engaged in some form of homosexual sex play at one time or another, relatively few experience feelings of romantic attraction. In a national survey of adolescents, 7.3% of adolescent boys reported such feelings, as did 5% of girls (Russell & Joyner, 2001). Among adults, the percentage of males or females who are exclusively gay or lesbian throughout their adult life is even smaller (Kinsey, Pomeroy, & Martin, 1948; Kinsey et al., 1953).

This last statistic introduces yet another factor that contributes to the fuzziness of these categories. Sexual attraction can change during one's lifetime. An additional complication is that sexuality cannot be reduced simply to behavior; it includes attraction and desire as well. One could, in other words, be celibate throughout one's life and still be straight or gay.

sexual orientation The attraction individuals feel for members of the same or the other sex.

heterosexual Sexual attraction toward individuals of the other sex.

homosexual Sexual attraction toward individuals of the same sex.

bisexual Sexual attraction toward individuals of both sexes.

Homosexuality

How is one to think of homosexuality, if having homosexual experiences does not necessarily mean that one is homosexual? In general, homosexuals are individuals who, for some extended period of their lives, are more attracted sexually to individuals of their own sex than to those of the opposite sex. This definition underscores several points. First, sexual attraction is as important in defining sexual orientation as actual behavior; and second, an isolated sexual experience does not mean one is homosexual: Sexual orientation reflects a prolonged sexual preference. Furthermore, many individuals are neither exclusively heterosexual nor exclusively homosexual.

Establishing a sexual identity is difficult for most adolescents, but especially so for those who wonder whether they're atypical. Many gay, lesbian, and bisexual adolescents report experiencing feelings that they recognized as atypical for their gender as early as the age of 10, which prompted a period of sexual questioning even prior to puberty. Even in late childhood, those who question their sexual identity report being more anxious about relationships with peers and are less accepting of themselves (Carver, Egan, & Perry, 2004; Egan & Perry, 2001).

Being different is never easy, especially when it places one in a group that is viewed negatively by many segments of society. Sexual-minority adolescents indicate being more depressed and anxious; and some research, though not all, reports lower self-esteem than for heterosexual peers (Diamond & Lucas, 2004; Hart & Heimberg, 2001). Lisa Diamond and Sarah Lucas (2004), at the University of Utah, found that loss of friends and worries about maintaining existing friendships accounted for many of the negative emotions experienced by sexual-minority youth. These investigators found that those who were younger (under 18) had lost more friends and had fewer close friends than their heterosexual peers. With age, however, this pattern changed, and older sexual-minority youth reported having more close friends than those who were heterosexual (Diamond & Lucas, 2004).

Prejudice and Discrimination

At a time when all adolescents, irrespective of their sexual orientation, face the developmental challenges of consolidating an identity, sexual-minority youth experience additional challenges in the form of societal prejudice concerning homosexuality. Harassment, being verbally or physically assaulted, avoided by classmates and neighbors, as well as unsympathetic or openly hostile reactions from family members, is experienced by substantial numbers of gay and lesbian adolescents. Additionally, government-funded education programs for schools neither mandate the inclusion of information related to sexual orientation, or counseling to students who might want to speak to someone, nor prohibit the inclusion of negative material about homosexuality, for example, some even teaching that homosexuality is unacceptable or "a criminal offense under the laws of the state" (Russo, 2006). These experiences may well account for the greater incidence of substance abuse, thoughts of suicide, and academic problems among sexual-minority youth (Rotheram-Borus, Rosario, Van Rossem, Reid, & Gillis, 1995; Russell & Joyner, 2001).

Biological and Psychosocial Bases of Sexual Attraction

What determines one's sexual orientation? Is sexual orientation biologically based? Can sexual attraction be traced to formative experiences, such as the type of family one is raised in or a first sexual encounter? We will look first at biological explanations and then at psychological ones.

Biological Factors J. Michael Bailey and Richard Pillard (1991) interviewed gay and bisexual men with twin brothers. Twins can be of two types. Identical (monozygotic)

Too few gay adolescents are like the young men and women in this group. Most have no one with whom to share concerns and questions about their developing sexual identity, and they must cope by themselves with the social prejudices against homosexuality.

twins share the same genetic makeup, having developed from the same cell (zygote). Fraternal (dizygotic) twins develop from separate cells and are no more similar genetically than other siblings. If there is a genetic contribution to sexual orientation, more identical twin brothers should both be homosexual than fraternal twin brothers. This study also included an additional, third group of gay and bisexual men; these men had adoptive brothers, that is, with no shared genetic background but who shared a similar environment. It was expected that the co-incidence of homosexuality would be lowest in this third group.

Bailey and Pillard found that over 50% of the identical twins whose brothers were homosexual were themselves homosexual, whereas only 22% of the fraternal twin brothers were and even fewer, 11%, of the adoptive brothers were.

A similar study of sexual orientation in females revealed comparable findings. Forty-eight percent of monozygotic twin sisters of gay women were also lesbian, in contrast to only 16% of dizygotic twin sisters and 6% of adoptive sisters (Bailey, Pillard, Neale, & Agyei, 1993).

Overall, these findings strongly suggest a genetic component to sexual orientation. Additional research suggests that the path of genetic transmission, at least for males, is likely to be through the mother. A higher percentage of maternal uncles of gay men, and cousins who are sons of maternal aunts, are gay than the base rate of homosexuals in the population. Higher rates are not found for paternally related males.

The precise means by which genes might influence sexual orientation is still being studied. One possibility is through hormones that are present in differing amounts in males and females. However, studies of gay males and lesbians and of heterosexuals do not find expected differences in the levels of circulating hormones (Money, 1988). Hormones might also affect prenatal brain development. One study found that a node of the hypothalamus, which is related to sexual behavior, is smaller in gay males than in heterosexual males (LeVay, 1991). However, differences in hypothalamic size due to other causes cannot be ruled out.

It is also possible that individuals may be genetically predisposed to homosexuality but nonetheless develop a heterosexual orientation because of the presence or absence of other contributing factors.

Psychological Factors Sexual orientation develops within a psychosocial environment. Freud assumed that children are initially bisexual and only gradually develop heterosexual interests through the resolution of the Oedipal or Electra complex in early childhood (see Chapter 2). Other theorists have suggested that homosexuality in males is due to a domineering, overprotective mother and a passive father. However, one would expect such family influences to affect siblings, and the incidence of homosexuality among brothers of gay males is no higher than in the population at large, with the exception of twins, as discussed earlier.

Family influences remain important, but not necessarily in expected ways. For instance, adolescents raised by same-sex couples have not been found to differ in either their romantic relationships or other measures of psychosocial adjustment from those raised by opposite-sex couples. Home atmosphere, nonetheless, was found to be important; it was the closeness of parents' relationships to children, however, that was associated with adjustment, and not their sexual orientation (Wainright, Russell, & Patterson, 2004).

All of this is not to say that psychosocial factors do not contribute to sexual orientation. Recall that even though 50% of the identical twins of gay men were gay, the other half were not. Rather, adolescents' sexual orientation results from a complex mix of environmental and genetic factors that are then shaped and molded to uniquely fit the perceived experiences of each adolescent.

Similar attempts have been made to trace lesbianism to traumatic early sexual experiences that may have turned these women away from males as objects of sexual desire. However, estimates of the frequency of such experiences are considerably higher than the incidence of homosexuality among females (see Chapter 12).

Sexual Health: Risks and Responsibilities

One might think that early sexual activity among adolescents would be accompanied by an equal sophistication concerning contraception, but data suggest this is not the case. Approximately 870,000 adolescent girls become pregnant every year (Centers for Disease Control and Prevention, 2004). Most of them do so unintentionally. Additionally, more than nine times that number become infected with a sexually transmitted disease each year (Alan Guttmacher Institute, 2004). Yet adolescents can select from a wide range of contraceptives. The most effective of these all but eliminate the possibility of pregnancy and are highly effective in protecting against sexually transmitted diseases (STDs). Why aren't they more effective for teenagers? The answer, it seems, is that many sexually active teenagers do not consistently use contraceptives.

Contraception

In a national survey of high school students, only 63% of those who were sexually active said they or their partner had used a condom before last having intercourse (Centers for Disease Control and Prevention, 2004). Why might contraceptive use be sporadic for so many adolescents? A number of possible reasons exist. Three of the more likely are lack of information, inability to accept one's sexuality, and cognitive-emotional immaturity.

Lack of Information Most adolescents are surprisingly misinformed about their own reproductive capabilities. For instance, many early adolescent girls believe it isn't necessary for them to take any precautions because they are too young to get pregnant, and many boys believe that withdrawal is an effective way to avoid pregnancy. Most adolescents similarly are unaware of the likelihood of becoming infected with a sexually transmitted disease. An equal number of adolescents appear to be so anxious about their sexual activities that they are not able to deal with the associated issues in any practical way.

Most adolescents do not receive much information about reproduction or contraception from their parents. Most are also not likely to disclose their concerns to their parents. How likely adolescents are to talk to their parents depends on the quality of the relationship they have with them and on their parents' willingness to talk when disagreements arise rather than avoid potential conflict (Papini, Farmer, Clark, & Snell, 1988; Troth & Peterson, 2000). Talking with parents depends as well on adolescents' levels of self-esteem and individuation (Papini, Snell, Belk, & Clark, 1988). This last point suggests that young adolescents especially will have difficulty bringing their sexual concerns to their parents, since they are still in the early stages of individuation.

Many adolescents also do not receive information about contraception at school. One in four teachers across the country are not allowed to teach about contraception, and 4 in 10 teachers either are not allowed to inform students about contraceptives or must teach that they are ineffective in preventing pregnancy or protecting against STDs, whereas, in fact, they are highly effective with respect to each of these (Alan Guttmacher Institute, 2004).

Does teaching adolescents about contraception increase the likelihood that they will become sexually active? Research finds just the opposite to be true. Sex education programs that provide adolescents with information about the use of condoms and other forms of contraception have been found to actually delay the initiation of sexual activity and to result in safer sex practices once adolescents become sexually active (Alan Guttmacher Institute, 2004; Kirby, 2002).

Inability to Accept One's Sexuality First sexual encounters can occasion considerable conflict in many adolescents, especially in girls. A number of reasons exist for this conflict. Sexual behavior is closely tied to religious and moral issues. In some homes, sexual matters are cloaked with secrecy, and discussions of sexual concerns are infrequent or absent entirely. Many adolescents simply are uncomfortable discussing their sexuality, even those who are sexually active. Adolescent girls who *can* accept and talk about their own sexual behavior are more likely to use contraceptives effectively (Tschann & Adler, 1997).

Cause for conflict among many adolescent girls also can be found in current stereotypes of femininity and masculinity. Compare these components of the feminine stereotype—yielding, shy, sensitive to the needs of others, childlike, and compassionate—with those of the masculine stereotype—makes decisions easily and is self-reliant, independent, assertive, and willing to take risks. Who is more likely to make decisions, be self-reliant, or assertively insist on the use of a condom? Many females fail to use a contraceptive because they simply think it isn't feminine to plan to have sex or to take precautions against getting pregnant.

Cognitive-Emotional Immaturity One of the hallmarks of cognitive development is the ability to think about things that have not been experienced. Thought that is limited by experience is limited to what has happened before. Most adolescents are just entering a form of thought in which they can consider events that may only exist as possibilities for them. Most have never been pregnant before either.

Despite the emergence of new mental skills that enable adolescents to imagine things they have never experienced, things that exist only as abstractions or possibilities, these skills appear at different times for different individuals. Some adolescents may be facing sexual decisions while still approaching daily problems in a concrete fashion, their thinking limited to what is immediate and currently apparent (see Chapter 4). Thus a 13-year-old girl flattered by the attentions of an older boy may not have the cognitive maturity, in the pressure of the moment, to consider distant consequences. The concrete problem is "What will make him like me now?" Pregnancy and disease belong to the world of tomorrow, and tomorrow is but dimly represented in concrete thought.

Even among those adolescents who can think more abstractly, the absence of practical experience and accurate information can make imagined consequences hard to evaluate. Many adolescents are able to conceive of problems intellectually yet feel personally immune to them. To these individuals, disease and pregnancy are possible but not real, and it's hard to take dangers seriously if they believe such things only happen to others.

Teenage pregnancies are due partly to a lack of information and partly to a denial of personal responsibility. Adolescents need help in learning how to make decisions about their sexual behaviors, especially those that could alter the course of their lives.

Early adolescents tend to think that other people are as interested in what they are thinking and doing as they are themselves (Elkind, 1967; Lapsley, FitzGerald, Rice, & Jackson, 1989). In doing so they create an imaginary audience. Imagining that others are aware of their feelings or activities can mean that their private fantasies about sex risk becoming public knowledge. The imaginary audience can also give adolescents the feeling that they are special (the personal fable). Why else would everyone be so aware of what they are feeling and doing? Being special carries the implication that what happens to others will not happen to you. Thus many adolescents believe they will not get pregnant or become infected with an STD even though their friends do.

Sexually Transmitted Diseases

Approximately nine million adolescents and young adults a year become infected with a **sexually transmitted disease (STD)** (Alan Guttmacher Institute, 2004). Because many STDs are asymptomatic, and because those with symptoms do not always seek treatment, the actual number of adolescents affected is almost surely greater than estimated.

What are sexually transmitted diseases? They are infections that are spread through sexual contact. Some STDs, such as syphilis and HIV infection, also can be acquired through blood transfusions. They range in seriousness from irritating itches to life-threatening infections. Some are reaching epidemic levels among adolescents. The most serious STDs are HIV infection, syphilis, and gonorrhea. Less serious infections range from genital herpes, for which there is no known cure, to pests such as pubic lice, which can be treated with a prescription shampoo.

Many adolescents mistakenly believe that *other* people get sexually transmitted diseases—not them. Well-dressed, neatly groomed teenagers assume they could never get anything like syphilis or gonorrhea, much less AIDS. Assumptions such as these couldn't be further from the truth. STDs are presently as American as apple pie and country music. The facts are simple: Most diseases have reached epidemic proportions,

sexually transmitted disease (STD) An infection that is spread through sexual contact.

and some are especially rife among adolescents. Adolescents who are sexually active are likely at some point to get a sexually transmitted disease.

STDs can be classified into one of two groups on the basis of how they are transmitted. HIV, chlamydia, and gonorrhea are known as **discharge diseases** because they are transmitted through genital secretions, for example, semen and vaginal fluids, and in the case of HIV/AIDS also through the blood of infected individuals. Genital herpes and syphilis are known as **genital ulcer diseases,** since they are transmitted through contact with sores or ulcers on the skin, or patches that appear normal but are nonetheless infected. Gential warts, or human papilloma virus, can be transmitted either by contact with infected areas of skin or by secretions (CDC, 2004c, 2005c).

We will begin by looking at the first category of STDs, starting with HIV/AIDS since this is the most serious of the STDs, even though the least frequent among adolescents in the United States.

HIV and AIDS The risk to adolescents in the United States of infection with **HIV** (human immuno deficiency virus), the virus that causes AIDS, is relatively slight compared to other sexually transmitted diseases. However, HIV remains the riskiest of all STDs because of its life-threatening nature (CDC, 2005c).

Certain ethnic minorities within the United States are disproportionately at risk for HIV infection. Over half of those diagnosed with HIV/AIDS are African American even though they represent only 13% of the population (CDC, 2006). Similarly, Hispanics are overrepresented among those diagnosed with HIV/AIDS. Rates of infection are also higher among American Indians and Alaska natives, given their proportions within the population; Asians and Pacific Islanders have the lowest rate of infection (CDC, 2006a). Because the incubation period from infection to the appearance of symptoms averages 10 years, it is likely that most adults with AIDS were infected when they were adolescents or young adults (NIAID, 2005). (See Figure 6.4.)

HIV is a virus that attacks the immune system, causing it to break down. This in turn leaves the body defenseless against infection, eventually resulting in death from any of a number of secondary, opportunistic infections. At present, there is no cure for this disease; however, great strides have been made in drug treatments that are effective in combating the development of secondary infections and in prolonging life. HIV infection progresses through several stages, the last of which is **AIDS** (acquired immune deficiency syndrome). The virus can be transmitted by exposure to infected blood, such as through sharing contaminated needles for injecting drugs or through blood transfusions from an infected person, as well as by sexual contact. However, most adolescent and young adult males become infected through sexual contact with other males, and relatively few through heterosexual contact or contaminated needles. Most females, though, become infected through heterosexual contact (CDC, 2006a).

What steps can adolescents take to protect themselves from HIV infection? The first step is simply a mental one, but it is as important as any that follow because adolescents are unlikely to take additional steps unless they begin with the realization that *anyone* can get AIDS, including themselves. Realizing they are at risk is not an easy step for many adolescents. Nancy Leland and Richard Barth (1993) asked 1,000 high school students how likely they thought it was for them to "get AIDS." Most adolescents did not think they were likely to be infected, as many as a third indicating there was "no chance."

For those who can narrow this mental distance, a number of practices can significantly reduce the risk of sexually transmitted HIV infection. Of course, the surest way is to avoid sexual contacts of any kind. We have seen earlier in the chapter, however, that a majority of adolescents are sexually active by the end of high school. Furthermore, most

discharge diseases Sexually transmitted diseases transmitted through genital secretions, for example, semen and vaginal fluids.

genital ulcer diseases STDs transmitted through contact with sores or ulcers on the skin, or even patches of skin that appear normal but are infected.

HIV Human immunodeficiency virus: a virus attacking the immune system, leading to AIDS (acquired immune deficiency syndrome).

AIDS Acquired immune deficiency syndrome: a sexually transmitted disease resulting from a virus that attacks the immune system; can also be transmitted through contaminated blood transfusions or from an infected pregnant woman to her fetus.

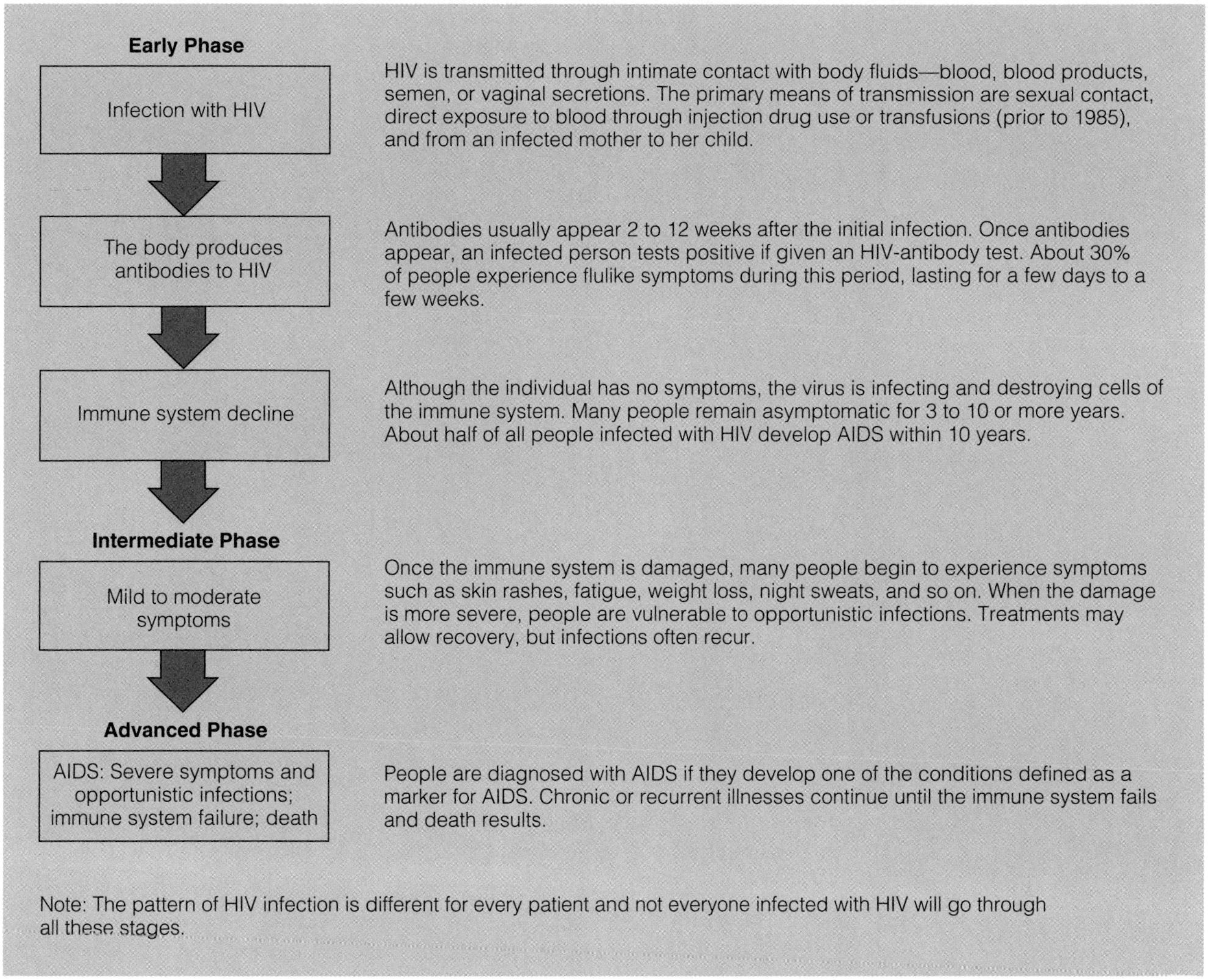

Early Phase
Infection with HIV
HIV is transmitted through intimate contact with body fluids—blood, blood products, semen, or vaginal secretions. The primary means of transmission are sexual contact, direct exposure to blood through injection drug use or transfusions (prior to 1985), and from an infected mother to her child.
The body produces antibodies to HIV
Antibodies usually appear 2 to 12 weeks after the initial infection. Once antibodies appear, an infected person tests positive if given an HIV-antibody test. About 30% of people experience flulike symptoms during this period, lasting for a few days to a few weeks.
Immune system decline
Although the individual has no symptoms, the virus is infecting and destroying cells of the immune system. Many people remain asymptomatic for 3 to 10 or more years. About half of all people infected with HIV develop AIDS within 10 years.
Intermediate Phase
Mild to moderate symptoms
Once the immune system is damaged, many people begin to experience symptoms such as skin rashes, fatigue, weight loss, night sweats, and so on. When the damage is more severe, people are vulnerable to opportunistic infections. Treatments may allow recovery, but infections often recur.
Advanced Phase
AIDS: Severe symptoms and opportunistic infections; immune system failure; death
People are diagnosed with AIDS if they develop one of the conditions defined as a marker for AIDS. Chronic or recurrent illnesses continue until the immune system fails and death results.
Note: The pattern of HIV infection is different for every patient and not everyone infected with HIV will go through all these stages.

FIGURE 6.4
The Progressive Course of HIV Infection. *Sources:* Adapted from R. Schwartz. (1992). *AIDS medical guide.* San Francisco: San Francisco AIDS Foundation and Centers for Disease Control. (1991). *HIV infection and AIDS: Are you at risk?*

will not marry until their mid 20s, resulting in a period of about 10 years during which the risk of acquiring an STD is relatively high (Alan Guttmacher Institute, 2004). The following precautions can significantly reduce the risk of exposure not only to HIV infection, but to other STDs as well.

1. *Use of a latex condom.* Latex condoms have been found to be highly effective in protecting against infection since the HIV virus, as well as pathogens causing other STDs, cannot pass through the wall of the condom. Nonlatex condoms, however, do not provide the same protection. Additionally, latex condoms are effective only when they are consistently and correctly used (CDC, 2004c).
2. *Avoid the exchange of body fluids.* Although HIV is most highly concentrated in blood and semen, it has also been found in other body fluids, for example, vaginal and pre-ejaculatory secretions. For infection to occur, the virus must enter the body through a break in the skin, usually a cut, tear, or sore, and from there reach the bloodstream. Vaginal intercourse, anal intercourse, and

For some adolescents, protecting themselves against HIV infection is not enough; many work for increased awareness and community support of effective intervention programs.

oral-genital sex all carry risk of exposure. Even intercourse without ejaculation carries some risk of infection because the virus can be present in pre-ejaculatory and vaginal secretions.

3. *Be discriminating.* Certain practices and lifestyles increase the risk of infection. Individuals who have had numerous sexual partners and those who have used drugs intravenously are more likely to have been infected. However, this doesn't mean that someone with a more conservative lifestyle may *not* be infected.

Those who maintain a monogamous sexual relationship with someone are at lowest risk of infection from the HIV virus or any other STD. However, only a blood test can establish whether an individual is free of the virus, since those who are not infected will not have antibodies in their blood. Simply asking someone, even a loving partner, does not guarantee a completely truthful answer.

How likely are adolescents to follow or even understand any of these precautions? A randomly sampled survey of 1,773 adolescents age 16 through 19 found that adolescents who have the most sexual partners (more than ten a year) are least likely to use a condom, yet these adolescents have the highest risk of infection (Hingson, Strunin, Berlin, & Heeren, 1990). Even understanding the risk of infection, however, is no guarantee that adolescents will avoid engaging in risky practices. Nearly a third of adolescents receiving treatment for substance abuse in one study indicated that even though they knew and were worried about the risk of HIV infection, they were likely to go ahead and have unprotected sex (Langer, Tubman, & Duncan, 1998).

All the factors that make it difficult for adolescents to use contraceptives in general apply equally to the precautions they must take against HIV infection. Lack of information among adolescents complicates the problem, even though most adolescents are taught about HIV in school. More than misinformation is at work with adolescents. Almost surely adolescents' cognitive immaturity sets limits on their ability to understand the seriousness of the disease or the precautions that need to be taken. So, too, does adolescents' sense that they are invulnerable.

Chlamydia **Chlamydia,** a bacterial infection, is one of the most common STDs among adolescents. It is referred to as a "silent" disease since most of those who are infected experience no symptoms and don't even know they are infected; this is especially true for females. Adolescents who do have symptoms may notice a discharge, or a burning feeling when urinating, or itching around the urethral opening.

If untreated in females, the infection can spread through the reproductive tract, causing pelvic inflammatory disease (PID). Inflammation of the tiny tubules of the tract leaves scar tissue and may result in infertility and increased risk of ectopic pregnancy (a pregnancy occurring outside the uterus). Even when chlamydia has spread, many females may remain symptom-free; others can experience abdominal or back pain, nausea, or fever, all symptoms of PID. Immediate treatment should be sought.

Because so many adolescents have no symptoms, and because the consequences of infection are potentially serious, those who are sexually active should be screened for the disease at least once a year, at least until age 25 (CDC, 2005c).

Gonorrhea Another common STD is **gonorrhea,** also a bacterial infection. Gonorrhea can be transmitted by many forms of sexual contact: intercourse, oral-genital sex, or even kissing. Anyone who is sexually active may be at risk for contracting this disease; however, those with the highest rates of infection are adolescents and young adults. Rates of infection are also higher among African Americans (CDC, 2005c). Many adolescents experience either no symptoms or very mild ones. In males, the most noticeable symptom is a watery discharge from the penis, and some may experience swollen testicles; females also may notice a discharge, and both may experience pain when urinating. Left untreated, the disease spreads through the reproductive system, leaving scar tissue that can block the tubules and cause infertility. Untreated cases of gonorrhea can also affect the joints, causing a type of arthritis, and the heart, affecting the valves.

Early adolescent females run a special risk because the immature cervix is especially vulnerable to infection by the bacterium causing gonorrhea. Early coital activity also appears to delay cervical development, as does the use of oral contraceptives. Thus early adolescent females who are using oral contraceptives are at greater risk of infection than those using other forms of birth control. Because the long-term consequences of infection for females include a higher risk of cervical cancer, those who have ever had gonorrhea should routinely get Pap tests (CDC, 2005c).

Both chlamydia and gonorrhea can be treated with antibiotics. Adolescents who discover they are infected should notify any sexual partner who is likely to have been infected or to have passed on the infection. They should also refrain from sexual contact until a checkup indicates that the infection is gone. Both steps are important in preventing the spread of these diseases.

Genital Warts **Genital warts** are caused by infection with the human papilloma virus (HPV). This STD is widespread among adolescents (CDC, 2005c). The warts are painless, dry, light-colored outgrowths on the genitals or rectum. HPV actually includes over 100 different strains of the virus, some of which are "high risk" in that they have a known relationship to cervical dancer (CDC, 2005c). Adolescent girls with HPV should have Pap tests at least once a year.

chlamydia A sexually transmitted disease, caused by a bacterium, that can affect the reproductive tract, possibly leading to pelvic inflammatory disease.

gonorrhea A sexually transmitted disease caused by a bacterium.

genital warts A sexually transmitted disease caused by the human papilloma virus.

Genital Herpes **Genital herpes,** another common STD, is caused by the herpes simplex virus. There are two types of herpes simplex virus, HSV-1 and HSV-2; genital herpes is most frequently caused by HSV-2. As with other STDs, most adolescents experience few or no symptoms. When symptoms occur, they appear as blisters, usually on the genitals or the rectum. The blisters break after several days, leaving small wet sores that dry up in a week or two. Even though the blisters eventually disappear, the virus remains dormant in the body, and outbreaks can recur at any time. Again, most adolescents may not develop sores or, if they do, these may be mild enough not to be noticed. Although infection can occur through exposure to the sores, a sexual partner with no apparent sores can still transmit the virus. No cure presently exists for herpes, although medication can control outbreaks and may help to reduce the risk of transmission to others (CDC, 2005c).

Syphilis Sexual contact is the most common way **syphilis** is transmitted, although this bacterial infection can also be transmitted through contaminated blood transfusions or passed from an infected pregnant woman to her fetus. Symptoms typically occur from one to three weeks, or even longer, following infection. In the *primary stage* of the disease, a small, usually painless sore, or possibly several, appears on the genitals, rectum, or lips, or in the mouth. These typically heal within several weeks, and unsuspecting adolescents may believe that whatever they had is gone.

If not treated, syphilis progresses to a *secondary stage* marked by symptoms including a rash, fever, headache, and sore throat. These symptoms are easily mistaken for flu, especially as they can come and go for several months. Once these symptoms disappear, the disease enters a *latent stage.* Although adolescents in the latent stage experience no symptoms, the disease continues its course within their bodies. Many who have syphilis remain in this stage and experience no further complications. Others can move into a *tertiary stage* in which damage to the heart, eyes, brain, and spinal cord can occur (CDC, 2005c).

Despite its highly destructive nature, syphilis is easily treated with antibiotics in the primary and secondary stages, and even in later stages is responsive to larger doses over longer periods.

Pubic Lice Frequently known as crabs, **pubic lice** are pests that are usually transmitted sexually but can also be transmitted via bedsheets or clothing. Lice live in the pubic hair, causing severe itching as they draw the blood on which they live. Bedding used by an infested person can remain infected for up to a week. A prescription shampoo (marketed as Kwell) kills the lice, but because eggs that drop onto bedding and clothing can survive for five or six days, clean sheets and clothing are important to prevent a recurrence.

Risks and Precautions The risk of acquiring an STD is often greater for an adolescent than it is for an adult. Adolescents are likely to have more sexual partners than are adults, and they are more likely to have unprotected sex. Additionally, adolescent girls are more susceptible biologically to certain STDs, such as chlamydia and gonorrhea, than are adults (CDC, 2005c).

Knowing the Risks One need not be promiscuous to run the risk of contracting an STD. Even adolescents who practice serial monogamy, limiting themselves to one sexual partner before becoming active with another, expose themselves to the sexual history of their partner—as well as the sexual history of each of their partner's partners, and so on. Like standing in a hall of mirrors, the regression is infinite. Because many diseases have

genital herpes A sexually transmitted disease characterized by recurring outbreaks of itching or burning blisters; caused by a virus that remains dormant in the body.

syphilis A sexually transmitted disease, caused by a bacterium, that can also be transmitted through blood transfusions or from a pregnant woman to her fetus; progresses over several stages.

pubic lice Pests that are usually transmitted sexually; sometimes called crabs.

TABLE 6.3 The Use of Condoms Among Sexually Active Adolescents Decreases with Age, as the Use of Birth Control Pills Increases

Grade	Condom Use During Last Sexual Intercourse	Birth control pill Use Before Last Sexual Intercourse
9	69.0%	8.7%
10	69.0%	12.7%
11	60.8%	19.6%
12	57.4%	22.6%
Total	**63.0%**	**17.0%**

Source: Centers for Disease Control (2004). Youth risk behavior surveillance—United States, 2003. *Morbidity and Mortality Weekly Reports, 53,* No. SS-2.

no symptoms following the initial infection, adolescents who are infected, even if well intentioned, can pass the disease unknowingly to future partners.

Information concerning how these and other STDs are transmitted, whether there are symptoms and what they may be, and what treatments are available for different STDs is available at the Web site for the Centers for Disease Control and Prevention and can be accessed at http://www.cdc.gov/std.

Taking Precautions Symptoms such as a discharge or the appearance of sores should receive immediate medical attention. Most STDs can be treated with an antibiotic if caught before complications develop. Honesty is important, and partners need to be informed so that they can get treatment, too. Routine medical checkups are especially advisable for sexually active females because they are not as likely as males to experience symptoms, and the health complications that arise when infections are left untreated can be considerable.

Adolescents who are sexually active should always use a latex condom. A condom is important even when another form of contraception is used, because it offers protection against STDs as well as pregnancy. Females and males can both assume responsibility here. But as simple as this precaution is, it still is not likely to be consistently followed. Many females feel they can engage in sex only if they are swept away in a moment of passion; pulling a condom out of a purse implies advance planning. Males may fear that stopping to put on a condom can break the mood. Using a condom, however, is the most effective precaution against STDs for sexually active teenagers. Even so, less than two-thirds of high school students indicated they had used one the last time they had sex (Centers for Disease Control and Prevention, 2004). Additionally, older adolescents are less likely to use a condom than are younger adolescents, perhaps because they are more likely to be in a steady relationship in which the adolescent girl assumes responsibility for contraception, primarily through the use of birth control pills (see Table 6.3). Effective as these may be in preventing pregnancy, they do not offer protection against STDs.

Difficulties to Confront Precautions that are relatively simple for an adult may be next to impossible for an adolescent. Many adolescents feel invulnerable to infection and may not take precautions. Others may be too frightened or embarrassed if symptoms do appear to get medical attention. Early adolescents frequently avoid seeking treatment, assuming the problem will go away by itself. Many are afraid their parents will discover their secret problem, and many more don't know how to get treatment or where to go, especially if they do not want their parents to find out. In addition, most don't have enough money to pay for a doctor's visit or for prescription medication. Transportation can be a problem, too, especially for those living in rural areas.

Shame, fear, or anger may prevent adolescents from informing a partner about their own symptoms. And partners who are told may likewise do nothing for the same reasons. Even adolescents who seek treatment will not necessarily comply with the directions they have been given, especially early adolescents who do not yet have an adult's concern about the future. They may fail to take medication as prescribed or discontinue use when symptoms first disappear; similarly, they may fail to abstain from sex or to return for a checkup to make sure they are clear of the infection. Clearly, for preventive programs to be effective, these programs need to address more than the misinformation and lack of information that currently exists among adolescents.

Teenage Pregnancies

Other countries such as England, Sweden, France, and Canada have rates of adolescent sexuality similar to those in the United States, yet they have lower pregnancy, birth, and abortion rates (CDC, 2005d). (See Figure 6.5.) Why might this be? Lisa Lottes, (2002), at the University of Maryland, summarizes a number of key differences.

Attitudes toward adolescent sexuality. These countries have identified teenage *pregnancy,* not teenage sexuality, as a social problem. In other words, it is believed that adults, not adolescents, are the ones to have children. Being adult is defined very much as it is in this country: in terms of completing one's education, getting a job, living on one's own, and being in a stable relationship (Darroch et al., 2001). Rather than denying adolescent sexuality, these countries offer programs that teach teenagers to assume responsibility for their sexuality, and more teenagers in these countries practice contraception effectively. As a consequence, there are far fewer instances of teenage pregnancies, parenting, or abortion, and far fewer adolescents become sexually active at a young age (Darroch et al., 2001).

Sex within committed relationships. Sexuality itself tends to be viewed differently in these countries, primarily as a healthy expression of one's feelings for another and not as a hedonistic source of pleasurable feelings for oneself. These feelings, in turn, are viewed as developing within the context of a committed and loving relationship. This view of sexuality is explicitly taught in schools (Lottes, 2002). In Sweden, for instance, courses in sex education include the following ethical principles:

> Nobody is entitled to regard and treat another human being simply as a means of selfish gratification.
>
> Sexuality forming part of a personal relationship has more to offer than casual sex and is therefore worth aspiring to (Swedish National Board of Education, 1986, as cited in Lottes, 2002).

Open discussion of sexual responsibility. These countries differ as well in viewing sexuality as a normal aspect of development. As such, there is no expectation that adolescents will remain abstinent until marriage, and educational programs do not attempt to pressure them to commit to this as a goal. Instead, adolescents learn from adults in their society that when they become sexually active, they are to do so responsibly, protecting themselves and their partner from unintended pregnancies and STDs. Thus, although these countries are more accepting of adolescent sexual activity, they are less accepting of adolescent pregnancy (Alan Guttmacher Institute, 2004).

Research with U.S. adolescents generally finds that those who can talk more freely with parents and sex educators are more likely to delay sexual initiation and be more

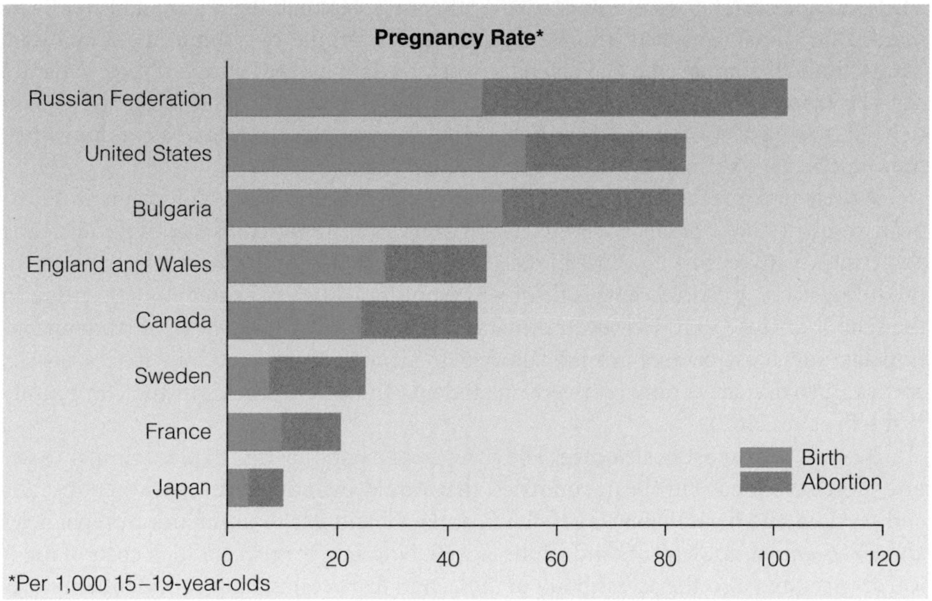

FIGURE 6.5
Teenage Rates of Pregnancy, Births, and Abortions. *U.S. teenagers have higher rates of pregnancy, birth, and abortion than teenagers in most other developed countries. Source:* Alan Guttmacher Institute. (2004). *Sex education: Needs, programs and policies.* Retrieved from http://www.guttmacher.org/presentations/sex_ed.pdf.

responsible when they become sexually active (Kirby, 2002; Meschke, Bartholomae, & Zentall, 2005; Rose, Koo, Bhaskar, Anderson, White, & Jenkins, 2005).

Accurate information. European countries provide adolescents with comprehensive sex education through schools and community health centers in which accurate information about effective methods of contraception is made available to them. In contrast, a majority of school districts in the United States promote abstinence over contraception (51%). An additional third (35%) of all school districts require teachers to present abstinence as the only option for unmarried teens, and either allow no discussion of contraception or allow a discussion of contraceptives only in terms of their failings. Only 14% of school districts in the U.S. teach abstinence as just one of several effective options (Alan Guttmacher Institute, 2004).

Although it is true that abstinence is the surest way to avoid STDs and unintended pregnancies, it is not accurate to teach that contraceptives are ineffective. Latex condoms, when consistently and correctly used, are highly effective. Additionally, the use of oral contraceptive pills or Depo-Provera, an injectable contraceptive lasting three months, virtually eliminates unintended pregnancies. Adolescents themselves must be added into the equation when presenting abstinence as a "sure way" to avoid these problems since many do not define abstinence the way federally funded government programs do. Many adolescents believe that one can be abstinent and still engage in oral sex, anal intercourse, or vaginal intercourse without full penetration (Bruckner & Bearman, 2005). Yet STDs can be transmitted through all of these activities, and pregnancy is possible with the latter since live sperm can be present in the lubricating fluid that appears at the opening of the penis.

Abstinence education also teaches that "sexual activity outside of the context of marriage is likely to have harmful psychological and physical effects" (Section 510(b) Title V, 1996). This assertion, again, is not accurate. Nicole Else-Quest, Janet Shibley Hyde, and John Delamater (2005), at the University of Wisconsin, compared the responses of nearly 3,500 individuals who either had premarital sex or abstained until marriage, and found no differences with respect to later sexual functioning, feelings of guilt about sex, or their overall physical health. Although those who abstained had fewer

STDs, other research has not found such a difference. Hannah Bruckner and Peter Bearman (2005), analyzing data from a large national sample of adolescents and young adults, found that those who had taken pledges to remain virgins until marriage had rates of STDs comparable to non-pledgers. Most likely this is because 88% of pledgers go on to have sex before marriage and are not as likely as non-pledgers to use a condom when they first become sexually active (Bruckner & Bearman, 2005).

Access to contraceptives and reproductive health services. Adolescents in European countries have better access to health services offering contraceptive counseling and contraceptives than do those in the United States. One of the most effective ways of providing access to adolescents is through school-based health centers located either in the school or close to it. However, centers such as these serve only 2% of students nationally, and most centers are not allowed to provide contraceptive services on-site and can provide these only by referring students to other agencies in the community (Santelli et al., 2003).

Access to low cost health care. The absence of a national health plan, similar to the one present in most European countries, that would include contraceptive counseling and services, and be available to all, significantly contributes to unintended pregnancies and STDs among adolescents and adults as well. Not only the present high costs of medical services, but also the accessibility of these, and fears concerning confidentiality prevent adolescents from seeking the reproductive counseling and services they need (Averett, Rees, & Argys, 2002).

Better access to clinics, more information, and promotion of contraceptive use in the media are important steps to be taken here at home. Yet teenage pregnancies are likely to remain a problem, especially among poor and low-income adolescents for whom the temptation to compromise future options—which may appear doubtful at best—for the immediate gains offered by sex can be hard to resist.

Teenage Parenting Pregnancy and child rearing present challenges for women of any age, but especially for adolescents. Adolescents are less likely to receive regular prenatal care, and they experience more medical complications during pregnancy. Children born to teenage mothers also experience more complications. The risk of premature birth, low birth weight, which is a general measure of infant health risk, and infant mortality is substantially higher. They also are at somewhat greater risk for neurological and behavioral problems (Klein, 2005). However, programs that target teenage mothers for prenatal care can be successful in reducing many of these risks (Barnet, Duggan, & Devoe, 2003; Grady & Bloom, 2004). Similarly, interventions following the birth of a child can reduce risks to the infant (Quinlivan, Box, & Evans, 2003).

As might be expected, teenage mothers are less ready for parenting and experience more stress in this role than women who are older. Family support is important, leading to better parenting (Bunting & McAuley, 2004a; Gee & Rhodes, 2003; Nadeem, Whaley, & Anthony, 2006). Support from the child's father or, in some cases, another male partner is also related to more effective parenting (Bunting & McAuley, 2004a; Krishnakumar & Black, 2003). Despite initial difficulties, most adolescent mothers successfully cope (Oxford, Gilchrist, Lohr, Gillmore, Morrison, & Spieker, 2005).

What do we know of teenage fathers? Country to stereotypes casting them as exploitive or uncaring, most remain psychologically involved with the mother through the pregnancy and for some time following the child's birth. Longitudinal research following teenage-mother families finds that most fathers become less involved over time, with only about a third remaining involved (Gee & Rhodes, 2003; Kalil, Ziol-Guest, & Coley, 2005). Most teenage fathers have less education and lower incomes than do those who postpone parenting, and many find it difficult to provide support for the mother and infant (Bunting & McAuley, 2004b).

Currently, there are few programs to help teenage fathers learn to be better fathers. Those in existence stress the importance of finishing high school and getting a job. Many provide job training as well as parenting classes, enabling teenage fathers to provide financial as well as emotional support.

Adolescents and Abortion Thirty-three percent of adolescents who become pregnant obtain an abortion, with younger adolescents being more likely to do so than older ones. Overall, the percentage of adolescents having an abortion has decreased over the last several decades, in large measure due to fewer teens becoming pregnant (Alan Guttmacher Institute, 2004).

A number of factors affect the decision to abort or to carry a baby to term. Important among these are family background variables and the influence of peers. Teenagers from middle-class homes are more likely to abort an unintended pregnancy than those living at the poverty level. White adolescents are also more likely to terminate a pregnancy than are African American or Hispanic adolescents (Strauss, Herndon, Chang, Parker, Bowens, & Berg, 2005). Personal variables such as religious beliefs and parents' attitudes also play a role in a teenage girl's decision to carry a baby to term or to abort. Girls who have strong religious beliefs are less likely to abort a pregnancy, as are those whose parents disapprove of abortion. Peers influence an adolescent's decision, too. Girls with friends who are single teenage parents are more likely to carry the pregnancy to term; those whose friends view abortion positively are more likely to terminate a pregnancy (Benson, 2004; Ellison, Echevarria & Smith, 2005).

Complicating decisions about abortion for many teenagers is the fact that many do not realize at first that they are pregnant. Young adolescents especially are likely to have irregular menstrual cycles, making it difficult to determine when they have missed a period. Still others may attempt to deny they are pregnant until it is no longer possible to hide from the truth. The difficulties adolescents experience in finding out where to go for health services and arranging transportation compound these problems. As a result, teenagers are somewhat less likely to have an abortion in early pregnancy than are women who are young adults (Strauss et al., 2005).

The issues surrounding abortion are magnified as the result of delay, because the timing of an abortion has both health and moral consequences. Early abortions carry less risk to the adolescent. Similarly, issues concerning the taking of a life are less clear-cut before the fetus becomes viable, or even earlier in the pregnancy, before the appearance of signs, such as brain-wave activity, that are used at the other end of the age spectrum in decisions to terminate life support.

Sex Education: What Adolescents Need to Know

Although many adolescents can talk with their parents about sex, most do not, leaving friends and school-based programs as the most common sources of information about sexuality. School-based programs can differ widely, both in what they cover and in how effective they are (DiClemente, 1998; Kirby, 2002). Programs are considered to be effective if they delay the onset of sexual activity among adolescents who are not yet sexually active, and lead to responsible sexual practices among those who already are. (See Figure 6.6.)

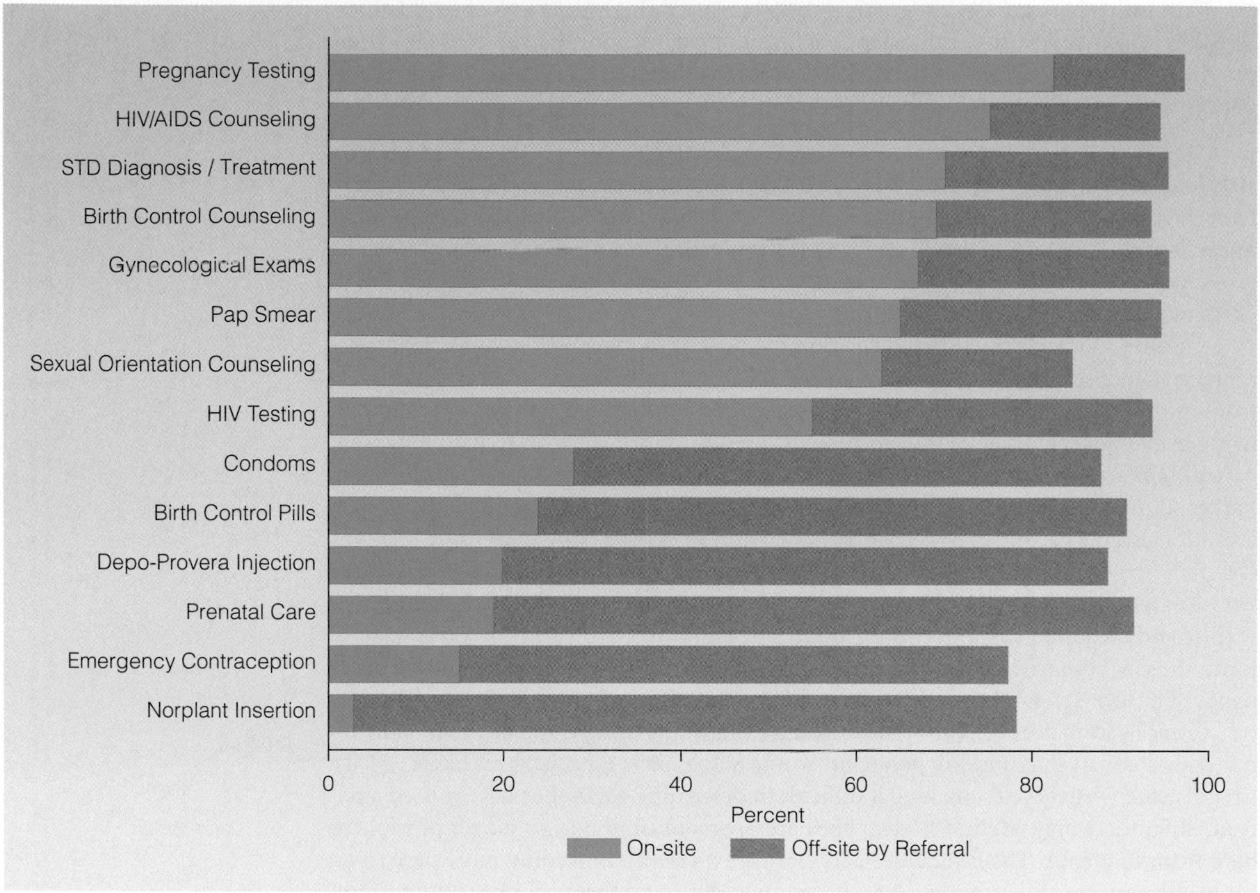

FIGURE 6.6
Reproductive Health Services Provided in School-Based Health Centers Serving Adolescents, 1998–1999. *One of the most effective ways of providing reproductive health services is through school-based centers; however, most of these are not allowed to provide contraception services on site and must refer students to other agencies in the community.* *Source:* J. S. Santelli, R. J. Nystrom, C. Brindis, L. Juszczak, J. D. Klein, N. Bearss, D. W. Kaplan, M. Hudson, and J. Schlitt. (2003). Reproductive health in school-based health centers: Findings from the 1998–99 census of school-based health centers. *Journal of Adolescent Health, 32,* 443–451.

The Effectiveness of School Programs

An important factor contributing to the success of a program almost surely is the degree to which it allows adolescents to actually practice the skills they will need either to abstain or to successfully use contraception. Richard Barth, Joyce Fetro, Nancy Leland, and Kevan Volkan (1992) incorporated homework assignments such as talking with parents, pricing birth control methods, and role playing sexual encounters in a comprehensive sex education program including information on abstinence and contraceptive information. Adolescents completing the program were no less likely to engage in sexual intercourse; however, they were more likely to use contraception.

A number of abstinence programs have reported some success in changing adolescents' attitudes. After taking such programs, students were found to view abstinence more favorably and to have less-favorable views of teenage sex (Maynard et al., 2005). However, these differences, although statistically significant, were actually quite slight. When attitudes regarding abstinence were assessed on a scale from 0 to 3, for instance, the means for students in the abstinence program versus those in the control program were 1.86 and 1.78, respectively! Additionally, it is not clear how effective such programs are in changing adolescents' behavior. To date, there is no evidence that abstinence-only programs are effective in delaying the initiation of sexual activity or reducing the risk of teenage pregnancies and STDs (Alan Guttmacher Institute, 2004). Just how successful these programs will be is likely to depend, at least in part, on how congruent they are with adolescents' own values and religious beliefs and with the values and beliefs held by their families and present in their communities.

Sex education programs that provide adolescents with information about the use of condoms and other forms of contraception, in addition to teaching abstinence, have been found to actually delay the initiation of sexual activity and to result in safer sex practices once adolescents become sexually active.

Programs that teach adolescents assertiveness and decision-making skills offer an attractive supplement to information-based programs. These programs approach sexual decision making by building interpersonal and problem-solving skills. Sex *is* problematic for most adolescents, and it is highly interpersonal. Many adolescents feel pressured into sexual encounters that they would otherwise avoid or postpone if they felt comfortable stating how they felt. These pressures affect adolescents of both sexes. Adolescent males, as well as females, frequently feel pressured into making sexual overtures simply because they assume it's expected of them or that everybody else is having sex. One of the ways in which sex education programs can be effective is to increase adolescents' self-efficacy. The data we have on assertiveness and decision-making programs suggest that they are effective. Problem-solving and communication skills improve, as does knowledge of reproduction; contraception use also improves among adolescents enrolled in such programs (Kirby, et al., 2004).

Comprehensive and Service Learning Programs

Research evaluating school programs generally finds two types of programs to be effective. These are **comprehensive sex education programs** and **service learning programs** (Kirby, 2002). Comprehensive sex education programs teach abstinence as a preferred approach and educate students concerning effective methods of contraception. Despite concerns among supporters of abstinence education that teaching contraception in the same program may be giving students mixed messages, research clearly shows that educating students about contraception does not lead adolescents to engage in sex at an earlier age or have more frequent sexual encounters. To the contrary, such programs are likely to reduce overall sexual activity among adolescents, and to reduce unprotected sex (Kirby, 2002; Kirby et al., 2004; Office of the Surgeon General, 2001).

Comprehensive sex education programs that incorporate service learning into the program are even more effective than those utilizing only classroom instruction. Service learning programs require students to work as volunteers in the community, doing things such as tutoring in classrooms or helping out in nursing homes. Students are also required to engage in structured reflection on their volunteer work, such as meeting for group discussions or journaling. A meta-review of research on various types of interventions suggests programs incorporating service learning are the most effective type of sex education program offered in school (Kirby, 2002).

comprehensive sex education programs Sex education programs that teach abstinence as a preferred approach and educate students concerning effective methods of contraception.

service learning programs Comprehensive education programs that include a community service component, requiring students to do volunteer work.

Low-income seventh- and eighth-graders attending public schools in New York City who participated in service learning along with their classroom instruction in health

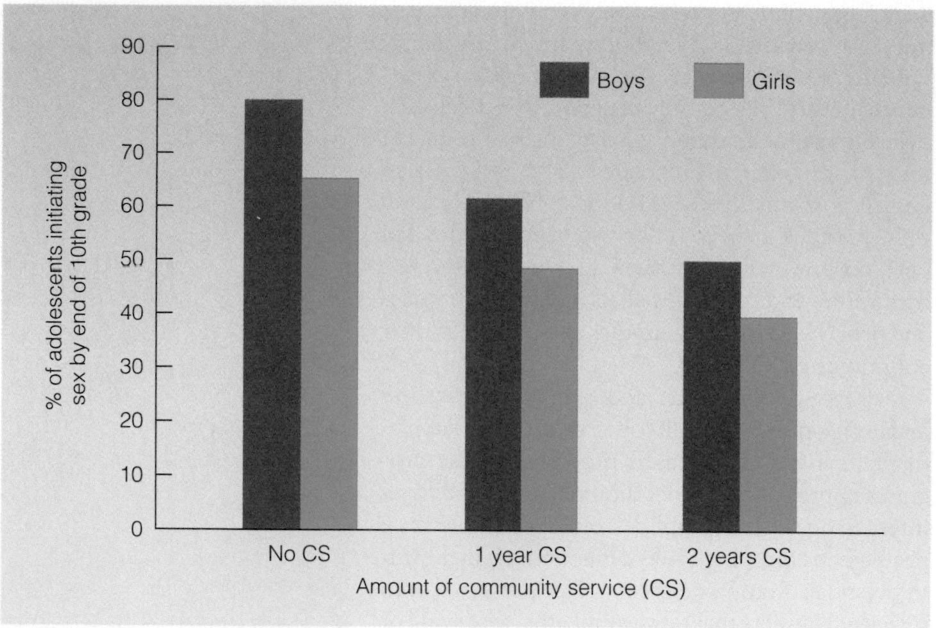

FIGURE 6.7 Reductions in Sexual Activity Among Adolescents in a Service Learning Program. *Percentage of adolescents initiating sex by the end of the tenth grade after completing a sex education program with no community service, one year of community service, or two years of community service.* Source: L. O'Donnell, A. Stueve, C. O'Donnell, R. Duran, A. San Doval, R. F. Wilson, et al. (2002). Long-term reductions in sexual initiation and sexual activity among urban middle schoolers in the Reach for Health service learning program. *Journal of Adolescent Health, 31,* 93–100.

education were found to be significantly less likely to engage in sexual activity than those who received only the classroom instruction (O'Donnell et al., 1999; O'Donnell et al., 2002). This research was notable in several respects, each of which makes the findings especially significant. Students were assigned at random (by classes) to either of the two conditions, making it unlikely that the findings could be attributed to any preexisting differences. Students were resurveyed, or followed up, two years later to determine the long-term effectiveness of the intervention. Finally, students in the participating schools were from low-income homes, placing them at even greater risk for early sexual activity.

As can be seen in Figure 6.7, the longer adolescents had participated in the health program that involved them in community service, the more likely they were to delay sexual activity. Additionally, adolescents who already were sexually active were less likely to have engaged in sex during the previous month. The findings of this research are of particular significance because they represent relatively large reductions in sexual activity, and also in long-term effects—the data shown in Figure 6.7 were collected two years *after* adolescents had completed the program (O'Donnell et al., 2002).

How might volunteering for others help adolescents make healthier choices for themselves? Definite answers can't be given. However, it's likely that the caring relationships these adolescents developed through their experiences contributed to their sense of competence and of self-worth.

An after-school program titled the **Children's Aid Society Carrera-Model Program,** or CAS-Carrera, also has been found to be highly effective in preventing teen pregnancy (Philliber, Kaye, & Herrling, 2001). Participants are recruited for the program when they are 13 to 15 and are encouraged to remain in it throughout high school. The approach of the program is holistic, providing not only sex education but also help with such things as schoolwork, finding part-time jobs, and getting into college. In all of this, the aim is to establish close, familylike relationships with the youth. Research evaluating the effectiveness of the program is methodologically sound. Three aspects of the research methodology lend special credence to the findings: Adolescents were randomly assigned to either the experimental program or a regular after-school program offered in their community; the effectiveness of the program was based on long-term assessments; and participants were drawn from high-risk, low-income populations.

Children's Aid Society Carrera-Model Program (CAS-Carrera) An after-school program that provides sex education as well as help with schoolwork, finding part-time jobs, and getting into college.

The CAS-Carrera after-school program has proved to be extremely effective in reducing teen pregnancy. For instance, girls enrolled in the program have been more than 50% less likely to become pregnant than those in the control group. Girls are also significantly more likely to delay sex and to use condoms or another effective contraceptive when they become sexually active (Kirby, 2002; Philliber et al., 2001).

Abstinence-Only Programs

Abstinence-only programs differ from comprehensive sex education programs by teaching that the only effective way for adolescents to avoid pregnancy and the risk of STD is to abstain from sex. Contraception is discussed only in terms of its failure to protect against pregnancy or disease rather than its effectiveness. Yet the chances of becoming pregnant within one year for a sexually active adolescent who does not use contraceptives are 90% (Alan Guttmacher Institute, 1999; Kirby, 2002). Additionally, abstinence programs that pressure teenagers to pledge virginity and fail to educate them about contraception may actually be harmful since those who subsequently become sexually active are less likely to use contraception initially, placing them at greater risk of pregnancy and STDs (Bruckner & Bearman, 2005).

Federal funding of abstinence-only programs has increased substantially despite the absence of research demonstrating the effectiveness of such programs in getting adolescents to postpone sex and in the face of research showing other programs to be more effective in reducing high-risk behavior (Kirby, 2002; Starkman & Rajani, 2002). The 1996 Welfare Reform Act, for instance, provides federal funds solely for abstinence-only programs. Since states receiving federal funds are required to supply matching funds, state support for comprehensive sex education programs has been decreased. Other recent legislation has provided additional federal funds for abstinence-only programs, resulting in an increase in funding for abstinence-only education by almost 3000% since 1996 (Starkman & Rajani, 2002).

A national survey found that 93% of adults support comprehensive sex education in the schools, indicating they want adolescents to be given information on contraception as well as abstinence (Haffner & Wagoner, 1999). Over 90% of teachers also favor teaching adolescents about contraception, although fully 25% of them indicate they are prevented from including this information in the programs they teach (Starkman & Rajani, 2002).

abstinence-only programs Sex education programs that teach that abstinence is the only way to avoid pregnancy and the risk of sexually transmitted diseases.

Summary

Sexual Identity

- Constructing a sexual identity introduces questions of what it means to be masculine or feminine. Adult sex roles, in the form of gender stereotypes, provide cultural answers. *Gender stereotypes* are the cultural expectations concerning which behaviors are appropriate for each sex. These stereotypes play an important role in self-definition as adolescents integrate questions posed by their sexuality into their developing sense of themselves.
- Sexuality embraces general aspects of one's sense of self, such as expressions of one's masculinity or femininity, the social roles one has within a family, and how one is seen in society. In constructing a sexual identity, adolescents are integrating sexuality into their sense of self.
- *Sexual scripts* are sets of guidelines concerning expected patterns of behavior in a sexual situation. Scripts inform adolescents not only of what they should do and feel, but also of what the person they are with is likely to do and feel. These scripts reflect masculine and feminine gender stereotypes.

Making Sexual Decisions

- Adolescents must revise their self-concepts to include new sexual feelings and behaviors. This process is problematic for those who experience conflict in leaving their childhood behind them. Adolescents who do not consciously think about the consequences of becoming sexually active may engage in sex without planning to and may do so irresponsibly.
- Attitudes surrounding sexuality are not likely to be openly discussed by adolescents and their parents. Adolescents who talk with their parents, however, tend to become sexually active later and to engage in sex more responsibly.
- Adolescents move through stages of sexual activity as they grow older. Most start with kissing, progress to petting, and then engage in intercourse and oral-genital sex. Boys begin their sexual experiences earlier than girls and have more positive feelings about their first intercourse than girls do. Although the number of adolescents who have had sexual intercourse increases with age, the percentage of adolescents who are sexually active has decreased over the past 15 years.
- A number of protective factors delay the initiation of sexual activity. Biologically based factors are late maturation, being female, and being intelligent. Psychological factors include strong religious beliefs and involvement in school. Social factors include parental monitoring, family religious beliefs, not dating steadily, and not using alcohol or drugs.
- The *sexual response cycle* consists of four phases: excitement, plateau, orgasm, and resolution. Similarities in the sexual response for each gender exist for all phases. Two processes, vasocongestion and myotonia, underlie the changes that occur in each phase.
- Adolescents have numerous misconceptions about sexual functioning. Many are not aware that the size of the male's penis is not important in sexual functioning or that females have the same capacity for sexual pleasure as males. Adolescents frequently do not know that individuals of either sex experience discomfort if orgasm does not follow the plateau phase. Adolescents as well as adults fail to distinguish cultural taboos from physical reasons for not engaging in intercourse during menstruation.

Sexual Orientation

- Adolescents who are homosexual are, for some extended period of their lives, more attracted sexually to individuals of their own sex than to those of the opposite sex. Gay, lesbian, and bisexual adolescents often go through a period of sexual questioning prior to puberty.
- Research comparing co-incidence of homosexuality among identical and fraternal twins and adoptive siblings suggests a genetic component to sexual orientation.

Sexual Health: Risks and Responsibilities

- Most adolescents do not systematically use contraceptives because they lack adequate information. Many also do not practice responsible sex because they are unable to accept their own sexuality. Many more engage in unprotected sex due to their cognitive and emotional immaturity.
- Approximately 9 million adolescents and young adults become infected with a *sexually transmitted disease (STD)* each year.
- Many STDs do not have well-defined symptoms and, if not treated promptly, can have serious health consequences.
- Sexually active adolescents have difficulty realizing that they run a high risk of contracting STDs, and many do not take precautions to prevent these diseases or get treatment when symptoms appear.
- *Human immunodeficiency virus (HIV)* attacks the immune system. Over a period of years the disease progresses to *AIDS*. There is no known cure for the disease; individuals die when the immune system fails. Prevention of HIV infection includes avoiding exchange of body fluids, using condoms, and being discriminating in sexual relationships.
- *Chlamydia* is one of the most common STDs among adolescents. It can affect the reproductive system and cause pelvic inflammatory disease in females.
- *Gonorrhea* results from a bacterial infection. Many individuals experience no symptoms, but if it is not treated, the disease can cause infertility, joint and heart problems, and cervical cancer.
- *Genital warts* are caused by human papilloma virus and can lead to cervical cancer.
- *Genital herpes* is caused by the herpes virus and can remain dormant in the body; no cure presently exists.
- *Syphilis* is a bacterial infection that progresses through three stages. If not treated, it can result in serious medical complications.
- *Pubic lice*, which can cause severe itching, are easily killed by medicated shampoo.

- Although the rate of teenage sexuality in some European countries and Canada is similar to that in the United States, the rate of teenage pregnancy is lower because those countries have identified adolescent pregnancy, not adolescent sexuality, as a social problem to be addressed by public policy. These countries also differ in their emphasis on the importance of a committed relationship, of open discussions of sexual responsibility, and providing accurate information about and access to contraceptives and reproductive services.
- Pregnancy and child rearing present challenges for women of any age, but especially for adolescents. Adolescents are less likely to receive regular prenatal care, and they experience more medical complications during pregnancy. This is especially true for younger adolescents.
- Children born to teenage mothers are more likely to experience complications such as prematurity, low birth weight, and neurological and behavioral problems. However, programs that target teenage mothers for prenatal care can be successful in reducing many of these risks.
- Most teenage fathers remain psychologically involved with the mother through the pregnancy and for some time following the child's birth. Many have less education and lower income than those who postpone parenting and find it difficult to provide support for the mother and infant.
- Approximately 30% of teenage pregnancies end in abortion. Decisions to abort or carry the pregnancy to term are related to socioeconomic status, race, and personal as well as parents' and friends' attitudes.

Sex Education: What Adolescents Need to Know

- School-based programs differ widely in what they cover and how effective they are. Effective programs delay the onset of sexual activity among adolescents who are not yet sexually active and lead to safer sexual practices among those who already are.
- School programs may be *comprehensive sex education programs, service learning programs, or abstinence-only programs.* The *Children's Aid Society Carrera-Model Program* is a comprehensive after-school program that has been found to be highly effective in preventing teenage pregnancy.
- Although federal funding for abstinence-only programs has increased dramatically, these programs have not been found to be as effective as comprehensive sex education programs in delaying sexual activity.

Key Terms

gender stereotypes
androgynous
sexual scripts
self-stimulation
vasocongestion
myotonia
sexual orientation
heterosexual
homosexual
bisexual
sexually transmitted disease (STD)
discharge diseases
genital ulcer diseases
HIV
AIDS
chlamydia
gonorrhea
genital warts
genital herpes
syphilis
pubic lice
comprehensive sex education programs
service learning programs
Children's Aid Society Carrera-Model Program
abstinence-only programs

CHAPTER OUTLINE

CHAPTER 7

Adolescents in the Family

Changing Roles and Relationships

CHAPTER OBJECTIVES

- To consider changing roles within the family and the implications these have for day-to-day interactions between adolescents and parents
- To examine characteristic styles of parenting and consider the potential ways these influence adolescent development
- To explore family factors in development, looking at the ways in which strengths of parents enable adolescents to become stronger, and at distinguishing features of families differing in ethnicity
- To consider the potential effects of divorce on adolescents and their parents, and changes in relationships within single-parent and blended families

Neena's mother knocked on the half-closed door and stepped in when she heard the soft "Com'n," careful to avoid the pile of clothes in her path and whatever lay beneath them. Surveying the room, she couldn't help but comment on the mess.

"Look, Mom, I know where everything is, honest," her daughter answered. What Neena really wanted to say was, "It's my room and I can keep it any way I like!" But she knew what her mom would say to that. Her mother, not to be dissuaded by pragmatic appeals to reason, pointed out that she had told Neena several times already to straighten up her room.

Looking at her mother's back, rigid with irritation as she left, Neena sighed inwardly. It seemed lately that the two of them couldn't agree on much of anything, even things Neena thought were rightfully hers to decide, such as what clothes she wore, what music she listened to, or the friends she had. Her little brother Joey, still in the fourth grade, got along great with Mom. Being an adolescent wasn't all that easy.

Chapter Overview

Does adolescence necessarily bring turmoil to families? Is conflict unavoidable? What does current research tell us? The first section of this chapter evaluates recent findings on adolescent–parent relationships; we then take a closer look at parenting styles.

In Chapter 5, we discussed the process of individuation, whereby adolescents distinguish themselves from their parents and clarify who they are as individuals.

Continuing that discussion, we consider in this chapter some additional factors related to the family that play a role in adolescent development, such as parents' ego development, levels of self-awareness and support, ethnicity, and the presence of siblings.

The structure of families has changed dramatically in the past several generations. Increasing numbers of adolescents experience divorce, live with a single parent, or have a stepparent join the family unit. Family relationships can be problematic even at their best; some require more coping skills than others. We will discuss the changing conditions of family life, examining in particular the effects of divorce and the challenge for dual-earner families, and the ways adolescents and their families cope with them.

Changing Relationships with Parents

Are mood swings and unpredictable behavior necessarily part of adolescence? Must relationships with parents be disrupted and distant? Or can adolescents continue to maintain positive and satisfying relationships with parents while developing as individuals?

Turmoil and Change

Psychoanalytic theorists maintain that adolescents must separate from their parents in order to develop as their own persons and that this separation is inevitably conflictual. Sigmund Freud believed that dramatic increases in hormones during adolescence reactivate earlier incestuous feelings and that adolescents' only defense against these repressed Oedipal impulses is to distance themselves from their parents (see Chapter 2). This distancing creates the emotional separation necessary for further psychological growth. Anna Freud (1969) felt so convinced that emotional turbulence was a natural consequence of adolescence that she considered it *ab*normal for adolescents to maintain their emotional balance. (See the Research Focus "Sampling" for a study of the emotional experiences of early adolescents.)

The psychoanalytic view received considerable support from clinical psychologists working with troubled adolescents and also from those working with adult patients who, during the course of therapy, referred to problems they experienced as adolescents. But how safe is it to generalize clinical data to a normal population?

Calm and Continuity

Research with normal adolescents gives us a different picture of adolescents' relationships with their parents. These studies point to continuing, close relationships (Larson, Richards, Moneta, Holmbeck, & Duckett, 1996; van Wel, Linssen, & Abma, 2000). Even though conflicts become more frequent in adolescence, they do not prevent adolescents and parents from remaining close. In fact, the most autonomous adolescents are also most likely to say that their parents remain an important influence in their lives and that they continue to seek their advice (Fuligni & Eccles, 1993).

In other research, most adolescents described themselves as happy and self-confident and did not feel that there were any major problems between themselves and their parents. They reported feeling close to their parents and believed their parents were proud of them. (Offer, Ostrov, & Howard, 1981). This positive regard for parents has changed little with time and characterizes adolescents today, just as it did a generation ago (van Wel, Linssen, & Abma, 2000).

RESEARCH FOCUS

Sampling: How Emotional Are Adolescents?

Do words such as *impulsive, moody,* and *intense* capture something special about adolescence as a time of life? Are adolescents more emotional than their parents? Parents and educators have come to expect emotional turmoil with the onset of adolescence, but what evidence is there that the daily emotional states of adolescents are different from those of children or adults?

Reed Larson and Maryse Richards (1994) tackled this difficult question in an unusual way. They asked fifth- to ninth-graders and their parents to wear beepers for one week. Each time they were beeped, they filled out a one-page form indicating their emotional state. You might ask, "How can we be sure these investigators caught all the emotional states adolescents and parents experience? If they beep each person only a few times each day, they will catch only a few emotional states and perhaps reach the wrong conclusions. How do we know the emotions they recorded are representative of all adolescents' and parents' feelings?"

"Beeping" adolescents and their parents is a way of *sampling* emotional states. Larson and Richards could not ask individuals to record each and every feeling every moment of the day. Instead, they sampled from this larger population of emotions. The *population* is the entire group of people or events, or, in this case, emotional states, in which one is interested. The *sample* is a subgroup drawn from this population. If the sample is drawn at random from the population, we can be reasonably certain that it will be *representative* of that population. This is because in random sampling, each person or event has an equal chance of being chosen. How might this procedure apply to emotional states?

Larson and Richards first limited the population to waking states between the hours of 7:30 A.M. and 9:30 P.M. They organized these into four 2-hour blocks of time from 7:30 A.M. to 3:30 P.M. and four 90-minute blocks between 3:30 P.M. and 9:30 P.M. (The more frequent sampling during later afternoon and evening hours provided better sampling of family time together.) They randomly beeped each adolescent once within each of the eight blocks of time. This procedure ensures that each of the 120, or 90, minutes within each block has an equal chance of being sampled. To imagine how this might work, think of a hat containing 120, or 90, slips of paper, one for each minute in the block of time. The time written on the slip you pull would be the time the adolescent is beeped.

What did the samples show? Are adolescents more emotional than their parents? These investigators found that adolescents are in fact more emotional than their parents. When sampled, adolescents reported extremes of highs and lows much more frequently. Adolescents reported feeling "very happy," for instance, five times more often than their parents did. Similarly, they reported more intense lows than their parents, their beepers catching them as "very unhappy" three times more often than their parents. Larson and Richards conclude that the inner life of adolescents differs significantly from that of their parents, adolescents "ascending higher peaks of rapture and tumbling into deeper crevasses of dejection" (p. 83). Differences such as these make it easier to understand how misunderstandings can so easily arise between adolescents and parents. As Larson and Richards put it, "They are on different wavelengths."

Source: Adapted from R. Larson & M. H. Richards. (1994). *Divergent realities.* New York: Basic Books.

Change and Continuity

Can both of these characterizations of parent–adolescent relationships be true? Are some changes so significant that to deny them is to deny what adolescence is all about, and do most adolescents remain close to their parents while going through these changes? Research answers yes. Relationships with parents remain important in adolescence, *and* these relationships are renegotiated (Baumrind, 1991a).

Reed Larson, Maryse Richards, Giovanni Moneta, Grayson Holmbeck, and Elena Duckett (1996) had adolescents wear pagers for a week, asking them to record what they were doing and how they were feeling when beeped at random intervals during the day and evening. Larson and his associates noted both dramatic changes as well as important continuities in the ways adolescents interacted with their families. Perhaps the most striking change was the amount of time adolescents spent with their families. In contrast to fifth-graders, who spent about 35% of their waking hours with their families, twelfth-graders spent only 14%. However, these investigators caution that the adolescents in this study were all from European American backgrounds, and this trend may not be characteristic of adolescents from other backgrounds. In fact, when adolescents from different countries are compared, they can be found to differ considerably in the amount of time they spend with their families (Claes, 1998).

Emotional Experiences Adolescents' emotional experiences when they are with their families also change with age—the positive feelings of fifth- and sixth-graders becoming negative by junior high, especially during conversations, only improving again toward the end of high school (Larson et al., 1996). Similarly, early adolescents report being less affectionate to their parents and less helpful than they had been as children or again as late adolescents (Eberly & Montemayor, 1999). As one might expect, how likely positive interactions are to remain in adolescence is a function of the trust and respect adolescents have had up to this point with their parents (Ducharme, Doyle, & Markiewicz, 2002).

Time Spent with Family Withdrawal from family life does not appear to be due simply to dynamics within the family. Decreases in family time were unrelated to increases in conflict, or to decreases in such things as family cohesion and closeness to parents, or even to the feelings adolescents had when they were with their families. Instead, other factors appeared to be responsible. The need to be alone was important for early adolescents, who spent much of their time alone in their rooms, even though they were not necessarily happier there than with the family. Once in high school, however, outside attractions, such as after-school activities and going out with friends, became more important. Having access to a car, a job, and permission to stay out later all related to decreases in family time.

The continuities? Adolescents and parents actually found ways to make up for the lost time together. Even though older adolescents participated less in family activities involving little or no communication, such as watching television, they spent just as much time as they had before in conversations with family members. In fact, twelfth-graders spent the same amount of time alone with each of their parents as fifth-graders did, suggesting that adolescents and parents actively attempt to maintain closeness. Maintaining closeness seems to be particularly important when this is with the parent of the same sex, and especially for girls, even in late adolescence (Buist, Dekovic, Meeus, & van Aken, 2002; Geuzaine, Debry, & Liesens, 2000).

Stability in Relationships Thus, despite changes in the pattern of adolescents' interactions with their families, there is considerable stability in what they want in their relationships. Furthermore, some of the most frequently expressed relationship concerns of adolescents remain true for young adults as well. Robert Waldinger and his associates (2002), at Harvard Medical School, interviewed individuals, first as adolescents (14–16 years) and then as young adults (25 years) concerning their relationships with parents, siblings, and friends. What individuals most frequently said they wanted, whether as adolescents or young adults, was to be close to others. They also expressed a desire for separateness, which, in adolescents, took the form of needing to be distant. Young adults, for whom closeness presumably was not as problematic with respect to maintaining a separate sense of themselves, were able to see others as more understanding than

Are disagreements between adolescents and their parents an inevitable part of growing up? Research says they are, but also that most adolescents and parents stay close despite conflict.

were adolescents, who were likely to see others as opposing them in one way or another and experience them as bad.

Increasing Mutuality Larson and his associates (1996) found that adolescents' interactions with parents became more mutual with age, older adolescents reporting, for example, that they could give direction to conversations as frequently as their parents. In short, even though the time adolescents spend with the family decreases with age, this time involves more direct, one-on-one interaction, greater mutuality, and, once the negativity of early adolescence is past, is experienced in even more positive ways than previously.

Relationships between younger children and parents, however, are relatively one-sided in their distribution of power and responsibility, even in families where parents involve the children in family decisions. Several conditions cause adolescents to press for change in this arena of family life.

Conditions Pressing for Change One condition is adolescents' new awareness of themselves. The ability to think abstractly contributes to this awareness (see Chapter 4). Teenagers can imagine how someone else might see their interactions with others. They can get a feeling for how their actions and intentions are seen not only by the person they are with, but by others in general. This ability sharpens their sense of themselves as separate from others. They begin to appreciate the many ways they are different, even though they do the same things, share the same tastes, and have similar preferences as their friends.

The very same ability that allows teenagers to see themselves through the eyes of others also allows them to see themselves with their parents in a new light. They see how their relationships with their parents differ from the ones they have with their friends (Eccles, Buchanan, Midgley, Fuligni, & Flanagan, 1991). The latter are egalitarian and mutual; friends arrive at decisions jointly. James Youniss (1980) suggests that adolescents

A messy room and a busy phone may be signs of a young adolescent moving toward autonomy rather than of innate sloppiness or irresponsibility.

become conscious that they live in two very different social worlds: one with friends, in which they participate on an equal footing, share in decision making, and negotiate differences; the other with parents, in which they have little power, make few decisions, and conform to parental expectations. Adolescents face the need to achieve a single sense of themselves that holds across *all* the social situations they enter; as a first step, they press for fuller participation in relationships within the family so that these more closely mirror those they have with their friends. Even so, adolescents are able to take into consideration the expertise that certain types of decisions require, such as curriculum decisions at school, and endorse a more authority-based approach to decisions in those contexts (Helwig & Kim, 1999).

Negotiating Family Conflicts

Perhaps at no time are their changing roles more evident than when parents and adolescents discuss their perceptions of family conflicts. Judith Smetana and Rusti Berent (1993), at the University of Rochester, asked seventh-, ninth-, and eleventh-grade adolescents and their mothers to respond to vignettes describing typical conflicts that occur at home, such as those involving household chores, keeping one's room clean, or personal appearance. Each conflict was presented both from the parent's perspective and the adolescent's, by giving justifications each might use in appealing to the other. (Table 7.1 shows the different perspectives.)

Perhaps not surprisingly, given their responsibility for maintaining family ways, mothers considered conventional justifications to be more adequate in resolving conflict than did adolescents. Adolescents, on the other hand, saw this type of reasoning as a source of conflict. This was especially true of mid-adolescent ninth-graders, for whom family conflict is likely to have reached a peak as gains in autonomy are won by questioning parental authority.

Mothers also considered appeals to authority and threats of punishment to be more effective in getting adolescents to comply with their wishes than did adolescents, a dif-

TABLE 7.1 Differences in the Parent's and the Adolescent's Attempts to Resolve Conflict

The examples below are responses to a typical conflict:
Mother wants Anne to wear something else, but Anne doesn't want to.

	Type of Justification	Example
PARENT	Conventional	Reference to behavior standards, arbitrarily arrived at by family members, e.g., "I'd be embarrassed if any of my friends saw you looking like that."
	Pragmatic	Consideration of practical needs or consequences, e.g., "You'll catch a cold."
	Authoritarian	Reference to authority and punishment, e.g., "I'm your parent, and I say you can't dress like that."
ADOLESCENT	Conventional	Reference to standards of behavior shared with peers, e.g., "My friends would think I'm weird."
	Pragmatic	Consideration of practical needs or consequences, e.g., "I'm comfortable in these clothes."
	Personal	Portraying the issue as one of maintaining personal jurisdiction in an area, e.g., "The way I dress is an expression of me and my personality."

Source: J. G. Smetana & R. Berent. (1993). Adolescents' and mothers' evaluations of justifications for disputes. *Journal of Adolescent Research, 8,* 252–273.

ference that increased with the adolescents' age. Adolescents, on the other hand, appealed to practical considerations, perhaps because such arguments are less likely to be challenged by parents. Judith Smetana has found that, although adolescents may believe their position can be justified by appeals to personal jurisdiction ("It's my room and I can keep it as I like"), they will use pragmatic reasons ("It doesn't matter if it's messy; I can find whatever I need") when arguing with a parent. Parents are not as likely as adolescents to view the behaviors in question as rightfully within the adolescents' purview (Smetana, Braeges, & Yau, 1991). Adolescent appeals to social convention in resolving family conflict are likely to generate more conflict than they settle, usually because the conventions referred to are those of their peers, perhaps already a sore point for many parents.

Domains of Authority The complexity derives from the fact that different domains of authority exist within the family. Only in some domains is there a shift in parental authority. In others, parents continue to be perceived as having a legitimate say, both by themselves and by adolescents. Judith Smetana and Pamela Asquith (1994) have found that conflict arises over which issues lie within which domains: Adolescents and parents, in other words, don't always see things eye to eye.

Smetana and Asquith (1994) asked sixth- through tenth-graders and their parents to indicate the legitimacy of parental authority concerning various hypothetical issues, shown in Table 7.2. Almost all adolescents and parents agreed that parents have the authority, even the obligation, to set rules concerning *moral issues,* in which a person's actions can affect the well-being of another. Similarly, most adolescents and parents considered *conventional issues* to be the legitimate province of parental decision making, although parents saw themselves as having more authority here than did adolescents.

TABLE 7.2 Issues Concerning Parental Authority

MORAL ISSUES	**FRIENDSHIP ISSUES**
Taking money from parents without permission	Going to a movie alone with a boyfriend or girlfriend
Hitting brothers and sisters	Seeing a friend whom parents do not like
Lying to parents	Having a party when parents are away
Breaking promises to parents	Inviting a boyfriend or girlfriend over when parents are away
CONVENTIONAL ISSUES	**PERSONAL ISSUES**
Not doing assigned chores	Watching cartoons on TV
Calling parents by their first names	Choosing own clothes
Eating with elbows on table	Spending allowance money on games
Cursing	Listening to heavy metal music
MULTIFACETED ISSUES	**PRUDENTIAL ISSUES**
A boy wearing an earring	Smoking cigarettes
A girl wearing heavy makeup	Eating junk food
Not cleaning one's room	Drinking alcohol
Not putting clothes away	Driving with friends who are new drivers

Source: J. G. Smetana & P. Asquith. (1994). Adolescents' and parents' conceptions of parental authority and personal autonomy. *Child Development, 65,* 1147–1162.

These perceptions, by the way, did not change with age, suggesting that parents are seen as rightfully the ones to establish and maintain the social as well as the moral order and adolescents as the ones seeking greater autonomy within this.

There was similar agreement between adolescents and parents about *personal issues,* both believing that adolescents should have the say concerning these. When disagreements arose, they were most likely to concern *friendship issues, multifaceted issues* (involving both personal and conventional concerns), and *prudential issues,* which involved adolescents' well-being or possible harm. Adolescents, for instance, believed their friendships to be matters of personal choice, whereas parents considered these to more legitimately fall within their domain, feeling obligated to step in when they disapproved of certain friends. Similarly, even though parents and adolescents agreed that parents had the authority and were even obligated to set down rules concerning prudential issues, disagreements arose over which specific issues fell within this domain, with parents seeing themselves as having more authority to govern adolescents' behavior than adolescents did. The large differences in parents' and adolescents' perceptions of these issues indicate where the struggle for autonomy is fought—not on moral or even conventional grounds, but on what constitutes the personal prerogatives of adolescents.

In general, for both adolescents and parents, the realm of issues considered to be properly the domain of adolescents increased with age, with more items being considered personal as adolescents got older, thus expanding the sphere of adolescent autonomy (Bosma et al., 1996; Smetana, 2000; Smetana & Asquith, 1994). Smetana and Asquith point out, however, that this sphere remains narrower for parents than for adolescents, the former continuing to see themselves as legitimately setting rules governing adolescents' bodies, physical appearance, and choice of friends.

Although parents are more likely to see older adolescents as having a right to privacy in personal matters than younger adolescents, they balance this right with what they see as adolescents' entitlement to proper care, even when this might entail a violation of

When parents and adolescents agree on domains of parental authority, adolescents are able to better communicate with their parents about issues that come up in their lives because they don't feel that their autonomy is threatened.

privacy. As one mother said, when asked whether her tenth-grade daughter had the right to have a private diary, "Yes, she should have that privacy, but it is also the parents' right to know what's going on in a child's life. She has the right to privacy but [some] secrets in there, mom has the right to know" (Ruck, Peterson-Badali, & Day, 2002, p. 392).

Cultural Contexts To what extent are adolescents' appeals to personal prerogative in resolving conflicts with their parents specific to our own highly individualistic culture? Can we generalize findings such as these to other cultures, such as Chinese or Hispanic cultures, which are more collectivistic and place a greater value on interpersonal obligations and harmonious relationships? Jenny Yau and Judith Smetana (1996) interviewed seventh-, ninth-, and twelfth-graders from Hong Kong, asking them to describe the types of conflicts they experienced with their parents and listening to the reasons they gave about why they and their parents felt as they did. They found that these Chinese adolescents talked about conflicts with their parents in very much the same way as North American adolescents, supporting their positions with appeals to personal jurisdiction. This finding suggests that bids for autonomy take place in similar ways despite other differences between these cultures. It should be noted, however, that although these adolescents talked about conflicts with their parents in much the same way as did North American adolescents, they reported far less conflict—just under two disagreements per month—as compared with nearly four and a half for North American adolescents. Even so, when conflicts occurred, they involved the same kinds of ordinary, everyday issues as those between parents and adolescents in North America: what they could do in their free time, chores, homework, friends, and the like.

Developmental Context Samuel Vuchinich, Joseph Angelelli, and Antone Gatherum (1996), at Oregon State University, followed 63 families in a two-year longitudinal study of family problem solving, making their first observations when the children were in the fourth grade. These investigators found that the struggle for autonomy begins in preadolescence, even before the ages observed by Smetana and Asquith. Families were videotaped as they discussed an issue that had been a problem in the family during the past month. As preadolescents got older, from 9½ to 11½ years, problem solving became less effective, with family members finding it more difficult to reach a solution or even take the other's perspective. With age, preadolescents became more negative. Fathers, especially, appear to react negatively to this, mothers being more the "peacemaker." Consistent with the findings of Smetana and Asquith, difficulties in communicating were not so much a matter of *what* was being discussed, mundane issues generating as much difficulty as significant ones, as was the age of the child.

Emotional Climate of Families

In general, however, it is not children but their parents who are responsible for changes in the emotional climate within the family. Reed Larson and David Almeida (1999) point out that this climate changes as emotions are transmitted from one person to another through daily interactions. In fact, one can actually follow the path of an emotion as it moves through a family. A parent, for instance, might come home after work tense and irritable, yell at a child, who then fights with a sibling.

Research on such **emotional transmission** reveals a number of characteristic patterns. First, negative emotions are more easily transmitted than others. It is easier to pass on anger, anxiety, or depression, for instance, than joy or peacefulness, or as Larson and Almeida put it, "Negative emotions may trump positive ones." In general, however, families with greater psychological resources are less likely to experience the transmission of negative emotions than those with fewer resources.

Second, some members of the family are more likely than others to transmit emotions. The flow of emotions from one person to another is often unidirectional rather than reciprocal. Specifically, the emotions of men are more likely to affect their wives and children than vice versa. It is unclear whether this pattern reflects individuals' relative power within the family or, with respect to women, a greater sensitivity to the emotional states of others as well as a greater responsiveness to these. Emotions are also more likely to flow from parents to children than vice versa (Larson & Gilman, 1999). However, when they do, these are more likely to be the father's emotions than the mother's. This is not to say that mothers do not pass on their emotional states at the moment to their children; they are just less likely to do so.

Many of the negative emotions fathers pass on can be traced to stresses they experience at work (Repetti, 1994). Mothers seem to be better at keeping such stresses from spilling over into the emotional life of the family; they may even become more responsive to their children when stressed at work. Marital tensions, on the other hand, are likely to be transmitted by mothers and fathers alike (Almeida, Wethington, & Chandler, 1999).

Finally, it is common for an emotion that is passed from one person to assume a different form in the next person. Thus, the transmission of anger on the part of a parent may result not in anger in an adolescent, but in anxiety. In this way, the effects of "secondhand" emotions on children can include physiological symptoms and patterns of behavior as well as emotional states. Thus, adolescents can experience nervous stomachs or headaches, form "defensive alliances" within the family, or simply experience anxiety.

The way adolescents react to the emotions of others depends in large measure on the way in which they interpret these emotions. Adolescents actively construct, or make sense of, the emotional states of others just as they do other aspects of their world. Simply because an emotion is expressed does not mean that it will be experienced in the same

emotional transmission The transmission of emotions from one person to another within a family.

TABLE 7.3 Parenting Style and Social Competence

Parenting Style	Characteristics	Adolescent Social Behavior
Authoritative	Demanding, encourages independence; responsive, warm, and nurturing; disciplines with explanation; maintains open dialogue	Social competence and responsibility
Authoritarian	Demanding; consistent in enforcing standards; restrictive, controlling	Ineffective social interaction; inactive
Indulgent	Responsive, warm, and nurturant; undemanding; uses punishment inconsistently and infrequently; exercises little control	Social competence, well adjusted; peer oriented; misconduct
Neglectful	Unresponsive, little warmth or nurturance; undemanding, sets few limits, and provides little supervision	Poor orientation to work and school; behavior problems

Source: Adapted from D. Baumrind. (1991). The influence of parenting style on adolescent competence and substance use. *Journal of Early Adolescence, 11,* 56–95.

way by different individuals. Geraldine Downey, Valerie Purdie, and Rebecca Schaffer-Neitz (1999) compared anger transmission from mother to child in mothers who experienced chronic pain and those who did not. They found that anger in the latter was likely to result in consequent anger in the child, but not in families in which the mother experienced chronic pain. This appeared due in part to the way in which the children of these mothers interpreted their anger. These children simply did not interpret the anger the same way as they would were it not for the pain, that is, as a statement about themselves.

Parents and Adolescents

Parents themselves initiate many of the changes that occur in relating to their adolescent children. They expect adolescents to be more assertive and independent than when they were younger. They think teenagers should get around more on their own, whether going to the library or to a part-time job, and have ideas of their own, from what to wear to how to study for a test. Even so, many parents react with ambivalence to adolescents' bids for independence. For some adults, their sense of themselves is strongly tied to their parenting roles, and to include adolescents in more family decisions, they must redefine those roles.

Styles of Parenting

Diana Baumrind (1967, 1971, 1991a), at the University of California, Berkeley, has distinguished four *styles of parenting* in terms of differences in parental responsiveness and demandingness (shown in Table 7.3). *Responsiveness* refers to how sensitive, supportive, and involved parents are, and *demandingness* to the degree to which parents hold high expectations for their adolescents' behavior and supervise their activities, monitoring them in terms of where they are going and who they are with.

authoritative parenting Parenting that stresses self-reliance and independence; parents are consistent, maintain an open dialogue, and give reasons when disciplining.

Authoritative parents are both responsive and demanding. They are warm and nurturant, listen openly to their children's ideas and plans, and yet are willing to assert their own authority and do so by consistently enforcing their standards. These parents stress self-reliance and independence, maintain an open dialogue with their children,

Authoritative parents, in contrast to authoritarian and permissive ones, try to balance tradition with innovation, cooperation with autonomy, and tolerance with firmness. The children of such parents tend to be socially competent and responsible.

and give reasons when they discipline. **Authoritarian parents** are equally demanding but less responsive than authoritative ones. They, too, are consistent in enforcing their standards but, perhaps because they value obedience over self-reliance, are less open and responsive to the other's perspective. Instead, they expect their children to do as they are told and not to question them. Rather than backing up their discipline with reasons, they are more likely to use force. **Indulgent parents** are responsive to their children, as are authoritative parents; however, they are not demanding. These parents are warm and nurturant, making few demands for responsible behavior, punishing infrequently and inconsistently, and exercising little control or power over their children's decisions. A fourth group of parents, **neglectful parents,** are neither responsive nor demanding. These parents provide little nurturance or supervision, are cold and uninvolved, and set few limits, letting their children do whatever they choose.

Both authoritarian and authoritative parents provide strong models, but in different ways. Authoritarian parents attempt to control their children, authoritative ones to guide them. In line with this difference, the latter place greater value on autonomy and self-discipline and the former on obedience and respect for authority. Both types of parents define limits and set standards. Authoritative parents, however, are more willing to listen to reasons and arguments, tending to draw the line around issues rather than set absolute standards.

authoritarian parenting Parenting that stresses obedience, respect for authority, and traditional values.

indulgent parenting A style of parenting characterized by warmth and nurturance (high responsiveness) but little supervision (low demandingness).

neglectful parenting A style of parenting characterized by little warmth or nurturance (low responsiveness) and little supervision (low demandingness).

Authoritative parenting carries clear advantages, which persist into adolescence. Adolescents raised in authoritative families are more socially competent, more self-reliant, do better academically, and have a better work ethic. They also show fewer signs of psychological distress, such as anxiety or depression, and fewer problem behaviors, such as truancy or the use of drugs (Kurdek & Fine, 1994; Slicker, 1998; Steinberg, 2001). Laurence Steinberg, Susie Lamborn, Nancy Darling, Nina Mounts, and Sanford Dornbusch (1994) found these advantages to remain relatively stable during the high school years. Similarly, the profile of adjustment for adolescents reared by authoritarian parents changed little during high school. These adolescents continued to do well in school and had few behavior problems but were less self-reliant and had less positive conceptions of themselves.

A different picture emerges over time for adolescents raised by indulgent parents. These adolescents are well adjusted and socially competent and, if anything, even more oriented toward their peers than other adolescents. However, during high school, their interest in school declined, and forms of misconduct, such as truancy, increased. The most serious declines, however, occurred among adolescents reared by neglectful parents. These adolescents showed even poorer orientations over time toward work and school and significantly more problem behaviors, suggesting a downward trajectory of disengagement at school and emerging behavior problems (Steinberg et al., 1994).

Despite the superiority of authoritative parenting, this type of parenting is not simple, nor is it stress-free. In fact, parenting authoritatively seems to be distinguished by the presence of tensions produced by the need to balance opposing forces: tradition with individualistic innovation, cooperation with autonomous behavior, and tolerance with principled firmness.

At times it may seem easiest to simply appeal to authority or threaten punishment, both characteristic of authoritarian parenting. Smetana and Berent (1993) found that, although each of these alternatives has the short-term payoff of being effective in achieving compliance, adolescents and parents alike see them as having the potential for causing conflict, especially with older adolescents.

As a group, children of authoritative parents are more competent and independent, and are less likely to be rebellious, than those of other parents (Baumrind, 1991b). Their parents have stressed self-reliance and have paved the way for independence by involving their children in decision making from early childhood on. Interestingly, the conditions that lead to rebelliousness in adolescence, or childhood, are not necessarily rigorous demands, but arbitrary ones. Parental strictness per se does not appear to be the issue; rather, it is the willingness, or lack thereof, to give adolescents a voice in decision making (Fondacaro, Dunkle, & Pathak, 1998). Andrew Fuligni and Jacquelynne Eccles (1993), at the University of Michigan, found that early adolescents who perceive their parents as unwilling to relax their control or allow them to participate in decisions often turn to friends for support and advice, even when maintaining such relationships involved some personal cost. Parents encounter rebelliousness, it seems, when they fail to leave room for autonomy, do not give reasons for their actions, or are inconsistent in their punishment. Inconsistency can also take the form of different parenting styles from each parent, as when one parent is authoritative and the other permissive. This type of inconsistency is associated with lower self-esteem and lower school achievement in adolescents (Johnson, Shulman, & Collins, 1991).

Parenting styles vary little with the gender of adolescents, but they do change with their age. In a study of nearly 8,000 high school students, Sanford Dornbusch and his colleagues (1987) found that authoritarian parenting decreases as adolescents get older; similarly, permissiveness increases. Interestingly, authoritative parenting does not vary with adolescent age. The reason, Dornbusch and his associates suggest, is that authoritative parenting reflects an ideological commitment on the part of parents and is not a simple response to what adolescents do. Also, being more democratic than authoritarian parenting, it continues to be appropriate in adolescence.

Styles of Parenting and Ethnicity

Research with European American adolescents clearly links measures of adjustment and school success to parenting styles, with authoritative parenting being the best predictor of adolescent adjustment and authoritarian parenting more frequently being associated

Chinese American parents may appear to be controlling or strict, but they differ from authoritarian parents in that control is bidirectional.

with negative outcomes. Many ethnic minority families prove an exception to this general finding. Yet it has been difficult to determine what might be responsible for the differences. To what extent, for instance, are the cultural differences associated with ethnicity responsible? Or are the differences due to the resources of one's community, resources—such as the quality of schools, libraries, and parks—that also frequently differ with ethnicity?

Susie Lamborn, Sanford Dornbusch, and Laurence Steinberg (1996) assessed adjustment in more than 3,500 African American, Asian American, European American, and Hispanic 14- to 16-year-olds over a two-year period. These investigators drew their samples of adolescents from two types of communities: ethnically mixed communities and predominantly White, somewhat more affluent, communities. They found little to support the possible mediating role of community context. Instead, the advantages of authoritative parenting were equally visible for African American adolescents, whether they came from one type of community or the other, and the disadvantages associated with authoritarian parenting were similar for European American adolescents, irrespective of their community. Authoritarian parenting was unrelated to adolescent adjustment for either Asian American or Hispanic adolescents, for either type of community.

Ruth Chao (1994), at the University of California, Los Angeles, argues that parenting styles cannot be separated in any simple way from their cultural contexts. She points out that Chinese American parenting, often referred to by developmentalists as "authoritarian," "controlling," or "strict," nonetheless is very different from the authoritarian style of parenting identified by Baumrind. "Strictness" and "control" simply do not exist as ways of interacting for most Asian parents. For instance, control, instead of taking the form of a unidirectional exercise of power by parents over the child, in Asian cultures is bidirectional, carrying with it an obligation to nurture and support the child. Thus, parents are as much governed by the child's needs as the child is under the control of the parents. This manner of parenting, by the way, is associated with high levels of academic achievement among Asian American students.

Chao refers to this harmonious parenting relationship as *chiao shun,* or child "training." In practice, this type of parenting takes the form of providing an exceptionally supportive environment for the child. If anything, it comes closer to authoritative parenting, as this is practiced by European American parents, which is also characterized by high degrees of responsiveness and support and high expectations in terms of the child's behavior. Chao, in fact, found that the immigrant Chinese American mothers she studied did not differ from European American mothers in the degree to which they endorsed statements indicative of authoritative parenting. David Crystal and Harold Stevenson (1995) have found as well that adolescents in China do not differ from European American adolescents in their perceptions of the disruptiveness of conflict in the family, suggesting that Chinese parents may be more open to dialogue with adolescents (also a characteristic of Baumrind's authoritative parents) than previously thought.

Parenting is not an activity limited to mothers and fathers; many ethnic minority, as well as majority, families include a grandparent or other relative living in the home. Adolescents who have contact with grandparents, aunts, and uncles, whether under the same roof or close enough to visit, typically benefit from their support. Ronald Taylor (1996), at Temple University, found that adolescents whose families frequently got together with relatives, and who could count on them for advice and support, were more self-reliant and successful in school and had fewer problem behaviors.

Robin Jarrett (1995), at Loyola University, identifies such supportive adult networks as a key element for low-income families, an element that can make a difference in buffering the adolescent from the risks associated with poverty. The excerpt that follows describes such a relationship between an adolescent girl, Ruth, and her oldest sister, who already has two children of her own:

> Ruth's siblings have been an important influence in her life. Her oldest sister, Mary, is twenty-five and an unmarried mother of two. When asked about her relationship with Mary, Ruth says, "We have a good relationship. Not only is she my oldest sister, but she is also my second mother. As a child she was our mother while our real mother was working. She spanked and chastised us just like my mother. Mary and I have a relationship that I wouldn't trade in for anything." (Williams & Kornblum, 1985, p. 24, as cited in Jarrett, 1995)

Finally, parenting is not an activity that is limited to interactions in which the parent is physically present. Parents can monitor their children's behavior during hours when they themselves may not be at home to supervise their activities. **Parental monitoring** refers to parents' awareness of their children's activities, of the friends they spend their time with, and whether other adults are present. For instance, a mother may require her ninth-grade son to call her at work whenever he will be staying after school for an activity, and to tell her whose parent will be driving him home, and when. This only works, of course, if his mother knows the friend and has met the parent. But if she's good at monitoring, she will. She'll also call home at the time he's said he'll be back to check that he is. Parental monitoring contributes significantly to adolescents' well-being. Adolescents whose parents monitor their activities more closely are better adjusted and have fewer problems than those whose parents do not (Frabutt, Walker, & MacKinnon-Lewis, 2002; Galambos & Maggs, 1990; Mounts, 2001; Pettit, Bates, Dodge, & Meece, 1999).

parental monitoring The practice in which parents monitor their children's behavior when they are not physically present to supervise their activities.

The Contexts of Parenting: Genetic and Environmental Contributions

To what extent can the correspondence between parenting styles and the characteristics of adolescents be attributed to parenting per se, and to what extent can this correspondence be attributed to what parents and adolescents have in common to begin with? Families share more than living spaces and meals together. They also share a gene pool. Is reliance on reason and consistency when disciplining, for instance, the *cause* of adolescents' competence and achievement in school? Or might a more complex interplay between parents and adolescents be present, one in which both the parents' and the adolescents' behavior is due to similarities in their genetic environments?

Sandra Scarr (1992, 1993), at the University of Virginia, takes a constructive approach in explaining the interplay of genetic and environmental factors, arguing that adolescents construct their realities from many possible realities that are latent in their environments. The events that make up their daily lives, for instance, can be perceived in quite different ways by different adolescents; consequently, these events will not have the same impact from one adolescent to the next. For instance, Matt McGue, Anu Sharma, and Peter Benson (1996) found that measures of adolescent adjustment among adopted siblings—children who were not biologically related yet were reared in the same home—were quite low, indicating that their shared environment contributed little to their adjustment.

Scarr adds that not only do environments not exist for adolescents apart from being constructed by them, but also the processes adolescents bring to bear in doing so are themselves influenced by genetic factors, making it impossible to separate environmental and genetic contributions to development. An adolescent's genotype, in other words, will predispose that adolescent to take in certain environmental experiences and not others, even though the latter may be equally present. Such experiences simply will not be as salient for an adolescent with that genotype.

Scarr distinguishes three ways in which genotypes structure environments: passive, evocative, and active.

Passive. Because parents are responsible for both the adolescent's genes and the home environment in which the adolescent grows up, the adolescent's genes and environment will be correlated. For instance, parents who enjoy reading will enjoy things such as talking about books and watching educational programs on television. In this way, the parents' own enjoyment of reading, which may be genetically influenced, in turn influences both the adolescent's environment and the adolescent's genotype.

Evocative. In this pattern of influence, genetically influenced behaviors, such as sociability, mood, or intelligence, evoke responses in others that contribute to the adolescent's interpersonal environment and to the adolescent's self-image. It is possible, for instance, that parents' behavior is more similar with siblings who are themselves more similar, such as is the case with identical twins. Genetically influenced traits serve as self-fulfilling prophecies. For instance, children with sunny personalities elicit positive responses in others, which in turn occasion positive moods in the children; fussy children, in contrast, are more likely to experience negative reactions in others, which contribute to their negative moods.

Active. Adolescents select environments that fit their genetically influenced personalities. Thus, the way in which adolescents spend their time, either with others or alone, and what they do will reflect their personalities and talents. Adolescents will sort themselves into different types of environments based

Parents influence their adolescents in multiple ways. Do these adolescents enjoy roller-blading because they have shared other activities like this with their parents? Or do they share similar activities with their parents because they also share a gene pool?

on the interests and abilities resulting from different genotypes. This third way in which genetic predispositions structure adolescents' experiences, sometimes called "niche picking," is increasingly likely to occur with age, as children have more opportunities to choose their own activities.

The notion that adolescents create their own environments runs counter to many parents' beliefs concerning the importance of their influence. Yet research examining similarities among siblings differing in degrees of relatedness supports substantial genetic contributions (Plomin & Daniels, 1987). Scarr (1992) points out that the variability among children from the same family is as great as that among children from different families. This observation suggests that family environments have fewer important effects on children than have been supposed, providing, of course, that the family environments are sufficient to support the development of genetically influenced individual differences. In other words, Scarr believes that differences in environments, given that these are "adequate," are not important determinants of differences among children. Some parents, at least, may find comfort in Scarr's words, namely that "children's outcomes do not depend on whether parents take children to the ball game or to a museum so much as they depend on genetic transmission, on plentiful opportunities, and on having a good enough environment that supports children's development to become themselves" (1992, p. 15).

Genetic Relatedness Support for Scarr's position comes from research examining similarities in the way children perceive their family environments as a function of the degree to which the children are genetically related to one another. When identical twins (100% genetic relatedness), fraternal twins (50% relatedness), full siblings (50% relatedness), half siblings (25% relatedness), and genetically unrelated children (0% relatedness) were asked to evaluate their family environments along a number of dimensions, such as parental warmth and the way parents monitor their children's behavior and deal with conflict, investigators found significant genetic effects for most of their measures. That is, the closer the genetic relatedness among the siblings, the more similar the siblings' perceptions of their environments. In general, over 25% of the variance of environmental measures was attributable to genetic similarities among children (Plomin, Reiss, Hetherington, & Howe, 1994).

Yoon-Mi Hur and Thomas Bouchard (1995) also examined identical and fraternal twins' perceptions of their childhood family environments. However, the twins they studied had been separated early in childhood (mean age at separation was 1 year) and grew up in different homes. Even so, these investigators found that identical twins were much more likely than were fraternal twins to share similar perceptions of parental support. With respect to issues of parental control, however, genetic contributions were minimal. Because the twins grew up with different sets of parents and in different homes, these findings suggest a very real biological basis to differences among individuals in the ways in which they perceive, or construct, their surroundings. They suggest, in other words, that children help to create the environments that they experience.

What's Good Enough? A number of scholars have criticized Scarr's position (Baumrind, 1993; Jackson, 1993). Diana Baumrind (1993) has argued that Scarr has not made clear what makes a family environment "good enough." In the absence of specifying what contributes to a family's environment, Scarr's argument that certain factors (such as parental disciplinary patterns or family income) are not important, loses its force. In fact, Baumrind's point is underscored by Hur and Bouchard's finding that children's perceptions of certain dimensions of the family environment, such as parental support, reflect a biological component, whereas other dimensions, such as parental control, do not. Baumrind also argues that research into genetic and environmental contributions to development is limited by the inadequacies of the instruments currently available for measuring family environment. The research of Baumrind and others on parenting styles clearly underscores parents' contribution to developmental outcomes such as social competence and independence (Baumrind, 1991a; Smetana & Berent, 1993).

In general, parents who are responsive, consistent, willing to listen, and willing to give adolescents a voice in decision making will have healthy relationships with their adolescents. All this may sound good in theory; however, many parents may be at a point in their own lives in which responsiveness, consistency, and a willingness to listen—let alone sharing responsibility—are especially difficult, if not outright problematic. They, too, are facing a crisis—that of middle age.

Whose Identity Crisis? Parents and Middle Age

Middle-aged parents face the downward side of the developmental curves their adolescent children are climbing. Each of the developmental tasks facing adolescents comes up for review again in the middle years. Figure 1.5 (page 15) lists these tasks, along with those of middle age.

Just as puberty marks the beginning of adolescence, physical changes alert parents that they are entering middle age, and many find these changes difficult to accept. Perhaps the first sign of aging for most adults appears when they step on the bathroom scales. Middle age brings an increase in body weight and a change in its distribution. The face becomes thinner, as do legs and arms. But what is lost in the extremities is gained through the middle. Bob Hope once quipped that "middle age is when your age begins to show around your middle." Changes such as these are difficult at any age, but the kicker for most parents is the timing: Most adults begin to experience these changes just when their adolescent children are developing beautiful bodies and fantastic physiques.

How might these and other physical changes affect the willingness of parents to listen to or share responsibility for decision making with adolescents? An everyday example such as buying clothes provides some insights. Although bathing suits are merely swimwear to parents of preteens, to parents of adolescents they can raise issues of sexuality or even competition. Adolescents' arguments that suits of the same style are worn by young children can go unheard, if parents are alarmed by their adolescent's obvious physical maturity or their own feelings of physical decline and undesirability.

Middle-aged parents face another assault on their egos. The functioning of the reproductive organs begins to decline, marking a period of life known as the **climacteric.** Women experience **menopause**, a cessation of menstrual periods, somewhere between ages 48 and 52. As the body decreases its production of estrogens, sexual functioning can be affected (Stevens-Long & Commons, 1992).

The climacteric in men is not as noticeable as in women, though it does affect them as well. Middle-aged men also are likely to experience a change in sexual functioning. Erections and orgasms take longer to achieve. For both sexes, there may be a slight diminishment of the intensity of orgasm (Masters, Johnson, & Kolodny, 1988). Thus, when their children reach sexual maturity, middle-aged parents face a sexual identity crisis—or at least a serious inventory taking. Changes in sexual function can affect parents' sense of themselves as sexually desirable partners. For increasing numbers of middle-aged adults, these changes come at a time when they face the loss of a marriage partner through divorce and the doubts and anxieties raised by dating. Parents may view their adolescents' dates and romantic involvements with more concern—or perhaps vicarious pleasure—than they would if their own sexual functioning and prowess were not as salient a concern to them.

Similarly, just when adolescents begin to think about future careers, many middle-aged parents begin to review their own careers and question whether the jobs they have been pursuing all these years have been worth the effort they have put into them. Many adults may face the realization that they will never advance beyond their present position. This realization can be especially painful if they see opportunities for their children that offer more promise than the jobs they presently have. Listening to plans about the future can be difficult as parents face hard facts about their own present realities.

Each of these areas of change is a source of stress in the lives of parents and adolescents. The fact that the changes experienced by one generation complement so neatly those experienced by the other almost guarantees that relationships will be more stressful.

Families and Adolescent Development

As noted in Chapter 5, the process of individuation occurs within the context of the family and is facilitated by family interactions that promote both individuality and connectedness. Here, we consider some additional factors related to the family that affect adolescent development.

Family Factors in Development

Ego Development of Parents and Adolescents Measures of ego development of parents and adolescents find complex relationships between the level of development in parents and that of their children. **Ego development** refers to increases in the complexity and integration of thought and judgment that occur with age. Stuart Hauser, Emily Borman, Alan Jacobson, Sally Powers, and Gil Noam (1991) found that parents' ego

climacteric Gradual decline in functioning of the reproductive organs in middle age.

menopause A cessation of menstrual periods in middle age.

ego development Increases in the complexity and integration of thought and judgment that occur with age.

development, especially that of mothers, predicted ego development in adolescents, as measured by the coping strategies adolescents used. These investigators suggest that coping styles in parents, just as in adolescents, reflect the level of their ego development. By observing and interacting with their parents, adolescents adopt coping styles that reflect the interactional patterns that characterize their family life.

Supporting these observations, research finds that ego development in adolescents relates to the parents' use of cognitively stimulating behaviors and to their supportiveness. Adolescents with the highest levels of ego development are most likely to come from families with a high degree of noncompetitive sharing of perspectives and support. There is little distortion (inaccurate portrayal of another's view or the task) or avoidance (distracting attention from the problem) and little rejection (trying to close off discussion without exploring differences) (Powers, Hauser, Schwartz, Noam, & Jacobson, 1983).

How might such a family operate when faced with a problem? First, they might not see the problem as having a single solution and are likely to agree to disagree. This approach should not be confused with a dismissal of the problem. Each person thinks carefully about his or her own position and the positions of others. But if they cannot resolve their differences, they are comfortable letting things rest there. They are likely to openly discuss their differences without criticizing each other's remarks. As a result, they aren't defensive with each other. The stress is on clarifying one's position relative to another when differences arise. Members of the family listen a lot to each other, though they are not necessarily swayed from their own ideas. There is also obvious emotional support for each other. Parents are genuinely proud of adolescents for knowing and standing by what they believe (Powers et al., 1983).

We can compare the above family's approach with that of a family in which adolescents are likely to have low ego development. We also see much noncompetitive sharing of perspectives, but there is also high avoidance, distracting attention from the problem. Even though family members may share opinions, they avoid discussing them; they are not able to explore their differences long enough to reach an understanding of each other's position.

Self-Awareness Other investigators have found similar dimensions of family interaction to be important for the development of individuation. David Bell and Linda Bell (1983) emphasize the importance of self-awareness and support. They find that adolescents with high degrees of self-awareness are more accepting of themselves. Accepting oneself means that one can be aware of needs and motives that one might otherwise feel a need to deny or distort, sometimes by attributing them to others. Thus, self-awareness clears the way for more accurate perceptions of others. Self-aware adolescents are also in a better position to appreciate their own complexity and to acknowledge complexity in others. Insight into themselves and others makes it possible for them to validate the other person's experiences. Others, in turn, are more likely to validate theirs. Being able to communicate that you have heard another person, for example, allows that person to relax and listen to you. This process of mutual validation promotes self-awareness in each person by providing accurate feedback to each (Bell & Bell, 1983).

A negative converse to this bright picture exists for other adolescents. The inability to understand one's own complexities makes it likely that one's approach to others will be simplistic. Adolescents who do not understand their own actions will make inaccurate observations about the reactions of others. Motives unrecognizable in themselves will color their perceptions of others. Neither the adolescents themselves nor those with whom they interact are likely to receive validation through their encounters with each other, further perpetuating this negative cycle.

Warm and loving relationships within the family help adolescents individuate and develop self-esteem. Without family members who believe in them and stand by them, teenagers may lose faith in themselves and drop out of school long before graduation day.

Family Climate Bell and Bell believe that supportive—that is, warm and loving—relationships within the family are central to the development of positive self-regard and hence of individuation. It is possible, of course, for families to be supportive and yet not be validating. Such families might be warm and loving, for example, but not comfortable with their differences. Because they are threatening, differences of opinion are avoided. Validating another person merely requires that one be aware of and comfortable with differences between oneself and others, making it possible to listen without the expectations that reflect one's own needs. One can hear what the other is saying more accurately. An accurate reading of another person does not, however, signal agreement or even liking: A family can be validating yet not supportive.

To test their ideas, Bell and Bell observed adolescent girls and their families interact in a "revealed differences" task, designed to reveal differences in the way members of a family answered various questions (for example, "We fight a lot in our family," or "We really help and support one another"). As family members tried to reach agreement on items on which they had disagreed, a research team coded their exchanges for support and acknowledgment of what each person said.

These investigators found, as had Powers and her associates, that the effect of parental ego development on adolescents' ego development is not direct, but is mediated by a family climate characterized by accurate interpersonal perception. Thus, parents' ego development is positively related to an accurate perception of others, which in turn is related to adolescent ego development. It is the family *process,* not a modeling of parental behavior, that promotes ego development in adolescence. The best climate is one in which people accurately read their own and others' actions, in which they are not excessively concerned with others' reactions, and in which there is little covert conflict. Both parental ego development and family comfort with differences facilitate the development of such a climate (Bell & Bell, 1983). However, even with optimal family climates, parents can still wish at times that they had known more about adolescence, as discussed in the In More Depth box.

The findings of studies such as these emphasize the need to consider the family system as a whole rather than focus on individuals. Parents' personalities do not directly affect adolescent development; it is the family system that mediates the effect of parental ego development and parental self-regard. However, individual characteristics of parents can contribute to the family climate, which then affects the parents' behavior and the adolescent's personality (Bell & Bell, 1983).

Families and Ethnicity

Ethnicity is an important factor contributing to the impact of the family on adolescent development. Over recent decades, the number of ethnic families in the United States has increased dramatically, from just over 10% of the population in 1950 to over 40% projected by 2020 (U.S. Census Bureau, 2004).

IN MORE DEPTH
What Parents Wish They Had Known About Adolescence

"They seem to get caught up in fads in junior high. They do certain things . . . to be part of the crowd. I wish I'd known how to handle that. At what point are these fads okay, because it's important to identify with your peer group, and at what point do you say no? If they are really dangerous, then it's easy; but with a lot of them, it's a gray area, and I wish I'd known what to do better."—*Father*

"I wish I had realized that she needed more structure and control. Because she had always been a good student and done her work, I thought I could trust her to manage the school tasks without my checking. But she lost interest in school, and I learned only very gradually that I had to be more of a monitor with her work than I had been in the past."—*Mother*

"I wish I had known more about the mood swings. When the girls became 13, they each got moody for a while, and I stopped taking it personally. I just relaxed. The youngest one said, 'Do I have to go through that? Can't I just skip that?' Sure enough, when she became 13, she was moody too."—*Mother*

"I wish I'd known how to help the boys get along a little better. They have real fights at times, and while they have a lot of fun together and help each other out, I wish I knew how to cut down on the fighting."—*Father*

Source: Adapted from J. Brooks. (1999). *The process of parenting* (5th ed.). Mountain View, CA: Mayfield.

Asian American Families Just under 5% of adolescents in the United States are Asian and Pacific Islander American (U.S. Census Bureau, 2004). Asian traditions emphasize the importance of the group rather than the individual, and Asian American adolescents feel strong loyalties to their families. Roles in Asian American families tend to be more rigidly defined than in Western families, and relationships are vertically, or hierarchically, arranged, with the father in a position of authority at the top. Family relationships are likely to reflect the roles of members more than in individualistic, Western cultures. An aspect of the children's role is to care for their parents. This sense of responsibility to the family characterizes Asian American adolescents (Fuligni, Yip, & Tseng, 2002). Socialization practices emphasize duty, maintaining control over one's emotions and thoughts, and obedience to authority figures within the family. Chinese American adolescents, for example, indicated, when asked, that they would meet parental expectations rather than satisfy their own desires when these conflicted. However, many of those responding to such questions cited practical reasons for doing so in addition to respect for cultural traditions, saying it would increase the likelihood that they would be given permission to do something else they might want to do (Yau & Smetana, 1993).

African American Families Approximately 13% of adolescents in the United States are African American (U.S. Census Bureau, 2004).

Family roles tend to be more flexible and less gender specific than in the dominant culture, with parents assuming responsibilities within the household according to work hours and type of task rather than according to gender-based roles. Parents also show less differentiation in the roles and tasks they assign to children of either sex. Support from extended family members is also more common than in majority families (Levitt, Guacci-Franco, & Levitt, 1993).

Considerable diversity exists in income levels, and in associated educational attainment and other indices of well-being, among African Americans. Despite the massive inroads made against discrimination in jobs, schooling, and housing in the 1960s, many forms of covert discrimination still exist. Rates of unemployment are higher and median earnings are lower, for instance, than for White workers (NCCP, 2004).

For bilingual adolescents, intergenerational conflicts over differences between their native culture and the majority culture of their peers are underscored by the different languages spoken in each sphere.

Despite Erik Erikson's (1959) concern that Black adolescents would have difficulty developing a positive identity due to negative images of Blacks in the dominant culture, the self-esteem of Black adolescents is higher than that of adolescents from other ethnic backgrounds and of Whites (Twenge & Crocker, 2002).

Hispanic Families Just over 15% of U.S. adolescents are Hispanic (U.S. Census Bureau, 2004). For adolescents from Spanish-speaking homes, the sense of being between two cultures is especially strong. Traditionally, Hispanic families tend to be patriarchal; however, roles have changed as more Hispanic women find work outside the home. Employment is associated with higher status for the wife and greater decision making in the family (Herrera & DelCampo, 1995). Adolescents tend to be socialized into well-differentiated gender roles (Casas, Wagenheim, Banchero, & Mendoza-Romero, 1994; Ramirez, 1989). As do African American families, Hispanic families enjoy greater extended family support than do majority families. Also, as with African American families, more Hispanic families are low-income than are nonminority families (NCCP, 2004).

Native American Families Only slightly more than 1% of adolescents are Native Americans (U.S. Bureau of the Census, 2001c). Over 500 different native entities are recognized by the federal government. Each has its own customs and traditions, and over 200 Native American languages are spoken today.

Siblings

Another aspect of the family system that affects adolescent development is its size. Adolescents growing up with sisters and brothers experience a different family life, and are affected differently by it, than those without siblings. Over three-quarters of adolescents have at least one sibling. Most adolescents find that despite the conflicts that inevitably arise, they develop close bonds of affection with siblings, and these increase with age

(Buist et al., 2002). Gene Brody, Zolinda Stoneman, and Kelly McCoy (1994), at the University of Georgia, followed 70 families over a four-year period, assessing the quality of sibling relationships. In general, siblings reported that their relationships with each other improved over time. However, as siblings reached early adolescence, they reported relationships with other children in the family as being more negative, a finding that corroborates that of Larson and associates (1996), who also found adolescents' emotional experiences, when they were with their families, to become more negative by junior high.

Older siblings are models for younger ones. Through their interactions with parents and others, they illustrate expected forms of behavior and family standards. Their achievements influence younger siblings' aspirations and interests. An adolescent girl's interest in sports, for example, will be influenced by having an older sister on the varsity field hockey team. She sees the interest her parents take in her sister's activities and the pride her sister has in her team role. The girl takes it for granted that girls participate in sports and intends to try out for the swimming team herself when she reaches junior high.

Older siblings are also likely to serve as caretakers for younger children in the family. Having to watch out for a younger sister or brother can increase an adolescent's sense of responsibility, usefulness, and competence. If these caretaking activities are too demanding and take time away from schoolwork or friends, however, they can result in frustration, anger, and lowered self-esteem (Hetherington, 1989). Adolescents in single-parent homes are more likely than those from intact families to be given responsibility for watching over younger siblings.

Siblings provide emotional support, friendship, and company for each other (Seginer, 1998; Tucker, Updegraff, McHale, & Crouter, 1999). Because they are closer in age to each other than to a parent, they are often more in touch with the problems each faces and can frequently offer better advice than a parent. An older brother can advise a 12-year-old girl that the hazing she is experiencing in the first weeks of junior high will soon end. He knows, because that was his experience a year ago when he started junior high. A parent would be less likely to have this information.

Siblings in blended families may experience somewhat more conflict than those in intact families. However, relationships frequently improve with time and may reach the level of those in intact families (Hetherington & Kelly, 2002).

Families in Transition

Several major social trends affect the lives of adolescents. Increasing numbers experience divorce, single parenting, and stepparenting, and more live in homes in which both parents are wage earners.

Changing Family Structures

Divorce Adolescents today are more likely to experience divorce than were their parents or grandparents. Approximately half of marriages in the United States end in divorce (Munson & Sutton, 2005). What impact does divorce have on adolescents? Simple answers don't exist. Its impact will vary for each adolescent, based on a host of conditions: the family situation prior to the divorce, the adolescent's coping skills, the degree of family conflict, the adolescent's age and gender, the availability of social supports such as friends and extended family, the amount of time spent with the noncustodial parent, the quality of the relationship with the custodial parent, parental monitoring of activities, whether the divorce involves economic hardship, moving to a new neighborhood or new school, and so on. E. Mavis Hetherington, a developmentalist who has followed numerous families through divorce, remarks that one of the most notable things she has observed is the tremendous diversity in the responses of parents and children (Hetherington, 1989; Hetherington, Hagan, & Anderson, 1989; Hetherington & Kelly, 2002).

Even relatively amicable divorces can be emotionally charged and stressful events. As a consequence, developmentalists have not been surprised to find a number of negative effects associated with its occurrence. Adolescents from divorced homes frequently have lower academic self-concepts than those from intact homes; as a group, they are more likely to use substances such as cigarettes, alcohol, or marijuana, and to engage in sexual intercourse at an earlier age. Other, more global measures such as self-concept, self-esteem, social competence, happiness, and maturity have been found to differ for those from divorced homes (Hetherington & Kelly, 2002; Ge, Natsuaki, & Conger, 2006; Sun, 2001; Wallerstein & Lewis, 2004).

How extensive are these problems? Hetherington, who has studied almost 1,400 families, many of them for more than three decades, has found that 25% of children whose parents are divorced experience one or more of these types of problems, in comparison to 10% of those whose parents are not. Looked at another way, however, one can say that 75% of youth do not experience serious problems, and a small minority actually come through their parents' divorce even stronger than they had been before (Hetherington & Kelly, 2002).

Conditions Contributing to Stress Perhaps because these findings support popular stereotypes of children with divorced parents, developmentalists have been relatively slow to look beneath surface statistics to determine what factors other than *not* living with a father in the home (the usual custodial arrangement) might be contributing. One of the first studies to follow children of divorce over time discovered a number of conditions contributing to stress, not the least of which is divorce's effects on the parents (Hetherington, Cox, & Cox, 1982). Subsequent research has supported these observations (Hetherington & Kelly, 2002). Recently divorced parents, for example, report more depression and have poorer parenting skills than those not divorced. Difficulties in adjusting among their children can be traced, in part, to the parents' reactions to the divorce. Divorce can be highly damaging to a parent's self-esteem and sense of worth. Many leave a divorce with a sense of failure, not just in the relationship, but as individuals. Most experience depression and increased tension as they adjust to their changed life circumstances. Parents can become preoccupied with their own problems and consequently less responsive to the needs of adolescents who are also adjusting to the divorce (Hetherington & Kelly, 2002). Adolescents whose parents remain as caring and supportive as they were previously are less likely to be affected by marital discord or divorce (Davies & Windle, 2001; Dunlop, Burns, & Bermingham, 2001).

Divorce also is frequently accompanied by less intimate relationships between parents and children (Sun, 2001). Fathers in particular are seen as less caring (Dunlop et al., 2001), and adolescents' relationships with fathers are likely to further deteriorate over time (Gunnoe & Hetherington, 2004; Burns & Dunlop, 2001). Two years following a divorce, for instance, only 25% of noncustodial fathers saw their children once a week, with most seeing them biweekly or even monthly (Hetherington & Kelly, 2002).

Not only the quality of relationships is likely to suffer, but initially so is the effectiveness of parenting. Fathers become more permissive, perhaps reluctant to spoil their available time on a dispute over discipline, and mothers become more inconsistent,

Parenting changes following a divorce. This father is likely to be less consistent and effective than he was previously, or will be again.

at times ignoring infractions and other times reacting more severely. Each of these changes adds to the level of stress. Parents who are consistent and firm in their discipline, while maintaining warm and supportive relationships with their children, are the most successful in helping adolescents adjust to a divorce (Hetherington & Kelly, 2002).

Life evens out within a two- to three-year period following the divorce. Parents and adolescents regain much of their earlier emotional stability, and each is better able to "be there" for the other. Christy Buchanan, Eleanor Maccoby, and Sanford Dornbusch (1992), at Stanford University, interviewed over 500 adolescents four years following their parents' divorce. They found that the most important predictors of adolescents' adjustment were their closeness with the parent they were living with and that parent's monitoring of their activities, such as knowing where they were after school, how they spent their time and money, and who their friends were.

Because divorce is more common today than in previous generations, adolescents are less likely to experience any stigma associated with it. Many of their friends have gone through a similar experience, and natural support groups exist in which adolescents can air their feelings and gain perspective on their situation.

Holding On, Letting Go, and Staying in Place Divorce can also be difficult because it introduces changes in the family just at the time adolescents themselves are in the process of changing. It's hard to push off from something, in other words, when it is moving away from you. Robert Kegan (1982) speaks of three functions that the environment must serve, at any age. The first is *holding on;* the environment needs to support, nourish, and sustain the adolescent. Individuals—such as parents, siblings, and teachers, who make up the adolescent's environment—must "be present" for the adolescent, recognizing and accepting what the adolescent is going through. The second function is *letting go,* or assisting the adolescent in establishing the ways in which she or he differs from others, helping the adolescent find her or his own way. These two functions parallel the dimensions of family interaction referred to earlier as individuality and connectedness. A final function of the environment is *remaining in place,* thereby permitting the adolescent to reintegrate aspects of the self that have become differentiated. Kegan notes that "it takes a special wisdom for the family of an adolescent to understand that by remaining in place so that the adolescent can have the family there to ignore and reject, the family is providing something very important, and is still, in a new way, intimately and importantly involved in the child's development" (1982, p. 129). Were the family to "move away," as opposed to remain in place, those aspects of the self that the adolescent has thrown off can become lost to the adolescent and be more difficult to reintegrate into new ways of relating to others.

Conflict Marital conflict and not just divorce per se contributes heavily to the stress adolescents experience (Amato & Afifi, 2006; Turner & Kopiec, 2006). Conflict most likely affects adolescents by affecting the quality of parent–child relationships (Fauber, Forehand, Thomas, & Wierson, 1990; Sun, 2001). Adolescents are more likely to experience problems when their parents divorce relatively late rather than early, when they were children (Needle, Su, & Doherty, 1990; Smith, 1990). Adolescents whose parents divorce late experience more years of marital conflict. A three-year longitudinal study of over 1,000 seventh-, ninth-, and eleventh-graders found that conflict within the family, not divorce, was associated with negative effects such as depression, anxiety, and physical symptoms. Adolescents from intact homes with high levels of conflict showed lower levels of well-being than those in low-conflict divorced homes on all measures that were used (Mechanic & Hansell, 1989). A full 25% of the adolescents reported that their parents' divorce was a positive change.

Exposure to conflict need not always be negative; sometimes it is the only way of working through differences. But how sensitive are adolescents to cues, such as conciliatory or angry tones of voice, versus the actual content of what is said in resolving conflict? Kelly Shifflett-Simpson and Mark Cummings (1996), at West Virginia University, had 5- to 7-year-olds and 9- to 12-year-olds watch videotaped arguments between a couple, systematically varying the endings in terms of emotional tone and content. Thus, an argument might end in a sarcastic apology ("I'm *so* sorry I wasn't more sensitive to your needs," said in a negative tone of voice) or a genuine one (the same words spoken in a positive tone of voice). Adolescents are better at discerning what is actually taking place than are children, reacting emotionally to both the content and the emotional tone of the argument. Children, on the other hand, are more literal, responding simply to the verbal content of the message.

Adverse effects of divorce decrease as adolescents reach early adulthood (Ge, et al., 2006). In other ways, the increasing divorce rate in society may affect all adolescents. Perhaps the issues facing this generation of adolescents will be to find meaning in relationships and institutions that previous generations accepted as givens. The prevalence of divorce, even when not personally experienced, can raise issues of intimacy and family relationships for all adolescents.

Single-Parent Families About half of the adolescents who live in single-parent families do so because of divorce; most of them (80%) live with their mothers (U.S. Bureau of the Census, 2002). One of the most noticeable differences between these adolescents and those from intact homes is their economic well-being. Approximately half of all families headed by a single female parent live below the poverty level, compared to only 10% of two-parent families (U.S. Bureau of the Census, 2002). For many adolescents, this income level is a dramatic change. One year following a divorce, a single mother's income is likely to have dropped to 67% of the total household income before divorce, whereas the father's income is likely to drop only to 90%. The initially lower earning capacity of most women, along with frequent lack of child support and little state support, contributes to this pattern. Economic hardship can contribute to adolescents' distress in intact families as well.

Adolescents in single-parent families face the need—some for the first time—to take on part-time jobs to pay for things they previously took for granted. There are advantages and disadvantages in this situation, as in almost any other. On the positive side, adolescents stand to gain in autonomy and independence through being more responsible. Hetherington finds that adolescents are given greater responsibility, have a greater role in family decision making, and are given more independence than in intact families. Potential disadvantages can result when responsibilities exceed

Adolescents in single-parent families must often take on new roles and responsibilities, such as part-time jobs and additional chores around the house. In return for greater responsibility, however, they gain in autonomy and independence.

adolescents' capabilities or keep them from normal activities, such as schoolwork and social participation.

Many adolescents face additional changes immediately after a divorce. Thirty percent of adolescents move within the first year following a divorce; for many this means adjusting to a new neighborhood and a new school and making new friends. Less-frequent contact with old friends is an additional loss. Frequently, divorced mothers will change their employment within the same time period, adding to the general level of stress within the family. Divorced mothers report lower levels of psychological well-being and more concerns than mothers in two-parent families. Adolescents living with divorced mothers are likely to enjoy the same family support as before, yet they typically have less contact with their neighbors than those living in two-parent families. Most divorced mothers, however, are relatively successful in establishing the social supports they need (Hetherington & Kelly, 2002).

On the positive side, relationships between adolescents and mothers often become stronger in the process of coping with these conditions; relationships become closer and less hierarchical. Mothers and daughters especially are likely to find these relationships satisfying, with the exception of early maturing girls, for whom family conflict increases. Adolescents living with their mothers may also develop more liberal attitudes regarding work and gender roles. Daughters living with their divorced mothers report high expectations from their mothers for them to attend college. Divorced mothers may see a need for their daughters to be economically and socially independent, in case of similar circumstances (McLanahan, Astone, & Marks, 1988; Sessa & Steinberg, 1991).

Paternal Custody An increasing number of divorced fathers receive custody of their children, although this arrangement is still relatively uncommon. Of all children living with a single parent because of divorce, 80% live with their mothers and 20% live with their fathers (U.S. Bureau of the Census, 2002). Perhaps because of the special circumstances under which fathers are likely to be awarded custody, more fathers experienced difficulty. For instance, hostility between parents remained higher when fathers had custody; fathers with custody also worked more hours per week than did mothers with custody, and residential arrangements changed more frequently following the divorce than in the other two types of custody arrangements.

Other things being equal, however, fathers have been found to adjust to their custodial role well. A survey of over 1,000 single fathers found them to be relatively comfortable in their roles. Those who were most comfortable were the ones who had been at it the longest; presumably they had worked out the kinks and developed their own successful routines over the years. Those who were satisfied with their social lives also reported more satisfaction with their roles, as did those who had higher incomes and rated themselves high as a parent (Greif & DeMaris, 1990).

Remarriage and Blended Families Parents who divorce are likely to remarry and to introduce a stepparent into their children's lives. Close to 20% of children under the age of 18 live with a stepparent, who in most cases is a stepfather. Remarriage usually occurs soon on the heels of the divorce, typically within three years. Many stepparents bring a stepsibling or two (residential or weekend) in the process. For adolescents, this series of events comes on top of the changes introduced by puberty, moving to a new type of school, and rapidly changing social relations. Fewer changes would still be enough to disrupt anyone's equilibrium. Yet many families weather the stresses of these new relationships, and some even thrive. Success cannot be rushed, however, and more typically than not comes only after years of relationship building.

What makes the difference between success and failure? A number of general statements can be made.

Role Clarity Perhaps the first thing to emphasize is the importance of **role clarity,** the understanding among family members regarding each person's role and how it affects the others (Hetherington & Kelly, 2002). Agreement as to what these roles are is often difficult, since roles that are acceptable to a parent or stepparent may not be acceptable to the children, who, as Hetherington notes, may not even view the stepparent as a member of the family. Adolescence introduces its own confusions into roles and the issues that surround them, such as being a child versus an adult, being dependent versus independent, being autonomous versus emotionally connected. The addition of stepparents to this confusing mix creates the potential for real drama. An adolescent who bridles at suggestions from his mother can refuse to even listen to a stepfather. If a 6-foot-tall, strapping, 15-year-old male is confused about his role as a "child" to a biological parent, magnify that confusion by an order of 10 when you add a stepfather who is 3 inches shorter, 20 pounds lighter—and an emotional rival.

Things may be no clearer to the stepparent. As one stepfather remarked, "I have no idea how I'm supposed to behave, or what the rules are. Can I kiss my wife in front of my stepchildren? Do I tell my stepson to do his homework, or is that exceeding my authority? Can I have my own kids over for the weekend, or is that going to be an imposition? It's hard living in a family where there are no clear rules or lines of authority" (Hetherington & Kelly, 2002, p. 181). Families with the most ambiguity in roles are those with a stepmother and at least one child in common. The difficulties facing stepmothers are especially acute, because they are likely to oversee the management of the household, a role that can bring them into direct conflict with stepchildren who may resent their presence.

Ordinary family problems are magnified in blended families. The most successful families establish clear guidelines for parenting. The same type of parenting that works

role clarity Clear understanding among family members concerning the nature and responsibilities of each one's role.

best in intact families, authoritative parenting, is also best in blended families. The catch is that it's harder to be authoritative if you're a stepparent. Hetherington and Kelly (2002) estimate that only a third of stepfathers, and even fewer stepmothers, become authoritative. Rather than a direct hands-on approach, it is better for stepparents to support the biological parent's use of discipline and to work on building trust and friendship with the stepchild (Moore & Cartwright, 2005).

Timing of Remarriage Another factor contributing to the success of remarriage and building successful relationships is the age of children when the stepparent arrives on the scene. Remarriages are most likely to be successful when they take place either before children reach the age of 10 or after 15. With younger children, roles are easier to define. Similarly, older adolescents can appreciate having a stepparent as an emotional support for the biological parent as they begin to think about leaving home, either to go to college or to start work and live on their own. However, early adolescents are attempting to establish their autonomy and may feel threatened by the presence of another adult with whom they may need to negotiate this. Also, early adolescents who have been living with a single parent are likely to have enjoyed a greater role in family decision making than age-mates from intact families and may resent losing this role to a new stepparent (Hetherington & Kelly, 2002).

On the positive side, younger and older adolescents alike can appreciate the benefits of having a parent remarry when this is successful. Not only are financial problems likely to be lessened, but the biological parent is likely to be happier. As one child put it, "Mother's not worrying so much and working so hard now. I've never seen her really happy before. She's a different person. I realize now how tough things were for her" (Hetherington & Kelly, 2002, p. 191). Many adolescents also appreciate having a stepparent fill what previously had been a void in their lives. As one boy said, "I love Mom, but it's different having a dad in the family. Nick throws a football around with me and he's teaching me to fly-fish and we go to basketball games together. We do guy things I couldn't do with Mom. I talk about different things with Nick" (Hetherington & Kelly, 2002, p. 191).

Rituals In addition to role clarity and the timing of a remarriage, a third factor contributes to the success of blended families. Successful families are those that establish their own rituals. These can range from everyday routines, such as sitting down for breakfast together or taking a walk with the dog each night, to family traditions, such as piñatas at birthday parties, backpacking on weekends, or barbecues on the Fourth of July. Rituals provide a family with shared experiences and foster a sense of belonging (Hetherington & Kelly, 2002).

Dual-Earner Families

In most families with children under the age of 18, both parents are employed (U.S. Bureau of the Census, 2005). Despite the fact that having two working parents in the home is normative for adolescents, most research on dual-earner families has focused on the effects of maternal employment.

What effect *does* maternal employment have on adolescents? Research addressing this question suggests that *whether* mom works is not as important as the *conditions* that are present when she does (Gottfried, Gottfried, & Bathurst, 2002; Joebgen & Richards, 1990). Joebgen and Richards (1990), for example, periodically contacted adolescents and parents throughout the day (they wore beepers) to sample their activities and their moods. They found the match between the mother's level of education and her employment to be most predictive of her self-esteem and well-being. This in turn related to well-being in adolescents. Maternal employment per se was not important; what mattered in terms of both her well-being and the adolescent's emotional adjustment was the match between the mother's interests and abilities and the work she did during the day—whether inside or outside the home.

Studies of working mothers and their adolescents find few consistent relationships between maternal employment and indicators of adjustment in adolescents, such as academic achievement, emotional development, or social competence (Armistead, Wierson, & Forehand, 1990; Bird & Kemerait, 1990; Keith, Nelson, Schlabach, & Thompson, 1990). Problems, when they arise, are related more to parental monitoring than to maternal employment per se (Jacobson, 2000). Similarly, parent–adolescent relations are most likely to be affected when *both* parents experience work-related stress (Galambos & Maggs, 1990; Galambos, Sears, Almeida, & Kolaric, 1995). Job-related stresses of employed mothers do not seem to spill over to their relationships with their adolescent children, or to affect the latter's psychosocial adjustment, or to differ significantly from those of working fathers (Schwartzberg & Dytell, 1996).

Gender Roles The effects of mom's joining the workforce appear to be more positive than negative. Maternal employment has a liberalizing effect on gender roles in the household. In single-earner families, with the traditional model of fathers as "breadwinners" and mothers as "homemakers," fathers spend more time with their sons than their daughters, while in dual-earner families they spend equivalent amounts of time with each (Crouter & Crowley, 1990). Even though traditional, single-earner families expect daughters and sons to spend equal amounts of time doing household chores, they assign work in gender-stereotypic ways. Girls, for example, might be expected to clear the table, do dishes, or watch younger siblings; boys might mow the lawn, wash the car, and take out the garbage. In other respects, dual-earner families mirror for daughters the social realities facing employed mothers. Just as the workload of employed mothers increases when they work outside the home (because they continue to be responsible for work within the home), daughters actually do 25% more work in dual-earner homes than in traditional families (Benin & Edwards, 1990).

Maternal Well-Being Maternal employment may affect the mother's sense of well-being more than the children's during adolescence. A study of over 100 families with adolescents between ages 10 and 15 found that parents who were positively invested in their jobs weathered the stresses of parenting adolescents better than those who were not (Silverberg & Steinberg, 1990). As adolescents enter puberty, begin dating, and engage in more activities outside the home, parents face midlife identity issues and frequently a drop in self-esteem and life satisfaction. Parents who are involved in their work roles, however, show increases in self-esteem and life satisfaction and have fewer midlife concerns when their children start to date (Silverberg & Steinberg, 1990).

Maternal employment can relate to well-being in yet another way. As adolescent autonomy increases, conflicts with parents increase, especially with mothers. The stability of work roles outside the home, in which established patterns of authority and decision making are not questioned, can buttress parental self-esteem in the face of changing relationships at home (Gottfried, Gottfried, & Bathurst, 2002).

Summary

Changing Relationships with Parents

- Psychoanalytic theory expects adolescence to bring about emotional turmoil and distancing from parents. Large-scale studies of normal adolescents find that even though conflicts increase, adolescents continue to maintain close relationships with parents. These relationships are renegotiated as adolescents press for more mutuality and fuller participation in family decision making.
- Several domains of authority exist within a family, and parental authority shifts in only some of them. Conflicts arise when parents and adolescents do not agree about which issues should remain under parental authority and for how long.

Parents and Adolescents

- Four styles of parenting have been identified:
  - *Authoritative* parents are both responsive and demanding; they take their children's ideas into account but are also willing to assert their own authority and to enforce standards of behavior.
  - *Authoritarian* parents are as demanding as authoritative ones but less responsive; they value obedience over self-reliance.
  - *Indulgent* parents are responsive to their children but are not demanding; they seldom express expectations for responsible behavior.
  - *Neglectful* parents are neither responsive nor demanding; they are relatively uninvolved in their children's lives.
  - Authoritative parenting fosters competence, self-reliance, and academic achievement.
- Styles of parenting must be considered within the context of ethnicity.
  - Authoritative parenting has been shown to be an effective style of parenting for African American, Asian American, and Hispanic adolescents, as well as for European American adolescents.
  - The parenting characteristic of Chinese Americans has been described as authoritarian, but in reality is closer to authoritative parenting.
- A supportive adult network of relatives and friends can ensure a better outcome for poor children by helping to buffer against the risks they face.
- An adolescent's behavior may be influenced as much by parenting style as by similarities in genotype between parents and adolescents, which in turn can influence how an adolescent perceives events and experiences. Environmental and genetic contributions to development interact with each other, and their influence on children's outcome cannot be identified or measured separately.
- Most parents face middle age just when adolescents reach puberty. This particular combination of developmental changes and identity crises can heighten the tensions within families with adolescents.

Families and Adolescent Development

- The process of individuation, whereby adolescents distinguish themselves from their parents and clarify who they are as individuals, takes place within the context of the family. The quality of adolescents' interactions with their parents, as well as personality characteristics of the parents themselves, are important to ego development in adolescence.
- Ethnicity contributes to the impact of the family on development. Adolescent–parent relationships typically take different forms in families with differing cultural backgrounds.
- Family size also affects adolescent development. Over three-quarters of adolescents have at least one sibling. Most develop close bonds of affection despite the inevitable conflicts. Older siblings serve as models for younger ones; they are also likely to serve as caretakers. Siblings provide friendship and company for each other.

Families in Transition

- Increasing numbers of adolescents experience divorce. The impact of divorce depends on conditions in the adolescent's life, such as age, gender, amount of marital conflict, support from family and friends, and economic stability. The effectiveness of parenting drops in the first years following divorce.
- Marital conflict, rather than divorce itself, contributes heavily to the stress adolescents experience, but exposure to conflict need not always be negative.
- Most parents who divorce will remarry. Role clarity facilitates interaction in blended families. Factors contributing to successful blended family relationships include authoritative parenting by the biological parent, supported by the stepparent; the

age of the children (remarriages are more successful if the children are under 10 or over 15); and family rituals.

- In most families with children under 18, both parents are employed. The effects of maternal employment on adolescents are mediated by several factors, one of the most important being the mother's satisfaction with her work. Maternal employment may liberalize gender roles in the family and increase a parent's sense of well-being.

Key Terms

emotional transmission
authoritative parents
authoritarian parents
indulgent parents
neglectful parents
parental monitoring
climacteric
menopause
ego development
role clarity

CHAPTER OUTLINE

CHAPTER 8

Adolescents and Their Friends

CHAPTER OBJECTIVES

- To examine the function of friendships in adolescence: furnishing a group identity, supporting steps toward a personal identity, and solidifying feelings of self-worth
- To identify patterns in friendships that are traceable to differences in age, social status, gender, ethnicity, and sexual-minority status
- To distinguish different types of peer groups and to relate these to the transition to dating
- To explore the contributions to a youth culture made by schools, youth organizations, peers, and family

"Hey, Jenny!" Alisa tossed her books on the table and perched on the chair beside her friend. "I saw Sylvan today. Think he'll ask you to the rally Friday night?"

"What if he did?" asked Jenny. "I wouldn't be able to go. My parents won't let me date until . . ."

"Sure, I know—until you're 15. That's what mine said."

"If only! They won't even say. Dad just says 'When we marry off your older sister.' Too bad I don't have an older sister, it might make things easier."

"I do. It doesn't . . . just makes them nervous."

"What a bummer."

"Uh-huh," agreed Alisa.

"Anyway, Sylvan's not that hot."

"Forget you!" exclaimed Alisa. "You were so distracted yesterday you put your clothes on over your gym shorts."

"Yeah," smiled Jenny, "but, you know what I mean. . . . It's just like he's not, well . . ."

"Yeah, I understand."

"I know you do, kiddo. That's what's so great."

Chapter Overview

Friends are important at any age, but especially in adolescence when so many things are new. Friends are emotional supports to whom adolescents turn with their concerns, triumphs, secrets, and plans. In larger numbers, they are socialization agents, guiding

Early adolescents come to see themselves in terms of what they share with other members of their group, making possible a new kind of identity.

adolescents into new, more adult roles. And one on one, they are mirrors into whom adolescents look to glimpse the future within.

Dramatic hormonal and physiological changes literally transform the emotional and social arenas of adolescents' lives. Ironically, adolescents are least able to turn to their parents in the face of these changes, because relationships with parents are part of the changes. Peers step into the void. Changing relationships with parents, together with their need for belonging, underlie the psychosocial task of forming a group identity in early adolescence. Distinctive themes distinguish friendships in early adolescence from those in preadolescence. These themes reflect the concerns of each age. Preadolescents are concerned with being accepted by others; adolescents with discovering—and accepting—themselves. The first section of this chapter addresses these aspects of friendships and ends with a discussion of their impact on self-esteem.

The next section examines the varying patterns to adolescent friendships. Early adolescents, for instance, have friends who are almost exclusively the same sex as they, whereas late adolescents are likely to have friends of both sexes. Adolescents who are considered popular by their peers can say and do things that other adolescents would be shunned for. Friendship patterns, then, can be seen to differ with age and social status; they also differ with gender, ethnicity, and sexual orientation.

The chapter then moves to peer groups: their organization and the functions they serve. Small groups bridge adolescents' first steps outside the family. Larger groups provide a social setting in which adolescents try out more adult social roles. One of the functions of the larger peer group is to facilitate the transition to mixed-sex interactions and dating. This section closes with a discussion of dating.

The culture in which adolescents move throughout the day, though similar in important respects to that of their parents, younger siblings, and neighbors, is also different in many ways. Their experiences at school or after school, in informal groups or youth organizations, with friends on the phone or out on a date, define them as a distinct group. We look at the attitudes and behaviors adolescents share with their friends, and consider whether these conflict with those shared with parents. In the process, we will take a look at conformity during adolescence.

Many parents voice concerns over peer pressure. Even though all of us are influenced by our friends, parents of adolescents seem particularly distrustful of their influence. Although peers exert more influence than parents do in some areas of adolescents' lives, parents continue to influence their children more than friends do in other areas.

The Importance of Friendships

Adolescents gain a sense of who they are and what their lives are about through seemingly small and insignificant daily encounters with friends and members of their families (Erikson, 1968). They try out new aspects of themselves in the relative safety of close relationships. As a consequence, adolescents are often just as interested in what they discover about themselves as in what they find out about each other. This is especially true for friendships during early adolescence.

Adolescents experiment with new behaviors as they face a pressing need to discover what is acceptable and what is not. They know, for example, that they cannot be as dependent as before, but neither are they totally self-reliant. And what about their emotions? Sentimentality is "uncool," but do they have to put a cap on all emotion? Friends provide essential feedback. Adolescents try on new behaviors much as they do clothes on a shopping spree. Which ones fit? Which make them look better? Friends become mirrors in which they can see themselves as they imagine they must look to others. The ability of adolescents to consider the thoughts of others gives early friendships this special reflective quality.

Group Identity

Barbara Newman and Philip Newman (2001), at the University of Rhode Island, argue that early adolescents experience a heightened need for connection and belonging, and that they seek to affiliate themselves with, not distinguish themselves from, others. The psychosocial task facing early adolescents, they argue, is one of forming a **group identity,** not one of achieving a personal identity. Only when issues related to affiliation and belonging have been resolved will they be ready, in mid-adolescence, to address the differences in interests, values, and skills that distinguish them from others, that is, to address issues related to an individual identity.

Seeing the self as a member of a group is not peculiar to early adolescence, of course; belonging to a family has been central to children's experience of themselves. What is different, however, is the group to which they see themselves belonging and, with this, what belonging means. Unlike one's family, in which parents remain, in some ways, larger than life, and in which siblings' ages and interests only imperfectly match one's own, the peer group is composed of others whom one sees to be very much like oneself, making possible a new kind of identity. Early adolescents come to see themselves in terms of what they share with other members of the group. Only later will they begin to see how they are different from, as well as similar to, others in their group and, with this, be ready to address issues related to a personal, as opposed to a group, identity (Newman & Newman, 2001).

Seeing the self in relation to the group can also lead to feelings of alienation. Most obviously, these can come from seeing others as part of something to which one does not belong. However, belonging to the group does not in itself protect against alienation. It

group identity A psychosocial task of early adolescence that entails the resolution of issues related to affiliation and belonging.

is still possible for adolescents to feel cut off, or alienated, from themselves while a member of the group. Adolescents must learn, for instance, how to be a member of a group without losing themselves to the group, and how to enjoy shared interests without succumbing to pressures to conform. Failure to master these skills also can lead to alienation, with adolescents feeling themselves forced into roles or positions they do not support or that are counter to their values.

Gossip and Self-Disclosure

Friendships change with age, taking on themes that characterize the concerns of each age group. Preadolescents want to be understood and accepted by others; adolescents want to understand themselves—and different processes facilitate both of these concerns. **Gossip** helps preadolescents establish norms and avoid being rejected; self-disclosure helps adolescents define themselves. Friendships reflect these themes in characteristic patterns of interacting.

Preadolescence Preadolescents spend a lot of time comparing themselves to others. In fact, being accepted by others is one of their central concerns. Peer reactions figure heavily in determining preadolescents' levels of self-esteem and self-definition. The cognitive changes discussed in Chapter 4, especially being able to assume the perspective of another, contribute to their awareness of the importance of socially appropriate behavior and the need for "impression management." Fear of rejection and ridicule, and jockeying for position in friendships, characterize relationships among this age group (Parker & Gottman, 1989). Keller and Wood (1989) found that most of the preadolescents they interviewed mentioned trust as the most important issue in their friendships.

Insecurity regarding one's social position is perhaps best reflected in a characteristic mode of interaction: gossiping. Even though gossip is an unreliable source of information and is generally considered inappropriate, almost all preadolescents gossip (Kuttler, Parker, & La Greca, 2002). Gossiping is important to preadolescents with good reason: It discloses the attitudes and beliefs that are central to the peer group (Parker & Gottman, 1989). This function is vital when we realize that these behaviors are the basis for being accepted or rejected by the group. Listen in on the following conversation as two friends discuss telling lies, something friends are not supposed to do with each other:

Dari: Barb said that her mom gave her $300 to buy a dress and shoes for the dance, and that the dress, the yellow one she showed us, remember? Well, that that dress cost over $200.
Tracey: That yellow dress she took out of the closet? It was ripped. I saw it!
Dari: Yeah. Under the arm. I saw it too.
Tracey: That wasn't a new dress. There was a stain on it.
Dari: She told us she bought it for $200. But I think her sister gave it to her, the one who's married.
Tracey: Yeah. She gives her a lot of clothes.

Notice that in gossiping about Barb, Dari and Tracey affirm the norms of the group; that is, friends don't lie to each other. They also communicate to each other that they adhere to these norms.

Mutual disclosure and affirmation of group norms through gossip allows preadolescents to reaffirm their membership in the group. This is especially important because preadolescents are often insecure about their social status and their general acceptability. Much of the energy that goes into friendship is devoted to solidifying their position and protecting themselves against rejection (Parker & Gottman, 1989).

gossip A process by which preadolescents establish group norms.

Gossip serves another important function. It allows preadolescents to explore peer attitudes in areas where they lack clear norms, without actually committing themselves to a position. Because many of the behaviors in question are not common among their peers, gossip frequently involves well-known older adolescents, as in the following example, or even popular figures such as rock musicians and movie stars:

Brian: They say Dale [captain of the varsity football team] uses steroids every football season.
Andy: A lot of athletes do. It helps them build up muscle.
Brian: Steroids are really drugs, you know.
Andy: You think the coach knows?
Brian: Nah. How could he and still let Dale do it? He might lose his job.
Andy: Yeah.

Neither Brian nor Andy directly stated an opinion about using steroids or drugs in general. Yet by the end of the conversation, they had established that athletes who use them have to hide that fact from others and consequently it must be wrong to use them. As demonstrated in this example, gossiping is a low-risk way of determining the attitudes of one's peer group. Neither boy had to reveal a view of his own in order to discover the position taken by the other. Their conversation affords them a way of sampling the reactions and attitudes of peers regarding behaviors that are not yet common to their group (Parker & Gottman, 1989).

Preadolescents are still learning which emotions are appropriate for them and what rules exist for displaying these. By monitoring feedback from peers in social situations, they gain invaluable information regarding each of these aspects of social competence. Even so, their rules for emotional expression are rough at first. Perhaps their most salient guideline is to avoid sentimentality at all costs, especially when with one's friends. The rule of thumb is to be rational, cool, and in control.

Adolescence Adolescents' friendships reflect different concerns, which at this stage take the form of defining who they are and what they are going to be in life. Friends get together to discuss the mix of experiences offered up each day. The remarks of classmates, teachers, and parents and the successes and failures of the day are expressed, taken apart, analyzed, and reanalyzed. Friends provide the support—and sometimes the challenge—that adolescents need in order to meet the new and untried, as the following conversation illustrates (Parker & Gottman, 1989):

James: So we're watching the game last night and my dad says, "You need to think about your future." Like, I don't know what I want to do but it doesn't really bother me. [Laughs.]
Sam: [Returns laughter.]
James: [Laughs again.] It's my life and it bothers my dad more than me that I haven't got my future planned.
Sam: My dad's the same. I tell him: "I know I'll be doing *something*."
James: Right, *something!* [Laughs nervously.]
Sam: "*Que sera*," you know?

Exploring uncharted territories in one's life is never easy, as the nervous laughs of these two adolescents suggest. Yet adolescents are peculiarly well equipped for the task. In many ways, they have reached the pinnacle of thought and can think easily in the abstract, reasoning about the possibilities in their lives and those of their friends (see Chapter 4). Rather than seeing themselves as limited to their present circumstances, they can see their present realities as reflecting a limited sample of the many possible alternatives that exist. Parker and Gottman (1989) note that adolescents are uniquely qualified to

Whereas younger children derive much of their sense of self-worth from their parents, adolescents receive validation primarily from their friends.

help each other through indecisions such as these, and do so with genuine concern, even seeing this as one of the obligations of friendship.

They take this obligation seriously. When adolescents are with their friends, they are most likely to talk about themselves rather than gossip about others. Just as gossip serves the very real needs of preadolescents—affirming group norms and group membership—self-disclosure serves the needs of adolescents. It is one of the primary means by which they discover themselves. **Self-disclosure** is an intimate sharing or exchange of thoughts, feelings, and otherwise undisclosed aspects of the self with another person. It takes a very different form in adolescence than in childhood or preadolescence. Adolescents respond to disclosures with an honest, almost confrontational examination of the issues raised. They accept these offerings of the self in the spirit in which they are given—as problems to be addressed and solved—whereas self-disclosures among preadolescents are more likely to evoke feelings of solidarity, such as "Me, too." With age, adolescents get increasingly better at establishing intimacy this way (McNelles & Connolly, 1999; Parker & Gottman, 1989).

Adolescent friendships reflect considerable emotional development beyond those of preadolescents. Adolescents begin to master the rules for emotional display and feeling that so mystify preadolescents. Adolescents are comfortable expressing a range of emotions, which preadolescents would likely deny. They have moved beyond cool to compassion or any of the many other emotions that might be called for in a situation. They understand that actions can be motivated by several emotions. What remains to refine is an understanding of the potential impact of emotion on their relationships. Many of their conversations are about losing control of an emotion—exploding at someone or just "blowing it"—and the effects this can have (Parker & Gottman, 1989).

Friends and Well-Being

self-disclosure A process by which adolescents understand and define themselves through an intimate sharing of thoughts and feelings.

Self-Esteem Friendships bear a special burden at first, as significant sources of adolescents' feelings about themselves. Children derive feelings of self-worth from the simple fact that their parents love them; adults additionally derive much of theirs from their work. Adolescents can neither turn to their parents with the simple needs of children nor feel the strength they will later experience through their jobs and families of their own. Friends help them bridge this difficult passage and make them feel good about themselves. In this respect, having close friends, even if only a few, is better than being popular. The latter, although not to be slighted, may make adolescents feel socially competent, but it does not contribute to **self-esteem,** as do friends (Keefe & Berndt, 1996; Rubin, Dwyer, Booth-La Force, Kim, Burgess, & Rose-Krasnor, 2004). Friends, especially same-sex friends, affirm adolescents' sense of self. They do this simply by enjoying each other's company, by "being real" with each other.

Ideal Self-image Just as individuals pull in their stomachs and stand a bit straighter when passing a mirror, adolescents see more than their present selves reflected by their friends. By imagining themselves as other than they are, adolescents can rehearse new roles, set goals, and plan ways of attaining them. They can try out ways they would like to be—an **ideal self-image.** This image includes more than the roles they are refining; it anticipates the adult roles they will assume (Bybee, Glick, & Zigler, 1990; Dunkel & Anthis, 2001). We see the importance of the ideal self-image in studies relating it to other measures of adjustment. Adolescents with high ideal self-images are better adjusted: They are more reflective, do better in school, tolerate frustration better, and are more resilient to stress.

How positive adolescents feel about themselves affects the quality of their relationships with others. As the quality of their relationships improves, these improved relationships contribute to even more positive feelings about themselves (Berndt, Hawkins, & Jiao, 1999). Adolescents who feel inadequate and are unsure of themselves find it difficult to believe that others will like them any better than they like themselves. Conversely, adolescents who have positive self-attitudes anticipate positive reactions from others.

Gossip is a favorite pastime of preadolescents, and it has a developmental purpose. From discussions of other people's behavior, they learn social norms to guide their own behavior.

Parents and Well-Being

Self-Esteem Relationships with parents are also important. Interactions that communicate support, affection, and encouragement promote self-esteem (Colarossi & Eccles, 2000; Quatman & Watson, 2001). Families in which these qualities exist support each other, even when they disagree (see Chapter 7). Adolescents still see their parents as major sources of support (Levitt, Gaucci-Franco, & Levitt, 1993); in fact, relationships with parents become closer with age, with high school seniors reporting greater intimacy with each of their parents than eighth-graders report (Rice & Mulkeen, 1995). Adolescents who are close to their parents report being more satisfied with themselves and having

self-esteem The individual's overall positive or negative evaluation of herself or himself.

ideal self-image The individual's idealized image of the self, including anticipated as well as actual ways of being.

Although girls generally find it easier than boys to share their innermost thoughts, disclosure to a close friend is one of the most important ways that older adolescents learn about themselves.

closer relationships with friends than those who are not close to their parents (Hodges, Finnegan, & Perry, 1999; Raja, McGee, & Stanton, 1992). Adolescents who have a good relationship with their parents are also more likely to seek friends for support, perhaps because they have learned from their families that others can be helpful in solving problems.

Attachment Although it might seem that adolescents' well-being and **attachment** to parents are incompatible states, nothing could be further from the truth. Attachment theory assumes that we form working models of relationships, in the form of expectations, based on our earliest experiences of acceptance or rejection. These expectations promote a readiness to perceive the actions of others either positively or negatively and, when positively, to feel secure in new situations (Bowlby, 1969). Attachment, then, simply refers to the enduring emotional bonds we form, first with parents and siblings, and then with friends and romantic partners (Ainsworth, 1989).

Adolescents who perceive their parents as supportive feel better about themselves (Rubin et al., 2004). Research following ninth- and tenth-graders over a two-year period has found that those with mothers who are supportive, even when disagreeing with them, show increases in security. Those who became entangled in disagreements, on the other hand, show decreased security. Despite the demonstrated importance of this relationship, stressful conditions, such as poverty, can undermine adolescents' ability to draw strength from attachment relationships, leaving them more vulnerable to stress. The potentially damaging effects of poverty on adolescents' ability to cope should not be surprising given the frequent moves, changes in schools, disruption of friendship networks, lack of medical services, tensions within the family, and frequently unsafe neighborhoods that are associated with this (Allen, McElhaney, Kuperminc, & Jodl, 2004).

Friendship Patterns

attachment The enduring emotional bonds formed first with parents and siblings and then with friends and romantic partners.

What do adolescents want from their friends? Emotional support, intimacy, and advice. They get these in somewhat different ways depending on their sex. The major activity in girls' friendships is talking. Girls develop close friendships primarily by sharing their feelings. Self-disclosure contributes to emotional closeness in boys as well, but they also develop emotional closeness through sharing experiences, such as sports and other activities (Camarena, Sarigiani, & Petersen, 1990; Frankel, 1990; McNelles & Connolly, 1999).

Same-sex friendships become more intimate and affectionate with age and become increasingly important as sources of emotional support. Whereas parents are the primary source of support for children, mid-adolescents are as likely to confide in their same-sex friends as in their parents, and late adolescents indicate that friends are more important in this respect than the parents (Furman & Buhrmester, 1992; Levitt, Guacci-Franco, & Levitt, 1993). Not surprisingly, adolescents spend a lot more time with friends than they did as children.

The number of friends also increases in adolescence, especially for girls. The percentage of these friends whom mothers know (40%) remains about the same as in childhood; however, because the circle of friends widens in adolescence, the actual number of friends whom mothers do not know increases substantially (Feiring & Lewis, 1993).

Elizabeth Douvan and Joseph Adelson (1966) interviewed over 2,000 adolescents across the United States, asking them about their friendships. After more than four decades, these interviews still offer one of the most complete and informative studies of how adolescents feel about their friends. These investigators discovered three distinct phases to adolescent friendship, corresponding to early, middle, and late adolescence. These phases reveal characteristic gender differences.

Age Differences in Friendship Patterns

Early Adolescence Elizabeth Douvan and Joseph Adelson found that during early adolescence, friendships focus on the activities that bring friends together. Although friendships are more intimate than in childhood, they are less so than they will be in middle or late adolescence (Berndt, 1982; Furman & Buhrmester, 1992). When asked to say what is important in friends, early adolescent girls say less about their personalities than about the things they do together. After listening to these girls talk about their friends, one has the feeling that friendships are not emotionally relevant at this age. If anything, distinct personalities of friends appear to be a disadvantage to the extent that they might interfere with activities. These early friendships are almost always with someone of the same sex (Camarena, Sarigiani, & Petersen, 1990; Lempers & Clark-Lempers, 1993).

Boys' friendships in early adolescence, just as those of girls, are almost exclusively with others of the same sex. Boys report feeling close emotionally with their friends, but they achieve closeness in somewhat different ways. They spend less time talking about their feelings than do girls and more time sharing activities that cement friendships (Camarena, Sarigiani, & Petersen, 1990). Even so, when adolescents are asked to evaluate their friendships, girls consistently rate theirs higher in intimacy than do boys (Rice & Mulkeen, 1995).

Middle Adolescence Douvan and Adelson found friendships in mid-adolescence to focus on security; girls want friends they can trust. Friendships lose their earlier, superficial quality and involve emotional sharing and mutuality. Mid-adolescent girls are more aware of their friends' concerns than they were a few years earlier (Berndt, 1982; McNelles & Connolly, 1999). There is also more concern with personal qualities of friends. Girls are particularly concerned with having a friend in whom they can trust and confide. It is especially important to them that their friends not disclose their secrets to others or talk about them behind their backs (Berndt, 1982). Frankel (1990), for example, found that the most common stresses in friendships come from not keeping secrets and talking behind a friend's back.

For girls in their early and middle teens, friends are reflections of themselves. They tend to pick friends primarily on the basis of obvious similarities, especially of style and status.

These concerns fall into place when we consider the dramatic physical changes and sexual interests that occur during puberty, which adolescents attempt to understand by sharing their feelings and observations with their friends. Finding out that others are going through the same changes assures them that they are normal and that nothing is wrong with the way they feel. In disclosing their feelings, however, they are turning over a part of themselves to their friends, perhaps the part about which they are least secure. Naturally they don't want their confidences divulged to others.

Most girls start to date in mid-adolescence, and friends become especially important in making sense of the emotions they encounter. (Dating is discussed in more detail later in the chapter.) Dating can also be a source of tension among friends. Girls experience more conflict with their friends than boys do when moving into opposite-sex relationships, conflicts frequently centering on fears of disloyalty and competition. Relatively few girls develop close friendships with boys at this age, friendships with other girls remaining more important for the majority (Hogue & Steinberg, 1995; Lempers & Clark-Lempers, 1993).

Anxieties about friendships peak in mid-adolescence. The most common anxieties reflect more general insecurities about the changes adolescents are experiencing. They are midway through puberty, renegotiating relationships with their parents, facing a more impersonal and challenging school setting, and beginning to date. These teenagers need the emotional support of friends, and anything that appears to threaten that support causes anxiety.

Douvan and Adelson found that in mid-adolescence, boys' friendships have many of the same characteristics as do those of girls in early adolescence, although girls rate their friendships more positively (Brendgen, Markiewicz, Doyle, & Bukowski, 2001). Friendships increase in intimacy and affection for boys, as they do for girls, although increases are less pronounced (Furman & Buhrmester, 1992). Boys are looking for someone with whom they can do things. Like girls in early adolescence, they appear to have little interest in the personal characteristics of their friends as long as these do not interfere with the activities they are enjoying together. They have less concern than girls for sharing feelings or being understood. They want someone who is easy to get along with and who enjoys doing the same things they do. Perhaps because they do not self-disclose as much as girls, mid-adolescent boys are not as concerned that friends not betray their confidences. However, they expect their friends not to "squeal" about things they have done together (Bukowski, Newcomb, & Hoza, 1987; Douvan & Adelson, 1966; McNelles & Connolly, 1999).

In early and middle adolescence, boy achieve closeness by sharing activities, such as scouting or sports, rather than talking about their feelings, as girls do.

Late Adolescence Girls' friendships in late adolescence focus more on personalities. Some of the earlier intensity is gone, but intimacy continues to grow. Late adolescent girls have more stable identities and better social skills. Being more secure with both themselves and others may make them better able to tolerate individuality in their friends. They no longer need friends to reflect themselves as they did in mid-adolescence. Instead, friends can be appreciated for who *they* are. Self-disclosure is still important, but each friend is able to appreciate the unique qualities the other brings to the relationship (Douvan & Adelson, 1966; Thomas & Daubman, 2001).

Douvan and Adelson did not interview late adolescent boys. However, subsequent research has found that boys are less likely than girls to establish intimacy through self-disclosure, instead achieving this through shared activities (McNelles & Connolly, 1999). Same-sex friendships continue to be important for boys, but older adolescent males also report rewarding friendships with female friends (Thomas & Daubman, 2001).

The friendship patterns described by Douvan and Adelson are as characteristic of adolescents today as they were then. They differ only in their timing: Adolescents begin the sequence somewhat earlier today. The secular trend may be partially responsible for this difference, in that puberty occurs earlier for adolescents today than it did in the past, and the social and emotional pressures that puberty brings are certain to be reflected in adolescents' friendships.

Social Competence

As with so many of their activities, adolescents' ability to make and keep friends involves a number of skills. These skills involve the way they assess situations, how they respond to them, and how they approach relationships.

The first component of **social competence,** assessing the situation, is to see what's going on and adapt one's behavior accordingly. In a sense, joining a social group involves some of the same skills adolescents learn when driving. One has to judge the speed of the ongoing activity, accelerate, then move into the thick of things. Pulling onto a freeway at 10 miles per hour requires everyone else to slow down to your speed: It doesn't work.

When adolescents "pull into the fast lane" with a remark such as "What are you doing?" they're asking others to stop for them, an unlikely response if they are enjoying themselves. Entry remarks that call attention away from the ongoing activity are likely to be rebuffed. Similaly, remarks about oneself are usually unsuccessful ways of getting a

social competence Skills enabling individuals to accurately assess social situations and respond adaptively.

Joking around with casual acquaintances doesn't come easily to every adolescent. For most, however, social competence increases with age and experience.

group's attention. Instead, fitting into a group appears to be a matter of figuring out what the group is doing. Those who are better at this are more popular. Simply put, one needs to be able to know what the group is doing in order to join in (Dodge, 1983; Putallaz, 1983).

The second component of social competence involves how adolescents respond to others' behavior. Prosocial behaviors, such as fairness, being willing to listen, or ready to help someone who's in trouble, and speaking up for others, are characteristic of adolescents who are well-liked. They're also more fun to be around. They're better at keeping things going, and others appear to have a better time with them (Dodge, 1983; Pakaslahti, Karjalainen, & Keltikangas-Jarvinen, 2002; Rose & Asher, 2004).

The third component of social competence involves how adolescents approach relationships. Those who are well-liked recognize that relationships take time to develop; they understand that the best way to reach a goal is sometimes an indirect one. For example, they might ask someone over after school or suggest going to the library to study together.

Social Status: Who's In and Who's Not

popular Adolescents nominated by their classmates as those they most like.

social preference An index of popularity measuring how much an adolescent is liked by others.

social prestige An index of popularity measuring how much an adolescent is looked up to by others.

prosocial behaviors Positive behaviors such as cooperativeness, kindness, and trustworthiness.

Popularity One might think that adolescents who are liked most by their classmates would also be the most **popular** ones at school. But such is not always the case. Simply put, there's more than one way of being popular. Popularity can refer to **social preference,** how much others like you, or to **social prestige,** how much others look up to you. Social preference is assessed by asking adolescents to list the classmates they "like the most." Adolescents who emerge as popular using this measure are characterized by **prosocial behaviors,** such as being cooperative, kind, trustworthy, and friendly. Measures of social prestige, on the other hand, ask adolescents who "the most popular" classmates are. Using this measure, the popular adolescents tend to be athletic, attractive, influential—and frequently aggressive.

Aggression is relatively easy to recognize when it's physical; examples of **physical aggression** would be actions such as pushing or starting fights. **Relational aggression** is more subtle. Adolescents who engage in this type of aggression affect peers by manipulating their relationships, such as excluding them from a group, divulging their secrets, or spreading rumors. In a longitudinal study that followed adolescents from the ages of 10 to 14, adolescents who were perceived as popular were found to use both types of aggression, especially relational aggression (Cillessen & Mayeux, 2004). These adolescents apparently use aggression as a way of maintaining their privileged status as well as a means of achieving this in the first place (Cillessen & Mayeux, 2004; Rose, Swenson, & Waller, 2004; Xie, Cairns, & Cairns, 2002).

At the other end of the social spectrum are **rejected adolescents**. These adolescents are rarely mentioned by classmates as someone they "like the most" and are frequently mentioned as someone they "like the least." Rejected adolescents engage in relatively few prosocial behaviors and also appear to lack the social skills that would enable them to get along better with peers. Although not all rejected adolescents are aggressive, many are (Friman et al., 2004; Pakaslahti, Karjalainen, & Keltigangas-Jarvinen, 2002).

Controversial adolescents are both highly liked and highly disliked by their peers, frequently being mentioned as a best friend and just as frequently by others as someone they "like the least." They tend to be confident, sociable, and socially skilled (Pakaslahti et al., 2002). However, they can also be aggressive and are more likely than popular adolescents to engage in problem behaviors (Miller-Johnson, Costanzo, Coie, Rose, Browne, & Johnson, 2003).

Average adolescents, as the term suggests, are moderately popular with their classmates and moderately disliked as well. They are more friendly and cooperative than rejected or neglected peers, but less so than popular or controversial peers. In terms of social skills, they are similar to popular adolescents (Pakaslahti et al., 2002).

Neglected adolescents are neither highly liked nor disliked, rarely being identified as someone others "like the most" or identified as disliked. Some neglected adolescents have difficulty making and maintaining friends due to their poor social skills. However, others may have adequate skills, yet fail to approach others because of their negative self-image and fears of rejection. The status of these adolescents is more dependent on their social context than that of other adolescents. In a supportive peer environment, their behavior is closer to that of average adolescents. However, when challenged by peers, they tend to withdraw; this, in turn, creates a self-fulfilling prophecy in which others, by not spending time with them, reinforce their initial self-perceptions (Caldwell, Rudolph, Troop-Gordon, & Kim, 2004; Gazelle & Rudolph, 2004).

Intervention Programs Failure to fit in with peers can be especially painful for adolescents. As we have seen, a number of factors can cause problems in peer relationships, such as having poor social skills, being overly aggressive, or having a negative self-image. Although interventions can be tailored to particular problems such as these, approaches that are multifaceted are generally most successful (Spence, 2003; Sukhodolsky, Kassinove, & Gorman, 2004).

Social skills training is part of many interventions since poor social skills contribute to a number of social and emotional problems. Social skills training uses a variety of techniques, including direct instructions on how to do something (e.g., initiate a conversation), the use of others to model how it's done, role-playing the behavior in question, and getting feedback (Spence, 2003). **Social-cognitive intervention** programs address how accurately adolescents perceive the intentions and behaviors of others. An example would be training in which adolescents are asked to identify situations or emotions that have been problematic for them, and then asked to think of all the ways they

physical aggression Aggressive actions involving physical contact, such as pushing or hitting.

relational aggression Aggression achieved by manipulating relationships, such as by excluding someone from a group or spreading rumors.

rejected adolescents Adolescents frequently mentioned by classmates as someone they least like and rarely mentioned as someone they most like.

controversial adolescents Adolescents frequently mentioned by classmates as someone they least like and by others as a best friend.

average adolescents Adolescents who are moderately popular with their classmates and moderately disliked as well.

neglected adolescents Adolescents who are rarely mentioned by their classmates as someone they most like or as someone they least like.

social skills training A component of social-cognitive intervention programs.

social-cognitive intervention An intervention program based on social-cognitive learning principles.

could have responded to these and to predict how others would react to each of these alternatives. Interventions such as this have been found to be effective in reducing subjective anger and aggressive behavior (Sukhodolsky, Kassinove, & Gorman, 2004; van Manen, Prins, & Emmelkamp, 2004).

Reputation may also be more important than previously thought. For instance, similar behaviors in popular and rejected youth can be responded to differently, adolescents reacting more positively to those who are popular, even when they are aggressive, than to others. Although it is certainly possible that adolescents' reactions can be traced to subtle differences in the behaviors themselves, it is also possible that they are reacting not just to the momentary exchange, but also to a history of interactions. The status of neglected adolescents, for example, frequently changes when they enter a different peer setting.

Interethnic Friendships

Most friendships among adolescents are with peers of the same ethnic and cultural backgrounds (Hamm, 2000; Hartup, 1993). As a consequence, the sheer number of adolescents at school who share one's ethnic background is likely to be important in forming friendships. When African Americans are a minority within a school, for instance, they are less likely to be members of cliques, or small groups of close friends; similarly, when European Americans are a minority within a school, *they* are the ones less likely to belong to cliques (Urberg et al., 1995). This is particularly true of European American and African American adolescents. Jill Hamm (2000), at the University of North Carolina at Chapel Hill, studied friendship patterns among adolescents from a number of ethnically diverse high schools in California and Wisconsin. She found that 80% of European American and African American adolescents indicated as their best friend at school someone from the same ethnic group as themselves; in contrast, only 60% of Asian American adolescents did so.

Even so, Andrea Smith (2000), at the University of Toronto, found that, with respect to ethnicity, adolescents are more inclusive than exclusive in their choice of friends. Similarly, Jean Phinney and Nancy Cobb (1996) found that nearly 75% of the adolescents they interviewed indicated they would favor including a peer from an ethnic group other than their own in a club, even if that club were made up exclusively of students from their own background. However, even though the number of adolescents in favor of including such a student did not differ for Hispanic and European American adolescents, the reasons given for refusing membership—for those who thought the student should not be included—did differ. Hispanic students more frequently mentioned cultural barriers to friendship, whereas European Americans cited rights and rules. It is likely that Hispanics, because of their experience as members of a minority group, were more aware of cultural differences than European Americans, who, for the most part, need only be familiar with their own, the dominant, culture.

Generally, adolescents are likely to have friends who live in the same neighborhood, go to the same school, and share other things in common—including ethnic background. Of those who live in ethnically mixed neighborhoods and have classes together, many form friendships with those from other groups. Adolescents report these friendships to be close, although they may not see these friends with the same frequency outside of school as they do friends of the same ethnic group (DuBois & Hirsch, 1990; Hallinan & Teixeira, 1987).

Several conditions affect the formation of friendships between adolescents from different ethnic backgrounds. Classroom climates have been found to affect the sociability of White adolescents toward Black peers. Classrooms where students work together,

Friendships among members of different ethnic or cultural groups are most likely among those who go to the same school and live in the same neighborhood. Adolescents usually form their closest friendships with people of the same ethnicity and socioeconomic status.

such as those in which teachers assign students to small working groups, have more interethnic friendships. These friendships are most likely to develop when academic competition is deemphasized and learning per se is emphasized in the classroom (Hallinan & Teixeira, 1987).

In general, it appears that the more positively adolescents regard their own ethnic group, the more positive are their attitudes toward those who belong to other groups. Jean Phinney, Debra Ferguson, and Jerry Tate (1997) found this relationship to be mediated by adolescents' ethnic identity. Adolescents who were secure in their own ethnicity, in other words, were likely to regard other members of their group positively. These positive in-group attitudes, in turn, were related to more positive attitudes toward classmates who were members of other groups. These investigators also found that each of the ethnic minorities they studied tended to perceive their own group more favorably than the other groups. They point out that this bias, commonly referred to as ethnocentrism, rather than contributing to negative attitudes toward other groups, actually appeared to support their development of positive intergroup attitudes.

How favorably adolescents viewed students from other ethnic minorities is also related to how much contact they have with them outside of school (Phinney, Ferguson, & Tate, 1997). Neighborhood conditions affect the likelihood of such friendships as well. Most adolescents who attend integrated schools report having at least one close friend at school who belongs to another group, but less than one-third of these see the friend outside school. Those who do are more likely to live in integrated neighborhoods and are also less likely to be White. Black adolescents are almost twice as likely as Whites to maintain school friendships with those from another group outside of school. Blacks have more close neighborhood friends in general than Whites (DuBois & Hirsch, 1990).

Interethnic friendships face special challenges, not the least of which are differences in the enculturation experiences of adolescents from different backgrounds. **Enculturation** is the acquisition of the norms of one's ethnic group. It differs from acculturation, which is the acquisition of the norms of the larger society. The norms of their group shape adolescents' expectations and reactions to others. The Mexican American culture, for example, stresses group affiliation, interdependence, and cooperation. The African American culture, in contrast, places greater emphasis on individualism and independence. Mexican American adolescents tend to be brought up in homes with clear

enculturation Acquiring the norms of one's social group.

Adolescents who are secure in their own ethnic identity are able to have close friends who are members of other ethnic groups, particularly if they live in the same neighborhoods.

hierarchical family relationships and are expected to accept and show respect for authority figures. African American adolescents grow up in more egalitarian homes that permit questioning of authority (Rotheram & Phinney, 1987). We might expect these enculturation experiences to affect the way adolescents from either culture react to social situations, and they do.

Mary Jane Rotheram-Borus and Jean Phinney (1990) showed videotapes of social encounters to African American and Mexican American children and adolescents. The videotapes were of everyday scenes. In one, a student asked a peer for lunch money; in another, a student witnessed a fight; and in another, a student needed materials that a classmate had in order to complete a class assignment.

Clear ethnic differences emerged in reactions to these scenes. The responses of Mexican American adolescents reflected the emphasis their culture places on the group. They were more likely, for example, to say that a peer should share lunch money with someone who had lost theirs, even when the latter was disliked. They also expected others to anticipate their needs (as they would the needs of others) and would wait for others to notice what those needs were. In response to the video in which two peers working at the same table with the supplies that both needed beyond the reach of one and close to the other, Mexican American adolescents saw no problem with the situation, expecting the other person to hand over the supplies. African American adolescents indicated they would be upset and were likely to reach over and get what they needed for themselves. A small difference? Not really. These are just the types of situations that create misunderstandings and lead to hurt feelings among friends.

Another sequence showed a boy being rejected for a team. African American students reported they would get angry or leave; not one of them said they would feel badly. Two-thirds of the Mexican American adolescents said they would feel hurt, but almost none of them would leave, and relatively few said they would be angry. These differences translate easily into the failures of understanding that test friendships. Consider an example in which Eddie, a Hispanic, tries out for football but gets cut early in the tryouts. He doesn't seem especially angry and doesn't say much about it. His friend Joe, who is African American, thinks Eddie must not care and offers no consolation. Eddie, who has been waiting for his friend to say something, doesn't understand Joe's ostensibly callous attitude and begins to question whether he's really his friend. Joe, assuming that Eddie would react as he would if he minded being cut (by being angry, not silently hurt) has no way to anticipate his friend's growing resentment toward him.

Gender and Friendships

As with ethnicity, most close friendships are with peers of the same gender, especially in early adolescence. This being said, there are few differences in the number of friends that adolescents of either sex have or in the amount of conflict they experience in their friendships. However, they're likely to handle conflict in different ways. Anne Bowker (2004), at Carleton University, found that boys' friendships tend to be more stable when they minimize conflicts, whereas girls' friendships fare better when they confront their friends and let them know they're upset. These differences are consistent with other research that finds that girls talk more about their feelings than do boys.

Boys friendships tend to last longer than girls (Hardy, Bukowski, & Sippola, 2002). This difference is surprising given that girls evaluate their friendships more positively than do boys, seeing them as stronger, more supportive, and more rewarding (Brendgen et al., 2001; Engels, Deković, & Meeus, 2002; Thomas & Daubman, 2001). Not only do they evaluate their friends' behavior more positively than do boys (Bradley, Flannagan, & Fuhrman, 2001), their own behavior is more positive when interacting with their friends than is boys' (Brendgen et al., 2001). Yet despite all this, girls report their friendships as being more stressful than do boys (Thomas & Daubman, 2001). Perhaps this is because they don't minimize the conflicts that occur. Or it may be that having higher expectations for friendships also means that it is more difficult for friends to live up to these (Hardy et al., 2002).

Friendships and Sexual-Minority Youth

Sexual-minority youth are adolescents whose sexual orientation is not exclusively heterosexual. These adolescents share the same friendship concerns as heterosexual youth, with some additional ones thrown in. When questioned about their friendships, Lisa Diamond and Sarah Lucas (2004), at the University of Utah, found sexual-minority adolescents to have more fears and concerns about relationships with their peers, to have experienced a greater loss of friends, and to have smaller peer networks. By late adolescence, however, sexual-minority adolescents actually had more close friends than heterosexual youth. Furthermore, they did not differ from heterosexual adolescents in how connected they felt to their friends or in how much control they had over their relationships.

These investigators also found that sexual-minority youth who were "out," that is, who openly disclosed their sexual orientation to heterosexual peers, had more friends, but had also lost more friends. Overall, however, these investigators found that it was the quality of adolescents' relationships with their friends, rather than their sexual identity per se, that contributed to their sense of well-being (Diamond & Lucas, 2004).

The Peer Group

A Malayan proverb counsels that one should trumpet in a herd of elephants, crow in the company of cocks, and bleat in a flock of goats. This pretty much sums up the behavior of adolescents with their peers. The **peer group** is one of the most important socializing forces in the lives of adolescents, regulating the pace as well as the particulars of the socialization process. Adolescents who fall behind their friends in social skills are dropped

sexual-minority youth Adolescents whose sexual orientation is not exclusively heterosexual.

peer group A group of individuals of the same age; a social group that regulates the pace of socialization.

from the group, just as are those who move ahead too quickly. Similarly, those whose tastes and attitudes fail to match the group's are likely to be considered nerdy, geeks, or just "out of it." The cost of bleating when others are crowing can be high.

The peer group assumes special importance in adolescence for a number of reasons. Adolescents are moving toward greater autonomy and independence, and peers provide much-needed emotional and social support. Adolescents also learn many social skills with peers that they would not learn from parents or teachers. Peers reward each other with potent reinforcers: acceptance, popularity, and status (Muuss, 1990).

Cliques and Crowds

Most adolescents move in two types of groups: the **clique** and the crowd. A clique consists of the close friends with whom adolescents spend most of their time. Cliques can be as large as ten or as small as three. These friends are usually the same sex and age, are in the same class in school, share the same ethnic background, and live relatively close to each other. Similarities in the composition of boys' and girls' cliques are striking. Aaron Hogue and Laurence Steinberg (1995), at Temple University, asked over 6,000 high school students to name their closest friends at school. Sixty-five percent of boys' cliques and 63% of girls' cliques were made up exclusively of same-sex friends, and 85% of boys' and 86% of girls' cliques had no more than one friend of the opposite sex.

Even though cliques are the most common type of social grouping, only about half of students belong to a clique. What about the other half? Two other types of peer relationships, liaisons and isolates, are also common. **Liaisons** are adolescents who are socially active and have friends in a number of cliques but do not themselves belong to any one of these. These students serve the important function of bringing together groups of adolescents who otherwise would have few channels of communication—in a sense, plugging these cliques into the larger social network within the school. For instance, one of an adolescent's best friends may have been in several school plays with him and another may be on the baseball team. When he gets together with these friends, each of them may occasionally bring one of their friends along, with the result that members of the baseball team and the class play now give each other "high fives" when they meet, whereas previously they would not have known each other. **Isolates,** on the other hand, have few friends, either within a clique or outside it, having few links to other adolescents in the social network (Ennett & Bauman, 1996).

A **crowd** is larger than a clique and more impersonal. Crowds usually number about 20. Not all the members of a crowd are close friends, but each is someone other members feel relatively comfortable with. Crowds usually consist of several of the friends in one's clique along with adolescents from several other cliques. For about half of the adolescents, their best friend is also in the same crowd. It is relatively unlikely for an adolescent to be a member of a crowd without belonging to one of these cliques; however, many adolescents belong to a clique and not to a crowd (Urberg et al., 1995).

The functions of cliques and crowds differ. Crowd events provide the settings in which adolescents try out new social skills. Clique activities provide feedback about the success of these skills and advice when skills fall short. If the crowd has a single purpose, it is to help adolescents move from same-sex to mixed-sex interactions (Dunphy, 1963). Many adolescents need all the help they can get.

clique A peer group made up of one's best friends, usually including no more than five or six members.

liaison Adolescents who have friends in several cliques but do not themselves belong to any one of these.

isolate Adolescents who have few friends, either within a clique or outside it, and who have few links to other adolescents in the social network.

crowd A peer group formed from several cliques of the same age group.

Adolescents spend most of their time talking about crowd activities when they are with members of their clique, either planning the next event or rehashing the last one, gathering valuable information from such "pregame" and "postgame" analyses. The feedback comes from specialists—other adolescents who know just how difficult a social maneuver can be and who can recommend something that has worked for them in similar situations.

If clique activities are coaching sessions, crowd events are the game itself. Adolescents enter the field ready to try out new social moves. Reflecting their specialized nature, crowd and clique activities take place at different times during the week. Crowd events, just like actual games, occur on weekends, and clique activities, like other coaching sessions, take place throughout the week.

Developmental changes occur in the structure of peer groups just as they do with friendships. Both cliques and crowds evolve as adolescents face different issues; so does the importance of being in a group. Belonging to groups is most important to early and middle adolescents, and less so for preadolescents, for whom they are not yet needed, or late adolescents, who no longer need them. Initially adolescents move in isolated same-sex cliques. The first movement toward heterosexual encounters occurs with the emergence of the crowd. Members of unisex cliques get together in crowds made up of cliques of both genders. Adolescents consider these initial interactions to be daring and engage in them only in the safety of groups. The author can attest to the accuracy of this observation. At a party given by her sixth-grade daughter, one of the girls hung some mistletoe. Within minutes the boys had fled the house and milled about in the yard in the dark, returning only after the mistletoe had been removed. Yet reports that filtered back over the week indicated the boys had had a *great* time and wanted to know when there would be another party.

These two girls are likely to belong to the same clique, and are not likely to include an outsider in their intimate conversation.

Late adolescents are comfortable with others of the opposite sex, and the crowd disintegrates into loosely grouped cliques of couples who are "going together." Cliques also become less important with age. The number of adolescents belonging to a clique declines from the sixth to the twelfth grades. As the Research Focus "Longitudinal Design" discusses, however, the membership of a clique tends to be stable over time.

All crowds are not created equal. Ask any adolescent. Some are more prestigious than others. A "leading crowd" exists at most schools. Students in this crowd are held in high regard by others, sometimes even to the point of envy. Almost always the members of this crowd feel good about themselves as well, having higher levels of self-esteem than students in less-prestigious crowds (Brown & Lohr, 1987). All the students at any school know what it takes to be a member of the leading crowd. For boys, being good at sports is important; for girls, it is being a social leader. Students in the leading crowd are also likely to be leaders in the school and even to have teachers look to them for help with extracurricular activities.

At crowd events, such as high school football games, where various cliques mingle, adolescents can practice new social skills and new roles with new people.

Other crowds form a loose status hierarchy below the leading crowd. Adolescents receive constant reminders at school of their status. Who sits with them in the cafeteria, who can cut in front of whom in line, which clubs and activities are open or closed to them—all confirm the loose pecking order that reflects the relative prestige of their particular crowd. One might think that the only ones to escape with their self-esteem intact would be those from the leading crowd. However, adolescents from other crowds appear to fare just as well if they like the crowd to which they belong. This suggests that although peer group membership is important for adolescents, it is a sense of belonging rather than the status of the group itself that is critical.

Crushes and Dating

Even before dating begins, adolescents go through a stage in which they develop crushes. A **crush** involves an idealized fantasy about another person, and it is rarely reciprocated. The other person remains distant, even if it's someone just two seats away in the same class. The absence of reciprocity and the distance factor in crushes are important features, because they allow adolescents to explore new role possibilities at a safe distance (Erikson, 1950, 1968).

Even so, it is common for early adolescents to get together in various types of mixed-sex activities. In one study, fifth- through eighth-graders were questioned at the beginning and again at the end of each school year concerning the extent to which they participated in various types of mixed-sex activities. These could range from simply hanging out together, to dating, to having a girlfriend or boyfriend (Connolly, Craig, Goldberg,& Pepler, 2004). By the sixth grade, the amount of time students spent in mixed-sex activities had increased, and for seventh- and eighth-graders, **dating** had increased by the end of the school year.

Dating is so much a part of the cultural scene one might assume it has always been practiced. Yet it is a relatively recent phenomenon. Prior to the early 1900s, couples dated primarily to determine their suitability for marriage. Before that, girls were given in marriage by their families to suitable partners; young couples had little say over the choices of their prospective mates.

Dating today serves a number of functions, of which the selection of marriage partners is only one. A very important function for adolescents when they first begin to date is simply recreation: Dating is fun—or at least it's supposed to be. Adolescents also report feeling nervous and apprehensive. Dates can have awkward moments. Many adolescents fear rejection and are uncertain about how to act on a date. Should the boy or the girl open the car door? One girl explained, "You just sort of walk along and if he walks the other way, you know you have to open it yourself." Should the boy help the girl

crush An idealized fantasy about another person that is rarely reciprocated.

dating A social activity that typically begins in mid-adolescence.

RESEARCH FOCUS

Longitudinal Design: Friendship Patterns

How stable are adolescents' friendships? Are the kids that make up an adolescent's closest circle of friends likely to be in that same circle a year later? For that matter, how common is it for adolescents to have a group of intimate friends instead of, say, a single best friend or few close friends at all?

Studies of adolescents' friendships have identified a number of friendship patterns, but until recently we have not known how common or stable each of these patterns was. One friendship pattern is the *clique.* A clique is a small group of intimate friends who are similar in sex, age, ethnicity, and social status. Friends who belong to the same clique spend much of their time together. A second type of friendship pattern is that of the *liaison.* Adolescents who are liaisons have a number of close friendships, but these are with adolescents who belong to several different cliques. Thus, liaisons open channels of communication between cliques, increasing the likelihood that adolescents from different cliques will do things together. A third friendship pattern, that of *isolates,* characterizes adolescents who are not members of a clique and, unlike liaisons, have few friendships in general.

Susan Ennett and Karl Bauman (1996) asked adolescents to name their best friends—first when they were in the ninth grade and a year later when they were in the tenth grade. These investigators used a *longitudinal design.* In this type of research, one studies a single *cohort,* a group of individuals all the same age, and takes several measurements, each at different ages. Ennett and Bauman selected two *times of measurement,* assessing adolescents' friendships in the ninth and tenth grades.

By following the same individuals over time, we can see patterns to development that we might otherwise miss. And because we are comparing the adolescents with themselves at each age, we minimize the problem of having equivalent samples. Are there any problems with this type of research? Unfortunately, the answer is yes. To understand what these problems are, we must define three terms: age changes, time of measurement differences, and confounding.

Age changes are the biological and experiential changes that always accompany aging. They occur in all cultures and at all points in history. We assume that age changes have a biological basis (although we are not always able to identify them) and should therefore be universal; that is, they should occur in all people no matter what their social or cultural background. A good example of an age change is the neural development that continues into adolescence (see Chapter 4) and presumably underlies the development of increasingly abstract thought.

Time of measurement differences reflect social conditions, currents of opinion, and historical events that are present when we make our observations and that can affect attitudes and behavior. When we study age changes by repeatedly observing the same group of individuals over time, we can mistake time of measurement changes for age changes. It's always possible, for example, that transition from a middle school to a high school setting could disrupt existing friendship patterns.

Confounding occurs when observations reflect systematic differences in more than one variable, with the result that we cannot separate the effects of one from those of the other. Longitudinal research frequently confounds age changes with time of measurement differences, making it impossible to conclusively separate the effects of age from those due to time of measurement. Do changes in friendship patterns over adolescence reflect differences due to age or to disruptions due to transitions from one school setting to another?

Longitudinal research can suffer from other problems as well. It is difficult to keep in touch with individuals over the years. Maintaining elaborate records, and the staff required for this bookkeeping, can be expensive. Longitudinal research is also time-consuming. We must wait while individuals age. And there is no guarantee that we will outlive them. A more serious problem than any of these is the nearly inevitable loss of subjects over time. People move away, die, or for other reasons are not available for study. This loss is called *subject mortality* and is almost always systematically related to age. In other words, the individuals who remain in the study are not necessarily representative of those their age in the general population, because the less healthy and otherwise less fortunate are the first to leave the sample. (Perhaps adolescents with few friends do not want to be reminded of this and drop out of the study.)

(continued)

RESEARCH FOCUS *(continued)*

With these cautions in mind, let's go back to Ennett and Bauman's study and see what they found about adolescents' friendships. Consistent with the findings of other studies of friendships, these investigators found that the most frequent type of friendship pattern was the clique, with 44% of adolescents belonging to a clique. Additionally, significant numbers of adolescents were isolates (27%) and liaisons (29%).

What about the stability of these friendship patterns over time? These investigators found that, for any adolescent, both those who were clique members and those who were isolates at the first time of measurement were more likely to have the same status one year later than were those who were liaisons. These findings may not be that surprising, especially when we learn that clique membership itself tends to be stable over a year's time. Also, adolescents who have already experienced difficulty integrating themselves into a social group may not find it that much easier to do so a year later. Liaisons, on the other hand, have already had close friendships in one or more social groups and can more easily move into any one of them, changing their characteristic friendship pattern to that of a clique member.

Source: S. T. Ennett & K. E. Bauman. (1996). Adolescent social networks: School, demographic, and longitudinal considerations. *Journal of Adolescent Research, 11,* 194–215.

on with her coat? "I act like I'm having problems, and if he doesn't notice, I forget it," suggested one teenager (Place, 1975). Yet despite the uncertainties, most adolescents find dating enjoyable.

Related to these uncertainties is another important function of dating: Dating enables adolescents to explore a new role, namely, the adult sexual role they will assume. When adolescents date, in other words, they find themselves in a role that is significantly different from that of any other they have previously assumed, whether as child, friend, student, or employee (Dowdy & Kliewer, 1998). Dating, as a consequence, is fraught with uncertainty and excitement.

When Dating Begins Adolescents start to date between the ages of 12 and 16 (Adams, Laursen, & Wilder, 2001). Girls go out on first dates somewhat earlier than boys (they also enter puberty earlier). Most girls start to date by the age of 14, although age itself is not the only indicator. One can better predict whether an adolescent is dating by knowing whether friends have begun to date than by knowing the adolescent's age or even sexual maturity (Dornbusch et al., 1981). Parents seem especially subject to a form of peer pressure all their own in this respect. As one adolescent girl remarked when she explained how she got her parents to consent to letting her go on a date, "If your girlfriends are not going out, forget it. I just gave examples of who was going out." Another ice-breaker was a strategy learned from childhood:

Daughter: Dad, can I go to the movies with Eddie?
Father: I don't know; ask Mom.
Daughter: Mom, Dad said Eddie and I can go to the movies if you say it's okay.
Mother: Okay, then, you can go.
Daughter: Dad, Mom said it's okay.

The peer group regulates the pace of socialization into more adult roles. Adolescents who don't begin dating when their friends do may be dropped from their peer groups. Adolescent girls frequently report friction with their friends when they begin dating. These conflicts often involve concerns of disloyalty and competition. Boys, on the other hand, experience fewer of these difficulties (Roth & Parker, 2001).

When they are just beginning to date, most adolescents worry about awkward moments and fear rejection. Once they do date someone regularly, however, the self-consciousness diminishes and they can relax and have fun.

A Youth Culture

In certain respects, adolescents are no different from individuals of any age. Most of us spend our free time with those who enjoy the same things, laugh at the same jokes, and share similar beliefs as to what's really important in life. When you think of it, this is also how we've talked about culture—in terms of the shared customs and beliefs among members of a group. How, then, do the company of friends and the society of peers influence adolescents, and does their influence create cultural barriers that parents and others find difficult to cross?

School

A concern among some parents and educators is that adolescents place less importance on academic achievement than they should, presumably due to competing values held by their peers. In a classic study, students at ten different high schools were asked to identify which of their classmates they most admired (Coleman, 1961). For boys at every school, the best athletes were also considered to be the most popular. Athletes were twice as likely to be in the leading crowd as were those who did well in school. Perhaps not surprisingly, when boys were asked how they would like to be remembered, 44% of them said as an athletic star. For girls, being a leader in school activities contributed most to popularity and was the way they wanted to be remembered.

This picture appears to have changed little over the years. However, one noticeable change is that girls value good grades more than they did a generation ago, even though they do not see these as valued by peers any more than in previous years (Hopmeyer Gorman, Kim, & Schimmelbusch, 2002; Quatman, Sokolik, & Smith, 2000; U.S. Department of Health and Human Services, 2002c).

Even though adolescents think good looks are important, physical attractiveness probably contributes to popularity only for those adolescents at either extreme. For those in between—and this would be most adolescents—other factors are more important. Conversely, academic achievement is probably more important than most research has suggested. Part of the difficulty in interpreting the findings on academic achievement may be due to the way questions have been worded. When asked, "How would you like to be remembered?" boys say as an athletic star and girls as a leader in activities. But when asked, "How would you rank the following in importance to you?" most adolescents will put getting good grades above being good in sports or being a social leader (Quatman et al., 2000).

The importance of athletic ability, school activities, and academic achievement also varies from one school to another. Athletic ability tends to have more importance, for example, in rural communities and in schools drawing from lower socioeconomic levels, whereas in urban settings or in communities with more highly educated parents, it is less important.

Conformity and Peer Pressure

Friends draw adolescents into realms beyond the family that highlight differences between themselves and their parents. These differences become important ways of organizing their individuality; however, they can leave adolescents with feelings of loneliness. Peers provide the emotional support that contributes to feelings of self-worth. Peer expectations for well-defined standards of speech and dress also establish outward behaviors that define the group and establish a sense of belonging among its members. Adolescents consider it a bargain to give up some of their individuality for the security that comes with belonging to a group.

Conformity peaks in early adolescence when adolescents begin to experience their separateness from their parents. Studies of conformity show that early adolescents are most influenced by others' judgments, sometimes even changing their answers when they are obviously right to conform to those of the group. By mid-adolescence, conformity has already begun to decrease, and by late adolescence it has decreased even more (Gavin & Furman, 1989). Figure 8.1 shows this trend. With respect to age-linked behaviors such as smoking and drinking, however, adolescents' concerns about what their friends might think peak somewhat later (Hendry, Glendinning, & Shucksmith, 1996).

Conformity isn't limited to adolescence; it characterizes behavior at every age. Nor is conformity necessarily bad. It is simply a tendency to go along with the standards and norms of one's group. Trends in fashion, food, and recreation are as apparent among 50-year-olds as among 15-year-olds. We notice conformity, however, when the norms for one group run counter to those of another, as sometimes occurs with adolescents and their parents. Different behaviors and skills contribute to acceptance more by peers than by adults. These differences increase with age in early adolescence.

Not all adolescents are equally likely to conform to the opinions of others. Those who have high status in their peer group are less likely to show conformity. The same is true for adolescents who have a well-developed sense of themselves. In general, adolescents who have a firm sense of who they are, and are held in high regard by others, are less influenced by others' opinions. The same has been found to be true for adults (Harvey & Rutherford, 1980; Marcia, 1980).

conformity The tendency to go along with the norms and standards of one's group.

Conformity also reflects adolescents' relationships with their parents. Parents who have encouraged adolescents to take part in responsible decision making within the family, who provide reasons when disciplining, and who encourage a verbal give-and-take with their children—that is, authoritative parents, as discussed in Chapter 7—have adolescents who show the least conformity. Adolescents from these homes have more positive self-concepts and a better-developed sense of self. Further, they have learned from childhood to live with the consequences of their decisions, even when these have been as simple as deciding not to clean their rooms and choosing to be grounded instead. They have also learned that even when their parents disagree with them, they still have their emotional support.

However, even authoritative parents can worry that peers will have more influence than they on their children's values and activities. Adolescents are beginning to spend more time with their friends than with their families. Perhaps, too, parents realize that the decisions adolescents make can affect their futures in ways decisions rarely do for children. Even so, adolescents report that parents are the best all-around source of support, whether emotional or informational, in the form of advice (Reid, Landesman, Treder, & Jaccard, 1989).

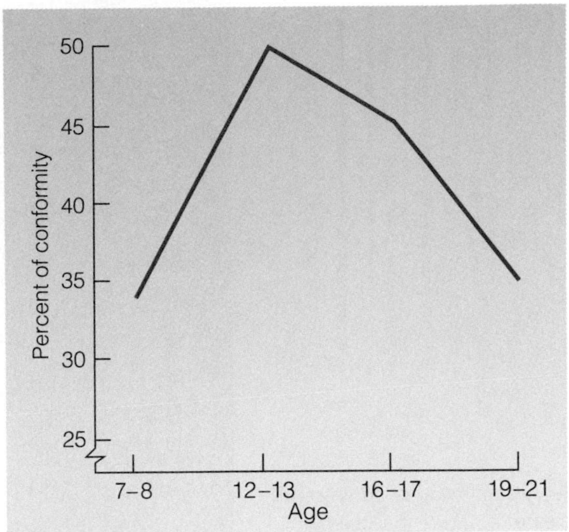

FIGURE 8.1
Changes in Percent of Conformity with Age. *Source:* P. R. Costanzo. (1970). Conformity development as a function of self-blame. *Journal of Personality and Social Psychology, 14,* 366–374.

Fashion fads such as pierced eyebrows, spiked hair, and baggy jeans do little to alleviate parents' fears that they have lost their children to an alien culture. But even flagrant differences such as these do not mean that parents no longer influence their children's values. If they did not, adolescents would not have to go to such extremes to assert their individuality. Nor do obvious differences in taste, as in music and clothes, reflect a shift in underlying values. This is not to say that adolescents are not influenced by their peers. They are. But the extent to which they are and the way this occurs cannot be thought of simply as an either-or contest between the values of parents and those of peers.

Adolescents experience **peer pressure** as a pressure to think and act like their friends. The price of belonging to a group is to maintain the ways of the group. This pressure changes with age. One of the primary functions of the peer group is to help adolescents gain their footing as they step outside the family. As adolescents become more sure of themselves, pressures to maintain the norms of the group lessen. Peer pressure is strongest in early adolescence, when adolescents most need the support of a well-defined group. Conformity is also greatest then. As adolescents become more sure of themselves, the peer group becomes less important. As a result, the need to define group membership through rigidly prescribed standards of dress, speech, and so on lessens (Clasen & Brown, 1985).

With age, too, adolescents become more comfortable in thinking for themselves and arriving at their own decisions. They are less likely to look to their parents *or* their friends for advice, and when they do seek advice, they are better able to weigh the opinions of others and arrive at their own decisions. This confidence reflects a new level of security in their values and how they arrived at them.

Values

If anything, the values of peers and parents are likely to complement each other rather than conflict. Friends typically share similar experiences; they live nearby, come from families of about the same income level, and are likely to share the same ethnic background. Friends' parents are also important in maintaining the values established by an adolescent's parents, primarily, it seems, by influencing the behavior of the adolescent's friends. Socially and academically competent adolescents are likely to seek the company

peer pressure Experienced pressure to think and act like one's friends.

Every generation of adolescents creates a culture that seems wholly foreign to older generations. And yet, despite their untraditional tastes, adolescents' values remain surprisingly similar to those of their parents' and grandparents' generations.

of similar adolescents. These interactions, in turn, often amplify the initial advantages of each. Anne Fletcher, Nancy Darling, and Laurence Steinberg, at Temple University, and Sanford Dornbusch, at Stanford University, (1995) studied a large sample of 14- to 18-year-olds, looking in particular at the way adolescents' friends described their parents. In general, adolescents whose friends described their parents as authoritative had more positive attitudes toward school and were less likely to use substances such as alcohol or cigarettes. For boys, authoritative parenting among their friends' parents was also associated with behavioral measures, such as greater resistance to conformity and lower levels of misconduct, and for girls, this parenting style was associated with measures of psychosocial adjustment, such as higher levels of self-reliance and self-esteem.

Of course, some differences between parents and peers can be expected. And when they occur, the reference group that adolescents turn to will depend on a number of factors, one of which is the type of decision to be made. Adolescents generally look to their friends for short-term decisions, such as whether to go to a party or what clothes to buy. They turn to their parents for decisions about their futures: plans for education, marriage, or choosing an occupation. Thus, parents have more influence over the larger decisions of life, and friends over the day-to-day particulars of living it.

Important life decisions reflect values, and adolescents are likely to share these with their parents—values about education, relationships, and work. But values as broad as these do not translate easily into the language of daily affairs. They say little about how one spends an afternoon or which movie to see. With respect to actual behaviors such as these, friends have more influence.

Deviant Behavior

The support of friends remains important with respect to deviant behavior. Adolescents seek out friends who engage in similar activities and, in turn, are influenced by the activities of their friends. In an early study of 2,000 adolescents, no other single activity or

Most adolescents spend more time talking with their friends than with their parents and are more influenced by their friends about day-to-day decisions. But the background and the values of an adolescent's friends tend to be similar to those of the adolescent's parents.

attitude was found to be as likely to be shared by friends as the use of recreational drugs (Kandel, 1978). Similarly, Kathryn Urberg (1992) followed pairs of friends over a two-year period and found that individual friends, not the social crowd, were the major influence in whether adolescents were likely to smoke. Kimberly Henry, Michael Slater, and Eugene Oetting (2005), at the University of Colorado, also followed adolescents and their friends over a two-year period, and found not only that adolescents' use of alcohol reflected the number of their friends who drank, but that changes with time in their drinking corresponded to similar changes in their friends' use of alcohol over time. Before concluding that adolescents are likely to do whatever their friends are doing, it should be pointed out that the influence of peers was moderated by adolescents' own beliefs and personalities. Thus, those who viewed drinking as harmful were less influenced by drinking among their friends. Similarly, more general aspects of adolescents' personalities, such as level of autonomy or willingness to take risks, moderate peer influence (Allen, Porter, & McFarland, 2006).

In part, similarity in the use of recreational drugs reflects adolescents' perceptions of their friends as more deviant than they actually are. Comparisons of adolescents' estimates of their friends' use of substances, such as cigarettes or alcohol, with actual reports from their friends find that adolescents overestimate the extent to which their friends engage in deviant behavior. Adolescents' use of these substances, nonetheless, is likely to correspond more closely to their perceptions of what their friends are doing than to their friends' actual behavior (Bauman & Fisher, 1986). Adolescents *are* influenced by their friends, but they also appear to select friends based on their perception of similar characteristics—especially as these characteristics relate to deviant behaviors (Cleveland, Wiebe, & Rowe, 2005).

Actual pressure from friends to misbehave may be relatively slight. A survey of nearly 700 junior high and high school students found little pressure from friends for misconduct—for example, drug or alcohol use or sexual intercourse—and much actual discouragement by friends. Different crowds exert pressure in different areas of adolescents' lives, of course, and the "druggie-toughs" surveyed in this study experienced more pressure for misconduct than did "jock-populars" or "loners" (Clasen & Brown, 1985).

What are adolescents likely to do if approached by a friend to engage in some deviant activity? Adolescents of either sex feel different pressures. Boys are more likely to agree or disagree because of the anticipated outcome; they will say no because they're not interested or they think they might get in trouble. Peer approval and friendship are more important sources of pressure for girls. Girls are more likely to agree even when they anticipate a negative outcome, citing friendship or peer approval as reasons (Pearl, Bryan, & Herzog, 1990; Treboux & Busch-Rossnagel, 1990).

How much influence parents retain with their teenagers when deviant behaviors or conflicting values arise depends in large measure on the quality of the relationship they have with them. For instance, Andrew Fuligni and Jacquelynne Eccles (1993), studying a sample of over 1,700 sixth- and seventh-graders, found that adolescents who perceived themselves as having little opportunity to participate in decision making, and who believed their parents to be overly strict, were less likely than other adolescents to seek advice from their parents and more likely to turn to their peers. They were also more likely to sacrifice significant aspects of their own lives, such as keeping up with schoolwork or developing their talents, in order to be popular with friends.

Parents who are overly permissive or authoritarian are least effective. Adolescents are most likely to listen to parents who have involved them since childhood in decision making in the family and have held them responsible for their actions. These parents are also most likely to give reasons for family rules and to maintain an open dialogue with their children. Adolescents from families such as these, with a strongly developed sense of self, are less likely to be pressured by peers to misbehave.

It is easier for adolescents to listen to their parents' views when they are sure of their own autonomy. The quality of the relationship between adolescents and their parents, not the existence of another reference group, determines whether adolescents will remain close to their parents and seek them out for advice in decisions about their lives.

It should be clear at this point that the relative influence of parents and peers cannot be thought of as a simple tug-of-war with the adolescent in the middle (Kandel, 1996). The values of friends frequently overlap with those of parents, minimizing conflict when it occurs. Parents may occasionally even look to an adolescent's friends to determine what is normative when they are uncertain about what adolescent behaviors are appropriate, for example, when to wear lipstick or when to get a part-time job. Also, the values of parents and peers influence different types of decisions, leading to less conflict than many parents anticipate. Finally, adolescents vary considerably among themselves in the extent to which they are influenced by the attitudes and behaviors of others, whether these be parents or peers.

Are adolescents and parents likely to experience conflict? Probably. Does conflict weaken the relationship? Not necessarily. Conflict can help adolescents restructure and strengthen relationships with parents. Parents are likely to participate in this restructuring process as well. Even as they attempt to get teenagers to agree with them, parents also encourage adolescents to think for themselves and to speak their own minds. Honest exchanges such as these frequently lead to the evolution of joint views shared by both (Youniss & Smollar, 1989).

Youth Organizations

In addition to informal get-togethers with peers and the more formal world of school, many adolescents devote their time to another aspect of youth culture: youth organizations. Adolescents belong to clubs, are members of teams, and participate in volunteer work in their communities. **Structured voluntary activities,** such as sports, the creative arts, or volunteer work, are part of most adolescents' worlds and are thought to contribute substantially to their well-being. Reed Larson (2000), at the University of Illinois, argues that because such activities are intrinsically motivating and challenging, and because they demand adolescents' concentrated attention, they build skills and develop initiative. They also have a spillover effect, promoting other positive qualities such as self-control, assertiveness, and even improved grades (Hattie, Marsh, Neill, & Richards, 1997).

Sizable numbers of adolescents participate in after-school activities. Some, but not all, of these activities are school-related. For instance, approximately 25% to 40% of high school seniors indicate being involved in sports, the creative arts, academic clubs, or other school activities (Youth Indicators, 2005). Additionally, many adolescents belong to national youth organizations such as the Scouts or 4-H and to local community organizations. A substantial number of adolescents are involved in religious activities; 33% attend religious services weekly, and many of these also attend weekly youth groups (Huebner & Mancini, 2003; Youth Indicators, 2005). Additionally, many adolescents are involved in various types of community volunteer work, 34% doing so at least once or twice a month (Youth Indicators, 2005).

Activities such as these also fill the hours after school lets out but before working parents typically return home. Sara Goldstein, Pamela Davis-Kean, and Jacquelynne Eccles (2005), at the University of Michigan, followed adolescents from the seventh to the eleventh grade, determining, among other things, how they spent this time. These investigators found evidence that by the eighth grade, unsupervised and unstructured time spent with peers was associated with problem behavior in the eleventh grade.

Despite the increasing importance of friends in adolescents' lives, parents continue to remain significant sources of strength and influence. Both parents and peers contribute to adolescents' ability to face changes in yet another area of their lives—school. We will analyze these changes in the next chapter.

structured voluntary activities Activities that are intrinsically motivating and challenging that build skills and foster initiative.

Summary

The Importance of Friendships

- Adolescents experiment with new behaviors with their friends and, in doing so, discover new things about themselves.
- The psychosocial task in early adolescence may be more one of forming a *group identity* than of achieving a personal identity. The latter task assumes salience in mid-adolescence when issues related to affiliation and belonging have been resolved, and adolescents are ready to address the differences that distinguish them from others.
- Friendships change with age. Those of preadolescents reflect a concern with being accepted. Preadolescents use gossip as a way of affirming group norms and their membership in the group. Adolescent friendships reflect a concern with self-discovery; self-disclosure becomes important to this process.

- Friends contribute to adolescents well-being; they facilitate the formation of an ideal self-image and are important sources of self-esteem.
- Parents also contribute to well-being. Interactions that communicate support, affection, and encouragement promote *self-esteem.*

Friendship Patterns

- Patterns of friendship differ with the age and sex of adolescents. Early adolescent girls' friendships focus on the activities that bring friends together. Friendships in mid-adolescence for girls are concerned with the personal qualities of friends more than before. Girls want friends they can confide in and trust. Friendships in late adolescence focus more on personalities. Intimacy continues to grow and more friends are of the opposite sex.
- Boys' friendships in early adolescence are also centered on shared activities. By middle adolescence, their friendships are as close emotionally as girls' friendships but involve less discussion of feelings.
- There are several dimensions to *social competence:* assessing a situation, responding to it, and knowing that relationships take time to develop. Competent adolescents are better able to see what is going on in a social situation and adapt their behavior accordingly. They also realize that developing friendships takes time.
- Popularity can refer to social preference, how much others like you, or to social prestige, how much others look up to you. Popular adolescents who enjoy social prestige often use either physical or relational aggression to both achieve and maintain their status within the group.
- Adolescents can be categorized into five social statuses based on the frequency with which classmates nominate them as someone they "like the most" or "like the least." *Rejected* adolescents are rarely mentioned as someone liked the most and frequently mentioned as someone liked the least. *Controversial* adolescents are both highly liked and highly disliked. *Average* adolescents are moderately popular and moderately disliked as well. *Neglected* adolescents are neither highly liked nor disliked.
- Training in *social skills* is part of many intervention programs designed to facilitate better peer relationships, and social-cognitive programs address how accurately adolescents perceive the intentions of others.
- Interethnic friendships form when adolescents live in integrated neighborhoods and attend integrated schools. Classroom climates affect the formation of such friendships, which are likely to develop when students are assigned to small groups to work together in a noncompetitive atmosphere. Interethnic friendships face challenges posed by different enculturation experiences. Adolescents of different backgrounds can perceive and react to the same situation differently; misinterpretations and hurt feelings can result.
- As with ethnicity, most close friendships are with peers of the same sex. There are few differences in the number of friends adolescents of either sex have or in the amount of conflict they experience; however, boys tend to minimize conflicts and girls to confront their friends.
- Sexual-minority youth have more fears and concerns about relationships with their peers and experience more friendship loss. However, by late adolescence, they have more close friends than heterosexual youth.

The Peer Group

- The peer group regulates the pace of socialization. Adolescents who either fall too far behind or move too far ahead of their friends are dropped from the group.
- The most common type of peer group is the *clique*, a small group of friends. Adolescents not in cliques may be liaisons, who are socially active and have friends in several cliques, or isolates, who have only a few individual friends and are not part of the social network.
- *Crowds* are groups of about 20. Adolescents try out new social skills at crowd events, the most important of which involve the opposite sex. The crowd is primarily important in helping adolescents move into mixed-sex interactions, whereas clique activities provide feedback about the success of new social skills.
- Cliques and crowds change in importance as adolescents age. They are most important in mid-adolescence and become less so as adolescents begin to form couples who are "going together."
- Before dating begins, adolescents go through a stage in which they develop crushes. Dating begins anywhere between the ages of 12 and 16. Girls start somewhat earlier than boys. The most important

determinant of when they start to date is whether their friends are dating.

A Youth Culture

- School provides adolescents with a society of their peers. Adolescents may value academic achievement less than athletic achievement or being involved in many school activities.
- *Conformity* peaks in early adolescence. Adolescents with high social status and a well-developed sense of self are less likely to conform. Authoritative parenting also gives adolescents skills that help them make decisions for themselves.
- The values of peers and parents more frequently complement each other than conflict. Most adolescents have friends with values similar to theirs.
- When adolescents seek advice from parents and friends, they are more likely to seek parental advice concerning long-term life decisions and the advice of friends in daily matters. With age, adolescents become more comfortable in making their own decisions.
- Peers have an important influence on deviant behaviors. Gender differences exist in response to *peer pressure;* boys consider the anticipated outcome more, and girls consider peer approval and friendship more. Despite the importance of the peer culture, adolescents and parents share many basic values.
- Many adolescents participate in *structured voluntary activities* such as sports, the creative arts, or volunteer work. These activities build skills and develop initiative because they are intrinsically motivating and challenging, and because they demand adolescents' concentrated attention.

Key Terms

group identity
gossip
self-disclosure
self-esteem
ideal self-image
attachment
social competence
popular
social preference
social prestige
prosocial behaviors
physical aggression
relational aggression
rejected adolescents
controversial adolescents
average adolescents
neglected adolescents
social skills training
social-cognitive intervention
enculturation
sexual-minority youth
peer group
clique
liaison
isolate
crowd
dating
crush
conformity
peer pressure
structured voluntary activities

CHAPTER OUTLINE

CHAPTER 9

Adolescents in the Schools

CHAPTER OBJECTIVES

- To look more closely at adolescents as students and at how best to structure their classroom experiences
- To distinguish characteristics of effective schools: skilled teachers, small classes, supportive school climate, and multiple services for students and their families
- To look at violence, bullying, and peacemaking in schools
- To examine the relationship between academic achievement, socioeconomic status, gender, and culture
- To examine programs for gifted adolescents and those with learning disabilities
- To consider factors related to dropping out or completing school, and ways of assessing the success of schools

"Oh, no! Here he comes," I muttered.

"Move over, slime ball. Thanks for the place in line."

The kid was huge and his breath was fogging up my glasses. No food was worth this. I stepped out, and he stepped in line. From what I could see of the steam table, I was ahead on this one.

"Aren't you going to fight him?" nudged Erin.

"Sure, Erin. You want me to end up in the tossed salad?"

"This is too much!" she rasped. "The morning has gone from bad to awful—I want out!"

"Me too," I nodded. "But I don't think I could find my way. I got lost three times already today. If I'm late to another class, I'll have detention—and it's still the first week! Four minutes to get to classes! What are they training us for, the track team? I can't even open my locker that fast."

"Some ninth-grader slammed mine shut this morning—just as I popped the combination."

"Welcome to scrubs-ville, Erin."

"If this is what it's going to be like, I'm out of here!" she vowed.

Chapter Overview

Secondary school is a new experience for early adolescents, one that most will never forget. Some adolescents leave elementary school for a middle school, and others go to a junior high, but for all, the pace of learning will quicken. How well adolescents keep up will depend on many things. We will look at what adolescents bring to the classroom and at the learning environments they are entering.

We turn next to the characteristics that distinguish effective schools. These schools have skilled teachers and small classes, and are designed to meet the needs of early versus late adolescents. They also offer a variety of programs in addition to academic coursework, serving as a base for services ranging from health care to parent education.

We look next at school violence and bullying, and at characteristics of bullies and victims, before turning our attention to intervention programs that are effective in reducing bullying in schools. We then look at programs for resolving conflict that are designed for all adolescents.

Not all students have the same interests and not all learn at the same rate. We will look at ways for meeting the needs of diverse groups of students, such as mixed-ability grouping, tracking, and parental involvement in the schools. We will then turn our attention to how well schools are meeting the needs of female and male students, and the needs of adolescents from ethnically and culturally diverse backgrounds.

In the next section of the chapter, adolescents themselves step into the spotlight. Some rise to the occasion, meeting their own and others' expectations, while others lag behind. We will look first at proficiency in basic subjects and then at patterns of achievement among different groups of students. We then move to a consideration of students at the edge—those who are gifted, those who have learning disabilities, and those who drop out of school.

In the last section of the chapter, we consider ways of measuring the success of schools. Research into effective schools raises the question of whether changes that are necessary in order to reach alienated minorities are also necessary to effectively teach mainstream adolescents.

Educating Adolescents

The growth of **secondary education** in this country, that is, of middle schools, junior high schools, and high schools, has been nothing short of phenomenal given that fewer than 5% of the population completed high school in the early 1900's. Yet the successes of secondary education have been punctuated by crises as well, and by questions as to how best to educate adolescents.

Structuring the Learning Environment

secondary education Middle schools, junior high schools, and high schools.

direct instruction Instruction directed toward the mastery of basic skills; all students are involved in the same activities at any given time.

School districts and teachers face choices as to how best to structure classroom learning. We can distinguish two broad approaches to instruction. **Direct instruction** has as its goal the mastery of basic skills. Teachers work with the class as a whole, involving all students in the same activities at any given time during the class. Students spend class time working on tasks assigned by the teacher, covering basic disciplines such as math, literature, and science. Students typically work individually at their desks, while the teacher circulates around the room giving feedback or answering questions. Teachers offer direct instruction, providing students with necessary facts and illustrating solutions to problems. A basic assumption is that by having students work an all aspects of each lesson, each student will be given the opportunity to master all the elements of the assignment.

Differentiated instruction assumes that learning is not so much getting the facts straight as knowing what they mean; in that sense, this approach reflects the constructivist perspective described in this text. Since no two students are assumed to share the same learning profile of abilities and interests, classrooms are structured so that students have multiple ways of gaining information and of making sense of what they are learning. Classroom structure is flexible. At any one time, various groups of students can be working on a number of different projects; at other times, teachers may use whole-class discussions to relate the different projects to a common theme (Hall, 2002). Learning is seen as an active process, discovering solutions rather than being shown them. Consequently, students are encouraged to help plan the learning tasks they will study, set goals, and define the ways they will approach these.

Classroom learning can be structured in different ways. In this classroom, students work individually at their desks and the teacher offers direct instruction, providing them with necessary information and help when needed.

A central assumption of differentiated instruction is that students have different learning styles. **Learning styles** can be distinguished in terms of students' preferences for various elements of the learning situation. For instance, some students prefer to work for extended periods of time and others need frequent breaks. Some students prefer to work alone and others in groups; groups can be further distinguished by whether students work in pairs or as part of a team. Yet another difference concerns the modality in which information is presented. Some students learn best when information is presented visually, as in reading, whereas others do better if they can listen to a lecture (Dunn & Dunn, 1993; Lovelace, 2005).

Preparing for High School: Junior High or Middle School

Another choice facing school districts concerns the type of school adolescents enter once they leave elementary school: a **middle school** (fifth or sixth through eighth grade) versus a **junior high school** (seventh through eighth or ninth grades). Two events focus educators' concerns: Adolescents enter puberty during these years, and they leave one form of school for another. Puberty introduces intellectual, emotional, and psychological changes as well as physical ones. A change in school settings confronts adolescents with a more impersonal environment than the one they have previously known. Will one type of school ease the stresses of puberty more than the other? Also, which arrangement of grades will best facilitate the transition to high school (Epstein, 1990)?

Because of the secular trend, sixth-graders today are physically more like seventh- and eighth-graders than like schoolchildren a year behind them. Sixth-graders are also

differentiated instruction Flexible classroom structure providing multiple formats for gaining information.

learning styles Students' preferences concerning various aspects of the learning situation, for example, working individually or in groups, getting information by reading or listening to a class presentation.

middle school A secondary school that includes the fifth or sixth through the eighth grades.

junior high school A secondary school that typically includes the seventh through the ninth grades.

The structure of this classroom reflects the assumption that students differ in their interests and abilities; consequently students are given multiple ways of gaining information and of making sense of what they are learning.

intellectually and emotionally more mature. Most have begun to use formal thought, and patterns of friendship are changing (see Chapter 8). Students at the highest grades in middle school, those in seventh and eighth grades, are still experiencing pubertal changes and just moving into mixed-sex relationships. Middle schools place students going through similar changes in a single setting. Although some educators argue on this basis that sixth-, seventh-, and eighth-graders' needs are best met in a middle school, others voice concerns that by placing sixth-graders with older adolescents, they are rushed into more mature forms of behavior. These latter educators want to protect early adolescents from growing up too fast.

In actuality, decisions about middle schools and junior high schools are more likely to be made on the basis of local demographics than educational policy, but because comparisons of these two school settings reveal more similarities than differences, this fact loses much of its importance (Kohut, 1988). Similarities of both types of schools include the curriculum, teaching practices, and extracurricular activities.

Few consistent differences emerge in academic achievement between the two types of schools. Also, attitudes and behaviors among students attending each do not differ consistently. When differences emerge, they usually favor middle schools (Lipsitz, 1984). Students at middle schools have more positive attitudes about school, and about themselves, their peers, and their teachers, than do junior high students. Teachers' attitudes are more positive, too, in many of the comparisons.

Even though junior high schools and middle schools are designed specifically to meet the needs of early adolescents, the transition from elementary school to either one of these still can be difficult. Adolescents leave behind the comfortable familiarity of elementary school: a classroom they knew as well as their living room and a teacher they saw more often than their parents. And instead of being the oldest and biggest kids at school, they are once again the youngest and smallest.

Perhaps we shouldn't be surprised, then, by research showing that students' grades drop when they leave elementary school, for either a junior high school or a middle school. It's unclear what may be responsible for this drop since their achievement test

Whether they graduate to a junior high or a middle school, the transition from elementary school is a big step for young adolescents. No longer do they stay in the same classroom with the same teacher; now they have to find their way around campus and manage their time so that they carry out assignments from several teachers.

scores do not show a comparable drop in knowledge (Eccles, 2004). There is some evidence that performance is more disrupted in White students than in Black or Latino students; however, the reasons for this are unclear since grades for the latter were already significantly lower than for the White students, suggesting that for minority students, problems affecting their performance are already present in elementary school (Kuperminc, Blatt, Shahar, Henrich, & Leadbeater, 2004).

Problems adjusting to secondary school may reflect students' response to the more impersonal classroom environment they enter when they leave elementary school. Secondary schools typically are larger and classroom environments less supportive than in elementary schools (Barber & Olsen, 2004). Also, teachers involve students less in classroom decision making, which collides with young adolescents' press for greater autonomy (see Chapter 7). Perhaps because of this, Kuperminc et al. (2004) found students' sense of efficacy to drop with the transition, despite no change in feelings of self-worth. Finally, recall that this transition coincides with the onset of puberty, which, like toppling a row of dominoes, has a cascading effect extending to all areas of adolescents' lives.

What Makes Schools Effective?

What types of learning environments are likely to be most effective for young adolescents? Effective schools have skilled teachers, they are smaller or establish small learning communities within larger schools, they provide a supportive school climate, and they involve parents and the community in the services they offer.

The most important characteristic of an effective school is teachers who care about their students and have high expectations for them.

Skilled Teachers

One factor consistently distinguishes effective schools: the beliefs of the teaching staff that all students are capable of learning. Teachers at effective schools have high expectations. They interact with students more, reward them more, and have friendlier classrooms (Teddlie, Kirby, & Stringfield, 1989). Research constantly underscores the potent effect that individual teachers can have on their students (Crosnoe & Needham, 2004; Schoon, Parsons, & Sacker, 2004). Expecting the most from students and letting them know when they have succeeded are just as important as the latest in software and the number of books on the shelves. Students in classrooms where progress is monitored and positive feedback is given as to how well they are doing adjust better academically, and have higher achievement levels (Wentzel, 2002). In fact, the characteristics of effective teachers are similar to those of effective parents. Effective teachers are supportive and encourage their students, have organized classrooms in which students know what is expected of them, and make effective use of feedback in guiding students' activities. Such environments, whether in the classroom or at home, facilitate adjustment by enabling adolescents to regulate their own behavior (Brody, Dorsey, Forehand, & Armistead, 2002; Wentzel, 2002).

Skilled teachers are also able to present material in ways that can be understood by all of their students. Consider a science class in which, to solve a problem, students must hold all of the conditions constant except the one they are considering. The development of hypothetical thought enables adolescents to do this. Because not all students develop at the same rate, skilled teachers are likely to combine abstract approaches that illustrate isolating variables with concrete examples to bring their points home to less advanced thinkers as well. The example in the In More Depth box illustrates this point. Notice how the discussion revolves around common objects such as a Frisbee, a shoebox lid, and the cover to a tin can. Even concrete thinkers can wrap their minds around these examples.

IN MORE DEPTH

Science in the Classroom: Analysis of a Frisbee

The teacher in this science class has told students to bring in something that flies. One student brought in a Frisbee.

Teacher: Okay, let's consider some explanations now. Why is the Frisbee built this way? Look back at our list of structural features on the blackboard. . . . Why is the Frisbee designed the way it is? I'd like to see almost everyone's hand up with one idea.

Student 1: Well, it's round so you can spin it.

Teacher Okay. Now let's take this a little bit further. Could you spin it if it weren't round?

Student 1: No. Well, I guess you could. But it wouldn't work very well. It would flop around; it wouldn't sail smoothly.

Teacher: Can anyone think of an example of something shaped like a Frisbee . . . ? What has a rim like a Frisbee but isn't round?

Student 2: Maybe the lid of a shoe box. You know, it's shaped like a rectangle but it has sides like a Frisbee.

Teacher: And what would happen if you spun it like a Frisbee?

Student 2: Well, it wouldn't go very far. The air slows it down maybe.

Teacher: Good. Anyone else have some ideas about why it slows down?

Student 3: It doesn't spin well because the sides of the box lid hit the air.

Teacher: Good point. When it's not round, the sides hit the air and slow it down. That's a reason for a Frisbee being round. But that leads to another question: Why is spin so important? What happens if you throw a Frisbee without spinning it, versus throwing the Frisbee with a spin?

Student 4: It flops if you don't spin it. So I guess the spinning keeps it straight.

Teacher: Very good. So a Frisbee is round so it can spin fast without slowing down when its edges hit the air. And it needs to spin to keep it from tumbling. What about some other feature on the structure list? Who has an explanation for something else? . . .

Student 5: It's rounded on top. I mean it isn't perfectly flat. That maybe helps it to fly.

Teacher: A very interesting idea. So a Frisbee is a kind of spinning wing. The spinning keeps it straight and the wing shape helps it to stay up. Can anyone think of other things you can throw? . . .

Student 6: A discus.

Student 7: A tin-can lid. You can throw those by spinning them.

Teacher: Interesting examples. I wonder if we can see whether the rounded shape of a Frisbee really gives it more lift than something that's flat.

Student 8: But a discus is pretty heavy; so are tin-can lids.

Teacher: That's a good point. . . . When you're making a comparison, you want it to be fair. If you're comparing how much the rounded top helps, you don't want the comparison messed up by other differences, like weight. Is there any way we could make a fairer comparison? Could we test the Frisbee against itself somehow?

Student 9: How about throwing it upside down? If the rounded top really helps it to stay up, it shouldn't fly as well upside down.

Teacher: That's a good idea. Is it a fair comparison?

Student 9: Sure, because it weighs the same right-side up and upside down.

Teacher: Okay, so we have a good idea for controlling the variables. It's a fair test because everything is the same except what we're interested in—the rounded top. We have a Frisbee here, so let's try the experiment.

Source: D. N. Perkins. (1987). Knowledge as design: Teaching thinking through content. In J. B. Baron & R. J. Sternberg (Eds.), *Teaching thinking skills: Theory and practice*. New York: Freeman.

Secondary school students are often divided into vocational and college-bound tracks. The mere assignment to one track or the other can profoundly affect students' performance and teachers' expectations.

Smaller Schools and Smaller Communities for Learning

The size of schools is known to affect behavior at school—inside and outside class. Adolescents from smaller schools have more positive interactions with each other, fewer discipline problems, less absenteeism, and fewer dropouts. The critical size for a school is about 500 students. Once that number is reached, further increases don't have much effect (Garbarino, 1980).

Small schools can be more flexible in responding to the needs of adolescents. Anthony Bryk and Stephen Raudenbush (1988) analyzed data from a national survey of over 1,000 schools. They found that smaller schools can overcome differences related to social class, academic background, and personal factors more readily than large schools. Programs on drug use, multicultural education, and cooperative learning are easier to set in motion and to change in response to student needs. Students in small schools have more opportunity to participate in activities. The particular type of activity is not important—yearbook staffing, hall monitoring, cheerleading, or peer counseling. Each one gives students a sense of belonging and a way of identifying with school.

Although it is not possible to eliminate large schools, it is possible to create smaller "communities for learning" within them. These smaller environments can be just as responsive to students' needs as small schools are (Herlihy & Kemple, 2005). Small classes, in particular, may be especially important in facilitating learning. A comparison of ninth-grade students who had been randomly assigned to one of several class sizes for the first four years of their schooling found that those assigned to smaller classes performed significantly better in mathematics—six years later. Those who benefited most from smaller classes were minority students (Nye, Hedges, & Konstantopoulos, 2001).

School Climate

Unique characteristics of schools may be at least as important as their size. The relationship between school input variables—number of students per classroom, computers per student, or books in the library, for example—and school output, in the form of student achievement, is not a simple one. Schools with similar resources can differ markedly in their effectiveness. Process variables that reflect the qualities of a school, such as differences in social and academic climates among schools or differences in their teaching staffs, must also be entered into the equation. Achievement is determined not so much by how many computers are in a classroom or how many books are in the library, but by how effectively these resources are integrated into the instruction. In this respect, the relationships teachers have with their students are of vital importance. Teachers who are supportive and fair and have clearly defined expectations for their students contribute substantially to a school's climate (Barber & Olsen, 2004; Gottfredson, Gottfredson, Payne, & Gottfredson, 2005). Relationships among students, such as perceived friendliness and noncompetitiveness, also contribute to a school's climate (Loukas & Robinson, 2004). Additionally, schools that involve parents, either as classroom aides or tutors or as members of governing committees making schoolwide decisions, are more effective, especially in low-income districts where continuity between the home and the classroom needs bridging (Hill et al., 2004).

Schools that place as much value in educating students in music or drama as in college algebra or literature promote higher levels of achievement among all students. Often this requires a redefinition of values among teachers, staff, and parents. Our society has come to define intelligence in terms of verbal and mathematical abilities (see Chapter 4). In emphasizing these abilities, we have slighted others such as mechanical, interpersonal, or musical, in which students can also excel.

Full-Service Schools

Full-service schools collaborate with community agencies to provide a variety of health and social services for students and their families (Dryfoos & Maguire, 2002; Smith, 2000, 2004). Some of these services are offered on the school campus and others are available through referrals. Examples of these services are health clinics, ESL (English as a Second Language) classes, and family welfare services. Such "one-stop" schools support students by supporting their families. They also strengthen ties between the school, parents, and the community, and are one of the policy recommendations made by the Carnegie Corporation (1989) as a way of improving education.

Parental Involvement

Effective schools also work to involve parents in their children's education. Adolescents whose parents are involved have more positive attitudes toward school, higher achievement scores, and higher educational aspirations (Fan & Chen, 2001; Hill et al., 2004). Parental involvement at school can take many forms, from volunteering in the classroom or cafeteria to sitting down with teachers and administrators to discuss educational issues, to participating in parent–teacher organizations.

School Violence

More important than a school's size or climate or the attitudes of its teachers is its ability to provide an environment in which students feel safe. In the past, safety was simply taken for granted. It no longer can be. Among the top disciplinary problems listed by teachers in the 1940s were chewing gum and running in the halls. In the 1990s, teachers had to be concerned about assault, rape, drug abuse, and robbery.

Teachers' concerns reflect students' realities. As can be seen in Table 9.1, approximately 23% of ninth-grade males report having been in physical fights at school, over 15% said they had been threatened or injured with a weapon, and 7% reported that they sometimes felt too unsafe to go to school (Centers for Disease Control and Prevention, 2004). Differences among ethnic groups and between sexes are large. An even more startling statistic is that over 6% of ninth-grade males and 10% of twelfth-grade males said they had carried a gun or other weapon to school (Centers for Disease Control and Prevention, 2004).

What are the sources of these fears and behaviors? A number of factors suggest themselves. Violence for many begins in the home: An estimated 10 million children witness domestic violence in their families every year, and estimates of various forms of

full-service schools Schools that provide a variety of health and social services to students and their families in collaboration with the community.

TABLE 9.1 Percentage of Adolescents Experiencing Violence While at School, 2003

	9th Grade		12th Grade	
	Female	Male	Female	Male
Felt too unsafe to go to school	6.6%	7.1%	3.9%	3.8%
Carried a weapon such as a gun, knife, or club	3.8	6.6	2.6	10.2
Been threatened or injured with a weapon	8.3	16.4	3.9	8.5
Been in a physical fight	12.2	23.3	4.7	9.6

Source: Centers for Disease Control and Prevention. (2004). Youth risk behavior surveillance—United States, 2003. *Morbidity and Mortality Weekly Reports, 53* (No. SS-2).

neglect and abuse are as high as 1 in 25 children and adolescents. These figures cut across ethnic and class lines, affecting all segments of society (see Chapter 12).

Many adolescents watch three or more hours of television nightly (Centers for Disease Control and Prevention, 2004; U.S. Department of Health and Human Services, 2002c), hours that are filled with violence. Before leaving elementary school, children will have watched approximately 8,000 murders and 100,000 violent acts (Toch, 1993). Figures such as these are disturbing, given the suggestive nature of research demonstrating the effects of viewing aggression (see Bandura, Chapter 2). The ability of television to teach—whether for good or bad—is well established (Beentjes & van der Voort, 1993; Ward, 2002).

Connecting copycat acts of violence with ones portrayed in the media is relatively easy because of their uniqueness. But what of the common, ordinary acts of violence in which one person pulls a gun on another—and pulls the trigger? Rather than being seen as the exception, copycat violence can just as easily be seen as supporting research which shows that children will copy acts of violence they have viewed on film, whether inside or outside a research laboratory (Bandura, Ross, & Ross, 1963).

Media modeling of violence is not in itself the cause of the increased violence we are currently experiencing as a society. Significant here are the devastating effects of poverty and discrimination so many adolescents experience, together with very real threats to personal safety both at home and at school. These factors, combined with the accessibility of guns, add up to a national problem. Seventy-eight percent of youth homicides involve firearms (CDC, 2005e). Nevertheless, complete explanations for school violence, especially school shootings, are elusive; see In More Depth "Columbine: The Imaginary Audience and a Real Stage."

Bullies and Victims

For some students, violence takes another form—it's not the possibility there will be a shooting one day, but the probability of being harassed any day. **Bullying** is a fact of life for a significant number of adolescents. For instance, a nationally representative sample of over 15,000 sixth- through tenth-grade students in schools throughout the United States found that 16.9% of those sampled had experienced moderate or frequent bullying (Nansel et al., 2001).

bullying Repeated aggressive behaviors or remarks occurring over an extended period of time that the victim finds difficult to defend against.

What *is* bullying? Dan Olweus (1978, 1993, 2001), a pioneer researcher in this field, defines bullying as repeated aggressive behaviors or remarks directed against a student by one or more others over a period of time, and against which the victim finds it difficult to defend himself or herself. There are three things to note in this definition of bullying: The actions are hurtful, they are repeated over time, and there's an imbalance of power between the aggressor and the victim. The import of being bullied, in other words, is not simply that one has been hurt in some way by another. Rather, it is that one can expect this to occur again and that there is little one can do to prevent it. As a consequence, victims of bullying never feel completely "safe" at school.

Among adolescents, middle schoolers are much more likely to be bullied than are high schoolers (Craig, Pepler, Connolly, & Henderson, 2001; Nansel et al., 2001; Pellegrini & Long, 2002). Nansel and her associates (2001) found that 13.3% of sixth-graders reported being bullied on a weekly basis and another 10.9% reported occasional bullying. Given figures such as these, it should come as no surprise that middle schoolers list bullying as one of their major concerns. In contrast, the corresponding percentages for tenth-graders were 4.8% and 4.6%, respectively.

Bullying is likely to take a different form among boys than among girls. With boys, acts of direct physical aggression are common. Examples can range from knocking a book or cafeteria tray out of a victim's hands to pushing, tripping, or hitting him. Direct verbal aggression, such as name-calling or teasing, is also common. Among girls, indirect forms of aggression are more typical, such as spreading rumors or excluding another girl from a group, although girls are just as likely as boys to experience verbal bullying (Nansel et al., 2001).

Given the importance to early adolescents of connection with one's peers and of belonging to the group, that is, of establishing a group identity, bullying can have genuinely harmful effects. Students who are bullied report experiencing anxiety, depression, feelings of loneliness, and a loss of self-esteem (Graham & Juvonen, 2002; Nansel et al., 2001; Olweus, 2001). They find it harder to make friends, and they do more poorly in school (Nansel et al., 2001).

Some adolescents are more likely to be bullied than others. The classic profile of a victim is an adolescent who is anxious and insecure and has low self-esteem (Olweus, 1978). Conversely, adolescents who are easygoing and friendly are less likely to be victimized (Jensen-Campbell, Adams, Perry, Workman, Furdella, & Egan, 2002). Also, bullying is somewhat more common among males than among females. Adolescent males typically react to bullying in one of two ways: passively or provocatively. Passive victims tend to be sensitive and quiet boys who are somewhat depressed and anxious, don't feel that they are liked by their peers, and have low self-esteem. All of these characteristics make them an "easy mark." They are not likely to retaliate on their own or to rally support among their peers. Not all boys who are bullied are passively submissive.

Some victims are actually aggressive, being easily provoked by others and reacting angrily, their outbursts apparently targeting them for retaliation. These provocative victims, who make up a much smaller percentage of victims, share many of the characteristics of passive victims but differ from them in being hyperactive and more likely to engage in aggressive behavior. Their aggression differs from that of those who bully them, however, taking the form of unwitting emotional outbursts rather than being used intentionally to dominate others (Olweus, 1999, 2001; Salmivalli, 2001).

One might think that bullies would be rejected by their peers due to their aggressive behavior, but that typically is not the case (Olweus, 2001). Bullies do not stand out from their classmates in terms of popularity, but they do stand out in other ways. They tend to be more impulsive and aggressive than their peers and, at least among boys, to be somewhat bigger and stronger than their victims. Bullies and victims alike tend to score lower on measures of psychosocial adjustment, such as ease of getting along with others, social problem solving, and managing feelings of depression (Haynie et al., 2001; Nansel

IN MORE DEPTH

Columbine: The Imaginary Audience and a Real Stage

With Michael Wapner

The columbine is a flower. But for many of us the word no longer evokes images of blossoms. Instead, we associate it with students cowering under desks or fleeing for their lives as two of their fellow students hunted them down, eventually killing 12 and a teacher, at Columbine High School in 1999. We have other names that evoke images of violent death—Dallas, Waco, Oklahoma City. But Columbine doesn't belong to that group. Columbine is the name of a school, and the images it evokes—of both killers and killed—are those of adolescents. Tragically, Columbine has come to stand for a new collection of events—shootings in which students murder other students at school.

In one sense the image of school as a place of violent death is all out of proportion. Less than 1% of homicides involving school-age children occur in or near school (Healthy Youth, 2005). On the other hand, 1% is an alarming figure given the circumstances that have given rise to it.

How can we begin to understand this rash of deadly violence? Can we even group into a single category the events at Columbine High School in Littleton, Colorado, and at schools at West Paducah, Kentucky, at Jonesboro, Arkansas, and Springfield, Oregon? A number of elements are certainly common to all, but they seem few indeed, perhaps because of their very ordinariness. The killers were all males, all were teenagers, as were almost all of their victims, all carried out their deadly acts at school, and all used guns to do it. Also common to these events was what was missing: the conditions or characteristics one might expect to find in the lives of violent youth. In none of these cases do we find uncaring or incompetent parents, substance abuse, domestic violence, poverty, or a crime-infested environment. Columbine, like the other shootings, defies easy answers to our questions.

We are unlikely to find a single cause for events such as those that took place at Columbine. Parenting, for instance, is only one of many influences in a child's life and can be expected to interact with many other influences, such as the child's own temperament, the changing developmental challenges faced by a child at different points in life, and the larger culture into which that child steps. This may be especially true for children who by temperament are less easygoing, more negative in their moods, or less flexible in adapting to change (Garbarino, 1999).

Temperament can similarly interact with another environment, that of school. Examples of friendly, nurturing support among students are everywhere to be found—but so are bullying, teasing, name-calling, and petty exclusiveness. Unfortunately, boys who already feel resentful and unaccepted are much more likely to receive and notice the latter. If one expects to be hurt, there is no place like a schoolyard or cafeteria to have those expectations fulfilled. Adolescents with extremely sensitive temperaments, either violently excessive or coldly deficient, do not easily form friendships or achieve a sense of belonging, making it even more difficult for them to buffer themselves from rejection. But there are other contexts in which such boys may come together—in clubs organized around hate (e.g., neo-Nazi or racist groups), violence (e.g., guns, martial arts), or provocative deviance (e.g., outrageous dress). Or they may find one or two other youths with similar outlooks. The affiliation of several resentful, marginal young men who encourage each other to act out their violent fantasies is particularly dangerous.

Bumper stickers may say that the best revenge is living well. But that's not what Rambo says. And that's not what thousands of movies, television programs, and video games say. Culture is the medium that gives form to feelings. Marginal, hypervigilant young men have plenty of feelings. And when the forms provided by the culture feature automatic weapons and high explosives to "blow away" your antagonist, the mix is dangerous. Adolescents are steeped in violence, not only in the commercial images of films, television, and song lyrics, but also in the reality of their lives, from verbal and physical skirmishes at school to nightly statistics on the evening news.

et al., 2001). The similarities don't end there. Many bullies are themselves victims of other bullies (Haynie et al., 2001; Nansel et al., 2001).

Intervention Programs For an intervention program to be effective, teachers, staff, and parents, as well as students, must be aware of what is going on and must be involved. Intervention programs typically involve actions to be taken at several levels. One of these

The United States leads other nations in homicides to a staggering degree (see Figure 9.1). Of all the factors contributing to the lethal nature of violence in this nation, the most important of these is the accessibility of firearms. Individuals are not necessarily more aggressive in the United States than in other countries, but they do have readier access to guns, a difference that can be lethal. A comparison of two demographically similar cities, Seattle and Vancouver, conducted over six years, offers strong support for the position that accessibility of firearms is causally related to the greater incidence of homicide in the United States. Seattle had virtually no restrictions governing gun possession and use, whereas Vancouver had many. Despite similar rates of conviction for violent crime in each of the cities, rates of homicide were nearly twice as high in Seattle (Sloan et al., 1988).

A last factor to consider in school shootings involves the characteristics of adolescent thought. In particular, cognitive development enables adolescents to react intellectually and emotionally in new ways. Adolescents' ability to interpret the actions of others enables them to assign more than the obvious meaning to any social encounter. Further, their heightened awareness of themselves makes it likely that they will relate these actions to themselves. As a consequence, adolescents are more likely to experience emotions such as moodiness, depression, or resentfulness than are children or adults.

In the case of Columbine, the motivation seems to have been not just retaliation, but also a desire for celebrity. Why wouldn't students who said they were enraged at athletes who had taunted them place their bombs in the locker room? FBI agent Mark Holstlaw suggests that instead of revenge, they were looking for a way to be famous. This particular shooting may have been influenced by the media, but not in the way typically assumed, which presumes the media to be the *cause* of the violence. Instead, knowing that the media would be drawn to their violence, these students may have *used* the media in an attempt to become celebrities, even going so far as to imagine that famous directors would fight for the chance to make a movie of their story.

If true, this concern with celebrity reflects another quality of adolescent thinking—the tendency to act for an imaginary audience. Adolescents' capacity for abstract thought enables them to think not only about their own thoughts but about the thoughts of others as well. David Elkind suggests that adolescents frequently lack perspective about what concerns them and what concerns others, leading them to believe that everyone is as interested in them as they are and that others are continually noticing them. The imaginary audience gives adolescents an exaggerated feeling of self-consciousness and self-importance.

What factors contribute to school shootings such as at Columbine? None of the ones we have considered, either separately or in some complex mix, explains why adolescents such as these act as they do while other adolescents, sharing many of their experiences and backgrounds, do not. We frequently think we understand youth violence, at least with respect to those instances in which adolescents come from bad homes or otherwise bad environments. Yet even "predictable" violence such as this leaves us with few explanations when we are asked to consider the many nonviolent youth from those very same homes and neighborhoods who lead caring, disciplined, and considerate lives. The actions of these latter youth are unrecorded, their names absent from police blotters or reports on the evening news. Contributing factors offer no more complete explanation, in other words, for violence that fits the mold than for violence that breaks it. In each case, one is left to explain why a handful of adolescents acted as they did, while others did not.

Sources: A. Goldstein, M. Harrington, and R. Woodbury. (1999). National School Safety Center. (1998). Total school-associated violent death count: July 1992 to Present [Online]. Updated June 18, 1998. Retrieved from http://www.nccsl.org. J. Sloan, A. Kellermann, D. Reay, J. Ferris, T. Koepsell, F. Rivara, C. Rice, L. Gray, & J. LoGerfo. (1988). Handgun regulation, crime, assaults, and homicides. *New England Journal of Medicine, 319,* 1256–1262.

programs, implemented by Olweus in the Norwegian school system, has been highly effective, reducing bullying by as much as 50% to 70% (Olweus, 2001). The program identifies actions at three levels: the school, the class, and the individual.

Measures at the School Level The first step in reducing bullying is to provide individuals with information about the frequency with which this occurs. Many teachers and

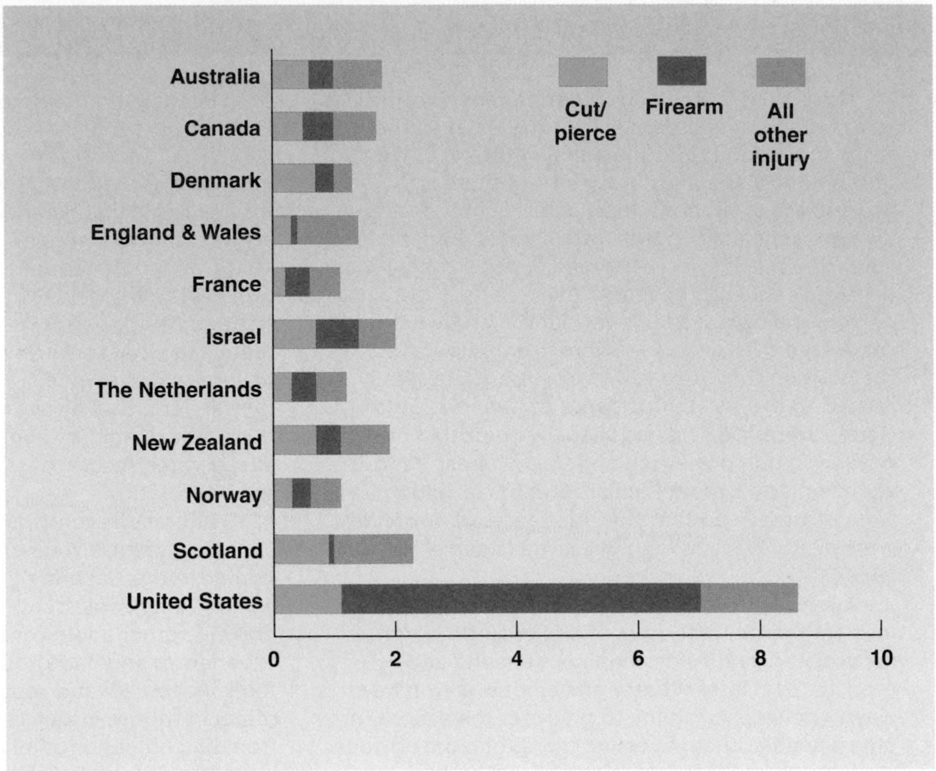

FIGURE 9.1
International Homicide Rates.
Source: L. A. Fingerhut, C. S. Cox, & M. Warner. (1998, October 7). International comparative analysis of injury mortality. *Advance Data from Vital and Health Statistics, 303.*

staff are unaware of the extent of victimization among students. Questionnaires filled out anonymously by teachers, students, parents, and staff can give accurate information about the frequency of bullying, and about where and when this is most likely to occur, as well as who is most likely to be involved.

Also important are measures that enable individuals to identify bullying when they see it. This step entails coming up with a definition of bullying that everyone can understand (see In More Depth) and then engaging in a dialogue. The objective of such a dialogue is to formulate school policies that promote healthy relationships among students, which of course would include ways of preventing bullying and victimization.

Olweus stresses the importance of a schoolwide conference day devoted to the issue of bullying. Intervention programs work, in other words, not simply because they affect the behavior of individual students or teachers, but because they result in a "restructuring" of the entire school environment. Usually included during this day are statements concerning students' right to feel safe at school and how the school will deal with bullying.

Once teachers, staff, and students are more informed about bullying, it becomes possible to provide better supervision of interactions among students, especially during relatively unstructured times, such as lunch breaks, free periods, and before and after school.

Measures at the Class Level Olweus (1999) recommends the use of materials such as videos that show everyday occurrences in the lives of children who are bullied. Videos can serve as a format for class discussion both by helping students recognize bullying and by enabling them to identify with the effects of bullying. Students typically react to bullying in a number of ways, from taking an active part themselves in the bullying to actively trying to help the victim. Olweus conceptualizes these roles in terms of a "bullying

IN MORE DEPTH

Definition and Forms of Bullying

We say *a student is being bullied when another student, or several other students*

- say mean and hurtful things or make fun of him or her or call him or her mean and hurtful names
- completely ignore or exclude him or her from their group of friends or leave him or her out of things on purpose
- hit, kick, push, shove around, or lock him or her inside a room
- tell lies or spread false rumors about him or her or send mean notes and try to make other students dislike him or her
- and do other hurtful things like that.

When we talk about bullying, these things happen repeatedly, and it is *difficult for the student being bullied to defend himself or herself*. We also call it bullying when a student is teased repeatedly in a mean and hurtful way.

But we *don't call it bullying* when the teasing is done in a friendly and playful way. Also, it is *not bullying* when two students of about the same strength or power argue or fight.

Source: D. Olweus. (2001). Peer harassment: A critical analysis and some important issues. In J. Juvonen & S. Graham (Eds.), *Peer harassment in school: The plight of the vulnerable and victimized* (pp. 3–20). New York: Guilford Press.

circle" (see Figure 9.2), which he uses in classes to stimulate discussions of ways of getting students to move from the left in the circle to the right. Through such discussions, students are encouraged to speak up about their concerns and to assume responsibility to try to stop bullying when they see instances of it.

Measures at the Individual Level Talking with bullies works best when they do not have their support group present, that is, by meeting with them one-on-one. Once alone with a teacher or counselor, bullies are more likely to accept responsibility for their actions, especially if they are invited to think of ways of changing the situation rather than simply being blamed for what they have done (Rigby, 2001). In other words, issues related to bullying, just as parenting, are resolved best when approached in an authoritative, not an authoritarian, way. In an approach referred to as a method of "shared concern" (Pikas, 2002), first the bully and the victim are spoken with individually. The teacher or counselor serves as a mediator, often talking a number of times with each student, in order to bring the concerns of each to the other, before the students themselves meet to formally agree to what they have worked out. Typically, some training is needed for teachers or counselors to learn effective mediation procedures.

Teaching Peace

Morton Deutsch (1993) argues that schools can encourage values and provide experiences that promote constructive, rather than destructive, means of resolving conflict. Four elements are critical to "teaching peace": cooperative learning, training in conflict resolution, putting controversy to constructive use, and creating conflict resolution centers.

Cooperative Learning Students learn interpersonal skills in cooperative learning classrooms; goals are shared by members of a group, reducing competition. Students are more helpful and caring in these learning environments than in the more traditional, individualistic, and competitive ones.

Conflict Resolution Training These programs teach students to perceive a conflict as a problem to be solved mutually, one in which all participants can come out ahead, instead of solved competitively, in which some win and others lose.

cooperative learning Placing students of different ability levels together in small working groups.

conflict resolution training Programs designed to teach students to view conflict as a problem to be solved mutually, with a win-win outcome.

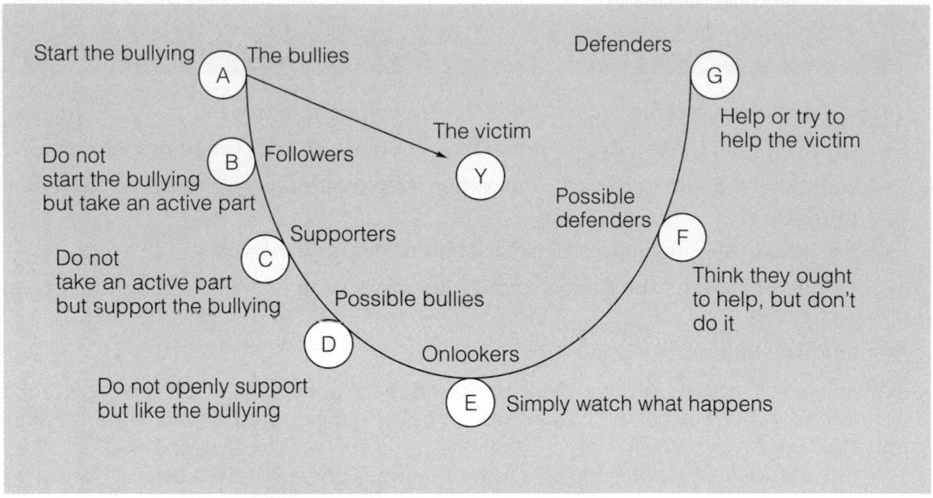

FIGURE 9.2 The Bullying Circle: Possible Student Responses to Bullying. *Source:* Adapted from D. Olweus. (2001). Peer harassment: A critical analysis and some important issues. In J. Juvonen & S. Graham (Eds.), *Peer harassment in school: The plight of the vulnerable and victimized* (pp. 3–20). New York: Guilford Press.

Students also learn to identify potential causes of violence and, knowing its consequences, to discover alternatives (see Chapter 12).

Constructive Controversy Controversy, in itself, is not undesirable. It can actually stimulate students to think about problems and come up with creative solutions when shown how to do so. One way of doing this is to have students work in small groups in which pairs alternately argue for opposing positions and then reverse their arguments, taking their opponents' position and arguing as earnestly as they can for that. Finally, all work toward reaching a consensus.

Conflict Resolution Centers Some schools have established mediation programs in which both teachers and students are trained in listening skills and conflict resolution.

Education for All

One of the challenges facing secondary schools is to reach students with different interests, backgrounds, and abilities using methods and materials that capture interest and fire imagination. However, some schools still use materials that exclude half their students from the most exciting adventures.

Gender in the Classroom

From Hamlet to Tom Sawyer, most of the characters adolescents read about in classics or see in films are males. School materials also take their readers to high adventure most readily if they are males. These trends begin in elementary school and continue into high school.

constructive controversy A technique using controversy to stimulate solutions to problems by having students alternately argue their own and the opposing position to a conflict.

conflict resolution centers Mediation programs in which teachers and students are trained in listening skills and conflict resolution.

Visual Materials One survey of children's textbooks found that males are pictured more often than females and shown in more adventurous roles. Although female characters appear as often as male characters, they still appear in fewer occupations and need rescuing more frequently (Purcell & Stewart, 1990).

Even so, these comparisons represent a giant step away from the disparities that characterized school materials 25 years earlier. A similar survey conducted in 1972 found the same trends but differences that were even more exaggerated (Women on Words and Images, 1975).

About 90% of students' time in school is spent with various types of educational materials such as books, films, or class handouts. Even though many states have introduced regulations to ensure that the portrayal of females and males in textbooks is balanced, many schools do not buy new books until the old ones need replacing.

Materials that show women and men in nontraditional roles or filling roles in proportion to their actual numbers in the workforce lead to greater flexibility in sex-role attitudes among students. Thus, students who read about females who are doctors or postal carriers and males who are telephone operators or daycare directors are less sex-typed in their approach to occupations in general and in their personal interest in these professions.

Language A second form of bias occurs through the gender characteristics of language itself. English, for the most part, either ignores females or treats them as exceptions. **Male generic language** uses the pronoun *he* to refer to an individual of either sex and uses words such as *man* or *mankind* to refer to all people. When individuals are identified as female, it is often to call attention to the fact that they are *not* male, such as in terms like *woman doctor* or *actress.* These usages suggest not only that doctors and actors ordinarily are males, but also that when they are females, they are different enough from "regular" doctors and actors to require different labels (Lips, 2005).

A formidable array of research shows that male generic language causes people to think of males, not of people in general (Kennison & Trofe, 2003; Liben, Bigler, & Krogh, 2002). In one study, seventh-graders completed a story about a student's first day in their class. Some students read a story referring to the new student as "he"; others read stories in which the student could be of either sex. When the subject was referred to as "he," all the males and 80% of the females wrote stories describing the student as a male. When "he or she" or "they" were used, significantly fewer students referred to the new student as a male. Those most affected by the use of inclusive language ("he or she" or "they") were females; whereas 80% wrote stories in which the subject, when referred to as "he," was a male, 21% and 12% wrote about a male when the subject was referred to as "he or she" or "they," respectively (Switzer, 1990). When we realize that teachers are just as susceptible to the influence of male generic language as students, the implications of these findings assume even larger proportions.

Male generic language also affects adolescents' judgments of how competent a woman is in different types of jobs. When students are asked to consider how well a woman might perform a fictional job (for example, a "surmaker"), their evaluations are influenced by the sex of the pronouns used to describe the characters performing the job. Women are thought to be least competent for the job when the surmaker is referred to as "he" and most competent when referred to as "she." Referring to doctors, mechanics, scientists, or artists as "he" has clear implications not only for adolescent females' ability to see themselves in those professions, but also for all students' evaluation of the relative competence of the men and women in those occupations (Hyde, 1984; Lips, 2005).

Multicultural Education

LaRue glanced briefly at his group as Mr. Brooks, his physical science teacher, finished giving the assignment: to study the activity of gases. That shouldn't be too difficult, he thought. But what would he do for his part? He had to think of common examples

male generic language Use of the pronoun *he* to refer to an individual of either sex, and use of words such as *man* or *mankind* to refer to all people.

Learning in a group can be more interesting than learning on one's own. Students work in small groups that are balanced for both ability and for gender and ethnic or racial background.

illustrating the properties of gases. Paulo had an easy part to present to the group; all he had to do was describe their chemical properties. Becky's part would be interesting: identifying the gases that are present in different substances. He could imagine the fun Yinpeng would have with that one. He liked his group. They worked well together, and it was more interesting than working on their own. But what could he contribute? Then he remembered the canned drinks he had put in the freezer—the juices had burst open but the soda hadn't. Of course, gases constrict and liquids expand when cold.

LaRue's physical science class is organized as a **jigsaw classroom.** Students work in small groups that are balanced for ethnic background and ability. Each student in the group contributes a different part of the lesson. The parts fit together, much like the pieces of a jigsaw puzzle: One needs each part to get the whole picture. This approach to classroom learning fosters cooperation among students and promotes better relations among adolescents from different ethnic and cultural backgrounds (Aronson, 2002, 2004).

jigsaw classroom A classroom organized into small, ethnically balanced working groups in which each student contributes a different part of the lesson.

Even in classes that foster cooperative and friendly relations, minority adolescents often face problems that don't exist for those from the dominant culture. They need to find a way to reconcile the often contradictory perspectives presented at school with their own life experiences. Comedian Dick Gregory once remarked that he and his friends used to root for the Indians against the cavalry, because they didn't think it was fair for textbooks to characterize the cavalry's winning as a great victory and the Indians' winning as a massacre. Many minority adolescents would agree. For them, life experiences frequently run counter to what they must learn at school. Will *Tom Sawyer* or *Huckleberry Finn* be read with the same interpretation, or with sensitivity to the same issues, by African American, Asian American, or Native American adolescents as by European American adolescents? Which students' experiences are more likely to be reflected by their teachers?

Similarly, carpetbaggers have traditionally been portrayed as low-life opportunists who turned the chaos following the Civil War to personal advantage. Yet if one believes that members of the White majority at that time, or the present, have opportunistically taken advantage of minorities, this portrayal does not raise meaningful distinctions, or at least does not evoke the same sensitivities as it would for those whose views reflect the dominant culture.

Consider the westward expansion on the North American continent. Numerous treaty violations with Native Americans led to the eventual decimation of these people. The internment of Japanese Americans during World War II violated all of their civil rights. How are these events covered in most U.S. history books? Do textbooks, or teachers, simply adopt the dominant cultural perspective, and if they do, can we expect minorities to understand the facts presented in class as easily as students for whom these facts present no cultural conflict?

Textbooks used in courses such as history and literature frequently present a narrative account that evolves from a single frame of reference—a European American perspective. Many teachers uncritically adopt this same perspective. Students who do not share this view of history, as many minorities do not, will fail to experience these courses as "making sense." Yet teachers and textbooks are the authoritative sources, and students who cannot remember the facts as presented will be seen as problems.

In studying the westward expansion, for instance, asking adolescents to describe the experiences of the pioneers, the American Indians, and the Mexicans turns this problem into an advantage. The introduction of a multicultural perspective enriches all students' understanding of the issues surrounding westward expansion.

Most minority students face instances of prejudice and discrimination on at least some occasions. Interviews with Black adolescents who attended predominantly White high schools revealed a number of ways of coping with their minority status. One way was to be a "model" student. Students who chose this coping style made good grades, studied for college, and participated in school activities. Many also earned the resentment of their Black friends for "acting White." One model student had this to say:

> They . . . prefer to be black, they want to just hang around with the blacks, they don't want nothing to do with the whites. . . . I'm not like that. . . . I attended the ski club and I asked if anyone else wanted to get into it, and you should have seen their faces, it was hysterical. What is this kid talking about, the ski club? It's a bunch of "honkies" gonna be there. (R. Miller, 1989, p.181)

Other students coped by forming friendships across groups and becoming members of popular crowds at school. Still others became involved in many different school activities. Not all the Black adolescents preferred attending an integrated school to a predominantly Black school. Some who were bused from inner-city schools to suburban ones made few friends and felt little connection with the school. When asked why they attended, they mentioned getting a better education and having more opportunities (R. Miller, 1989).

In the classroom, unfamiliar patterns of communication complicate learning for some minority students. The simple matter of asking questions is a case in point for many African American students. Teachers ask questions in very different ways than do adults in the community (Brice-Heath, 1982). Teachers use questions to stimulate classroom discussions and to focus ongoing behavior. It's common to ask about things the class has already discussed. Adults typically ask questions only when they want information they do *not* have. They rarely use questions as a way of discussing issues or of channeling ongoing behavior into more desirable forms (as a teacher might, by asking a question of a student who is talking with a classmate to get that student to pay attention). Consequently, students may misunderstand questions regarding material the class

Minority students from cultures that value the group more than the individual may pay as much attention to the feelings of others as to the task at hand. This orientation can frustrate teachers, but is serves the students well in group-learning situations and in the world outside the classroom.

has already covered ("What is she asking for? We've gone over that"). Effective intervention depends on discovering differences such as these. The solution in this instance is for everyone—teachers, parents, and students—to be made aware of the different rules that regulate language in class and at home (Slaughter-Defoe, Nakagawa, Takanishi, & Johnson, 1990).

Other problems arise from lack of familiarity in using Standard English, the language used in the classroom. Some minority students—such as Hawaiians, Native Americans, and Alaska Natives—can understand Standard English well enough but still not be at ease speaking it in front of classmates if they speak a dialect at home. Using different languages at home and in school limits opportunities to practice the way ESL students need to speak at school and can cause them to be silent for fear of embarrassing themselves. Even written schoolwork becomes problematic for students who have difficulty translating the ideas they frame easily in the intimate language of their home into Standard English. Additional complications arise when corresponding terms are not available in the two languages (Feldman, Stone, & Renderer, 1990).

Examining the Differences

The increasing ethnic diversity of our society makes it difficult to characterize students in terms of simple behavioral and motivational profiles. Recognizing the distinctive approaches that characterize different ethnic groups can be a start and can be used to advantage in the classroom. Research on ethnic groups reveals distinct differences along four dimensions of personal interaction: group versus individual orientations, active versus passive coping styles, attitudes toward authority, and expressive versus restrained mannerisms.

Group Versus Individual Orientations Some cultures, such as Japan and Mexico, stress affiliation, interdependence, and cooperation. Other cultures, such as the United States, stress individual achievement, independence, and competition. Within the United States, ethnic differences emerge along this dimension. Chinese, Hispanic, and African American adolescents, for instance, are more group oriented than those from the dominant culture (Sedikides, Gaertner, & Vevea, 2005). These adolescents are more attentive to the feelings and expectations of others than their White counterparts are. A Hispanic or an African American adolescent may pay as much attention to the feelings of others as to the demands of the task at hand, an orientation many teachers may not understand or appreciate. However, in learning situations that require students to work together, this orientation will serve these students as well inside the classroom as outside it (Kernan & Greenfield, 2005).

Active Versus Passive Coping Styles Cultures characterized by active coping styles stress the importance of controlling one's environment and being productive. Those with passive styles place more emphasis on being than on doing. The sense of the present is greater in the latter and of the future in the former. These differences—like those of group versus individual orientation—can translate into either strengths or weaknesses in the classroom. Adolescents with a take-charge attitude may find it difficult to wait for others or to take enough time to explore all the issues. The strength of this approach is the way that it fosters achievement.

The strength of the passive approach is the freedom it gives students to turn themselves over to the moment and learn what it can teach them. The disadvantages to this coping style are most apparent in classrooms structured according to active coping strategies. Adolescents from cultures with a passive coping style are not as likely to ask for help or materials, and if teachers and classmates assume that no help is needed unless asked for, these students will not receive the help they need (Rotheram & Phinney, 1983).

Attitudes Toward Authority Clear ethnic differences exist for this dimension. Hispanic and Asian American adolescents, for instance, are more likely to have been raised in authoritarian homes (see Chapter 7) and taught to be respectful and not to question those in authority. Certain Native American and many White adolescents have been socialized to make decisions for themselves and are less accepting of authority (Rotheram & Phinney, 1987). It should not be surprising that some students want to be told what to do and do their best work under those conditions, whereas others want to make decisions for themselves and do not fare well with authoritarian teachers.

Expressive Versus Restrained Mannerisms Interactions in some cultures are informal and open, and in others are ritualized and private. The former is more characteristic of African American and White adolescents, the latter of Asian American adolescents. African American adolescents express their feelings even more openly than Whites; theirs is a high-intensity culture, in which feelings are given more open expression. An Asian American student might easily misread an African American student's expressions of anger as aggression or a White student might regard an Asian American's reaction to an incident as timid simply because each is not familiar with the other's culture.

Adolescents are not very accurate in predicting how those from another culture will react. Differences along each of these dimensions underscore the importance of developing cross-ethnic awareness among adolescents as well as teachers.

Many minority adolescents have difficulty predicting their own experiences as they move from home, to school, to community. As we saw in Chapter 1, Urie Bronfenbrenner (1979b) describes the experiences that make up one's reality in terms of overlapping spheres of influence. At the most immediate level, the *microsystem,* are one's firsthand experiences—interactions at home, in the classroom, and with friends. The *mesosystem* arises from interactions among the different microsystems of which one is a part. Minority adolescents frequently experience problems with interactions involving the mesosystem. They may see their parents distrust the system, or teachers communicate less respect for their parents than for those of other students.

Adolescents experience the *exosystem* at the level of their communities. Available housing and the types of schools they attend reflect decisions made at the community level but influence their lives directly. The *macrosystem,* which consists of the underlying social and political climate, is even further removed from adolescents' daily experiences, yet it impinges on their realities in very real ways. Laws concerning compulsory education, the mainstreaming of students with special needs, and the separation of grades into elementary, junior high, and high schools all illustrate the direct ways the macrosystem can affect the lives of adolescents. A less observable, but no less real, effect of the macrosystem is experienced in the form of beliefs, biases, and stereotypes. The values of the macrosystem can be at odds with those of the home microsystem for adolescents from some minority groups.

John Ogbu (1981, 1992) offers a disturbing analysis of the plight of many minority students. He notes that educational programs have assumed that the problems many minorities experience at school (poor attendance, high dropout rates, low achievement) should be addressed at the level of the microsystem—by improving the home environment or enriching educational experiences. Ogbu suggests that the problem is generated at the macrosystem level and can be solved only by changes introduced at that level. He attributes poor academic performance and high dropout rates among minorities to a "job ceiling," or discrimination in job opportunities, and to their perception that members of their own families have not been rewarded for their achievements.

If all adolescents progressed through the same *social mobility system,* one in which mobility, or social class, reflects their abilities, then the most effective method of intervention for minorities who are failing would be at the microsystem level, reaching into the home or classroom to bring their abilities and skills up to the level of the others. But *do* all members of our society move through the same mobility system? Is there more than one system, similar to academic tracking, but with respect to economic rather than educational opportunities?

If there is more than one mobility system, what factors other than ability and skill determine the system in which individuals participate? Notice that if we have more than one social mobility system, social class is an *effect* rather than a cause, and the problems of minorities must be addressed at another level. Social status among minorities, argues Ogbu, reflects the realities of a job ceiling: a consistent set of social and economic obstacles preventing equal selection based on ability imposed on certain minorities at birth, that is, a society stratified by ethnic and racial castes as well as by class. The problems of minority groups need to be addressed at multiple levels, at the macrosystem level as well as that of the microsystem.

Academic Achievement

In this section, we will look at some of the factors that affect students' achievement. One of the single most important factors contributing to differences in achievement is socioeconomic level. As we will see, proficiency in basic subjects also differs from one country to the next. Within the United States, differences in achievement correspond to students' beliefs as well as their study habits.

Socioeconomic Status

Students attending schools in low-income neighborhoods are likely to have overcrowded classrooms, fewer resources such as computers, and teachers who are less well trained in the subjects they are teaching.

Family income is consistently related to academic achievement. Students from low-income families score lower on achievement tests, get lower grades, and are less likely to finish high school (Felner, Brand, DuBois, Adam, Mulhall, & Evans, 1995; McLoyd, 1998). The reasons for these differences are many and varied. Low-income students are likely to have poorer nutrition and less-adequate health care. Living spaces are more crowded, making it more difficult to find quiet places to study, and more activities, such as caring for a younger sibling, compete with schoolwork. More frequent residential moves disrupt schooling and decrease the likelihood of parental involvement with their adolescent's school.

Additionally, low-income students have access to fewer resources such as books, computers, transportation for school events, or help with homework. They also are less likely to have role models in either their families or neighborhoods who have completed high school and gone on to college. Moreover, higher rates of unemployment in low-income neighborhoods offer less incentive for getting an education.

The quality of schools serving low-income versus middle- or high-income neighborhoods also differs, in both teaching staff and physical facilities. Schools in low-income neighborhoods are more likely to have teachers who are less experienced and are less well trained in the subjects they are teaching. For instance, there are fewer teachers with master's degrees than in middle- or high-income schools. Also, substantially more teach subjects in which they have not majored or for which they are not certified. These disparities are even greater for high-poverty schools, in which classes in math and science are two to three times more likely to be taught by someone not trained in the field. Schools in low-income neighborhoods are more likely to be overcrowded and have larger classes and fewer resources, even basic ones such as textbooks and supplies, not to mention computer or science labs. Furthermore, differences such as these in the quality of schools are likely to have been present for low-income students in the elementary grades as well, resulting in lower scores in basic skills even before they enter secondary schools (National Center on Education Statistics, 2003).

Existing public programs, however, can be effective in countering the effects of economic adversity on academic achievement. "Wraparound" early childhood intervention programs that continue into the second or third grade, as opposed to ending in kindergarten, are particularly effective. Arthur Reynolds and Judy Temple (1998) found that students who had been in such programs had higher achievement scores in the seventh grade in reading and math and were less likely to have repeated a grade. Students in such programs are also less likely to need special education and more likely to finish high school (Reynolds, Ou, & Topitzes, 2004; Reynolds, Temple, Robertson, & Mann, 2001).

Academic Tracking

academic tracking The assignment of students to one of several courses of study in high school on the basis of criteria such as academic interests and goals, past achievement, and ability.

Academic tracking is a common solution to problems created by the diverse interests and abilities of students. **Academic tracking** is the practice of offering students several

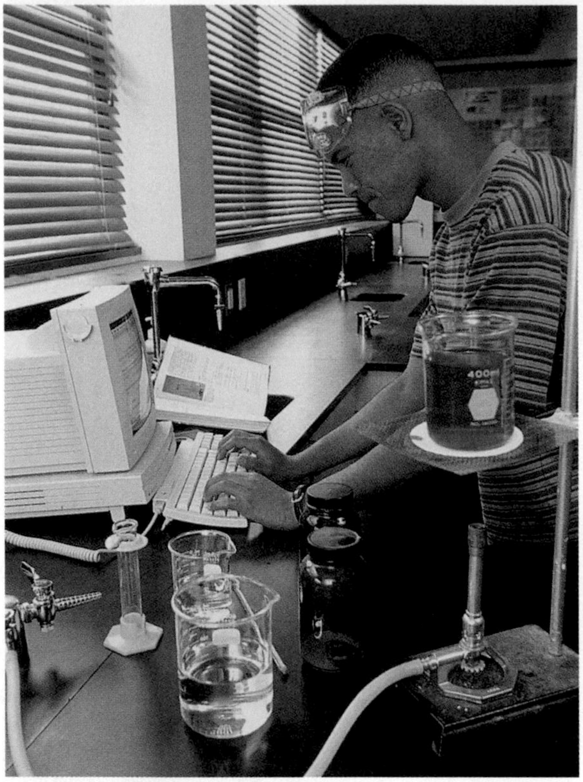

Task-oriented students, who focus on the task to be learned and work to increase their mastery and competence, are more likely to succeed than are students who are primarily concerned with the performance aspects of learning.

programs of study, with assignment to these based on prior achievement, stated goals, and the evaluations of counselors.

Most high schools offer at least two tracks—college preparatory and noncollege—and many offer other options. Students in different tracks frequently do not take classes together even for the same course. Educators assume that multiple tracks allow students to work at different paces and teachers to adjust the content of the courses to match differing interests. These assumptions make tracking seem a reasonable approach for teaching students with very different abilities and interests.

However, tracking may contribute to the problems it was designed to correct. Adolescents from minority groups and low-income families are more likely to be in noncollege than in college tracks. Of the students in noncollege tracks, more lose interest in school and drop out than those in college-preparatory tracks. Some research suggests that assignment to a lower track makes it more likely that students will work toward lower goals, proceed at a slower pace, have fewer opportunities to learn, and achieve less than students in higher tracks (Raudenbush, Rowan, & Cheong, 1993; Snow, 1986). Not all data support this conclusion. A nationwide study comparing students of similar ability levels attending schools in which tracking was either practiced or not practiced suggests that tracking may actually benefit students by enabling them to more favorably compare themselves with those of similar interests and abilities (Catsambis, Mulkey, & Crain, 2001).

An alternative to tracking for dealing with diversity is to place students of different ability levels together in small working groups. This approach, known as cooperative learning, gives students recognition for both their individual performance and that of the group. Power relationships subtly shift, placing the responsibility for learning on students rather than the teacher. Cooperative learning increases achievement in many students and has eased tensions in multicultural classrooms as students learn to work together (Slavin, 1985; Slavin, Hurley, & Chamberlin, 2003).

Another powerful alternative is the involvement of parents in the educational process. Parents can be involved in a number of ways: instructing students in the classroom, helping them at home, participating in school governance, and becoming involved in community service. James Comer and his colleagues (1985, 1988, 1996), at Yale University, have created a program in which parents, along with teachers, administrators, and staff, are responsible for administering the activities of the school. This program addresses the social and developmental, as well as the educational, needs of students. Comer believes, for instance, that social skills and ties to the community are as important as academic subjects, especially for lower-income students, who often lack these assets. In two inner-city schools using Comer's model, student performance so improved that the schools tied for third and fourth place in the district, with the students testing up to a year above the average for their grade! Attendance also improved dramatically, and behavior problems practically disappeared.

It is easy to understand why such a program could work: Teaching becomes more relevant when academic subjects are translated into the daily concerns of students and their families. In turn, what is learned in the classroom receives the support of parents who are committed to educational programs they help plan.

Despite their proven success, alternatives such as cooperative learning and Comer's model will not be beneficial unless teachers and staff are trained to use them effectively. Cooperative learning, for example, is a relatively complex technique to implement, requiring in-service training. Similarly, parental involvement can be cumbersome and can even increase conflict if parents' and teachers' views of education conflict.

Another alternative combines assignment to noncollege tracks with actual work experience for which students receive academic credit. This approach also addresses the financial difficulties many low-income students face. Innovative use of computers is a promising alternative for students who are "light-sensitive"—that is, who get most of their information through visual media such as television or the Internet and spend little time reading (Solomon, 1990).

Why are some students engaged in school and others unmotivated? One of the key contextual factors is beliefs about the future consequences of success or failure in school.

Proficiency in Basic Subjects

In terms of mathematics proficiency, the average 17-year-old can work with decimals and fractions, calculate areas of geometric figures such as rectangles, and work with signed numbers, exponents, and square roots. Students showing the greatest improvement on recent national tests in mathematics are minority youth—African American and Hispanic adolescents (Snyder & Tan, 2005). International comparisons of mathematical abilities of high school seniors find that U.S. adolescents place just below the international average in proficiency in mathematics and science, and somewhat above the national average in reading proficiency (Snyder & Tan, 2005). Comparisons with students in other countries are shown in Figures 9.3 and 9.4. The tremendous diversity of students attending high schools in the United States is certainly a factor contributing to the difficulties in meeting common educational goals. In contrast, some countries minimize diversity by giving students a qualifying exam prior to entering high school and placing them in different educational settings based on their performance.

Academic Success

Laurence Steinberg, Bradford Brown, and Sanford Dornbusch (1996) studied over 20,000 adolescents, talking as well with parents and teachers, in an effort to discover why some adolescents succeed in school and others do not. These investigators worked with an ethnically diverse sample, with nearly 40% of the adolescents from African American, Asian American, and Hispanic families, approximately the percentage that will soon characterize the general U.S. population. A number of their findings are disturbing; others are equally encouraging.

One of the more disturbing findings is that many high school students are disengaged from school. Over a third said they spend much of their time during the school day "goofing off with their friends," and many admitted to cheating on their schoolwork. On average, these students spent only four hours a week doing homework, a figure that is roughly equivalent to the number of hours *per day* spent by students in other

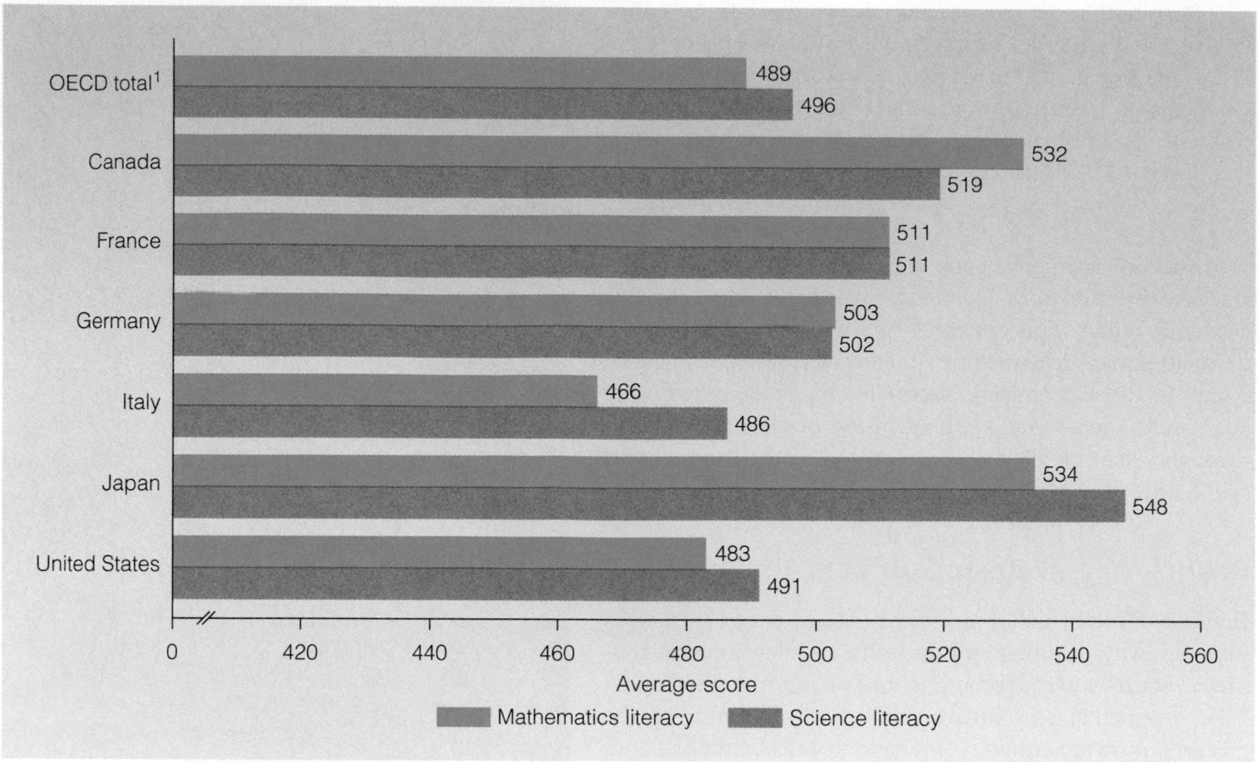

FIGURE 9.3
Average Scores on Mathematics and Science Literacy Assessments Among 15-Year-Old Students in Selected Countries: 2003. *Source:* Organization for Economic Cooperation and Development (OECD). (2004). *Learning for tomorrow's world: First results from the OECD Programme for International Student Assessment (PISA) 2003.*

[1]*Refers to the average for OECD countries as a single entity, to which each country contributes in proportion to the number of 15-year-olds enrolled in its schools.*

Note: The scale range is from 0 to 1000. The scale was designed to have an average score of 500 points, with approximately two-thirds of students achieving between 400 and 600 points.

industrialized nations. In addition to spending time with friends outside of school, two-thirds of high school students had part-time jobs, many working more than 15 hours a week and many intentionally taking easier classes to reduce their workload while maintaining their grades.

These investigators suggest that the problems in secondary education are due not so much to what is taking place in the classroom as to what is going on outside the classroom—at home, with friends, and in the community. This is not to say that the quality of schooling does not matter; rather, it points to the importance of the larger context in contributing to the influence schools can have. What contextual factors might be supporting this disengagement from school?

One factor appears to be students' beliefs about how important it is for them to do well in school in order to be successful once they graduate. In a nationwide survey, only about 40% of White high school seniors indicated that good grades were of great importance to them. In contrast, about 60% of Black students believed this to be of importance (U.S. Department of Health and Human Services, 2002c). These investigators found that although students believe that future success is related to graduating from high school, they do not relate success to how well they did in their classes. In other words, they believe that having a *diploma* is important, rather than what they have learned. Given this belief, it is not surprising that many put so little work into their classes. In motivational

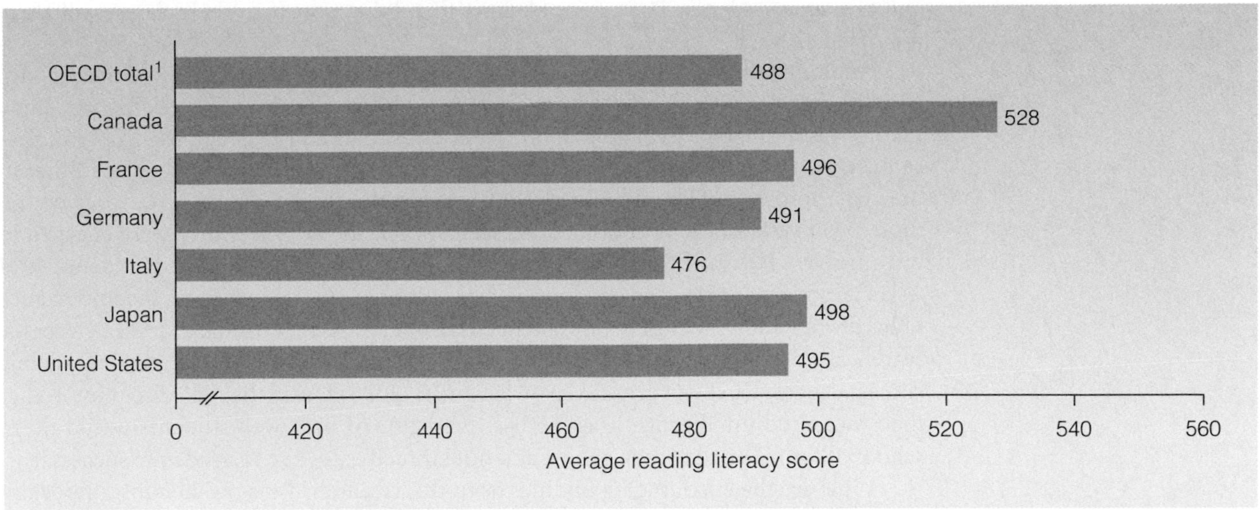

■ **FIGURE 9.4**
Average Scores on Reading Literacy Assessments Among 15-Year-Old Students in Selected Countries: 2003. *Source:* Organization for Economic Cooperation and Development (OECD). (2004). *Learning for tomorrow's world: First results from the OECD Programme for International Student Assessment (PISA) 2003.*
[1]*Refers to the average for OECD countries as a single entity, to which each country contributes in proportion to the number of 15-year-olds enrolled in its schools.*
Note: The scale range for the Program for International Student Assessment (PISA) is from 0 to 1000. The scale was designed to have an average score of 500 points across OECD countries, with approximately two-thirds of students achieving between 400 and 600 points.

terms, many students appear to be motivated more by the need to avoid failing, or the fear of not graduating, than by the need to get something out of their classes.

How might one change this motivational pattern? Several answers were suggested, interestingly, by differences in achievement among adolescents from different ethnic backgrounds. Specifically, Asian American adolescents consistently outperformed European American adolescents, who performed better than African American or Hispanic adolescents. These differences existed even after other factors that are known to relate to academic success, such as family income or parental education, had been controlled for. In fact, ethnicity was more importantly related to academic achievement than any other factor, including affluence. As these investigators note, mention of ethnic differences in academic achievement is a sensitive subject, leading as it does to questions of differences in native ability. A more probable explanation than native ability, however, is that Asian American students simply work harder and have more adaptive attitudes toward school. In fact, however, if they really were superior, they would not put in twice as many hours on homework as other students.

So, what is it that contributes to the academic success of Asian American students? We've mentioned one factor—effort. They spend more time on schoolwork than their peers. Differences in their beliefs, however, are also important. Steinberg and his associates found that students from different ethnic backgrounds differed little in their beliefs about school success, about the importance of getting a good education, but they did differ in their beliefs about failing in school. When asked, for instance, if they thought that not doing well in school would interfere with their ability to get a good job, striking differences emerged. Asian American students, more so than any others, believed that not doing well would hurt their chances for later success. These investigators point out that it is excessive optimism, not pessimism, that is the problem for many African American and Hispanic students: They do not believe that doing poorly in their classes will affect their later success.

Asian American adolescents have also been found to report more positive feelings when engaged in activities they perceive as "worklike," indicating they feel happier, enjoy themselves more, and feel better about themselves than do European American adolescents. Over 60% of the time these activities were related to school, taking place either in the classroom or outside it, such as with homework. Their feelings, however, were no more positive than those of other adolescents when the activities they were engaged in were unrelated to work. Such findings suggest that, in part, the greater academic success of Asian Americans reflects having internalized cultural values concerning the importance of hard work and academic achievement (Asakawa & Csikszentmihalyi, 1998). Other research, as well, underscores the importance of hard work and self-discipline for academic success. Angela Duckworth and Martin Seligman (2005) found that self-discipline, rather than measured intelligence, was the best predictor of how well students would do in school. In other words, work habits, and not ethnicity, are key to academic success.

What are the encouraging findings from this research? Perhaps the most important is the power for change that lies within the reach of parents (Sorkhabi, 2005; Steinberg, Brown, & Dornbusch, 1996). Most parents value education and want their adolescents to succeed in school. However, not all ways of parenting are equally effective in promoting academic achievement. The most effective parents are accepting (versus rejecting), are firm (versus lenient), and encourage autonomy in their children (versus controlling them). This type of parenting is known as *authoritative parenting* (see Chapter 7). Authoritative parenting, in addition to promoting competence, maturity, and academic success, can also offset negative peer influences. Parental expectations, and adolescents' perceptions of these, contribute significantly to academic achievement. When parents become engaged, their children become engaged as well, and academic achievement improves (Comer, Haynes, Joyner, & Ben-Avie, 1996; Hill et al., 2004).

Patterns of Achievement

The power of positive thinking is getting some scientific backing. The attitude adolescents take toward their successes and failures is an important determinant of future success. It's not so much whether they fail or succeed—we all experience our share of both; it's what adolescents attribute their failure or success to that determines whether they will persist and eventually achieve. Research distinguishes two quite different patterns of achievement behavior: one defined by a focus on the task and what it takes to master it (a **task-mastery orientation**) and the other by a focus on one's performance or ability (a **performance-ability orientation**). The first approach is adaptive; the second is not (Dweck, 2002; Midgley, Arunkumar, & Urdan, 1996). We saw these two patterns earlier in this chapter in the discussion of school climate; schools also define success and achievement in these ways.

Adolescents who are task, or mastery, oriented enjoy situations that challenge them, and they work at them even when they are difficult. They even take pride in how much effort they have to put into mastering something new. Adolescents who are performance, or ability, oriented avoid challenging situations and show little persistence in the face of difficulty.

task-mastery orientation A motivational pattern in which students focus on the task they are learning and work to increase their mastery and competence.

performance-ability orientation A motivational pattern in which students focus on their own performance, using it as a way of assessing their ability.

Performance-oriented adolescents tend not to pursue challenging material unless they're sure they will succeed. They choose situations that will not reveal what they regard as their lack of ability. These students are likely to prefer tasks that are either very easy or very difficult; failure at the first is unlikely, and failure at the second cannot be taken as a measure of their ability. Even above-average students who are performance oriented will avoid situations that involve risk in preference to those where they can perform effortlessly and thereby feel smart. In doing so, however, they can miss situations that promote further understanding (Grant & Dweck, 2003).

Carol Dweclk (1999; Dweck & Molden, 2005) focuses on students' beliefs about the nature of intelligence in explaining different patterns of achievement. Differences between students who allow themselves to be challenged by difficult tasks and those who shy away from these can be traced to underlying beliefs about intelligence. Those who believe that their intellectual skills can actually be developed by working through difficult tasks are likely to be mastery oriented. Conversely, those who view intelligence as something one is born with, that's fixed and can't be changed, are more likely to be performance oriented. These adolescents are likely to be disrupted by failure, frequently to the point of giving up. Because they interpret failure to mean that they lack the ability for what they have attempted, they defensively withdraw in the face of it. To believe that failure means that one lacks ability is also to believe that trying harder isn't going to help. Rather than trying harder, these students are more likely to explain their failure as bad luck or the task's being too difficult. For them, having to work hard to achieve is dangerous; it's just another way of calling their ability into question.

Carol Midgley, Revathy Arunkumar, and Timothy Urdan (1996) examined the use of *self-handicapping strategies* among African American and European American early adolescents. Such strategies are behaviors—such as not studying until the last minute or partying the night before a test—that could be seen as a cause of poor performance when students do not do well. Like achievement attributions, students may use strategies such as these to explain their performance in achievement situations; however, self-handicapping strategies are put into play before, rather than after, a student experiences success or failure. Thus, instead of explaining why one failed to pass a test that one had actually studied for by saying that one hadn't studied hard enough (achievement attribution), one might intentionally not study until the night before (self-handicapping strategy), using inadequate time to study as an excuse for failing. Self-handicapping strategies hold the allure of a win–win situation: If one does poorly, those strategies provide an excuse, and if one does well, they make one appear even smarter. The disadvantages to their use are two-edged as well: Not only do they actually handicap students, making failure more likely; they also interfere with the use of adaptive ways of coping with achievement demands.

Given what we know of the ways adolescents interpret failure, we might suspect that some are more likely to self-handicap than others. Midgley and associates found, as suspected, that adolescents who adopt a performance-ability orientation to achievement situations more frequently report using these strategies. Additionally, even though the grade-point averages for African American and European American students did not differ, African American students who adopted a performance-ability orientation were more likely to self-handicap than were European American students. This difference is particularly surprising because African American adolescents were more positive in their self-esteem and certain attitudes toward school than European American adolescents were. Claude Steele (1992; Steele & Aronson, 1995) suggests a possible explanation. Steele argues that African American students face an additional challenge to their ability, which he terms *stereotype threat*. Stereotype threat is the risk of confirming a negative stereotype about one's ethnic group, and hence about oneself, a threat that may increase the use of self-handicapping strategies as a self-defense.

Gender Differences and Achievement

Gender, as well, is related to perceptions of academic competence (Johns, Schmader, & Martins, 2005; Ryan & Ryan, 2005). Jennifer Steele, Jacquclyn James, and Rosalind Barnett (2002) found that female college students also experienced stereotype threat when taking courses in traditionally male-dominated fields such as math, science, and engineering. Furthermore, beliefs about competency in different domains are established early (Hyde & Durik, 2005; Tenenbaum & Leaper, 2003). David Cole and his associates (1999), at Notre Dame, followed children and early adolescents over a three-year period, starting in the third and sixth grades, periodically obtaining estimates of their competency beliefs. By the fourth or fifth grade, differences associated with gender emerged, with boys overestimating their abilities and girls underestimating theirs. These differences increased with age through early adolescence. Similarly, Jennifer Herbert and Deborah Stipek (2005) found that by the third grade, girls evaluated their competency in math lower than did boys even though they performed at the same level.

Dweck (2002) points out that teachers and parents can help male and female students alike adopt more adaptive achievement motives by focusing on their efforts and not on their successes. Students who are praised for sticking with a challenging task until they eventually master it, learn to value the effort that's often needed to solve new tasks. Giving them feedback about the strategies they're using is important since this focuses them on the process of learning and what they can do to improve this. Students who are praised for the strategies they come up with when faced with challenging tasks, and not for how smart they are when they quickly solve problems, will actually enjoy having to work at something until they discover an approach that is successful.

Females frequently respond to success and failure in different ways than do males. Males are likely to attribute their successes to their ability and their failures to lack of effort. What this means, of course, is that males will persist at a problem until, more likely than not, they get it right. Females are more likely to attribute their successes to hard work, luck, or the ease of the task, and their failures to lack of ability, thereby discounting their successes and taking responsibility only for their failures. This interpretation can make females helpless in the face of success; they're not sure how they did it and unsure whether they could do it again. It was luck or an easy grade, they tell themselves, attributing their success to factors other than their own skill. Females can be equally helpless in the face of failure. Because they attribute it to their inability, they have little recourse but to give up and try something new (Dweck, 1986, 2002).

Of all adolescents, those who are most likely to show maladaptive achievement behavior are females of high ability. Licht, Linden, Brown, and Sexton (1984) found a gender difference in response to failure *only* among the brightest students: The performance of the most able females was disrupted and that of males was actually facilitated. Bright females are more likely than males of equal ability, or students of either sex of average ability, to avoid challenge, to attribute their failure to inability, and to withdraw in the face of failure.

Similarly, bright females who experience initial confusion at a task are less likely to do well than less capable females. Specifically, the brighter the female, the less likely she is to master a task if she encounters initial problems with it. If she experiences no initial confusion, however, her mastery is directly related to ability. A similar pattern does not exist for males. In fact, males are slightly more likely to master tasks when they experience some initial confusion. This is especially true for those of high ability (Dweck, 1986, 2002).

These motivational patterns frequently become evident only when adolescents enter junior high. Prior to this point, course material may not be sufficiently challenging to prompt defensive withdrawal. Mathematics represents a case in point. Girls and boys perform equally in math throughout elementary school. Carol Dweck (1986, 2002) notes that achievement in math takes a new turn in junior high, one that is likely to call into play the gender differences in motivational patterns that we have been discussing. Dweck points out that math, unlike verbal tasks, often requires students to determine which solutions are appropriate to which problems. In verbal tasks they can follow the same approach with new material as with the old. Whether a word is *dog* or *dogmatic*, if it is unfamiliar, the solution is the same: Look it up in the dictionary. New problems in math often require students to adopt a different approach, and they are likely to make errors at first. The initial confusion that results is more likely to interfere with the performance of girls than with that of boys.

A study by Byrnes and Takahira (1993) points to the importance of cognitive operations, in addition to motivational processes, in explaining gender differences in mathematics. These investigators focused on high school students' performance on the math section of the Scholastic Aptitude Test (SAT), in which males typically outperform females by over 40 points. Students were given five math problems from the SAT. Prior to taking the test, all students completed a measure testing their knowledge of the concepts that would be needed to solve the problems, and immediately after, they indicated which strategies they had used. Even though males did no better on the test assessing mathematical concepts, they outperformed females on the SAT items. Their superiority on these was explained by differences in the way they put to use what they knew.

Female students, even gifted ones, are more likely than male students to attribute initial confusion about a task to their own inability rather than to the nature of the task itself and consequently to withdraw in the face of failure.

Attitudes toward math almost surely are important, and females develop a less positive attitude toward math with age. In a longitudinal study following females from middle school to high school, Klebanov and Brooks-Gunn (1992) found that females' attitudes about math became less positive, even though their grades did not change. These investigators note the importance of socialization in contributing to attitudes toward math, showing that mothers' attitudes toward their daughters' achievement corresponded to how well they did in middle school. By high school, females' own attitudes toward math became more important, reflecting sex-role stereotypes in which math achievement is perceived as masculine. College students as well share these attitudes (Nosek, Banaji, & Greenwald, 2002).

Dweck (2002) cautions that maladaptive motivational approaches can have cumulative effects. They can lead female adolescents to take fewer math courses and consequently to become less skilled than males in math. Math is a "gateway" subject, opening up possibilities in fields such as medicine, engineering, and most branches of science.

Adolescents at the Edge

Three quite different groups of students have special needs and frequently find themselves out of step with the rest of the class. These adolescents come from all backgrounds. They are the gifted, those with learning disabilities, and those who drop out.

Gifted Adolescents

In 1925 Lewis Terman, of Stanford University, defined the gifted as those who place among the top 2% on a test of intelligence. Today, as well, the most common criterion for placing students in special educational programs is still a score on an intelligence test: 130 or higher. The following descriptions come close to what the average person is likely to think of as gifted: the super smart, the ones who ace school, the kids behind the books.

In 1981 Congress passed the Education Consolidation and Improvement Act, which defines giftedness more broadly. The **gifted** and talented are those "who give evidence of high performance capability in areas such as intellectual, creative, artistic, leadership capacity, or specific academic fields, and who require services or activities not ordinarily provided by the school in order to fully develop such capabilities" (Sec. 582).

Howard Gardner (2006) also includes more than traditional measures of intelligence in defining giftedness. Gardner considers seven domains of intelligence: musical, bodily-kinesthetic, logical-mathematical, linguistic, spatial, interpersonal, and intrapersonal (discussed in Chapter 4). Adolescents can be creative in any of these different domains, and for Gardner, creativity is the highest form of functioning. Creativity and giftedness, however, are not neatly related. Many gifted individuals are also highly creative, but many are not. Also, many creative people are not intellectually gifted.

Identifying Gifted Students Perhaps because intelligence reflects our personalities, gifted adolescents fail to fit any stereotype. It is easy to identify those who have large vocabularies or who top out on standard tests of achievement. But what about the ones who never see things the way others do, have zany senses of humor or vivid imaginations, those who get bored easily or who, when they can't do things perfectly, fail to do them at all? Gifted adolescents are likely to fit any of these descriptions as well.

Barbara Clark (1988), an educator at California State University, Los Angeles, offers the characteristics listed in the In More Depth box as indices of cognitive giftedness. Many of these characteristics would not be taken as signs of unusual talent or intelligence by most of us. Some, in fact, seem to signal just the opposite.

Gifted adolescents not only excel academically; they typically apply their intelligence to advantage in other areas of their lives as well. They tend to be more mature, have better social skills, and be more self-confident, responsible, and self-controlled. So much for the negative stereotypes of the gifted as bookworms and wimps.

Being gifted does not offer immunity to social and emotional setbacks. In fact, it may make them harder to take. Social injustices can be especially difficult for those concerned with social or political problems, and slights can easily be exaggerated by those who react to life intensely and with passion. Adolescents who sailed through grade school with nothing lower than an A can be devastated when they get their first B. And gifted adolescents—just like others—must cope with emotions and concerns magnified by the changes of puberty.

Educating Gifted Students Educational programs follow one of two alternatives: enrichment or acceleration. The goal of **enrichment** is to provide gifted students with more opportunities and experiences than they would normally get, without moving them to a higher grade. An example would be offering special courses in literature, math, science, or the arts, along with their normal course of studies. **Acceleration** allows gifted students to advance beyond their grade level at a faster than normal rate, that is, skipping grades. Advocates of enrichment point to the social and emotional needs of gifted students, arguing that these are best met by keeping them with others their age. Although many gifted adolescents are socially and emotionally more advanced than their peers, this argument is especially compelling for late maturers, especially boys.

gifted Adolescents who place above a predetermined cutoff point on intelligence scales or who demonstrate special talents in diverse areas.

enrichment Providing gifted adolescents with additional opportunities and experiences.

acceleration Allowing gifted adolescents to advance beyond their grade level at a faster than normal rate.

IN MORE DEPTH

Some Characteristics of Gifted Students

Asks many questions	Completes part of an assignment and leaves it unfinished for something else
Has much information on many topics	Continues to work on an assignment when the rest of the class moves on to something else
Adopts a questioning attitude	Is restless
Becomes unusually upset at injustices	Daydreams
Is interested in social or political problems	Understands easily
Has better reasons than you do for not doing what you want done	Likes to solve problems
Refuses to drill on repetitive tasks	Has own ideas as to how things should be done
Becomes impatient when can't do an assignment perfectly	Talks a lot
Is a loner	Enjoys debate
Is bored and frequently has nothing to do	Enjoys abstract ideas

Source: B. Clark. (1988). *Growing up gifted* (3rd ed.). New York: Macmillan.

On the other hand, failure to advance the highly gifted can present as many problems as acceleration. Adolescents who experience little or no intellectual challenge in their classes and feel they are simply "marking time" can face intellectual stagnation, loneliness, and apathy—difficulties as serious as any introduced by moving ahead of their age-mates.

Adolescents with Learning Disabilities

For some students, marking time takes a very different form. They, too, have difficulty maintaining interest in their classes but for reasons very different from those of gifted students. These students have experienced difficulty in school almost from the beginning. Many live with the bewildering sense that something is wrong, though they can't say what. Most feel stupid, though they are not. These adolescents have a **learning disability**.

Defining Learning Disabilities Who are these students, and what special problems do they face? Answers focus on three defining features of learning disabilities: (1) a discrepancy between expected and actual performance, (2) difficulty with academic tasks that cannot be traced to emotional problems or sensory impairment, and (3) presumed neurological dysfunction.

First, learning-disabled students show a *discrepancy between expected and actual performance*. Students with a learning disability are of average or above-average intelligence but don't perform at the level one would expect based on their intelligence; they frequently fall at least two grade levels behind their peers in academic skills. Second, their *difficulty with academic tasks* cannot be traced to emotional or sensory dysfunction. They may experience difficulty in one or more specific areas (for example, reading or math) or in the general skills needed for many areas, such as being able to pay attention or to monitor their performance (such as remembering which subroutines they have completed in a math problem in order to begin the next). They do not have a learning disability if the source of the difficulty is an emotional problem, problems at home, or a sensory impairment, such as a hearing loss. Finally, students with a learning disability are

learning disability Difficulty with academic tasks that is not due to emotional or sensory problems and presumably reflects neurological dysfunction.

RESEARCH FOCUS

Within-Subjects Design and Attention Deficit Disorder: "Can't I Stay Home? I Think I Don't Feel Well."

Robbie hated going to school. He didn't *dislike* going to school. He actually hated it. And Monday mornings were the worst. He hadn't always felt this way. As a matter of fact, he had liked school at first. But things had started to change soon enough. He never could seem to finish his work on time, couldn't concentrate, and was continually distracted by events around him. The least little thing would pull his attention away from what he was doing—someone walking outside the classroom, a fly buzzing overhead, even the sound of someone else's pencil. He had trouble remembering things, too. He would forget assignments or lose the ones he had done. Sometimes he even had difficulty recalling what an assignment had been about. Yes, school made him feel crazy. And it made him feel stupid.

Robbie was anything but stupid. Like 3–5% of those in school, Robbie suffered from attention-deficit hyperactivity disorder (ADHD), a learning disability more common among males than females (American Psychiatric Association, 1994). Students with ADHD have difficulty sustaining their attention on the task at hand, are easily distracted by what is going on around them, and often act impulsively, saying or doing whatever comes to mind. Many, though not all, are also hyperactive. ADHD is most likely multiply determined. A number of factors, both genetic and environmental, have been identified as contributing to this disorder. Thus, students identified with ADHD are likely to find that others in their family are also affected. Environmental factors have also been found to be important, reflecting a wide range of experiences, from prenatal exposure to teratogens, or factors that interfere with normal development, to the amount of structure adolescents experience at home or in their classrooms.

Steven Landau, Elizabeth Lorch, and Richard Milich (1992) investigated the effects of one type of structure, the presence or absence of distractors in the room, on ADHD boys' ability to sustain attention to an outgoing task. These investigators reasoned that if boys with ADHD attend significantly less to a task than do other boys when distractors are present but show little difference when they are absent, the difficulties they experience reflect problems not so much in sustaining attention as in selective attention, or screening out distractions. To this end, they had ADHD subjects and control subjects watch two segments from the television show "3-2-1 Contact." While the boys were watching one segment, no distracting toys were present; while they were watching the other, they were available. The researchers measured both the percentage of time boys attended to the programs and how much they remembered of the programs. Finally, each group of boys was divided into younger (6–9 years) and older (10–12 years) subjects.

These investigators used a within-subjects design, in which each subject experienced each of the distraction conditions (toys present, toys absent). This design can be compared with a between-subjects design in which each subject would experience only one condition (see the

presumed to have some *neurological dysfunction*, because they are of at least average intelligence and their difficulties are not primarily the result of sensory, emotional, or cultural causes (Lenz & Deshler, 2005).

Addressing Problems Learning-disabled adolescents face problems both inside and outside the classroom. In the classroom, problems can range from difficulty paying attention or following class discussions to failure to turn in written assignments. Learning-disabled students have difficulty keeping up with classmates. A national study of 30,000 tenth-graders found that twice as many students with a learning disability as nondisabled students placed in the bottom 25% of their class (Owings & Stocking, 1985). Performance for learning-disabled students is likely to be anywhere from two to four grades for junior high students and can be even greater for high school students. In addition, most learning-disabled students have poorer study habits, are less likely to do their homework,

Research Focus "Between-Subjects Design" in Chapter 6). Within-subjects designs are *economical,* requiring fewer subjects, because the same subjects react to all conditions. They are also *sensitive.* A design is sensitive to the extent that it can pick up, or detect, differences resulting from the experimental treatment. Within-subjects designs are sensitive because they use the same subjects in all conditions, thus reducing variability due to individual differences.

Despite these important advantages, this type of design has several serious disadvantages. First, there is the risk of *carryover effects*, in which the effect of one treatment is still present when the next is given. In this example, subjects who previously watched the program with attractive toys present in the room may be distracted by thoughts of playing while viewing the subsequent program even though there are no distractors present. Carryover effects are not necessarily symmetrical for each of the orders in which different subjects watch programs under different conditions; watching with no distractors present first might have no effect on subsequent viewing. In addition to carryover effects, there can be *order effects* with this design. These reflect systematic changes in performance over time due to factors such as practice, fatigue, boredom, and so on. Both carryover and order effects introduce the potential for *confounding*. Confounding exists when the difference between treatments can be explained in more than one way, that is, when an experiment lacks internal validity (see the Research Focus "Internal and External Validity" on the Web site).

Landau, Lorch, and Milich *counterbalanced* the order in which subjects experienced the two distractor conditions. Counterbalancing presents each condition an equal number of times in each order, thus balancing any effects due to order equally across conditions.

What did they find? First, with respect to attending to the program, the ADHD boys did not differ from the control boys in the percentage of time they attended to the programs when no distractors were present. However, when distractors were present, they spent only half the time attending to the programs that the other boys did. Age was also a factor with respect to length of attention, with older boys paying more attention, but only when distracting toys were present. When there were no distractors in the room, younger boys were as attentive as older ones. With respect to remembering what they had seen, ADHD boys did not differ from controls in their ability to recall aspects of the programs they had watched. Further, having distractors present interfered with recall only for the younger boys. These findings suggest that environmental structure, in the form of removing potential distractors, may be useful in helping students with ADHD attend to the tasks at which they are working. Medication, in the form of stimulants such as Ritalin, has also proven helpful in improving attention (Barkley, 1990). Such treatment, however, is most effective when used in conjunction with programs that teach adolescents how to structure their learning environments so as to support the behaviors they will need to maintain.

Sources: American Psychiatric Association. (1994). *Diagnostic and statistical manual of mental disorders* (4th ed.). Washington, DC: Author. R. A. Barkley. (1990). *Attention deficit hyperactivity disorder: A handbook for diagnosis and treatment.* New York: Guilford Press. S. Landau, E. P. Lorch, and R. Milich. (1992). Visual attention to and comprehension of television in attention-deficit hyperactivity disordered and normal boys. *Child Development, 63*, 928–937.

and, when it comes to demonstrating what they *have* learned, have poorer test-taking skills. Frequently, nonattendance, incomplete assignments, and failure to turn in homework contribute to their failure in a course as much as their scores on tests do (Lenz & Deshler, 2005). For a look at the effect of distractions on boys with learning disabilities, see the Research Focus "Within-Subjects Design and Attention Deficit Disorder."

The problems of learning-disabled adolescents don't end when they leave the classroom. As a group, they have poorer social skills than other students. They are less likely to pick up on another's mood and respond appropriately, and they are less aware of the effect their behavior has on others. Subtle cues can go right by them. The same problems that make it difficult for them to understand what their teachers are saying in class can affect their interactions with friends. They may miss nuances of conversation and respond inappropriately or miss rule changes in a game and feel they've been taken advantage of when the old rules no longer apply. Frequently, they prefer the company of those who are younger, just because they are more compliant.

Learning-disabled students are less likely to be involved in extracurricular activities than other students. Perhaps this fact reflects their general disenchantment with school. Or it may reflect a poorer self-image and expectations of failure in these activities as well. Increasing learning-disabled students' involvement in extracurricular activities such as teams, clubs, and music and drama productions might be one of the most important ways of increasing their participation and their motivation to stay in school.

Schooling Learning-Disabled Adolescents **Mainstreaming** places learning-disabled adolescents in regular classes. The most common accommodation teachers make is to adjust their grades. Perhaps because so little is done to meet the special needs of the learning-disabled in most classrooms, mainstreaming can introduce special problems of attendance. A growing number of schools that mainstream learning-disabled students provide a **special education consultant** who meets with regular teachers to discuss ways of managing the needs of these students. This procedure allows students to attend classes with their peers while receiving materials designed by someone who has specialized in learning disorders.

The other extreme from mainstreaming places learning-disabled students in **special education classes**. The obvious advantages of such an approach are small classes in which materials can be personalized to the needs of students and a teacher who is experienced in the special needs of the learning-disabled. A disadvantage is that special education teachers may not be as well versed in all subjects as regular high school teachers. Association with nondisabled students who might serve as positive role models is limited, and teachers may not hold learning-disabled students to the same standards that are required of other students.

Dropping Out

Dropping out, for most students, is the last step on a path begun years earlier. These students are likely to have experienced more school failure than their classmates, to have been held back a grade, and to have higher rates of absenteeism (General Accounting Office, 2002). Disproportionate numbers of students who fail to complete high school are economically disadvantaged. Dropout rates are also strikingly higher for students who belong to an ethnic minority, with the exception of Asian American students (see Figure 9.5.) In addition to low income and ethnicity, a number of conditions both at home and at school are associated with dropping out. Parents' educational level is important (Connolly & Snyder, 2005). Parents serve as models for educational success; adolescents with parents or older siblings who have dropped out of high school are more likely to drop out. The relationship between parental education and socioeconomic status is equally important. Socioeconomic status confers numerous advantages as one moves up the economic ladder. Adolescents from higher-income homes have broader cultural experiences, attend better schools, have parents with more time (and skills) to help with homework, and experience lower levels of stress within the family. Not surprisingly, family income level is associated with achievement and staying in school (Snyder & Tan, 2005).

Parental attitudes toward education are also important. Interviews of Black and Hispanic mothers revealed that they place a high value on getting good grades—often a higher value than does the dominant culture (Figure 9.6). In addition to the value placed on education in Black and Hispanic families, these differences may reflect an awareness of the greater need for their children to achieve in order to overcome existing social biases (Stevenson, Chen, & Uttal, 1990).

Level of stress within the family is another important predictor of dropping out, as is the number of parents living in the home (Barton, 2005). On average, female-headed

mainstreaming Placing learning-disabled students in regular classrooms.

special education consultant A consultant who meets with teachers to discuss ways to meet the needs of learning-disabled students who are mainstreamed.

special education classes Classes for learning-disabled students that are tailored to the needs of each student.

households have significantly lower incomes than those with both parents present. When the stresses that accompany low-income living are factored in, family configuration (female-headed households versus two-parent ones) has little bearing on school performance (Entwisle & Alexander, 1990; McLanahan & Booth, 1989).

Students' experiences within the classroom also relate to dropping out. Lack of basic skills is one of the most important. Adolescents who have difficulty with their coursework, who have failed a course, or who have stayed behind a grade are at risk (Connell, Halpern-Felsher, Clifford, Crichlow, & Usinger, 1995). Many of these adolescents are in noncollege tracks, a factor that in itself contributes to dropping out (Gamoran & Mare, 1989). Many also have changed schools frequently. Other predictors of dropping out are low self-esteem and disruptive behavior (Nelson, 1988; Tidwell, 1988).

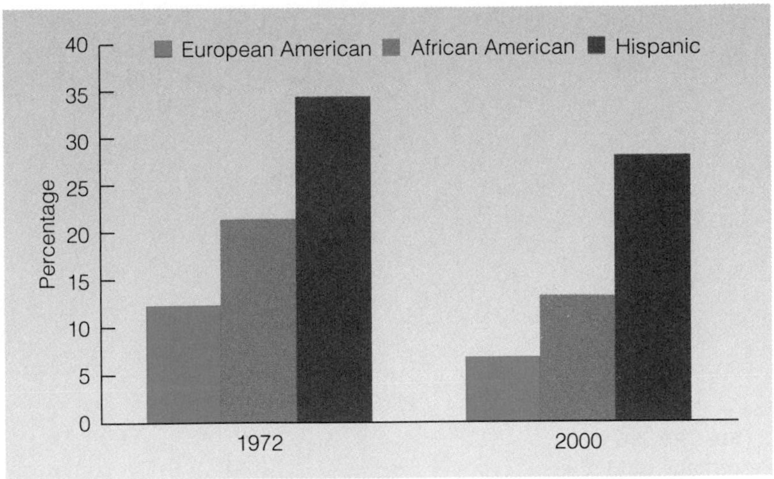

FIGURE 9.5
Percentage of High School Dropouts, 1972 and 2000.
Source: T. C. Snyder & C. M. Hoffman. (2002). *Digest of education statistics, 2001* (NCES 2002-130). Washington, DC: U.S. Department of Education, National Center for Education Statistics.

Peer influence is also important. A study of tenth-grade inner-city Hispanic youth found that those at low risk for dropping out had experienced less pressure to join a gang and had fewer friends in gangs than those who were likely to drop out. The low-risk students also reported more satisfaction with school (Reyes & Jason, 1993). Similarly, Jane Corville-Smith, Bruce Ryan, Gerald Adams, and Tom Delicandro (1998) found that a handful of factors allowed them to distinguish with 90% accuracy students with high rates of absenteeism from those who attended school regularly. Specifically, absentee students perceived their school experience less positively; they experienced less consistent discipline at home and more family conflict and parental control. They also felt inferior academically and less competent socially.

Interviews with adolescents who have dropped out of high school corroborate these findings (Tidwell, 1988). When asked why they dropped out, they mentioned poor grades, dislike of school, trouble with teachers, and financial problems. Many mentioned home responsibilities, pregnancy, and marriage. Almost all said they would not recommend dropping out to a friend or sibling.

Effective Programs Peter Coleman (1993), at Simon Fraser University, contends that rather than seeing dropouts as a problem within the school system, they are instead a measure of its quality. Because dropouts are part of the system, programs that reach them should benefit all students.

At this point, we have some idea what makes schools more effective. We know, based on Comer's model, described earlier in this chapter, that schools which train students in social skills and establish ties with the community are more successful. So too are those that involve parents in the educational process. Comer directly invited parents to participate; however, parents also become more involved when schools collaborate with agencies in the community to provide a variety of school-based or referral services to students and their families, as they do in full-service schools. Each of these practices makes classroom experiences more relevant to experiences outside the classroom, whether with peers, parents, or the community.

Coleman found, from interviews with several hundred parents, that most of their interactions with schools are not instructionally focused. Yet most parents believe that

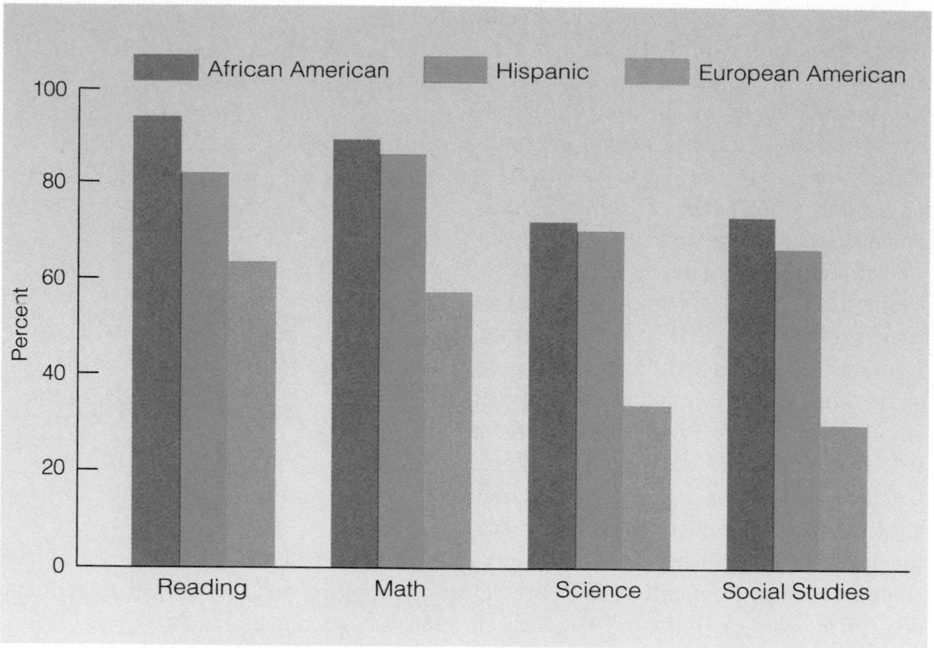

FIGURE 9.6 Percentage of Mothers Placing High Value on Academic Achievement.
Source: H. W. Stevenson, C. Chen, & D. H. Uttal. (1990). Beliefs and achievement: A study of black, white, and Hispanic children. *Child Development, 61,* 508–523.

they could help their children if they were allowed to participate more actively. Coleman points out that because parents' attitudes exert such a strong influence on children's attitudes toward school, reaching out to parents and working collaboratively with them is one of the most effective ways schools can increase students' commitment.

Early childhood intervention programs, particularly those that continue through the second or third grade, both improve academic performance in grade school and increase the likelihood of completing high school. Once again, parents become more involved. They participate more in school activities, volunteer in the classroom, and network with other parents. They're also more likely to monitor their child's activities and know what assignments are due and when (Reynolds & Temple, 1998; Reynolds et al., 2001).

Among programs designed specifically for students who drop out, the most effective are those that simultaneously address the many problems these adolescents face at home as well as at school. Many adolescents, especially those from low-income families, need to work to help support themselves and their families. Innovative work–study programs that combine academic coursework with work in job settings for which students also receive academic credit have been successful, as have those that establish for students the connection between finishing high school and making a living. Almost all at-risk students need individual attention.

One program illustrates many of these points with notable success. Jefferson County High School in Louisville, Kentucky, has enrolled over 5,000 former dropouts, and in its first four years, it graduated 1,100 of them. A number of features that are especially important for schooling at-risk adolescents distinguish this high school. The school offers an individualized program to every student, ensuring that they complete each unit of coursework with 70% mastery before moving on to the next. The latter requirement guarantees their success at what they attempt next. Students receive hands-on vocational guidance, in which they complete a battery of tests using manipulative materials. After reaching the end of these, they know what jobs they would like and which ones they would be good at. This high school puts as much emphasis on placing students in the right career track as on getting them ready for college (Gross, 1990).

TABLE 9.2 National Graduation Rates By Race and Gender

By Race/Ethnicity	Nation	Female	Male
American Indian/AK Nat	51.1	51.4	47.0
Asian/Pacific Islander	76.8	80.0	72.6
Hispanic	53.2	58.5	48
Black	50.2	56.2	42.8
White	74.9	77	70.8
All Students	**68**	**72**	**64.1**

Source: Urban Institute. (2005). *Education in the age of accountability.* Available at www.urban.org/content/IssuesInFocus/EducationintheAgeofAccountability/Education.htm

Many students who drop out work, and many have children. Schools that allow them to fit their classes into their other schedules minimize the conflicts that might otherwise keep students away from school. Much of Jefferson County High School's flexibility comes from its use of **computer-assisted instruction** (CAI). CAI provides printouts showing a student's trouble spots, so teachers know where to help. CAI also centralizes bookkeeping so that students can pick up where they left off even after an absence—an important plus for students who need to take time off to complete a job or stay home with a sick child.

Another approach to getting students who drop out back on track utilizes community colleges. The Gateway to College program at Portland Community College in Oregon enables dropouts to earn a high school diploma while accumulating college credits. This program places students first in small learning communities, or cohorts, where they get individualized support and receive concentrated instruction in basic skills. Following this, students meet with a resource specialist who helps them select college courses that will simultaneously satisfy the requirements for their high school degree as well as meet requirements for their community college degree. Courses are offered during the day and evening, providing the flexibility that students need to avoid conflicts with their work or child-care schedules. This program currently is being replicated in other states because of its success (Gateway to College, 2005).

Measuring Success

Effective as the above programs are, broad social policy changes are needed to ensure that all students receive a good education. The U.S. faces a crisis in secondary education—almost a third of students do not graduate high school with a diploma (Barton, 2005). Percentages are even lower for low-income and minority students (see Table 9.2). The extent of this problem has frequently been obscured since states have been able to report higher than actual graduation rates by using formulas that enable them to count a percentage of students who do not graduate as having transferred to other schools. For instance, California's reported graduation rate of 87% for 2002 was actually closer to 71%. When this figure was broken down for minority students, rates for African Americans (56.6%) and Hispanics (60%) were even lower (Civil Rights Project, 2005). Additionally, there are wide variations in completion rates from state to state, from a high of 88% to a low of 48% (Barton, 2005).

computer-assisted instruction The use of computers to monitor the progress of students.

Testing and Public Policy

The standards-based educational reform, No Child Left Behind, enacted in 2002, is designed to strengthen academic achievement for all children and to decrease the disparity in achievement that currently exists between children from high- and low-income families and between European American children and those belonging to an ethnic minority. Schools are held accountable for making progress toward meeting higher proficiency levels, and parents are given the option of choosing another school if the one their child attends fails to meet these standards. Critics of this legislation argue that the federal funds which schools receive must go to support increased standardized testing, with little left over for programs that actually change the quality of education, such as teacher training and support, and smaller class sizes. Additionally, in many urban areas, there are not enough high-performing schools for parents to actually have a choice (Urban Institute, 2005).

Solutions to problems in education will need to focus on more than the schools themselves. Schools' successes in graduating more of their students, in the end, must be accompanied by society's success in providing these students with decent-paying jobs. The schools that are in greatest need, with the highest dropout rates, are low-income inner-city schools in neighborhoods with high rates of unemployment. Until programs bring jobs back to inner cities, educational reforms are not likely to succeed (Wilson, 1996).

What will work? Funding for "wraparound" early childhood intervention programs so that children from low-income families are brought up to speed in the skills they need for school; funding for teacher training, basic resources, and improving the physical facilities of schools, especially for impoverished inner city schools; implementing the recommendations of the widely respected Carnegie Council on Adolescent Development (1989), such as establishing small communities for learning and strengthening ties between schools and the community; and giving more local authority to schools to make the changes they need to make to reach students more effectively.

Summary

Educating Adolescents

- School districts and teachers face choices as to how to structure classroom learning. Teachers using a *direct instruction* approach work with the class as a whole, involving all students in all aspects of each lesson. Teachers using *differentiated instruction* structure classrooms so that students work in groups on different projects, giving them multiple ways of gaining information and of making sense of what they are learning.
- Differentiated instruction assumes that students have different *learning styles* distinguished by the conditions under which they learn best, such as working for concentrated periods of time or needing frequent breaks, working alone or in groups, with materials presented visually or auditorially.
- Even though junior high schools and middle schools are designed to meet the needs of early adolescents, students' grades drop when they leave elementary school. Difficulties may reflect more impersonal classroom environments and teachers involving students less in classroom decision making.

What Makes Schools Effective?

- Effective schools have skilled teachers who have high expectations for all students, monitor their progress, and make effective use of feedback in guiding students' activities.
- Smaller schools can overcome differences related to social class and academic background better than large schools; students have more positive interactions, fewer discipline problems, and less absenteeism. It is possible to create smaller

communities for learning within large schools that can be responsive to students' needs.

- Effective schools have a supportive school climate that promotes achievement through the way they integrate resources into instruction and emphasize diverse types of achievements.
- Effective schools are *full-service* schools that collaborate with community agencies to provide a variety of health and social services for students and their families.
- Effective schools involve parents in their children's education.

School Violence

- A number of factors are likely to contribute to the presence of violence at school: societal attitudes toward violence, domestic violence, media modeling, poverty and discrimination, and the accessibility of guns.
- Many students do not feel safe at school because they are victims of *bullying*. Adolescents in middle school are more likely to be bullied than are those in high school.
- Intervention programs that involve parents, teachers, and staff, as well as students, have been found to be effective in reducing bullying.
- Schools can promote peace through *cooperative learning*, through *training in conflict resolution and constructive controversy*, and by establishing *conflict resolution centers*.

Education for All

- Some gender-role stereotyping still exists in teaching materials. In textbooks, males are likely to be pictured more frequently, appear in more diverse occupations, and need rescuing less frequently. Even so, large advances have been made in reducing stereotyping.
- The use of *male generic language* represents another form of bias. Using the masculine pronoun generically predisposes students and their teachers to think of males, not of individuals in general. Their evaluations of the competence of students of either sex for different types of work are thereby skewed.
- *Jigsaw classrooms*, where students work in small groups, each contributing a different part of the lesson, foster cooperation and promote better relations among students from different ethnic backgrounds.
- Presenting material from several cultural perspectives is helpful to minority students who may not always share the perspective assumed in the textbook or other materials used.
- Communication problems arise for some minority students when language is used differently at school and at home. Four distinctive approaches characterize different ethnic and cultural groups: group versus individual orientations, active versus passive coping styles, attitudes toward authority, and expressive versus restrained mannerisms. Intervention programs that heighten teacher and student awareness of these differences improve the quality of multicultural education.
- Most intervention programs have focused on problems minority students may experience at the level of the microsystem, that is, in the home and the classroom. Problems of poorer achievement and higher dropout rates may have to be addressed at the level of the macrosystem, that is, the society. The assurance of equal opportunity for jobs may be the most effective form of intervention.

Academic Achievement

- Students from low-income families score lower on achievement tests, get lower grades, and are less likely to finish high school. Home conditions are less conducive to studying, they have access to fewer resources, high rates of unemployment offer less incentive for completing school, and they attend schools in which teachers are less likely to be experienced or trained in the subjects they teach.
- Existing public programs, such as early childhood intervention programs, have been found to be effective in countering the effects of economic adversity on academic achievement.
- *Academic tracking* is a common solution to diverse interests and abilities among students, but tracking may contribute to differences in achievement and dropout rates among those assigned to college and noncollege tracks.
- Alternatives to tracking include forming small *cooperative learning* groups in the classroom and involving parents in the educational process. Work–study programs and computer-assisted instruction offer additional alternatives.
- U.S. students place somewhat below students in other industrialized countries in mathematics and science and somewhat above the international average in reading proficiency. The cultural and socioeconomic diversity of the U.S. student population and the amount of time students spend watching television are assumed to contribute to overall proficiency levels.

- Spending time with friends, participating in sports, and working are also higher priorities for many U.S. adolescents than school. Not all students believe that doing well in high school is related to their future success. Consequently, they may be motivated more by the fear of failing than by the desire to learn. Academic achievement is strongly correlated with authoritative parenting in terms of involvement, communication, and expectations.
- Adolescents can be distinguished in terms of achievement motivation patterns. Task-oriented adolescents focus on the task and work to increase their mastery. Performance-oriented adolescents focus on their performance and use it as a measure of their ability. Task-oriented adolescents are less likely to be disrupted by initial failure, believing it to result from lack of sufficient effort rather than inability. Performance-oriented adolescents are likely to withdraw in the face of failure and attribute it to an external cause rather than their own lack of effort. Some may preemptively use self-handicapping strategies to provide an excuse for failing.
- Gender differences reveal more adaptive motivational patterns for males. Gender-role stereotypes contribute to the less positive attitudes that affect females' motivation. These differences often do not appear until adolescents enter junior high and encounter work that is challenging enough to prompt defensive withdrawal.

Adolescents at the Edge

- Adolescents who score 130 or above on an intelligence test or who have creative, artistic, leadership, or other special talents are defined as *gifted* and talented. Educational programs for the gifted offer *enrichment,* providing them with more experiences than they would ordinarily get, or *acceleration,* allowing them to advance beyond their grade level.
- Adolescents with *learning disabilities* are of average or above-average intelligence who show a discrepancy between expected and actual performance. They have difficulty in academic tasks that presumably can be traced to a neurological dysfunction. Learning-disabled high school students can fall two or more grade levels behind classmates in some subject areas and generally have poor study habits and test-taking skills. Social skills are also affected for many.
- *Mainstreaming* places learning-disabled students in regular classes with their classmates. A *special education consultant* may advise regular teachers on the special needs of these students. At the other extreme, learning-disabled students may be placed in special education classes with specially trained teachers. Each of these educational options has different advantages.
- Dropout rates are related to low socioeconomic status and ethnicity. Parents' or siblings' failure to complete high school and family stress also are predictive of dropping out. School variables that predict dropping out are a history of difficulty or failure, low self-esteem, assignment to a noncollege track, and behavior problems.
- Early childhood intervention programs improve academic performance in grade school and increase the likelihood of completing high school.
- Programs that are effective in helping at-risk students involve parents, provide individualized counseling, and help students meet their financial as well as academic needs, as in work–study programs for which students receive academic credit.
- Community college programs that enable students who have dropped out to earn a high school diploma while accumulating college credits are also effective.

Measuring Success

- Broad social policy changes are needed to ensure that all students receive a good education. Presently, nearly a third of U.S. adolescents fail to graduate high school with a diploma. Percentages are even higher for low-income and minority students.
- Standards-based education reform is designed to strengthen academic achievement for all children by holding schools accountable for making progress toward meeting proficiency levels and giving parents the option of placing their children in better schools if their present schools fail to meet proficiency standards.
- Critics of this reform argue that federal funding primarily supports assessment, with little for program improvement.
- Solutions to problems in education will need to address high rates of unemployment and improving the quality of schools serving low-income inner-city youth.

Key Terms

secondary education
direct instruction
differentiated instruction
learning styles
middle school
junior high school
full-service schools
bullying
cooperative learning
conflict resolution training
constructive controversy
conflict resolution centers
male generic language
jigsaw classroom
academic tracking
cooperative learning
task-mastery orientation
performance-ability orientation
gifted
enrichment
acceleration
learning disability
mainstreaming
special education consultant
special education classes
computer-assisted instruction

CHAPTER OUTLINE

CHAPTER 10

Work, Careers, and College

New Decisions, New Ways of Thinking

CHAPTER OBJECTIVES

- To look at part-time employment and spending patterns among adolescents
- To consider explanations for why individuals choose one type of work over another
- To look at the types of jobs that are available for those entering the workforce and at inequities in the opportunity structure associated with gender, race, and socioeconomic level
- To determine the similarities and differences between formal thinking and structural analytic thinking
- To examine differences in the ways in which college students approach knowledge, and how these may vary with gender
- To look at how adolescents think about practical problems in daily settings

Kip leaned on the horn and cursed his friend's ability to sleep through an alarm. "Late one more time and you'll be docked in pay," Mr. Perkins had said.

Sam flew out the door with a sandwich in his mouth and a sweater half over his head.

"Climb in," shouted Kip, as he threw the car in gear and spun away from the curb.

"Gi-yugh," spat Sam, "I got jelly on this sweater."

"Don't worry, no one will notice."

"Not on the outside, fool. It's inside the sleeve!" griped Sam.

"Serves you right," Kip said. "You're the only one I know eats in his clothes—and I mean inside 'em."

"So what was I supposed to do with the sandwich while I was putting on the sweater?"

Sam changed the subject. "How much longer on this shift?"

"It's a killer, isn't it? Sometimes I wonder if these wheels are worth it," Kip replied.

"Can you see doing this the rest of your life?" Sam asked from under the sweater, turning the sleeve inside out for repairs.

"I'm already tired of working and I've just started," answered Kip, as he wheeled into the last parking space and switched off the ignition. "Let's go. Sooner begun, sooner done, or something like that, as my dad says."

"You wonder how they do it," Sam replied. "Year after year at the same old job. Is this what it's gonna be like for the next fifty years?"

Chapter Overview

What it's like for the next fifty years, give or take ten for most people, will depend on a number of things, many of which get sorted out in adolescence. This chapter opens with a look at adolescents in the workplace. Increasing numbers of adolescents work while still in high school. Others start full-time jobs after graduating, and still others will work while they go to college. For those who never finish high school, occupational choices are more limited. We will consider high school students, those who drop out, and work in the opening section of the chapter.

Why do individuals choose one type of work and not another? Explanations for vocational choice differ. Social-cognitive theory looks at environmental variables that influence career decisions—such as parents' occupations and the salience of models in different occupations. The developmental theories of Eli Ginzburg and Donald Super identify stages of occupational choice. Ginzburg, for example, believes that realistic decisions occur fairly late in the process, and Super links occupational choice to the development of the self-concept. Finally, John Holland identifies different personality types that are suited to different types of work.

What happens to young workers once they are on the job? Many need additional training beyond high school. Business and industry increasingly find that they must pick up the tab for the education of their newest workers, often having to train them in basic skills such as reading and math. Ironically, many of the nation's newest full-time workers must continue their education on the job. Adolescents in the workforce is the subject of the next section.

Many factors affect adolescents' decisions about the type of work they will do. Not least among these are gender and ethnicity. Some adolescents never even consider certain jobs because they rarely see individuals of their gender or race in them. Even when adolescents do consider a wide variety of jobs, the opportunity structure all too frequently reflects inequities associated with gender, ethnicity, and socioeconomic level. Gender and ethnicity are considered as they relate to occupational choice in adolescence. Intervention programs aimed at changing belief structures about career opportunities have been effective in helping adolescents realistically evaluate the opportunities available to them.

Many adolescents will go off to college instead of beginning work. They too will face new experiences; these can change the way they think about themselves, even the way they think about knowledge itself. Is it possible to discover truth? Or does truth, like beauty, exist only in the mind of the beholder? Some adolescents attempt to discover absolute truths in their classes; others view truth as relative. Still others achieve ways of reconciling the alternative truths of relativism. This progression takes different forms in male and female adolescents, and we will chart changes in knowing separately for each.

Real-life problem solving is not as straightforward as logicians would have us believe. For instance, adolescents, like everyone else, think most efficiently and in more sophisticated ways in areas that interest them, and problems arising in the context of one's culture are solved more efficiently than similar problems that do not utilize culturally specific knowledge. Cultural knowledge is a form of expertise in which natives think like experts and strangers like novices.

The final section of the chapter addresses the way adolescents think through practical problems in daily settings. As with other aspects of reasoning, success increases with age.

Adolescents at Work

Continuity of Attitudes Toward Work over the Lifespan

Attitudes toward work and leisure show surprising continuity through large segments of the lifespan. Many of the attitudes adults hold toward work, for instance, can first be seen by the time children enter adolescence. Adults who are asked to report how they feel about what they are doing at the moment, if asked this while they are at work, are likely to indicate they would rather be doing something else. Yet these same individuals acknowledge that work, more than leisure, contributes significantly to their sense of self and frequently is more deeply satisfying (Csikszentmihalyi, 1997).

In a similar fashion, 10- and 11-year-olds report activities they label as work as being less pleasurable than those they label as play, even though they acknowledge that the former more frequently contribute to feelings of high self-esteem. Adolescents as well, when asked to indicate how they feel while they are working, report they are less happy than if doing something else, even though their feelings of self-esteem are higher when they are working than at other times and even though they are likely to regard what they are doing as important (Csikszentmihalyi, 1997).

Children's chores, as well as adolescents' part-time work, anticipate the gender divisions that characterize work among adults, with girls performing more of the inside chores and boys doing more outside chores. For example, over 80% of boys versus 50% of girls reported having to take the trash out (Entwisle, Alexander, Olson, & Ross, 1999). Thus, not only attitudes toward work but also patterns of work show continuity through the lifespan.

Part-Time Employment

Many high school students have part-time jobs. Predictably, this number increases with age. Whereas just under 10% of 15-year-olds are likely to be employed in any month during the school year, slightly over 25% of 16-year-olds are, and nearly 40% of 17-year-olds are likely to be employed (U.S. Department of Labor, 2000). These figures, as one would expect, increase during the summer months. Even more adolescents would be working if they could find jobs. The unemployment rate for 16- to 19-year-old White adolescents seeking but unable to find work is 15%. However, for minority adolescents, the percentage is much higher. For example, unemployment rates among African American and Hispanic adolescents are 33% and 20%, respectively (Fox, Connolly, & Snyder, 2005). These differences persist into early adulthood, as can be seen in Figure 10.1.

Spending Patterns Adolescents with jobs spend their money in different ways than they will as adult workers. Most of what they earn they spend on personal items such as clothes, CDs, and entertainment (Figure 10.2). Because over half of those who work earn more than $50 a week, adolescents can engage in a fair amount of conspicuous consumption. The price of clothes is high if one buys designer labels—and many adolescents do. Popular name-brand athletic shoes go for $100 and even $200. One might imagine that at those prices, few adolescents would buy name-brand athletic shoes. But increasing numbers of adolescents choose to work in order to spend money on personal items such as these. Jeans, a staple wardrobe item for most adolescents, are also expensive, many starting at $50 a pair and working their way up, depending on extras such as acid-washes, type of cut, and so on. The cost of an outfit can add up, and we haven't even gotten above the belt in this example.

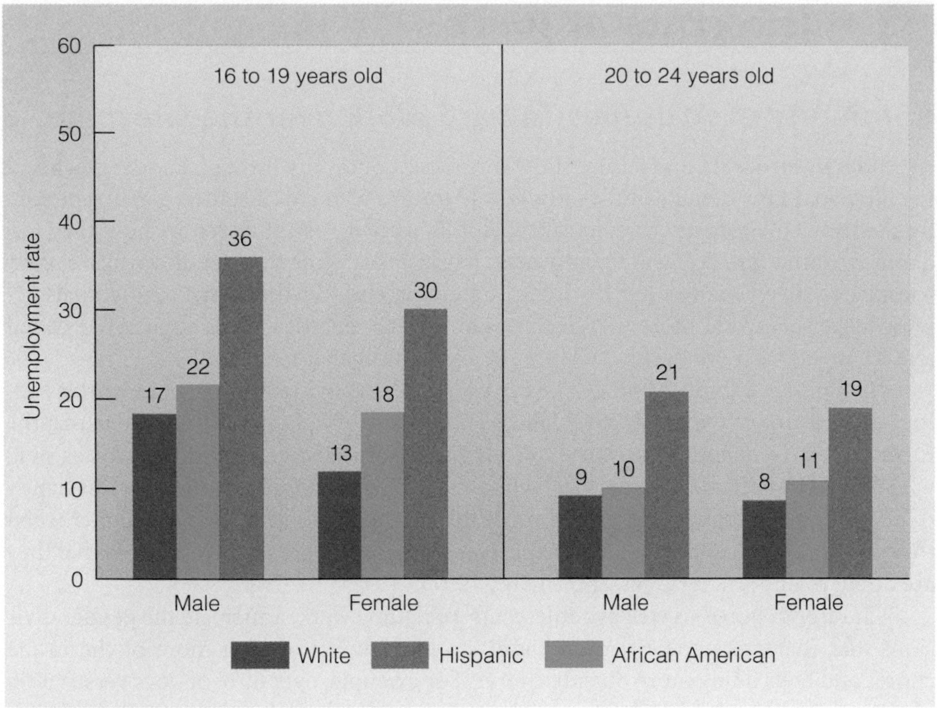

■ **FIGURE 10.1**
Unemployment Among European American, Hispanic, and African American Youth.
Source: M. A. Fox, B. A. Connolly, & T. D. Snyder. (2005). *Youth indicators 2005: Trends in the well-being of American youth (NCES 2005-050).* U.S. Department of Education, National Center for Education Statistics. Washington, DC: U.S. Government Printing Office.

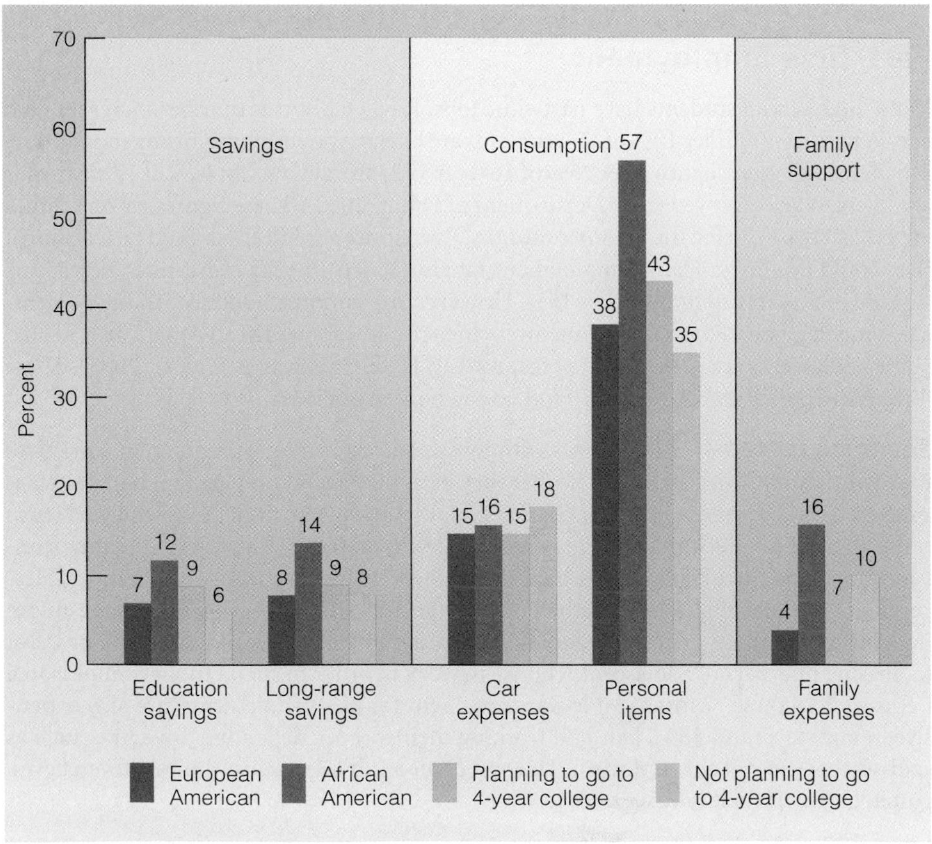

■ **FIGURE 10.2**
How High School Seniors Spend Their Money.
Source: University of Michigan, Institute for Social Research, *Monitoring the future, 2001.* In *Youth indicators: trends in the well-being of American youth.* (2005). Washington, DC: U.S. Government Printing Office.

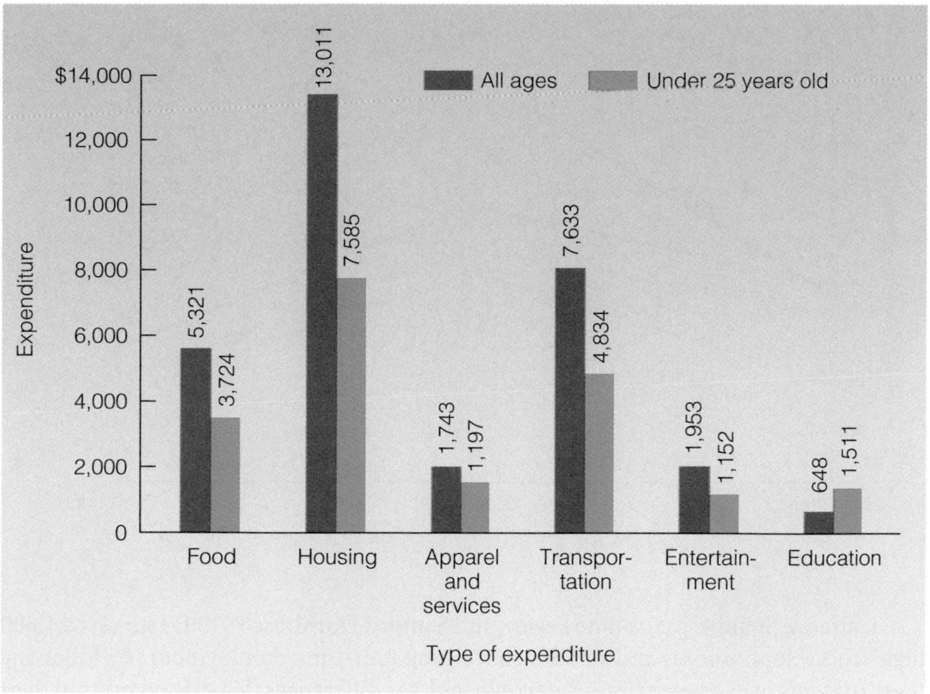

FIGURE 10.3 Spending Patterns of People 25 Years of Age and Under Compared to Those of All People. *Source:* U.S. Department of Labor, Bureau of Labor Statistics. *Consumer expenditure survey: Integrated survey, 2001.* In M. A. Fox, B. A. Connolly, & T. D. Snyder. (2005). *Youth indicators 2005: Trends in the well-being of American youth (NCES 2005-050).* U.S. Department of Education, National Center for Education Statistics. Washington, DC: U.S. Government Printing Office.

Adolescents also spend money on entertainment. A simple date, such as a movie and hamburger afterward, can cost $20 or more apiece: $6 to $12 for tickets, another $5 to $10 at the concession stand, and a whopping $10 to $15 more for hamburgers and drinks afterward—and this doesn't include the cost of the round-trip gas. Special events, such as rock concerts, can be four to five times as expensive. Even though most adolescents go to concerts infrequently, they go to other events, such as school dances or get-togethers after games, regularly—and these all add up. Just spending an evening with a friend or two can be expensive. When adolescents get together, they eat. Two or three adolescents can kill several 2-liter bottles of cola in a night and munch through several bags of chips at $2 to $3 a bag.

The above expenses can be minor compared to those for a car. Car expenses are a significant item for many adolescents as Figure 10.2 shows. A sizable number of adolescents—18%—spend from half to all they make on their cars.

Many adolescents save their money, as well as spend it. Teen Research Unlimited, a large market research firm, found that over 67% of the adolescents surveyed in a nationally representative sample had savings accounts, 18% had stocks or bonds, and 8% had mutual funds (Teen Research Unlimited, 2001). High school seniors who are planning to attend a four-year college are, predictably, more likely to put more of their money into savings for education than those without plans for college. Some also contribute to their families' expenses (Youth Indicators, 2005).

Disadvantages and Advantages of Part-Time Employment Some researchers question whether part-time employment exposes adolescents to an unrealistic standard of living. They point out that most teenagers are allowed to spend what they earn as discretionary income; as we have seen, only a few contribute to family expenses. As a result, few adolescents are prepared for the realities that confront employed adults, such as the costs of housing, food, transportation, and health care. Figure 10.3 presents a comparison of spending patterns of people under 25 to overall spending patterns.

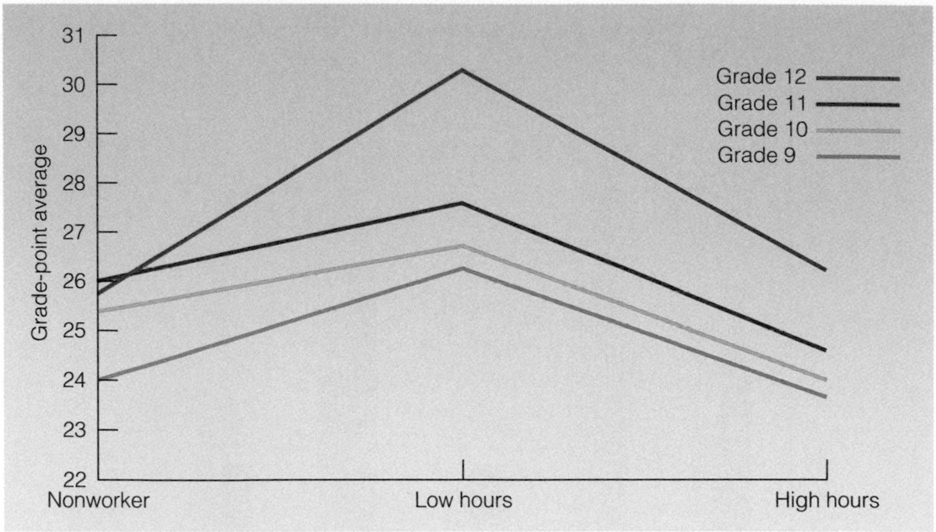

■ **FIGURE 10.4**
Grade-Point Average by Work Hours, Grades 9 to 12.
Source: J. T. Mortimer, M. D. Finch, S. Ryu, M. J. Shanahan, & K. T. Call. (1996). The effects of work intensity on adolescent mental health, achievement, and behavioral adjustment: New evidence from a prospective study. *Child Development, 67,* 1243–1261.

Laurence Steinberg, Suzanne Fegley, and Sanford Dornbusch (1993) surveyed 1,800 high school sophomores and juniors concerning part-time employment. By following these students over a year's time, they could look for differences that existed prior to their part-time employment, as well as compare adolescents who worked with those who did not. These investigators found that adolescents who work are less invested in school than their peers, even before beginning to work, and that working contributes to their disengagement from school, especially if they work more than 20 hours a week. Conversely, adolescents who work moderate hours and then quit their jobs show improved performance in school.

Jaylen Mortimer and associates (1996) also found that low work hours were associated with better performance in school. However, grades for these students were also higher than for those who did not work at all (Figure 10.4). It is possible that employment fosters work habits and personal discipline that carry over to their studies. Or, conversely, it may be that students who work accommodate for the demands on their time by taking less rigorous classes (Steinberg, Fegley, & Dornbusch, 1993). Mortimer and associates (1996), who also studied a large representative sample, did not find evidence of working students taking easier classes, however. Clearly, simple answers concerning the relationship of part-time employment to success in school are not forthcoming.

Nor, for that matter, is the relationship any clearer between part-time employment and measures of mental health. Although part-time employment is consistently related to increased use of alcohol (Mortimer, Finch, Ryu, Shanahan, & Call, 1996; Steinberg, Fegley, & Dornbusch, 1993), evidence of its relationship to other criteria of mental health is not that consistent. Whereas Steinberg, Fegley, and Dornbusch found adolescents who do not work to be better adjusted than those who do—having higher self-esteem, greater self-reliance, and less delinquency—Mortimer and associates found no difference in self-esteem or in other measures of adjustment.

The types of jobs adolescents fill, in addition to the hours they work, also need to be considered. In this respect, at least, a clearer picture emerges. Most adolescents are employed in high-turnover positions, with little pay, little authority, and relatively little opportunity for advancement. The work is often simple and repetitive and requires little skill or training. Such jobs are associated with negative consequences for workers, whether adolescents or adults (Mortimer, Finch, Shanahan, & Ryu, 1992).

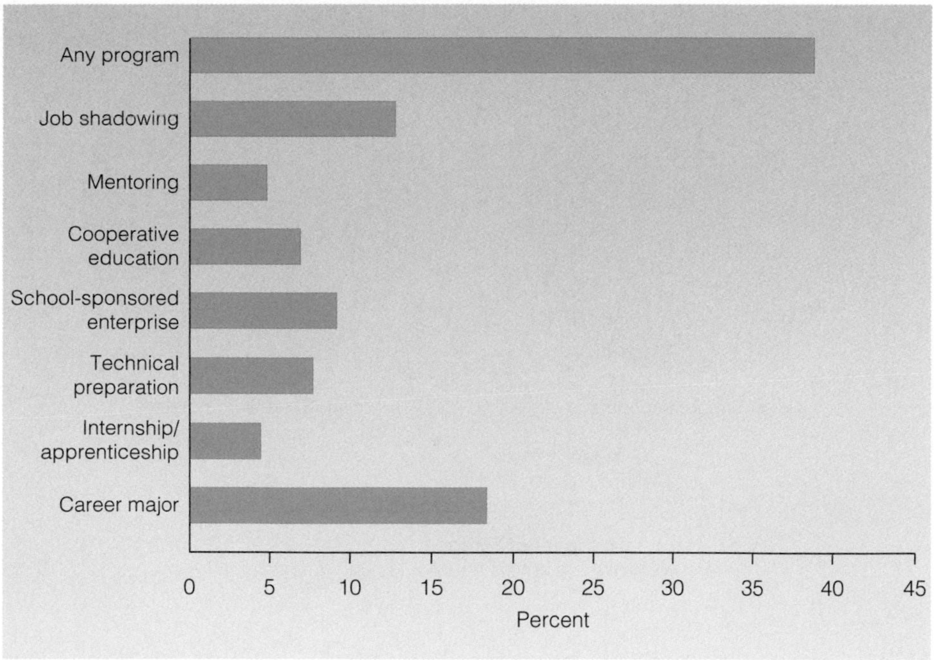

FIGURE 10.5 Percentages of Adolescents Participating in School-to-Work Programs, Grades 9 through 12. *Source:* U.S. Department of Labor. (2000). *Report on the youth labor force.* Retreived from http://www.bls.gov/opub/rylf/rylfhome.htm

When adolescents perceive their work as contributing to skills they could later use, however, part-time employment has been found to be associated with a number of measures of well-being (Mortimer et al., 1992). Holding a job can help adolescents develop a sense of responsibility and give them a feeling of being productive. Work can also develop general skills, ranging from interpersonal ones, such as getting along with coworkers, to personal ones, such as managing time. Some jobs may help adolescents discover where their interests lie, even if by exclusion—they may discover, for example, that they would not enjoy the same work in a full-time capacity.

Many adolescents are able to discover more about what they *would* like to do through school-to-work programs that help them step into the work world from the world of school (Legters, 2000). These programs can take a number of forms (see Figure 10.5). In **job shadowing,** students spend part of their school day in a work setting, following the activities of one or more workers there, whereas in **mentoring,** students work with someone who, in addition to overseeing their work and offering advice, serves as a role model. In some schools, students are encouraged to do an **internship** or apprenticeship in which they spend time working at a job. **Cooperative education** focuses on making education relevant to jobs in a particular field by enabling students to combine vocational studies with on-the-job experience. Other programs, such as technical preparation and career major, help students define career goals and determine the educational programs necessary for achieving these. Approximately 40% of high school students participate in a school-to-work program (U.S. Department of Labor, 2000).

For some adolescents, such a discovery is a luxury. Adolescents who drop out of high school find it difficult to obtain work even under the best of circumstances. Many cannot afford to be choosy. We turn to this group of workers next.

job shadowing A school program in which students spend part of the school day in a work setting following the activities of one or more employees.

mentoring A school program in which students work with someone who serves as a role model.

internship A school program in which students spend time working at a job.

cooperative education A school-to-work program that combines vocational studies with on-the-job experience.

Adolescents Who Drop Out and Employment

Adolescents who drop out of high school are about twice as likely to be unemployed as those who graduate (U.S. Department of Labor, 2000). Because future jobs will require

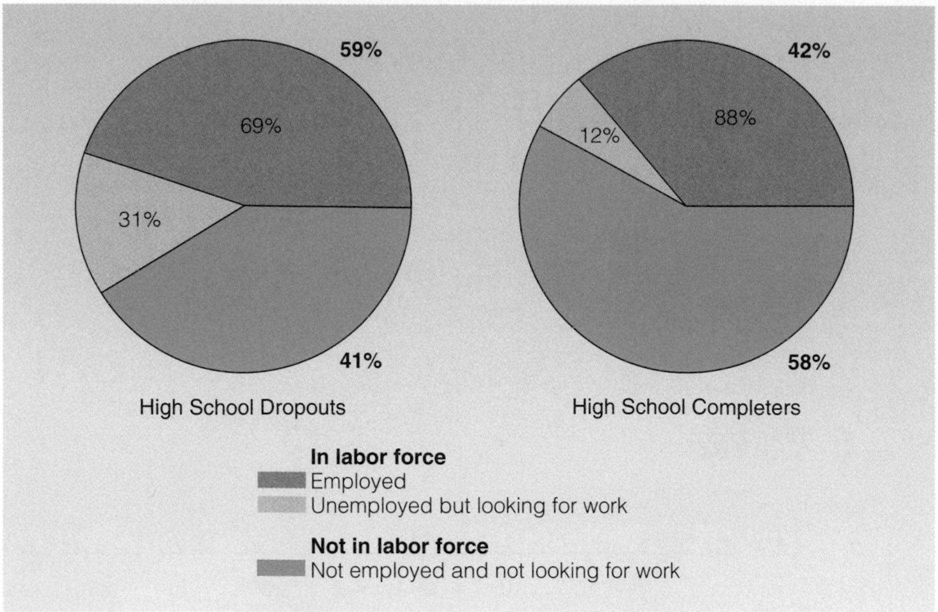

FIGURE 10.6 Employment Status of High School Dropouts and High School Completers. *Source:* M. A. Fox, B. A. Connolly, & T. D. Snyder. (2005). *Youth indicators 2005: Trends in the well-being of American youth (NCES 2005-050).* U.S. Department of Education, National Center for Education Statistics. Washington, DC: U.S. Government Printing Office.

even more education and preparation, adolescents who fail to complete high school will find it harder to compete for these jobs than in the past. Figure 10.6 shows the proportions of those who drop out who are employed or unemployed. Differences do not end there, however. Even when employed, high school dropouts earn less money, are less satisfied with their working conditions, see less opportunity for promotion, and experience less security and permanence in their jobs (Youth Indicators, 2005; Kaufman, Alt, & Chapman, 2001). Given the importance of finishing high school, one looks for programs that have been successful in working with adolescents at risk of dropping out (see Chapter 9). Several successful programs share a number of features.

First, high schools that are effective in keeping at-risk adolescents in school establish the connection between having a diploma and earning money. Although the actual amount of money earned by high school graduates versus those who drop out is not always large, the likelihood of *having* a job is significantly greater if one has a diploma. Successful programs offering work opportunities that provide on-the-job experience have been particularly successful. Most also give intensive training in basic skills, increasing the likelihood of success both at school and on the job. Many programs also prepare students to take the GED, a test that, when passed, gives them the equivalent of a high school diploma.

Second, effective programs usually have lower student–teacher ratios, smaller campuses, and an atmosphere that communicates the message that any student who wants to can be successful. Teachers have more time to interact with students. Many schools also provide infant care for adolescent mothers returning to school.

Additionally, many students who fail to graduate have a history of school failure and are demoralized by the time they reach high school. Effective programs integrate computers into their instructional programs, using them for individualized instruction in basic skills. Remedial programs in reading and math help break self-defeating cycles in which students avoid work at which they feel inadequate, causing them to fall even further behind.

Finally, successful schools often involve individuals from the community, such as civic leaders and local businesses and industry, in their programs. Students learn about resources in the community. Parents are an important part of any coalition, and these

Schools that are effective in reaching potential dropouts communicate to students that they care. These schools typically integrate computers into their instructional programs, and support teacher involvement by reducing class workloads so that teachers can have more time to interact with students.

programs involve parents in the students' progress (see Chapter 9). Frequently, too, counseling for emotional problems is available to students who need it.

Successful programs increase the motivation of the students enrolled in them. They also help students set realistic goals. These two benefits are almost surely related. Students' motivation to do well in their courses will increase as they see the relationship between their own success and what they need for specific jobs. More generally, these programs have an impact on students' self-esteem; when one likes oneself, one does not have to have fantasy-level aspirations about a job—reality does quite well (Bloch, 1989). (For a look at the effect of other factors on adolescents' future aspirations, see the Research Focus "Correlational Research."

Choosing a Vocation

At-risk students face one problem in common with other students. Almost all adolescents have difficulty discovering the type of work for which they are best suited or would enjoy most. We look first at social-cognitive theory for an explanation of how adolescents select the type of work they will engage in for most of their adult lives, and then at the theories of Eli Ginzburg, Donald Super, and John Holland.

Social-Cognitive Theory

Why do individuals choose the occupations they do? Social-cognitive theory, which emphasizes the role of observational learning and modeling, focuses on complex interactions between the inborn talents, the environmental conditions in which these are played out (for example, demographic trends affecting the availability of jobs or social policies regulating equal employment opportunities), the unique learning histories of each person, and the skills with which individuals approach their work (see Chapter 2).

Adolescents observe themselves and note how well their skills, interests, and values match the requirements of the situation. These observations have consequences for the

RESEARCH FOCUS

Correlational Research: Hangin' out on a Friday Night

It's Friday night and a group of 16-year-olds are sitting around the television, talking, channel surfing, and working their way through a bag of chips. Periodically, one of them will call the others' attention to something on the screen or mention some event that happened last week at school, but as the evening wears on, the conversation gets more serious. They talk about being friends, about what they've been through together, and what lies ahead for each of them.

Despite their casual appearance, adolescents have a lot on their minds. Mixed in with studying for tests, picking up the latest CD, or hanging out on a Friday night are their concerns about the future—their futures. One of the major tasks facing adolescents is that of identity formation, gaining a sense of themselves that reflects what they value and want to be and, in turn, is valued by those whom they respect (see Chapter 5). One might suspect, as a consequence, that adolescents' aspirations would be related to those of their friends. But are they? Are other factors involved? And how might one go about finding answers to questions such as these?

One would first need to measure both adolescents' and their friends' aspirations, as well as any other factors one thinks might be related. Then one could look for relationships among these variables. When changes along one variable correspond to changes along another, the variables are said to be *correlated. Correlation coefficients* are statistics that reflect the degree of relationship between variables. Scatterplots show this relationship pictorially. In the figure, the scatterplot on the left illustrates no relationship ($r = 0$); the one on the right shows a strong relationship ($r = +1.00$). One could have an equally strong relationship but in the opposite direction ($r = -1.00$); that is, variables can be either positively or negatively correlated. In the case of positive correlation, increases along one variable match increases along the other. When variables are negatively correlated, increases along one are accompanied by decreases along the other. Let's look at how one team of investigators used this approach to determine whether adolescents' future aspirations are related to various characteristics of their friends, such as their friends' ambitions, beliefs, and use of drugs.

Judith Stein and Michael Newcomb (1999) gave seventh- through ninth-graders a measure of their future aspirations (Positive future aspirations), asking them how well they were doing in school, what their educational aspirations were, and what their ambitions were. They also questioned them about their friends (Conventional friends). Specifically, they asked how much they talked with their friends about their homework, what grades their friends got, whether

types of work they think they might be good at. They are also related to what they are interested in and what they value (Mitchell & Krumboltz, 1990). Let's take a look at how social-cognitive theory puts these various factors together in explaining career choices.

Consider the case of a fictitious adolescent, Carlos, age 17. Carlos grew up in a quiet, ethnically mixed neighborhood; his mother is native-born, and his father came to this country as a young boy. Both parents are hardworking; his father is a contractor and his mother a daycare worker. Carlos was quiet in elementary school and received little attention from his predominantly European American teachers. He often heard his father say that "White teachers think Mexican kids aren't that smart." He began to perceive his teachers as different from himself, and he emotionally shut down when interacting with them. Nothing in elementary school disproved what he had learned from his father.

In junior high, Carlos's English teacher noticed that his creative stories were well written and that he had an unusually large vocabulary for his age. She displayed his work in the classroom. Carlos felt proud, and his classmates often asked him for help. Carlos began to think that not all teachers are alike—some think he is smart.

Carlos tells himself that he might not tell stories as well as his grandma, but he knows he's better than the other kids in his class. Carlos enjoys writing and wonders if their friends planned to go to college, and what their parents thought of their friends. In addition, they assessed how conventional adolescents' attitudes were, asking about law abidance, liberalism, and religiosity (Social conformity). Finally, they assessed their use of drugs (Drug use).

Are adolescents' future aspirations related to characteristics of their friends? Absolutely. These investigators found that adolescents' high future aspirations correlated positively with having conventional friends and with greater social conformity. Conversely, high future aspirations correlated negatively with drug use.

This research is further distinguished by the fact that these investigators followed these same adolescents into adulthood, testing them again 13 years later when they were young adults and again 20 years later when they reached middle adulthood. Tracing the paths of these adolescents into adulthood revealed that those who had positive goals for themselves in adolescence (Positive future aspirations) showed more efficacy and agency as young adults. Further, both efficacy and agency in early adulthood predicted greater fulfillment and satisfaction with life in middle adulthood.

Source: J. A. Stein & M. D. Newcomb. (1999). Adult outcomes of adolescent conventional and agentic orientations: A 20-year longitudinal study. *Journal of Early Adolescence, 19,* 39–65.

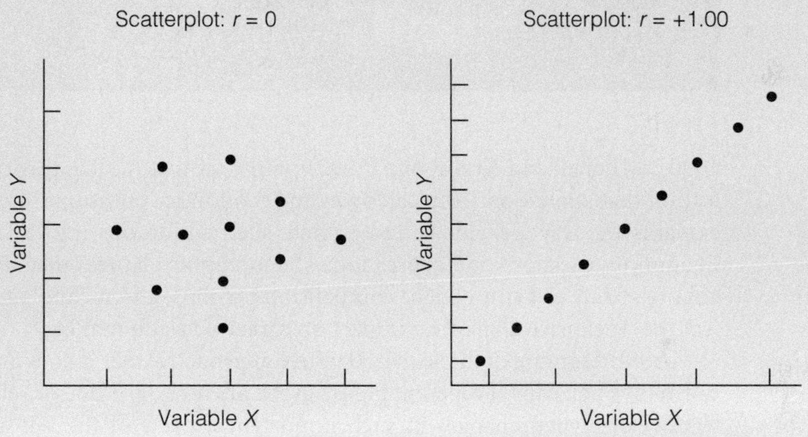

he's good enough to get paid for doing it for a living. He also questions whether he would enjoy it more than being a contractor. When he has worked for his father, he has always felt competent. He wonders which occupation would be best for him and decides to take some creative writing courses and talk to his father about a summer job.

Environmental events such as higher interest rates on loans (and a drop-off in construction) and a TV writer's strike can affect vocational decision making. Even though social-cognitive theory emphasizes individual learning experiences, many of which are planned (such as taking a writing course), it acknowledges the impact of unplanned events like an economic recession and its effect on the construction industry, or a screenwriter's strike and national awareness of the importance of writers (Mitchell & Krumboltz, 1990).

Critique of Social-Cognitive Theory A strength of social-cognitive theory is its use of learning principles to explain individual choices, yet doing so without portraying individuals as automatons. Social-cognitive theory recognizes that people actively attempt to understand the consequences of their actions and use this understanding in ways that change their environments to better meet their needs (Mitchell & Krumboltz,

Vocational development can be viewed as a progressive narrowing of choices in the search for the best fit between one's goals and self-concept and the opportunities that actually exist.

1990). Mitchell and Krumboltz (1990) point out that, unlike theories of vocational selection that analyze sociological forces and economic conditions, social-cognitive theory explains the way individuals incorporate such conditions into their decision making. Economic recessions and depressions, demographic changes that affect the size of one's cohort group and consequent competition for jobs, and technological changes that affect the workplace all have an impact on career decision making.

A shortcoming of the social-cognitive approach is that it does not give us a model of normative behavior at different points in the life cycle, nor does it relate decision making to developmental changes in such important aspects of the self as identity and self-concept (Brown, 1990). For a developmental approach to vocational choice, we turn to the theories of Ginzburg and Super.

Ginzburg: Vocational Stages

Eli Ginzburg (1972) views vocational development as a progressive narrowing of choices that at first reflect only fantasy but with age come to be based on reality. Choosing a career is an adaptive process in which individuals continually seek the best fit between their own goals and the opportunities that actually exist. The process unfolds over three stages: fantasy, tentative, and realistic.

Three Vocational Stages The **fantasy stage** lasts through childhood. During this time, children imagine themselves in the roles of those with whom they identify. These figures can be as real as parents, teachers, even ballerinas or sports heroes, or as fantastic as the cartoon characters they see on television. This stage involves no real assessment of what one might be good at or what the actual requirements of an occupation might be. Children respond to visible aspects of jobs—uniforms, fire trucks, and ballet slippers. Ginzburg (1990) notes that the 5-year-old son of a banker may say he wants to be a policeman when he grows up, because the uniform and activities of a policeman are understandable in a way that those of a banker are not.

fantasy stage Ginzburg's first stage of vocational development, characterized by focus on highly visible aspects of vocations and no assessment of personal qualifications.

In the **tentative stage** (from about age 11 to age 17), career thoughts begin to reflect adolescents' own interests, abilities, and values. At first, however, only their *interests* are important. One adolescent may plan to be a jockey because she loves horses, or another a musician because he is interested in jazz. With time, adolescents become aware that their interests change and, more important, that they may not match their *abilities*. A boy who lives for basketball may fail to make the team at school, or a girl who wants to be a jockey may find that at 12 she is already larger than most professional jockeys. In other words, adolescents discover that interest alone is not enough. Eventually, adolescents think of work in terms of what they *value*. They question how important it is to make a lot of money, whether their work will contribute to society, or how much they value free time, independence, or security. As they think through the things that are important to them, they let certain choices slide in favor of others that better fit their values and abilities.

Late adolescents enter the **realistic stage** when they *explore* the tentative choices they have been considering. For college students this means taking courses in a specific field. Some will find these courses interesting and challenging and will go on to major in that field, whereas others may find they are not sufficiently interesting or challenging and look for another field in which to concentrate. Similarly, students who start to work after high school will find out whether the jobs remain interesting or whether they need to look for different ones.

Following exploration, adolescents pull together, or *crystallize*, the many factors bearing upon a career choice: the required training, their own interests and talents, and the actual opportunities that exist. This integration results in commitment to a particular vocational path. College students will complete the required courses in their major; adolescents working at a job will finish the training programs needed for advancement. Finally, individuals *specialize* within their field. Students preparing to teach, for instance, will decide whether to do so at the elementary or the secondary level; an auto mechanic will decide whether to specialize in foreign or domestic cars.

Critique of Ginzburg's Theory Developmental data support Ginzburg's distinctions between fantasy, tentative, and realistic bases for thinking about work. We know, for example, that children understand their world in terms of its visible and tangible properties long before they appreciate its more abstract qualities (see Chapter 4). Similarly, adolescents begin to think of themselves in terms of their psychological characteristics—interests, abilities, and values—as in Ginzburg's tentative stage; even so, Monica Johnson (2002), at the University of North Carolina, found that adolescents' work values are not nearly as realistic as they will become with time. Finally, the commitment to an occupation that occurs in Ginzburg's realistic stage is an integral part of the identity formation process of late adolescence.

A weakness of Ginzburg's theory is his failure to give an explanation for movement from one stage to the next. He does not, in other words, explain the process responsible for developmental change. An example of such a process in another well-known stage theory, that of Piaget, is the cycle of assimilation and accommodation that accounts for the growth of thought from one stage to the next (see Chapter 4). The process responsible for change in Ginzburg's theory remains unclear.

Also, Ginzburg based his theory on data collected exclusively with males. Although it is true, as John Holland (1987) points out, that basing a theory on observations only of men does not invalidate the theory or even mean it can't be used to make statements about women, limiting one's sample to men raises the strong possibility that interesting data may have been missed that might permit a better description of the career plans of women and perhaps of some men.

tentative stage Ginzburg's second stage of vocational development, in which vocational choice is directed more by interests than capacities.

realistic stage Ginzburg's third stage of vocational development, characterized by exploration of and commitment to a vocational path.

Super: Careers and the Self-Concept

Donald Super (1981, 1990) suggests that people choose occupations that are consistent with the way they see themselves, that reflect their interests, values, and strengths. Choosing an occupation means finding a match between the self-perceptions that make up one's self-concept and the actual requirements of the jobs one is considering, a process that in some ways is like reaching for a brass ring on a carousel—both you and the ring are moving, but not at the same speed or necessarily in the same direction. Adolescents' views of different occupations and of work itself change as they age, as do their self-concepts. An adolescent may have only the vaguest idea of what a psychologist does after speaking with one at school. She may think that all psychologists work in schools testing students. Several years later, that same adolescent may have discovered that some psychologists counsel people with personal problems, that others work in industry, and even others work in laboratories collecting and analyzing data. Meanwhile, this adolescent's sense of herself may have changed from someone who wanted to help others to someone who is more interested in ideas than in people. How suitable she sees psychology as an occupation depends on how her perceptions of the discipline have evolved as she has changed.

Five Vocational Stages Super describes five stages of vocational development. In the **growth stage,** adolescents discover more about themselves than about an occupation. Super (1990) feels that the major developmental task in this stage is simply to develop a realistic self-concept. At the same time, adolescents are also developing a feeling for what work involves.

In the **exploration stage,** adolescents begin to make choices that relate to their future work. Choosing courses in school is part of this process. This stage unfolds as adolescents move from plans that reflect only their interests (what they would *like* to be), to those that reflect a growing awareness of their abilities (and how well these match their interests), to a realistic appraisal that includes the availability and accessibility of certain jobs.

For Super, choosing a vocation marks the beginning of a process that typically lasts through early adulthood. In the **establishment stage,** individuals settle into their work. Even if they change jobs, they are likely to find the same form of work in another setting or office.

The years of middle adulthood, from about 45 to 65, are devoted to maintaining one's occupational position, the **maintenance stage.** Super speaks of the developmental task in these years as "holding one's own against competition," whether in the form of others who are involved in the same type of work, or maintaining the same level and quality of the work as in the past. Finally, the **decline stage,** which occurs in late adulthood, involves retirement for most workers and the need to find other roles through which to express themselves.

growth stage Super's first stage of vocational development characterized more by discovery about oneself than about vocations.

exploration stage Super's second stage of vocational development, in which one begins to make choices related to their future work.

establishment stage Super's third stage of vocational development, in which one settles into one's work.

maintenance stage Super's fourth stage of vocational development, in which one maintains one's occupational skills and position.

decline stage Super's fifth stage of vocational development, in which one retires.

Critique of Super's Theory Super's theory is one of the most widely cited and influential theories of vocational development. It is also one of the most interesting psychologically, in that it traces vocational development through the life cycle by relating it to changes in the self-concept and the roles one fills at different ages. Super's theory enjoys considerable research support (Osipow, 1983).

The process Super uses to account for development is similar to the homeostatic or equilibrium model in other organismic theories, such as Piaget's. A match between self-perceptions and the requirements of one's work results in vocational stability; this

Why do some adolescents pursue a career in science versus other fields? A combination of personality type as well as factors such as an inspiring teacher, gender, and ethnicity influences most adolescents' vocational choices.

stability is maintained until changes in self-perceptions or work requirements create a mismatch. Mismatches produce instability and the need to repeat elements of the larger cycle until individuals find another type of work that suits them (Super, 1990).

Holland: Personality Types and Work

Picasso once said, "When I work I relax; doing nothing or entertaining visitors makes me tired." Picasso illustrates Holland's explanation for vocational success: His personality type corresponded to the type of work he did. John Holland (1985a) classifies individuals into one of six types. Different work environments either complement or oppose the qualities that make up any type. As an artist, Picasso excelled; as a banker, he would have been a flop.

realistic personality types In Holland's typology of vocational interests, individuals who prefer situations that are explicitly defined and require few interpersonal skills, for example, mechanic, computer programmer.

investigative personality types In Holland's typology of vocational interests, individuals who prefer work requiring intellectual curiosity, for example, scientist, mathematician.

artistic personality types In Holland's typology of vocational interests, individuals who prefer work requiring imagination and creativity, for example, graphic artist, poet.

social personality types In Holland's typology of vocational interests, individuals who prefer work involving them with people, such as counseling or teaching.

Six Personality Types **Realistic personality types** are practical and down to earth. They prefer problems that can be explicitly defined and that yield to an orderly approach, as opposed to those that require abstract or creative approaches. Their interpersonal skills are weak, and they like work that does not involve them with people. These types prefer occupations such as mechanic, farmer, construction worker, engineer, or surveyor.

Investigative personality types are as curious as realistic types are practical. They delight in situations that call for a creative or analytic approach. They are thinkers rather than doers, and their approach is intellectual and abstract. They enjoy being by themselves and getting caught up in their own world of ideas. Investigative types make good scientists, doctors, computer programmers, and writers.

Artistic personality types are original, imaginative, and creative. They prefer situations that are relatively unstructured and allow them to express their creative talents; they do well as painters, writers, or musicians.

Social personality types are understanding, friendly, and people oriented. They have the verbal and interpersonal skills that allow them to work well with others. They

Creative adolescents are both reflective and spontaneous. They are less likely to conform to accepted practice and more likely to try new ways of doing things than their less creative peers. These two teenagers in the Bronx used their spray cans to transform a crumbling concrete wall next to an empty lot.

are comfortable with their own and others' feelings, often approaching problems in terms of feelings rather than seeking an intellectual solution. They make good counselors, ministers, teachers, and social workers.

Enterprising personality types are gregarious and dominant. They have strong interpersonal skills and enjoy work that brings them into contact with others in ways that allow them to express their assertiveness. Fields such as real estate, management, law, or sales suit their ambitious temperament.

Conventional personality types are efficient and tidy. They like well-defined tasks in which their conscientious approach is likely to bring success. They are followers—of rules and authority figures—and seek out highly structured environments in which they need not be leaders themselves. Occupations for which they are suited include banking, accounting, and secretarial services.

Holland believes these personality types reflect different learning histories and inborn talents that together shape patterns of success, resulting in preferred approaches to problems or tasks.

Critique of Holland's Theory Perhaps the strongest features of Holland's theory are its usefulness and the extent to which it has stimulated research in the field of vocational choice. The Strong-Campbell Interest Inventory (Campbell, 1974) and the Vocational Preference Inventory (Holland, 1985b), both based on Holland's typology, are widely used measures of vocational preference (Donnay & Borgen, 1996). Holland himself considers the usefulness of a theory to be one of its most important features.

enterprising personality types In Holland's typology of vocational interests, individuals who prefer work involving interpersonal skills and assertiveness, such as management, law, or sales.

conventional personality types In Holland's typology of vocational interests, individuals who prefer highly structured environments and well-defined tasks.

However, Holland's theory has not given sufficient consideration to social context variables such as gender and ethnicity. Holland predicts that personality types influence the work one chooses, yet for many adolescents vocational choices are limited by variables such as sex, ethnicity, and socioeconomic level. For instance, African American and Hispanic men are overrepresented (considering their actual numbers relative to other groups) in low-level realistic jobs and underrepresented in all other types of jobs. All women, regardless of their ethnic background, are overrepresented in conventional and social jobs, and African American and Hispanic women are particularly overrepresented in low-level realistic types of work (Arbona, 1989).

Despite the realities of the work world, however, Jennifer Ryan, Terence Tracey, and James Rounds (1996), at the University of Illinois, nonetheless found the interests of African American and White high school students to be highly similar when assessed with Holland's Vocational Preference Inventory. As for gender, Holland's model was found to fit the interests of high school females somewhat better than males. With college students, though, gender differences do emerge, with females expressing more confidence on the realistic and social themes and males on the enterprising, investigative, and conventional (Betz, Harmon, & Borgen, 1996).

Ryan, Tracey, and Rounds's research is important in another respect, as well. The career interests of these minority adolescents did not differ from those of Whites. Because minority students are likely to experience barriers in pursuing their occupational objectives, it is important for school counselors to help students identify the source of the difficulties they are experiencing and to suggest possible ways of dealing with them. Differences in the levels of occupation they actually attain underscore the need for approaches to career counseling developed especially for minority students (Arbona, 1989).

Joining the Workforce

Job Availability

What kinds of jobs await youths who are about to join the workforce? Among the top ten fastest-growing occupations, over half are related to health care and computers (see Table 10.1) (U.S. Bureau of Labor Statistics, 2005a). These figures may be somewhat deceptive, however, because the fastest-growing occupations do not necessarily provide the largest number of jobs. There are far more salesclerks, cashiers, janitors, waiters, and home health aides than there are systems analysts and computer engineers.

In many respects, the picture is a bright one for youth entering the workforce. Even though the group of workers aged 16 to 24 will increase more rapidly than the rest of the labor force, many jobs will be available for those from every educational background. (U.S. Bureau of Labor Statistics, 2005a). Some of the fastest-growing occupations, such as technical jobs, require more education, but many others require only short-term training.

Despite the availability of jobs, unskilled workers will be looking for work in an increasingly automated, technological workplace. Even though most adolescents will replace workers in existing jobs, the qualifications for these jobs will increase as technology and foreign trade affect the workplace. Twenty years ago, an auto mechanic had to master only 5,000 pages of service manuals to work on any car on the road, compared to today, when 465,000 pages of service manuals exist for the hundreds of models sold in this country. Equally demanding changes are taking place in service sector jobs:

> The secretary who once pecked away at a manual typewriter must now master a word processor, a computer and telecommunications equipment. Even the cashier at the 7-Eleven store has to know how to sell money orders and do minor maintenance jobs on the Slurpee and Big Gulp machines. ("The Forgotten Half," 1989, p. 46)

Many of the newly created jobs will require more skill than did jobs in the past. Peter Coleman (1993) estimates that approximately 40% of new jobs will require more

TABLE 10.1 Occupations with the Largest Job Growth, Projections to 2012

Occupation	Employment[1] 2002	2012	% Change	Postsecondary Education	Earnings Quartile
Medical assistants	365	569	59	Moderate-term on-the-job-training	$$
Home health aides	580	859	48	Short-term on-the-job training	$
Computer software engineers, applications	394	573	46	Bachelor's degree	$$$$
Personal home care aides	608	854	40	Short-term on-the-job training	$
Computer systems analysts	468	653	39	Bachelor's degree	$$$$
Postsecondary teachers	1,581	2,184	38	Doctoral degree	$$$$
Security guards	995	1,313	32	Short-term on-the-job training	$
Management analysts	577	753	30	Bachelor's or higher degree, plus work experience	$$$$
Receptionists and information clerks	1,100	1,425	29	Short-term on-the-job training	$$
Registered nurses	2,284	2,908	27	Associate degree	$$$$

[1]Numbers in thousands of jobs.

Source: U.S. Department of Labor Statistics (2005a). Available at http://www.bls.gov/emp/emptab4.htm

than 16 years of preparation and training. Even so, the greatest challenge facing our nation is to meet the needs of adolescents who will *not* be college graduates.

Although unemployment among young workers has increased since 2000, this increase has not been uniform across all adolescents, and many minority youth face significantly higher rates of unemployment than the White majority. Among inner-city minority youth, unemployment can reach staggering proportions, exceeding 70% in some inner-city areas (Panel on High-Risk Youth, 1993; U.S. Bureau of Labor Statistics, 2002). These inner-city youth face not only joblessness but also poverty, poorly equipped schools, increased drug use, and high rates of violent crime. Furthermore, many businesses have left the cities, making employment even less accessible. Job-training programs have offered one of the few opportunities to change the life circumstances of these youth, but federal funding for these tends to fluctuate with the political climate. For these youth to begin to realize the promise of the talents within them, they need programs to help not only with jobs, but also with the host of conditions that attend joblessness, both at the individual and community level.

Gender in the Workplace

In past generations, the type of jobs people held could be predicted more easily than today by knowing their sex. The terms *pink collar* and *blue collar* refer to occupations that are female- or male-dominated. Females were more likely to work in service occupations—clerical and salesclerk positions or child care—and males as craftsmen, machine operators, technicians, farmers, or laborers. This is still the case, but the divisions are not

TABLE 10.2 Percentage of Men's Annual Earnings Earned by Women as a Function of Educational Level

	Years			
Educational Level	'91	'94	'97	'00
Less than 9th grade	0.689	0.701	0.725	0.753
High school	0.689	0.717	0.695	0.730
Some college	0.687	0.707	0.713	0.703
Associate's degree	0.741	0.718	0.742	0.723
Bachelor's or higher	0.717	0.709	0.710	0.714
Master's	0.705	0.731	0.727	0.723
Doctorate	0.735	0.771	0.718	0.736
Professional	0.618	0.670	0.696	0.614

Source: Adapted from H. M. Lips. (2003). The gender pay gap: Concrete indicator of women's progress toward equality. *Analysis of Social Issues and Public Policy, 3,* 87–109.

as distinct as previously. Occupational planning among high school seniors is less sex-typed. The percentage of high school females planning for professional occupations or thinking of entering male-dominant occupations has increased dramatically, as has the percentage of males entering careers in female-dominant professions such as nursing or teaching.

Despite these changes, the gender gap in pay remains significant. For instance, with the exception of younger workers, who make considerably less irrespective of their sex, women earn approximately 73% of what men earn (U.S. Bureau of Labor Statistics, 2005c). This gap in pay remains even when level of education is equated and even in female-dominant occupations, thus ruling out possible artifacts due to qualifications or to occupational choice (Lips, 2003). (See Tables 10.2 and 10.3.)

Even though more female adolescents today aspire to high-level jobs than in previous generations, they will still have to battle many assumptions about women's ability to function as effectively as men in high-power positions.

Advancement Opportunities The upward mobility of entrants to the labor force is limited by the large numbers of baby boomers already there (see Chapter 1). Shifts in patterns of employment are not likely until these baby boomers reach retirement age, beginning in 2011. The relatively large numbers of middle-aged boomers also cuts down on advancement opportunities for youth who are starting work now, because they will still be in the workforce when the latter are ready to move up to more advanced positions (Toossi, 2004).

The problem for females is not so much getting work as it is getting *quality* work. Females still have difficulty entering certain occupational areas and getting jobs from which they can advance. Until recently, career counselors focused primarily on external

TABLE 10.3 Women's Median Weekly Earnings as a Percentage of Men's in 10 Most Female-Dominated Occupations[1]

Occupations	Percentage of Women in the Occupation	Women's Percentage of Men's Earnings
Legal assistants	84.0	95.8
Miscellaneous administrative support occupations	84.2	84.0
Data-entry keyers	84.6	91.3
General office clerks	86.0	96.0
Health service occupations	87.8	89.0
Information clerks	88.2	81.0
Nursing aides, orderlies, and attendants	89.0	89.7
Financial records processing	90.6	92.3
Registered nurses	91.0	87.9
Bookkeepers, accounting and auditing clerks	92.2	93.7

Note: Occupations were selected from approximately 166 (of some 330) containing complete data for both women and men in U.S. Bureau of Labor Statistics (2002) tables.

[1]Very highly female-dominated occupations (such as pre-kindergarten and kindergarten teachers, librarians, secretaries, stenographers, and typists) were not included, because they fail to meet the Bureau of Labor Statistics' minimum criterion of at least 50,000 participants of each sex for comparison purposes.

Source: Adapted from H. M. Lips. (2003). The gender pay gap: Concrete indicator of women's progress toward equality. *Analysis of Social Issues and Public Policy 3,* 87–109.

barriers to equal employment—active or passive discrimination. Such barriers will continue until eradicated by social movements; however, internal barriers in the form of self-limiting expectations are also present. An immediate advantage to focusing on these barriers is to place the forces of change in the hands of the individual. Change through broad social movements such as legislation will of course remain important.

Self-Limiting Expectations One of the primary internal barriers adolescent females face when they begin a job is the value they assign to their work. Females place less value on their work than do males; as a consequence, females expect to be paid less—and are. An office worker who sees the importance to a company of maintaining files and records (invoices, shipments, and so on) will value the work he or she does and expect to be paid accordingly. This person might argue, with reason, that the company's income depends on how effectively records are kept. Those who consider their work to be important are likely to show initiative and creativity—important for pay increases and advancement to higher positions. Most, if not all, of the self-limiting expectations females have are learned (Major & Forcey, 1985).

A number of factors distinguish females who expect to pursue nontraditional occupations (the ones that also pay more) from those who stay in traditional types of work. The influence of significant others, including role models, is important. So, too, is the anticipated cost of education (Davey & Stoppard, 1993). Information about the availability of jobs and the many types of jobs that exist is also vitally important. But for such information to have an effect, adolescent females must see it as relevant to their own career plans—that is, that *they* can be a botanist, beautician, electrician, ship loader, teacher, or business owner.

Many of the problems women face in the workforce are shared by minorities. We turn to a consideration of minorities in the workforce next.

Minorities and Work

Whitney Young, a prominent African American leader, once remarked, "The trouble is that blacks are so visible. You hire one secretary and it looks like a whole lot of integration." As Young reminds us, we are still at the "token" stage with respect to the full range of job opportunities open to minority adolescents. One African American or Hispanic in the office may look like a lot of integration, but that token minority person is usually a secretary, not the boss.

Minority youth start out with career aspirations as high as those of youth from the dominant culture, but they encounter numerous social, cultural, and personal barriers to success. Despite the landmark legislation in the 1960s and 1970s that paved the way for equity in employment, progress has been slow. Figure 10.7 shows the percentages of African Americans and European Americans employed in different types of occupations in 2001.

More high school students work today than a generation ago. But their jobs are usually for minimum wage and provide few opportunities to move up to more responsible and challenging positions.

Poverty The high incidence of poverty among minority adolescents is a common link among the factors that affect their eventual employment; among the most important factors are staying in school, receiving quality education, and making informed decisions about their futures. The rate of poverty can be more than twice as high among minorities as among Whites (National Center for Children in Poverty, 2004). Poverty in relation to education is much like oil in relation to water—the two don't mix. Low-income students are significantly more likely to drop out of high school as their upper-income counterparts, and those who remain in school are more likely to be tracked in non-college-preparatory and vocational courses (see Chapter 9).

Poverty is also related to lower academic performance. Low-income students are not as likely to achieve at the same levels as middle-income and upper-income students, nor are the educational programs they receive of the same quality as those provided to middle- and upper-income youth (see Chapter 9). Poverty is unevenly distributed, tending to be centralized in urban and inner-city schools, where minority students make up most of the student body.

Programs Some programs are more important to occupational success than others. Math and science courses provide a gateway to many of the higher-level jobs. Preparation in both of these areas is generally poorer among minority students. African American and Hispanic students, for instance, take fewer math courses and do more poorly in them than European American students (Fox, Connolly, & Snyder, 2005). They also have less actual experience with science either inside the classroom (for example, watching chicks hatch, growing a plant from seed, studying an ant colony) or outside it (such as trips to museums and science fairs) and, not surprisingly, can think of fewer uses for science. With the exception of Asian Americans, all minorities are underrepresented in science, math, and engineering, and these are the fields preparing students for the high-level jobs of the future.

On an encouraging note, significantly more minority high school students are entering college than a generation ago and more are completing college. Among African

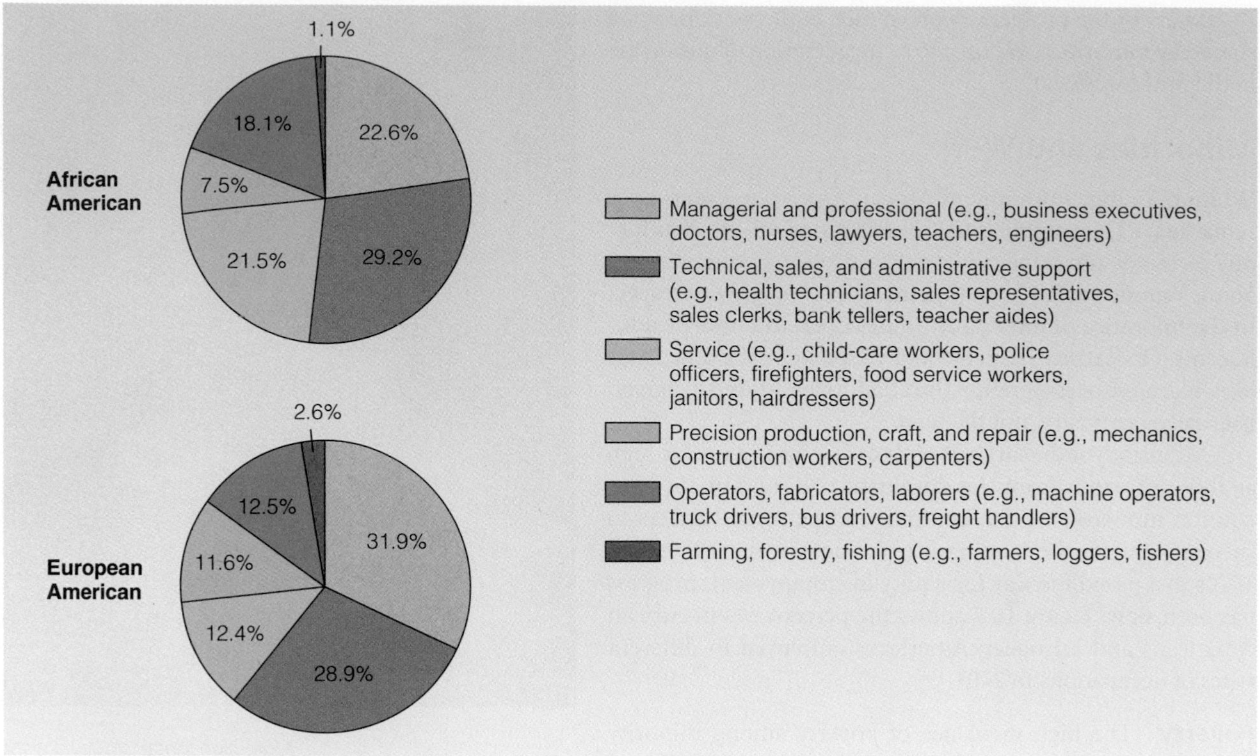

FIGURE 10.7
Employment by Occupational Category, African American and European American Workers, 2001. *Source:* Adapted from U.S. Bureau of Labor of Statistics. (2001). *Annual average: Household data.* Retrieved from http://www.bls.gov/cps/cpsaat10.pdf

American youth, for instance, more than four times the number of individuals completed four years of college in 1995 than in 1960 (*Digest of Education Statistics,* 1996).

Positions Most minority youth are all too aware of the barriers to equal employment, and both African Americans and Hispanics adjust their expectations accordingly. Thus, Hispanic students have just as high career *aspirations* as do European Americans, but lower expectations of achieving them (Arbona, 1989). Similarly, African Americans students are aware of the existence of barriers (Howell, Frese, & Sollie, 1984). Perhaps no statistic speaks more clearly to this issue than unemployment rates: Unemployment among African Americans who graduated from high school in 1997 was somewhat higher (22.2%) than among European Americans who dropped out of school (17.4%) (U.S. Bureau of Labor Statistics, 1998).

Intervention Programs: Strategies for Change

Adolescent females, minority students, and the counselors who work with them need to increase their awareness of the problems, and opportunities, these youth face in making career decisions.

Counselors as Change Agents

Having a teacher or a counselor who believes in them is an important element contributing to their eventual success for many minority adolescents.

Because the opportunity structure for minority adolescents, and for females, is not the same as that for White, middle-class males (see Chapter 9), counselors may have to become active "change agents" in order to effectively prepare students for jobs (Brooks, 1990; Ogbu, 1992). Linda Brooks (1990) suggests that counselors leave their offices and meet with parents, teachers, and local businesses to combat the inequities that minority youth face. Many minority adolescents are not as well prepared as their nonminority counterparts for the careers that have traditionally been held by White males. Many have fallen below competitive levels in basic skills such as reading and math. Counselors may need to act as student advocates, working with teachers and schools to develop effective intervention programs that prepare minority youth for the full range of careers open to others.

An example of one such program is currently under way at California State University, Los Angeles (Wapner, 1990). The university established a contractual agreement with a local, predominantly Hispanic, junior high school. All students who participate in a precollege program in the sciences are guaranteed admittance to the university. Junior high school teachers, counselors, university professors, and administrators meet with students and parents to familiarize them with the program. Students receive tutoring in basic math and reading skills while taking science courses in junior high and, later, high school. Programs such as this one have been started at a number of universities across the country.

Before counselors can assume the role of active change agents, many need to face their own biases. A counselor who accepts a talented minority girl's statement that she is interested in working with children as an aide or a helper in a classroom or playground, without suggesting other career opportunities that also involve helping people (such as medicine, psychology, social work), reveals an insensitivity to the existence of very real gender or culturally based conflicts (Brooks, 1990).

Would it be too intrusive to direct this student to consider other career options? Brooks argues that counselors *must* begin directing minority and female students' attention to areas other than the role-traditional ones in which they express an initial interest. Those who have doubts about the appropriateness of such actions should consider what the same counselor would be likely to do if a talented White male student with similar interests said he wanted to be a teacher aide or helper (Brooks, 1990).

Irrational Beliefs and Maladaptive Myths

Students frequently approach career decisions with maladaptive beliefs and myths (Krumboltz, 1991; Luzzo, Funk, & Strang, 1996). These can be about themselves ("I'm not very smart"), a profession ("You have to be self-confident to be a nurse"), or the

IN MORE DEPTH

Myths That Interface with Adaptive Career Decision Making

- "I have to know exactly what I want to do before I can act."
- "Choosing a career involves making just one decision."
- "If I change my mind once I've picked a career, I'm a failure."
- "If I can only be good in nursing [construction, management, and so on], then I will be content."
- "Work satisfies all of a person's needs."
- "If I work hard enough, I can be successful at anything."
- "How good I am at my job determines my worth as a person."

Source: L. K. Mitchell & J. D. Krumboltz. (1987). The effects of cognitive restructuring and decision-making training on career indecision. *Journal of Counseling and Development, 66,* 171–174.

conditions that lead to satisfaction with a career ("I wouldn't be happy in a profession unless I made a lot of money at it"). The In More Depth box identifies types of myths that keep many people from trying interesting careers.

Intervention Techniques One approach to counseling students with career indecision, known as **cognitive restructuring,** recommends confronting them with their irrational beliefs. Confrontation can result in cognitive restructuring, making more adaptive decision making possible. A female, for instance, may think that her parents "would have nothing to do with her" if she didn't become an elementary school teacher. Because she has little interest in teaching, she finds it difficult to plan for college or think about a career.

Intervention in the form of cognitive restructuring would encourage her to look at the evidence supporting the belief that her parents would sever their relationship if she did not become a teacher (she might find little to support this belief). A counselor might then give her the assignment of talking to her parents about her future. She discovers they are concerned only that she will be able to support herself in a secure job. She is also assigned the task of interviewing five women in different professions and asking them the most satisfying and frustrating aspects of their work. She finds that accounting, career guidance, and being a teacher (surprise!) are all attractive alternatives. She decides to apply to college. Lynda Mitchell and John Krumboltz (1987) report that cognitive restructuring helps reduce students' anxiety when thinking about career planning, consequently making it easier for them to think about their futures.

A related approach, termed **attributional retraining,** focuses students' attention on the way they explain career-related outcomes. Do they attribute career outcomes to conditions for which they are responsible and over which they have control, conditions that will yield to their efforts? Or do they see career outcomes as being influenced more by circumstances beyond their control, where their efforts will do little to change the situation? The former beliefs are adaptive, whereas the latter are not (Luzzo & Ward, 1995).

Darrell Luzzo, at Auburn University, and Tammy James and Marilyn Luna, at the University of North Alabama, (1996) showed students with maladaptive beliefs an attributional retraining video containing adaptive attributional statements such as the following:

> I realized as I was growing up that anything worthwhile in terms of my career was going to take effort and hard work. I pretty much took control over my career decisions. I've worked hard . . . and it has helped me. If I hadn't taken the time and put forth the effort that I did, I wouldn't be doing as well as I am now. (p. 417)

cognitive restructuring A counseling technique that confronts individuals with their irrational beliefs.

attributional retraining A career counseling technique that focuses on individuals' explanations for anticipated career-related successes or failures.

After attributional retraining, these students were significantly more likely to believe that they had control over career decisions, and that the more work they put into these, the more successful they would be. Furthermore, a six-week follow-up showed these differences to persist over time.

At present we need much more information about the effectiveness of the many programs that exist to help minority youth and adolescent females combat the internal and external barriers they face in attaining career goals. What is clear so far is that most teachers, parents, counselors, and students need to expand their thinking beyond role-traditional careers for minorities and females.

Adolescents and College: Thinking About Ideas

With age, adolescents get better at solving life's problems. Is this simply because they can bring more experiences to bear on any decision? Or do their experiences contribute to new ways of thinking, ways that allow them to see that what they presently face often has much in common with problems they solved in the past?

New Solutions to Old Problems: Structural Analytical Thinking

What form might thinking take if it were to move beyond the formal thinking that emerges in early adolescence? Remember, formal thought enables adolescents to stretch their minds beyond a physical world defined by their senses to a world of possibilities that exists first and foremost in their minds, a process that enables them to think of all the possible forms a problem could assume. Formal thought is thought that generates a system, a set of all possible alternatives.

Commons and Richards (1982) suggest a way of thinking that allows individuals to relate two or more systems. Just as formal thinking generates a single system, **structural analytical thinking** identifies parallels between several systems by noting relations that are common to each.

Does structural analytical thinking sound like something only philosophers and metaphysicians engage in? Don't be too quick to say yes. You have already used this way of thinking yourself when reading Chapter 4. Piaget himself has provided us with an example of structural analytical thought: He had to think in a structural analytical way to envision the characteristics of formal thinking. Piaget had to see, in other words, how each of several quite different problems required the same operations for their solution. Whether determining what form life might take on a newly discovered planet or which combination of chemicals produces a yellow liquid, one must isolate the relevant variables, generate all the possible combinations, and systematically test each combination. To see each problem as a reflection of formal thinking, one must think at a structural analytical level.

Structural analytical thinking has a distinct advantage over formal thinking: It gives one a perspective from which to view the problems one is attempting to solve. Unlike formal thinking, which is limited to solving problems within the systems that define them, structural analytical thinking makes it possible to mentally step outside any particular system and consider another approach.

structural analytical thinking A stage of cognitive development characterized by the ability to relate two or more systems of thought.

Propositional and Dialectical Reasoning Stepping outside a system and seeing things from another perspective touches all areas of adolescents' lives, not just the intellectual. Not every adolescent (or even every adult) can do this; it requires reasoning in a new way. Klaus Riegel (1973) distinguishes this reasoning, which he terms *dialectical reasoning,* from the propositional reasoning that develops with formal thinking. Both types of reasoning start with a set of premises, or assumptions that are accepted as true. As these assumptions are put to the test, in the course of thinking through numerous life problems, they are either supported or refuted.

In **propositional reasoning,** these premises are never questioned, even though any number of situations may reveal them as wrong. In *dialectical reasoning,* the premises are put into question if, over time, actions based on them are not supported. What does it mean to question our most basic assumptions? We must be able, if only for the moment, to assume another perspective, another view of reality. We must be able to move beyond our worldview to frame questions about the assumptions that underlie it. **Dialectical reasoning** provides a means by which we can gain a perspective on the system we use to define our world.

Formal and Structural Analytical Thinking Compared Consider two adolescent females as each realizes that even though her parents have always told her that she was free to do or be whatever she wanted, they do not accept her plans for her life. Each has introduced to her parents a young man she intends to marry and has found that they do not approve of her choice.

Connie is upset and confused. She can think of only two explanations for her parents' reaction: Either she is wrong or her parents are wrong. Either her parents *are* willing to accept the choices she makes, but this choice is so outrageous that no parent could support it, or her parents have been living a lie—it's not all right with them for her to be anything she wants to be if that means being different from them. She reacts with hurt and anger and can think of nothing to say to them or to her fiancé.

Janice recognizes her hurt and anger at her parents and begins to think about the differences in their values and hers. She recognizes that people's values influence their actions, but that in acting, people change events, and these changes frequently lead to new awareness and new values. Her parents' affirmation of her freedom to be herself has allowed her to be the person she is—a person who is quite different from them. Janice knows that because her parents have valued her, they valued her freedom to make her own decisions, and that because of this freedom she has had experiences they never had. She realizes that these experiences have changed her view of the world and allow her to see things in others that her parents are not able to recognize. Although Janice is sad that her parents cannot appreciate the qualities in her fiancé that she values, she is grateful she had the opportunity they gave her to be herself (Basseches, 1984).

Connie and Janice have each dealt with a painful situation in different ways. Connie's approach reflects formal thinking. She believes there are a set of truths that are described by a point of view. She can evaluate situations and events from this point of view but has no way of reconciling differences that may challenge it. Thus, either she or her parents must be wrong. Janice can step outside her beliefs and see how they have evolved from those of her parents. Her ability to see evolution and change as a natural part of people and relationships may help her find ways to reestablish a new relationship with her parents.

We have discussed the ability to move from one perspective to another, noting differences and finding relationships between them, as an intellectual feat—that is, as structural analytical thinking. Yet more than intellect may be involved. The ability to stand back from one's own way of thinking while viewing that of others may reflect one's

propositional reasoning Reasoning from a set of premises that themselves are not questioned even when not supported by tests derived from them.

dialectical reasoning Reasoning that questions the premises on which it is based when tests of the premises are not supported.

personality as much as one's intellect. There's a risk in letting one's beliefs be put to the test in this way. We examine the implications of this very personal stance on knowledge in the next section.

How College Changes the Way Adolescents Think

William Perry (1970), of Harvard University, identified important changes during the college years in the way adolescents think about ideas. These changes reflect their beliefs about the nature of truth as much as their ability to think in general. Perry conducted his observations among college men. However, individuals in any setting should experience similar changes if they let their experiences challenge their ideas. Perry identified three major forms of thought: dualism, relativism, and commitment in relativism.

Dualism: Looking for Answers **Dualistic thinking** is the belief that problems are simply solved by finding the right answer, that is, by discovering the truth. Dualistic thinkers have not yet encountered differences of perspective or belief that are so great they could not be bridged by a single set of answers. They operate, in other words, within a single frame of reference. For them learning is mostly a matter of acquiring the facts; it does not require evaluation of the facts. Adolescents who function at this level tend to view ideas, and people, as right or wrong, as good or bad. Ideas that are familiar—that can be assimilated into their belief system—are accepted as legitimate; those that violate their beliefs are regarded as illegitimate or, at the very least, suspect (Perry, 1970).

Although a job can help older adolescents develop structural analytical thinking and dialectical reasoning, college courses provide more systematic opportunities for cognitive growth, as can discussions with friends outside the classroom.

Adolescents who function at this level have rarely experienced ways of life that are different from their own. To them, issues are straightforward, and problems yield to discipline and hard work. The following is an adolescent's description of life in his hometown:

> Well I come, I came here from a small town. Midwest, where, well, ah, everyone believed the same things. Everyone's Methodist and everyone's Republican. So, ah, there just wasn't any . . . well that's not quite true . . . there are some Catholics, two families, and I guess they, I heard they were Democrats, but they weren't really, didn't seem to be in town really, I guess. (Perry, 1970, p. 70)

One of the central experiences of adolescence is the discovery that others have points of view different from one's own. This discovery is pivotal in moving out of the first of Perry's levels. Here is what the same adolescent had to say about diversity:

dualistic thinking The first of Perry's three forms of thought: the belief that truth is independent of one's frame of reference.

> So in my dorm I, we've been-ah a number of discussions, where, there'll be, well, there's quite a variety in our dorm, Catholic, Protestant, and the rest of them, and a Chinese boy

> whose parents-ah follow the teachings of Confucianism. He isn't, but his folks are. . . . And a couple of guys are complete-ah agnostics, agnostics. Of course, some people are quite disturbing, they say they're atheists. But they don't go very far, they say they're atheists, but they're not. And then there are, one fellow who is a deist. And by discussing it-ah, it's the, the sort of thing that, that really-ah awakens you. (p. 70)

Relativism: Losing Oneself to Ideas Perry (1970) points out that the steps from dualism to relativism require courage. It's an uncomfortable journey. Instead of accepting simple answers, adolescents must learn to rely on their own judgment and risk their own ideas. Students know that this process is difficult. As one student said, "Every now and again you do, do . . . do meet p-people who just give up and try and find 'answers' . . . I mean . . . it's hopeless" (p. 107).

Relativistic thinking compares ideas instead of looking for the single one that is right. Relativistic thinkers become aware that what they had accepted as facts are actually interpretations that make sense within some frame of reference, whether a theory presented in a class or the perspective offered by the culture. They also know that more than one frame of reference exists and that each represents a legitimate point of view. From Perry's description of these characteristics, it sounds as if students are moving from formal thought, in which they are operating within a single frame of reference, to structural analytical thought, in which they can compare several worldviews or frames of reference. The development of dialectical reasoning may be pivotal to this change, as this would allow students to evaluate their assumptions as they go along.

One student had this to say about the change to relativistic thought:

> I think the main thing that was interesting this year was questioning basic assumptions. . . . It was interesting in anthropology, particularly, which I didn't go into very deeply, but what I saw as the very basic differences, things that never occurred to me to question before, I don't know whether I'm questioning them now, but at least I know that it's possible to question. (p. 117)

Students experience a new freedom in these discoveries: a freedom to see that they can decide for themselves which ideas are best rather than try to discover what has made most sense to someone else. Learning becomes personally relevant, as they shift their focus from the facts they have been amassing to the process of thinking itself. Relativistic thinking carries a distinct advantage: Students can discover *themselves* in addition to the concepts and theories they are studying. Looking back on this discovery, one student remembered his first year in college as follows:

> I remember my first Christmas vacation home from college. Nobody could say anything about the world that I didn't say was just an hypothesis. My Dad and I argued all the time. He'd say something was an established scientific fact, like gravity or the world being round, or anything else that most people believe, and I would answer that a "fact" is just an hypothesis that hasn't been disproved yet. I know I must have been a pain in the butt to everybody but I had discovered relativism. I "knew" that what people believed to be true, including scientists, was what fit their experience. And since different people had different experiences—and even the same people had new experiences—nothing was true for everybody for all time. I'm a little embarrassed now when I think back to how I must have sounded, but I sure thought that I had found the philosophical answer to everything. (Wapner, 1990)

relativistic thinking The second of Perry's three forms of thought: awareness of more than one frame of reference by which ideas can be evaluated.

Commitment in Relativism: Finding Oneself Erik Erikson (1959) has said that one's sense of identity requires a feeling that what "I" know is also what "I" value.

Relativism challenges this equation as students cut themselves adrift from the moorings of ideas and values they once accepted as absolutes. The danger of relativism is the potential loss of identity that adolescents face. If knowledge reflects different contexts, adolescents will experience discontinuity in what they believe and value as they move from one context to the next.

The pathway out of this maze is choice. Adolescents move beyond relativism by making commitments, becoming agents, choosing, investing themselves, and affirming their experiences. Perry notes that choice and **commitment in relativism** create meaning that would not otherwise exist in a relativistic world; reason alone offers little basis for commitment to any particular worldview. Paradoxically, intellectual development lies in going beyond reason, in taking a position despite one's knowledge that reason alone does not justify this position over others. This step, in a very real sense, involves an act of faith, just as the previous one involved courage. Adolescents move from first defining themselves through individual commitments, such as a career or a mate, to the realization that commitment has come to characterize a way of living.

Gender Differences in Intellectual Development

Does the preceding description fit the intellectual journey of college women as well as men? We simply don't know. Perry included a small number of women in his sample, but he referred only to interviews with males in validating his scheme of intellectual development. Although the females he interviewed conformed to this progression, he may have missed other progressions that better describe intellectual transitions in college women. To explore a fuller sample, Mary Belenky, Blythe Clinchy, Nancy Goldberger, and Jill Tarule (1986) conducted a similar study with women.

Unlike Perry, these investigators did not interview a homogeneous sample of students in a university setting. One-third of their sample was composed of mothers facing the real life challenges of parenting. Belenky and her associates point out that it is easiest to see a sequence such as the one Perry observed when the sample is homogeneous and the context in which development takes place does not vary. Only future research will tell us whether females move through a similar intellectual progression. Meanwhile, the comparisons Belenky and her colleagues provide with Perry's data are indeed interesting.

They note, first, that females do not think in ways neatly described by Perry's categories. Differences emerge from the very beginning. Let's look again at the first step males take. Belenky and her associates (1986) note that the adolescent male, once he discovers the multiplicity of truth,

> foresees his own future as an authority and stakes his claim to the intellectual terrain. . . . [His] perception of the multiplicity of truth becomes a tool in the process of his separation and differentiation from others. His opinion distinguishes him from all others and he lets them know it. (p. 64)

Adolescent females take a different first step. Those who begin the intellectual journey move from subjective knowledge (realizing that truth is relative) to procedural knowledge (assuming responsibility for what they know) to constructive knowledge (being aware that knowledge is constructed by each knower). Not all complete this journey.

commitment in relativism The third of Perry's three forms of thought: committing oneself to a point of view from which one can derive meaning.

Subjective Knowledge: Agreeable Dissent Adolescent females with **subjective knowledge** appreciate that the multiplicity of truth frees them from traditional authority; but they are cautious about embracing an intellectual position. Unlike males, who have been rewarded for testing the status quo, females have been rewarded for being

subjective knowledge The first of Belenky and associates' three forms of thought: covert examination of issues while maintaining a surface conformity to traditional ideas.

Many female adolescents maintain a surface conformity, becoming polite listeners and spectators. Rather than asserting their abilities, many experience intellectual loneliness and become silently alienated from the learning process.

quiet, predictable, and agreeable. Speaking up, taking a stand, or disagreeing with others runs counter to all they have learned. Female adolescents repeatedly express concern that, in taking an intellectual stand, they will isolate themselves from others. Thus their relationships constrain them from forming and defending ideas that would distinguish or separate them from other people. They experience few expectations about, and get little support for, this type of intellectual risk taking (Belenky, Clinchy, Goldberger, & Tarule, 1986).

Rather than speaking out, many maintain a surface conformity while they covertly examine issues. "They become the polite listeners, the spectators who watch and listen but do not act" (Belenky et al., 1986, p. 66). Belenky and her associates note the intellectual loneliness of these female adolescents:

> The tragedy is that [they] still their public voice and are reluctant to share their private world; ultimately this hinders them from finding mentors who might support their intellectual and emotional growth. [They] can be silently alienated . . . , knowing somehow that their conformity is a lie and does not reveal the inner truth or potential they have recently come to value. (p. 67)

In speaking up, males lay claim to an intellectual terrain that has been staked out for centuries as theirs. There are few equivalent intellectual domains for females, and few means are identified for their use in defining one. Instead of reason—the ultimate analytic tool—females have been told their strength lies in intuition, which in relation to reason is like a divining rod compared to a surveyor's level. Instead of mapping out ideas, many learn to wait for the gentle tug of mind in an otherwise silent trek across an uncharted terrain.

In becoming skilled listeners to themselves and others, some women come to see the contradictions of their stance. Their observations make it possible for them to develop the more critical thought that characterizes the next step they take.

Procedural Knowledge: Stepping Out Intellectually Females who step out intellectually—with **procedural knowledge**—assume responsibility for discovering things for themselves. Some do this by mastering the facts in an area, whether it be political economics, nursing, or managing a home. Others adopt a more subjective approach to what they are learning, approaching ideas for what they have to say about their lives. The understanding these women gain is more intimate and personal than that of the first group. Only the first approach is characteristic of Perry's males. For those who adopt it, doubting becomes an important way of putting ideas on trial, and bull sessions provide a forum in which individuals attack each other's position to hone the cutting edge of their logic. Belenky and her associates (1986) note that

> women find it hard to see doubting as a "game"; they tend to take it personally. Teachers and fathers and boyfriends assure them that arguments are not between *persons* but between *positions,* but the women continue to fear that someone may get hurt. (p. 105)

procedural knowledge The second of Belenky and associates' three forms of thought: independent thought that is nonetheless limited to a single frame of reference.

Conversations for females serve the function of bull sessions for males. Belenky and her associates give an example of a young Ethiopian college student who explained in one

Research supports the observation that the rich get richer, at least with respect to increasing expert knowledge. Students who know a lot about a subject organize information about it differently and make better use of it than do students who know less.

such conversation with an American friend why her country had adopted communism. They note the following:

> These young women did not engage in metaphysical debate. They did not argue about abstractions or attack or defend positions. No one tried to prove anything or to convert anyone. The Ethiopian articulated her reality, and the American tried to understand it. They did not discuss communism in general, impersonal terms, but in terms of its origins and consequences among a particular group of real people. (p. 114)

Though more advanced than subjective knowledge, procedural knowledge operates within a system of knowledge that cannot examine itself. Females who think in either of these ways

> can criticize a system, but only in the system's terms, only according to the system's standards. Women at this position may be liberals or conservatives, but they cannot be radicals. If, for example, they are feminists, they want equal opportunities for women within the capitalistic structure; they do not question the premises of the structure. When these women speak of "beating the system," they do not mean violating its expectations but rather exceeding them. (Belenky et al., 1986, p. 127)

For females to move beyond these forms of knowing, they need more than formal thought.

Constructive Knowledge: Examining the Self Young women who move into **constructive knowledge** report a period of self-examination in which they experience being out of touch with parts of themselves. "During the transition into a new way of knowing, there is an impetus to allow the self back into the process of knowing, to confront the pieces of the self that may be experienced as fragmented and contradictory" (Belenky et al., 1986, p. 136). These females ask themselves questions such as "Who am I?" and "How will I approach life?"

constructive knowledge The third of Belenky and associates' three forms of thought: an awareness that knowledge is constructed; the ability to examine one's beliefs.

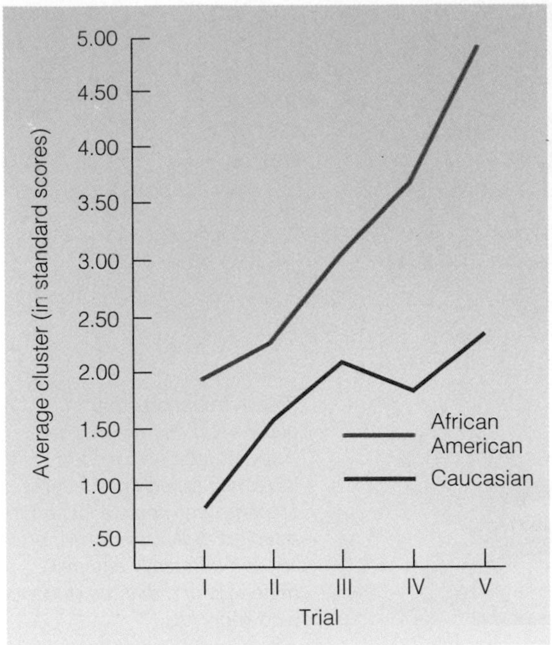

FIGURE 10.8
Clustered Recall of Words by African American and Caucasian Adolescents.
Source: A. J. Franklin. (1985). The social context and socialization variables as factors in thinking and learning. In S. F. Chipman, J. W. Segal, & R. Glaser (Eds.), *Thinking and learning skills* (Vol. 2). Hillsdale, NJ: Erlbaum.

Questions such as these echo the concerns of Perry's young males who experienced the need for commitment in their relativistic thought. Belenky and her associates note that these females experience a "heightened consciousness and sense of choice" about the ways they examine their world and who they will become. They become aware of the fact that given a different perspective or even a different point in time, they could come up with different answers to the same questions (Belenky et al., 1986). This awareness leads to the central truth of constructed knowledge: that knowledge is constructed and hence relative, and the knower is an intrinsic part of the process. This position allows these females to examine a set of beliefs from a perspective outside that system. Something like structural analytical thinking almost surely is present at this point.

In addition to their general approach to knowledge, how much adolescents know about the subject they are studying affects how they think about it and how much they will remember of what they learn. We turn to research on cultural influences on learning next.

Knowledge of One's Culture: Everybody's an Expert

What adolescents know can affect how easily they learn even more. Expertise in an area makes studying related material easier than material with which they're less familiar. All adolescents are experts in one area: their own culture. This expertise makes it easy to assimilate information that is consistent with what they know based on their experiences. Information that is inconsistent is not easy to learn, because they must change the way they understand things in order to accommodate a new perspective. Consequently, it is difficult to learn concepts and facts that violate one's cultural perspective or are incongruent with one's experiences.

Anderson Franklin, at the City University of New York, put these observations to the test in a simple experiment. Franklin (1985) assumed that African American adolescents would have an advantage over White adolescents in remembering words common to the African American culture but not common outside it. Franklin interviewed 75 urban African American teenagers to obtain commonly used slang terms. He constructed lists of categories of words using the terms they supplied, together with words common to both African Americans and European Americans.

As shown in Figure 10.8, African American adolescents remember more words than European American adolescents do. In fact, if one did not know how the list of words had been derived, one might assume that African American adolescents have better memories than do European Americans. Based on similar comparisons, some investigators have assumed that European Americans are more intelligent than African Americans and other minorities because they score higher on measures common to intelligence tests. In doing so, these investigators have failed to take into account that minorities may not be familiar with all the items included in the tests (see Chapter 4). Franklin noticed that African American adolescents were also better at recalling items that were equally familiar to the European American students. African Americans were more likely to categorize items into related clusters, a strategy that vastly improves memory when it is used. The presence of unfamiliar items may have led the European American adolescents to believe that the words were unrelated. Familiarity with all the words, which was the case only for the African American adolescents, had allowed them to see that the words could be easily categorized (Franklin, 1985).

Adolescent Decision Making

Intellectual changes during adolescence have very real implications for daily living. How effective do adolescents perceive themselves to be? What are they willing to attempt? How motivated are they to pursue different goals? How successful will they be? The answers to these and similar questions reflect their burgeoning intellectual skills.

Personal Effectiveness

Feelings of personal effectiveness reflect how much control adolescents feel they have in a situation, which stems directly from their ability to predict the outcome. The ability to predict is an intellectual skill. "If I tell Gina that the junior she has a crush on asked me out, she'll flirt with my boyfriend." Or, "If I work all the different types of algebra problems in this chapter, I'll be able to pass the test on it." Adolescents who know the consequences their actions will have are in a better position to control what happens to them by doing or not doing certain things. Predicting outcomes involves the same type of analytic thinking (if . . . then . . .) adolescents use in the classroom: inductive and deductive reasoning.

Adolescents can think about outcomes of their actions probabilistically, a development that accompanies formal thought. They also realize that events can have more than one cause (for example, "Gina might also flirt with my boyfriend because she thinks he's cute") and that the same event can contribute to different outcomes (for example, "Gina might even spend more time with me . . ."). In addition to intellectual skills, how much adolescents believe in themselves also affects their approach to any situation, in this case, by the type of outcomes they anticipate. Those who perceive themselves as effective anticipate positive outcomes. They mentally rehearse adaptive solutions, which help them find their way through problems more effectively (Bandura, 1989; Zimmerman, Bandura, & Martinez-Pons, 1992).

The type of outcome adolescents anticipate also affects their motivation to engage in an activity. In other words, the goals they set reflect their appraisal of their ability to meet them. Those who doubt themselves are likely to give up when they face some difficulty; adolescents who believe in themselves work harder. Belief in self has other effects as well; it can determine how much stress one can tolerate. Those who think they can cope with something do not anticipate all the possible negative outcomes that others with self-doubts imagine. As a consequence, they don't have to deal with the negative emotional side effects such fantasies may produce (Bandura, 1989).

Bandura points out that, at times, inaccurate self-assessments can actually *help* adolescents when making decisions. Optimistic evaluations of competence—if not too far off the mark—can help for all the reasons just reviewed. A less optimistic, if truer, judgment can be self-limiting, failing to motivate adolescents to stretch beyond their present performance.

Feelings of competence or incompetence can be general or quite specific. Are some adolescents more likely than others to react to failure with general feelings of inadequacy? Poole and Evans (1988) had adolescents rate their competence in several life skill areas

The demands of school and homework are relatively inflexible compared to the negotiated settlements that can be reached with friends and parents.

(such as use of time, setting goals, making choices, social awareness). In general, adolescents view themselves as being competent at the things they value, though not always as much as they might desire. Important gender differences exist in self-perceptions. Females view themselves as less competent than males overall and as competent in fewer areas, even though an objective measure that all adolescents completed showed females doing slightly better (Poole & Evans, 1988). Do female adolescents' lower ratings of themselves limit their actual competence in any way? At the very least, we might expect their lower ratings to affect the goals they set for themselves.

Dealing with Everyday Problems

Most of the thinking adolescents do is directed at solving the problems of life—*their* lives. Most of these take the form of daily hassles, that is, interpersonal problems such as an argument with parents or a misunderstanding with friends. Several skills help adolescents negotiate successful resolutions to interpersonal problems. Not unexpectedly, late adolescents are better at these than early adolescents (Berg, 1989; Mann, Harmoni, & Power, 1989).

Any of three general strategies can be attempted when a problem arises. Adolescents can alter their behavior so that it better fits their environment, they can attempt to change the environment so that it better fits their behavior, or they can select another environment (Sternberg, 1985). A number of additional steps are important. The first is simply to plan to take action. Also helpful is to get more information and to change one's perception of the problem. Sometimes redefining the problem, looking at it in a different way, is all that is needed to emotionally defuse it.

Each of these steps underscores the importance of flexibility when faced with a problem, and flexibility increases with age. When asked, "What does a good decision maker do when making a decision?" late adolescents are more likely to mention generating options, and they are better at doing this themselves. They are also more likely to take into consideration the consequences of following any of the options and to check the advice or information they get (Mann, Harmoni, & Power, 1989).

Cynthia Berg (1989) asked adolescents to evaluate the effectiveness of these strategies when faced with a problem such as the following:

> Your parents have become more strict in what time you must be home at night. On Friday and Saturday nights you have to be home by 12:00. You and your friends want to go out to a movie on Friday night that will not be over until 12:30, so you won't be home until 1:00. You find out from the movie theater that the movie will be showing at the theater for one more week. Rate how good each of the answers is in allowing you to see the movie and be home by 12:00. [The curfew for fifth-, eighth-, and eleventh-graders was 9:30, 10:30, and 12:00, respectively.]
>
> Ask your friends if they have a strict time that they must be home at night. (Get more information)
>
> Decide that seeing the movie is really not worth causing problems with your parents. (Redefine the problem)
>
> Wait to see the movie on Saturday afternoon. (Alter behavior)
>
> Persuade your parents that the new rule is not fair. (Change the environment)
>
> Spend Friday night at the house of a friend who does not have to be home so early. (Pick another environment)
>
> Plan how you could both see a movie and be home by 12:00. (Plan a course of action) (p. 618)

Late adolescents choose more effective strategies than early adolescents, and females do so more than males. As obstacles are introduced or removed, less-effective problem solvers are likely to radically alter their approach. The best problem solvers change their strategies relatively little. This difference suggests that interpersonal problem solving is a skill that, once learned, adolescents can apply across a variety of settings. Supporting this interpretation is Berg's finding that using strategies effectively is related to adolescents' own evaluations of their practical intelligence, as well as that of their teachers' and parents', and to their actual achievement (in the form of grades and achievement test scores).

The effectiveness of strategies varies with the setting in which problems arise. Adolescents believe, for example, that the problems they encounter at school (for example, getting into a special class, resolving a grade discrepancy) are best handled either by redefining their perception of the problem or by simply selecting another environment. An adolescent who receives a C on an essay that she feels deserves a B might think the teacher is biased against her. Most adolescents in high school realize that the best way to resolve grade discrepancies is to find out what the teacher wanted (that is, redefine the problem from an interpersonal one to an academic one) or try to get another teacher next time (select another environment).

When problems arise outside of school, planning and getting more information are seen as most effective. Opting for different approaches in either setting itself reveals knowledge of effective strategies. School settings are relatively inflexible compared to the environments where one can negotiate settlements, such as with friends or parents. Late adolescents are more likely to realize this difference than early adolescents (Berg, 1989).

In all, whether it be thinking through academic arguments and abstract ideas or facing everyday decisions, adolescents use increasingly sophisticated strategies.

Summary

Adolescents at Work

- Most high school students have part-time jobs, and more want to work than can find jobs. Unemployment among minority adolescents is higher than among majority youth. Most adolescents spend their money on personal items such as clothes, entertainment, and cars. Smaller numbers save for education or other long-term plans. Students who work part-time spend less time on schoolwork and with families, but they develop a sense of responsibility and feel productive.
- Students who drop out of high school are about twice as likely to be unemployed as graduates. Programs that are successful in preventing at-risk students from dropping out communicate the importance of having a degree for making money. These programs create an atmosphere of caring and involvement, provide individualized instruction through computerized programs, and involve the community and parents.

Choosing a Vocation

- In explaining vocational choices, social-cognitive theory emphasizes the interrelationships among inborn abilities, one's particular environment and unique learning history, and one's skills.
- Developmental theories trace occupational choices over stages. Ginzburg views vocational development as a progressive narrowing of choices that at first reflect only fantasy, then tentative career choices, and, with increasing age, realistic choices.
- Super assumes that people choose occupations that reflect the way they see themselves. Because the self-concept changes with age, so will occupational plans. In the *growth* stage, adolescents develop a realistic self-concept; in the *exploration* stage, they begin to make choices related to future work. Individuals settle into their work as early adults in the *establishment* stage, maintaining their occupational position through middle adulthood in the *maintenance* stage. The *decline* stage involves retirement.
- Holland classifies individuals into six personality types; different work environments either complement or oppose the qualities that make up any type. *Realistic* types prefer orderly, structured work. *Investigative* types prefer work that involves analytic skills. *Artistic* types do best in unstructured situations that let them express their creativity. *Social* types have good interpersonal skills. *Enterprising* types enjoy work that brings them into contact with others in ways in which they can express their assertiveness. *Conventional* types prefer to work under the direction of others.

Joining the Workforce

- Most of the fastest-growing jobs are in health, technology, and the service occupations; many of these jobs require more skills than in the past. These are not necessarily the most numerous jobs, however, and many of the latter do not require more skills than previously. Employment opportunities of any kind for inner-city minority youth are scarce, however.
- More female adolescents plan to work in professional jobs than before. Sex segregation still exists in the workforce, and advancement opportunities for females are limited. Female adolescents also have internal barriers to advancement that take the form of lower expectations for pay and lower valuation of their work; these barriers are learned.
- Minority adolescents face problems similar to those of females; in addition, poverty contributes heavily to the problems they face. Minority adolescents' career aspirations are as high as those of majority adolescents, but their lower expectations reflect social barriers to equal employment opportunities.

Intervention Programs

- Because of inequities in the opportunity structure for minority adolescents and females, counselors may need to become active change agents to prepare these students for the full range of jobs that exists. Effective intervention programs work with local businesses, parents, and teachers as well as the students. Counselors often must first address their own biases.
- Students frequently approach career decisions with maladaptive beliefs and myths. Intervention programs based on cognitive restructuring and on attributional retraining effectively address these as the first step to vocational counseling.

Adolescents and College

- Some developmentalists believe a new form of thinking develops in late adolescence. *Structural analytical thinking* builds on the achievements of formal thought and allows adolescents to find parallels among different views of a problem.

- *Dialectical reasoning* is necessary for structural analytical thought, just as propositional reasoning is necessary for formal thought. In *propositional reasoning,* the premises are not questioned even when they are not supported. In dialectical reasoning, one questions the premises if, over the course of time, actions based on them are not supported.
- William Perry has identified three major forms of thought in college men: (1) *Dualistic* thinkers approach problems in a straightforward manner and look for the right answer. They operate within a single frame of reference that allows them to view ideas as either right or wrong. (2) *Relativistic* thinkers are aware that what they previously accepted as facts are actually interpretations that make sense within a given frame of reference. They are aware that more than one frame of reference exists and that each represents a legitimate point of view. (3) Relativists who commit themselves to a point of view create new meaning through anchoring their beliefs in a committed style of life.
- Female adolescents think in ways other than those captured by Perry's intellectual progressions: (1) *Subjective* knowers covertly examine issues while maintaining a surface conformity to traditional ideas. (2) *Procedural* knowers own the responsibility of discovering things for themselves, but their thought is limited by the confines of formal thinking. (3) *Constructive* knowers are aware that knowledge is constructed and hence relative, and that the knower is an intrinsic part of the process. They can examine their beliefs using structural analytical thought.
- Adolescents who know a lot about a subject organize information more efficiently and recall it better.
- A form of expertise that does not involve academic learning comes from knowledge of one's culture. This expertise makes it easy for adolescents to assimilate information consistent with cultural experiences but difficult to learn material that runs counter to their experiences.

Adolescent Decision Making

- Adolescents' intellectual skills contribute to their sense of personal effectiveness. The control they feel in situations stems directly from their ability to predict outcomes, which involves the same types of analytical thinking used in the classroom.
- Most of the intellectual skills put to use outside the classroom are directed at solving interpersonal problems. Adolescents get better at this with age.

Key Terms

job shadowing
mentoring
internship
cooperative education
fantasy stage
tentative stage
realistic stage
growth stage
exploration stage
establishment stage
maintenance stage
decline stage
realistic personality types
investigative personality types
artistic personality types
social personality types
enterprising personality types
conventional personality types
cognitive restructuring
attributional retraining
structural analytical thinking
propositional reasoning
dialectical reasoning
dualistic thinking
relativistic thinking
commitment in relativism
subjective knowledge
procedural knowledge
constructive knowledge

CHAPTER OUTLINE

CHAPTER 11

Facing the Future

Values in Transition

CHAPTER OBJECTIVES

- To look at the values of adolescents and how they are influenced by their parents and their culture
- To compare theories of moral development with respect to how they explain developmental changes in moral reasoning and behavior
- To examine adolescents' religious beliefs and their importance to their lives

White-lipped and shaking, Sarah replaced the receiver with exaggerated care, as if each movement could restore order to her world.

"So what's the word? Are you or aren't you?" asked Gina in a voice tight with urgency.

"I'm not," replied her friend.

"So, then, what's the problem?"

"I'm not sure," began Sarah, "but until now I don't think any of this has been real to me."

"You mean," interrupted Gina, "that a minute ago you weren't afraid you might be pregnant?"

"Hey, I was. I just didn't feel anything. But when I heard that the test was negative, I felt empty . . . sad . . . and happy and angry . . . all at once. It's strange. When I thought I might be pregnant, I felt nothing, but now that I know I'm not, I have all these feelings."

Gina looked at her friend with concern. "How could you have taken care of a baby?"

"I sure can't imagine myself as a mother," agreed Sarah,with a wry look on her face.

"You would've had to forget about plans for college and working with abused children."

"That's a laugh!" Sarah answered bitterly. "How can I put those two parts of myself together—the one that thought about giving the baby away or even getting an abortion and the other that wants to help children whose parents hurt them?"

"You have a responsibility to yourself as well," offered Gina.

"Sure, but how do I balance that against my responsibility to someone else? Would it have been responsible to give the baby away if I couldn't have taken care of it properly? Or was it wrong to have even thought of it?"

"Was Eddie any help in thinking about this?" asked Gina.

"We were both too numb to think very clearly," answered Sarah. "But the few times we talked, we seemed to be discussing different problems altogether."

"I can relate to that!" snapped Gina. "At times J.J. doesn't even seem to speak the same language."

"Eddie talked about whether the fetus was a person, and whether it had the same rights that we had. It sounded so impersonal. All I could think of was whether I could take care of it and still take care of myself," Sarah replied quietly, as she broke another toothpick and absently added it to the pile in front of her.

Chapter Overview

Many adolescents find themselves face-to-face with problems like Sarah's and Eddie's. In this chapter, we will look at the standards adolescents use in making decisions—decisions that increasingly affect others as well as themselves. Changing roles, untrodden rights, and uncharted responsibilities create a compelling need for a system of values to guide decisions. Beliefs that have worked all through childhood come up again for review in adolescence. Many will withstand close scrutiny; others will not. All will be tested against a developing system of values as adolescents face the challenge of defining themselves.

Self-definition means that adolescents must distinguish values and beliefs that are unique to them from those they acquired from their parents. Many begin by scrutinizing their families' values to see which ones they will accept for themselves. Some adolescents forgo this process and continue to live by standards set by others. The development of values is an integral part of one's identity.

What criteria distinguish moral concerns from social convention? From religious beliefs? Some developmentalists consider early experiences within the family to be pivotal to later moral development, whereas others stress the importance of interactions with peers. Do females and males approach moral issues differently? Are there progressions in religious development as there are in moral development? Developmentalists, as well as the families they study, frequently arrive at different answers to questions such as these. Their answers will structure our discussion of moral development.

The Values of Adolescents

The values of adolescents have changed little over the years. Most adolescents today consider having a good marriage and family life, and being successful in their work to be extremely important, just as their parents did when they were adolescents. They also consider it important to have money and contribute to society. With respect to the latter, adolescents act out their values; over a third are active in community affairs or do volunteer work at least once or twice a month, as shown in Figure 11.1 (Fox, Connolly, & Snyder, 2005, U.S.; Department of Health and Human Services, 2002c).

Values: Adolescents and Parents

Most adolescents hold attitudes that are in substantial agreement with those of their parents. Close to 90% of adolescents and their parents have similar attitudes concerning the value of an education, and nearly 75% agree with parents on big questions such as what to do with one's life. Similarly, high agreement exists concerning religion, work ethic,

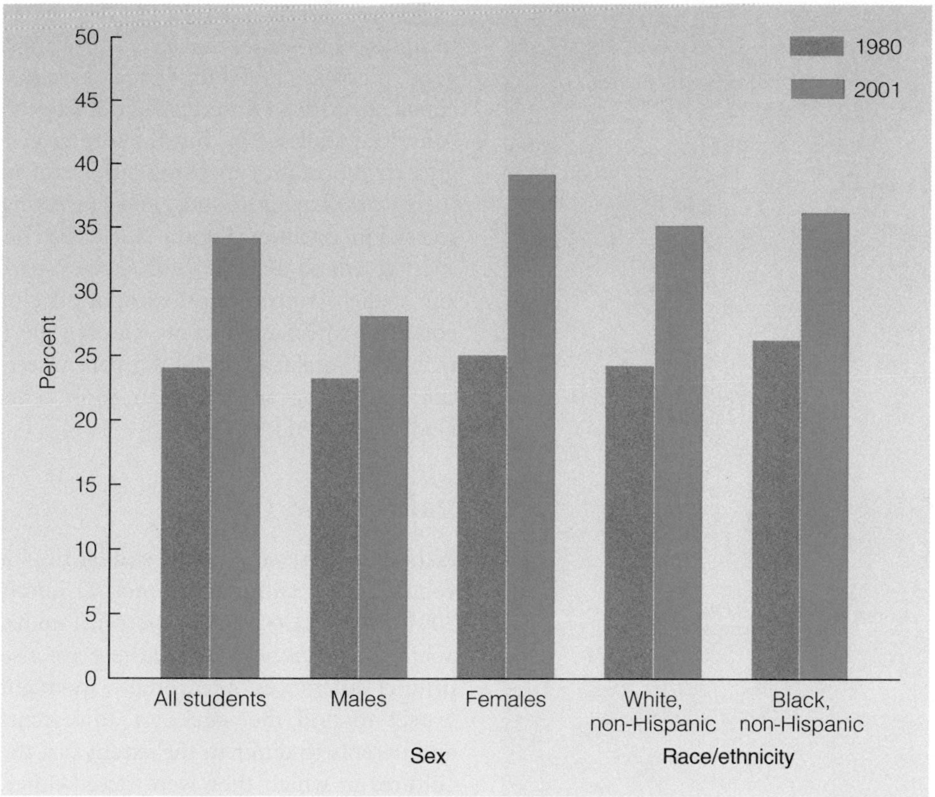

FIGURE 11.1 Percentage of High School Seniors Who Participated in Community Affairs or Volunteer Work at Least Once or Twice per Month, by Sex and Race: 1980 and 2001.
Source: University of Michigan, Institute for Social Research, *Monitoring the future,* various years. In M. A. Fox, B. A. Connolly, & T. D. Snyder. (2005). *Youth indicators 2005: Trends in the well-being of American youth (NCES 2005-050).* U.S. Department of Education, National Center for Education Statistics. Washington, DC: U.S. Government Printing Office.

racial issues, and certain conventional behaviors, such as how to dress (ter Bogt, Raaijmakers, & van Wel, 2005).

This shouldn't be surprising since parents transmit their values to their children in myriad ways, influencing their children's values both explicitly through what they say and implicitly through what they do. With respect to academic achievement, for instance, parents' values have been found to directly predict those of their adolescent children (Jodl, Michael, Malanchuk, Eccles, & Sameroff, 2001). Thus, parents of adolescents who valued education and believed their children could succeed academically were more likely to have adolescents who saw education as important (for example, "I have to do well in school if I want to be a success in life.") and who had higher educational expectations. These expectations, in turn, were positively linked to adolescents' professional, that is, white-collar, career aspirations for both African American and European American adolescents. Thus, parents appear to influence adolescents' career aspirations by transmitting values concerning the importance of education (Jodl et al., 2001).

Values: Gender and Race

More similarities than differences also exist in the values held by adolescent females and males. In comparison to adolescents a decade ago, adolescent females in 2000 were just as likely as males to say that being successful in one's work was "extremely important." Differences appear when it comes to marriage and family and making money: Among high school seniors, females are more likely than males to indicate that marriage and family are important, and males are more likely to place a higher value on having a lot of money. In other respects, the values of each are remarkably similar. (U.S. Department of Health and Human Services, 2002c).

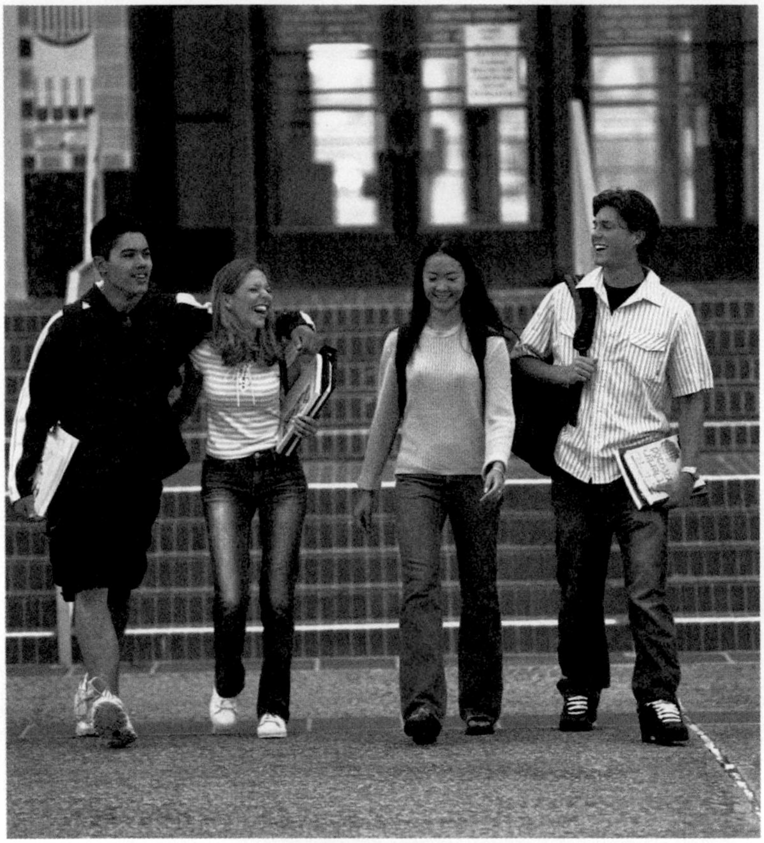

The parents of today's teenagers aren't as different as their children sometimes think. Their attitudes are quite similar with regard to life goals, the value of an education, and the importance of relationships.

There also are relatively few differences in adolescents' values due to race. Having a good marriage and family life is valued equally by African American and European American adolescents, but the former give greater importance to being successful in their work, having money, and correcting societal inequalities (Figure 11.2). With respect to what's necessary for success, parents' beliefs concerning the importance of education affect adolescents' career expectations in similar ways for African American and European American adolescents (Jodl et al., 2001).

Values and Culture

Although there are many similarities in values across cultures (Diener & Lucas, 2004; Schultz, Gouveia, Cameron, Tankha, Schmuck, & Franek, 2005), there are also distinct differences. Accordingly, we might expect to find the values of adolescents and parents to differ to the extent that the cultures in which they were raised differ. Asian American (Cambodian, Laotian, Vietnamese, and Hmong) parents and first-generation adolescents growing up in the United States were asked to discuss what it means to be a good parent and to be a good adolescent. Discussion revealed that values reflected both the cultural traditions of the parents and the American values that the adolescents were acquiring (Xiong, Eliason, Detzner, & Cleveland, 2005).

What might these different cultural traditions be? Cultures can be broadly distinguished with respect to the value they place on **individualism** versus **collectivism** (Triandis, 1988). Individualistic cultures, such as the United States, Canada, and Great Britain, value independence, self-reliance, individual achievement, and self-expression. Collectivist cultures, such as Mexico, Japan, and many other Asian cultures, value interdependence, cooperation, working for the success of one's group, and maintaining harmonious relationships. It's important to keep in mind, however, that these portrayals are broad generalizations, and adolescents within any culture can differ among themselves as much as adolescents might from different cultures.

Values and Identity

Individualism Valuing independence, self-reliance, individual achievement, and self-expression.

collectivism Valuing interdependence, cooperation, group success, and harmonious relationships.

Adolescents' values shape their sense of themselves. Erik Erikson believed values are an important component of our identity. A sense of identity allows us to make countless daily decisions, to take ourselves for granted, as Ruthellen Josselson (1987) puts it. Like much of the way we function, our identity remains largely unavailable for inspection—until we hit a snag.

Developmental snags await us all. They take the form of age-related changes in the expectations that we and others hold up to ourselves. Erikson (1956, 1968) refers to these

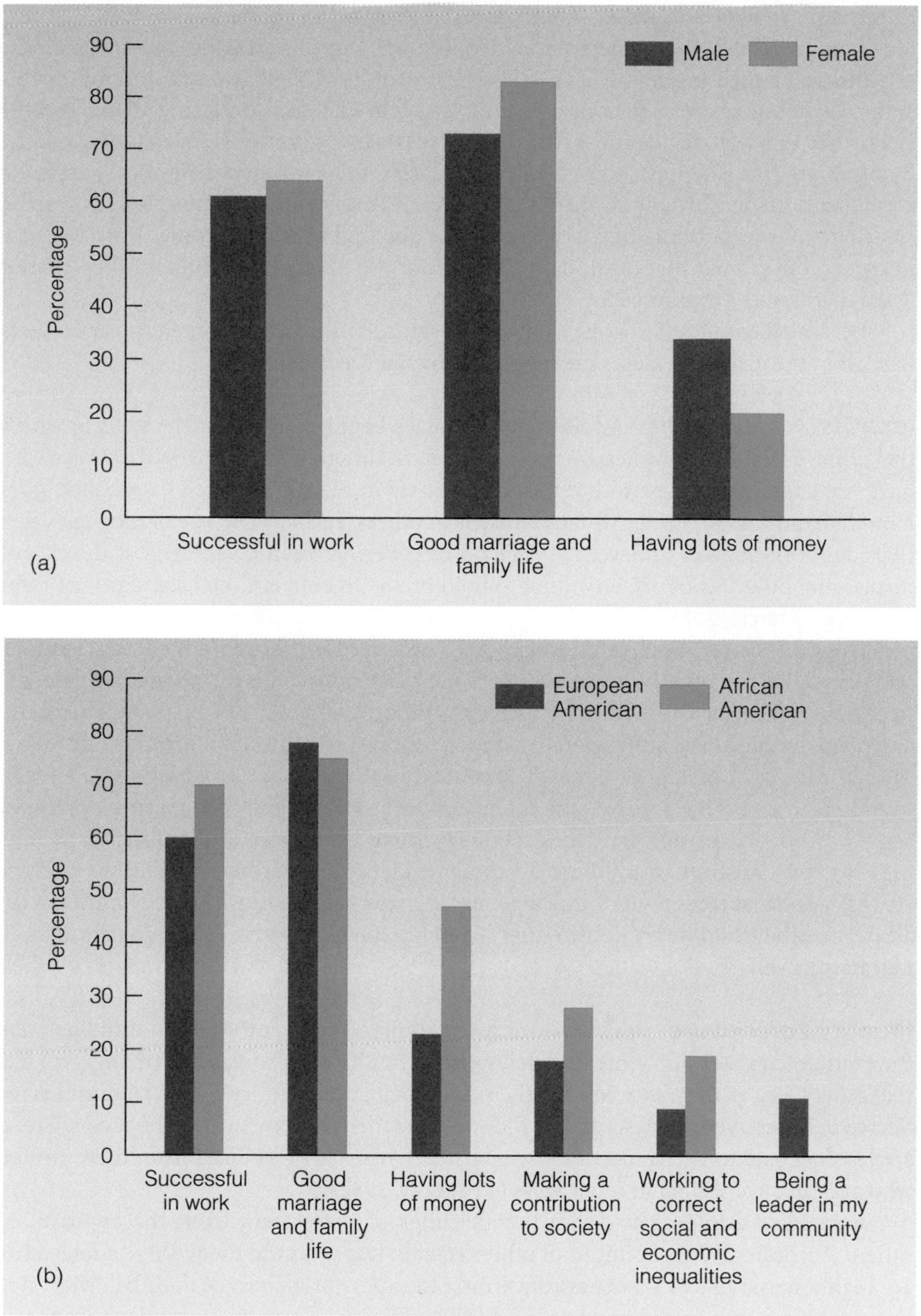

FIGURE 11.2 Values of High School Seniors. *(a) Percentage of male and female high school seniors indicating life goals as "Extremely Important." (b) Percentage of African American and European American high school seniors indicating life goals as "Extremely Important."*
Source: U.S. Department of Health and Human Services. (2002). Social development and behavioral health. In *Trends in the well-being of America's children and youth, 2001* (sect. 4). Retrieved from http://aspe.hhs.gov/hsp/01trends/contents.htm#SD

changes as psychosocial crises. Crises arise when physical maturation, together with changing personal and cultural expectations, lead individuals to reexamine their sense of who they are and what they are about. "Taking oneself for granted," because it flows from one's identity, is precisely what most adolescents find hardest to do: Most of them are continually revising their sense of themselves (see discussion of identity statuses in Chapter 5).

Prior to adolescence, the elements that contribute to identity are ascribed (Josselson, 1987). For example, children have few choices in such matters as where they live, go to school, worship, and so on. Adolescents can begin to explore possibilities that differ from those chosen by their parents. Some will continue to live out the patterns established by their parents. This is still a choice, although adolescents who follow this path may not be aware of making a decision as such. The decision facing all adolescents is whether they will decide things for themselves or live with decisions made by others. Being aware that one has choices, and considering the various possibilities, can make adolescents uncomfortably aware of themselves. Erikson considers this discomfort to be central to one's experience of crisis. By crisis he does not mean that adolescents' lives are in pieces, but simply that until identity decisions are firmly behind them, they cannot "take themselves for granted."

Because identity reflects one's values, the stance toward values taken by adolescents in each of the identity statuses described in Chapter 5 will differ.

Identity Achievement Adolescents who have begun to discover the ways in which they differ from their families are more tolerant of differences in others than those who have not experienced a period of crisis. Openness in examining one's own beliefs goes hand in hand with accepting different beliefs in others. Perhaps because of the high value that identity-achieved adolescents place on discovering themselves, even at the risk of displeasing others, they are unwilling to hold others to conventional standards of right or wrong (Marcia, 1988).

Does this description sound too good to be true? Keep in mind that conscientious and principled behavior is not necessarily what most adults label as "good." Adolescents in search of themselves are likely to question and experiment. They may dress flamboyantly, act outrageously, and generally adopt a "show me" attitude. They may not follow in their parents' footsteps or be ready to settle down when others their age have already found their way. The positive side to this picture is that these adolescents develop a sense of who they are and translate that image into effective strategies for living, including close relationships with others. The independence they achieve reflects an internal struggle, one that frees them for change, not an external one in which they must act on all the possibilities they are considering (Cramer, 2000; Schwartz, Mullis, Waterman, & Dunham, 2000).

Identity Foreclosure Identity-foreclosed adolescents are more rule-bound and authoritarian than identity-achieved adolescents. They have a strong sense of duty and feel that others, just as they, should obey the rules. Their respect for rules and tradition is reflected in the conventional standards they hold for their own and others' behavior. These adolescents tend to be critical of those whose behavior or ideas differ from their own or who are unconventional in other ways (Josselson, 1987).

Foreclosed adolescents derive their feelings of self-esteem from the approval of others. Accordingly, the opinions of others remain important to them; these adolescents are highly sensitive to social cues concerning the appropriateness of their behavior. Actions or beliefs that might cause conflict will be rejected. Security, not independence, is their overriding concern (Cramer, 2000; Marcia, 1980).

Moratorium Moratorium adolescents, like foreclosed adolescents, seek others to complete themselves. However, instead of seeing others as sources of security, they look to them as models. Like identity-achieved adolescents, they realize that their own values are not any more right than those of others, but unlike identity-achieved adolescents, who experiment until they find their own way, moratorium adolescents set out on a "kind of crusade, determined to discover what is 'really right'" (Josselson, 1987). Josselson points out that theirs is an impossible quest, made all the harder because they hold

Identity-achieved and moratorium adolescents do not automatically define themselves according to convention, and they are tolerant of others who are unconventional.

back from experiences that would define them, always leaving a back door open through which to escape if they make a wrong choice. Josselson (1987) writes:

> Often, we unconsciously arrange for someone to function as a kind of savings bank. We deposit our old self in them for safekeeping, trusting them to hold it for us if we decide to come back to claim it. Many of the moratorium women spoke of this process. In describing the ways in which they thought their parents expected them to be, they were describing old selves, ways they used to be. They could, then, have the luxury of experiencing their growth as an external battle, between themselves and their parents, rather than inside themselves. In addition, they knew that their parents were holding the old selves for them, just in case they ever decided to return, which is exactly what many of them did. (p. 138)

Perhaps because moratorium adolescents live with so much indecision themselves, they are tolerant of differences in others. Their ability to question, and to tolerate the uncertainty of not having all the answers, a characteristic they share with identity-achieved adolescents, allows them to transcend the thinking of the group and move beyond social convention. Adolescents who have not examined their values—foreclosed adolescents—are more likely to live lives of conformity and be bound by the expectations of others (Berzonsky & Kuk, 2000; Josselson, 1987).

Identity Diffusion Identity-diffused adolescents, rather than confront issues head-on, tend to avoid them (Berzonsky & Ferrari, 1996; Berzonsky & Kuk, 2000). These adolescents are, in large measure, defined by the absence of strong commitments of their own and by their dismissal of the importance of commitment in others. Their actions, rather than reflecting beliefs or values, are likely to reflect the demands of the situation or the moment. These adolescents are neither rule-bound and authoritarian as are foreclosed adolescents nor truly tolerant as are identity-achieved and moratorium adolescents. Tolerance of differences in both of the latter implies a tension arising out of these differences that is not present in diffused adolescents, because others' ways do not conflict with clear-cut beliefs of their own (Cramer, 2000; Schwartz, Mullis, Waterman, & Dunham, 2000).

A Developing Morality

Adolescents differ from children in important ways with respect to a developing **morality.** Adolescents evaluate others' actions in terms of internalized standards; children do not. Adolescents take the intentions of others into consideration; children judge actions in terms of their consequences. Adolescents can question values; children adopt a fixed standard of right and wrong. How are we to understand these developmental changes?

Answers differ, depending on who is speaking. In the sections that follow, we will consider four approaches to the development of morality: Social-cognitive theory derives from the environmental model; Kohlberg's and Gilligan's approaches reflect the assumptions of the organismic model, as does Freud's.

Social–Cognitive Theory and Moral Development

Why do adolescents internalize the standards of their communities? Why do they become law-abiding citizens? Social-cognitive theorists look to principles of learning for explanations (Bandura, Caprara, Barbaranelli, Pastorelli, & Regalia, 2001; Mischel & Mischel, 1976).

Internalizing Standards

Those who adopt the social-cognitive approach assume that rewards and punishments regulate behavior. These incentives are initially effective in young children only when other people, such as parents and teachers, are around to administer them. As children imitate adult models, they also tell themselves when they have been good or bad, administering their own rewards and punishments.

Community standards determine which behaviors are to be rewarded and which ones punished. In learning the consequences of their behavior, children also acquire the standards of the group. These internalized controls tend to be concrete at first. Children learn specific actions and their consequences; they learn to say thank you, for example, or not to interrupt. In time they also acquire the principles behind these actions. Being polite, for instance, can take the form of a thank-you or considering others' feelings by not interrupting. Thus, social-cognitive theory offers an explanation for internalizing the standards of one's community.

Considering Intentions

How does social-cognitive theory explain age-related changes in moral thought? Children at first do not take the intentions of others into consideration; they judge actions in terms of their consequences. This literal focus is one of the facts that any theory of moral development must address. Social-cognitive theorists point out that the experiences of children make this type of reasoning likely. Adults rarely give children reasons for doing things, often simply relying on physical restraints. Because physical rewards and punishments are common with young children, they are more likely to attend to the re-

morality The development of standards of right and wrong.

wards or punishments that follow what they do than to the reasons that directed their actions.

Parental reactions to damage and messes probably contribute to children's literal focus. Most parents become more upset over big messes than small ones, even though both can be equally unintentional. Consider a child who, keeping out of his mother's way as she fixes dinner, attempts to pour himself a glass of milk. His grip slips as he positions the milk carton, and he watches, transfixed, as a stream of milk sends the cup scudding, flooding the countertop with milk. Is this mother likely to comment on his thoughtfulness at not disturbing her? Probably not. This child, like most, will be scolded for making a mess. It makes sense that children fail to understand that intentions can enter into one's evaluation of a situation when their intentions are so imperfectly considered.

Questioning Values

Social-cognitive theory also explains the questioning of values that occurs in adolescence. Parents and teachers expect adolescents to start thinking for themselves, to evaluate ideas on their merit instead of accepting the endorsement of authorities. Social-cognitive theorists argue that we subtly reward adolescents for questioning the very ideas we taught them to uncritically accept as children. Similarly, learning experiences explain the relativistic form of thought that emerges in many adolescents as they near their twenties. Exposure to new values challenges them to consider their own values as one of a number of possible belief systems.

Acting Morally

How likely are adolescents to act in ways that reflect their moral understanding? In part, it depends on the incentives. *Incentives* are the rewards and punishments for acting in particular ways. Martin Ford and his associates (1989) asked adolescents to indicate how they would respond in a situation involving conflict (for example, giving a friend exam questions versus abiding by the school's honor code) if they could be sure that nothing bad would happen to them if they acted irresponsibly, and then to imagine what they would do if there were negative social consequences (such as getting grounded, peer disapproval). As expected, adolescents were considerably more likely to choose the socially responsible alternative when there would be negative consequences for not doing so; the results are shown in Figure 11.3. The emotions motivating their choice reflected both external consequences, like fear of negative sanctions, and internalized ones, such as anticipated guilt and empathic concern. Choices were more likely to be motivated by self-interest or concern with peer approval when negative consequences were not anticipated.

When they were younger, these rollerbladers, along with many skateboarders, probably enjoyed the thrill of skating where they weren't supposed to if they knew they wouldn't be caught. Now, because their moral reasoning is more mature, they are more likely to limit their rollerblading or skateboarding to legal sites.

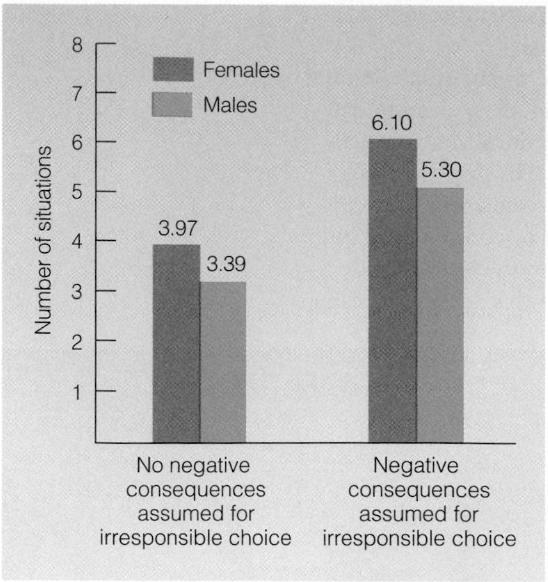

FIGURE 11.3
Mean Number of Situations in Which Adolescents Choose to Act Responsibly.
Source: M. E. Ford, K. R. Wentzel, D. Wood, E. Stevens, & G. A. Siesfeld. (1989). Processes associated with integrative social competence: Emotional and contextual influence on adolescent social responsibility. *Journal of Adolescent Research, 4,* 405–425.

Factors other than incentives also affect the likelihood of action. Adolescents are more likely to imitate the actions of prestigious people than of those whom they don't regard as important. Models who are nurturant are also more likely to be imitated, perhaps because we like them more than less nurturant people and want to be like them. Models who are similar to us in one or more ways are also likely to be imitated, again perhaps because we can imagine being like them.

Moral Virtues

Although psychology as a discipline has tended to focus more on negative emotions and behaviors than positive ones, especially with respect to adolescents, the recent positive psychology movement (Seligman & Csikszentmihalyi, 2000) has refocused our attention on human virtues such as gratitude, forgiveness, self-control, and hope (Emmons & Paloutzian, 2003). Michael McCullough and Robert Emmons and their associates (2001), for instance, consider gratitude to be a moral reinforcer, in that individuals are more likely to engage in prosocial behaviors when others express gratitude to them for what they have done. Thus, individuals are likely to choose to act in prosocial ways not only because there may be negative consequences for not doing so, but also because their actions are reinforced by others through their expressions of gratitude. These investigators also view gratitude as a motivator, in that individuals who experience gratitude are inspired to act in more positive ways toward others (McCullough, Emmons, & Tsang, 2002).

Critique of Social-Cognitive Theory

How well does this approach explain how adolescents actually act in a moral situation? Let's look at a common behavior among students—academic cheating. High school students report that they frequently cheat even though they consider it wrong to do so (Davis, Grover, Becker, & McGregor, 1992). Social-cognitive theory reminds us, however, that what people do is not necessarily what they believe is right. Instead, whether adolescents are likely to cheat is influenced by situational factors such as the normative behavior of classmates (Eisenberg, 2004; Vowell & Chen, 2004) and the amount of risk involved (Eisenberg, 2004; Underwood & Szabo, 2003). What is rewarded in the classroom also influences the likelihood of cheating; students are less likely to cheat in classrooms that reward mastery of the material than the grade one gets on a test (Anderman & Midgley, 2004; Murdock, Miller, & Kohlhardt, 2004). Students' attitudes concerning the seriousness of cheating are also important, with those judging it to be less serious engaging in cheating more often (Jensen, Arnett, Feldman, & Caufman, 2002).

Little mention has been made about conscience in this discussion. Social-cognitive theory suggests that many internalized controls are not necessarily related to moral values or to conscience; they simply reflect conditioning. Adolescents become helpful or law-abiding in order to avoid the anxiety they associate with doing otherwise. Conscience, when it does apply to behavior, is merely the set of standards one internalizes with the learning process. For social-cognitive theorists, there is no inner voice other than the echo of the voices around them.

Kohlberg: The Development of Moral Reasoning

What makes one moral? Is it simply that one internalizes the standards of one's community? Is it ever possible for individuals to function at a higher level than the society in which they live? Where does a sense of justice come from if it is not present in the social order? Lawrence Kohlberg's theory of moral reasoning addresses these questions.

Kohlberg's (1976, 1984) theory bases its assumptions about moral development on the organismic model, stressing the importance of the inner forces that organize development. The most important of these forces is a sense of justice, which underlies the highest forms of moral thought.

Kohlberg's theory traces moral reasoning over a number of discrete stages. Movement from one stage to the next is prompted by the need to resolve conflict. This conflict arises when one realizes that others view things differently. Individuals gain insight into the perspectives of others through increases in role-taking skills. As they become able to put themselves in the place of another, they can see things as that person does. Cognitive maturity—the ability to think about and balance the competing demands produced by examining several perspectives—also contributes to moral development. Kohlberg assumes that one's level of cognitive development places limits on the sophistication of moral thinking (Kohlberg, 1976, 1984).

Kohlberg traces moral development over three levels of moral reasoning, with two stages at each level. The levels reflect the stance adolescents take in relation to the standards of their community. Not all standards reflect moral issues. Some standards exist as laws, others simply as conventions or customary ways of behaving. It is the law, for example, that one not take another person's life; it is customary that one not giggle when hearing of another's death. Both of these reflect a common value—the sacredness of life. But only when adolescents reach the postconventional level of moral reasoning do they distinguish social convention, whether codified as laws or customs, from the values these conventions reflect. And only then, according to Kohlberg, can they distinguish conventional concerns from moral ones. The In More Depth box presents Kohlberg's levels of moral development and corresponding stages of moral reasoning.

Children at the level of **preconventional moral reasoning** want only to satisfy their needs and not get punished while doing so. At this level, they have not internalized the standards of their community even though they know what these standards are. They abide by the rules only when someone else is around. The "rule enforcers," and not the rules, constrain their actions. In the absence of the former, anything goes as long as you don't get caught (Kohlberg, 1984).

By adolescence, most adopt the standards of their community and reach the level of **conventional moral reasoning**. Simply observing the behavior of individuals at the first of Kohlberg's two levels does not reveal underlying differences. Kohlberg stresses the importance of the motives behind actions, not just the actions themselves, when evaluating moral conduct. Those at the conventional level want to live up to the standards of their group and are not motivated simply by the desire to avoid punishment. These standards have become their own; they are no longer other people's rules. In one sense, though, their behavior still lacks internal control, because the standards they live by are set by others rather than by themselves.

Only at the level of **postconventional moral reasoning** do adolescents and young adults develop genuine inner controls over behavior; the principles by which they live are self-derived standards rather than the conventions of their community and are assumed

preconventional moral reasoning Kohlberg's first level of moral reasoning, characterized by the absence of internalized standards.

conventional moral reasoning Kohlberg's second level of moral reasoning, in which moral thinking is guided by internalized social standards.

postconventional moral reasoning Kohlberg's third level of moral reasoning, in which moral thinking is guided by self-derived principles.

IN MORE DEPTH

Kohlberg's Stages of Moral Reasoning

Preconventional Level of Moral Reasoning

Stage 1: Obedience

Perspective	Only one's own
Motive	To satisfy one's needs; avoid punishment
Standards	The rules of others
Criteria	Consequences

Stage 2: Instrumental

Perspective	One's own and a second person's
Motive	To satisfy one's needs and those of the other
Standards	The rules of others
Criteria	Fairness

Conventional Level of Moral Reasoning

Stage 3: Conformist, or "Good Boy, Nice Girl"

Perspective	A third person's
Motive	To receive approval from others
Standards	Internalized rules
Criteria	Living up to expectations

Stage 4: Social Accord, or "Law and Order"

Perspective	The community's
Motive	To uphold the law
Standards	Rules codified as laws
Criteria	Compliance with the law

Postconventional Level of Moral Reasoning

Stage 5: Social Contract

Perspective	Society's, as seen by someone from another society
Motive	To maintain the social order
Standards	Laws as agreements among those governed
Criteria	Justice

Stage 6: Universal Principles

Perspective	Any society's as seen by humankind
Motive	To ensure human rights for all
Standards	Personal principles
Criteria	Universal moral values

to reflect values that are universal and common to all cultures. Motives, as well, reflect a sense of obligation to live within a code that is determined by one's principles. Thus, Kohlberg distinguishes levels of moral development in terms of both a progressive internalization of standards for behavior and motives for living according to these standards (Hoffman, 1980; Kohlberg, 1984).

Preconventional Moral Reasoning

Stage 1: Obedience Individuals at this stage (usually children) assume that everyone sees things as they do, not realizing that their view of a situation is just one of several possible perspectives. Consequently, they experience little or no conflict in their interactions with others. Their actions reflect only a need to satisfy their own desires, without getting punished for doing so. Stage 1 morality is not reflective; individuals do not take motives and intentions into consideration (they do not understand others' feelings and points of view easily). They judge behavior simply in terms of its consequences. Actions that are rewarded must have been good; those that were punished, bad. Read the dilemma presented in the In More Depth box "Rachel's Dilemma" before continuing, then consider how a stage 1 adolescent might respond to this situation.

What should Rachel do? Kohlberg reminds us that it is the reasoning rather than the answer itself that reveals the stage at which an adolescent is functioning. Adolescents at stage 1 might not report Elsie to the school counselor, fearing that the counselor would

IN MORE DEPTH

Rachel's Dilemma

Rachel didn't know what to do. Elsie looked so whacked out she could hardly put one foot in front of the other. Was it lack of sleep? (Elsie *did* party a lot.) Or was she actually on something? They had experimented with marijuana together, and Rachel suspected that Elsie had tried other drugs. Elsie had once started to talk about her friends and the parties they went to. It sounded like they did a lot of drugs. Elsie had gotten nervous when Rachel asked her about this. She'd changed the subject, and Rachel never heard any more about it. Elsie no longer wanted to get together with Rachel and their old friends, even referring to them as "small time" once. Rachel could see even from here that Elsie's eyes looked funny, like she was having a hard time focusing, even though it was only second-period gym class. She was perspiring, too, and the air conditioning was on. Should she tell her counselor that she thought Elsie was on drugs? Elsie and she had once promised each other they would never betray their confidence about smoking marijuana. And if she reported Elsie, her parents would almost surely find out that she also had experimented with drugs. She could forget about that lifeguard job this summer. They'd never let her out of their sight. Then again, drugs could kill.

discover that they, too, had used drugs and that punishment would result. Conversely, they might report her, fearing that they would be punished if they didn't. There is nothing in this reasoning to indicate conflict over which course of action is *right;* decisions are based on the potential impact the actions have for oneself.

Stage 2: Instrumental, or Considering Intentions As adolescents become better able to put themselves in the place of another person, they can see things as the other person would. Adopting the other's perspective gives them two points of view and, in turn, the likelihood that they will experience conflict. Which perspective is right? They can understand the reasons for the other person's actions and know that the other can understand theirs—that each of them can consider the intentions of the other. Adolescents who reason at this level don't have to rely on others' reactions to evaluate behavior. They can look at the motives behind an action. Even though fairness is central to reasoning at this stage, morality is still preconventional because adolescents consider only the actions and intentions of those they are with and not the rules or laws of the group, whether the school or community.

What would Rachel do? First consider the reasoning that would lead a stage 2 adolescent to believe Rachel should not report Elsie. This adolescent knows it's the rule to report anyone using drugs. However, Elsie and Rachel had made an agreement never to tell on each other. It's only fair for Rachel to live up to that promise. Besides, if she reported Elsie, she'd almost surely get caught herself. Best to let everyone take care of themselves in this case. The reasoning that might lead an adolescent to say that Rachel should report Elsie is similarly self-serving. Rachel might be rewarded in some way for reporting her friend; even if the authorities found out that she, too, had experimented with drugs, they would not punish her as severely as if she didn't indicate her respect for the rules by reporting those who she knew were breaking them.

Conventional Moral Reasoning: Internalizing Standards

Stage 3: Conformist, or "Good Boy, Nice Girl" The self-reflection that comes with formal thought makes it possible for adolescents to see themselves as they imagine others would. This third-person perspective forms the basis for taking the norms of their group, in the form of concern with what others think of them, into consideration, and

RESEARCH FOCUS

Statistical Tests of Significance: What Do a *Huai Haizi*, a *Warui Ko*, and a Bad Kid Have in Common?

None of the students seemed to notice the chatter of birds outside the classroom window, or other signs of spring in Taipei, as they bent over their desks, completing the questionnaire. These Chinese adolescents had been asked to think of someone they knew who was a *huai haizi*, a "bad kid," and to describe what kind of person that was. In another classroom nearly a thousand miles away, Japanese students were asked to describe a *warui ko* (bad kid), as were yet other students, American adolescents in Minneapolis, who were similarly asked to describe a "bad kid."

How comparable were the descriptions of these adolescents? To what extent do perceptions of deviance reflect the social values of one's culture? Are the behaviors that American teenagers think of as bad similarly bad in other cultures?

David Crystal and Harold Stevenson (1995), at the University of Michigan, set out to get answers to such questions by asking Chinese, Japanese, and American eleventh-graders what a "bad kid" meant to them. After coding their responses to the open-ended questions (see the Research Focus "Coding Descriptive Responses" on the Web site) into 12 types of behavior, they found that 40% of the Chinese students mentioned society-related behaviors, such as "rebels against society," "makes trouble for society," or "is a member of a street gang," whereas only 29% of the American adolescents described a bad kid this way, and even fewer Japanese students did (14%). Other interesting differences emerged. The most frequently mentioned behaviors by Japanese students (84%) made reference to disruptions of interpersonal harmony, such as "hurting other people's feelings," "being argumentative and starting fights," and "speaking badly of other people"; only 50% and 53% of Chinese and American adolescents, respectively, mentioned such behaviors. American adolescents, on the other hand, were most likely to mention behaviors related to self-control, 38% referring to being "weak-willed," "childish," or "immature"; in

here adolescents move into conventional reasoning. This concern about the opinions of others adds a new dimension to morality: the need to live up to the expectations of others. Kohlberg believes that stage 3 reasoning is dominant during adolescence and even common in adulthood (Kohlberg, 1984). The prevalence of stage 3 reasoning helps to explain adolescents' sensitivity to the approval of peers. Rather than thinking through a situation in terms of the claims of those involved, adolescents are likely to be swayed by the opinions of their friends.

How would stage 3 adolescents reason about Rachel's dilemma? Reasoning that leads to not reporting Elsie would focus on loyalty among friends—how would Rachel look turning in a friend? Reasoning that leads to reporting her would focus on what her teachers and parents would think of her for *not* reporting Elsie. The decision turns on which reference group the adolescent considers: that of friends and peers or that of teachers and parents. The Research Focus "Statistical Tests of Significance" illustrates how cultural values can affect adolescents' evaluations of their own and others' behavior.

Stage 4: Social Accord, or "Law and Order" As the ability to think more abstractly increases, adolescents begin to see themselves as members of an invisible but nonetheless real community. As such, they realize the need to evaluate actions by the community's standards. Kohlberg believes that reasoning at the fourth stage is frequently the highest that most people reach.

Rachel's dilemma takes on new proportions for adolescents at stage 4. On the one hand, friendship demands that she not betray Elsie to the authorities; her duty is to be loyal to her friend. On the other hand, Rachel has a duty to live within the law and to see contrast, only 24% of Chinese and Japanese students did so.

What are we to make of these differences? Can we conclude that adolescents from each of these cultures differ in what they consider to be bad? How different must their answers be in order to support this conclusion? After all, each adolescent is an individual, and one can always expect slight variances simply as a result of individual differences. Unexplained variability, such as individual differences, that is not due to the variable being investigated is termed **random error.**

To determine whether a difference between two groups is due to random error or whether it reflects the variable being studied, one uses a **test of significance.** Common tests are chi-square, t-tests, and F-tests. If the value obtained is larger than a tabled value for the same number of participants, one can reject the assumption that random error was responsible and attribute the difference to the independent variable. Probability theory tells us that the likelihood that random error is responsible for the difference decreases with increases in the number of participants in each group. Thus, with larger numbers of participants, one needs a smaller difference to reject the assumption that random error was responsible.

Crystal and Stevenson's statistical tests comparing differences in the frequencies with which adolescents from the three cultures mentioned different types of behaviors were significant. Chinese students were significantly more likely to mention society-related behavior than American or Japanese students; Japanese students were significantly more likely to mention interpersonal behavior than were Chinese or American students; and American students were significantly more likely to mention self-control than were Chinese or Japanese students.

Bad kids—unlike roses, which, the poet tells us, would still be a rose by any other name—do not differ in name only. Each culture has its own profile of social values and, although there is considerable overlap from one culture to the next, what is considered to be "bad" differs to the extent that the most prominent values in a culture, but not necessarily those in another, are violated.

Source: D.S. Crystal & H. W. Stevenson. (1995). What is a bad kid? Answers of adolescents and their mothers in three cultures. *Journal of Research on Adolescence, 5,* 71–91.

that others do as well. After all, if everyone "did their own thing," the system would break down. Stage 4 reasoning is usually adequate for most situations. It breaks down, however, when laws conflict with human values. When this occurs, adolescents must develop a way to see their society in relation to the needs of others.

Postconventional Moral Reasoning: Questioning Values

Stage 5: Social Contract Kohlberg believes that adolescents move into stage 5 only when they have been exposed to other value systems, usually in late adolescence. Individuals who come to respect others' ways of life find it difficult to continue seeing their own as more valid. Once adolescents recognize that their society's conventions are in some sense arbitrary, they are forced to look beyond the conventions themselves to the function they serve. When they do, they discover that laws derive their importance because they represent agreements among people who live together, not because they are right in and of themselves. Members of a society enter into a contract with others in the society in which they agree to live within its laws, forgoing some individual freedoms, for the mutual benefit of all.

Stage 5 adolescents might reason that Rachel should not report Elsie because the way she has chosen to live her life reflects her values, and values are relative. They might add that Rachel is obliged to act in a way that protects each person's rights, including Elsie's, and might remind us that Rachel and Elsie had entered into a contractual agreement concerning their use of drugs. Reasons for reporting Elsie would stress that, as members

random error Unexplained and unsystematic variability.

test of significance A statistical procedure for determining whether group differences are due to random error or can be attributed to the variable being studied.

In the course of moral development, adolescents come to see themselves not only as members of the community but also as able to challenge community decisions that they feel are wrong. These high school students are attending a school board meeting to protest the dropping of a class.

of society, Rachel and Elsie have implicitly agreed to keep the laws of their community and that these laws must be upheld for the greater good of all.

Stage 6: Universal Principles This stage provides adolescents with yet another perspective: seeing past the mutual agreements shared by members of a society to the values these agreements reflect. The social contracts we enter into reflect underlying values such as truth, justice, honor, and the value of life itself. The step that late adolescents take in order to gain a perspective on their society removes them from the claims of time and circumstance. Kohlberg asserts that all societies throughout history have recognized these values—that they are, in fact, universal ethical principles. Those who reason at this final stage understand that societal conventions are imperfect reflections of these values and, consequently, individuals must look beyond conventions, and even laws, to their own principles when arriving at moral decisions (Kohlberg, 1984).

Why might Rachel not report Elsie to the counselor? Stage 6 reasoning stresses the honor among friends that would require Rachel to keep her word with Elsie. Conversely, those who reason that Rachel should report Elsie would be likely to mention the value of Elsie's life, which is threatened by her use of drugs. They might add that even if they were in Elsie's place, they would expect to be turned in by anyone else who opposes the use of life-threatening drugs. This last reason illustrates a point that Kohlberg makes about stage 6 individuals. He describes them as able to imagine themselves in the place of every other person in a situation and to impartially evaluate the rights of each. The image of the stage 6 person is that of the blindfolded figure of Justice who weighs the claims of each without knowing which person has made which claim. This ability is truly an idealized form of role-taking, and very few people function at this level (Kohlberg, 1984).

When Justice May Not Be Enough: Forgiveness

We know a lot about the development of justice in adolescents. But we know relatively little about forgiveness. Justice is a consideration of competing claims among individuals; it weighs them and makes a decision in favor of one or the other. Forgiveness is a decision to release a person from a claim that justice would honor.

How are forgiveness and justice related? Is forgiveness just a special case of justice, one in which the injured person turns over any claims for retribution? If forgiveness *is* different, does it develop with age and social understanding as does justice? Are these different moralities? To the extent that certain religions, such as Christianity, emphasize the importance of forgiving, will forgiveness be related to the practice of one's faith?

Robert Enright, Maria Santos, and Radhi Al-Mabuk (1989) presented individuals of several ages with situations in which justice or forgiveness were called for. One of these described the dilemma of a man whose wife is dying of cancer. The man unsuccessfully attempts to persuade a druggist who has patented an expensive drug to sell him enough at a reduced price to save his wife's life. The druggist refuses, pointing out that it is through the sale of the drug that he makes his livelihood. In the justice scenario, individuals consider the competing claims of life versus private property. In the forgiveness scenario, the druggist anticipates that the man will try to steal the drug and hides it. The wife dies. Individuals answer questions that reflect stages of forgiveness by the husband ranging from vengeful retribution to unconditional forgiveness based on a principle of love. The degree of religiousness for each individual was also measured.

These investigators found that reasoning about forgiveness, just as about justice, becomes more mature with age. Adolescents find it easiest to be forgiving when they know it's expected of them (expectational forgiveness). Children are likely to say they can forgive only if they first get back what they lost (restitutional forgiveness). Adults are likely to forgive because it is required by their religion, or to defer to a higher authority (lawful forgiveness). Their forgiveness, like that of adolescents, however, is conditional. With the latter, it depends on encouragement from others, mainly friends, and with the former, from a religious authority. Relatively few instances of *unconditional,* or principled, forgiveness (based on a principle of loving others) were found, and all of these occurred among adults. Other research as well has found that unconditional forgiveness is most likely to occur among adults; when it does, it is most likely to be evidenced by the elderly (Mullet & Girard, 2000).

In many ways, reasoning about forgiveness parallels Kohlberg's stages of moral reasoning about justice. Those who can forgive only after first punishing the offender or otherwise recouping their losses (the lowest stages of forgiveness) are also likely to reason at Kohlberg's lowest (preconventional) level of moral reasoning. The conditional forgiveness of adolescents and early adults reflects the conventional level of moral reasoning described by Kohlberg; both depend on social supports. Unconditional forgiveness, the highest stage, reflects a principled (Kohlberg's postconventional) reasoning that emphasizes the importance of loving others. These parallels suggest the contribution of similar role-taking skills for each type of reasoning. In addition, religious beliefs and practices appear to contribute to reasoning about forgiveness. Adolescents who practiced their faith, for example, attending church and Bible study groups, had more mature approaches to forgiveness. Among a sample of college students and parents, religiosity has been found to be unrelated to forgiveness when the offense has been committed by someone close, such as a family member or friend. However, when the offense has been committed by a more distant person, such as an employer or a general "other," those who indicated they practiced their religion were more likely to forgive (Subkoviak et al., 1995).

Research on forgiveness suggests that if adolescents are to learn to forgive, they need the support of friends who encourage them to adopt forgiveness as part of their approach to resolving interpersonal conflicts. Why forgive in the first place? Often other strategies of conflict resolution are equally appropriate. Many times, however, these leave the injured person with residual anger and resentment. The decision to release another from obligation, however, can free the person who has been injured from these feelings and open the way to restoring the relationship.

Critique of Kohlberg's Theory

Influence of Parents Versus Peers Kohlberg assumed that increases in role-taking skills contributed to moral reasoning and that these skills were gained primarily through interactions with peers. Specifically, in order to resolve conflicts, children and adolescents had to be able to integrate perspectives that differed from their own. Supporting this assumption, Kimberly Schonert-Reichl (1999) found that boys who reasoned at higher moral levels indicated that the conflicts they had with their friends took longer to resolve, suggesting that what they went through in resolving their disagreements contributed to their moral reasoning. It is also possible, of course, that adolescents who are better at reasoning will spend more time doing this, for the sheer enjoyment of the argument. With correlational data such as this, Schonert-Reichl points out, one can never be sure of the direction of effect.

Similar instances of perspective-sharing with parents may have comparable effects on adolescents' moral reasoning, despite Kohlberg's assumption that peers, rather than parents, are the ones to exert a major influence on moral development. In a two-year longitudinal study, early adolescents whose fathers extended, challenged, and clarified their reasoning showed gains in moral reasoning in late adolescence. In a like manner, those whose mothers were more open and responsive to their actions and ideas, showing more perspective-sharing and engagement, reasoned at higher levels as late adolescents (Pratt, Arnold, Pratt, & Diessner, 1999).

Evidence of Stages Kohlberg's is also a developmental theory, and, as such, one would expect older individuals to reason at higher stages than younger ones. Rosemary Jadack, Janet Shibley Hyde, Colleen Moore, and Mary Keller (1995), at the University of Wisconsin, Madison, asked students differing in age to consider dilemmas concerning sexual behavior in which a character must decide whether to tell a partner about the presence of a sexually transmitted disease. These investigators found that older college students (mean age 22 years) generally reasoned at a higher level, as assessed by a scoring system designed for use with Kohlberg's dilemmas, than did younger students (mean age 18 years). Younger students focused more on the likelihood of simply acquiring the disease, whereas older students introduced issues of responsibility and accountability.

Implicit in the assumption of developmental change is the expectation that reasoning can be characterized, at any point, as being at one stage or another. However, reasoning about different situations has often been found to reflect a number of adjacent stages (Jadack et al., 1985).

Moral Issues Versus Social Conventions Do most adolescents and adults reason at stages 3 and 4, as Kohlberg asserts? Snarey (1985) reviewed nearly 50 studies that had used Kohlberg's scale and found that 75% of the individuals who were interviewed reasoned entirely at the conventional level or at a combination of conventional and preconventional levels. Less than 10% functioned at higher levels. Similarly, Schweder, Mahapatra, and Miller (1987) reported that only 15% of the children and adults they interviewed treated conventional rules (such as those governing table manners or forms of greeting) as if they could be changed. These data suggest that most people do not distinguish moral issues from social conventions.

Joan Miller and David Bersoff (1989), of Yale University, questioned this conclusion. They found that adults and children alike considered the usefulness of social conventions before deciding whether they could be changed. Nearly 80% thought it wrong to violate conventions that are useful (those that maintain order, such as using properly marked exits), but less than 15% felt it wrong to violate ones with little usefulness (such as standards of dress). Rules with little utility were accepted only for private settings. Violating the same restrictions in a public setting was not considered wrong, whereas violating a moral rule was considered wrong irrespective of the setting—and by individuals of all ages (Miller & Bersoff, 1989).

Both morals and conventions set forth rules for behavior; however, each relates rules to behavior in different ways. Elliot Turiel (1983), a psychologist at the University of California, Berkeley, maintains that even very young children distinguish moral rules from conventional ones. Conventional rules reflect accepted ways of doing things. As these change, so do the rules. Standards of dress and speech reflect these flexible relationships. The rules relating moral concerns to behavior are inflexible. Moral rules reflect a concern for the well-being of others and do not change with climates of opinion.

Charles Helwig, Carolyn Hildebrandt, and Elliot Turiel (1995) interviewed first-, third-, and fifth-graders and found that nearly all the children agreed that moral acts such as pushing someone down would not be all right even in the context of a game that legitimized such actions. The youngest children, however, were less clear about acts leading to psychological harm, such as name-calling as part of a game. Similarly, Larry Nucci, Cleanice Camino, and Clary Sapiro (1996), interviewing 9- and 15-year-olds in Brazil, found that children as well as adolescents distinguished moral from conventional issues, agreeing that if there were no rules against doing so, it would be all right not to wear a school uniform, but not to hit or steal. These data indicate that even children distinguish moral from conventional concerns; Kohlberg assumes that one makes this distinction only with the fifth stage of reasoning.

If even children can distinguish moral issues, how can we explain the developmental progression that Kohlberg has noted? Martin Hoffman (1980) answers that we socialize children in either of two very different ways: One way stresses being obedient and following the rules; the other emphasizes altruism and a concern for others. Hoffman points out that it is possible for young children to comply with both sets of demands because the behaviors called for by either usually apply in different settings. However, older children frequently experience conflict between the demands for living by the rules and their prosocial concerns. Hoffman suggests that the emergence of truly moral concerns in adolescence is actually a resurgence of earlier prosocial ones that had been channeled into conventional behavior in middle childhood in the course of acquiring society's norms (Hoffman, 1980, 1988).

In addition to assuming that the level at which individuals reason increases with age, Kohlberg has assumed that the highest levels of moral reasoning reflect universal values that are common to all cultures. Research on moral behavior and judgment, however, finds evidence for cultural differences in values. Cooperation, maintaining harmonious relations with others, and working for the common good, for instance, are more highly valued in Hispanic and Asian cultures than in Western European ones. Thus, social context appears to influence moral development more than Kohlberg initially had assumed (Carlo, Fabes, Laible, & Kupanoff, 1999).

Kohlberg's theory, despite the debate it has occasioned, enjoys wide support. His theory has an intrinsic elegance. Each of the six stages is a logical extension of the preceding one, and the progression is systematically related to new role-taking skills and cognitive maturity. But there may be another reason to account for the popularity of this theory: Kohlberg has given us a sympathetic view of human nature. He accounts for our ability to control our behavior in terms of the development of an inner sense of justice, rather than the "carrot and stick" approach of social-cognitive theory.

Carol Gilligan questions whether justice is the highest arbiter of moral issues. She finds that an ethic of care, rather than a morality of justice, is more characteristic of females. She points out that Kohlberg developed his theory based on interviews with only males. Like many developmentalists before him, Kohlberg equated the male perspective with development in general (see Chapter 2).

Gilligan: An Ethic of Care

Carol Gilligan (1982, 1989a, 1996), of Harvard University, gives a fresh perspective on moral development, one that balances male-oriented theories such as Kohlberg's and Freud's with insights gained from interviews with females. Gilligan found that most females think of morality more personally than males do; they adopt an **ethic of care.** They speak of morality in terms of their responsibilities to others rather than as the rights of individuals. Their moral decisions are based on compassion as well as reason, and they stress care for others as well as fairness.

Gilligan traces these approaches to differences in the way females and males define themselves in relation to others. Whereas males tend to view themselves as separate from others, females see themselves in terms of their relationships with others. These themes of separation and connectedness translate into different approaches to morality. The assumption that one is separate from others highlights the need for rules to regulate the actions of each person with respect to the other; the assumption that one is connected to others emphasizes the responsibility each has to the other (Gilligan, 1982).

Gender differences also exist in the way individuals think of responsibility (see Chapter 2). Males tend to think of responsibility as *not* doing something that would infringe on the rights of others, such as not hurting them. Females think of responsibility in terms of *meeting* the needs of others, that is, as something to be done. Both males and females are concerned with not hurting others, yet each sex thinks of this in a different way. Gilligan points out that, given differences such as these, attempts to chart moral development as a single sequence are bound to give us only half the picture.

Gilligan traces moral development in females through three levels, each of which reflects a different resolution to the conflict between responsibility to self and responsibility to others. Movement from one level to the next occurs in two transitional periods. At the first level, the primary concern is with oneself. Transition to the next level occurs when one sees caring only for oneself as selfish and at odds with responsibility to others. At the second level, females equate morality with goodness and self-sacrifice—caring for others. Transition to the third level occurs when they experience problems in their relationships that result from excluding themselves from their own care. At the third level, they equate morality with care for both themselves and others.

Level 1: Caring for Self (Survival)

The primary concerns at this level of moral development are pragmatic: What's best for me? The motivation is survival. Actions are guided by self-interest and self-preservation. Gilligan (1982) says of this perspective that "the woman focuses on taking care of herself because she feels that she is all alone. From this perspective, *should* is undifferentiated from *would,* and other people influence the decision only through their power to affect its consequences" (p. 75). Gilligan notes that the issue of "rightness" is considered only when one's own needs are in conflict and force the individual to consider which need is more important. Otherwise, there is little conflict over making the right decision.

Why might individuals function at this level? Gilligan believes that a preoccupation with one's needs reflects feelings of helplessness and powerlessness. These feelings have

ethic of care Gilligan's description of a morality based on responsiveness to and care for others.

Because females define themselves in relation to others and males define themselves as separate from others, the course of their moral development is different, according to psychologist Carol Gilligan.

their origin in being emotionally cut off, or *disconnected,* from others. The young women she interviewed who were at this level had frequently experienced disappointing relationships in which they had been hurt by others. These women often chose to hold themselves apart from others rather than experience further pain. Feeling alone and cut off from others, they were left with the sense that they had to look to their own needs, because no one else would (Gilligan, 1982).

This first level is similar to Kohlberg's preconventional level of moral reasoning. In neither level do individuals consider others except for their possible reactions to what they do, that is, except as potential consequences for their actions. Conflict is also absent in both levels, and self-interest, rather than the need to make the right decision, dictates what one does.

Transition: From Selfishness to Responsibility Individuals begin to move beyond the first level when they experience a discrepancy between the way they are and the way they feel they ought to be, that is, between self-concern and responsible concern for others. A certain amount of self-worth is needed in order to move through this transitional phase. One must feel sufficiently good about oneself in order to see oneself as having the capacity for good and to be included in the social group (Gilligan, 1982).

Level 2: Caring for Others (Goodness)

Gilligan assumes that females move to a second level of moral development when they internalize social conventions. The progression is similar to that described by Kohlberg for movement from preconventional to conventional reasoning. Gilligan (1982) notes that in the first level,

> morality is a matter of sanctions imposed by a society of which one is more subject than citizen, [and in the second] moral judgment relies on shared norms and expectations. The woman at this point validates her claim to social membership through the adoption of societal values. Consensual judgment about goodness becomes the overriding concern as survival is now seen to depend on acceptance by others. (p. 79)

Transition: From Conformity to Choice The equation of morality with conventional feminine goodness is a step toward repairing the failed relationships that led to a preoccupation with the self at the first level. But this equation creates a second imbalance that itself is in need of repair. Conventional images of feminine goodness center on the care of others. They also involve self-sacrifice. Females at the second level of morality purchase membership in the larger community at the cost of caring for themselves. The price of membership is costly and introduces tensions that, for some, will prompt movement to the third level. These individuals realize that excluding themselves from their own care creates as many problems as excluding others had done previously; in other words, goodness results in as much hurt as selfishness (Gilligan, 1986). This realization is an important step in moving to an ethic of care that includes themselves as well as others. Gilligan, like Kohlberg before her, believes that many females do not take this step and do not develop beyond conventional forms of thought.

Level 3: Caring for Self and Others (Truth)

To move into the third level, females must move beyond the conventional wisdom that tells them to put the needs of others above their own. In doing so, they must reformulate their definition of care to include themselves as well as others. As females reconsider their relationships with others, they once again must consider their own needs. Questions such as "Is this selfish?" again arise. Because these occur in the context of relationships with others, they also prompt a reexamination of the concept of responsibility.

When one moves beyond conventional forms of wisdom, one finds there is no one to turn to for answers but oneself. Females at this level cannot rely on what others might think; they must exercise their own judgment. This judgment requires that they be honest with themselves. Being responsible for themselves, as well as for others, means they must know what their needs actually are. As Gilligan (1982) asserts, "The criterion for judgment thus shifts from goodness to truth when the morality of action is assessed not on the basis of its appearance in the eyes of others, but in terms of the realities of its intention and consequence" (p. 83). The bottom line is simple: To care for oneself, one must first be honest with oneself and acknowledge the reasons behind one's actions.

Individuals at this level adopt an inclusive perspective that gives equal weight to their responsibility to themselves and to others. Care extends to all. To exclude the self would introduce pain that could otherwise be avoided, and their commitment to minimizing pain requires a new balance of concern for self with responsibility for others.

Although Gilligan and Kohlberg document developmental sequences that parallel each other in many respects, a critical difference separates these two accounts. Kohlberg believes that his sequence is a path universally trodden by all individuals as they move into adulthood. He assumes that this sequence takes the form it does because it reflects developments in cognitive maturity that have a strong biological component (see the discussion of Piaget in Chapter 2). Gilligan is not equally convinced that the sequence she documents in adolescent girls and young women is developmentally necessary. She does not believe the sequence to be "rooted in childhood," as does Kohlberg. She suggests, instead, that it is a response to a crisis, and that the crisis is adolescence itself (Gilligan, 1989a).

Gilligan proposes that leaving childhood is problematic for girls in ways that it is not for boys. The problem lies with the culture each enters. Adolescence introduces the expectation that children will assume the conventions of their society, whether these be adult gender roles, the knowledge that forms the basis of cultural wisdom, or behaviors that fit prescribed definitions of "goodness" and "rightness." Why should this expectation present more problems for girls?

Gilligan's answer is powerful. The most visible figures populating the landscape of adulthood are males—whether plumbers, politicians, poets, or philosophers—and their collective experiences form its norms. Girls risk losing themselves as they relax the intimate bonds of childhood to embrace a larger world of experience. Gilligan (1989b) writes:

> As the river of a girl's life flows into the sea of Western culture, she is in danger of drowning or disappearing. To take on the problem of her appearance, which is the problem of her development, and to connect her life with history on a cultural scale, she must enter—and by entering disrupt—a tradition in which "human" has for the most part meant male. Thus a struggle often breaks out in girls' lives at the edge of adolescence. (p. 4)

The problem is pervasive because it is woven into the very fabric of cultural thought. Even formal education, Gilligan suggests, presents a challenge to female identity: "In learning to think in the terms of the disciplines and thus to bring her thoughts and feelings into line with the traditions of Western culture, . . . she also learn[s] to dismiss her own experience" (p. 2).

Gilligan traces the crisis of connection for girls to their ability to find a "voice" with which to speak and a context in which they will be heard. The culture they are entering has not been equally responsive to the voices of women and men, "or at least has not been up to the present. The wind of tradition blowing through women is a chill wind, because it brings a message of exclusion. . . . The message to women is: keep quiet and notice the absence of women and say nothing" (Gilligan, 1989a, p. 26).

Critique of Gilligan's Theory

What evidence is there for gender differences in moral concerns? Although a **meta-analysis** of research on gender differences in moral reasoning found differences favoring a care orientation for females and a justice orientation for males, these differences were small, and there were more similarities in the reasoning of females and males than there were differences (Jaffee & Hyde, 2000). In fact, considerable research suggests that individuals take both care and justice issues into consideration when thinking through moral issues.

In fact, the type of problem individuals are asked to think about appears to be more important than their gender in determining which perspective participants use. Dilemmas that approximate real life situations, such as those studied by Gilligan, rather than the more impersonal dilemmas of Kohlberg, are more likely to prompt a care perspective. Rosemary Jadack and her associates (1995) found that females and males differed little in the extent to which they adopted a care or a justice orientation in reasoning about real life types of dilemmas. In fact, individuals of either sex frequently used reasoning characteristic of both approaches, suggesting that these are not competing perspectives. Similarly, Eva Skoe and associates (2002a) have found more care reasoning and more emotional involvement with relational, real life dilemmas than with nonrelational ones (2002b).

Finally, it may be that moral reasoning is related not to gender per se, but to one's gender-role orientation, that is, not to whether one is female or male but to how feminine or masculine one is. Skoe and her associates (2002a) found that not just women but individuals scoring higher in femininity on a measure of gender-role identity were more likely to engage in care reasoning. A study of Brazilian adolescents also found those with a feminine orientation to be more likely to be sympathetic to another's plight and more likely to assume the other's perspective (Eisenberg, Zhou, & Koller, 2001).

meta-analysis A statistical procedure for reaching conclusions regarding an area of research by combining the findings from multiple studies.

Individuals, male and female, with a justice orientation are more likely to protest low wages of immigrant workers, whereas those with a care orientation are more likely to express their concern by providing a helping hand.

It appears, then, that individuals use both care and justice perspectives in thinking through moral situations, and that which perspective is more likely to influence their reasoning will depend on how the situation is presented as well as on their gender-role identification.

Finally, Gilligan views the developmental sequence that she catalogues as complementing that of Kohlberg's, not as an alternative (Gilligan & Attanucci, 1988). She points out, however, that the care orientation would have been missed had she and others not studied females as systematically as Kohlberg studied males.

Comparison of Kohlberg's and Gilligan's Approaches

Internalizing Standards Both Kohlberg and Gilligan assume that initially individuals act primarily out of self-interest, with little thought to how their actions affect others. For Kohlberg, this stance reflects the individual's limited role-taking and cognitive skills; Gilligan attributes it to feelings of being cut off from others, leaving one to take care of one's own needs.

For Kohlberg, the development of abstract thought enables adolescents to imagine how others view their actions; because they are concerned about the opinion of others, they want to live up to the standards of their group. Gilligan assumes that as adolescents feel accepted by and connected to others, they take on the values of their group.

Considering Intentions The same cognitive growth by which Kohlberg explains the internalization of group standards is also responsible for considering others' intentions when evaluating their actions. As adolescents become able to take the perspective of others, and understand that others can do the same with respect to their own behavior, motives or intentions become important in evaluating the acceptability of their own and others' actions. For Gilligan, seeing oneself as a member of the social group leads women to evaluate their actions in terms of how "good" they are, with goodness being defined conventionally by taking care of others.

Questioning Values Kohlberg believes that exposure to other value systems, usually in high school or at work, gives adolescents a new perspective from which to view their own values and, with this, to examine and question them. Gilligan believes that individuals question conventional definitions of goodness when they begin to experience the tension created by caring for others to the exclusion of caring for oneself.

Freud: Morality and the Superego

For Freud, responsibility for moral behavior resides with the superego, which emerges, at about age 5, as the child identifies with the same-sex parent, thus resolving the Oedipal complex (see Chapter 2). Identification is the process by which the child internalizes or appropriates the values and behaviors of the parent. These values form the superego, which includes the conscience, and serve as the basis for an internalized set of standards for behavior.

Prior to the development of the conscience, Freud assumed that children are governed only by the desire to win parental affections and the fear of being rejected for wrongdoing. Like social-cognitive theorists and Kohlberg, Freud believed that an internalized code or ethic is not present in early childhood.

The final step in moral development occurs in adolescence when puberty threatens the surface tranquility achieved through repression and identification. Freud assumed that adolescents emotionally distance themselves from their parents to defend against newly awakened sexual desires. In doing so, they have to toss out the parental figures they had internalized in childhood. Adolescence becomes a time for reworking the parental standards that were uncritically accepted as part of these figures (Josselson, 1980, 1987).

Critique of Freud's Theory

Freud believed that the absence of castration anxiety in females and the presence, in its stead, of penis envy resulted in a weaker superego in females and differences in their moral behavior. Freud (1925b) wrote:

> I cannot evade the notion (though I hesitate to give it expression) that for women the level of what is ethically normal is different from what it is in men. Their superego is never so inexorable, so impersonal, so independent of its emotional origins as we require it to be in men. Character traits which critics of every epoch have brought up against women—that they show less sense of justice than men, that they are less ready to submit it to the great exigencies of life, that they are more often influenced in their judgment by feelings of affection or hostility—all these would be amply accounted for by the modification in the formation of their super-ego which we have inferred. (pp. 257–258)

These assumptions concerning the basis for gender differences in moral behavior have not received empirical support. Research on the internalization of moral standards does not find males to have stronger superegos than females. Nor do differences in behavior, when they occur, favor males. They are, if anything, as likely to favor females (Ford et al., 1989; Silverman, 2003).

Research has similarly failed to support other of Freud's assumptions related to the development of morality. For instance, adolescence is not a period of emotional turmoil for most teenagers. Also, large surveys of normal adolescents do not find they are preoccupied with sex or with controlling their impulses. Nor do most adolescents have weak egos, nor have they cut emotional ties with their parents (see Chapter 7).

Internalizing Standards How does Freud explain the facts that other theories of moral development have addressed? Like social-cognitive theorists (as well as Kohlberg and Gilligan for conventional standards of morality), Freud assumes that individuals acquire their values and their sense of right and wrong by internalizing society's norms. The conditions that prompt children to internalize parental standards differ for each theory, however. Freud traces internalization to resolution of the Oedipal complex and identification with the parent of the same sex. Social-cognitive theory speaks of the child's ability to reinforce itself, rather than having to receive praise or punishment at the hands of others. Both theories must address the central problem with internalization as an explanation for moral conduct: If one's culture is the ultimate source of moral authority in an individual's life, how does a person ever reach a level higher than that which characterizes the society? Gilligan and Kohlberg both view the internalization of social conventions as an intermediate step in moral development. Gilligan believes that females take this step when they experience a discrepancy between their self-concern and concern for others. Kohlberg traces this step to increases in cognitive maturity.

Considering Intentions For Freud, the emergence of the superego explains the child's shift from evaluating behavior in terms of its consequences to the motives that underlie it. Social-cognitive theorists, in contrast, explain this shift in terms of the social-learning experiences of the child, but frequently fail to take into consideration the child's own motives and intentions or the expectation that adolescents will begin to think for themselves. Kohlberg attributes this shift to new levels of cognitive maturity and role-taking skills. Gilligan's analysis of morality begins with individuals who have already made this transition.

Questioning Values And how might Freud explain the flexibility that characterizes the moral thought that develops in some with late adolescence? Rather than refer to changing social expectations, increasing cognitive maturity, or the need to repair relationships, psychoanalytic thought attributes flexibility in moral judgments to the work of the ego in balancing the demands of the id and superego. Individuals who remain relatively inflexible are those dominated by a threatening superego. The ability to evaluate a situation, to develop coping strategies, and to delay gratification of one's impulses are all functions of the ego and characterize mature moral functioning.

Adolescents' Religious Beliefs

Do adolescents think of God the same way children do? Or do the intellectual developments that occur in adolescence affect their views of God and religion just as they affect their views of so many other things? James Fowler (1981, 2001) suggests that they do. He identifies stages of religious belief that parallel the stages of moral development discussed earlier (see Table 11.1).

TABLE 11.1 Fowler's Six Stages of Faith Development

STAGE 1: INTUITIVE-PROJECTIVE FAITH (EARLY CHILDHOOD)

Children's grasp of religious concepts is intuitive and personal, based largely on their own experiences and on narratives of good and evil. Thinking is dominated by imagination and fantasy, and religious beliefs reflect the qualities of Piaget's pre-operational thinking.

STAGE 2: MYTHIC-LITERAL FAITH (MIDDLE CHILDHOOD)

As logical thought develops and supplants intuition, children appropriate the religious beliefs of their community. However, religious concepts are interpreted literally, as is characteristic of concrete operational thought.

STAGE 3: SYNTHETIC-CONVENTIONAL FAITH (EARLY ADOLESCENCE)

Abstract thought enables adolescents to integrate previously unrelated narratives and beliefs into a single system of beliefs. Since these beliefs are not explored for their personal relevance, faith is largely conformist, reflecting the unexamined tenets of one's religious community. Fowler assumes that many adults do not progress beyond this stage.

STAGE 4: INDIVIDUATIVE-REFLECTIVE FAITH (EMERGING ADULTHOOD)

As late adolescents and emerging adults assume responsibility for the decisions of life, they take responsibility for their beliefs as well, examining these for their relevance to other life commitments. Commitments in one area have implications for decisions in another, and individuals become aware of tensions in life, e.g., individualism versus belonging to a group, or putting oneself first versus putting others first.

STAGE 5: CONJUNCTIVE FAITH (MIDDLE ADULTHOOD)

Whereas the previous stage is characterized by a need to resolve life tensions, this stage is characterized by an openness to the tensions that result from conflicting claims within different arenas of life. Individuals become able to view their beliefs as one of many belief systems, and they recognize that each of these is incomplete and relative. Fowler believes that few adults reach this stage.

STAGE 6: UNIVERSALIZING FAITH (MIDDLE OR LATE ADULTHOOD)

Individuals at this stage experience themselves as being at one with God and with others; differences in beliefs and practices are no longer seen as important, with the result that previously experienced tensions dissolve. These individuals work for the good of all irrespective of group membership, frequently at risk to their own personal safety.

Children's views of God reflect the concrete nature of the way they think in general. To them, God is someone with a human form who sits celestially enthroned above them. This figure is typically masculine, whereas adolescents are more likely to have a gender-neutral image of God (Ladd, McIntosh, & Spilka, 1998). Children accept the teachings and stories of their religion literally and do not question them, other than to try to fit them into their current ways of understanding, such as wondering how God can be everywhere at the same time (Fowler, 1981).

The ability to think abstractly that comes with adolescence transforms these views, enabling adolescents to appreciate abstract qualities of God, such as righteousness, compassion, and mercy. Bradley Hertel and Michael Donahue (1995) analyzed the responses of fifth- through ninth-graders to nine descriptors of God. Two dimensions emerged. One described God in terms of love, and the second described God in terms of authority. Items related to the first of these, for instance, described God as loving someone irrespective of what that person had done, whereas those related to the second dimension described God in terms of rules and punishing wrongdoers. Of these two dimensions, the image of God that predominated among these youth was overwhelmingly that of a loving God. This was true, by the way, for their parents as well.

These two dimensions suggest parallels to the moral perspectives discussed earlier. In fact, many biblical narratives of conflict between individuals and God lend themselves to either a justice or care interpretation. For instance, one could view the behavior of Adam and Eve from a justice perspective and argue that by eating fruit they had been told not to eat, they broke a rule. However, one could as easily view the transgression from a care perspective and see their actions as a betrayal of trust in that the fruit had been left within their reach. Similarly, the narrative of the exodus from Egypt, in which the Israelites worshipped a golden calf, might be viewed from either perspective. Worshipping the calf clearly violated the commandment not to worship idols; however, worship is a relational act and, as such, constituted a betrayal of the special relationship the Israelites had with God.

Nancy Cobb, Anthony Ong, and Jerry Tate (2001), at California State University, Los Angeles, examined late adolescents' and early adults' perceptions of biblical and moral wrongdoings in which the characters' actions could be seen to simultaneously violate a rule and betray a trust. When participants were asked to describe the nature of the transgression in each case, they defined the wrongdoing from a justice perspective, speaking of it as breaking a rule. However, when asked what mattered most to the party that had been wronged, they more frequently mentioned the relationship, irrespective of whether this had been God or another person. Given the commonality between religious and moral domains, in that both teach about right and wrong conduct, perhaps these findings should not be that surprising.

Thus, adolescents can engage in sophisticated reasoning about religious, as well as moral, issues. Adolescence is also a time when they may begin to question religious beliefs. "If God is all-powerful, why is there suffering and evil in the world?" The answers adolescents arrive at reflect an increasingly personalized faith much as Kohlberg's and Gilligan's final stages (Fowler, 1981, 2001).

This increasing sophistication is reflected in adolescents' prayers, which include petitions such as to "better understand your holy will" or to "deal better with my anger." Even so, the social identity reflected in adolescents' prayers is, for the most part, limited to family and friends and only occasionally extends beyond these to the larger community (McKinney & McKinney, 1999).

With respect to **religious identity,** one also sees evidence of a clear developmental trend. In a series of studies, David Elkind (1961, 1962, 1963) asked Catholic, Jewish, and Protestant children and adolescents how they could tell whether a person was of the same religion that they were. By middle childhood, children identified members of religious groups in terms of concrete behaviors and characteristics. Thus, one who is Catholic might be identified as someone who goes to Mass every Sunday, or one who is Jewish as a person who goes to temple and attends Hebrew school. Such an understanding, as Elkind points out, highlights the differences between religions. That is, if one is attending Mass, one cannot also be going to temple. One is either one religion or the other, and the two are noticeably different.

Adolescents, however, are able to appreciate the commonalities to different religions, understanding that one can worship God irrespective of whether one does this in a church, a temple, or a mosque. In this stage, adolescents identify their religion in terms of abstract beliefs. Thus, Protestants might describe someone in their faith as "a person who believes in God and Christ and is loving to others," whereas those who are Jewish might describe themselves as "a person who believes in one God and doesn't believe in the New Testament" (Elkind, 1961, 1962, 1963).

How important, one might ask, *is* religion to one's sense of self? When asked to describe themselves, in other words, how likely are individuals of different ages to mention their religion? Rachel Royle, Martyn Barrett, and Eithne Buchanan-Barrow (1998) asked

religious identity An awareness of belonging to a religious group.

participants of various ages, religions, and nationalities, all of whom lived in London, to sort cards into either of two boxes, one labeled "Me" and the other "Not Me." Each card identified some single aspect of identity, such as gender, ethnicity, language, age, or religion. Once participants had finished this initial sort, they were asked to go through the "Me" cards again and select the one that was most descriptive of themselves. This card was removed and they selected the next most descriptive card, continuing in this way until each of the terms had been ranked in order of importance.

Religion is a significant part of their identity for many adolescents.

Religion emerged as a significant aspect of identity, being among those most likely to be selected as "Me." Furthermore, its importance to a sense of self increased with age. Children were most likely to identify themselves in terms of their gender or their nationality; however, by early adolescence, religion was more important and was mentioned more frequently than sex, age, or nationality. Religion contributed to identity more heavily for some participants than it did for others, possibly reflecting the minority status it conferred on them. A similar trend has been found for ethnicity, in which individuals who are members of a minority are more aware of their ethnicity than those belonging to the majority, the latter frequently not even having a sense of being a member of an ethnic group (Phinney, 1989). So, too, with religion. For Muslims living in London, for instance, religion was more salient than it was for Christians.

Thus, religious beliefs reflect more than adolescents' ability to think in certain ways. The processes of exploration and commitment that are central to identity formation also contribute to differences in religiosity. The ability to think abstractly may make it possible for adolescents to entertain questions such as why God would tolerate suffering, but this ability alone is not enough to determine that they will.

Acceptance of religious tenets has been viewed by some as a means of controlling the ultimate risks of life, risks such as those introduced by disease and natural disaster (Malinowski, 1925). From this perspective, those who reject religious beliefs become the risk takers. However, as we have seen with other aspects of identity exploration, a determination of what is risky cannot be made in any simple way without reference to the particular contexts of an individual's life. In this respect, risk taking in religious beliefs, just as in the vocational and social domains of identity, takes the form of daring the unknown. Thus, it would be equally risky for an adolescent whose parents are avowed atheists to explore a belief in God as it would for an adolescent coming from a deeply religious background to reject those religious beliefs.

The very same willingness to consider the unfamiliar, whether in terms of a career or a lifestyle, is also at the heart of religiosity. Will adolescents give themselves the freedom to explore their religion? Some will; others will not. Adolescents can remain committed to traditional religious beliefs without ever examining them. These adolescents can be said to be foreclosed in their religiosity. Conversely, adolescents can explore their beliefs, asking questions to which they do not have simple or familiar answers, and be identity-achieved (Markstrom-Adams, Hofstra, & Dougher, 1994; Markstrom-Adams & Smith, 1996).

One cannot distinguish either type of adolescent simply by looking at their beliefs. It is not so much a question of *what* adolescents believe as it is the *process* by which they have gotten to these beliefs. Just as with the broader process of identity formation, the beliefs one ends up with can remain essentially unchanged. It is the believer who has changed. One index of religious exploration, for instance, is switching one's church affiliation due to dissatisfaction with its teachings. Individuals who switch have been found to be more actively involved in their religion subsequent to switching than those whose beliefs have remained unexamined (Hoge, Johnson, & Luidens, 1995).

The extent to which adolescents are involved in their religion also has been found to relate to measures of psychosocial maturity. Carol Markstrom (1999) found that late adolescents who more frequently attended religious services and participated in a Bible study or youth group scored higher on various measures of ego strength, such as hope, will, purpose, fidelity, love, and care, than adolescents who were less involved.

The extent to which adolescents have a strong religious identity is also related to their concern for others (King & Furrow, 2004; Furrow, King, & White, 2004). Michael Kerestes, James Youniss, and Edward Metz (2004), at Catholic University of America, followed students from their sophomore to their senior year of high school and found that those who maintained a strong religious identity were more likely to be involved in prosocial activities, for example, volunteering in the community, demonstrating for causes they believed in, and helping others.

The Importance of Religion

How important is religion in the lives of adolescents? Nearly a third of high school seniors in a nationally representative sample indicated that religion is very important in their lives and attend religious services weekly (Fox, Connolly, & Snyder, 2005). Additionally, one-quarter of high school seniors have attended a religious youth group for all four years of high school and nearly another third have attended from one to three years (Smith, Denton, Faris, & Regnerus, 2002).

The importance of religion in adolescents' lives differs by gender, with religion playing a more significant role in the lives of adolescent females than males. Differences associated with race are even greater. Significantly more African American adolescents attend weekly services than do European American adolescents, and more than twice as many African American as European American adolescents indicate religion is very important in their lives, 57% versus 26% (U.S. Department of Health and Human Services, 2002c). As can be seen in Table 11.2, religion is an important aspect of adolescents' lives.

Furthermore, most of these adolescents put their religious beliefs into action (Youniss, McLellan, Su, & Yates, 1999). Religious adolescents are nearly three times as likely to be involved in some form of voluntary community service as are adolescents for whom religion is not important. For instance, approximately three-quarters of high school seniors who indicated that religion was important in their lives engaged in volunteer work, either monthly or more frequently. In comparison, only a quarter of those who said that religion was not important volunteered for such work (Youniss, McLellan, & Yates, 1999).

Are adolescents today as religious as adolescents have been in previous generations? In terms of attending religious services, one might think not. Surveys show that fewer adolescents attended religious services on a weekly basis in 2001 than two decades earlier. Even so, the importance of religion in adolescents' lives has, if anything, increased somewhat. Approximately a third of the adolescents who were surveyed in 2001 reported that religion was "very important" to them, and just under 30% indicated that religion was "pretty important." Given the importance of religion to so many adolescents, more

TABLE 11.2 Religious Practices and Beliefs Among High School Seniors, 1981 to 2001

	Percentage of Seniors		
Religious Activity and Level of Interest	1981	1991	2001
FREQUENCY OF ATTENDING RELIGIOUS SERVICE			
Weekly	40.0	31.2	32.8
1–2 times a month	17.0	16.8	16.1
Rarely	33.5	37.6	34.2
Never	9.5	14.4	16.9
IMPORTANCE OF RELIGION IN LIFE			
Very important	30.5	27.7	32.3
Pretty important	32.8	30.0	27.9
A little	26.0	27.0	24.4
Not important	10.7	15.3	15.5

Source: University of Michigan, Institute for Social Research, *Monitoring the future,* various years. In Fox, Connolly, & Snyder (2005). *Youth Indicators 2005: Trends in the Well-Being of American Youth.* (NCES 2005-050). U.S. Department of Education, National Center for Education Statistics. Washington, DC: U.S. Government Printing Office.

research on religious beliefs and practices is needed for a fuller understanding of adolescent development.

We have considered in this chapter the ways in which adolescents' values relate to their identity and to a developing system of moral and religious beliefs. In the next chapter, we will look at the crisis of values in adolescents' lives—at alienation, delinquency, violence, and substance abuse.

Summary

The Values of Adolescents

- Most adolescents place a high value on having a good marriage and family life, and being successful in their work, much as their parents did a generation ago.
- Most adolescents hold values that are in substantial agreement with those of their parents.
- With respect to gender, more similarities than differences exist in the values held by adolescent females and males. There are also few differences in adolescents' values due to race.
- Although there are many similarities in values across cultures, there are also differences. *Individualistic* cultures value independence, self-reliance, individual achievement, and self-expression. *Collectivist* cultures value interdependence, cooperation, working for the success of one's group and maintaining harmonious relationships.
- The way adolescents approach both their own and others' values reflects identity issues. Identity-achieved and moratorium adolescents have explored issues for themselves and are tolerant of similar explorations and differences in others. Foreclosed adolescents tend to be more rule-bound and authoritarian than identity-achieved or moratorium adolescents. They are more likely to be critical of those who are different from them.
- Adolescents differ from children with respect to a developing *morality* in three primary ways: internalizing the standards of their community, considering the intentions of others, and questioning society's values.

Social-Cognitive Theory and Moral Development

- Social-cognitive theory assumes that children eventually internalize controls that initially are effective only when enforced by others. In doing so, children acquire their community's standards. Age-related changes in considering the intentions of others and questioning values are explained by referring to the experiences that make different forms of thought most likely at different ages.
- Research on variables predicting cheating supports social-cognitive theory.

Kohlberg and Moral Development: Morality as Justice

- At the *preconventional* level of moral reasoning, individuals lack internalized standards of right and wrong; their motives are only to satisfy their needs without getting into trouble.
- At the *conventional* level of moral reasoning, individuals have internalized the standards of their community and are motivated to live according to the standards of their group.
- At the *postconventional* level of moral reasoning, individuals live according to self-derived principles rather than the conventions of their community.
- Forgiveness is a decision to release a person from a claim that justice would honor. Reasoning about forgiveness, just as about justice, becomes more mature with age.
- Although some studies find that many individuals reason at adjacent stages about different situations, critics of Kohlberg's theory argue that individuals can usually distinguish conventional from moral issues even as children.

Gilligan: An Ethic of Care

- Gilligan asserts that most females think of morality more personally than do males. She finds that an ethic of care characterizes females' approach to moral decisions; this ethic emphasizes compassion and a sense of responsibility to others in contrast to the justice orientation of Kohlberg, which emphasizes reliance on rules and reason.
- Gilligan traces gender differences in moral reasoning to differences in ways of viewing the self. Females define themselves in relation to others; from this comes a sense of responsibility of each to the other. Males define themselves as separate from others; the assumption of separateness highlights the need for rules to regulate the actions of each with respect to the other.
- Gilligan traces moral development in females through three levels, each reflecting a different resolution to their conflict between responsibilities to themselves and to others. In level 1 the primary concern is care for oneself. Females soon see this as selfish and move to level 2, in which they equate morality with care of others. Only as they encounter problems that result from excluding themselves as legitimate recipients of their own care do females move on to level 3, in which they equate morality with care both of themselves and of others.
- Research finds that women and men take both care and justice issues into consideration when thinking through moral issues, and that the type of moral dilemma influences their moral reasoning more than their gender. Additionally, moral reasoning is more closely related to gender-role orientation than it is to gender itself.

Freud: Morality and the Superego

- Freud placed the responsibility for moral behavior in the superego, an aspect of the personality that embraces cultural standards of right and wrong. The superego develops when the young child identifies with the same-sex parent. Freud assumed the superego of females to be weaker than that of males because they are not as motivated to resolve Oedipal tensions.
- Despite the usefulness of Freud's theory to clinicians, his assumptions concerning gender differences in moral development have not been supported by research.

Adolescents' Religious Beliefs

- The intellectual changes that occur in adolescence make it possible for adolescents to view God in new ways and to question beliefs they once accepted uncritically.
- As with identity status, processes of exploration and commitment determine the form beliefs will take. For more than 60% of adolescents, religion remains very to moderately important in their lives.

Key Terms

individualism
collectivism
morality
preconventional moral reasoning
conventional moral reasoning
postconventional moral reasoning
random error
test of significance
ethic of care
religious identity
meta-analysis

CHAPTER OUTLINE

CHAPTER 12

The Problems of Youth

CHAPTER OBJECTIVES

- To examine common problem behaviors that can arise in adolescence, and distinguish those that are likely to disrupt the course of healthy development from those that are not
- To look at adolescent runaways and the types of support available to them and their parents
- To examine the nature of maltreatment in adolescence and discover the conditions under which this is likely to occur
- To look at delinquent behaviors in adolescence, identifying behaviors that are normative and those that are not
- To study gangs and see how these have changed over time and what functions they serve
- To look at the use of various drugs by adolescents and the potential risks involved
- To identify common eating disorders in adolescence
- To look at depression and suicide in adolescence

"No, don't! . . ." Abbie bolted upright in a sweat. She sat in the dark, the dream swirled around her, its sharp pain softening with each panting breath.

"Too much!" she cried, slipping her feet over the side of the bed and starting for the bathroom.

As her foot hit the dresser, she hissed angrily, "Why isn't anything where it's supposed to be?" Then, blindly feeling for the light switch and finding nothing, she remembered where she was. This wasn't her room. She was in her stepsister's bedroom at her father's house. Her mom had thrown her out. She had forgotten the reason for the fight; they had thrown things, said things.

As the heavy reality of her world closed in on her, she slipped to the floor sobbing—the angry words, fists, and ashtrays flying, her friends so far away, her father nervous, on edge, his wife distant and formal—and no place to call her own. She suddenly felt that she could bear none of it anymore.

Calvin and Hobbes
by Bill Watterson
LET'S SAY LIFE IS THIS SQUARE OF THE SIDE-WALK. WE'RE BORN AT THIS CRACK AND WE DIE AT THAT CRACK.
© 1991 Watterson/Distributed by Universal Press Syndicate
NOW WE FIND OURSELVES SOME-WHERE INSIDE THE SQUARE, AND IN THE PROCESS OF WALKING OUT OF IT. SUDDENLY WE REALIZE OUR TIME IN HERE IS FLEETING.
IS OUR QUICK EXPERIENCE HERE POINTLESS? DOES ANYTHING WE SAY OR DO IN HERE REALLY MATTER? HAVE WE DONE ANYTHING IMPORTANT? HAVE WE BEEN HAPPY? HAVE WE MADE THE MOST OF THESE PRECIOUS FEW FOOTSTEPS ??

Part of the appeal of the Calvin and Hobbes *cartoons for adults is nostalgia for the innocence of childhood. (CALVIN AND HOBBES © 1991 Watterson. Distributed by Universal Press Syndicate. Reprinted with permission. All rights reserved.)*

Chapter Overview

Adolescents face many pressures. Abbie is one of those with more than her share. Most adolescents will cope in one fashion or another; Abbie may, too. Relatively few will fail to cope. In this chapter we will consider first the problems of those for whom coping has become the ultimate test, the alienated and abused, looking at runaway adolescents and those who are maltreated, and at the supports that are available to them and their parents.

The term "juvenile delinquent" calls to mind images of angry youth; however, many forms of delinquency involve relatively minor offenses. Although a majority of adolescents indicate having engaged in some form of delinquent activity, we will see that disproportionate numbers of minority youth enter the juvenile justice system.

The chapter moves to a discussion of gangs and youth violence before turning to a consideration of adolescents' use of drugs and effective intervention programs. In a final section of the chapter, we examine eating disorders, depression, and suicide.

Alienation and the Failure to Cope

Some of the most common stressors in adolescence reflect the absence rather than the presence of something. Adolescents frequently feel cut off from themselves and others, emotionally distanced from their world, observers rather than participants in their own reality. Feelings of **alienation**—a sense of estrangement and loss—can be common in adolescence. These feelings are to be expected, given the many changes adolescents experience; however, when alienation becomes the predominant focus of an adolescent's experience, he or she is in trouble.

Loss is central to alienation, and it is always the loss of something important. Reactions to this loss can range from hostility to sadness to indifference—from anger to a defensive "What does it matter anyway?" The alienated who cannot replace their loss with the sense of a competent self, linked to a social order that gives meaning to their lives, surround the void without filling it.

alienation Indifference where devotion or attachment formerly existed; estrangement.

Adolescent runaways face numerous problems, and the availability of support, in terms of meals and a place to stay, varies from one community to another. The National Runaway Switchboard provides crisis intervention and a message center for adolescents and parents.

Runaways

For some adolescents, the loss is of something they never had. Anywhere from 1.3 million to just under 2 million adolescents run away from home before they reach the age of 18 (National Assembly of Health and Human Service Organizations, 1999; National Runaway Switchboard, 2004). Some run away in the hopes of finding something, but most are running *from* something—frequently from neglect or abuse. Table 12.1 shows the types of family problems reported by adolescents in runaway and homeless youth centers.

Despite the uniqueness of individuals when looked full in the face, the profile of runaways is disturbingly similar: low self-esteem, depression, poor interpersonal skills, insecurity, anxiousness, impulsiveness, and little sense of control over life's events. Most do poorly in school, many run into trouble with the law, and 20% attempt suicide (Leslie, Stein, & Rotheram-Borus, 2002). Almost all experience conflict within their families, and for many this includes abuse or neglect. With an average age of 15, runaways can be from any socioeconomic level.

Running away is clearly not the answer to their problems. It is equally clear that these adolescents are unable to face their problems and come up with any reasonable solution at the moment. Running away is almost never well planned. Two-thirds, for example, leave home with less than a dollar in their pocket. Many stay with friends or relatives, some seek out youth shelters, and others are homeless. Most return within the first week, and 40% the same day. Nearly 90% will run away again in the future (Farber, 1987).

Home life for most runaways is chaotic. The problems from which they are running (and to which almost all will return) have usually existed for years, yet the solutions remain as distant as ever. The dynamics of family life that would offer an answer to the problems are the very same ones that foster personal development in family members. Thus, most runaways lack a sense of who they are or what they can become, in large part because the development of their sense of self and of their potential has not been

TABLE 12.1 Common Problems Reported by Adolescents in Runaway and Homeless Youth Centers

Type of Problem	Total	Female	Male
FAMILY PROBLEMS*			
Emotional conflict at home	41%	43%	39%
Parent too strict	21	24	18
Parental physical abuse	20	23	18
Parental neglect	20	19	21
Parent drug or alcohol problems	18	19	17
Family mental health problems	11	12	11
Parental domestic violence	10	10	10
None of the above	16	13	19

*Because multiple responses are permitted, totals exceed 100%.

Source: Adapted from K. Maguire, A. L. Pastore, & T. J. Flanagan (Eds.). (1993). *Sourcebook of criminal justice statistics 1992.* U.S. Department of Justice, Bureau of Justice Statistics. Washington, DC: U.S. Government Printing Office.

supported within their families (Repetti, Taylor, & Seeman, 2002). Runaways are in need of programs that give them the interpersonal skills they did not develop within their families: skills in communicating thoughts and feelings, negotiating conflict, and making responsible decisions (see Chapter 7).

Edward Farber (1987) notes that many more services are available to abused youth than to runaways; society tends to see the former as victims and the latter as merely unruly. Yet in a study of runaways, Farber and his associates found these adolescents had experienced the same amount of violence as had a similar group of adolescents identified as abused. Rather than being the problem itself, running away is a symptom of other problems. One cannot expect such troubled adolescents to return home without first addressing the problems of family conflict and, for some, domestic violence they would face upon their return.

Support for Adolescent Runaways and Parents

Adolescents who do not return home right away face a number of problems. First among these are the basics—finding a safe place to stay, food, and clothing. Life on the streets poses dangers of its own. Runways, almost by definition, are in a one-down position, having exhausted all other means of coping, and are at risk for victimization. They are exposed to possible physical and sexual assault, are more likely to use and abuse drugs and to trade sex for food or shelter. They are also at high risk for exposure to the HIV virus through drug use and risky sexual practices (Rotheram-Borus, Song, Gwadz, Lee, Van Rossem, & Koopman, 2003.

The availability of immediate supports varies from one community to the next. Nearly all urban centers, however, have federally and privately funded shelters. Most of these offer short-term help (e.g., 30 days) in the form of meals and a place to stay; some also offer diagnostic and counseling services. The Internet is a valuable tool for finding shelters and one with which most adolescents are familiar. For instance, the International Homeless & Homelessness Directory lists shelters by city and state within the United States and in other countries (www.homeless.org.au /directory/shelters.htm). Additionally, the National Runaway Switchboard, a 24-hour national hotline for adoles-

IN MORE DEPTH

Types of Maltreatment

ABUSE

- *Physical abuse:* Involves substantial injuries that last for at least 48 hours and often, as in the case of burns, broken bones, or internal injuries, longer. Examples might include bruises or fractures from being hit or punched.
- *Sexual abuse:* Involves exposure, molesting or fondling, or actual penetration. Examples might include a daughter being molested by her mother's live-in boyfriend.
- *Emotional abuse:* Involves behavior that undermines an adolescent's sense of well-being and self-esteem. Examples could include denigrating or derisive remarks ("You stupid brat!").

NEGLECT

- *Physical neglect:* Involves a failure to provide for an adolescent's physical or medical needs, or for adequate supervision. Examples might include failure to provide treatment for a medical condition or not attending to obvious hazards around the home.
- *Educational neglect:* Involves permitting truancy (approximately 5 days/month) or keeping an adolescent home to care for other siblings.
- *Emotional neglect:* Differs from emotional abuse in that it is a passive emotional rejection of the adolescent, taking the form of giving little or no emotional support, attention, or affection.

Source: National Clearinghouse on Child Abuse and Neglect Information. (2005). Washington, DC: U.S. Department of Health and Human Services. http://nccanch.acf.hhs.gov/topics/prevention

cent runaways and parents, offers crisis intervention, a message center, and referrals (www.nrscrisisline.org/).

Longer-term interventions can take the form of counseling and parenting classes, offered by many communities through full-service schools (see Chapter 9, and Chapter 7 for parenting). Skill-focused prevention programs based on social-cognitive theory (see Chapter 2) have been successful in reducing the use of alcohol and drugs and reducing risky sexual behavior among runaways (Rotheram-Borus et al., 2003).

Maltreatment: Abuse and Neglect

Maltreatment refers to instances of harm that are nonaccidental and avoidable; these can occur either from abuse or neglect. Abuse can be physical, sexual, or emotional in nature, and often involves some combination of these. Similarly, neglect is distinguished as to whether it is a failure to provide for an adolescent's physical, educational, or emotional needs. The In More Depth box distinguishes among these types of maltreatment.

It is difficult to say precisely how many adolescents are maltreated, since different studies have used different methods of conducting surveys and have asked questions concerning different types of maltreatment (Amaya-Jackson, Socolar, Hunter, Runyan, & Colindres, 2000). Most studies, however, have obtained figures for physical and for sexual abuse. With respect to the former, estimates vary widely. For instance, in one study of eighth-, tenth-, and twelfth-grade adolescents attending over 40 schools in Washington State, 11% indicated they had been physically abused (Bensley, Eenwyk, Spieker, & Schoder, 1999). In a national survey of adolescents, however, this figure was 22% (Kilpatrick, Acierno, Saunders, Resnick, Best, & Schnurr, 2000). Statistics concerning sexual abuse are somewhat more consistent, with approximately 3% of adolescent males and 9% of females saying they had been sexually abused (Amaya-Jackson, et al., 2000). We know also that cases of abuse are somewhat less likely to be reported for adolescents than they are for children (Jonson-Reid, 2002).

maltreatment Instances of harm to children or adolescents that are nonaccidental and avoidable; they can be due to either abuse or neglect.

Cases of adolescent abuse and neglect are likely to follow one of three patterns: a continuation of earlier child abuse, a change in the type of punishment used by parents, and neglect related to the onset of adolescence (Doueck, Ishisaka, & Greenaway, 1988).

Continuation of Earlier Maltreatment The maltreatment some adolescents experience continues a pattern of earlier child maltreatment within the family. These adolescents typically come from families with many long-standing problems: violence between parents, alcoholism, financial instability, few social supports, and physical isolation from others. The maltreatment these adolescents suffer is not much different from that experienced when they were younger, and it reflects the inadequate coping skills of the parents and the generally dysfunctional nature of the family.

Abusive Punishment A second type of maltreatment, physical abuse, involves a change in the type of punishment used. In this instance, parents who have used physical punishment since childhood have increased the intensity of the punishment in an attempt to control adolescent misbehavior. Families in which this form of mistreatment occurs are typified by controlling, rigid parents who become even more controlling, to the point of abuse, when faced with adolescent bids for greater autonomy and independence and the loss of their own control (Doueck, Ishisaka, & Greenaway, 1988).

Neglect Precipitated by Adolescence A third type of mistreatment is brought about by the onset of adolescence itself. In this type of neglect, parents mistakenly conclude that because children have reached adolescence, they are able to be on their own and care for themselves.

Characteristics of Maltreating Parents What leads parents to be abusive or neglectful? No simple answers are to be found. Most of these parents love their children and experience genuine remorse for what they do. Similarly, relatively few would be diagnosed as suffering from a mental illness. Nor could one predict maltreatment simply by knowing their life circumstances. In fact, research on maltreatment has failed to identify any single factor that necessarily leads to maltreatment (Cicchetti & Lynch, 1995). In many ways, maltreating parents are not that different from average parents.

In other respects, however, important differences have been found. One difference concerns the way they respond under stress. Parents who engage in maltreatment appear to experience more difficulty coping with stress than do other parents. Not only are they likely to find the normal stresses of life more aversive than are other individuals, but they also tend to overreact when they are stressed, experiencing more difficulty controlling their impulses. In addition, maltreating parents are more likely to interpret events as being outside their control, and to react angrily and defensively, than are other parents (Brunquell, Crichton, & Egeland, 1981). Thus, although these parents may behave in ways that are similar to other parents under most circumstances, they are likely to respond differently when stressed.

Maltreating parents also appear to differ in what might be termed their worldview. They are less likely to have a positive outlook on life, seeing the world instead as a hostile place and life as a struggle, with them on the defensive. This defensive attitude can extend to their interactions with their children, in which they are more likely than are other parents to interpret an adolescent's behavior as intentionally disobedient or otherwise "aimed" at them. With their own feelings so much in the foreground, it also becomes easy for parent–child relationships to undergo a reversal in which the adolescent is expected to be responsive to the parent's feelings and meet the parent's needs. This reversal of roles, in which the child is **parentified,** or functions as a parent, places the burden for caring for the parent's needs on the adolescent. In fact, maltreated adolescents frequently are more nurturing than are their parents (Cicchetti & Lynch, 1995).

parentified A reversal in the parent–child relationship in which the burden of caring for the parent's needs is assumed by the adolescent.

Maltreating parents also tend to hold inappropriate expectations concerning what can reasonably be expected of adolescents. These unrealistic expectations can fuel their tendency to perceive an adolescent's behavior as willfully disobedient rather than as normal for someone of that age. They differ as well in the types of discipline they are likely to use, being less likely to use effective parenting styles. Instead, they are more likely to punish or threaten, and less likely to use reasoning. They are also less consistent in their discipline and less warm and affectionate in general in their relationships (Cicchetti & Lynch, 1995).

Finally, maltreating parents not only are able to bring fewer personal resources to bear when facing stressful life events, but also have fewer interpersonal resources on which they can rely. Perhaps the most important of these for most parents is their relationship with their spouse. Partners of maltreating parents have been found to be less supportive and warm, as well as more aggressive, than those of comparison parents (Cicchetti & Lynch, 1995; Howes & Cicchetti, 1993). In general, relationships within the home, whether with a spouse or an adolescent, are less positive and warm than in other homes.

None of these characteristics, in themselves, can be regarded as responsible for maltreatment. Maltreatment typically results from a combination of conditions rather than a single factor. Thus, a parent who has difficulty coping with stress may still be able to function adequately unless something untoward happens. The loss of a job, however, or a child entering a "difficult" developmental stage may be enough to precipitate maltreatment. One such condition that places families under significant stress is poverty. Although maltreatment is by no means limited to low-income families, it is unusually high among such families. Life below the poverty line can involve cascading stress on an almost daily basis. A case in point might involve something as simple as an appliance needing repair. A refrigerator breaking down can mean spoiled food. But when money is short, the food that has spoiled may have been purchased with the last of the food stamps. To repair the appliance would leave nothing for groceries; however, without a refrigerator, frequent trips to the market become necessary, taxing the reserves of an already overtaxed parent. Coupled with an unsupportive spouse or inadequate transportation, an event that might have been an ordinary stressor in another family can precipitate maltreatment in an impoverished one.

Positive actions for parents to take, information on parenting resources, and hotline numbers are available on the Internet through a Web site sponsored by the Centers for Disease Control (http://www.cdc.gov/ncipc/dvd/PAFP.htm).

Juvenile Delinquency

Juvenile delinquency involves illegal actions committed by a minor; the actions can be as serious as homicide or as relatively trivial as shoplifting a candy bar. Some actions, such as homicide, rape, or robbery, are illegal at any age; these are termed **index offenses.** Other actions, termed **status offenses,** are behaviors that are illegal when engaged in by minors but perfectly legal for adults. Running away and truancy are status offenses. Adults are free to choose where and with whom they will live and when they will leave. There's no such thing as a 40-year-old runaway—not legally, at least. Similarly, once adolescents reach the legal age set by their state, they are no longer considered truant even though they may not attend school.

Age Differences in Delinquency

The types of delinquent acts adolescents engage in varies with age. Many minor forms of delinquency—such as running away, violating curfews, or smoking marijuana—begin in early adolescence but decrease by adulthood. More serious types of crimes—like robbery or violent offenses—are generally more common in adulthood than in adolescence (Snyder, 2004).

juvenile delinquency Illegal actions committed by a minor.

index offenses Actions that are criminal at any age, for example, homicide, burglary.

status offenses Actions that are illegal when engaged in by minors but legal for adults, for example, truancy, drinking alcohol.

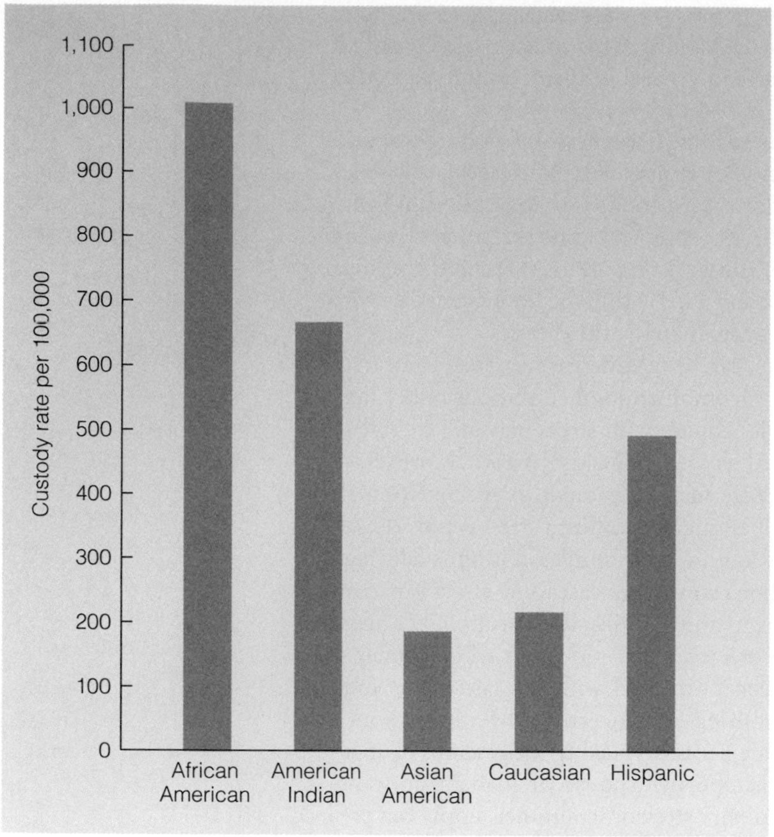

FIGURE 12.1
Custody Rates of Juveniles as a Function of Ethnicity.
Source: M. Sickmund. (2004). Juveniles in corrections. *National Report Series Bulletin.* Retrieved from Office of Juvenile Justice and Delinquency Prevention, U.S. Department of Justice Web site: http://www.ojp.usdoj.gov/ojjdp

There is little evidence to suggest that minor forms of delinquency predict a shift to more serious crimes later on, even for multiple offenders. The pattern instead suggests a small subgroup of delinquents who start early and account for a relatively high proportion of criminal activity (Henggeler, 1989).

Gender Differences in Delinquency

Females are less likely to engage in delinquent activities than are males, accounting for only 29% of juvenile arrests (Snyder, 2004). The size of the gender difference varies with the type of crime. Females are much less likely to commit violent crimes than males; only 18% of juveniles arrested for violent crimes are females. Females are most likely to be arrested for running away, sexual offenses, unruly behavior, and theft (Snyder, 2004).

Ethnic Differences in Delinquency

Large differences exist in the numbers of adolescents from different ethnic backgrounds who enter the juvenile justice system. Minority youth are significantly more likely to be arrested than are European Americans (Sickmund, 2004). Furthermore, with the exception of violent crimes, this is true even when it is for the same offense (Juvenile Justice Evaluation Center, 2004). Custody rates also differ for adolescents of different ethnic backgrounds. The custody rate for African Americans, for instance, is nearly five times that for European Americans and more than twice that for Hispanics (see Figure 12.1) (Sickmund, 2004). Self-report comparisons for African American and European American high school seniors, however, fail to reveal differences in delinquent activities that would be expected given figures such as these (*Sourcebook of Criminal Justice Statistics 2003*), strongly suggesting that arrest and detention rates reflect biases within the juvenile justice system (Juvenile Justice Evaluation Center, 2004).

Recent amendments to the Juvenile Justice and Delinquency Prevention Act require states to examine the way minority youth are dealt with, from the very first contact up to decisions regarding sentencing, to discover where problems exist in the treatment of minority youth and how these can be corrected (Juvenile Justice Evaluation Center, 2004).

Delinquency and Social Class

The effects of ethnicity and social class are difficult to separate. Arrest rates for minority adolescents are higher than those for nonminority youth, as are arrests of adolescents from lower-income versus middle-income homes. Disproportionate numbers of minority youth come from lower-income homes, and factors common to poverty are related to delinquency apart from ethnic status. Unemployment, poorer academic and vocational preparation, and fewer social and family resources are just a few of these factors. In addition, much middle-income delinquency is never reported; families are able to intervene, and youth authorities are more willing to release offenders to their parents' custody.

Even so, some types of delinquent activity vary with social class. Middle-income youth are less likely to commit violent crimes (such as aggravated assault, rape, robbery) or crimes against property (for example, auto theft, burglary) than are lower-income youth. Status offenses and minor delinquent acts such as creating a public nuisance, drunkenness, and disorderly conduct are as common among middle-income as lower-income adolescents.

Understanding Delinquency

How are we to understand delinquency? Can we trace delinquency primarily to individual differences, that is, to characteristics of individual adolescents? How important are the social contexts of adolescents' lives, such as those provided by family and peers? Once again, depending on whom one asks, different answers are given.

Middle- and lower-income youth are equally likely to commit status offenses and minor delinquent acts, such as vandalism. Adolescents from lower-income homes are more likely, however, to commit violent crimes or major crimes against property, such as auto theft or burglary.

Those who assume delinquency can be traced to individual differences cite stable traits and characteristics, such as poor self-control, impulsivity, and neurological deficits, that increase the likelihood of deviant behavior (Moffitt, 1997). Qualities of family life and parenting practices are assumed to be important either by promoting traits such as self-control, which should decrease deviant behavior or, conversely, by failing to curtail an adolescent's tendencies toward antisocial behavior (Repetti, Taylor, & Seeman, 2002). Peers, on the other hand, are not assumed to directly influence delinquent behavior. Although it is acknowledged that delinquent adolescents are more likely to associate with peers who engage in similar activities, those who adopt this perspective assume that these adolescents seek out peers who engage in similar behavior, rather than being influenced by them (Scaramella, Conger, Spoth, & Simons, 2002).

A social-contextual perspective on delinquency assumes that parents not only shape certain traits in their children but shape as well their children's social environments through their choice of the neighborhoods in which they live, the schools they attend, and how they spend their time outside of school. In other words, it is assumed that parents influence the choice of peers with whom adolescents spend their time and, in doing so, affect the type of influence peers have. Although there is support for both of these perspectives, the social-contextual approach has been found to explain developmental outcomes somewhat better than an individual differences one (Scaramella et al., 2002). What is clear from either perspective, however, is the importance of nurturant and involved parenting for decreasing the risk of delinquency. Parents who are warm, nurturant, supportive, and consistent in their discipline and who monitor their children's activities reduce the risk for delinquency (Ge, Brody, Conger, Simons, & Murry, 2002; Scaramella et al., 2002).

Parents frequently need help in providing the environments that will support healthy choices. It is encouraging to find that federally funded early childhood intervention programs, designed initially to give low-income preschoolers the skills necessary to succeed in school, have far-reaching and wide effects, affecting parents as well as children and extending into adolescence. "Wraparound" early childhood intervention programs that continue into the second or third grade, as opposed to ending in kindergarten (see Chapter 9), are associated not only with improved academic performance, but also with preventing juvenile delinquency in adolescence (Reynolds, Ou, & Topitzes, 2004; Smokowski, Mann, Reynolds, & Fraser, 2004). Children who participate in these programs have better mastery of basic skills and lower rates of grade retention. Important as both of these are, however, it is the impact these programs have on parents' involvement in their children's lives that is key to lowering rates of juvenile arrests. The support these programs offer families results in improved parenting practices and greater parental involvement, lessening the likelihood of antisocial behavior (Reynolds et al., 2004).

Gangs

As individuals, delinquent adolescents can cause considerable harm to others and themselves. As a group, their presence in a community can be disastrous.

The number of gangs has risen dramatically over the last several generations. In 1960, for instance, 58 cities reported the presence of gangs. In 1992, this figure had increased to 769 cities (Klein, 1995). By 2000, 86% of cities with a population of at least 100,000 reported the presence of gangs, as did 100% of all larger cities. The presence of gangs is very much tied to the size of the community, with up to 60% of smaller cities (less than 25,000) and rural communities reporting no gang presence (Egley, 2002).

The implications of gang presence are considerable, both for adolescents and for the communities they live in. Membership in a gang is associated with higher rates of criminal activity (Huff, 1996). Thornberry, Krohn, Lizotte, and Chard-Wierschem (1993) found that rates of delinquency were approximately four to five times higher for gang members. Because these investigators followed the same adolescents over several years, they could compare rates of delinquency for these adolescents prior to joining a gang with rates when they were members of a gang. The researchers found these adolescents did not have higher rates of delinquency than other adolescents prior to becoming gang members; furthermore, once they left the gang, their rates typically dropped. Only when they were in a gang did they have a high rate of delinquency.

Not only the number but also the nature of gangs has changed with time. In previous generations, gangs arose from the spontaneous associations of neighborhood males, and gang activities were primarily oriented toward defending the neighborhood territory or turf. Membership was almost exclusively limited to males and to those of the same ethnic group. Rumbles with rival gangs defined the territories of each and gave status to gang members. The leader of the gang carried a gun, but most members did not (Kratcoski & Kratcoski, 1986). Since the 1980s, gang members have had access to sophisticated weapons and have used them freely. As one former gang member from Detroit remarked,

> When I grew up we had it out with our hands. Maybe we'd steal a car and go for a ride. Now they steal a car and rip somebody off or shoot somebody. I'm afraid to walk down the street at night. I've never seen it like this. (Kratcoski & Kratcoski, 1986)

Gangs are still formed from neighborhood associations, and gang activities still involve defense of turf, but gangs are more likely to be linked with organized crime than

TABLE 12.2 Reasons for Staying in Gangs, as Reported by Members of Early (Prior to 1980) and Contemporary (Since 1980) Gangs

	Early Gangs (n=18)		Contemporary Gangs (n=30)	
Reason	n	Percentage	n	Percentage
Career	0	0%	9	30%
Economic	2	11	7	23
Political	2	11	2	7
Social	14	78	12	40

Source: J. P. Evans & J. Taylor. (1995). Understanding violence in contemporary and earlier gangs: An exploratory application of the theory of reasoned action. *Journal of Black Psychology, 21,* 71–81.

in the past, and making money, primarily through the sale of narcotics, is one of their major activities. Joseph Sheley and his colleagues (1995), at Tulane University, point out that gang activity tends to be more or less specialized in, or limited to, one or two types of criminal activities regularly committed. These investigators surveyed adolescent males in correctional facilities in four states, asking them if they had been members of a gang and what types of activities their gang had been involved in. They found that over 40% of the gangs could be categorized in terms of the criminal activities in which they engaged. For 20% of these gangs, this specialty was armed drug-selling. Another 16% were involved in some other single activity, and another 4% were involved in some combination of two activities. Among the 22% of respondents who indicated their gangs had regularly been involved in three types of activities, it was found, on closer inspection, that most of these activities were related to the sale and use of drugs, thus supporting the notion that gangs are specialized in the activities in which they engage. The implications of these findings, beyond their obvious link of gangs to criminal activities, is that gangs are more than just youth from a neighborhood who band together for social or defensive purposes (Sheley, Zhang, Brody, & Wright, 1995).

If the purpose of gangs has shifted from defending turf to developing criminal enterprises, then what types of functions do gangs serve in the lives of their members, and how have these changed over the past generation? Judy Evans and Jerome Taylor (1995), at the University of Pittsburgh, interviewed members of early gangs (46 to 55 years old) and contemporary gang members (15 to 20 years old), asking them why they belonged to a gang and what their role was in the gang. For both early and contemporary gang members, the most frequently given reason for gang membership was social (for example, "I see my homies every day"). Social reasons, however, were far more important for early gang members than contemporary ones, who also indicated career and economic reasons ("It's how I make my money") for belonging to a gang, as shown in Table 12.2.

A second difference to emerge between early and contemporary gang members is in the nature of the violence they engage in. For early gang members, violence took the form of fighting, with 56% saying this had something to do with their role in the gang. In stark contrast, none of the contemporary gang members said that fighting had anything to do with what they did as a gang member. Rather, violence for these gang members took the form of shooting, with 26% indicating this as their role within the gang. By way of contrast, none of the early gang members indicated shooting as an activity they engaged in, as shown in Table 12.3.

Table 12.3 also reveals another striking difference between early and contemporary gangs. The former had virtually no involvement in drug-related activities, whereas 93%

TABLE 12.3 Distribution of Roles Reported by Members of Early (Prior to 1980) and Contemporary (Since 1980) Gangs

	Early Gangs (n=18)		Contemporary Gangs (n=30)	
Reason	n	Percentage	n	Percentage
Fighting	10	56%	0	0%
Scouting	0	0	4	13
Dealing	0	0	16	53
Robbing	4	22	2	7
Shooting	0	0	8	27
None of the above	4	22	0	0

Source: J. P. Evans & J. Taylor. (1995). Understanding violence in contemporary and earlier gangs: An exploratory application of the theory of reasoned action. *Journal of Black Psychology, 21,* 71–81.

of the activities of contemporary gang members are drug related, 13% being involved in scouting for new members, 53% in dealing, and 27% in shooting. The corresponding percentage for each of these drug-related activities for earlier gang members is 0% (Evans & Taylor, 1995).

A final, and important, difference concerns the relative loyalty of gang members to family or their gang. Fully 100% of the early gang members said that, if they had to choose, they would protect their families before protecting their gang. Eighty percent of contemporary gang members, however, said they would protect their gangs before protecting their families.

C. Ronald Huff, at Ohio State University, and Kenneth Trump, at Tri-City Task Force (1996), note that gang activities are not limited to the streets but permeate the school system as well. Huff (1996), based on interviews of gang members from three metropolitan areas, reports that over half of the gang members interviewed admitted that members of their gangs had assaulted teachers, and approximately 70% indicated that gang members had assaulted students. Furthermore, over 80% said members of their gangs had taken guns to school, with nearly as many taking knives onto school campuses. Over 60% said their gangs had sold drugs at school.

What attractions do gangs hold for their members? It has been suggested that gangs serve as surrogate families, offering an intense intimacy, emotional support, protection, and a feeling of belonging (Henggeler, 1989; Vigil, 1988). Research has found, for instance, that parents of gang members do not monitor their children's activities closely and that their families are less cohesive (Henggeler, 1989). Parental absence, in the form of long work hours, or a single parent, or simple neglect, is also more common. In general, positive role models are less in evidence. Gang membership is also believed to confer a sense of identity, something especially important in adolescence. Members dress alike and adopt unique identifying behaviors they share with their gang, even being tattooed with gang insignia. The violence, too, can be an attraction, providing feelings of power and excitement to members.

Jean-Marie Lyon, Scott Henggeler, and James Hall (1992) found only partial support for the above assumptions. In a study comparing gang and non-gang members on a number of measures, these investigators found no difference between the two groups in measures of family relations such as parental acceptance or in peer relationships such as emotional bonding in friendships. In fact, friendships among gang members were more aggressive and less mature than those of nonmembers. The constant need of gang

Today's gangs are more likely to be linked to organized crime and the sale of drugs than in the past.

members to prove themselves to maintain their status within the gang also argues against emotional intimacy.

Youth and Violence

Violence is not restricted to inner-city youth or gangs; it extends to the suburbs and to middle-income families. At school, 17% of high school students indicate carrying some type of weapon, such as a knife, club, or gun to school; and 30% reported having something of theirs stolen or deliberately damaged while at school (Centers for Disease Control and Prevention, 2004). In their neighborhoods, teenagers are nearly twice as likely to be victims of a violent crime such as assault, robbery, or rape as are young adults 25 to 34 years old (Fox, Connolly, & Snyder, 2005).

Across all ethnic groups, homicide is the second leading cause of death for youth. And for those 13 years old or older, 78% are killed with a firearm (CDC, 2005e; Snyder, 2004). Minority males are most at risk: Native Americans are more than twice as likely to die violently as White males their age, Hispanic males are three to four times more likely, and African American males are nine times more likely than their White counterparts to die violently.

Adolescents in all segments of society risk becoming desensitized to violence. Television programming is saturated with murders, rapes, and kidnappings, and box-office stars offer images of bare-chested bodybuilders with semiautomatic weapons. Television programs, video games, and movies model graphic acts of violence as well as provide violent role models with whom adolescents can identify (Browne & Hamilton-Giachritsis, 2005). An anecdote offers an interesting, if chilling, example of the way in which television and the movies contribute to our images of violence. My niece reported she had recently been in a bank when it was held up by two armed men. She noted that on hearing "Everyone down," people knew immediately what to do—lie face down on the floor, not crouch or kneel, and not look at the robbers' faces—because they had all seen this on the screen. However, after the robbers left, no one knew what to do—the TV and movie cameras always cut to the getaway and chase.

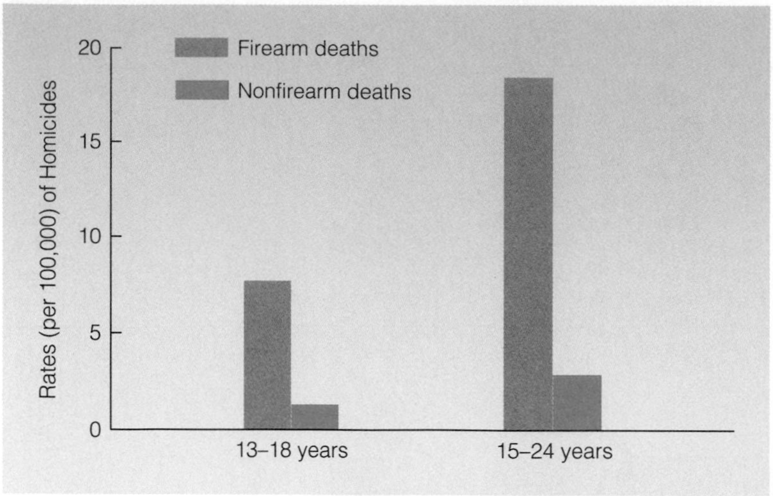

FIGURE 12.2
Rate of Firearm and Nonfirearm Homicides Committed by 13- to 18-Year-Olds and by 15- to 24-Year-Olds. *Source:* Centers for Disease Control. (2005). National Center for Injury Prevention and Control. WISQARS. Available at http://webappa.cdc.gov/sasweb/ncip/mortrate10_sy.html

One of the most important factors contributing to lethal violence is the accessibility of firearms (see Figure 12.2). Not only handguns but sophisticated semi-automatic weapons are readily available to those who would have them. The most frequently used weapon in the United States is a gun, accounting for nearly 80% of homicide victims 10 to 24 years of age (CDC, 2005e). Studies tracking the relationship between firearms and homicides in the United States find these to be predictably related; the rate of homicides by youth that involve firearms is six times that of those not involving a gun (CDC, 2005e). Further support for the relationship between accessibility of firearms and gun deaths comes from international comparisons of gun homicides in countries with strong firearms regulations with gun homicides in the United States, a country with weak regulations (see Table 12.4).

Social factors contributing to violence cannot be discounted. The poverty and hopelessness confronting inner-city youth, their daily exposure to community and family violence, and the reality of unemployment and racism for minority adolescents are powerfully related to violence. In the end, however, some adolescents choose violence and others do not. Most who engage in violent crimes have law-abiding siblings with whom they have eaten at the same family table and shared relatives, friends, and life experiences.

Do violent scenes in the movies and on television desensitize adolescents to violence or make them more likely to act violently? One of the most important factors contributing to lethal violence is the accessibility of firearms.

TABLE 12.4 International Comparisons of Firearms Regulations and Gun Homicides

Country	Licensing of Gun Owners	Registration of Firearms	Other	Gun Homicide (per 100,000)	Gun Suicide (per 100,000)	Total Intentional Gun Death Rate (per 100,000)
Japan	Yes	Yes	Prohibits handguns with few exceptions	0.03	0.04	0.07
England/ Wales	Yes	Yes	Prohibits handguns	0.07	0.33	0.4
Germany	Yes	Yes		0.21	1.23	1.44
Canada	Yes	Yes		0.60	3.35	3.95
France	Yes	Yes except sporting rifles		0.55	4.93	5.48
U.S.A.	In some states	Handguns in some states	Some weapons in some states	6.24	7.23	13.47

Source: W. Cukier. Firearms regulation: Canada in the international context. *Chronic Diseases in Canada,* April 1998 (statistics updated to reflect most recent figures, January 2001).

Adolescents and Drugs

As Ferris Bueller says, "Life moves pretty fast. If you don't stop and look around once in a while, you could miss it." He's right. If anything, it's faster now than ever before: instant messaging, e-mail, faxing, 24-hour markets, fast foods, and five-lane expressways. Stimulants, tranquilizers, sedatives, and alcohol fit neatly into the pace of our lives—they instantaneously pick us up, settle us down, mellow us out, or just blur the edges.

Today's adolescents expect fast results, and drugs are part of society's response to that expectation. Millions of people in the United States find it impossible to get started in the morning without coffee or a cigarette, or to relax in the evening without a drink. Millions more take medication for pain, pills to sleep, laxatives to correct faulty diets, pills to suppress appetites, and vitamin supplements when they fail to eat enough. Adolescents see quick pick-me-ups and instant remedies modeled everywhere around them. It is little wonder that by their senior year in high school, a majority of adolescents have experimented with drugs. The drugs adolescents most frequently try are the ones most frequently found in their homes—alcohol and cigarettes. Three-quarters of adolescents have used alcohol and nearly 60% have smoked cigarettes. The only other substance that is tried by a substantial percentage of adolescents is marijuana. Relatively few adolescents, less than 5%, experiment with other drugs (Centers for Disease Control and Prevention, 2004).

Adolescents try drugs for many reasons, of course; the prevalence of drugs in society is just one of them. Adolescence itself is a time of experimentation, and many adolescents explore substances as well as roles and ideas. Part of the attraction of legal drugs such as cigarettes and alcohol is that they are used by adults; when adolescents use them, they feel more adult. Also, advertisements make their use look glamorous. Many adolescents experience peer pressure to use substances, and countless other adolescents use substances to boost low self-esteem, dull pain, feel more confident, or compensate for poor social skills. Like any quick remedy, the promise far exceeds the payoff, and with some substances, even casual experimentation carries substantial risk.

Our discussion of drugs follows their pattern of use by adolescents. We will look first at alcohol and cigarettes and then at marijuana, the three most commonly used substances.

What Is Dependence?

Drug addiction and **drug dependence** are interchangeable terms. Both refer to a physical dependence on a substance. Not all drugs lead to dependence; one could take an aspirin a day for months or years with no such effect (although there might be other effects), and many individuals are dependent on prescribed drugs for their health. With respect to substance abuse, however, the drug must be **psychoactive:** one that is self-administered, that alters one's mood, and that comes to control behavior in such a way that one is no longer free *not* to use it (Surgeon General's Report, 1988). Dependence on a drug always involves developing a tolerance for it; the body requires increased amounts of the drug to achieve the same effect. Dependence also results in withdrawal symptoms whenever use is discontinued. Drug dependence can interfere with school, work, and relationships (American Psychiatric Association, 1994). The criteria for drug dependence appear in the In More Depth box.

Alcohol

Alcohol is typically the first drug adolescents try, and 65% do so before they reach high school (Centers for Disease Control and Prevention, 2004). Many people do not think of alcohol as a drug because its use is so embedded in the context of everyday life, but it is a powerful central nervous system (CNS) depressant, loosening inhibitions. As a result, adolescents are likely to become more talkative, feel more confident, and feel more at ease socially after having a drink. However, as blood alcohol level rises, activities controlled by the central nervous system are increasingly affected; thinking becomes disorganized and reactions slowed. Even small amounts of alcohol, depending on the adolescent, can be enough to affect activities requiring coordination and judgment.

Despite, or perhaps because of, its powerful effects, many high school students (45%) drink with some regularity. Just under 30% are likely to have engaged in heavy drinking, having five or more drinks in a row, within the last month (Centers for Disease Control and Prevention, 2004). Adolescents need not be chronic drinkers for alcohol to carry the potential for serious harm to themselves and others. Twenty percent of high school seniors admit to driving after drinking, and 30% of adolescents say they have ridden with someone who had been drinking (Centers for Disease Control and Prevention, 2004). And adolescents who have been drinking, irrespective of their blood alcohol level, are more likely than drivers of other ages to be involved in an accident (CDC, 2005e).

Cigarettes

Although many drugs carry the potential for great harm, the percentage of adolescents experimenting with them is relatively small, and the numbers of those habitually using these is even smaller. The one substance, however, that a sizable number of adolescents use on a daily basis is cigarettes (Centers for Disease Control and Prevention, 2004). Because of this, cigarettes pose one of the most serious, if not *the* most serious, health risks of all drugs to adolescents. Approximately 440,000 people die each year due to smoking or to exposure to cigarette smoke—and most of them started smoking as adolescents (Armour, Woollery, Malarcher, Pechacek, & Husten, 2004).

Most adolescents who smoke start before they reach high school. By the time they are seniors, 20% will be smoking on a regular basis (Centers for Disease Control and Prevention, 2004). Longitudinal data confirm that smoking is a difficult habit to break, even

drug dependence Physical dependence on a substance, such that one develops a tolerance and experiences withdrawal when use is discontinued; also known as drug addiction.

psychoactive A drug that alters mood.

alcohol A drug that functions as a central nervous system depressant.

IN MORE DEPTH

Criteria for Drug Dependence

Drug dependence is present when at least three of the following seven criteria are present:

1. Development of tolerance so that more of the substance is needed to achieve the same effect.
2. Physical and/or cognitive withdrawal symptoms if use of the substance is discontinued.
3. Use of the substance in larger amounts or over a longer period than was intended.
4. A persistent desire or unsuccessful attempts to cut down or control substance use.
5. Significant amounts of time devoted to obtaining and using the substance and recovering from its use.
6. Giving up or reducing important social, occupational, or recreational activities because of substance use.
7. Continuing to use the substance in spite of knowing that it contributes to a psychological or physical problem (such as cocaine-induced depression or an ulcer aggravated by alcohol).

Source: Adapted from *DSM-IV: Diagnostic and statistical manual of mental disorders* (4th ed.). (1994). Washington, DC: American Psychiatric Association.

among adolescents. Over 50% of adolescents who smoked half a pack or more a day said they had tried to quit and had not been able to. Nearly 75% of those who smoked in high school on a daily basis were still doing so ten years later, although only 5% thought they would continue when they began (Johnston, O'Malley, & Bachman, 1989). These figures are not surprising, given the withdrawal symptoms adolescents experience when attempting to stop: irritability, nervousness, anxiousness, impatience, difficulty concentrating, increased appetite, and weight gain.

The psychoactive agent in cigarettes is **nicotine,** which is both a stimulant and a depressant. Smokers feel both more alert and more relaxed when they smoke. These pleasures come with a heavy price tag. Smoking increases heart rate and blood pressure and carries an increased risk of heart disease. It also increases the risk of lung cancer and respiratory diseases such as emphysema and chronic bronchitis.

Pregnant adolescents who smoke jeopardize the health of their babies as well as their own health. Smoking during pregnancy is associated with prematurity, low birth weight, spontaneous abortion, and perinatal problems. These complications are especially disturbing, because females are just about as likely to smoke in high school and early adulthood as are males (Centers for Disease Control and Prevention, 2004).

Marijuana

By the time they reach the twelfth grade, 40% of adolescents have tried **marijuana** at least once and a quarter report current occasional use (Centers for Disease Control and Prevention, 2004). Use of marijuana, however, has declined in recent years and students are more likely to perceive its use as dangerous than previously (Johnston, O'Malley, Bachman, & Schulenberg, 2005).

Marijuana comes from the *Cannabis sativa* plant, which contains the psychoactive substance THC. This substance produces a high characterized by feelings of relaxation and peacefulness, a sense of heightened awareness of one's surroundings and of the increased significance of things. Marijuana can distort perception, affect memory, slow reaction timc, and impair motor coordination, especially for unfamiliar or complex tasks. The principal physical effects are an increase in heart rate, reddening of the eyes, and dryness of the mouth. Because marijuana affects perception, reaction time, and coordination, it impairs one's ability to drive. Yet adolescents under the influence of marijuana

nicotine The psychoactive substance in cigarettes that is both a stimulant and a depressant.

marijuana A mild hallucinogen from the plant *Cannabis sativa;* the psychoactive substance is THC.

The drugs adolescents are first likely to use are the ones they find at home, such as alcohol with these adolescents, and cigarettes.

experience heightened confidence in their abilities and are likely to take greater risks while driving, despite their impaired functioning (Insel & Roth, 2000).

Long-term heavy use of marijuana carries a number of potential health risks. The smoke from marijuana causes irritation of the bronchia and can lead to chronic bronchitis. Marijuana smoke also contains considerably more tar than does smoke from even high-tar cigarettes, and 70% more benzopyrene, a known carcinogen.

Age, Ethnicity, and Gender

There are significant age trends as well as ethnic and gender differences with respect to each of these drugs. First, the use of all three substances increases with age. Over a third of ninth-graders indicate having had a drink within the preceding month in contrast to over a half of twelfth-graders. Similarly, less than 20% of ninth-graders had smoked a cigarette or had marijuana in the preceding month, but over a quarter of twelfth-graders had. This trend is true for all drugs, with the exception of inhalants, which are most likely to be used by younger rather than older adolescents (Centers for Disease Control and Prevention, 2004).

There are ethnic differences as well in the use of drugs. African American adolescents are significantly less likely to drink than are European American or Hispanic adolescents, and even less likely to engage in heavy drinking. They are also less likely to have smoked than are European American or Hispanic adolescents; among the latter, European Americans are the more likely to smoke. Only with the use of marijuana do ethnic differences disappear (Centers for Disease Control and Prevention, 2004).

Overall, more females report using alcohol than males; however, this difference is largest among ninth- and tenth-graders, and most likely reflects the tendency for girls to date boys who are a year or two older. This trend in the use of alcohol is troublesome in that drinking in early adolescence can be problematic for girls since it has been found to affect pubertal development (see Chapter 3). Adolescent females are as likely to have smoked as males, but less likely to have used marijuana (Centers for Disease Control and Prevention, 2004).

Patterns of Drug Use

As we have seen, there is a pattern to the order in which adolescents experiment with different substances. The first drug they are likely to use is alcohol, followed by cigarettes, which in turn are followed by marijuana. This pattern has led to the **gateway hypothesis,** which assumes that adolescents' involvement in drugs progresses through a sequence of stages, with the use of one type of drug providing a pathway, or opening the door, to the use of other drugs (Kandel, 1975). Denise Kandel, at Columbia University, states, however, that this theory is often misunderstood. She points out that although using certain drugs precedes the use of other drugs, progression to the next stage isn't inevitable. That is, many adolescents drink without ever smoking; similarly, experimenting with marijuana does not mean that an adolescent will try other illegal drugs; and, in fact, most don't. As a logician might put it, although the use of alcohol and cigarettes might be a necessary condition for progression to the next stage, it is not a sufficient one (Kandel, 2002).

More important than *whether* adolescents have used a particular drug is how heavily involved they are in its use. Kandel notes that increased involvement with a drug generally precedes progression to a higher stage. For instance, it's not simply the use of alcohol and cigarettes that precedes more advanced drug use; rather, it's excessive drinking (Kandel, 2002). The question of involvement, however, leads us to the issue of risk factors, and protective ones, associated with substance abuse.

Risk and Protective Factors

Risk factors, recall, are the conditions present either as characteristics of adolescents themselves, or their families, or communities that place them at risk for substance abuse. In the case of personality characteristics, adolescents at risk for drug abuse tend to be less well adjusted and more impulsive and to have low self-esteem (Bryant, Schulenberg, O'Malley, Bachman, & Johnston, 2003; Shedler & Block, 1990; Siewert, Stallings, & Hewitt, 2003). They are also likely to do more poorly at school, experience more problematic relations with their peers, and have friends who use drugs (Bryant et al., 2003; Shedler & Block, 1990; Urberg, 1992).

Families also exert an important influence: Adolescents who are substance abusers are likely to have less nurturing parents and to experience less consistent parenting; they also are more likely to have parents who abuse substances themselves (Chassin, Flora, & King, 2004). There is evidence of a genetic component, as well, to a number of the problem behaviors seen in adolescent substance abusers (Siewert, Stallings, & Hewitt, 2003). Finally, communities in which there is more violence and in which drugs are more available place adolescents at greater risk of drug use (Lambert, Brown, Phillips, & Ialongo, 2004).

Protective factors are the conditions that provide adolescents with the resources they need for healthy development. These factors, too, can be grouped in terms of

gateway hypothesis The assumption that drug use progresses through stages in which the use of one type of drug provides a pathway to the use of other drugs.

characteristics of the adolescents, their families, and their communities that protect against substance abuse. With respect to the first of these, having high self-esteem and good social skills is associated with decreased involvement with drugs, as is involvement in church and religious activities and having friends who do not abuse drugs (Bottvin & Griffin, 2004; Huebner, Shettler, Matheson, Meszaros, Piercy, & Davis, 2005; Oman, Vesely, Aspy, McLeroy, Rodine, & Marshall, 2004). Adolescents who maintain good grades in school and who feel emotionally connected to their school are also less likely to abuse drugs (Huebner et al., 2005; Marsiglia, Miles, Dustman, & Sills, 2002; Skal, Ireland, & Borowsky, 2003).

Parents play a key role in protecting adolescents from drug abuse. Parents who are warm and understanding, with whom adolescents feel they can talk about their problems, are less likely to have adolescents who abuse drugs, as are parents who monitor adolescents' activities, knowing where they are and who they are with. These qualities, you may recall from reading Chapter 7, are characteristic of authoritative parents (Hays, Hays, & Mulhall, 2003; Huebner et al., 2005; Oman et al., 2004; Skal et al., 2003).

Finally, media campaigns affecting addolescents' perception of the harmfulness of drugs, at least with respect to marijuana, appear to have had some effect in reducing its use (Johnston et al., 2005). With respect to cigarettes, however, the sheer cost of cigarettes may be an important factor discouraging adolescents from smoking; since 1997, the price of cigarettes has increased 88% (Allen et al., 2003; Huebner et al., 2005).

Trends Over Time

The proportion of adolescents using drugs has continued to decline over the past decade. With the exception of alcohol, tobacco, and marijuana, less than 5% of high school seniors said they had used any drug within the preceding month (see Figure 12.3). Most of the drugs that had been used were used by less than 2% of seniors (Johnston et al., 2005). The greatest decline has been in marijuana, perhaps reflecting national media campaigns against this drug and increased perception among adolescents of its harmfulness (Johnston et al., 2005). Cigarettes, however, remain a much larger drug problem, being responsible for most substance-related deaths (Allen et al., 2003). Notwithstanding, states have cut spending on preventive programs aimed at tobacco use, whereas the amount spent by the tobacco industry on marketing *doubled* in 1997 through 2001, presumably in an effort to counteract the effect of public messages (Allen et al., 2003). The one disturbing exception to the downward trend in drug use was an increase in the use of inhalants by eighth-graders, who were less likely than previously to see these as dangerous (Johnston et al., 2005).

Prevention Programs

Efforts to prevent adolescent drug abuse have taken a number of forms, such as controlling adolescents' access to drugs, media campaigns, and school-based educational programs. When it comes to preventing drug abuse among adolescents, however, there is no "silver bullet." For programs to be maximally effective, the combined efforts of parents, schools, the community, and our society become important (Johnston et al., 2005).

Adolescents' access to drugs can be affected in a number of ways. Perhaps the most obvious of these is through stricter enforcement by communities of existing laws prohibiting the sale of alcohol and cigarettes to minors. For instance, a quarter of eleventh- and twelfth-graders who smoked within the past month said they had purchased cigarettes at a store or gas station, as did 12% of ninth-graders (Centers for Disease Control

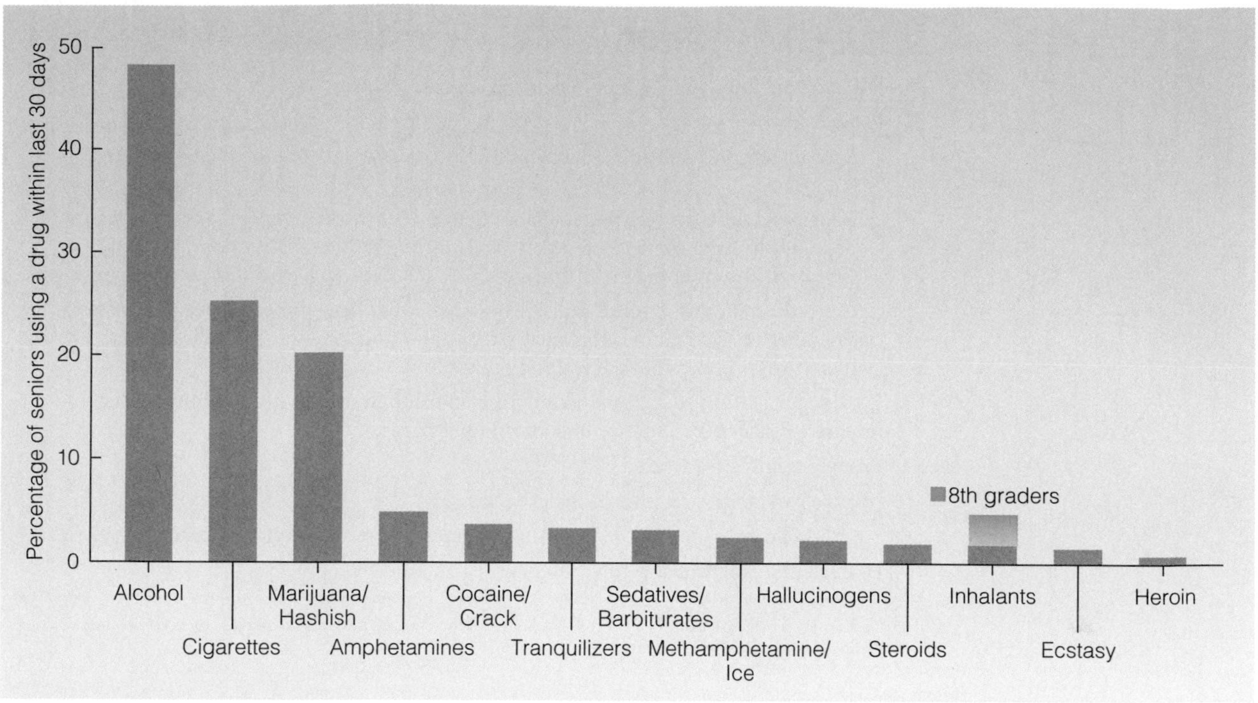

FIGURE 12.3
Percentages of High School Seniors Using Various Drugs Within the Past Month. *Source:* L. D. Johnston, P. M. O'Malley, J. G. Bachman, & J. E. Schulenberg (2005). *Monitoring the Future national results on adolescent drug use: Overview of key findings, 2004.* Available at www.monitoringthefuture.org

and Prevention, 2004). Similarly, access to these drugs can be limited through adolescents' pocketbooks; increases in the price of both cigarettes and alcohol have been accompanied by decreased use of these substances (Johnston et al., 2005; Ling & Glantz, 2002).

Media campaigns directed at both adolescents and their parents have been credited with reductions in adolescent drug use (Johnston et al., 2005; Office of National Drug Control Policy, 2005). A federally funded program targeting use of marijuana appears to have been largely responsible for recent declines in the use of marijuana, most likely by increasing adolescents' perception of its harmfulness (Johnston et al., 2005). Antismoking ads are similarly thought to have contributed to decreases in the percentage of adolescents who smoke. Johnston and his colleagues at the University of Michigan's Institute for Social Research note:

> Whether we will see teen smoking continue to decline in the future is likely to depend on what actions society and the tobacco companies take. The fact that a number of states have reduced their allocations of tobacco settlement monies to smoking prevention is likely to have an adverse effect, as is the scheduled decline in funding for the national anti-smoking campaign sponsored by the American Legacy Foundation. (Johnston et al., 2005, p. 3)

The American Legacy Foundation is a public health foundation funded by the settlement agreement with the tobacco industry. There is a downside to the effectiveness of media campaigns, however. Tobacco companies spend 12.7 billion dollars a year in marketing!

TABLE 12.5 Guidelines for School Health Programs to Prevent Smoking

1. Develop and implement a schoolwide smoke-free policy.
2. Provide instruction in
   a. Recognizing and refuting tobacco-promotion messages from the media, adults, and peers.
   b. Behavioral skills for resisting social influences that promote tobacco use. Programs should help students develop refusal skills through direct instruction, modeling, rehearsal, and reinforcement, and should coach them to help others develop these skills.
   c. General personal and social skills. Programs should help students develop necessary assertiveness, communication, goal-setting, and problem-solving skills that may enable them to avoid both tobacco use and other health risk behaviors.
3. Provide prevention education in kindergarten through twelfth grade, with especially intensive instruction in junior high or middle school.
4. Provide training for teachers.
5. Involve parents and families in the program.
6. Support efforts to stop smoking among students and school staff who currently smoke.
7. Evaluate the program at regular intervals.

Source: Centers for Disease Control. (1994). Guidelines for school health programs to prevent tobacco use and addiction. *Morbidity and Mortality Weekly Reports, 43,* 1–18.

School-based programs based on social-cognitive principles (see Chapter 2) that provide adolescents with the skills to recognize media messages for what they are, and with the resources for making competent decisions, also have been found to be effective in reducing drug use. These programs are most effective when combined with community and media support (CDC, 2001; McDonald, Colwell, Backinger, Husten, & Maule, 2003). Example of two effective programs are the Life Skills Training Program and Project Toward No Drug Abuse (http://modelprograms.samhas.gov/pdfs/FactSheets/ProjectTND.pdf), both identified by the Centers for Disease Control as programs that work (CDC, 2001).

Amazingly, despite the demonstrated effectiveness of social-cognitive interventions, these programs are not the ones being funded and used in most schools. The most widely used and heavily funded program is DARE, used in approximately 80% of school districts in the United States. Evaluations of DARE, however, have found it to be ineffective in reducing drug use (D'Amico & Fromme, 2002; General Accounting Office, 2003; Perry et al., 2003).

For a closer look at an effective program, we can look at Oregon's Tobacco Prevention and Education Program (Ronde et al., 2001). This program was funded by a 1996 ballot initiative that increased the state cigarette tax, and it illustrates the effectiveness of a school-based program when supported by local communities and the media. The program included a statewide media campaign, a "quitline," and a school-based prevention program, offered in a percentage of schools throughout Oregon, that was built around guidelines incorporating social-cognitive principles established by the Centers for Disease Control (see Table 12.5). The increased tax on cigarettes, by the way, also made these less accessible to adolescents who could not afford the additional cost.

All students throughout Oregon were exposed to the same media campaign and all had access to the quitline; however, only a portion of the students also participated in the school-based prevention program. Averaged over all schools, students who participated in the school prevention program were 20% less likely to smoke than those who attended schools that did not offer the program. Furthermore, the decline in smoking among participating students was "dose-dependent," being greatest for those whose schools

Although adolescents continue to try illegal drugs, use among high school seniors has dropped in recent years. Drug education programs are at least partially responsible for having made adolescents more cautious about using drugs. Although the use of many illegal drugs has increased, most adolescents do not use these substances. (This photo shows a mural being painted by the late Keith Haring.)

implemented all of the guidelines (42.2%), less when schools implemented fewer guidelines (21.9%), and least when schools implemented the fewest guidelines (6.6%) (CDC, 2001). Thus, when programs are properly implemented and given local and media support, smoking among teens can be decreased by over 40%!

Most adolescents will experiment with at least some drugs before they reach adulthood. A positive note is that most will not abuse them. However, even casual experimentation with some substances carries substantial risks. How best can society protect adolescents from the potential hazards of experimentation? Is the most effective approach to bombard them with information concerning the dangers of drugs such that they never take that first sip, puff, or pop? Given the pleasurable effects of drugs and the powerful pressures to use them, as well as the excitement of daring the forbidden, scare programs are not likely to keep most adolescents from experimenting. Candid discussions that acknowledge the pleasurable effects of drugs as well as their potential for abuse promise a better safeguard for adolescents. Establishing trust through open communication makes it possible for adolescents to approach adults when they need information or even help.

Eating Disorders

With physical maturation, adolescents experience increases in both height and weight. Some adolescents mistake the natural changes of maturation for unwanted fat; others, perhaps unsure whether they are ready for adulthood, attempt to delay its appearance by literally starving themselves. Still others turn to food when stressed and become obese. We will look at eating disorders next: bulimia, anorexia, and overweight. Anorexia and bulimia are more common among female adolescents than among males; overweight is more common among males (CDC, 2004a).

With respect to the first two disorders, adolescent females today face a standard of beauty that is considerably thinner than in the past. Models of feminine beauty—whether actresses, performers, or individuals advertising products—are thin indeed, compared to their curvaceous counterparts of generations past. The flapper era of the 1920s was the only other time during the past century when the popular images of women were as thin as they are at present. Developmentalists note with some alarm that eating disorders became epidemic among young women then and warn that, with respect to eating disorders, history may be repeating itself.

Anorexics severely limit their intake of food; however, they have a distorted body image. Even though they look dangerously emaciated to friends and family, to themselves, they still do not look thin enough.

Bulimia and Anorexia

Bulimia is characterized by binge eating, consuming large amounts of food in a short time, usually in less than two hours. Binges are usually accompanied by the fear that one cannot stop oneself and are followed by self-deprecating thoughts and compensatory behaviors to prevent gaining weight, such as self-induced vomiting or the use of laxatives.

Anorexia is a disorder in which individuals severely limit their intake of food, weighing less than 85% of what would be expected for their age and sex, have a distorted perception of their body weight, and are fearful of gaining weight. Severe weight loss has mental and emotional, as well as physical effects, and anorexics can be apathetic and irritable. Due to the loss of body fat, anorexics frequently become amenorrheic, ceasing to have menstrual periods.

Most bulimics are aware that their eating patterns are abnormal, and most make continued attempts to lose weight through highly restrictive diets, self-induced vomiting, and use of laxatives or diuretics. Anorexics deny that they have any problem and reject help (American Psychiatric Association, 2000).

Among high school students, somewhat less than 5% become bulimic (Centers for Disease Control, 2004; Stice, Killen, Hayward, & Taylor, 1998); the percentage of those who are anorexic is even smaller. Whereas anorexia is more common in young adolescents, bulimia is more common in older adolescents and young women.

Although bulimics can be of any weight, they are rarely fat (Ledoux, Choquet, & Manfredi, 1993). Usually their weight fluctuates widely, sometimes by as much as 20 to 30 pounds over a relatively brief period. Anorexics are excessively thin, frequently losing up to 25% of their body weight.

Anorexia and bulimia are closely related disorders. Both involve an obsession with food and a morbid fear of being fat. Both also share an obsessive need to be thin. Many anorexics engage in bingeing and purging, and many bulimics start with an initial anorexic phase. Most bulimics usually begin self-induced vomiting a year or two after they start bingeing. Due to the large numbers of calories bulimics consume, they can maintain their weight only by alternating binges with highly restrictive diets or by purging what they have eaten through self-induced vomiting, laxatives, or diuretics.

bulimia An eating disorder characterized by bingeing and then purging; more common in females.

anorexia An eating disorder characterized by severely limiting the intake of food; more common in females.

Bulimics are likely to live with the disorder for a number of years before seeking help. During that time they suffer physical as well as emotional symptoms, such as fatigue, weakness, and constipation. Dental caries and erosion of the enamel of the teeth are also common from frequent contact with stomach acids through self-induced vomiting. Anorexics have a distorted body image and are not likely to seek help even when they become emaciated through self-starvation (Stice, 2002).

Bulimics often have low self-esteem and a history of depression (Ledoux, Choquet, & Manfredi, 1993; Zaider, Johnson, & Cockell, 2000). These adolescents are likely to feel self-conscious around others, be sensitive to rejection, and have difficulty expressing their feeling directly. Both bulimics and anorexics are likely to have high standards and expectations for themselves and to be overly critical when they fail to meet them (Polivy & Herman, 2002).

Frequencies of bulimia and anorexia differ with ethnicity, most likely because body-type preferences differ among ethnic groups. Anorexia is less common among African American adolescents than among European American adolescents. Bulimia also is less common among African Americans, although not among Hispanic adolescents (Granillo, Jones-Rodriquez, & Carvajal, 2005; Mulholland & Mintz, 2001). Both disorders require professional intervention. Each is a serious threat to health and reflects underlying emotional problems that need treatment (Tobias, 1988).

Eating Disorders and Family Conflict Amy Swarr and Maryse Richards (1996) followed a sample of adolescent girls over a two-year period and found that adolescents who enjoyed close positive relationships with their parents had healthier attitudes both toward their weight and toward eating. Eating disorders, when they occur, hide deeper, underlying problems in which family experiences play an important role. Four characteristics of families that lead to the expression of psychological problems as physical symptoms frequently characterize the families of anorexics and bulimics (Minuchin, Rosman, & Baker, 1978; Tobias, 1988). *Enmeshment* exists when boundaries between family members are not clear. In enmeshed families. Everyone is involved in everyone else's life, making it difficult to be independent or autonomous. *Overprotective* families show an inappropriate concern for the welfare of family members. Families characterized by *rigidity* have a need to maintain the status quo and are unable to face change. These qualities make adolescence, a time of many changes, especially difficult. Finally, families in which there is *inadequate conflict resolution* avoid conflict, with the result that differences are never cleanly resolved and members continue to impinge on each other. An eating disorder may be the only way in which adolescents from such families can gain a sense of maintaining control over their lives (Tobias, 1988). The Research Focus "Bias and Blind Controls" describes research studying the families of girls with eating disorders.

Overweight

Physical appearance is perhaps never more important than during adolescence. Body image contributes significantly to self-image for most adolescents. Those who are **overweight** (see Chapter 3 for a more in-depth discussion on weight) tend to have less-positive self-images and lower self-esteem than adolescents of average weight (Miller & Downey, 1999). The prevalence of overweight youth has risen steadily in the United States over the past decade, affecting individuals of all ages (Wadden, Brownell, & Foster, 2002). A number of factors are most likely responsible for this trend, among the most important being changes in eating habits and in patterns of physical activity (CDC, 2004a; Troiano & Flegal, 1998). With respect to eating habits, a greater reliance on fast foods, which are higher in fats and sugars and lower in dietary fiber, and a tendency to snack more frequently throughout the day have led to an increase in the average daily energy intake. This increase has gone hand in hand with a decrease in physical activity, or

overweight Individuals are considered to be overweight when their weight is at or above the 95th percentile for their body mass index.

RESEARCH FOCUS

Bias and Blind Controls: Eating Disorders

"You always shut yourself off in your room," her mother said, somewhat angrily.

"I just want to be left alone," she pleaded, the hint of a whine in her voice. The teenager was 17, and her dark eyes communicated a sulky resentment.

The research assistant on the other side of the one-way mirror quickly coded the girl's response: "asserting," "appeasing," "separating," and "interdependent."

"Some message!" he thought, as he watched the family in front of him.

The girl was trim, neither overweight nor underweight. He couldn't tell from her appearance which type of disorder she suffered from; he only knew that this project was about adolescents with eating disorders. For all he knew, she could be part of the control group.

Why keep this graduate student in the dark about the families he is observing? Why not assume that the more he knows, the better he'll understand and more accurately record their behavior? Investigators have found from painful experience that their expectations all too often influence what they see—sometimes even causing them to read things into a person's behavior that just aren't there. Their expectancies can *bias*, or systematically alter, the results of the study.

Whenever investigators know the condition of which a subject is part, they can bias the outcome of the research either by unconsciously treating subjects in that condition differently or by interpreting—that is, scoring—their behavior differently. If, for example, this graduate student believed that the parents of girls with a certain type of eating disorder were harsh and demanding, he might read hostility into their remarks even when it wasn't there, or perhaps be less friendly with them when introducing them to the experiment. The latter difference might lead to tensions in family interactions that otherwise would not be present, thus unintentionally confirming initial expectations.

Investigators can eliminate experimenter bias by conducting the experiment "blind." Unlike a *single-blind control* procedure, in which only the subjects are unaware of which condition they have been exposed to, in a *double-blind control,* such as the one described here, the experimenter also is ignorant of which condition each subject is in. In this way, the experimenter's expectations cannot contribute to any of the observed differences. Double-blind controls are frequently used in drug studies in which it is necessary to control for the doctor's as well as the patients' expectations that they will get better if they take an experimental medication. In double-blind drug studies, all subjects are given a pill, but half receive a *placebo,* or sugar pill.

Let's get back to the other side of the one-way mirror. Do families of girls with different eating disorders interact in characteristically different ways? Laura Humphrey (1989) observed 74 adolescent girls with their parents. Sixteen were *anorexic,* 16 were *bulimic,* 18 were both *bulimic and anorexic,* and 24 were normal controls. All of those in the first three categories were patients who had been hospitalized long enough so that one could not distinguish the anorexics by their appearance.

Parents of anorexics were both more nurturing and comforting *and* more ignoring and neglecting than were those of bulimics or controls. The anorexic girls were the most submissive of the group when they were with their parents. Bulimics and their parents were more likely to engage in mutual grumbling and blaming and to exchange disparaging remarks. Interactions of normal controls and their parents were characterized more by helping, protecting, trusting, and simple enjoyment of each other.

These findings underscore the importance of treating the family as a whole, as well as working individually with the adolescent when treating eating disorders. Most eating disorders are associated with a pattern of disturbed family interactions.

Source: L. L. Humphrey. (1989). Observed family interactions among subtypes of eating disorders using structural analysis of social behavior. *Journal of Consulting and Clinical Psychology, 57,* 206–214.

in the amount of energy actually expended. As a consequence, the resulting excess energy is stored as fat.

Additionally, the eating patterns of overweight adolescents differ from those who are of average weight. Overweight adolescents are more likely to eat irregularly, missing meals and snacking instead. These habits make it difficult to maintain a balance between hunger and satiation. They are also more likely to eat rapidly, to eat somewhat larger portions, and to eat food that is denser in calories (Wadden et al., 2002). But perhaps the biggest difference between overweight adolescents and those of average weight is in how active they are, not how much they eat. Overweight adolescents are considerably less active than their peers of average weight and thus are less likely to burn off the excess calories they are taking in.

The relationship between overweight and inactivity highlights the importance of exercise in weight reduction programs. Exercise increases the body's metabolism, allowing the body to burn excess calories more rapidly; in moderate amounts, exercise also depresses appetite. Dieting alone can have paradoxical effects, frequently causing a preoccupation with food, which in turn can prompt reactive overeating. Ellen Satter (1988) recommends programs that incorporate procedures which foster a reliance on internal cues rather than on external constraints, such as counting calories and diets. The latter force one to continually think about food and ways of avoiding it.

Adolescents attempting to lose weight often have unrealistic expectations. Many view their weight as central to all of their problems and expect that once they lose weight, their problems will be solved—they will become popular, make the team, and so forth. When their problems do not roll away with the pounds, adolescents can become frustrated and fall off their diets. The most successful programs are multifaceted. The success of a weight control program for adolescents almost always depends on successfully integrating the family into the treatment program (McVey, Pepler, Davis, Flett, & Abdolell, 2002). As with bulimia and anorexia, overweight is often a symptom of underlying conflicts within the family.

Depression

Emotions color experience and give meaning to life. For most individuals they are anchored in reality, tethered to the situations that prompt them. Some individuals are pulled past these to an inner world of thoughts and feelings that bear little resemblance to the situations that occasion them. These individuals suffer from **affective disorders,** disturbances that affect their mood. Mood is an enduring emotional state that varies along a continuum of depression to elation (American Psychiatric Association, 1994). Individuals who suffer from affective disorders live much of their lives at the extremes of this continuum.

Three Depressive Disorders

From time to time everyone feels sad. Those who live with **depression** can feel a crushing weight of hopelessness and despair. They may have any of three major forms of depression. Adolescents with **major depressive disorder** experience severe periods of depression lasting several weeks or more. These are accompanied by some or all of the following symptoms: difficulty concentrating, loss of pleasure, slowed speech and movements, and vegetative signs such as sleepiness, loss of appetite, and weight changes. Adolescents suffering from **dysthymia** have a less severe form of depression but one that generally lasts much longer. The third form, **adjustment disorder with depressed mood,** is brought on by stress and is relatively brief (Petersen et al., 1993).

Feelings of sadness, loneliness, and despair become common by mid-adolescence. Nearly half of all adolescents report experiencing some of the symptoms that characterize depression—sadness, crying spells, pessimism, and feelings of unworthiness. Even so, the prevalence of major depressive disorder among adolescents is relatively

affective disorders Disorders whose primary symptoms reflect a disturbance of mood, such as depression.

depression An affective disorder that may take a number of forms, all of which are characterized by a disturbance of mood.

major depressive disorder A period of severe depression requiring hospitalization or other treatment.

dysthymia A form of depression in which the primary symptoms are unhappiness and dissatisfaction with life, often not traceable to particular events.

adjustment disorder with depressed mood A form of depression, for example, manifest in difficulty carrying out ordinary tasks of life and unsatisfactory social relations.

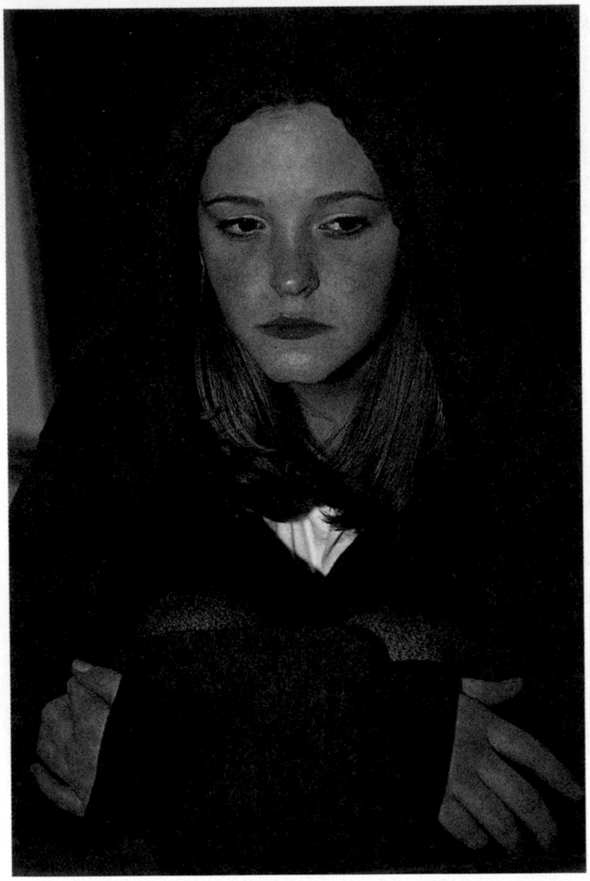

Nearly half of all adolescents report experiencing some of the symptoms that characterize depression: sadness, crying spells, pessimism, and feelings of unworthiness.

low—about 5%—with most of those affected being female (McFarlane, Bellissimo, Norman, & Lange, 1994).

Adolescents who suffer from depression share with adult depressives feelings of low self-esteem, pervasive sadness, hopelessness, and helplessness. A self-defeating cycle exists in which low self-esteem contributes to depression, which in turn fuels negative feelings about the self.

Masked Depression

Depression is often masked in early adolescence. Several symptoms signal **masked depression,** the most frequent being fatigue, poor concentration, and hypochondriasis (excessive concern with illness or health). Continual fatigue can reflect inner struggles with feelings that adolescents cannot put to rest or talk about with others. Similarly, difficulties in concentration can result from concerns they do not yet feel secure enough to articulate, and preoccupations with their health, or a seeming lack of it, may reflect fears of inadequacy or incompetence.

Each of these symptoms can be mistakenly interpreted as a natural part of adolescence. Fatigue is expected, given the accelerated growth of puberty and the demands of school, friends, and family. Similarly, poor concentration can easily be mistaken for problems with schoolwork ranging from boredom to being overwhelmed, and excessive concern with one's body is natural, given the changes that take place during puberty. Treatments that take into consideration the underlying source of an adolescent's depression will be more effective in combating these symptoms than those that are directed at the symptoms themselves: the fatigue, poor concentration, or excessive concern with health.

Irving Weiner (1980) suggests that adolescents may not be able to admit feelings of inadequacy and still accomplish the developmental tasks they face, such as achieving emotional independence, finding a sense of self, and developing intimate relationships. Any one of these would be difficult under the best of conditions and can be impossible with feelings of inadequacy. Early adolescents may also be more caught up in *doing* things than in reflecting about them. In either case, depression, or attempts to keep it at bay, are likely to at first assume a physical form in early adolescence.

Suicide

An alarming number of adolescents report thinking about suicide. In a national survey of high school students, 16.9% said that they had thought seriously about attempting suicide at some point during the past year, 16.5% indicating they had even made specific plans. A total of 8.5% actually attempt suicide; far more ninth-graders do so (10.1%) than do twelfth-graders (6.1%) (Centers for Disease Control and Prevention, 2004). Suicide is the third leading cause of death among adolescents.

masked depression Depression that manifests itself in ways other than depressed mood, for example, agitation, inability to sleep.

Startling as these figures are, they may underestimate the actual number of deaths by suicide because they don't include the many deaths recorded as accidents (for

TABLE 12.6 Percentages of African American, European American, and Hispanic High School Students Reporting Suicidal Thoughts and Behavior

Ethnicity	Suicidal Thoughts	Made a Suicide Plan	Attempted Suicide	Attempt(s) Requiring Medical Attention
African American	12.5	10.4	8.4	3.7
European American	16.5	16.2	6.9	1.7
Hispanic	18.1	17.6	10.6	5.0

Note: Questions asked whether students had seriously thought about attempting suicide at any time in the past year, whether they had made a specific plan, how many attempts they had made, and whether any of these attempts required treatment by a doctor or nurse.

Source: Centers for Disease Control and Prevention. (2004). Youth risk behavior surveillance—United States, 2003. *Morbidity and Mortality Weekly Report, 53.* May 21, 2004, Vol. 53, No. SS-2.

example, single-person car crashes, drownings, overdoses), which in some cases are misclassified suicides.

Gender and Ethnic Differences

Males are more likely than females to complete a suicide, despite the fact that females attempt suicide twice as often as males (Centers for Disease Control and Prevention, 2004). In part, this difference can be traced to the different methods chosen by males and females. Males are most likely to use a gun or attempt to hang themselves, both of which are more immediately lethal than ingesting harmful substances, the method most commonly used by females (Garland & Zigler, 1993). Among completed suicides, for both sexes, using a gun is the most frequent method. Although at first glance these gender differences would seem to suggest less ambivalence about dying among males, other factors are probably more important. Males, in general, are more impulsive and violent than females, qualities that are reflected in the methods they choose. Impulsivity may be a critical factor in most suicides, and males, because they are likely to choose a violent method, will complete more suicides (Garland & Zigler, 1993). Also, females may be able to seek out and use interpersonal supports more easily than males, who typically find it more difficult to reveal neediness or ask for help (Garland & Zigler, 1993).

Ethnic differences exist as well in suicidal thoughts and behavior. Table 12.6 summarizes the responses of high school students to questions concerning suicide. African American students reported fewer suicidal thoughts or attempts than either European American or Hispanic students, and Hispanic students reported the most (Centers for Disease Control and Prevention, 2004). Among all ethnic groups, the rate of suicide is highest for Native Americans. However, large differences exist between different tribes. The rate of suicide among Navajos, for instance, is close to that nationally, whereas the rate among Apaches is more than three times as high (Garland & Zigler, 1993). As a rule, tribes that are more traditional tend to have lower suicide rates, perhaps because they provide a greater sense of community and their members experience more support (Wyche, Obolensky, & Glood, 1990).

Warning Signs

Although every case of suicide is unique, a number of common warning signs exist. These include sudden changes in behavior, changes in patterns of sleeping or eating, loss

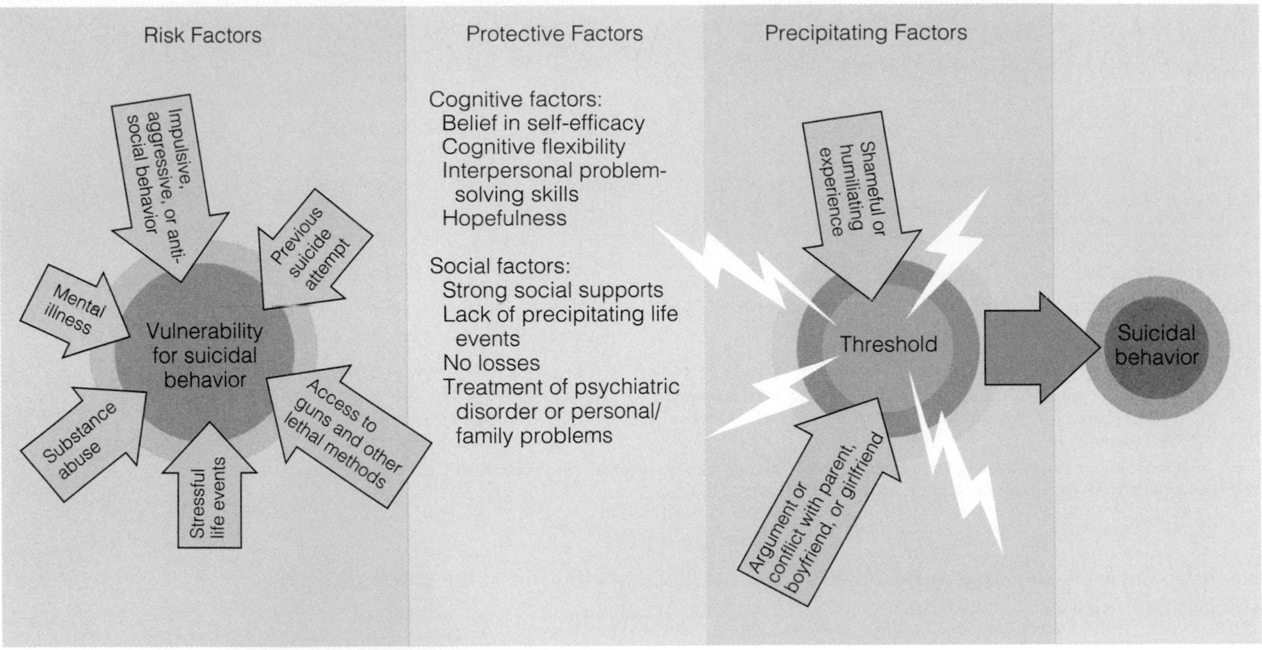

■ **FIGURE 12.4**
Factors Contributing to Suicide. *Source:* Adapted from S. J. Blumenthal & D. J. Kupfer. (1988). Overview of early detection and treatment strategies for suicidal behavior in young people. *Journal of Youth and Adolescence, 17,* 1–23.

of interest in usual activities or withdrawal from others, experiencing a humiliating event, feelings of guilt or hopelessness, an inability to concentrate, talk of suicide, or giving away one's most important possessions (U.S. Department of Health and Human Services, 2005). The presence of any one of these is a cause for concern; the presence of several is a clear signal that an adolescent may be in danger.

Risk Factors

Several factors are associated with an increased risk of suicide. Most of these characterize the person at risk, although some, such as substance abuse or exposure to suicidal behavior, can also involve elements of the family or the larger culture. Even though most suicides are associated with one or more of these risk factors, about one-third of youth suicides are associated with no risk factors at all; these youths come from loving and supportive homes.

Blumenthal and Kupfer (1988) classify risk factors into potentially overlapping domains. As the overlap among domains increases, so does the risk of suicide, as illustrated in Figure 12.4. According to this approach,

> the breakup of a relationship might be a final humiliating experience that triggers a depressive episode in a young person with a family history of affective disorder. Such an individual may also have poor social supports, which interact with the other identified risk factors to increase the individual's vulnerability for suicide. (Blumenthal & Kupfer, 1988, p. 4)

Cognitive factors that help to protect adolescents from the threat of suicide are feelings of self-efficacy, problem-solving skills, and hopefulness. Similarly, social factors

IN MORE DEPTH

A Poem Written by a 15-Year-Old Boy Two Years Before Committing Suicide

TO SANTA CLAUS AND LITTLE SISTERS
Once . . . he wrote a poem.
And called it "Chops."
Because that was the name of his dog, and that's
  what it was all about.
And the teacher gave him an "A"
And a gold star.
And his mother hung it on the kitchen door, and read
  it to all his aunts . . .
Once . . . he wrote another poem.
And he called it "Question Marked Innocence."
Because that was the name of his grief and that's
  what it was all about.
And the professor gave him an "A"
And a strange and steady look.
And his mother never hung it on the kitchen door,
  because he never let her see it . . .
Once, at 3 a.m. . . . he tried another poem . . .
And he called it absolutely nothing, because that's
  what it was all about.
And he gave himself an "A"
And a slash on each damp wrist,
And hung it on the bathroom door because he
  couldn't reach the kitchen.

Sources: A. Russell Lee, M.D., Director of Family Therapy Training, Pacific Medical Center, San Francisco, California, and Contra Costa, California, Mental Health Services; and Charlotte P. Ross, Executive Director, Suicide Prevention and Crisis Center, San Mateo County, Burlingame, California.

decreasing the risk of suicide are the presence of strong social supports, the lack of precipitating life events, and getting treatment or help for personal or family problems.

Among the most serious risk factors for suicide are depression and having made a prior attempt. Anywhere from 50% to 80% of all completed suicides by adolescents have been preceded by a previous attempt (Shafii, Carrigan, Whittinghill, & Derrick, 1985). Suicidal remarks or other warning signs among such adolescents assume added significance.

A common cultural stereotype of adolescent suicide attempts holds that these are shallow and impulsive bids for attention. Neither assumption is true. Adolescents who are suicidal are in personal pain and have usually sought a number of solutions to their present problems. Suicidal adolescents usually attempt to communicate their distress in a number of ways, and thoughts of suicide are often a last resort. The poem in the In More Depth box is a poignant illustration of this point.

In addition to a previous suicide attempt, other significant risk factors are depression, substance abuse, and aggressive or disruptive behaviors (American Psychiatric Association, 2005).

Adolescents who attempt or commit suicide commonly experience more life stress, more losses, and more changes within the family than those who do not. Frequently a humiliating event precipitates the suicide attempt, such as a crisis or an interpersonal problem involving parents or peers. Family life is more likely to be chaotic, relationships with parents are frequently problematic, and parental strife is more common. Suicidal adolescents generally have fewer social supports and personal resources while facing these added stresses (Blumenthal & Kupfer, 1988).

The availability of lethal methods, particularly firearms, is also a factor affecting suicide rates. Over half of all youth who commit suicide use a firearm (American Psychiatric Association, 2005).

Counseling and Prevention

The importance of communication cannot be stressed too much. Caring, open and supportive efforts to address problems on the part of those closest to the adolescent are vital. Yet important as these efforts are, they should never replace professional help.

Adolescents who are alienated, delinquent, depressed, or suicidal follow a different developmental path than most. But all adolescents share the need to be listened to and supported by those who are closest to them.

Frequently suicidal adolescents communicate with their peers. Frequently, too, peers are uninformed concerning warning signs of suicidal intent. Only half of one sample of adolescents knew, for instance, that remarks about wanting to die, seeming worried, or having problems in school or with a relationship might be related to suicidal behavior. Less than 20% knew that adolescents who are suicidal are likely to threaten they will kill themselves. Even more alarming was the finding that over 40% of these adolescents believed that such behaviors were *not* likely to be related to suicide (Norton, Durlak, & Richards, 1989).

What advice is there to give to those who fear that an adolescent close to them may be suicidal? Suicidal adolescents communicate their pain to those they are closest to. It is important to pick up on these signals. One should not be afraid to openly ask the adolescent if she or he has thought of self-destructive behavior. Listening to what the adolescent has to say can be painful, but it is vitally important. Attempting to deny the reality of the adolescent's pain through false assurances that everything will be okay only communicates that one has not heard the pain or the hopelessness. Serious thoughts of suicide require professional attention. Loving concern, though important in its own right, is not a substitute. Professional help should be obtained immediately.

Prevention Programs The most effective programs help suicidal adolescents face truths in their lives and have these work for them. Sometimes the truth can be as simple as learning how to say something and then make it happen. The approaches that work best are brief, crisis-oriented, and give adolescents skills they can apply in their ongoing relationships (Kerfoot, Harrington, & Dyer, 1995).

To be effective, programs must reach the adolescents who need them. Many adolescents who attempt suicide do not show up for therapy, or they drop out before they complete it. One study found that 20% did not keep any of the appointments they made, another 19% dropped out during the initial assessment sessions, and nearly one-third more discontinued the program before they finished (Trautman & Rotheram, 1986). Given the chaotic home lives of many of these adolescents, completing anything, even breakfast, can be an accomplishment. One program found it helpful to give adolescents who had been hospitalized for a suicide attempt a token that would give them readmission to the hospital on a "no questions asked" basis, should circumstances become intolerable (Cotgrove, Zirinksy, Black, & Weston, 1995).

The most effective treatments are highly structured programs that train adolescents in skills they can apply at home and in school. Most also teach adolescents to attribute their successes to their own efforts; they aim at getting them to a place where they can say, "I did that and I did it well."

Usually counselors help adolescents identify problem areas and generate alternative solutions. When adolescents can think of alternative solutions to conflicts and predict the effects of acting one way or another, they can cope more effectively. Even if the other person reacts negatively, being able to predict a response puts adolescents less "at the effect of" the other person. If adolescents can also anticipate their own feelings about negative reactions, they are in an even better place to control these feelings. In a sense, conflict management is a bit like surfing: You need to stay just behind the crest of the wave to keep it from crashing down on you.

Family Therapy Because many suicide attempts are precipitated by conflict with a parent, treatment that includes the family will almost always be the most effective. This type of therapy shifts the focus from the adolescent to family interactions that preceded the suicide attempt. Improving communication within the family is usually an important element to intervention programs (Kerfoot, Harrington, & Dyer, 1995).

Summary

Alienation and the Failure to Cope

- Feelings of *alienation* are common in adolescence. These can be triggered by pubertal changes, identity issues, and feelings of cultural estrangement.
- Many alienated adolescents are runaways. These youths are frequently abused or neglected. As a group they suffer from low self-esteem, depression, poor interpersonal skills, insecurity, anxiousness, impulsiveness, and lack of a sense of personal control over their lives. Home life for most is chaotic and characterized by violence.
- Three home-life patterns distinguish adolescents who are *maltreated.* The abuse may be a continuation of abusive patterns that started in childhood, it may reflect a change in the type of discipline used when they reach adolescence, or it may be occasioned by the onset of adolescence itself. Factors that, in combination, characterize maltreating parents include difficulty coping with stress; a negative, defensive worldview; inappropriate expectations of adolescents; less-supportive and warm partners; and poverty.

Juvenile Delinquency

- *Juvenile delinquency* involves illegal behavior committed by a minor. *Status* offenses are behaviors that are illegal when engaged in by minors but legal for adults. *Index* offenses are behaviors that are criminal at any age.
- The type of delinquent act varies with age. There is little evidence suggesting that minor forms of delinquency predict a later shift to more serious crime. The pattern instead suggests a small subgroup of delinquents who start early and account for a relatively large proportion of criminal activity.
- Gender, ethnic, and social class differences exist in delinquency. Females are less likely to engage in delinquent activities than are males and are less likely to commit violent crimes. Large ethnic differences exist in the numbers of adolescents from different ethnic backgrounds who enter the juvenile justice system. Although these differences are difficult to separate from social class differences, they strongly suggest bias within the juvenile justice system.
- The individual-differences perspective attributes delinquency to individual traits and characteristics, whereas the social-contextual perspective looks to parents' roles in shaping traits in their children and in shaping their social environment. From either perspective, nurturant and involved parenting decreases the risk of delinquency.
- Juvenile gangs have changed over the past generation. They are more likely to be linked to organized crime than in the past and are associated with more violent crimes and the sale of narcotics.
- The threat of violence is not limited to gang members. Teenagers are nearly twice as likely to be victims of violent crime as are young adults. Homicide is the second leading cause of death for all young people, and most are killed with a firearm.

Adolescents and Drugs

- Physical drug dependence occurs with *psychoactive* substances when they control behavior so that the individual cannot easily discontinue their use. Dependence on a drug involves developing a tolerance for it such that increased amounts are necessary to achieve the same effect, resulting in withdrawal when use is discontinued. Adolescents are likely to first try alcohol, then cigarettes, and then marijuana.
- *Alcohol* depresses the activity of the central nervous system; it loosens inhibitions and makes individuals feel more spontaneous. As blood-alcohol level rises,

activities controlled by the central nervous system are increasingly affected. Most high school seniors have tried alcohol and many do so with some regularity.

- *Cigarettes* are the only substance that a sizable number of adolescents use on a daily basis. Because of this, cigarettes pose one of the most serious, if not the most serious, health risks of all drugs to adolescents. Most adolescents who smoke start before they reach high school. Most adolescents who start to smoke have tried unsuccessfully to stop. The use of cigarettes and alcohol is associated with the use of other, illicit substances.
- *Marijuana* is a mild hallucinogen that affects thought, perception, reaction time, and coordination. Long-term heavy use carries a number of potential health risks. Of all illicit drugs, marijuana is the most frequently used by adolescents.
- There are significant age trends with respect to the use of alcohol, cigarettes, and marijuana, with the use of all three increasing with age. There are ethnic differences as well, with African American adolescents being less likely to drink alcohol or smoke cigarettes than European American or Hispanic adolescents. With respect to gender, early adolescent females drink more than males their age; overall, females are as likely to smoke cigarettes but less likely to have used marijuana.
- There is a pattern to the order in which adolescents experiment with drugs; alcohol is the first drug used, which is followed by cigarettes, which, in turn, are followed by marijuana. The *gateway hypothesis* assumes that involvement with drugs progresses through a sequence of stages, with the use of one type of drug providing a pathway to the use of other drugs. The extent to which adolescents become involved in the use of a drug is important in predicting progression to a higher stage.
- Factors that place adolescents at risk for substance abuse are being less well adjusted, being impulsive, having low self-esteem, doing poorly in school, having problematic relations with peers, and having friends who use drugs. Adolescents who abuse drugs are likely to have less nurturing parents, to have parents who abuse substances themselves, to live in more violent communities, and to have drugs more available.
- Protective factors include high self-esteem, good social skills, involvement in religion, friends who do not abuse drugs, and doing well in school. Also important are parents who are warm, communicate well, and monitor their children's activities. Media campaigns affecting adolescents' perception of the harmfulness of drugs have been effective as well.
- The proportion of adolescents using drugs has continued to decline over the past decade. With the exception of alcohol, cigarettes, and marijuana, most of the drugs adolescents report using were used by less than 2% of seniors.
- Efforts to prevent drug abuse include controlling access to drugs, media campaigns, and school-based educational programs organized around social-cognitive principles. Programs using a combination of these approaches are the most effective.
- Most adolescents will experiment with some drugs before they reach adulthood; most will also not use them frequently. Even casual experimentation with some substances carries substantial risks. Candid discussions that acknowledge the pleasurable effects of drugs as well as their potential dangers promise to be the most effective ways of providing help to adolescents.

Eating Disorders

- Standards for female attractiveness show thinner models today than in past generations. This trend is problematic in that eating disorders are more common among females.
- *Bulimia* and *anorexia* are closely related eating disorders. Bulimia is characterized by binge eating alternated with purging through self-induced vomiting, laxatives, or diuretics. Anorexia is an eating disorder in which food intake is severely limited to the point of self-starvation. Both disorders are more common among females than males and are more likely to occur in adolescents who come from families characterized by enmeshment, overprotectiveness, rigidity, and inadequate conflict resolution.
- *Overweight* adolescents are defined as being at or above the 95th percentile in weight for their age and sex. Overweight adolescents are likely to have parents who are overweight; they also eat irregularly, eat food that is denser in calories, and are more inactive than adolescents of average weight. Effective treatments include exercise and involve the family.

Depression

- Depression is an *affective disorder* that can take a number of forms. Adolescents with *major depressive disorder* suffer episodes of debilitating depression that can last for several weeks or more. Those with *dysthymia* experience less severe but longer-lasting symptoms. Those with *adjustment disorder with depressed mood* experience brief bouts of depression brought on by stress. Adolescents who suffer from depression have feelings of low self-esteem, sadness, hopelessness, and helplessness. Depression can be *masked* by physical symptoms in early adolescence.

Suicide

- Nearly 17% of high school students indicate having thought about attempting suicide at some point within the last year, and nearly 9% actually attempt suicide. Suicide is the third most common cause of death among adolescents.
- Warning signs include sudden changes in behavior, changes in sleeping or eating patterns, loss of interest in usual activities or withdrawal from others, experiencing a humiliating event, feelings of guilt or hopelessness, inability to concentrate, talk of suicide, or giving away important possessions.
- Factors that place adolescents at risk of suicide are depression, a prior suicide attempt, substance abuse, life stresses and chaotic family lives.
- The most effective treatment programs work with the family as well as the suicidal adolescent.

Key Terms

alienation
maltreatment
parentified
juvenile delinquency
index offenses
status offenses
drug dependence
psychoactive
alcohol
nicotine
marijuana
gateway hypothesis
bulimia
anorexia
overweight
affective disorders
depression
major depressive disorder
dysthymia
adjustment disorder with depressed mood
masked depression

CHAPTER OUTLINE

CHAPTER 13

Positive Development in Adolescence

Meeting the Challenges and Making It Work

CHAPTER OBJECTIVES

- To look at the conditions that support healthy development in adolescence:
  - Responsive and demanding relationships with parents
  - Safe neighborhoods characterized by social networks of caring neighbors
  - Schools in which adolescents feel safe and form meaningful relationships with teachers
  - Personal strengths such as an easy temperament, competence, and strong religious beliefs
- To look at how adolescents cope with stress
- To examine the development of prosocial behavior in adolescents
- To consider the importance of structured voluntary activities for the development of initiative in adolescents

What is it that we—as parents, teachers, employers, and members of the community—want of adolescents? What is the cultural agenda awaiting adolescents as they move into adulthood? Do we simply want them to settle down, do well at school, and get to work on time? Or do expectations run deeper than that? What does it take, in other words, for us to consider them "grown up"?

Robert Kegan (1994), at Harvard University, says that it takes a lot. Kegan asserts that we do not simply expect adolescents to change how they behave. We expect them to change how they *know,* to change the way they understand, or give meaning to, their experiences. Such a change requires adolescents to let go of their current grasp of the way things are, a grasp that includes the way they know themselves.

Consider Sylvia, for instance. Sylvia is 15 and she is having a bad day. She has cut her afternoon classes to go to the mall with her friends. Glancing up from the cosmetics counter where they've been trying on lipsticks, she looks into the face of her mother, who is looking back at her. Her flushed excuse of a short day at school doesn't change the set to her mother's mouth or the look in her eyes, a mixture of hurt and anger.

For her part, Sylvia's mother is wondering why she has bothered for the past five months to pick her daughter up from school when she can so obviously get where she wants to go on her own. Where is the child who used to hold her hand so sweetly

One of the major steps in growing up is developing a relationship with one's parents that is mutual and reciprocal.

whenever they'd leave the house? Not that she wants that in a 15-year-old. No, and as much as she values independence and planning in her children, Sylvia's mother does not feel like congratulating her daughter on the way she has planned her afternoon or gotten to the mall on her own. Not on your life! In fact, she feels like saying, "It's time you started taking your schooling more seriously, sister! You've got a future to think about. You're not a kid anymore. And how do you think I feel knowing you would have met me in the parking lot lying about where you'd been all afternoon!" (Kegan, 1994).

Sylvia's mother was disappointed in her. She expected so much more of her daughter than this. But just what is it that parents expect of their teenagers? Is it simply that they behave better than Sylvia did? Is it that we don't want them to cut class, lie about where they've been, or in other ways deceive us? The answer to that, of course, is yes, but it is also more. What we really want of adolescents has more to do with the reasons behind their actions. We want them to do what they do for the right reasons. Kegan points out, however, that reasons have to do with the way we understand the world. And for Sylvia to behave differently, and do so for the right reasons, she would have to understand her world, understand both herself and others, differently.

Sylvia has organized her meaning of self largely in terms of her relationship with her parents. If asked to recount what happened this day, Sylvia would probably talk more about her mother than herself, saying that her mother is always checking up on her or that she doesn't really understand how she feels.

What are we to make of Sylvia? Is she simply thoughtless and "bad," an adolescent with no sense of values? Actually, if you knew a little more about her, you would find her to be quite the opposite, to be affectionate and loving, helpful and polite, and genuinely so in all of these things. If asked, for instance, about her favorite memories, she would most likely talk about the family holidays, the times when they are all together, the big meals, noisy evenings, and quiet mornings with leftovers for breakfast instead of cereal.

The problem is not as simple as sorting the good kids from the bad kids. If it were, we would all have an easier time of it. Sylvia is, with a few exceptions, a good kid. This does not mean that skipping school or lying to her mother is acceptable or that her mother should let it pass with no consequences. In important ways, however, Sylvia's problem is larger than what happened at the mall. Her problem has to do with how she understands herself.

Sylvia has difficulty separating herself from her parents. For instance, in order for her to see her mother differently, to take her mother's feelings into account, she must come to see herself differently, to distinguish the way she is feeling at the moment from her larger sense of who she is, from her sense of self. Only then will she be able to coordinate her own needs with the needs of others. When adolescents can recognize the needs of others as well as their own and, with this, appreciate the obligations each has toward the other, they can step into relationships characterized by reciprocity and mutuality (Kegan, 1982). And this is a large part of what most of us mean by being "grown up." Mutuality means that one not only does the right things but does them for the right reasons.

A developmental step of this magnitude, even though we expect it of all adolescents, is not an easy one to take. In order for adolescents to move toward greater mutuality in their relationships, to become full members in the adult community, they need the support of that community (Zeldin & Price, 1995). To change the way they know themselves and understand their world, they must let go of themselves enough to grow into new ways of being.

For adolescents to do something as risky as letting go, someone else needs to be there to hold on. In order to "grow up," in other words, adolescents need to experience not only the challenge to grow but the support that makes this possible. The supports that "hold" adolescents as they take these steps toward greater maturity assume a number of forms. Adolescents are held, for instance, by their families. They are also held by their communities—by such things as schools and teachers, activities and clubs, parks, libraries, recreation centers, and places of worship. Adolescents are also sustained, as they construct a new understanding of themselves and their world, by the strengths within them, such as their temperament, attitudes, and religious beliefs.

Chapter Overview

This chapter looks first at the ways in which families provide support through authoritative parenting, the use of supportive adult network structures, and effective use of institutions in the community. From there we move to a consideration of the ways in which community resources promote healthy development before turning to a consideration of the personal strengths of adolescents, such as their outlook on life, competence, and religious beliefs, that sustain healthy development.

Even under the best of conditions, stress is a common part of normal life. Differences in the ways adolescents cope with stress, as well as learning to cope more effectively, receive attention. The chapter then moves to a consideration of adolescents who are distinguished by their remarkable prosocial behavior, and concludes with an analysis of the types of everyday activities that contribute to the development of initiative.

Protective Factors in Adolescence

Adolescents are supported by many protective factors in their environment. Each of these factors—whether aspects of their homes, schools, or communities—helps adolescents to redefine themselves, to change the way they know themselves, so that the self they bring to their encounters with others will be one that is capable of mutuality and one that can continue to grow.

Families

Among the most important sources of support in adolescents' lives are their relationships within the family (Dubow, Arnett, Smith, & Ippolito, 2001), especially with parents. These relationships can be characterized in terms of two broad dimensions: care and support, sometimes referred to as *responsiveness,* and discipline and monitoring of adolescents' activities, or *demandingness* (see Chapter 7). Each of these dimensions of families has been found to be related to healthy development.

Longitudinal research confirms the importance of responsiveness. Kristin Moore and Dana Glei (1995) followed a nationally representative sample of children from the ages of 7 through 11 to the ages of 18 to 22, interviewing both children and parents. These investigators found that adolescents who had warm and emotionally satisfying relationships with their parents in childhood and who experienced fewer family disruptions, such as marital conflict or divorce, were more likely to have a greater sense of well-being in adolescence and to avoid serious risk taking, such as dropping out, using cigarettes or other drugs, or engaging in delinquent behavior. Similar findings from other studies confirm the importance of caring and supportive relationships within the family as significant protective factors contributing to the well-being of adolescents, even when other family variables such as socioeconomic status and family structure are controlled for (Birndorf, Ryan, Auinger, & Aten, 2005).

In general, authoritative parenting, which is characterized by responsiveness and demandingness, is associated with adolescents' ability to listen to parents' advice when making difficult decisions (Mackey, Arnold, & Pratt, 2001). Kathleen Mackey, Mary Louise Arnold, and Michael Pratt (2001) interviewed adolescents about decisions in which they'd asked a parent for advice; they also assessed the style of parenting and parental influence on the decision. One adolescent with an authoritative parent had this to say:

> At the beginning of the semester, I was thinking of dropping my math class, and we went through that and we (she and mother) talked about all our options. . . . I'm not doing very well, but, we decided I would keep going, and she got a tutor and stuff. She saw how much trouble I was having with it, so she said, "I don't want you to stress yourself out over this, but if you need the course for later on, it's good to keep it." She was just telling me to stick with it . . . like she would have let me make my own decision. . . . She just told me what she thought, but if I had told her I'm dropping the class, she never would have objected. . . . I decided to stay in the class and get a tutor. It was kind of like it was all my decision, but it was tough. . . . I'm glad I stayed in, but I don't really have much of an interest in it. (p. 251)

We can see both responsiveness and demandingness in this mother. The daughter speaks of her mother as caring and supportive ("She saw how much trouble I was having . . ."), yet the quality of demandingness is also present in the mother's expectations for responsible behavior (". . . if you need the course for later on, it's good to keep it" and "She was just telling me to stick with it"). By supporting her daughter in making this decision (". . . she got a tutor and stuff"), she helped her daughter find her own strengths (". . . it was tough. . . . I'm glad I stayed . . ."). Not least among the strengths was the daughter's experience of having made a good decision.

Robin Jarrett (1995), at Loyola University, summarizes a number of family characteristics—illustrating the dimensions of responsiveness and demandingness—that enhance the development of youth. Although these strategies are ones that have been

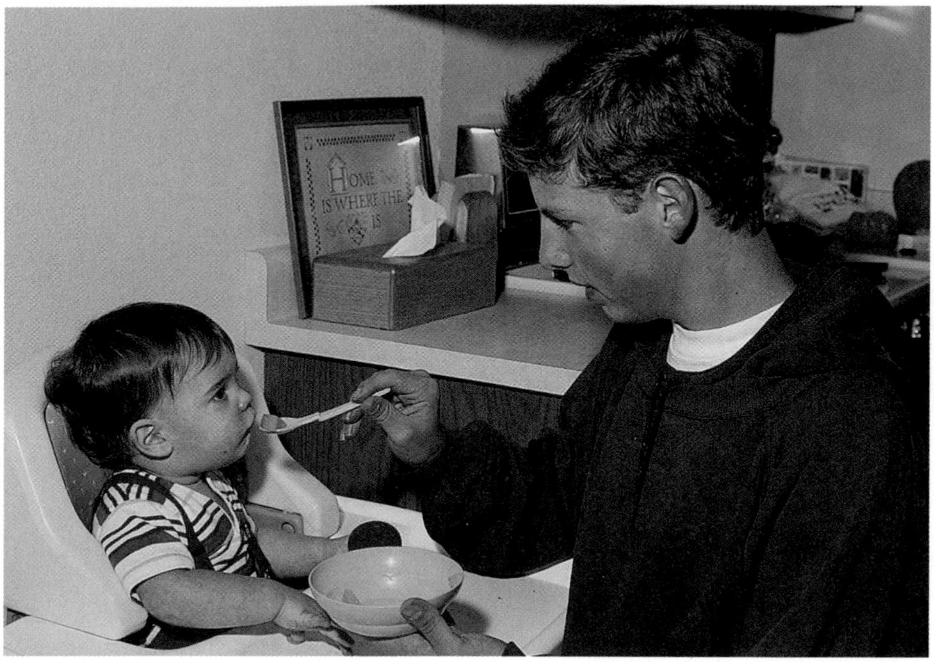

Being expected to help with family needs, such as caring for younger siblings, gives adolescents a sense of competence, an important factor in healthy development.

found effective specifically in counteracting the eroding effects of poverty among African American families, their wisdom cuts across income level and ethnicity, making them applicable in varying degrees to all families. For a look at other strategies used by African American families, read the Research Focus "Archival Research: Racial Socialization—Survival Tactics in a White Society?"

One of the first characteristics to emerge from the welter of research reviewed by Jarrett, a characteristic illustrating the dimension of responsiveness, involves the use of *supportive adult network structures.* These networks take the form of additional adults who can be called on to provide care. Adults, such as grandparents, godparents, or neighbors, provide resources that otherwise might not be available to these adolescents. The following excerpt illustrates this type of support:

> [Aunt] Ann . . . paid for [Ben's] class ring, his senior pictures, and his cap and gown. Ann did not see this as unusual behavior as it was exactly what Jean [her sister] had done for her a long time ago. She also pointed out that she had been helping to pay nominal school fees for Jean's children for several years. *(Zollar, 1985, p. 79, as cited in Jarrett, 1995)*

These successful families also made use of *supportive institutions within the community,* such as churches and schools. Churches were found not only to undergird these families spiritually but also to offer activities for youth in which they could form friendships and develop new skills. Religious beliefs and activities also foster self-respect, personal discipline, and a concern for others, as well as contribute to improvements academically, particularly for adolescents in low-income neighborhoods (Moore & Glei, 1995; Regnerus & Elder, 2003). Among adolescents girls, frequent attendance at religious services is also related to later ages for becoming sexually active (Jones, Darroch, & Singh, 2005).

Jarrett found that parental use of schools similarly took a number of forms. Parents collaborated with school personnel, attending parent–teacher meetings, serving on

RESEARCH FOCUS

Archival Research: Racial Socialization—Survival Tactics in a White Society?

With Michael Wapner

Parents reflect the values of their society and, in doing so, pass them on to their children. Psychologists refer to parents as socialization agents. As "agents" of society, they also communicate the statuses and roles that make up the social order and prepare their children to participate accordingly as adults. So far so good.

So what's the bad part? Minority parents face a special problem when they encounter societal values that can diminish the self-esteem of their children and, if internalized, could prevent them from realizing their potential. How do minority parents prepare their children for entrance into a society that frequently views their group negatively?

In a sense, they become "double agents." In addition to socializing their children into the values of the broader society, minority parents interpret that society's values in ways that shield their children from harm. By explicitly speaking against negative stereotypes, by serving as models themselves, and by exposing their children to cultural experiences that reflect the strengths of their own background, they inculcate feelings of worth and group pride. In African American society, this process is termed *racial socialization.*

The way Black parents perceive society, and communicate those perceptions to their children, should reflect their own position in it. Yet we know little about the influence of demographic variables on racial socialization. Frequently, a single study lacks the scope to address such issues. Tapping into existing databases, often collected from national samples, offers a useful alternative. **Archival research** does just that: It uses existing information to obtain answers to research questions.

Archives exist in many forms: Vast databases collected from national samples, written records such as books or newspapers, and publicly maintained records are examples. The databases maintained by the U.S. Census Bureau are an obvious source of archival information, illustrating the first of these forms. How might one use books or newspapers to answer research questions? Consider, for example, the question of whether school materials reinforce traditional sex-role stereotypes. To answer, one might sample textbooks and analyze their content for the frequency of female and male characters, their activities, and the settings in which they appear (such as home or work). Is living together prior to marriage more common today than a generation ago? One can look at marriage license applications for common addresses, to determine an answer.

An obvious advantage to archival research is *accessibility:* The data have already been collected. Another advantage is that many archives, such as the U.S. Census data, are more complete than any data that

committees, and maintaining close contact with their children's teachers. But parents were also willing to confront school personnel in order to ensure that their children received the attention they needed. As one mother explained, "This lady tells me that the principal doesn't have time to look at everybody's case. So I told that lady, 'that may be the case but this is one that he's going to look at.' . . . I was going to the Board of Education and everywhere I could think of to see that Marie could go ahead and graduate" (Clark, 1983, p. 41, as cited in Jarrett, 1995).

The strategies identified by Jarrett also illustrate the second dimension of family interaction: demandingness. For instance, Jarrett found parents to *monitor* their adolescents' activities and friendships, setting limits on whom they could associate with, what they could do, and when they were to get home. "Chaperonage" figured centrally in this monitoring, beginning in childhood as parents accompanied their children as they went into the neighborhood and taking a particularly inventive form in adolescence by having a younger sibling tag along on dates and other activities. Other research, as well, finds

archival research The use of existing data, such as public records, to provide answers to research questions.

could be collected in a single research study. A further advantage is that the measures are *unobtrusive.* Subjects do not know they are being studied and therefore do not change their behavior or their answers to questions (as they might, for instance, if asked whether they are living together). Unobtrusive measures are *nonreactive:* They do not change the behavior they are measuring.

Disadvantages to using archival data also exist. Information may be lost over time. The quality of record keeping can change with time, causing unsuspecting researchers to infer that changes have occurred when in actuality none have. Computers, for example, allow better record keeping by police. As a result, crime may appear to have increased, whereas in actuality it is only being recorded more precisely.

What does archival research tell us about racial socialization? Do most Black parents act as double agents to shield their children from harm by the larger society? Michael Thornton, Linda Chatters, Robert Taylor, and Walter Allen (1990), analyzing data from a national survey of African Americans, found that they do. Nearly two-thirds of all Black parents engage in some racial socialization. What demographic variables predict racial socialization? These investigators found that sex, age, marital status, and region of the country all predict the likelihood of racial socialization. Mothers are more likely than fathers to prepare their children for the realities of minority status. So, too, are older parents, those who are married (versus never married), and those who are more educated. Regional differences also predict socialization approaches. Black parents living in the Northeast, more so than those in the South, engage in racial socialization. Other research finds that racial socialization varies with the cultural diversity of the neighborhood. Boys are more likely to receive cultural pride messages when they live in ethnically mixed neighborhoods, whereas the opposite is true for girls, this being more likely when they live in predominately Black neighborhoods (Stevenson, McNeil, Herrero-Taylor, & Davis, 2005).

For most Black parents, race is a salient issue in the socialization process. Most feel the need to prepare their children for the minority experience of living in our society. Yet just like jewelers refining a precious metal, they may find that gold appears beneath the surface dross. The dross? Children learn of racially based restrictions, such as job and housing discrimination. And the gold? They learn that they must work hard, get a good education, and, above all, be proud of who they are.

What other groups can you name in which children and adolescents need *corrective socialization?* Can you think of any groups where it is needed but not generally available? Who teaches gay male and lesbian adolescents how to deal with negative stereotypes? Their heterosexual parents? What can mentally handicapped or intellectually gifted adolescents learn from their parents of average intelligence? Who socializes adolescents in more androgynous sex roles? Traditional parents?

Sources: M. C. Thornton, L. M. Chatters, R. J. Taylor, & W. R. Allen. (1990). Sociodemographic and environmental correlates of racial socialization by black parents. *Child Development, 61,* 401–409. H. C. Stevenson, J. D. McNeil, T. Herrero-Taylor, & G. Y. Davis. (2005). Influence of perceived neighborhood diversity and racism experience on the racial socialization of Black youth. *Journal of Black Psychology, 31,* 273–290.

that adolescents whose parents monitor their activities by asking where they are going and who they will be with have fewer problem behaviors (Richards, Miller, O'Donnell, Wasserman, & Colder, 2004; Waizenhofer, Buchanan, & Jackson-Newsom, 2004). This is so even though parents frequently do not know as much as they believe they do (Cottrell et al., 2003; Laird, Pettit, Bates, & Dodge, 2003).

Demandingness was also evident in parental expectations that adolescents assume *responsibility for helping with the family's needs,* whether economic or domestic. Thus, adolescents might be expected to have a part-time job to contribute to the family budget, do chores around the house, or help with younger siblings or an elderly grandparent. Such responsibilities not only contribute to family cohesion but also foster individual competencies and give a feeling of mastery (Jarrett, 1995).

Earlier in the text (Chapter 7), we discussed several aspects to family interactions that contribute to healthy personality development, specifically, to the development of individuation in adolescence. Harold Grotevant and Catherine Cooper (1986) identified two such dimensions of interaction: *connectedness* and *individuality.* The first of these reflects the degree of emotional support within the family, support that takes the form of openness to others' opinions (permeability) and respect for their ideas (mutuality). The dimension of connectedness is similar to the dimension of responsiveness that we mentioned earlier in the chapter. The second dimension—individuality—reflects the ability to function as an individual within this supportive context, to see how one differs from others and to express one's own ideas. There is a paradox to these findings, namely, that it is necessary to be held in order to be set free. Or, said another way, it is necessary to be supported by one's family in order to find oneself as an individual.

In a sense, these findings should not come as a surprise. Mary Ainsworth (1978, 1985) observed much the same thing in her studies of attachment in infants and toddlers. Infants whose mothers were sensitive and responsive to their needs—qualities, by the way, that are similar to the permeability and mutuality that comprise connectedness—were those who as toddlers were the most independent and curious. These were the ones who would be likely to disappear around a corner to explore, knowing that Mom or Dad would be there in a moment if they should call out. That, after all, is what they had learned: that it's safe to venture out on your own, because your parents will be there when you need them. To be held, or supported, by one's family does not create dependency in children. It frees them to develop as individuals.

Communities

Development, for adolescents, is a bit like banking; they need to make daily withdrawals to fund healthy growth. And someone needs to make deposits. The neighborhoods they live in, just as their families, fund reserves on which adolescents can draw. Michelle Kegler, at Emory University, and her associates (2005) found a number of neighborhood characteristics to contribute to youth assets. Foremost among these were the safety of a neighborhood and the services it provided, such as schools, places to shop, police protection, and sanitation. Neighborhoods with these qualities fostered the development of a number of youth assets. Adolescents in these communities were more likely to report relationships with adult role models who encouraged them and with peers who stayed out of trouble. They were also more likely to participate in organized activities after school and in religious activities.

Neighborhood effects such as these may be attributable directly to community resources such as the ones mentioned or may, as well, be due to the operation of more informal social networks and norms (Leventhal & Brooks-Gunn, 2000). Consider, for instance, a woman working in the corner grocery store who sees a young adolescent buying cigarettes. She doesn't know his name or where he lives, but she recognizes him from the neighborhood. Later that week, she mentions this to someone at church, also from the neighborhood, who says, "Oh yeah, that's Molly Beacon's son—she's the one we see at the co-op on Thursdays. Do you think she knows?" Molly is likely to hear that her son is smoking, and not just from one of these women, but from both. Hearing this from them communicates something else as well—their concern and their willingness to step in when they see a problem.

Dale Blyth and Nancy Leffert (1995), at the Search Institute in Minneapolis, compared over 100 communities in terms of the experiences of the adolescents living in them, to discover the ways in which communities support their youth. The healthiest communities were those in which adolescents were more likely to be "plugged in" to institutions within the community. Adolescents in these communities experienced their schools as caring and supportive and were more likely to attend religious services and to

Attending religious services and having spiritual values are among the protective factors that help adolescents weather the stresses of growing up.

participate in activities within the community. According to Blyth and Leffert, the strong relationship between active participation in religious and other community-based activities and the overall health of the community suggests that such extracurricular activities "may not be *extras*" after all. Their observation mirrors Robin Jarrett's finding about the way that successful families use institutions within their communities.

Blyth and Leffert note, too, that the adolescents who profit most from living in healthy communities are the ones who are most in need of support and who have the fewest personal resources. Even though similar findings have emerged from comparisons of adolescents from widely differing types of communities, such as inner-city versus suburban youth, Blyth and Leffert point out that they also hold true for communities that, on the surface, have few visible differences.

Schools

Just as with communities, schools contribute to positive development when they enable adolescents to feel safe and supported. That is, adolescents' perceptions of their schools as safe and their teachers as supportive make it possible for them to function more effectively (Colarossi, 2001; Ozer & Weinstein, 2004). Teachers, in addition to parents, offer emotional as well as informational support. In fact, the emotional support adolescents receive from teachers has been found to be importantly related to their achievement (Malecki & Demaray, 2003). This source of support can be especially important for adolescents who have problematic relationships with their parents and for those who are at risk academically (Brewster & Bowen, 2004; Crosnoe & Elder, 2004). It should be noted as well that teachers who are both supportive *and* demanding—qualities we see in authoritative parents—are most effective, particularly with students from low-income families (Gregory & Weinstein, 2004).

Personal Strengths: Temperament, Competence, and Religion

The personal qualities that adolescents possess also serve as protective factors, qualities such as temperament and outlook on life, intelligence, competence, attitudes about self-efficacy, and religious beliefs. Adolescents with easy temperaments—that is, those who react positively to new situations and who are sociable and moderate in their activity level—are more likely to ride out the stresses of daily living. Not only does their positive approach equip them to deal with problems better, but their engaging ways endear them to others, thus enabling them to recruit the support they need. Possessing at least average intelligence, being able to communicate well with others, and believing that they are in control of, rather than simply reacting to, the circumstances affecting their life (known also as having an internal locus of control) also serve as important protective factors (Lau & Lau, 1996; Laursen, Pulkkinen, & Adams, 2002; Werner, 1989).

Religious beliefs also are an important factor contributing to healthy development (Donahue & Benson, 1995; Emmons & Paloutzian, 2003; Frank & Kendall, 2001). For instance, Lloyd Wright, Christopher Frost, and Stephen Wisecarver (1993) found that adolescents who attend church frequently and for whom their religion gives their life meaning are also the least likely to suffer from depression. Similarly, Moore and Glei (1995) found that greater religiosity contributes to a sense of well-being in adolescents. Furthermore, religious involvement has been found to help adolescents in low-income neighborhoods stay on track in school (Regnerus & Elder, 2003), and to delay sexual initiation among adolescent girls (Jones, Darroch, & Singh, 2005). Jarrett (1995), reviewing numerous research studies, found attendance at church and spiritual values to contribute to healthy development, even in the face of the multiple risks associated with poverty. Emily Werner and Ruth Smith (1982, 1992) also noted the importance of a strong religious faith to the healthy development of resilient individuals from infancy to middle adulthood.

Adolescents need all the support they can get. Not only do they face the normative, developmental tasks of adolescence, each of which presses for a new understanding of some aspect of their lives (see Chapter 1), but they must also cope with numerous daily stressors, such as academic pressures and conflicts with parents or peers.

Stress and Coping

Bones mend and cuts heal, but worries fray the edges of the mind. Sometimes it's all one can do to keep from unraveling totally. Adolescence offers no immunity to life's stresses; in fact, the body's response to stress is remarkably similar at all ages. The only thing that changes is the way different individuals cope with stress.

Stress is a curious thing. For one thing, it's hard to predict what will be stressful. Trying out for a part in the class play or the debating team and not being picked is stressful, but so is getting the part or making the team. Similarly, losing one's job is an obvious stressor, but so is being promoted. These contrasts tell us something important about the nature of stress. What makes an event stressful is not necessarily the event per se. What is stressful is the need to accommodate, or adapt, to the changes brought about by that event. Generally, the more rapidly we need to adapt, the more stress we experience.

stress The body's response to an event that requires adapting to changes brought about by that event.

In the case of events that demand an immediate response, such as dangerous or threatening ones, chemical messengers ready the body for fight or flight. In other instances, bodily processes remain relatively unchanged (Selye, 1982). Adolescents have the option of interpreting many situations in ways that would make either reaction possible. Consider an example in which someone bumps into a boy's locker, knocking it shut. The adolescent can either swing around ready for a fight or simply ignore the incident. If he chooses to fight, chemical messengers will flood his body with adrenaline, pump blood into his muscles, stop his stomach from digesting his lunch, and heighten his awareness to all incoming stimuli. His blood pressure and heart rate will soar. These adaptations prepare him for a fight if one should occur, but they are also, to use Hans Selye's words, "biologically suicidal" when called upon too frequently.

Adolescents can also ignore potential stressors. In the above example, doing so would allow other chemical messengers to coordinate the adolescent's reactions, permitting him to reopen the locker, continue a conversation with a friend, and get on with digesting his lunch. The quality of life is determined not simply by the presence or absence of stressors, but by the way adolescents interpret and cope with them. In other words, it's not *what* happens but *how* one reacts to what happens that ultimately matters, illustrating again the way in which we construct meaning.

Adolescents who live in gang-ridden neighborhoods experience a high degree of stress. Some try to cope by looking for solutions to the problem; others try to minimize the emotional damage by joining a gang themselves or by emotionally withdrawing.

How Adolescents Cope with Stress

The preceding example highlights the distinction between stress and coping. A stressor is an event; **coping** is what one does about it. Adolescents can cope in either of two general ways. **Problem-focused coping** attempts to change the stressful situation; this approach is primarily offensive. **Emotion-focused coping** is directed at minimizing the impact of the stress and is primarily defensive. When adolescents cope in the first of these two ways, they are likely to look for additional information or come up with an alternative, less stressful approach to the problem. The process is an active one in which they evaluate information, make decisions, and confront the problem. Emotion-focused coping is *re*active rather than active. The focus, as the term suggests, is on minimizing the emotional damage of stress, not on changing the stressor. This approach more frequently takes the form of defensive measures such as wishful thinking, denial, or disengaging from the situation.

The ways adolescents cope reflect more general aspects of their personalities. Adolescents who repress or deny their problems will usually fail to process or deal with negative information. In contrast, those who are hypersensitive will typically focus only on the negative. Neither approach is adaptive, because adolescents need to be not only aware of situations that are potentially threatening but also able to see means of resolving them. Michael Berzonsky (1993; Berzonsky & Ferrari, 1996) distinguishes individuals in terms of their openness to information, whether in coping with stressors or in resolving identity issues (see Chapter 5). Those who seek out experiences that are relevant to the decisions or problems they face (information oriented) are most likely to adopt a

coping Strategies for managing stressful situations that tax personal resources.

problem-focused coping Attempts to reduce stress by changing a stressful situation.

emotion-focused coping Attempts to reduce stress by minimizing its emotional impact, for example, denials, wishful thinking.

problem-focused approach to coping. Conversely, those who are relatively closed to new information, relying instead on the standards of others (normative oriented), are more likely to use emotion-focused approaches, as are individuals who procrastinate and do nothing when faced with stress (avoidant oriented).

Gender and Ethnicity

Females have been found to be more likely to use emotion-focused coping than males, perhaps because this functions more effectively for them than it does for males (Phelps & Jarvis, 1994; Renk & Creasey, 2003; Wadsworth et al., 2004). Some research, however, finds no gender differences in the types of coping strategies likely to be used or in how successfully either gender copes, instead finding the effectiveness of coping to differ with personal strengths such as higher self-esteem and feelings of self-efficacy (Mullis & Chapman, 2000; Phinney & Haas, 2003).

Many of the stressors that adolescents face occur on a daily basis (de Anda et al., 2000). Among the most common sources of stress at school are aggression (whether actual or threatened), bullying, and fear of theft. These safety concerns are considerably higher among African American and Hispanic students than among European American ones. More than twice as many African American students and more than three times as many Hispanic students indicate that at times they have not gone to school because they felt unsafe (Centers for Disease Control and Prevention, 2004).

Common among all students, however, are concerns about career goals and grades. Most students set high goals for themselves and most believe they can achieve these (Adwere-Boamah & Curtis, 1993; Phinney, Baumann, & Blanton, 2001). Even so, minority adolescents are more likely to attribute success to hard work than they are to ability. This tendency underscores the importance of interventions in school counseling programs specifically designed to overcome internal barriers and of making clear to minority students the many academic and career paths that are available to them (see Chapter 10).

Despite these similarities in the experience of stress, some important differences exist as well. For instance, many of the situations that nonminority adolescents might find stressful, such as having to take care of younger brothers and sisters, were not perceived as stressful by the minority adolescents. Cultural expectations about extended families and child-care responsibilities rendered these situations normative rather than stressful. On the other hand, adolescents in immigrant families acquire the ways of their new culture more rapidly than their parents do, creating intercultural tensions in addition to the intergenerational tensions that all adolescents experience (Kwak, 2003; Phinney, Kim-Jo, Osorio, & Vilhjalmsdottir, 2005; Phinney, Ong, & Madden, 2000).

Learning Effective Coping Strategies

Coping with stress, like most of the activities adolescents engage in, requires skill; so, we can expect some to be better at it than others. Luckily, as with other skills, adolescents can learn to cope with stress more effectively. Social-cognitive intervention programs teach adolescents alternative ways of viewing potentially stressful situations, making them less stressful and improving the changes of coping successfully (see Chapter 8). Adolescents learn to identify and appraise stressful situations, anticipate their own reactions, and manage the resulting emotions (Meichenbaum, 1985).

Appraising the Situation Misinterpretations easily arise from personal blind spots that can cause adolescents to overestimate or underestimate potential stressors. Overestimation can turn what could have been a harmless episode into an interpersonal disaster, whereas underestimation can expose adolescents to potential harm. Only by appraising a situation correctly can adolescents predict the most likely set of events. Accurate prediction, in turn, puts them in a place where they can better influence the course of events. Appraisal becomes more accurate as adolescents learn to think of alternative interpretations for situations.

Adolescents can learn to challenge self-defeating interpretations. This learning requires adolescents to put their new intellectual skills to use (see Chapter 4). As adolescents bring new intellectual capacities to bear on problems, they're better able to revise their reading of ongoing situations and react appropriately; even with these, however, their cognitive appraisals of situations are likely to be less complex than those of adults (Rowley, Roesch, Jurica, & Vaughn, 2005). Frequently the most appropriate step is to get more information to find out which interpretation is the most reasonable. Sometimes this step can be as simple as asking the other person, "Did you really mean . . . ?"

Adolescents (like individuals of all ages) are likely to make an **attributional error** in which they overestimate the importance of *dispositional stressors* (presumed traits such as aggressiveness or anger) and underestimate the importance of *situational stressors* (such as tensions due to relationships or threats of personal violence). A girl who is dissatisfied with one of her friends because she sees her as aggressive and angry (dispositional stressors) may think there is little possibility of improving their relationship. By tracing her anger to situational factors—strife at home or hazing at school, for example—it becomes possible for her to think of ways to improve their relationship.

Adolescents frequently commit a second error when they notice only information that confirms their appraisal of a situation, or *confirmatory information.* An adolescent who expects a teacher to be unsympathetic or overly demanding is likely to act in a hostile way toward that teacher, provoking a reaction that confirms the expectation. Instead, adolescents can learn to look for, and even generate, behavior that disconfirms predisposing expectations. The above adolescent might, for example, thank the teacher in advance for her attention and time, thus creating a positive atmosphere in which the teacher will be more likely to listen to the student sympathetically.

Responding to the Situation Sometimes the response can be as simple as getting information or advice, or suggesting a talk with a friend. At other times the most effective action can be *no* action, like not shooting back an angry reply to a friend or parent. In most cases, skills related to assertiveness, communication, negotiation, and compromise are involved. Even adolescents who have these skills don't always think to use them. Under the stress of the moment, they may not use an approach that has worked for them in the past or they may fail to recognize which skills are called for. Sometimes, too, adolescents fail to respond effectively, because other, less adaptive responses are more dominant. Nonassertive adolescents might fail to speak up, for instance, simply because of concerns that inhibit assertive action.

The most effective responses are those that prevent stressful situations from occurring. Individuals create, as well as respond to, their environments. This fact makes preventive actions possible. Adolescents can pick up on social cues that bring out the best in others. Adolescents who develop these skills are more likely to bring out friendly, helpful behavior in others and less likely to cause the hostile or aggressive behaviors that typify stressful interactions.

Managing Emotions Even after successfully handling a stressful encounter, adolescents must still deal with the emotions caused by the situation. Adolescents differ widely in how quickly they get over feelings of anger or frustration. Mentally rehearsing one's successes or failures will either facilitate or interfere with the process of "unwinding."

attributional error An overestimation of the importance of dispositional stressors or an underestimation of the importance of situational ones.

Adolescents who have been trained in a stress-inoculation program involving the above three components (appraising, responding, and managing) have lower anxiety, less anger, and higher self-esteem (Hains & Szyjakowski, 1990).

Most research with adolescents has focused on the problems they face or on the ways in which they have been deficient in responding to these. A newer area of study is that of healthy adolescents who not only cope but make the world better in some way for others as well. Who are these adolescents, and what do we know about them?

Beyond Coping: Caring and Prosocial Behavior

Nearly a third of adolescents in the United States volunteer in charitable activities, working in after-school programs, food banks, libraries, senior centers, and the like (Rudder, 2002). They volunteer for many reasons: They believe they can make a difference in the lives of others; they want to be part of something bigger than themselves, to enrich the lives of others; and some volunteer simply because it's more interesting than anything else they might be doing.

Many of these youth go beyond volunteering to establishing organizations of their own. One adolescent started a program donating hats to cancer patients who were undergoing chemotherapy. It began when he was visiting his grandmother in the cancer ward and noticed many patients had lost their hair; he thought they might appreciate having a hat to wear. He got permission to place boxes in local businesses and schools for people to donate new hats, and then took these to the local hospital each week. Four years later, he had donated hats to more than 160 hospitals around the world, totaling over 40,000 hats (Heavenly Hats, 2005).

Another young woman, after working throughout her adolescence with youth in her community, started a youth program with two friends when she was 21. Their goal, as she puts it, "is to help children rescue their dreams deferred and to shape future leaders committed to making their community better for the next generation." They, too, started small, asking those who had just completed the program to volunteer with the next group of kids. As this young woman says, "I have had the pleasure of helping them realize that there is more to life than what they see. Just by showing them a difference and empowering them to make a choice allows them not only to change their world but mine as well" (A Different Side of the Game, Inc., 2005).

Daniel Hart, at Rutgers University, and Suzanne Fegley, at Temple University (1995), were interested in how adolescents who are distinguished by remarkable caring and prosocial behavior understand their world and themselves. These investigators studied a group of urban minority adolescents, African American and Hispanic, in an economically distressed northeastern city. These adolescents were remarkable in one way or another for their involvement in such things as volunteer work or unusual family responsibilities. (The sample was arrived at by contacting social agencies, church leaders, schools, and youth groups.) A comparison group of adolescents was matched for age, gender, ethnicity, and neighborhood. The latter adolescents were also well adjusted and attended school regularly, and many of them were also involved in volunteer activities, but not to the same degree. All adolescents were interviewed and completed a number of personality measures.

These investigators found, as anticipated, that the caring adolescents understood themselves quite differently than did the comparison adolescents. They were more likely to describe themselves in terms of their values and ideals. Also, their parents contributed more heavily to their sense of themselves than was the case for the comparisons, for whom best friends contributed most heavily. Differences between the caring and comparison adolescents, however, did not appear to be due to any single factor, such as overall maturity or sophistication of thought. The former did not, for instance, use more advanced moral reasoning or have more complex or sophisticated perceptions of others. Also, because these adolescents were not followed over time, one cannot say for sure whether the ways in which these remarkable teenagers saw themselves were responsible for the care they extended to others or whether their involvement in the care of others drew them away from friends, thus causing them to see themselves less in terms of their peers and more in terms of idealized figures.

Adolescents who distinguish themselves for community service and other kinds of prosocial behavior are likely to have experienced caring relationships with their parents or other adults.

P. Lindsay Chase-Lansdale, Lauren Wakschlag, and Jeanne Brooks-Gunn (1995) point to the importance of the family for the development of caring. The experience of being loved appears to be essential if one is to develop as a caring person. The research on attachment, beginning in infancy but extending throughout the lifespan (Ainsworth, 1985; Ainsworth, Blehar, Waters, & Wall, 1978; Bowlby, 1969), underscores the importance of the caregivers' sensitivity to the needs of the child and responsiveness in meeting these for healthy development. Children cared for in this way not only develop a sense of trust in their world but come to believe that others are trustworthy, and perhaps most important of all, come to believe that *they* are worthy of being cared for in this way (Erikson, 1968).

Not all adolescents are born into homes in which they will receive this type of care from their parents. What sort of chances do these adolescents have of developing into competent, caring adults? The research of Emily Werner and her colleagues (Werner, 1989; Werner & Smith, 1982, 1992) indicates that the chances are good—as long as there is at least one caring person in that young person's life, someone such as a grandparent, an aunt or uncle, or a sibling to love him or her (see Chapter 2).

Positive Youth Development

We began this chapter by asking what we want of adolescents—what, that is, do we take to be the markers of positive, healthy development? In asking this, we are speaking of healthy development as more than the *absence* of problematic behaviors such as those discussed in the previous chapter. Instead, Richard Lerner and his associates (2005) point to the presence of five qualities that together constitute a definition of positive youth development: competence, confidence, connection, character, and caring, or the five Cs. These qualities are presented in Table 13.1.

Reed Larson (2000), at the University of Illinois, believes that characteristics such as caring and prosocial behavior can be traced to the development of initiative in adolescents. The concept of **initiative** is closely related to the construct of agency (see Chapter 5) and describes behavior that is intrinsically motivated, or organized around

initiative Intrinsically motivated behavior that is organized around challenging and personally meaningful goals; closely related to agency.

TABLE 13.1 The Five Cs of Positive Youth Development

Five Cs	Definition
Competence	Viewing one's actions positively in different domains: social competence (e.g., resolving conflicts); cognitive competence (e.g., making good decisions); academic competence (e.g., getting good grades); vocational competence (e.g., establishing good work habits).
Confidence	Having an overall sense of self-worth and self-efficacy.
Connection	Having positive, mutually rewarding relationships with family members, peers, teachers, and members of the community.
Character	Respecting one's community's and society's standards; acting with integrity.
Caring	Having understanding and compassion for others.

Source: R. M. Lerner et al. (2005). Positive youth development, participation in community youth development programs, and community contributions of fifth grade adolescents: Findings from the first wave of the 4-H study of positive youth development. *Journal of Early Adolescence, 25,* 17–71.

challenging and personally meaningful goals. Larson considers initiative to be central not only to the development of altruistic behaviors, those directed toward helping others, but also to the development of a vision for one's own life and for the skills needed to realize this. Larson argues, in fact, that in the absence of initiative, adolescents may simply go through the motions without ever becoming invested in what they are doing. He regards the development of initiative, in other words, as essential if adolescents are to become socially competent and responsible adults. Yet Larson's research leads him to believe that the activities at which adolescents spend most of their time afford few opportunities to develop initiative.

The importance of discovering the ingredients to positive youth development became all too clear to Larson and his research associates when they studied the daily emotional states of a representative sample of working- and middle-class adolescents. Adolescents were given pagers to wear and were beeped at random moments throughout the day. When asked what they were doing and how they felt, adolescents indicated feeling bored 27% of the times they were beeped (Larson & Richards, 1991). Larson notes that the "litany of explanations for this boredom—'algebra sucks,' 'I'm always bored on Sunday,' 'there's nothing to do,' 'the *Odyssey* is boring'—reads like a script from Bart Simpson. They communicate an ennui of being trapped in the present, waiting for someone to prove to them that life is worth living" (Larson, 2000, p. 170).

Putting aside for the moment the possibility that algebra or the *Odyssey* may not offer excitement or challenge to all, Larson wondered what *would* need to be present in order for adolescents to become invested in what they were doing. Worded another way, what components of their ongoing experience would be needed to contribute to the development of initiative?

Larson identifies three conditions that are closely tied to the growth of initiative. The first of these is **intrinsic motivation.** Adolescents are most likely to experience initiative when they are able to work at things they find intrinsically motivating, or interesting in their own right. These are activities for which they need no reward other than the pleasure they get simply from doing them. Important as this type of activity is, however, intrinsic motivation by itself is not enough. A second component that Larson believes essential for the development of initiative is **engagement,** or concentration. Tasks that are sufficiently complex that they demand concentrated attention for their successful completion require adolescents to direct their thoughts and consciously plan what they

intrinsic motivation Motivation derived from the pleasure one experiences in an activity.

engagement Concentrated attention, necessary for the performance of complex activities.

will do next. These tasks, rather than simple ones, are most likely to engage adolescents. Finally, Larson believes that adolescents develop initiative when they work at projects that can be completed only over an extended period of time and that require them to *evaluate,* and then *adjust,* their performance in order to successfully accomplish what they initially set out to do.

To what extent are these three ingredients present in adolescents' daily experiences? The two contexts that comprise the bulk of adolescents' waking hours are schoolwork and leisure, accounting for 25–30% and 40–50% of their waking hours, respectively. Larson notes, however, that each of these contexts lacks one or more of the elements critical for the development of initiative. When adolescents are paged in the classroom or doing homework, for instance, they typically report feeling challenged but report little intrinsic motivation for what they are doing. They also find it hard to concentrate on the task at hand and, despite being challenged, say they are bored. Conversely, when adolescents are paged during leisure activities, they report relatively high intrinsic motivation for what they are doing but little challenge or concentration. Thus, neither of the two types of activities in which adolescents spend most of their time are ones that are likely to promote the development of initiative.

There is a third category of activities, however, that is intrinsically motivating to adolescents and also demands their concentrated attention. Larson refers to these activities as **structured voluntary activities;** examples include extracurricular sports, hobbies, or service learning programs (see Chapter 6). Even though adolescents spend relatively little time at these, the activities afford exposure to the ingredients Larson considers important for the development of initiative. Thus, when adolescents are paged during one of these activities, they report feeling highly motivated as well as needing to pay close attention to what they are doing. Although Larson's data do not directly provide a measure of change over time, other research suggests that this component is also present in such activities (Larson, 2000; Rogoff, Baker-Sennett, Lacasa, & Goldsmith, 1995).

What changes might we expect to see in adolescents' behavior as they participate in structured voluntary activities? A number of studies suggest that such participation can effect positive changes across a variety of domains in adolescents' lives, from improved grades and educational goals to increases in self-control, independence, and assertiveness (Eccles & Barber, 1999; Hattie, Marsh, Neill, & Richards, 1997; Marsh, 1992). Even adolescents' speech has been found to change over time as they participate in these types of activities. Instead of communicating boredom, passivity, or defensiveness, as Larson and others have noted, adolescents' speech is found to reflect a new sense of agency (Heath, 1993, 1994). Their use of language reveals that they begin to think in terms of the different outcomes that might result from acting in one way or another, and how best to achieve the outcomes they desire. As Larson (2000) comments, "The conditions that make structured youth activities a fertile context for the development of initiative, I believe, also make them a rich context for the development of an array of other positive qualities, from altruism to identity. Children and adolescents come alive in these activities, they become active agents in ways that rarely happen in other parts of their lives. This makes youth activities an invaluable laboratory for the study of processes of positive development, one that deserves much more scientific attention" (p. 178).

Love

Finally, one cannot overestimate the importance of being loved. Even though this is a truth we all live with, it is encouraging to see it find empirical support. Chase-Lansdale, Wakschlag, and Brooks-Gunn (1995) emphasize that just one caring relationship in an adolescent's life can make the difference between developing in a healthy or unhealthy

structured voluntary activities Activities that are intrinsically motivating and challenging that build skills and foster initiative.

way, even in the face of family conflict, poverty, parental psychopathology, and other formidable factors. Similarly, Werner and Smith (1982, 1992) found that the essential ingredient to healthy development in each of the individuals they studied, who were at risk for one or more reasons, was a "basic, trusting relationship" with someone who cared for them.

Perhaps Urie Bronfenbrenner (1990) summed it all up best when he said what adolescents need most is someone who finds them "somehow special, especially wonderful, and especially precious" (p. 31).

Summary

- A central difference between adolescents and adults is how they understand themselves. When adolescents recognize the needs of others as well as their own and appreciate their obligations to others, their relationships begin to be characterized by reciprocity and mutuality. In order for this to take place, adolescents not only need to be challenged but also need to be supported by their families, their communities, and the strengths within themselves.

Protective Factors in Adolescence

- From their families and their communities, adolescents need a combination of care (responsiveness) and discipline (demandingness). Responsiveness can be expressed not only by immediate family members but also by adult network structures and by community institutions. Demandingness is expressed through monitoring adolescents' activities and expecting them to help out with the family's needs. Family interactions that promote both connectedness and individuality also contribute to healthy personality development.
- Neighborhoods that are safe, that offer adequate services, and that provide informal social networks and norms for their residents foster the development of youth assets such as supportive relationships with adult role models, healthy relationships with peers, participation in organized activities after school, and participation in religious activities.
- The healthiest communities for adolescents are those in which adolescents are more likely to be involved in institutions within the community.
- Schools contribute to positive development when they enable adolescents to feel safe and when students receive emotional support from their teachers. Teachers who are both supportive and demanding—qualities found in authoritative parents—are most effective.
- In addition to characteristics of families, communities, and schools, the personal qualities of adolescents themselves are protective factors. Their temperament, intelligence, competence, sense of self-efficacy, and religious beliefs can help protect them against the stresses of daily life.

Stress and Coping

- What makes an event *stressful* is not necessarily the event per se, but the need to adapt to the changes it brings about. In general, the more rapidly one needs to adapt, the more stress one experiences. Many situations can be interpreted in ways that increase or reduce their stress potential.
- Adolescents typically *cope* with stress in either of two general ways. *Problem-focused* coping attempts to change the stressful situation; *emotion-focused* coping is directed at minimizing the impact of the stressful event. Gender differences have been found with respect to these forms of coping, with females being more likely to use emotion-focused coping than males.
- Common stressors are aggression, bullying, and fear of theft.
- Common among all students are concerns about career goals and grades; since minority students may be more likely to attribute success to hard work than ability, school counseling programs designed to overcome internal barriers are especially important.
- Adolescents can learn to cope with stress more effectively. By learning to appraise situations more accurately, adolescents can avoid common errors.
- *Attributional errors,* errors that overestimate the importance of dispositional stressors and underestimate the importance of situational stressors, and errors arising from a tendency to notice only confirming information frequently lead to

inaccurate appraisals and less-than-optimal coping strategies.

- The ways adolescents respond to stress can reduce it or increase it. Skills related to assertiveness, communication, negotiation, and compromise are most effective.
- Adolescents can also learn to anticipate and manage the emotions prompted by stress.

Beyond Coping: Caring and Prosocial Behavior

- Nearly a third of U.S. adolescents volunteer in charitable activities. Many of these youth go beyond volunteering to establishing organizations of their own.
- Prosocial adolescents are more likely than their peers to describe themselves in terms of their values and ideals; and their sense of themselves is more likely to come from their parents than from their peers. The experience of being loved, of having their needs met by someone in their life, appears to be essential for adolescents to develop into caring people.

Positive Youth Development

- Five Cs serve to define positive youth development: competence, confidence, connection, character, and caring.
- The development of *initiative,* intrinsically motivated behavior that is organized around challenging and personally meaningful goals, may be critical if adolescents are to develop a vision for their lives and the skills needed to realize this.
- The daily contexts in which adolescents spend most of their time, schoolwork and leisure, afford few opportunities to develop initiative.
- *Structured voluntary activities* incorporate the components thought to contribute to the development of initiative: intrinsic motivation, concentrated attention, and the need to evaluate and adjust one's performance to successfully accomplish a goal.
- Research shows that just one caring relationship in an adolescent's life can make the difference between developing in a healthy or an unhealthy way.

Key Terms

archival research
stress
coping
problem-focused coping
emotion-focused coping
attributional error
initiative
intrinsic motivation
engagement
structured voluntary activities

CHAPTER OUTLINE

CHAPTER 14

Studying Adolescence

Research Methods and Issues

CHAPTER OBJECTIVES

- To distinguish research strategies in terms of the number of participants that are studied and the degree of control the investigator exercises
- To compare the relative advantages and disadvantages of cross-sectional, longitudinal, and sequential designs
- To consider path analysis as a means of inferring causality with correlational data
- To illustrate the different types of measures that can be used in developmental research
- To understand research as a way of getting an unambiguous answer to a well-defined question
- To evaluate the importance of operational definitions, representative sampling, eliminating bias, using appropriate statistical tests, and following ethical guidelines
- To examine the advantages and disadvantages of between-subjects, within-subjects, matched-subjects, and factorial designs

Chapter Overview

In reading this text, you have been exposed to a host of statements summarizing research on adolescents, for example, "Adolescent boys have more positive body images than girls," "Authoritative parenting is superior to permissive parenting," "Adolescents experience more emotional highs and lows than do their parents." Each of these statements has been presented as trustworthy, something to be believed. Textbooks aren't alone in presenting information this way. Each day television, bloggers, and the nightly news flood us with information, most of it presented as factual. But how are we to know what is reliable? That is what distinguishes information gathered through research from information gleaned by other means, such as intuition, common sense, or reliance on an authority?

Scientific research is distinguished by its methodology. The **scientific method** differs from other methods by the systematic way in which it checks its conclusions against observable facts. Not all forms of inquiry check conclusions in this way. For instance, Aristotle, based on reasoning about what he termed the "qualities" of objects, concluded that heavy objects fall faster when they are dropped than do light objects because they possess more "earthiness" and are thus drawn more to the earth. This reasoning was

scientific method A method of inquiry in which conclusions are verified empirically by checking them against observations; a methodology for making observations that will support or refute hypotheses.

TABLE 14.1 Research Focus Boxes Included on the Web Site

RESEARCH STRATEGIES
Case Studies
DEVELOPMENTAL RESEARCH: ISSUES AND DESIGNS
Path Analysis
RESPONSE MEASURES IN DEVELOPMENTAL RESEARCH
The Dependent Variable
Questionnaires
Projective Measures
RESEARCH ISSUES
Internal and External Validity
Theory-Guided Research
Ethics
Confidentiality
RESEARCH DESIGNS
Matched-Subjects Design
Factorial Designs

accepted as fact until Galileo actually timed the speed of falling objects that differed in weight.[1] As one scientist said of Aristotle's assumption, "The important thing about this idea is not that it was wrong, but that it never occurred to Aristotle to check it" (Hungarian-American biochemist Albert Szent Gyorgyi).

In this chapter, we will look at various strategies used by researchers to check the accuracy of their conclusions. These strategies can be distinguished in terms of the number of individuals being observed and the degree of control the investigator has over the observations being made. As we shall see, strategies differ in terms of their effectiveness.

Developmental research, in which age is a variable, faces special problems. It is difficult to separate the effects of age from variables that may vary with age. Three research designs—cross-sectional, longitudinal, and sequential—are compared for their effectiveness in achieving this end.

The chapter then moves to a discussion of response measures and research issues, including internal versus external validity, operationalizing concepts, sampling, and ethics.

The last section of the chapter compares the relative advantages and disadvantages of between-subjects, within-subjects, matched-subjects, and factorial designs.

The Research Focus boxes that appear in each of the preceding chapters of the book have illustrated many different types of research that developmentalists employ in studying adolescents. Each box has introduced a particular research question concerning adolescents, then analyzed the research procedures that were used. Boxes focusing on additional aspects of research appear on the Web site. Table 14.1 lists these additional Research Focus boxes. Together, these boxes illustrate distinctions that are basic to an understanding of the methodology used by developmentalists. In this chapter we take a comprehensive look at these research methods and issues.

---

[1]The ultimate experiment was conducted on the moon by the *Apollo* astronauts who dropped a feather and a wrench and found that, in the absence of air resistance, both reached the ground at the same time.

Research Strategies

As mentioned, research strategies are procedures that scientists follow to safeguard against making faulty observations. Our discussion of these procedures will be organized in terms of (1) how many participants are studied and (2) the degree of control the investigator has over conditions that could affect the observations. With respect to the number of participants studied, strategies differ markedly. Researchers can limit their observations to a single individual, as in research involving case studies, or they can collect observations from hundreds or even thousands of people in survey research. Differences are equally large with respect to the degree of control. At one extreme is naturalistic observation in which researchers record behavior in natural, everyday surroundings. At the other extreme are experiments in which behavior is observed under the controlled and often highly artificial conditions of the laboratory. Between these extremes lie correlational research and quasi-experiments. Clearly, we are talking about very different procedures in each case. Each type of research carries a particular set of advantages, and each has its own problems.

Number of Participants

Case Studies In a **case study,** the investigator studies a single case extensively in order to arrive at a picture of the individual. The case is usually a person, although sometimes it might be a new program in a school, such as a jigsaw classroom (see Chapter 9), or even a school or work setting itself if it is unique in some way. Many clinical observations reflect the case study method. This method presents a detailed picture of the person. Freud, for example, saw many of his patients daily. The richness of the observations this method supplies is, in fact, one of its advantages. We might consider the case of a precociously gifted 13-year-old who is admitted to college because she has lost interest in her high school classes. Would such a course of action be beneficial to adolescents such as this? Typically, researchers might answer this question by comparing several groups of gifted adolescents, one of which would complete high school and the other would be admitted to college. But the number of precociously gifted adolescents is limited, and the number admitted to college without first finishing high school is even smaller—much smaller. It would be hard to answer this question using such a research strategy; there simply aren't that many gifted 13-year-olds attending college. Case studies provide an alternative research strategy for studying individuals or conditions that are highly unusual and can't be studied in large numbers. Through extensive observations of a single gifted 13-year-old attending college, one can gain insights leading to hypotheses that can be tested using other types of research. You can read an example of such an adolescent in the Research Focus "Case Studies" on the Web site.

Disadvantages to this approach concern the *generalizability* of the findings and the *objectivity* of the observations. How confident can we be that observations collected from a single individual are representative of others? This objection becomes especially critical when the individual is atypical. The concern, in fact, has been raised with respect to Freud's theory of psychosexual development (see Chapter 2). How reasonable is it to formulate a general theory of development based on the study of limited numbers of individuals, most or even all of whom suffered from psychological problems important enough to warrant psychoanalysis? Also, because the developmentalist collecting the observations works closely with the individual or program being observed, there is always the danger of losing one's objectivity and reading more into the behavior than is actually there.

case study Intensive observation of a single subject, such as an individual or a program.

Interviews and other self-report measures give researchers access to information that cannot be easily observed.

Surveys *Surveys* allow one to study large numbers of people through **self-report** measures such as *questionnaires.* In self-reports, the participants supply the information about themselves; the investigator does not observe their behavior directly. A distinct strength of this approach is the opportunity it provides to study behavior that could not be observed easily otherwise. For instance, information about adolescents' sexual attitudes or practices is obtained almost exclusively through surveys. So, too, is most information about drug use. A weakness to relying on individuals' reports about themselves is the opportunity for distortion, either through deliberately changing information or by failing to remember events as they actually happened. As Freud would remind us, memory is significantly better for pleasant events than for unpleasant ones.

Degree of Control

Research strategies also differ in the *degree of control* the investigator has over conditions that could affect the observations. Procedures vary from those that exercise no control, such as archival research or naturalistic observations, to those with a high degree of control over extraneous conditions—experiments. Between these extremes lie quasi-experimental designs and correlational procedures.

Archival Research **Archival research** uses data that already exist to answer questions posed by the investigator. Archival data exist in many forms, the most extensive source being the census. What percentage of adolescents live with a single parent? How many work at part-time jobs? What percentage of adolescents finish high school, go on to college, and so forth? To obtain answers to questions such as these, developmentalists can use census data and need not collect their own. Because census data are collected from large groups of individuals, they have the additional advantage of being representative of the population.

Other archival sources exist in the form of public records, such as birth certificates, marriage license applications, and applications for housing or welfare. Numerous public and private organizations maintain extensive archives; hospitals, housing and welfare

self-report Information supplied by participants about themselves, usually in response to interview or survey questions.

archival research The use of existing data, such as public records, to provide answers to research questions.

agencies, newspapers, and libraries are just a few examples. What diseases are most common among adolescents? Records maintained by local health agencies provide answers. Are males more prone to accidents than females? Hospital emergency-room records indicate that they are. Do more adolescents live in poverty today than 20 years ago? State and federal welfare agencies supply answers. For more on archival research, see the Research Focus "Archival Research" in Chapter 13.

Naturalistic Observation Perhaps the purest form of research is to directly observe participants in their natural settings. Developmentalists using **naturalistic observation** as an approach do not disrupt the natural flow of events; they simply watch and record behavior. Dian Fossey's research on the mountain gorilla of central Africa is a well-known example of this type of research. Pure though it may be, this research is often extremely difficult to carry out. Fossey's research illustrates this point well. Mountain gorillas live in the rain forest, making it impossible to observe them from a distance. Yet, if she attempted to get closer, the gorillas would notice her and either flee or attack. Her solution was to become a *participant observer,* observing their behavior by moving among them as just another member of the group. How does one do this? For Fossey this meant acting like a gorilla until they accepted her as one. Fossey describes beating her chest, vocalizing like a gorilla, and sitting for hours chewing on wild celery. The gorillas eventually accepted her, making it possible for her to live among them and observe their behavior. Coming a little closer to home, Dexter Dunphy (1963) conducted a classic study of adolescent peer groups using naturalistic observation. He, like Dian Fossey, simply "hung out" with those he was studying. He found two distinct types of groups: the clique and the crowd. As you may recall from Chapter 8, crowd activities provide a setting in which adolescents experiment with new social behaviors; cliques provide feedback about the success of these.

Naturalistic observation is most helpful when the investigator does not know much about the domain being studied. As Fossey's and Dunphy's research illustrate, naturalistic observation allows one to discover patterns in the observed behavior. These patterns frequently suggest hypotheses that can be tested with other forms of research. Although it gives richly detailed descriptions of behavior, naturalistic observation does not offer explanations for why the behavior occurs. Developmentalists arrive at explanations only when they can rule out competing alternatives. To do this, they must be able to control extraneous conditions that could affect the behavior. Only experiments provide this type of control.

Erikson's Psychohistorical Approach Erik Erikson developed a unique style of research that combined the tools of clinical analysis with those of fieldwork. His insights into human development reflected the psychoanalytic training he had received in working with Sigmund Freud and Anna Freud. Erikson applied these skills to an analysis of the relationship between the individual and the group. His observations of individuals from different groups—whether American teenagers or the Sioux and Yurok—convinced him that human development takes place within a social community. His willingness to study individuals in their natural communities contributed to his insights concerning the psychosocial nature of human development. This approach is discussed in the Research Focus "Erikson's Psychohistorical Approach" in Chapter 2.

Quasi-Experimental Designs **Quasi-experimental designs** work with existing groups, introduce a treatment, and look to see whether differences follow. This type of research differs from archival research and naturalistic observation in that the researcher intervenes in, or steps into, the flow of behavior. These designs differ from experiments

naturalistic observation The observation and recording of participants' behavior in their natural setting.

quasi-experimental design A research design in which participants are not randomly assigned to conditions, but in which preexisting groups are used, introducing possible confounding.

in that investigators do not randomly assign participants to the groups. Instead, they work with intact groups. Examples are groups of students in different academic tracks; social groups such as the populars, the brains, the jocks; and so on. Quasi-experimental research is common in applied settings in which developmentalists may want to observe the effects of a treatment but don't have control over all the conditions that might affect their observations.

The disadvantage to quasi-experimental designs is that one can't be sure that differences actually reflect the treatment. They may reflect differences that were present in the groups before the treatment was introduced. These disadvantages are discussed in the Research Focus "Randomized Versus Quasi-Experimental Designs" in Chapter 3. The presence of alternative explanations for observed differences is known as **confounding**. A number of potential confounds exist in quasi-experimental research. One of these, *maturation,* refers to systematic changes over time apart from those due specifically to the treatment under study.

Another type of confound common to quasi-experimental research is a **testing effect.** The performance of adolescents enrolled in special programs, for instance, may improve simply because they have been tested so often that they are better at taking tests than others whose performance is not being monitored so closely. Testing effects include both specific and general knowledge. For instance, pretests might include the same types of questions, covering the same information, as those included on tests given at the conclusion of the program. Adolescents enrolled in such programs would then be more familiar with these items and do better on tests including them. Also, general test-taking skills are acquired with frequent test taking. Students learn, for instance, whether to guess, how to manage their time, and how to stay on top of anxiety that might otherwise interfere with their performance.

Similarly, a **history effect** refers to confounding resulting from events that occur during the time in which adolescents are enrolled in a program to be evaluated and that can affect the behavior being measured. For instance, network channels might run a series of public service spots featuring well-known personalities who promote the value of a particular activity, such as staying in school or avoiding the use of drugs.

Statistical regression is yet another confound that can occur. This confound enters the picture when participants are selected because of their initial differences, because they are either behind or ahead of others in their group. For instance, students selected for a special program are more likely to have low scores on initial measures of their performance. When these students are retested at the conclusion of the program, the scores for most will be higher, but not necessarily because they have profited from the program. When they are tested at the end of the program, most scores will change somewhat simply because the two tests are not perfectly correlated. This change is to be expected because no tests ever are perfectly correlated. But for students who were initially at the bottom of the distribution, test scores can only go up. Because such a change is expected by those administering such programs, it is usually not questioned.

However, if one were to place another group of students who initially scored at the top of the distribution in such a program, their second test scores would drop, and for the same reason. Just as with the other students, there is only one direction in which their test scores could change, and for these students that would be down. In each case, scores on the second test drift toward the mean of the distribution, because this is where most of the scores are. In other words, to the extent that performance on the first test is unrelated to performance on the second test, chance influences the score a student gets. What score would a student be most likely to draw by chance? A score that occurs most frequently in the distribution—in other words, a score that is close to the mean, where most of the scores lie.

confounding The presence of additional factors other than the variable of interest that can account for observed differences.

testing effect Knowledge and skills acquired by taking similar tests over the course of a research study; a potential source of confounding.

history effect Any event extraneous to a research project that can affect the results and jeopardize the internal validity of the research.

statistical regression A potential confound in quasi-experimental research in which extreme pretest scores drift toward the mean of the posttest distribution.

Experiments **Experiments** start with equivalent groups of participants and treat each group differently. If the groups differ at the conclusion of the experiment, we can assume the difference is due to the way they were treated. To be confident about this assumption, we need to be sure that the groups are comparable at the outset. Given the myriad ways in which adolescents differ from each other, such an assumption might seem an impossible requirement.

Is it? Do investigators have a way of ensuring initial equivalence among their groups? The key to the solution is that the groups need not be identical, only equivalent. Rather than requiring that subjects be the same in each of the groups, an admittedly impossible requirement, we need only require that they not differ in any *systematic* way. They will, of course, differ in countless respects, but if each person has the same chance of being assigned to each group, and if enough people are assigned to each group, differences among people will soon be balanced across the groups. **Random assignment**—assigning participants in such a way that each has the same chance as every other of being assigned to any condition—distributes individual differences more or less evenly across the groups.

Let's say we want to determine the influence of a television model on adolescents' choice of reading materials. Specifically, we want to see whether adolescents will choose magazines that are described as appropriate to their gender and avoid those that are described as inappropriate. We can pretest a variety of magazines and select those for our experiment that appeal equally to either sex. In one part of the experiment, twenty 15-year-old girls will be randomly assigned to either of two groups. Each group is shown one of two videotapes in which the model describes several magazines. One videotape describes the magazines as appropriate for males; the other describes the same magazines as appropriate for females.

We could then have the girls wait for the next part of the experiment in another room with those magazines plus others on a table. We would record the amount of time they spent looking at the target magazines. Let's say we found that the girls spent more time looking at the magazines that were identified as appropriate for them. Because the only difference between the groups was the way the magazines were described, we could assume that the televised sequences had affected their behavior.

We said that an experiment treats two or more groups of individuals differently and looks for measured differences in their behavior. The treatment assigned to either group is called the **independent variable.** The independent variable in this experiment is the televised sequence viewed by each group. The measure of the effect of the independent variable is called the **dependent variable.** In a sense, the way individuals react "depends" on how they are treated. The dependent variable in this experiment is magazine choice. Which magazine the girls chose to look at depended on the way they had been treated.

We see the experimental approach illustrated in the research described in the Research Focus "An Experiment" in Chapter 1. Mary Lynne Courtney and Robert Cohen (1996) wanted to determine whether adolescents who had been told that two boys at play were friends, or been told that they were enemies, or been told nothing, would perceive the boys' actions differently. Adolescents were randomly assigned to groups, differing in what they were told about the boys.

Because participants had been assigned to groups at random, giving each individual the same chance as every other of being assigned to one of the three groups, these investigators could be confident that the three groups were equivalent. When enough participants are assigned to groups in this way, the likelihood of any systematic differences between groups is very low, and any resulting differences in perceptions of the boys' play between individuals in the three groups can be attributed to the information they were given.

experiment A research procedure in which participants are randomly assigned to groups that are then treated differently.

random assignment The assignment of participants to groups in such a way that each participant has an equal chance of being assigned to any condition.

independent variable The variable that is manipulated in an experiment, by randomly assigning participants to different levels of the variable.

dependent variable The measure used to determine the effect of the independent variable in an experiment.

TABLE 14.2 Comparison of Nonexperimental and Experimental Research Strategies

	Nonexperimental	Experimental
Degree of control	Low	High
Participants	Not randomly assigned to conditions	Randomly assigned to conditions
Variables	Classification variables	Independent variables
Conclusions	X co-varies with Y	X causes Y

Developmental Research: Issues and Designs

The experimental approach described above is often difficult to achieve in developmental research. Age is not a variable that can be manipulated. Individuals come to the laboratory with one age or another—they can't be assigned one. As a consequence, developmentalists face the central problem of separating genuine age changes from conditions that are likely to vary with age, namely, cohort differences and time of measurement differences (Schaie, 1965). These problems are illustrated in correlational research.

Correlational Research

Instead of working with an independent variable, one that can be assigned at random to different groups, **correlational research** works with **classification variables.** Developmentalists classify individuals according to age, or some other variable, and then see whether that variable is related to other differences. Table 14.2 presents the ways in which experimental research differs from nonexperimental research.

Let's say we want to know whether adolescents become more conscious of the sex-appropriateness of their behavior with age. We could show a group of 10-year-olds, a group of 15-year-olds, and a group of 20-year-olds video materials similar to those described above. Assume for the moment that we find that sex-appropriate choices of magazines increase with age. Is this because adolescents become more aware of the sex-appropriateness of their behavior with age? They may, in fact, but this is just one of several alternative conclusions.

These adolescents already differ in at least one respect: their age. They probably differ in other ways, too. Their age may be related to another condition that is causing the relationship we noticed. Benton Underwood, an author of several books on methodology, tells of a teacher in a private boys' school who observed that the best students all had very good vocabularies. This teacher suggested to a colleague that the school should require all students to take a course in developing their vocabularies. After a moment's thought, the colleague answered that he had noticed a relationship between the height of these students and the length of their trousers, but he doubted whether the school could increase their height by lengthening their pants.

We also have no way of knowing, in this hypothetical study of ours, if the relationship we observed is due to age itself. All we observed was a difference that corresponded to age.

correlational research A procedure in which subjects are assigned to groups on the basis of preexisting characteristics.

classification variable A variable, such as age, that cannot be manipulated by randomly assigning participants to levels of the variable, as can an independent variable.

This difference could be an age change, something we would see in any individuals the same age, regardless of their culture or the historical period in which they lived; or it could be either of two alternatives that are frequently confused with age in developmental research: cohort differences and time of measurement effects. Let's look at each of these more closely.

Age changes are the biological and experiential changes that always accompany aging; these occur in all cultures and all points in history. We assume that age changes have a biological basis (although we are not always able to identify it); therefore, these changes should be universal—that is, they should occur in all people no matter what their social or cultural background. A good example of an age change is the loss of high-frequency tones in hearing. If we notice that adolescents in all cultures become more aware of the sex-appropriateness of their behavior with age, we might be willing to say this awareness is a genuine age change. Even so, the difference could reflect either of two alternatives: cohort differences and time of measurement differences.

The only way we can observe age changes is to observe individuals of different chronological ages. The problem is that people who differ in chronological age also differ in other ways, namely, in their social and historical backgrounds. These differences don't always have to affect the way they respond to the measures we are taking, but they might. People of the same age belong to the same *cohort* group. Cohorts are more likely to have similar cultural experiences than people of different ages. Adolescents today live in an information-rich society in which cell phones, the Internet, and instant messaging are commonplace and contribute to rapidly changing fashions and attitudes. Adolescents born 30 years ago were less sophisticated technologically and society moved more slowly. Differences such as these appear in all sorts of attitudes and behaviors and can easily be confused with age changes; they are termed **cohort differences.**

If we return now to our hypothetical study, we can see how changing gender and work roles might lead to behavior that is less sex-stereotyped than before, with the consequence that older adolescents, who are further removed from these changes, may show more stereotyped behavior.

It is always possible, of course, to test a single group of 10-year-olds and then wait until they reach 15 and test them again, then wait and retest them again at 20. We wouldn't have any cohort differences, but we could have **time of measurement differences.** These differences reflect social conditions, currents of opinion, and historical events that are present when we make our observations and can affect attitudes and behavior. When we study age changes by repeatedly observing the same group of individuals over time, we can mistake time of measurement changes for age changes. It's always possible, for example, that researchers today are more aware of sexist attitudes and more likely to notice adolescents who label some things as appropriate only for one sex.

Developmentalists need to distinguish differences due to cohort effects and time of measurement from genuine age changes. We can evaluate the adequacy of three common developmental designs by their ability to do just this: cross-sectional, longitudinal, and sequential designs.

Cross-Sectional Designs

The **cross-sectional design** is one of the most common designs in developmental research. This design calls for testing several groups of individuals, each of a different age, at the same time. Going back to our hypothetical study, we would measure sex-appropriate choices for adolescents at each of three ages: 10, 15, and 20. There is but a single time of measurement in this design, but several cohort groups (Figure 14.1).

age changes Biological and experiential changes that accompany aging, irrespective of cultural or historical context.

cohort differences Experiential differences between groups of people born at different periods in time; these differences can be confounded with age changes.

time of measurement differences Differences due to social conditions, currents of opinion, and historical events that can affect observations in longitudinal research; such differences are confounded with age changes.

cross-sectional design A research design in which several age cohorts are compared at a single time of measurement.

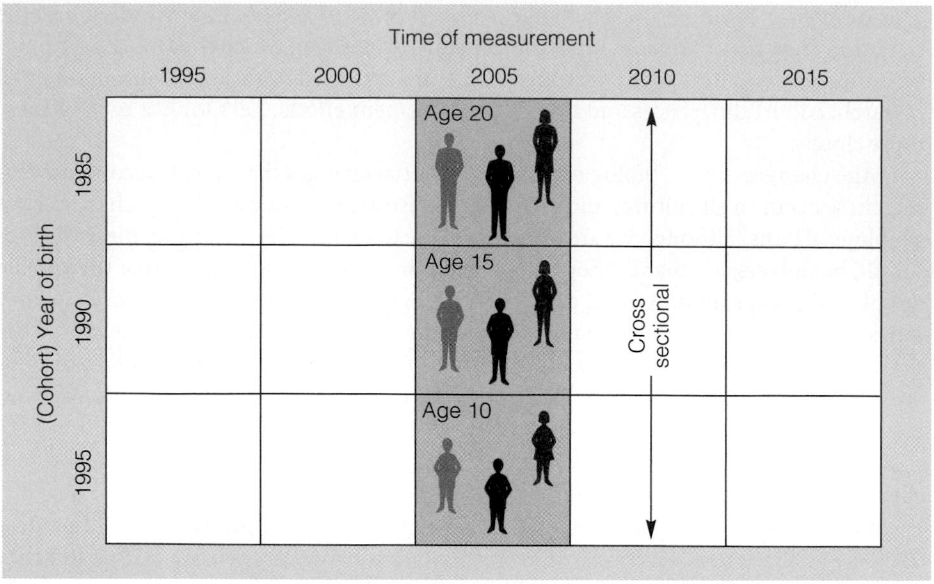

FIGURE 14.1
Cross-Sectional Design.
Source: Adapted from J. Stevens-Long & M. L. Commons. (1992). *Adult life: Developmental processes* (4th ed.). Mountain View, CA: Mayfield. Reproduced with permission of The McGraw-Hill Companies.

It is difficult to interpret cross-sectional data, because differences between the groups can reflect either age changes or cohort differences. Until fairly recently, however, we were unaware of this weakness in the design and used it regularly, mainly because it simplified data collection. We can obtain information about developmental differences relatively quickly, certainly in a matter of days as opposed to decades. The relative strengths and weaknesses of this design receive attention in the Research Focus "Cross-Sectional and Sequential Designs" in Chapter 4.

Longitudinal Designs

The **longitudinal design** studies a single cohort group of individuals over time, repeatedly observing its members as they age. Thus, we have a single cohort group but several times of measurement. We illustrated this design when we sampled a group of 10-year-olds, tested them, then retested them when they reached 15, and again at 20 (Figure 14.2). By following the same individuals over time, we can see patterns of development that we might miss with cross-sections. And because we are comparing individuals with themselves at each age, we minimize the problem of having equivalent samples.

This design, too, is seriously flawed, however, because it confounds age changes and time of measurement differences. It is impossible, in other words, to separate the effects of age from those due to time of measurement. The design suffers from other problems as well. Longitudinal research is very expensive because a large research staff is needed to maintain the elaborate records that must be kept to stay in touch with the individuals and maintain information about them over the years. Longitudinal research is also time-consuming. We must wait while individuals age—and there is no guarantee that we'll outlive them.

A more serious problem than either of these is the nearly inevitable loss of individuals with time. People move away, die, or for other reasons are not available for study. This loss is called **subject mortality** and is almost always systematically related to age. Thus, the individuals who remain are not representative of those their age in the population, because the less healthy and otherwise less fortunate are generally the first to leave the sample. The Research Focus "Longitudinal Design" appears in Chapter 8.

longitudinal design A research design in which a single cohort group is followed over time, tested at several times of measurement.

subject mortality In longitudinal studies, the loss of participants over time.

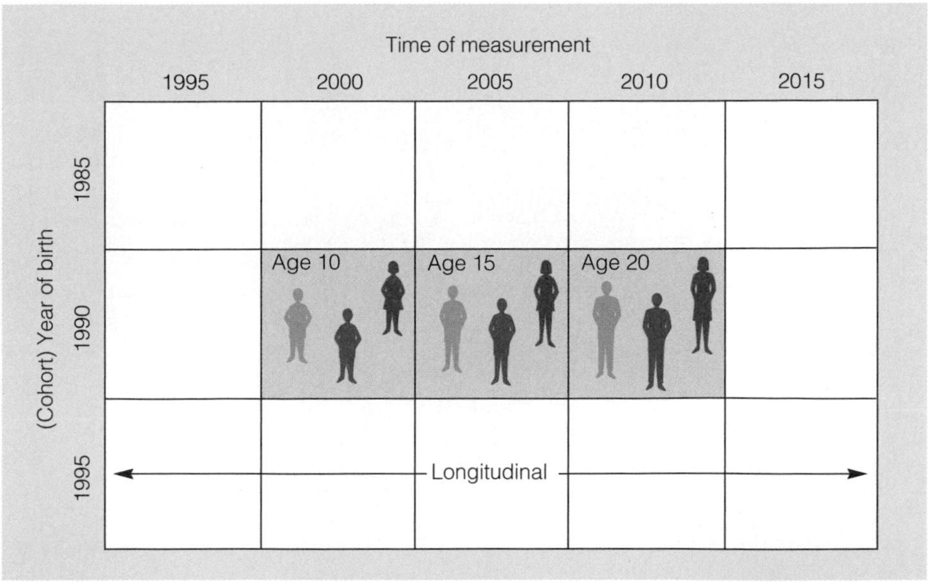

FIGURE 14.2
Longitudinal Design.
Source: Adapted from J. Stevens-Long & M. L. Commons. (1992). *Adult life: Developmental processes* (4th ed.). Mountain View, CA: Mayfield. Reproduced with permission of The McGraw-Hill Companies.

How does intelligence change with age? Are personality traits constant over time? To answer these kinds of developmental questions, researchers use various methods, such as studying twins or using longitudinal studies of the same individuals over a number of years.

Each of these designs has its own problems of interpretation, which we can see by looking at some of the research on age-related changes in intelligence. Cross-sectional studies for many years charted a marked decline in intellectual functioning after about age 30. It is likely, however, that most of this decline actually reflects cohort or generational differences. Our society changes significantly within our lifetimes, and individuals have different experiences than those born 20 or 30 years earlier. Longitudinal research shows that when we track the intellectual functioning of an individual over time, we fail to see real decline until advanced old age.

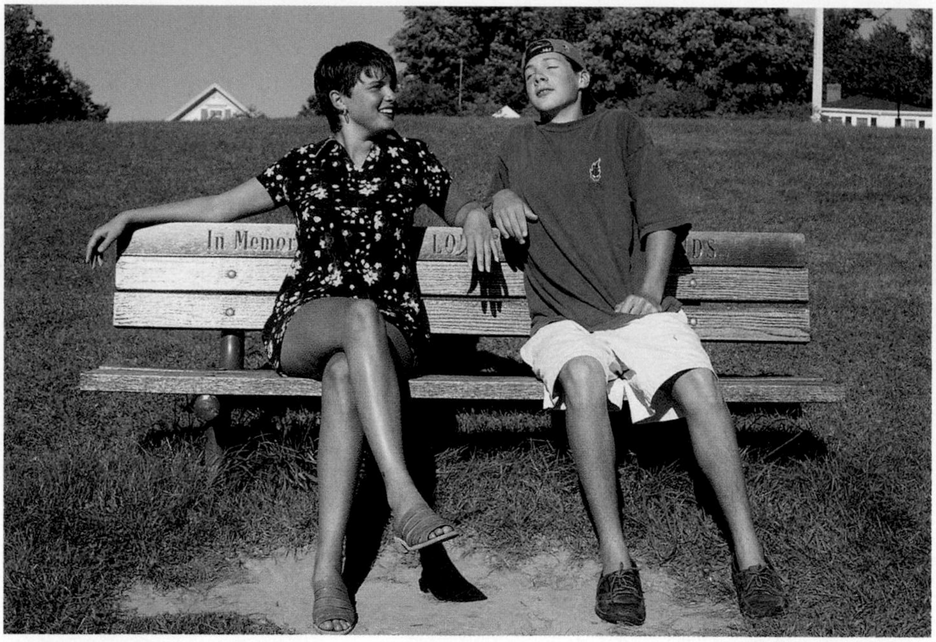

These adolescents differ in obvious ways, yet because they are the same age, they are members of the same cohort group and share many experiences in common.

Sequential Designs

A third design, the **sequential design** is the most successful in isolating age changes from cohort and time of measurement differences. This design tests several different cohort groups at several different times. In a way, the sequential design is a number of longitudinal studies, each starting with a different age group, as shown in Figure 14.3.

Let's suppose we want to see whether intelligence changes with age. By looking at the blocks that form the diagonals in Figure 14.3, we can compare 10-year-olds with 15-year-olds and 20-year-olds. The means for each of those diagonals will reflect age differences in intellectual functioning as well as cohort differences and time of measurement differences.

By taking an average of the scores for the blocks in the top row, we get a mean for the 1985 cohort. By averaging the scores for the blocks in the middle row, we get a mean for the 1990 cohort. And by averaging the scores for the blocks in the bottom row, we get a mean for the 1995 cohort. Differences among these three means provide an estimate of the amount of variability in intellectual functioning that is contributed by cohorts.

We can also estimate the effect of time of measurement. We can compare performance measured in 2000 (the blocks in the second column), for example, with performance measured in 2005 and 2010 (the blocks in the third and fourth columns). Thus, by using appropriate statistical techniques, we can isolate cohort and time of measurement effects and subtract these out; differences that remain reflect age changes.

Sequential designs signal an increasing sophistication in developmental research. Many problems of observation and data collection remain, of course, but we are still able to arrive at interesting observations about adolescents. The Research Focus "Cross-Sectional and Sequential Designs" appears in Chapter 4.

sequential design A research design in which several age cohort groups are compared at several times of measurement; essentially, a number of longitudinal studies, each starting with a different age group.

path analysis A statistical procedure that indicates the direction, or path, of effect with correlated variables.

Path Analysis

Path analysis is a statistical procedure that allows one to infer the path, or direction of effect in a relationship between variables using correlational data. For path analysis, one

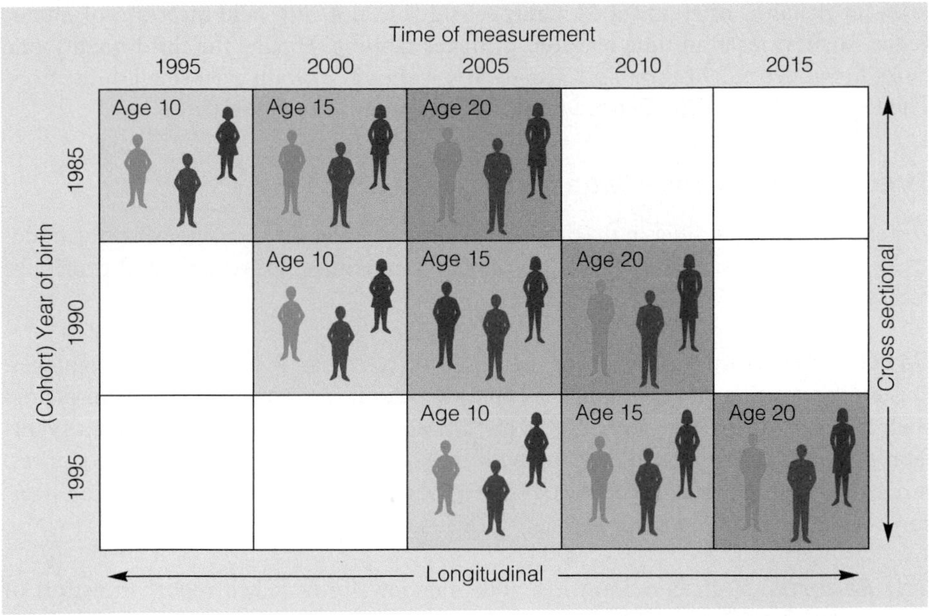

FIGURE 14.3
Sequential Design.
Source: Adapted from J. Stevens-Long & M. L. Commons. (1992). *Adult life: Developmental processes* (4th ed.). Mountain View, CA: Mayfield. Reproduced with permission of The McGraw-Hill Companies.

must have measures using the same variables taken at two separate times. Because we know that causes precede their effects in time, we can use this time difference to trace the direction of the relationship. Specifically, path analysis looks for differences in the strength of relationships according to which factor precedes the other. If television viewing is a cause of poor grades, for instance, these variables should be most highly correlated when the measure of television viewing precedes the measure for grades, that is, when television viewing at Time 1 is correlated with grades at Time 2. The opposite correlation, between grades at Time 1 and television viewing at Time 2, should be relatively weak. By using path analysis, developmentalists can look for causal relationships between classification variables. The Research Focus "Path Analysis" appears on the Web site.

Response Measures in Developmental Research

Dependent Variables

Recall that the scientific method is distinguished by the way in which conclusions are checked against observations. Dependent variables are the measures used in making these observations. Dependent variables can measure behaviors, feelings, or thoughts. Will viewing scenes of graphic violence cause adolescents to behave more aggressively? We can tally the frequency of their aggressive remarks or actions. Might adolescents feel more hostile or have more aggressive thoughts? Self-report inventories in which they rate their feelings and thoughts can provide answers. Tallies of their behavior and responses to self-report inventories are dependent variables. Each is a measure of the effect of the independent variable of viewing scenes of graphic violence.

What qualities does one look for in a dependent variable? **Reliability** is the first prerequisite; random variation should create little difference in a person's score from one occasion to the next. The second quality one looks for is validity. The **validity** of a measure refers to whether it measures what it was designed to measure. Early intelligence

reliability The extent to which the same observations are obtained each time a measure is used.

validity The extent to which the dependent variable measures what it was designed to measure.

tests, for instance, often included highly reliable but not very valid measures of intelligence, such as reaction time or speed of finger tapping. Finally, the third quality one looks for in dependent variable is **sensitivity;** it should pick up even small differences. The Research Focus "The Dependent Variable" appears on the Web site.

Types of Response Measures

Dependent variables differ in the degree to which they measure behavior directly; in decreasing order, these measures involve direct observations, self-reports, and projective measures.

Direct Observation Observing behavior directly has a number of advantages. **Direct observation** of an adolescent's behavior eliminates potential bias from factors such as selective memory or intentional distortions. Observers are trained to identify different types of behaviors and code them for frequency, context, and their consequences. A disadvantage to direct observation is that it takes a greater amount of time than measures relying on self-report.

Self-Reports Both questionnaires and interviews provide self-report measures of adolescents' behaviors, attitudes, and feelings. For instance, questionnaires have been used to obtain information about the relationship between adolescents' experience of "flow," or their immersion in an ongoing activity, and their relationship with their parents. Something such as flow is not as easily observed as it is reported. Subjective states such as flow are difficult to observe, so most of our information relies on self-report data. Self-report measures can tap feelings and states through questionnaires or interviews. A disadvantage to self-report data is the possibility of distortion, when subjects deliberately change information (as they might to questions such as "How many times have you used an illicit substance in the past year?") or when adolescents fail to remember or report events the way they actually occurred. The Research Focus "Questionnaires" appears on the Web site.

Projective Measures **Projective measures** consist of ambiguous stimuli to which subjects are asked to respond. Common projective measures are the Rorschach inkblot test and the Thematic Apperception Test (TAT). In the Rorschach test, individuals identify what they see in a series of inkblots. In the TAT, they are asked to tell a story about characters in pictures. Because the pictures themselves are unclear, it is assumed that subjects must project themselves into the situation they are describing and, in doing so, actually tell about their own thoughts and feelings. Projective measures have the advantage of tapping feelings and thoughts of which even the individual may be unaware. They suffer from the disadvantage of having relatively low reliability and validity. The Research Focus "Projective Measures" appears on the Web site.

sensitivity The extent to which the dependent variable can pick up very small differences due to the independent variable.

direct observation A response measure in which behavior is observed and recorded as it occurs.

projective measures Ambiguous images, such as inkblots or uncaptioned pictures, that participants are asked to describe; in doing so, they may reveal subconscious feelings and thoughts.

Research Issues

Internal and External Validity

Research is a way of asking and getting answers to questions. Thinking of it this way, we can evaluate just how good research is by the quality of the answers it gives us. Are these answers clear and unambiguous? Or can they be interpreted more than one way?

Research that provides unambiguous answers to the questions it was designed to address is said to have **internal validity.** Research in which competing explanations cannot be ruled out is confounded. Confounding exists when extraneous variables are not controlled.

A second criterion exists for evaluating any research study: How representative are its findings? Do they apply to other groups of adolescents than those who were studied? Research has **external validity** when its findings can be generalized to other populations and contexts. Frequently the conditions that are necessary to ensure internal validity conflict with those that promote external validity. Internal validity is easiest to achieve in laboratory experiments, in which the investigator has control over the conditions that can affect the observation. However, a laboratory setting is the very type of situation in which subjects are most likely to be on their best behavior—acting any way other than the way they normally would. On the other hand, external validity is virtually guaranteed for research conducted in natural settings, in which the investigator intervenes little in ongoing behavior. Yet these are the conditions that are rife with extraneous variables that can threaten the internal validity of one's observations. The Research Focus "Internal and External Validity," which appears on the Web site, provides examples of this continuing tension in developmental research.

Theory-Guided Research

Ideas for research come from many sources. One rich source is developmental theory, such as that of Erikson, Gilligan, Piaget, or Freud. Theories summarize specific facts under more general concepts that organize our understanding of development. Theories also make it possible to anticipate changes that would be congruent with the theory, even though they may never have been observed. The Research Focus "Theory-Guided Research" appears on the Web site.

Operationalizing Concepts

Operationalizing a concept defines it in terms of the methods that are used to measure it, that is, in terms of a set of operations that anyone can follow. **Operational definitions** make it possible to empirically investigate even abstract concepts, such as the growth of autonomy, popularity, or identity in adolescents. Operational definitions also make it possible for investigators working independently in different parts of the country to be sure they are studying the same concept, as long as they are using the same instrument or set of procedures to measure it. The Research Focus "Operationalizing Concepts" appears in Chapter 5.

Sampling

Most studies actually work with relatively small numbers of adolescents; yet each generalizes its findings to all adolescents, or to subgroups—for example, early adolescent females, or college-bound late adolescents, or late adolescent minority males. How can an investigator who observes or interviews a limited number of adolescents hope to generalize the findings from that study to adolescents in general? The answer comes from the way the investigator samples the subjects that are actually studied from the larger population. The **population** is the entire group of adolescents in which one is interested. The **sample** is a subgroup drawn from this population. If the sample is drawn at random from the population, we can be reasonably confident that it will be representative of

internal validity The extent to which a research study unambiguously answers the questions it was designed to address.

external validity The generalizability of research conclusions to other populations and contexts.

operational definition The definition of a concept in terms of the procedures used to measure it.

population The entire group of individuals in which an investigator is interested.

sample A subgroup drawn from the population that is the subject of research.

that population. When randomly sampled, each adolescent has the same chance of being chosen as every other adolescent. Consequently, as the size of the sample grows, it increasingly approximates the characteristics of the population from which it was drawn. The Research Focus "Sampling" appears in Chapter 7.

Bias and Blind Controls

Adolescents differ among themselves in countless ways. These individual differences are reflected in all types of research. Specifically, variability in subjects' responses that is not due to the variable being investigated is termed *random error.* Error obscures the effect of a variable. Despite this unwanted effect, there is no way to eliminate its presence from an investigation. As long as adolescents differ in individual ways, we will have random error. Investigators arrange their conditions of observation to minimize the presence of random error.

Bias, like error, reflects variations in subjects' responses that are not due to the variable being investigated. However, the similarity between bias and error ends here. **Bias** occurs when the source of variation is *differentially* present in one condition and not the other. Unlike error, which simply makes the effect of a variable more difficult to detect, bias actually distorts the effect of a variable. Investigators have only one option when facing the possibility of bias: to eliminate it. Bias threatens an investigation's internal validity.

Bias exists in many forms. The extraneous conditions that threaten the internal validity of quasi-experimental designs reflect different types of bias. Another common source of bias that can influence observations can be traced to what the experimenter expects to see. **Double-blind controls** eliminate the possibility of this source of bias by controlling for the experimenter's knowledge of which condition a participant is experiencing. The experimenter is blind with respect to the condition each participant is in. As a result, expectations cannot bias observations. The Research Focus "Bias and Blind Controls" appears in Chapter 12.

Tests of Significance

Will adolescents get a better grade in a course if they keep a log of the date, hour, and time spent studying each time they read their textbook or study for the course? One could assign students at random to two groups within the course. The experimental group is told they are part of a study on how adolescents learn and is given instructions on how to keep the log. The other group, the control, is merely told that they are part of a study examining how adolescents learn. Will the simple act of keeping a log improve the grade of students in the experimental group? How can we tell? How much better would these students have to do in the course to support this conclusion? Remember, too, that each student is an individual, and each will learn at a slightly different rate due to individual differences. Individual differences contribute heavily to random error.

To determine whether a difference between groups is due to random error or whether it reflects the variable being studied, one uses a **test of significance**. Common tests are chi-square, t-tests, and F-tests. If the value that is obtained is larger than a tabled value for the same number of participants, we can rule out random error as responsible for the difference and attribute it to the independent variable, in this case, whether students kept a log. The likelihood of random error being responsible for the difference decreases with increases in the number of participants in each group. The number of participants is reflected in the **degrees of freedom,** or the number of observations in a set that can vary without changing the value of the set. The Research Focus "Statistical Tests

bias Distortion of the effect of a variable due to research design or researcher expectations.

double-blind controls Research procedure in which neither the researcher nor the participants know which individuals have been assigned to which experimental conditions.

test of significance A statistical procedure for determining whether group differences are due to random error or can be attributed to the variable being studied.

degrees of freedom The number of scores in a set that are free to vary given certain constraints, such as a known mean.

of Significance" appears in Chapter 11. With larger degrees of freedom, one needs a smaller difference to reject the assumption that random error was responsible.

Ethics

What ethical concerns guide research? Like most professional organizations, the American Psychological Association provides guidelines governing the ethical conduct of research with human participants. The overriding principle governing any research with human participants is to protect the *dignity and welfare* of those who participate in the research. Other considerations follow from this concern. Participants are told, for instance, that their participation is *voluntary* and that they are free to leave at any point. They are also informed of anything in the research that could affect their willingness to participate.

Once participants agree to serve, investigators assume responsibility for protecting them from physical or psychological distress. After the data have been collected, the investigators debrief participants, informing them about the nature of the study and removing any misconceptions that may have arisen. If investigators suspect any undesirable consequences, they have the responsibility for correcting these. Any information gained about participants is confidential. The Research Focus on "Ethics" and on "Confidentiality" appear on the Web site.

Research Designs

Between-Subjects Designs

In a **between-subjects research design,** each participant experiences only one level of the independent variable. Consider an experiment in which participants read a description of a dating situation in which a male tries to kiss a female while they are at a movie together and, when she refuses, kisses her anyway. Some of the participants read that it was a first date; others read that they were married. The independent variable here is the couple's level of intimacy. Thus, some students experienced one level of the independent variable (first date), and other students experienced another level (married). (Margolin, Miller, & Moran, 1989).

Why might we care whether participants experience no more than one experimental condition? A major advantage to their not doing so is that investigators need not worry that participants responses will reflect the effects of any other condition that may still be present. What if students assigned to the "first date" condition had just previously read of a similar incident involving a couple who was married? Could we safely assume that these students would be able to separate their reactions to each situation? In a between-subjects design, one need not worry about such matters.

There is a second advantage to this design. Because participants can be assigned at random to conditions, investigators can be reasonably confident that groups don't initially differ before they experience the different treatments. Both advantages address the issue of internal validity; between-subjects designs are high in internal validity. The Research Focus "Between-Subjects Designs" appears in Chapter 6.

between-subjects design A research design in which each participant experiences only one level of the independent variable or one experimental condition.

within-subjects design A research design in which each participant experiences all levels of the independent variable.

Within-Subjects Designs

In a **within-subjects research design,** each participant experiences all of the experimental conditions in contrast to the between-subjects design, in which each participant experiences only one condition. Because of this, within-subjects designs are *economical.* They require fewer participants because the same individuals react to all the conditions. They are also *sensitive.* A design is sensitive to the extent that it can pick up, or detect, differences due to the experimental treatment when these exist. Within-subjects designs are sensitive because they use the same individuals in all conditions, thus reducing variability due to individual differences.

Despite these advantages, this type of design has a number of serious disadvantages. **Carryover effects** can occur in which the effect of one treatment is still present when the next is given. In addition to carryover effects, there can be **order effects** with this design. These reflect systematic changes in performance over time due to factors such as practice, fatigue, boredom, and so on. Both carryover and order effects introduce the potential for confounding, in that the difference between treatments can be explained in more than one way. The Research Focus "Within-Subjects Designs" appears in Chapter 9.

Matched-Subjects Designs

Participants in different groups can be *matched* for a number of variables, such as absence of father in the home, mother's age, or social class. To match participants along some variable, one first needs to rank the individuals in each sample according to the matching variable—for example, from oldest to youngest—and then draw pairs of participants that are the same or approximately the same age from the two samples. Using this procedure, one can be sure that the two groups will be equivalent with regard to the matching variable. If age is related to the independent variable, age is then equated for the two groups; that is, any differences between the groups cannot be due to age.

A **matched-subjects research design** carries an additional advantage. It reduces random error, or the amount of variability between groups that does not result from the independent variable. By reducing random error, one can more easily see the effects of the independent variable. Another way of describing this advantage is to say that matched designs are more sensitive than those in which each subject is randomly assigned to a condition.

Given the importance of these advantages, one might wonder why investigators don't routinely match subjects in all their experiments. Yet like other procedures, matching has its disadvantages. The most serious of these is a statistical one, concerning the degrees of freedom used when determining the significance of the tests that evaluate the research outcome. In designs that do not match, the degrees of freedom reflect the number of *participants.* In matched-subjects designs, they reflect the number of *pairs.* Matching cuts the degrees of freedom in half. This means that one must obtain a larger difference for this to reach statistical significance. The irony to this disadvantage is that matching is most advantageous when one is using few participants, because it increases the sensitivity of the design. But these are the very conditions under which one can least afford to lose degrees of freedom. Investigators should determine that the matching variable is highly correlated with the measure they are using before matching. Only in this way will matching effectively reduce unexplained variability and pay for the loss in degrees of freedom.

A second disadvantage is less serious. Matching designs are somewhat more time-consuming to conduct than are those involving simple random assignment of participants. One must first administer the matching variable and then rank individuals before they can be assigned to conditions. Extra expense may also be involved. A more serious disadvantage than either of these is the threat to *external validity* that occurs when indi-

carryover effects In within-subjects research designs, the effects of previous conditions that persist when subsequent conditions are given.

order effects In a within-subjects design, systematic changes in performance over time due to factors such as practice and fatigue.

matched-subjects design A research design in which groups are initially equated by matching participants according to a variable that correlates highly with the dependent variable.

viduals who cannot be matched must be discarded. Any loss of participants can affect the representativeness of the sample and the ability to generalize to the population from which it was drawn. Finally, investigators run the risk of *sensitizing* participants to the treatment by first pretesting them along a matching variable. Individuals who are sensitized become aware of the treatment in ways that other participants are not. Because they are sensitized to a variable, participants may respond to it in ways they might not, had their awareness not been initially raised. The Research Focus "Matched-Subjects Design" appears on the Web site.

Factorial Designs

In a **factorial design** two or more independent variables, or factors, are completely *crossed* so that each level of one variable is combined with each level of all the other variables. Factorial designs provide information about the effect of each of the independent variables alone, called a **main effect,** and information about the effect of a variable when another variable is present, called an **interaction.** An interaction exists when the effect of a variable changes when a second variable is present.

Consider an experiment examining the effect of ambiguous social cues on the distress experienced by adolescents who differ in their expectations of being rejected. To illustrate an interaction, we might find that when social cues make it clear that the refusal of a social overture is not personally motivated, all adolescents will experience minimal distress, but when social cues are ambiguous, adolescents with high expectations of being rejected find the refusal more distressful. The existence of an interaction means that we must qualify what we say about a variable. Is refusal of a social overture distressing to adolescents? It depends. For adolescents who have high expectations of being rejected, it can be. But for those who do not, there is little distress. The Research Focus "Factorial Designs" appears on the Web site.

factorial design A research design in which each of the levels of one independent variable are combined with each of the levels of all the other independent variables; provides information about the main effect of each independent variable and about interactions between these variables.

main effect In a factorial research design, the effect of each independent variable alone.

interaction An interaction exists when the effect of a variable changes when another variable is present.

Summary

Research Strategies

- Research strategies are procedures that social scientists follow to avoid making faulty observations. The strategies can be broadly distinguished in terms of two dimensions: the number of participants studied and the degree of control the investigator has over conditions that could affect the observations.
- In terms of number of participants, research can follow a single case, as in a case study, or can embrace large numbers of individuals, as in surveys. *Case studies* have the advantage of giving richly detailed data that can lead to hypotheses for future research but suffer from problems of generalizability and objectivity. *Surveys,* which rely on self-report measures obtained through either interviews or questionnaires, allow investigators to study behavior that is not open to direct observation, but they carry the risk of distortion.
- In terms of degree of control, both *archival research,* which utilizes existing records, and *naturalistic observation,* which involves observation of behavior as it occurs in a natural setting, involve no control by the investigator over conditions that might affect the observations, thereby reducing the chance that participants are responding to the particular procedure an investigator has chosen to use rather than the variables the investigator is interested in. Erikson's psychohistorical approach applies clinical skills in a fieldwork setting. These designs do not allow the investigator to make causal inferences concerning the relationships observed.
- *Quasi-experimental* designs involve more intervention, or control, than the previous

methods, but less than experiments. Potential *confounds* in quasi-experimental designs are maturation, testing and history effects, and statistical regression.

- *Experiments* offer the greatest control over possible confounds. In an experiment, the experimenter randomly assigns participants to groups, which are then exposed to different treatments. *Random assignment,* by distributing individual differences across groups, ensures that the groups are initially equivalent and allows the investigator to attribute any observed differences to the way the groups are treated.

Developmental Research

- Developmental research, in which age is a variable, faces problems of confounding. *Longitudinal* designs, in which a single cohort is repeatedly tested at different times of measurement, reveals patterns of developmental change but is time-consuming and expensive and potentially confounds age changes with time of measurement differences.
- Cross-sectional research, in which several age cohorts are tested at a single time of measurement, takes less time to complete but may miss developmental patterns and potentially confounds age changes with cohort differences.
- *Sequential* designs, in which several cohorts are each tested at several times of measurement, allow investigators to estimate time of measurement and cohort effects and to isolate these from age changes.

Response Measures

- Various types of response measures—direct observation, self-reports, and projective measures—have different advantages and disadvantages.

Research Issues

- Research is internally valid to the extent that it provides an unambiguous answer to the questions it was designed to address. *External validity* exists when the findings of a particular study can be generalized to other populations and contexts.
- Concepts can be operationally defined by defining them in terms of the operations that are used in their measurement. Operational definitions make it possible for investigators working in different laboratories to study the same concept.

Research Designs

- In a *between-subjects* research design, each participant experiences only one level of the independent variable.
- In a *within-subjects* research design, each participant experiences all of the experimental conditions. The latter design is economical and sensitive but runs the risk of carryover and order effects.
- *Matched-subjects* designs reduce variability due to individual differences by matching participants along a third variable, but they also reduce degrees of freedom by half, risk sensitizing participants to the intent of the study by pretesting them, and jeopardize external validity by not including individuals who cannot be matched.
- *Factorial* designs combine two or more independent variables and provide information about interactions.

Key Terms

scientific method
case study
self-report
archival research
naturalistic observation
quasi-experimental design
confounding
testing effect
history effect
statistical regression
experiment
random assignment
independent variable
dependent variable
correlational research
classification variable
age changes
cohort differences
time of measurement differences
cross-sectional design

longitudinal design
subject mortality
sequential design
path analysis
reliability
validity
sensitivity
direct observation
projective measures
internal validity
external validity
operational definition
population
sample
bias
double-blind controls
test of significance
degrees of freedom
between-subjects design
within-subjects design
carryover effects
order effects
matched-subjects design
factorial design
main effect
interaction

Glossary

abstinence-only programs Sex education programs that teach that abstinence is the only way to avoid pregnancy and the risk of sexually transmitted diseases.

academic tracking The assignment of students to one of several courses of study in high school on the basis of criteria such as academic interests and goals, past achievement, and ability.

acceleration Allowing gifted adolescents to advance beyond their grade level at a faster than normal rate.

accommodation Piaget's term for the process by which cognitive structures are altered to fit new events or experiences.

acculturation A socialization process by which members of a minority adopt the customs of the dominant group, while maintaining a separate cultural identity.

achieved ethnic identity A stage in ethnic identity formation in which one has a clear sense of one's ethnicity that reflects feelings of belonging and emotional identification.

adjustment disorder with depressed mood A form of depression, frequently manifested in difficulty carrying out ordinary tasks of life and unsatisfactory social relations.

adolescence The transitional and often ambiguous period of development between childhood and adulthood. The duration, characteristics, and even the existence of such a period depend very much on historical, social, cultural, and economic factors.

adrenal androgens Hormones produced by the adrenal glands that initiate the initial stage of puberty.

adrenarche The initial phase of puberty that involves activity of the adrenal androgens.

adult status hypothesis An explanation for the effects of asynchronous development that attributes the effects of timing to the status that awaits adolescents of either sex when they become adults.

affective disorders Disorders whose primary symptoms reflect a disturbance of mood, such as depression.

age changes Biological and experiential changes that accompany aging, irrespective of cultural or historical context.

agency An aspect of mature functioning characterized by assertiveness, mastery, and distinctiveness; the complement of communion.

AIDS Acquired immune deficiency syndrome: a sexually transmitted disease resulting from a virus that attacks the immune system; can also be transmitted through contaminated blood transfusions or from an infected pregnant woman to her fetus.

alcohol A drug that functions as a central nervous system depressant.

alienation Indifference where devotion or attachment formerly existed; estrangement.

androgens Male sex hormones.

androgynous Characterizing a personality in which there are both masculine and feminine attributes.

anorexia An eating disorder characterized by severely limiting the intake of food; more common in females.

anovulatory Menstrual cycles that do not include the release of an egg.

anterior pituitary A center within the brain that produces hormones that act on the gonads.

apprenticeship The process by which an individual internalizes cultural concepts and skills through association with more skilled members of a group.

archival research The use of existing data, such as public records, to provide answers to research questions.

artistic personality types In Holland's typology of vocational interests, individuals who prefer work requiring imagination and creativity, for example, graphic artist, poet.

assimilation Piaget's term for the process by which new events and experiences are adjusted to fit existing cognitive structures.

asynchrony Differences in the timing of pubertal changes within an adolescent or from one adolescent to the next.

attachment The enduring emotional bonds formed first with parents and siblings and then with friends and romantic partners.

attributional error An overestimation of the importance of dispositional stressors or an underestimation of the importance of situational ones.

attributional retraining A career counseling technique that focuses on individuals' explanations for anticipated career-related successes or failures.

authoritarian parenting Parenting that stresses obedience, respect for authority, and traditional values.

authoritative parenting Parenting that stresses self-reliance and independence; parents are consistent, maintain an open dialogue, and give reasons when disciplining.

automaticity The ability to perform highly practiced cognitive operations without conscious attention.

autonomy Being independent and responsible for one's actions.

average adolescents With respect to popularity, adolescents who are moderately popular with their classmates and moderately disliked as well.

behaviorism An approach to psychology that focuses on the observation and manipulation of behavior and deemphasizes the role of mind.

between-subjects design A research design in which each participant experiences only one level of the independent variable or one experimental condition.

bias Distortion of the effect of a variable due to research design or researcher expectations.

bicultural identity The process by which minority adolescents identify themselves with respect to the two cultures to which they belong.

bisexual Sexual attraction toward individuals of both sexes.

BMI Body mass index; one's weight in kilograms divided by the square of one's height in meters (kg/m^2); since body fatness varies with age and sex, percentiles for BMI are specific to age and gender.

body image Individuals' satisfaction or dissatisfaction with their image of their bodies.

bulimia An eating disorder characterized by bingeing and then purging; more common in females.

bullying Repeated aggressive behaviors or remarks occurring over an extended period of time that the victim finds difficult to defend against.

carryover effects In within-subjects research designs, the effects of previous conditions that persist when subsequent conditions are given.

case study Intensive observation of a single subject, such as an individual or a program.

castration anxiety In Freudian theory, a young boy's fear of being castrated by his father in punishment for the boy's sexual attraction to his mother.

cervix The opening to the uterus.

child labor laws Laws that specify minimum ages for various types of work.

Children's Aid Society Carrera-Model Program (CAS-Carrera) An after-school program that provides sex education as well as help with schoolwork, finding part-time jobs, and getting into college.

chlamydia A sexually transmitted disease, caused by a bacterium, that can affect the reproductive tract, possibly leading to pelvic inflammatory disease.

chronosystem The changing impact of the various environmental systems (micro-, meso-, exo-, macro) at different historical periods.

circumcision Surgical removal of the prepuce covering the glans of the penis.

classification variable A variable, such as age, that cannot be manipulated by randomly assigning participants to levels of the variable, as can an independent variable.

climacteric Gradual decline in functioning of the reproductive organs in middle age.

clique A peer group made up of one's best friends, usually including no more than five or six members.

clitoris That part of the external genitals in females that is the primary source of sexual stimulation.

cognitive psychology An approach to psychology that focuses on mental processes such as thought, memory, reasoning, and problem solving.

cognitive restructuring A counseling technique that confronts individuals with their irrational beliefs.

cohort differences Experiential differences between groups of people born at different periods in time; these differences can be confounded with age changes.

cohort group People born during the same historical period or undergoing the same historical influences.

collectivism Valuing interdependence, cooperation, group success, and harmonious relationships.

commitment in relativism The third of Perry's three forms of thought: committing oneself to a point of view from which one can derive meaning.

communion An aspect of mature functioning characterized by cooperation and union; the complement of agency.

comprehensive sex education programs Sex education programs that teach abstinence as a preferred approach and educate students concerning effective methods of contraception.

compulsory education laws Legislation making school attendance mandatory for children and adolescents until they graduate or reach a minimum age.

computer-assisted instruction The use of computers to monitor the progress of students.

concrete operational thought Piaget's third stage of intellectual development, thought to characterize middle childhood, during which knowledge is gained through mental operations.

conflict resolution centers Mediation programs in which teachers and students are trained in listening skills and conflict resolution.

conflict resolution training Programs designed to teach students to view conflict as a problem to be solved mutually, with a win-win outcome.

conformity The tendency to go along with the norms and standards of one's group.

confounding The presence of additional factors other than the variable of interest that can account for observed differences.

connectedness A quality of family interactions thought to be important for individuation, reflecting openness to and respect for others' opinions.

conscience That part of the personality that is concerned with issues of right and wrong; Freud believed the conscience to be part of the superego.

conservation The realization that something remains the same despite changes in its appearance.

constructive controversy A technique using controversy to stimulate solutions to problems by having students alternately argue their own and the opposing position to a conflict.

constructive knowledge The third of Belenky and associates' three forms of thought: an awareness that knowledge is constructed; the ability to examine one's beliefs.

constructive perspective The view that perception is an active, constructive process in which individuals interpret and give meaning to their experiences.

contextual perspective The view that development is influenced by one's ethnicity and culture.

continuity–discontinuity issue Disagreement as to whether the same set of laws is sufficient to explain behavior at all developmental levels and for all species (continuity assumption) or whether lawful relationships change with age and across species (discontinuity assumption).

controversial adolescents Adolescents frequently mentioned by classmates as someone they least like and by others as a best friend.

conventional moral reasoning Kohlberg's second level of moral reasoning, in which moral thinking is guided by internalized social standards.

conventional personality types In Holland's typology of vocational interests, individuals who prefer highly structured environments and well-defined tasks.

cooperative education A school-to-work program that combines vocational studies with on-the-job experience.

cooperative learning Placing students of different ability levels together in small working groups.

coping Strategies for managing stressful situations that tax personal resources.

correlational research A procedure in which subjects are assigned to groups on the basis of preexisting characteristics.

cross-sectional research A research design in which several age cohorts are compared at a single time of measurement.

crowd A peer group formed from several cliques of the same age group.

crush An idealized fantasy about another person that is rarely reciprocated.

cultural assimilation A socialization process by which members of a minority lose their distinctive characteristics as they assume the customs and beliefs of the dominant group.

cultural pluralism The coexistence of minority and majority groups within a society such that each participates fully in its political and economic systems while retaining cultural diversity.

culture The values, beliefs, and customs that are shared by a group of people and passed from one generation to the next.

culture-fair test A measure of intelligence that minimizes cultural bias by using materials or requiring skills not likely to be more familiar to one segment of the population than to another.

dating A social activity that typically begins in mid-adolescence.

decline stage Super's fifth stage of vocational development, in which one retires.

deductive reasoning Reasoning from the general to the particular.

degrees of freedom The number of scores in a set that are free to vary given certain constraints, such as a known mean.

dependent variable The measure used to determine the effect of the independent variable in an experiment.

depressants Substances that reduce or lower the activity of the central nervous system.

depression An affective disorder that may take a number of forms, all of which are characterized by a disturbance of mood.

developing countries Countries that have only recently begun to adopt modern technology, social forms, and means of production. Such countries were previously termed "third world" countries.

developmental contextualism The position that development must be studied in real life settings, thereby facilitating the integration of research with applied policies and programs.

developmental tasks Age-related norms that reflect social expectations for normal development.

dialectical reasoning Reasoning that questions the premises on which it is based when tests of the premises are not supported.

differentiated instruction Flexible classroom structure providing multiple formats for gaining information.

differentiation A process by which one distinguishes or perceives differences not previously recognized.

diffuse/avoidant orientation A style of information processing characterized by procrastinating and avoiding decisions.

direct instruction Instruction directed toward the mastery of basic skills; all students are involved in the same activities at any given time.

direct observation A response measure in which behavior is observed and recorded as it occurs.

discharge diseases Sexually transmitted diseases transmitted through genital secretions, such as semen and vaginal fluids.

double-blind controls A research procedure in which neither the researcher nor the participants know which individuals have been assigned to which experimental conditions.

drug dependence Physical dependence on a substance, such that one develops a tolerance and experiences withdrawal when use is discontinued; also known as drug addiction.

dualistic thinking The first of Perry's three forms of thought: the belief that truth is independent of one's frame of reference.

dysthymia A form of depression in which the primary symptoms are unhappiness and dissatisfaction with life, often not traceable to particular events.

early adolescence That period of adolescence between the ages of about 11 to 15, marked by the onset of puberty, changing gender roles, more autonomous relationships with parents, and more mature relationships with peers.

early maturation Pubertal maturation occurring earlier in adolescents than the norm for their sex.

ego The executive aspect of the personality in Freudian theory, which seeks to satisfy impulses in socially acceptable ways.

egocentrism The failure to realize that one's perspective is not shared by others.

ego development Increases in the complexity and integration of thought and judgment that occur with age.

Electra complex A Freudian concept in which the young girl is sexually attracted to her father and regards her mother as her rival.

emerging adulthood A period between adolescence and adulthood characterized by demographic unpredictability and increased opportunity for identity exploration.

emotional transmission The transmission of emotions from one person to another within a family.

emotion-focused coping Attempts to reduce stress by minimizing its emotional impact, for example, denial, wishful thinking.

encoding The process by which information is transferred from one form to another in memory.

enculturation Acquiring the norms of one's social group.

endocrine system The system of the body that includes the glands that produce hormones and those parts of the nervous system that activate, inhibit, and control hormone production.

engagement Concentrated attention, necessary for the performance of complex activities.

enrichment Providing gifted adolescents with additional opportunities and experiences.

enterprising personality types In Holland's typology of vocational interests, individuals who prefer work involving interpersonal skills and assertiveness, such as management, law, or sales.

environmental model A set of assumptions in which the environment is taken to be the primary determinant of psychological development.

epigenesis The emergence of new complexities in development that cannot be predicted from, or reduced to, earlier forms.

epigenetic principle Erikson's assumption that an internal ground plan governs the timing or period of ascendence for each new development.

equilibration Piaget's term for the balance between assimilation and accommodation that is responsible for the growth of thought.

establishment stage Super's third stage of vocational development, in which one settles into one's work.

estradial A sex hormone that is present in higher levels in females than males and contributes to breast development, distribution of body fat, and regulation of the menstrual cycle.

estrogens Female sex hormones.

ethic of care Gilligan's description of a morality based on responsiveness to and care for others.

ethnic identity An awareness of belonging to an ethnic group that shapes one's thoughts, feelings, and behavior.

ethnic identity search An intermediate stage in ethnic identity formation involving exploration of the meaning of one's ethnicity.

ethnicity The cultural group to which an individual belongs.

exosystem Contexts occurring at the level of the community, such as types of schools and housing.

experiment A research procedure in which participants are randomly assigned to groups that are then treated differently.

exploration stage Super's second stage of vocational development, in which adolescents begin to make choices related to their future work.

external validity The generalizability of research conclusions to other populations and contexts.

factorial design A research design in which each of the levels of one independent variable are combined with each of the levels of all the other independent variables; provides information about the main effect of each independent variable and about interactions between these variables.

fantasy stage Ginzburg's first stage of vocational development, characterized by focus on highly visible aspects of vocations and no assessment of personal qualifications.

federal minimum wage Federal policy determining the minimum wage to be paid workers.

female circumcision *See* female genital mutilation.

female genital mutilation Cutting out the entire clitoris, the primary source of sexual stimulation in females, and removing the inner labia and sewing shut most of the outer labia.

follicle-stimulating hormone (FSH) A gonadotropic hormone produced by the anterior pituitary that acts on the gonads.

formal operational thought Piaget's fourth stage of intellectual development, thought to characterize adolescence and adulthood, during which mental operations are extended to include thoughts in addition to concrete objects.

full-service schools Schools that provide a variety of health and social services to students and their families in collaboration with the community.

gateway hypothesis The assumption that drug use progresses through stages in which the use of one type of drug provides a pathway to the use of other drugs.

gender The cultural and psychological contributions to being female or male.

gender differences Culturally determined differences in masculinity and femininity.

gender stereotypes The cultural expectations concerning behaviors that are appropriate for each sex.

genital herpes A sexually transmitted disease characterized by recurring outbreaks of itching or burning blisters; caused by a virus that remains dormant in the body.

genital ulcer diseases STDs transmitted through contact with sores or ulcers on the skin, or even patches of skin that appear normal but are infected.

genital warts A sexually transmitted disease caused by the human papilloma virus.

gifted Adolescents who place above a predetermined cutoff point on intelligence scales or who demonstrate special talents in diverse areas.

glans The part of the clitoris or penis that is most sensitive to stimulation.

globalization The process by which expanding international trade, communication, and travel erases national and geographical boundaries.

gonadarche The second stage of puberty that is regulated by the neuroendocrine system.

gonadostat Cells within the hypothalamus that are sensitive to the level of circulating hormones and are part of the feedback system regulating the timing of puberty.

gonadotropin-releasing hormone (GnRH) A hormone released by the hypothalamus and involved in regulating the timing of pubertal events.

gonads The sex glands; the ovaries in females and the testes in males.

gonorrhea A sexually transmitted disease caused by a bacterium.

gossip A process by which preadolescents establish group norms.

group identity A psychosocial task of early adolescence that entails the resolution of issues related to affiliation and belonging.

growth spurt A period of rapid growth that often occurs during puberty.

growth stage Super's first stage of vocational development characterized more by discovery about oneself than about vocations.

guided participation Rogoff's term for the shared activity of a novice and one who is more skilled, in which both participate to decrease the distance between their respective contributions to the activity.

habituation Decreased responsiveness to a stimulus with repeated exposure to it.

hallucinogens Psychoactive substances that can produce altered states of awarcness, such as a distorted sense of time, hallucinations.

heterosexual Sexual attraction toward individuals of the other sex.

historical perspective An approach that considers the way patterns of individual development differ as a function of the historical context.

history effect Any event extraneous to a research project that can affect the results and jeopardize the internal validity of the research.

HIV Human immunodeficiency virus: a virus attacking the immune system, leading to AIDS (acquired immune deficiency syndrome).

homosexual sexual attraction toward individuals of the same sex.

hormones Chemical messengers that are secreted directly into the bloodstream and are regulated by the endocrine system.

hymen A fold of skin partially covering the opening to the vagina.

hypothalamus A center within the brain that regulates hormonal activity and regulatory activities such as eating, drinking, and body temperature.

id The primitive aspect of the personality in Freudian theory, which seeks immediate gratification of biological impulses.

ideal self-image The individual's idealized image of the self, including anticipated as well as actual ways of being.

identity The part of one's personality of which one is aware and is able to see as a meaningful and coherent whole.

identity achievement The resolution of the psychosocial crisis of identity through the formulation of personal goals and personally defined religious and political commitments.

identity diffusion The resolution of the psychosocial crisis of identity without the experience of crisis or commitment over identity issues.

identity foreclosure The resolution of the psychosocial crisis of identity through the assumption of traditional, conventional, or parentally chosen goals and values without the experience of crisis or conflict over identity issues.

identity formation In adolescence, a synthesizing of elements of one's earlier identity into a new whole; involves individuation.

imaginary audience The experience of being the focus of attention that emerges with adolescents' ability to think about thinking in others and their confusion of the concerns of others with their own preoccupation with themselves.

independent variable The variable that is manipulated in an experiment, by randomly assigning participants to different levels of the variable.

index offenses Actions that are criminal at any age, such as homicide, burglary.

individualism Valuing independence, self-reliance, individual achievement, and self-expression.

individuality A quality of family interactions thought to be important for individuation, reflecting the ability to express one's ideas and say how one differs from others.

individuation The process of distinguishing one's attitudes and beliefs from those of one's parents.

inductive reasoning Reasoning from the particular to the general.

indulgent parenting A style of parenting characterized by warmth and nurturance (high responsiveness) but little supervision (low demandingness).

information orientation A style of information processing characterized by actively searching for and evaluating information.

information processing An approach to cognition that focuses on the processes by which information is encoded, retrieved, and utilized.

inhalants Central nervous system depressants; obtained by inhaling fumes from substances such as glue, gasoline, paint thinner, and other solvents.

initiative Intrinsically motivated behavior that is organized around challenging and personally meaningful goals; closely related to agency.

intelligence The ability to profit from experience and adapt to one's surroundings; measured by intelligence tests.

interaction An interaction exists when the effect of a variable changes when another variable is present.

internal validity The extent to which a research study unambiguously answers the questions it was designed to address.

internship A school program in which students spend time working at a job.

intimacy The ability to share oneself with another; characterized by self-disclosure and mutuality.

intrinsic motivation Motivation derived from the pleasure one experiences in an activity.

investigative personality types In Holland's typology of vocational interests, individuals who prefer work requiring intellectual curiosity, for example, scientist, mathematician.

isolate Adolescents who have few friends, either within a clique or outside it, and who have few links to other adolescents in the social network.

jigsaw classroom A classroom organized into small, ethnically balanced working groups in which each student contributes a different part of the lesson.

job shadowing A school program in which students spend part of the school day in a work setting following the activities of one or more employees.

junior high school A secondary school that typically includes the seventh through the ninth grades.

juvenile delinquency Illegal actions committed by a minor.

juvenile justice Legislation instituting separate legal proceedings for juveniles and adults.

knowledge-acquisition components Cognitive mechanisms that, under the direction of metacomponents, acquire new information as needed.

late adolescence That period of adolescence between the ages of about 16 to 19 that is organized around the central task of achieving an identity, in which adolescents integrate their sexuality into their relationships, prepare for a vocation, and fashion a personal set of beliefs.

late maturation Pubertal maturation occurring later in adolescents than the norm for their sex.

laws Relationships that are derived from axioms and can be shown to be true or false.

learning disability Difficulty with academic tasks that is not due to emotional or sensory problems and presumably reflects neurological dysfunction.

learning styles Students' preferences concerning various aspects of the learning situation, for example, working individually or in groups, getting information by reading or listening to a class presentation.

leptin A hormone secreted by fat cells that may play a role in menarche.

liaison Adolescents who have friends in several cliques but do not themselves belong to any one of these.

libido The psychic energy Freud assumed is expressed through different body zones and motivates much of behavior.

lifespan perspective The view that development is characterized by continuity as well as change throughout life.

longitudinal design A research design in which a single cohort group is followed over time, tested at several times of measurement.

long-term memory A relatively permanent memory of unlimited capacity, in which information is organized according to meaning.

low-income families Families with incomes no greater than twice the federal poverty level.

luteinizing hormone (LH) A gonadotropic hormone produced by the anterior pituitary that acts on the gonads.

macrosystem The underlying social and political climate at the level of society.

main effect In a factorial research design, the effect of each independent variable alone.

mainstreaming Placing learning-disabled students in regular classrooms.

maintenance stage Super's fourth stage of vocational development, in which one maintains one's occupational skills and position.

major depressive disorder A period of severe depression requiring hospitalization or other treatment.

male generic language Use of the pronoun *he* to refer to an individual of either sex, and use of words such as *man* or *mankind* to refer to all people.

maltreatment Instances of harm to children or adolescents that are nonaccidental and avoidable; they can be due to either abuse or neglect.

marijuana A mild hallucinogen from the plant *Cannabis sativa;* the psychoactive substance is THC.

masked depression Depression that manifests itself in ways other than depressed mood, for example, agitation, inability to sleep.

masturbation Self-stimulation of the genitals.

matched-subjects design A research design in which groups are initially equated by matching participants according to a variable that correlates highly with the dependent variable.

maturational deviance hypothesis An explanation for the effects of asynchronous development that attributes the effects of timing to changing adolescents' status relative to their peers.

menarche The occurrence of a girl's first menstrual period.

menopause A cessation of menstrual periods in middle age.

mental operations Piaget's term for actions that can be carried out in one's head and then reversed or undone.

mentoring A school program in which students work with someone who serves as a role model.

mesosystem Social contexts involving interactions of several microsystems, such as when parents meet teachers.

meta-analysis A statistical procedure for reaching conclusions regarding an area of research by combining the findings from multiple studies.

metacognition Awareness of one's thinking, cognitive abilities, and style.

metacomponents Higher-order cognitive functions that select and monitor lower-order cognitive functions, for example, metacomponents are employed to determine which performance components are required to perform a task.

metamemory The awareness of one's memory and of those factors that affect it.

microsystem One's immediate social contexts, involving firsthand experiences, such as interactions at home or in the classroom.

middle school A secondary school that includes the fifth or sixth through the eighth grades.

minority A social group, distinguished by physical or cultural characteristics, that often receives differential treatment.

model A set of assumptions about reality in general and about human nature in particular from which theories proceed.

morality The development of standards of right and wrong.

moratorium The experience of conflict over the issues of identity formation prior to the establishment of firm goals or long-term commitments.

multiple intelligence The view that intelligence is comprised of a number of different capacities each relevant to a different domain—e.g., music, linguistics, mathematics, interpersonal relations. One's ability in each domain is not necessarily highly correlated with ability in others.

myelination The formation of a fatty sheath surrounding a nerve fiber (axon), which increases speed of neural conduction.

myotonia An increase in muscular tension.

narcotics Highly addictive opiates, such as opium and its derivatives, morphine and heroin.

naturalistic observation The observation and recording of participants' behavior in their natural setting.

nature–nurture controversy The controversy concerning the primary source of development: nature (heredity) or nurture (environment).

negative reinforcement An event that increases the frequency of the behavior on which its removal is made contingent.

neglected adolescents Adolescents who are rarely mentioned by their classmates as someone they most like or as someone they least like.

neglectful parenting A style of parenting characterized by little warmth or nurturance (low responsiveness) and little supervision (low demandingness).

nicotine The psychoactive substance in cigarettes that is both a stimulant and a depressant.

nocturnal emission A spontaneous ejaculation of seminal fluid during sleep; sometimes called a wet dream.

normative orientation A style of information processing characterized by reliance on social norms and the expectations of relatives and friends.

obesity An eating disorder in which one is 30% above the mean (average) weight for one's height.

object permanence Piaget's term for the infant's recognition that objects exist even when they cannot be seen.

observational learning A form of learning through which one acquires new behaviors by observing others.

Oedipal complex A Freudian concept in which the young boy is sexually attracted to his mother, and regards the father as his rival.

operant Skinner's term for actions that do not have identifiable stimuli eliciting them, that can be brought under the control of a reinforcing event.

operant conditioning A simple form of learning in which the probability of a behavior is affected by its consequences.

operational definition The definition of a concept in terms of the procedures used to measure it.

order effects In a within-subjects design, systematic changes in performance over time due to factors such as practice and fatigue.

organismic model A set of assumptions in which the unfolding of genetically organized processes is taken to be the primary determinant of psychological development.

outer labia The outer folds of skin surrounding the opening of the vagina and the clitoris.

ovaries Structures within the female reproductive system flanking the uterus that house the immature eggs and produce female sex hormones.

overweight Individuals are considered to be overweight when their weight is at or above the 95th percentile for their body mass index.

ovum (plural ova) The female sex cell, also called the egg; the male equivalent is sperm.

parental monitoring The practice in which parents monitor their children's behavior when they are not physically present to supervise their activities.

parentified A reversal in the parent–child relationship in which the burden of caring for the parent's needs is assumed by the adolescent.

path analysis A statistical procedure that indicates the direction, or path, of effect with correlated variables.

peer group A group of individuals of the same age; a social group that regulates the pace of socialization.

peer pressure Experienced pressure to think and act like one's friends.

penis The part of the external genitals in males that is the primary source of sexual stimulation.

penis envy In Freudian theory a girl's envy of, and desire for, a male sex organ.

performance-ability orientation A motivational pattern in which students focus on their own performance, using it as a way of assessing their ability.

performance components Cognitive mechanisms, selected by metacomponents, that operate directly on the information to be processed.

permissive parenting Parenting that uses little punishment, is accepting, makes few demands for responsibility, and exercises little control.

personal expressiveness A dimension of identity formation that distinguishes between seeking practical and personally fulfilling options.

personal fable The feeling of being special; thought to derive from the imaginary audience.

physical aggression Aggressive actions involving physical contact, such as pushing or hitting.

pituitary An endocrine gland located beneath the hypothalamus that is part of a feedback system regulating the hormonal control of puberty.

poor families Families with incomes below the federal poverty level.

popular Adolescents nominated by their classmates as those they most like.

population The entire group of individuals in which an investigator is interested.

positive reinforcement An event that increases the frequency of the behavior on which its occurrence is made contingent.

possible selves Life options that adolescents imagine for themselves; some are positive, or hoped-for, and others are feared, or negative, possibilities.

postconventional moral reasoning Kohlberg's third level of moral reasoning, in which moral thinking is guided by self-derived principles.

practical intelligence To be distinguished from "academic intelligence" or intelligence measured by IQ tests, practical intelligence requires the individual, rather than a teacher or an examiner, to define the problem to be solved and decide what constitutes a solution.

preconventional moral reasoning Kohlberg's first level of moral reasoning, characterized by the absence of internalized standards.

prefrontal cortex Region of the cortex located behind the forehead involved in abstract thought.

preoperational thought Piaget's second stage of intellectual development, thought to characterize toddlerhood and early childhood, during which experience is represented symbolically.

prepuce A thin skin covering the glans of the clitoris or penis.

primary sex characteristics Sex differences in the reproductive system that develop during puberty.

problem-focused coping Attempts to reduce stress by changing a stressful situation.

procedural knowledge The second of Belenky and associates' three forms of thought: independent thought that is nonetheless limited to a single frame of reference.

progesterone A sex hormone that is present in higher levels in females than in males and contributes to regulation of the menstrual cycle.

projective measures Ambiguous images, such as inkblots or uncaptioned pictures, that participants are asked to describe; in doing so, they may reveal subconscious feelings and thoughts.

propositional reasoning Reasoning from a set of premises that themselves are not questioned even when not supported by tests derived from them.

prosocial behaviors Positive behaviors such as cooperativeness, kindness, and trustworthiness.

protective factors Conditions present in individuals, families, communities, or society that promote healthy development.

pseudostupidity The inability to see the obvious by making a simple task more complicated than it is.

psychoactive A drug that alters mood.

psychometric approach An approach that focuses on the measurement of individual differences in abilities contributing to intelligence.

puberty Growth processes, including the skeletal growth spurt and maturation of the reproductive system, that begin in early adolescence and transform children into physically and sexually mature adults.

pubic lice Pests that are usually transmitted sexually; sometimes called crabs.

quasi-experimental design A research design in which participants are not randomly assigned to conditions, but in which preexisting groups are used, introducing possible confounding.

radical behaviorism A form of behaviorism that reduces the causes of behavior to contingencies of reinforcement.

random assignment The assignment of participants to groups in such a way that each participant has an equal chance of being assigned to any condition.

random error Unexplained and unsystematic variability.

realistic personality types In Holland's typology of vocational interests, individuals who prefer situations that are explicitly defined and require few interpersonal skills, for example, mechanic, or computer programmer.

realistic stage Ginzburg's third stage of vocational development, characterized by exploration of and commitment to a vocational path.

reciprocal determinism The two-way influence between person and environment; not only does the environment influence behavior but behavior changes the environment.

reductionism Explaining complex behaviors by reducing them to their simpler components.

rehearsal A control process used to prolong items in short-term memory by repeating them.

reinforcement Any event that when contingent on a behavior increases the probability of that behavior occurring again.

rejected adolescents Adolescents frequently mentioned by classmates as someone they least like and rarely mentioned as someone they most like.

relational aggression Aggression achieved by manipulating relationships, such as by excluding someone from a group or spreading rumors.

relativistic thinking The second of Perry's three forms of thought: awareness of more than one frame of reference by which ideas can be evaluated.

reliability The extent to which the same observations are obtained each time a measure is used.

religious identity An awareness of belonging to a religious group.

repression A Freudian defense mechanism that operates by relegating distressful thoughts and feelings to the unconscious.

respondent conditioning A simple form of learning in which simple behaviors are brought under the control of environmental stimuli that are associated with biologically significant events.

risk factors Conditions present in individuals, families, communities, or society that place adolescents at risk for developmental problems.

role clarity Clear understanding among family members concerning the nature and responsibilities of each one's role.

sample A subgroup drawn from the population that is the subject of research.
schemes Piaget's term for the precursors of concepts; ways of representing experience through one's actions.
schizophrenia A psychotic disorder characterized by disturbances of thought and perception.
scientific method A method of inquiry in which conclusions are verified empirically by checking them against observations; a methodology for making observations that will support or refute hypotheses.
scrotum The sac that hangs just beneath the penis and houses the testes.
secondary education Middle schools, junior high schools, and high schools.
secondary sex characteristics Differences between females and males in body structure and appearance, other than differences in the reproductive system; include differences in skeletal structure, hair distribution, and skin texture.
secular trend The earlier onset of puberty, faster growth, and larger size reached by adolescents today than in the past.
self-concept The individual's awareness of the self as a person; a theory about the self that explains personal experience.
self-disclosure A process by which adolescents understand and define themselves through an intimate sharing of thoughts and feelings.
self-esteem The individual's overall positive or negative evaluation of herself or himself.
self-report Information supplied by participants about themselves, usually in response to interview or survey questions.
self-stimulation Self-stimulation of the genitals.
semen A milky white fluid in which sperm are suspended.
sensitivity The extent to which the dependent variable can pick up very small differences due to the independent variable.
sensorimotor thought Piaget's first stage of intellectual development, assumed to characterize infancy, during which knowledge is based on perception and reflexes.
sensory memory A brief memory, usually lasting for less than a second, that preserves information during processing.
sequential design A research design in which several age cohort groups are compared at several times of measurement; essentially, a number of longitudinal studies, each starting with a different age group.
service learning programs Comprehensive education programs that include a community service component, requiring students to do volunteer work.
sex differences Biological and physiological differences distinguishing the sexes.
sexual dimorphism The physical differences that distinguish adult females and males.
sexually transmitted disease (STD) An infection that is spread through sexual contact.
sexual-minority youth Adolescents whose sexual orientation is not exclusively heterosexual.
sexual orientation The attraction individuals feel for members of the same or the other sex.
sexual scripts Learned expectations derived from cultural roles and gender stereotypes that guide behavior in sexual situations.
shaft The part of the clitoris or penis that becomes erect during sexual stimulation.
short-term memory A brief memory, limited in capacity to about seven items.
social-cognitive intervention An intervention program based on social-cognitive learning principles.
social competence Skills enabling individuals to accurately assess social situations and respond adaptively.
social personality types In Holland's typology of vocational interests, individuals who prefer work involving them with people, such as counseling or teaching.
social preference An index of popularity measuring how much an adolescent is liked by others.
social prestige An index of popularity measuring how much an adolescent is looked up to by others.
social skills training A component of social-cognitive intervention programs.
social understanding The ability to assume another's perspective and coordinate this with one's own.
special education classes Classes for learning-disabled students that are tailored to the needs of each student.
special education consultant A consultant who meets with teachers to discuss ways to meet the needs of learning-disabled students who are mainstreamed.
speed of processing The rate at which a cognitive operation (e.g., encoding, decoding, retrieval) or a combination of these can be performed.
sperm The male sex cell; the female equivalent is the ovum.
spermarche A boy's first ejaculation of seminal fluid.
stage A level of development that is assumed to be qualitatively different from the earlier level from which it evolves. Stages are assumed to occur in a fixed sequence and to occur universally within a species.
stage termination hypothesis An explanation for the effects of early maturation to not having as much time as needed to complete the developmental tasks of middle childhood.
statistical regression A potential confound in quasi-experimental research in which extreme pretest scores drift toward the mean of the posttest distribution.
status offenses Actions that are illegal when engaged in by minors but legal for adults, for example, truancy, drinking alcohol.

stimulants Substances that excite the central nervous system.

strategies Activities that organize cognition so as to improve performance, such as repeating a phone number or categorizing a list of things to be remembered.

stress The body's response to an event that requires adapting to changes brought about by that event.

stress-inoculation training A coping strategy that teaches ways to cognitively restructure stressful situations by identifying the stressful elements, anticipating one's reactions, and managing the emotions they occasion.

structural analytical thinking A stage of cognitive development characterized by the ability to relate two or more systems of thought.

structured voluntary activities Activities that are intrinsically motivating and challenging that build skills and foster initiative.

subjective knowledge The first of Belenky and associates' three forms of thought: covert examination of issues while maintaining a surface conformity to traditional ideas.

subject mortality In longitudinal studies, the loss of participants over time.

superego The aspect of the personality in Freudian theory that represents the internalized standards and values of society.

syphilis A sexually transmitted disease, caused by a bacterium, that can also be transmitted through blood transfusions or from a pregnant woman to her fetus; progresses over several stages.

task-mastery orientation A motivational pattern in which students focus on the task they are learning and work to increase their mastery and competence.

temperament The underlying predispositions contributing to an individual's activity level, emotionality, and sociability.

tentative stage Ginzburg's second stage of vocational development, in which vocational choice is directed more by interests than capacities.

test of significance A statistical procedure for determining whether group differences are due to random error or can be attributed to the variable being studied.

testes Structures within the male reproductive system contained in the scrotum that produce sperm and male sex hormones.

testing effect Knowledge and skills acquired by taking similar tests over the course of a research study; a potential source of confounding.

testosterone A sex hormone, present in higher levels in males than in females.

theory A set of testable statements derived from the axioms of a model.

time of measurement differences Differences due to social conditions, currents of opinion, and historical events that can affect observations in longitudinal research; such differences are confounded with age changes.

traditional cultures Cultures that have maintained their values and practices over long periods. These cultures often find themselves in conflict with other traditional or more rapidly changing cultures or with internal pressures for change.

unexamined ethnic identity An initial stage in ethnic identity formation that involves a lack of awareness of the issues related to one's ethnicity and a simple internalization of the values of the dominant culture.

uterus A muscular enclosure at the top of the vagina that holds the fetus during pregnancy.

vagina The muscular tube in females leading from the labia at its opening to the uterus.

validity The extent to which the dependent variable measures what it was designed to measure.

vasocongestion An accumulation of blood in the vessels serving the erogenous zones.

WAIS-R An intelligence scale for adults that is individually administered.

within-subjects design A research design in which each participant experiences all levels of the independent variable.

working memory A brief memory that holds information for less than a minute while further processing occurs.

zone of proximal development Vygotsky's term for the distance separating a novice's performance from what that performance might optimally be; for individuals to profit from working with those who are more skilled, their performance must already approximate that of the other person.

References

Adams, R. E., Laursen, B., & Wilder, D. (2001). Characteristics of closeness in adolescent romantic relationships. *Journal of Adolescence, 24,* 353–363.

Adams-Price, C., & Greene, A. L. (1990). Secondary attachments and adolescent self-concept. *Sex Roles, 22,* 187–198.

Adelson, J., & Doehrman, M. J. (1980). The psychodynamic approach to adolescence. In J. Adelson (Ed.), *Handbook of adolescence.* New York: Wiley.

Adwere-Boamah, J., & Curtis, D. A. (1993). A confirmatory factor analysis of a four-factor model of adolescent concerns revisited. *Journal of Youth and Adolescence, 22,* 297–312.

Aiken, L. R. (1987). *Assessment of intellectual functioning.* Boston: Allyn & Bacon.

Ainsworth, M. (1985). Attachments across the life-span. *Bulletin of the New York Academy of Medicine, 61,* 791–812.

Ainsworth, M. D. S. (1973). The development of infant–mother attachment. In B. M. Caldwell & H. N. Ricciuti (Eds.), *Review of child development research* (Vol. 3). Chicago: University of Chicago Press.

Ainsworth, M. D. S. (1989). Attachment beyond infancy. *American Psychologist, 44,* 709–716.

Ainsworth, M. D. S. (1993). Attachment as related to mother–infant interaction. In C. Rovee-Collier & L. P. Lipsitt (Eds.), *Advances in infancy research* (Vol. 8). Norwood, NJ: Ablex.

Ainsworth, M., Bleher, M. C., Waters, E., & Wall, S. (1978). *Patterns of attachment: A psychological study of the strange situation.* Hillsdale, NJ: Erlbaum.

Akers, J. F., Jones, R. M., & Coyl, D. D. (1998). Adolescent friendship pairs: Similarities in identity status development, behaviors, attitudes, and intentions. *Journal of Adolescent Research, 13,* 178–201.

Alan Guttmacher Institute. (1999, September). *Facts in brief: Teen sex and pregnancy.* Retrieved from http://www.agi-usa.org/pubs/fb_teen_sex.html

Alan Guttmacher Institute. (2004a). *Sex education: Needs, programs and policies.* Retrieved from http://www.guttmacher.org/presentations/sex_ed.pdf

Alan Guttmacher Institute. (2004b). U.S. teenage pregnancy statistics: Overall trends, trends by race and ethnicity and state-by-state information. Available at http://www.guttmacher.org

Alfieri, T., Ruble, D. N., & Higgins, E. T. (1996). Gender stereotypes during adolescence: Developmental changes and the transition to junior high school. *Developmental Psychology, 32,* 1129–1137.

Allen, J. A., Vallone, D., Haviland, M. L., Healton, C., Davis, K. C., Farrelly, M. C., Husten, C. G., & Pechacek, T. (2003). Tobacco use among middle and high school students—United States, 2002. *Morbidity and Mortality Weekly Reports, 52,* 1096–1098.

Allen, J. P., McElhaney, B., Kuperminc, G. P., & Jodl, K. M. (2004). Stability and change in attachment security across adolescence. *Child Development, 75,* 1792–1805.

Allen, J. P., Porter, M. R., & McFarland, F. C. (2006). Leaders and followers in adolescent close friendships: Susceptibility to peer influence as a predictor of risky behavior, friendship instability, and depression. *Development and Psychopathology, 18,* 155–172.

Allen, J. P., Weissberg, R. P., & Hawkins, J. A. (1989). The relation between values and social competence in early adolescence. *Developmental Psychology, 25,* 458–464.

Almeida, D. M., Wethington, E., & Chandler, A. L. (1999). Daily transmission of tensions between marital dyads and parent–child dyads. *Journal of Marriage and the Family, 61,* 49–61.

Alsaker, F. D. (1995). Timing of puberty and reactions to pubertal changes. In M. Rutter (Ed.), *Psychosocial disturbances in young people: Challenges for prevention* (pp. 37–82). Cambridge, England: Cambridge University Press.

Amato, P. R., & Afifi, T. D. (2006). Feeling caught between parents: Adult children's relations with parents and subjective well-being. *Journal of Marriage and Family,* 68, 222–235.

Amaya-Jackson, L., Socolar, R. R. S., Hunter, W., Runyan, D. K., & Colindres, R. (2000). Directly questioning children and adolescents about maltreatment. *Journal of Interpersonal Violence, 15,* 725–759.

American Association of Retired Persons. (1999). *Baby boomers envision their retirement: An AARP segmentation analysis.* Retrieved from http://research.aarp.org/econ/boomer_seq_1.html#UNIQEXP/

American Psychiatric Association. (1994). *Diagnostic and statistical manual of mental disorders* (4th ed.). Washington, DC: Author.

American Psychiatric Association. (2000). *Diagnostic and statistical manual of mental disorders* (4th ed., Text rev.). Washington, DC: Author.

Anastasi, A. (1988). *Psychological testing* (6th ed.). New York: Macmillan.

Anderman, E. M., & Midgley, C. (2004). Changes in self-reported academic cheating across the transition from middle school to high school. *Contemporary Educational Psychology, 29,* 499–517.

Anderson, K. J., & Cavallaro, D. (2002). Parents or pop culture? Children's heroes and role models. *Childhood Education,* 161–168.

Arbona, C. (1989). Hispanic employment and the Holland typology of work. *Career Development Quarterly, 37,* 257–268.

Archer, S. L. (1985). Career and/or family: The identity process for adolescent girls. *Youth and Society, 16,* 289–314.

Archer, S. L. (1989). Gender differences in identity development: Issues of process, domain, and timing. *Journal of Adolescence, 12,* 117–138.

Archer, S. L. (1992). A feminist's approach to identity research. In G. R. Adams, T. P. Gullotta, & R. Montemayor (Eds.), *Adolescent identity formation.* Newbury Park, CA: Sage.

Archibald, A. B., Graber, J. A., & Brooks-Gunn, J. (2003). Pubertal processes and physiological growth in adolescence. In G. R. Adams & M. D. Berzonsky (Eds.), *Blackwell handbook of adolescence* (pp. 24–47). Malden, MA: Blackwell.

Arehart, D. M., & Smith, P. H. (1990). Identity in adolescence: Influences of dysfunction and psychosocial task issues. *Journal of Youth and Adolescence, 19,* 63–72.

Aries, P. (1962). *Centuries of childhood.* New York: Knopf.

Armistead, L., Wierson, M., & Forehand, R. (1990). Adolescents and maternal employment: Is it harmful for a young adolescent to have an employed mother? *Journal of Early Adolescence, 10,* 260–278.

Armour, B. S., Woollery, T., Malarcher, A., Pechacek, T. F., & Husten, C. (2004). Annual smoking—attributable mortality, years of potential life lost, and productivity losses—United States, 1997–2001. *Morbidity and Mortality Weekly Report, 54,* 625–628.

Arnett, J. J. (2000). Emerging adulthood: A theory of development from the late teens through the twenties. *American Psychologist, 55,* 469–480.

Arnett, J. J. (2001). Conceptions of the transition to adulthood: Perspectives from adolescence to midlife. *Journal of Adult Development, 8,* 133–143.

Arnett, J. J., & Taber, S. (1994). Adolescence terminable and interminable: When does adolescence end? *Journal of Youth and Adolescence, 23,* 517–537.

Aronson, E. (2002). Building empathy, compassion, and achievement in the jigsaw classroom. In J. Aronson (Ed.), *Improving academic achievement: Impact of psychological factors on education* (pp. 209–225). San Diego: Academic Press.

Aronson, E. (2004). Reducing hostility and building compassion: Lessons from the jigsaw classroom. In A. G. Miller (Ed.), *Social psychology of good and evil* (pp. 469–488). New York: Guilford Press.

Artman, L., & Cahan, S. (1993). Schooling and the development of transitive inference. *Developmental Psychology, 29,* 753–759.

Asakawa, K., & Csikszentmihalyi, M. (1998). The quality of experience of Asian American adolescents in activities related to future goals. *Journal of Youth and Adolescence, 27,* 141–163.

Ashmore, R. D., Deaux, K., and McLaughlin-Volpe, T. (2004). An organizing framework for collective identity: Articulation and significance of multidimensionality. *Psychological Bulletin, 130,* 80–114.

Averett, S. L., Rees, D. I., & Argys, L. M. (2002). The impact of government policies and neighborhood characteristics on teenage sexual activity and contraceptive use. *American Journal of Public Health, 92,* 1773–1778.

Bailey, J. M., & Pillard, R. C. (1991). A genetic study of male sexual orientation. *Archives of General Psychiatry, 48,* 1089–1096.

Bailey, J. M., Pillard, R. C., Neale, M. C., & Agyei, Y. (1993). Heritable factors influence sexual orientation in women. *Archives of General Psychiatry, 50,* 217–223.

Bakan, D. (1966). *The duality of human existence.* Boston: Beacon Press.

Bakan, D. (1971). Adolescence in America: From idea to social fact. *Daedalus, 100,* 979–995.

Baldwin, S. A., & Hoffmann, J. P. (2002). The dynamics of self-esteem: A growth-curve analysis. *Journal of Youth and Adolescence, 31,* 101–113.

Bandura, A. (1986). *Social foundations of thought and action: A social cognitive theory.* Englewood Cliffs, NJ: Prentice-Hall.

Bandura, A. (1989). Regulation of cognitive processes through perceived self-efficacy. *Developmental Psychology, 25,* 729–735.

Bandura, A. (2004). Model of causality in social learning theory. In A. Freeman, M. J. Mahoney, P. DeVito, & D. Martin (Eds.), *Cognition and psychotherapy* (2nd ed., pp. 25–44). New York: Springer.

Bandura, A., Caprara, G. V., Barbaranelli, C., Pastorelli, C., & Regalia, C. (2001). Sociocognitive self-regulatory mechanisms governing transgressive behavior. *Journal of Personality and Social Psychology, 80,* 125–135.

Bandura, A., Ross, D., & Ross, S. A. (1963). Imitation of film-mediated aggressive models. *Journal of Abnormal and Social Psychology, 66,* 3–11.

Barber, B. K., & Olsen, J. A. (2004). Assessing the transitions to middle and high school. *Journal of Adolescent Research, 19,* 3–30.

Barkley, R. A. (1990). *Attention deficit hyperactivity disorder: A handbook for diagnosis and treatment.* New York: Guilford Press.

Barkley, T. J., & Procidano, M. E. (1989). College-age children of divorce: Are effects evident in early adulthood? *Journal of College Student Psychotherapy, 4,* 77–87.

Barnet, B., Duggan, A. K., & Devoe, M. (2003). Reduced low birth weight for teenagers receiving prenatal care at a school-based health center: Effect of access and comprehensive care. *Journal of Adolescent Health, 33,* 349–358.

Baron, J. B., & Sternberg, R. J. (1987). *Teaching thinking skills: Theory and practice.* New York: Freeman.

Barth, R. P., Fetro, J. V., Leland, N., & Volkan, K. (1992). Preventing adolescent pregnancy with social and cognitive skills. *Journal of Adolescent Research, 7,* 208–232.

Bartle, S. E., Anderson, S. A., & Sabatelli, R. M. (1989). A model of parenting style, adolescent individuation and adolescent self-esteem: Preliminary findings. *Journal of Adolescent Research, 4,* 283–298.

Barton, P. E. (2005). *One third of the nation: Rising dropout rates and declining opportunities.* Available at http://www.ets.org/research

Basseches, M. (1984). *Dialectical thinking and adult development.* Norwood, NJ: Ablex.

Bauman, K. E., & Fisher, L. A. (1986). On the measurement of friend behavior in research on friend influence and selection: Findings from longitudinal studies of adolescent smoking and drinking. *Journal of Youth and Adolescence, 15,* 345–353.

Baumrind, D. (1967). Child care practices anteceding three patterns of pre-school behavior. *Genetic Psychology Monographs, 75,* 43–88.

Baumrind, D. (1971). Current patterns of parental authority. *Developmental Psychology Monographs, 4,* 1–103.

Baumrind, D. (1986). Sex differences in moral reasoning: Response to Walker's (1984) conclusion that there are none. *Child Development, 57,* 511–521.

Baumrind, D. (1991a). The influence of parenting style on adolescent competence and substance use. *Journal of Early Adolescence, 11,* 56–95.

Baumrind, D. (1991b). Effective parenting during the early adolescent transition. In P. A. Cowan & E. M. Heatherington (Eds.), *Family transitions* (pp. 111–164). Hillsdale, NJ: Erlbaum.

Baumrind, D. (1993). The average expectable environment is not good enough: A response to Scarr. *Child Development, 64,* 1199–1217.

Beausang, C. C., & Razor, A. G. (2000). Young Western women's experiences of menarche and menstruation. *Health Care for Women International, 21,* 517–528.

Bedecarras, P., Gryngarten, M., Ayuso, S., Escobar, M. E., Bergada, C., & Campo, S. (1998). Characterization of serum SHBG isoforms in prepubertal and pubertal girls. *Clinical Endocrinology, 49,* 603–608.

Beentjes, J. W. J., & van der Voort, T. S. A. (1993). Television viewing versus reading: Mental effort, retention, and inferential learning. *Communication Education, 42,* 191–205.

Belenky, M. F., Clinchy, B. M., Goldberger, N. R., & Tarule, J. M. (1986). *Women's ways of knowing.* New York: Basic Books.

Bell, D. C., & Bell, L. G. (1983). Parental validation and support in the development of adolescent daughters. In H. D. Grotevant & C. R. Cooper (Eds.), *Adolescent development in the family.* San Francisco: Jossey-Bass.

Bem, S. L. (1974). The measurement of psychological androgyny. *Journal of Consulting and Clinical Psychology, 42,* 155–162.

Benin, M. H., & Edwards, D. A. (1990). Adolescents' chores: The difference between dual- and single-earner families. *Journal of Marriage and the Family, 52,* 361–373.

Bensley, L. S., Eenwyk, J. V., Spieker, S. J., & Schoder, J. (1999). Self-reported abuse history and adolescent problem behaviors: I. Antisocial and suicidal behaviors. *Journal of Adolescent Health, 24,* 163–172.

Benson, M. J. (2004). After the adolescent pregnancy: Parents, teens, and families. *Child & Adolescent Social Work Journal, 21,* 435–455.

Berg, C. (1989). Knowledge of strategies of dealing with everyday problems from childhood through adolescence. *Developmental Psychology, 25,* 607–618.

Berndt, T. J. (1982). The features and effects of friendships in early adolescence. *Child Development, 53,* 1447–1461.

Berndt, T. J., Hawkins, J. A., & Jiao, Z. (1999). Influences of friends and friendships on adjustment to junior high school. *Merrill-Palmer Quarterly, 45*(1), 13–41.

Berndt, T. J., & Hoyle, S. G. (1985). Stability and change in childhood and adolescent friendships. *Developmental Psychology, 21,* 1007–1015.

Berzonsky, M. D. (1989). Identity style: Conceptualization and measurement. *Journal of Adolescent Research, 4,* 268–282.

Berzonsky, M. D. (1992). A process perspective on identity and stress management. In G. R. Adams, T. P. Gullotta, & R. Montemayor (Eds.), *Adolescent identity formation.* Newbury Park, CA: Sage.

Berzonsky, M. D. (1993). Identity style, gender, and social-cognitive reasoning. *Journal of Adolescent Research, 8,* 289–296.

Berzonsky, M. D. (2004). Identity style, parental authority, and identity commitment. *Journal of Youth and Adolescence, 33,* 213–220.

Berzonsky, M. D., & Ferrari, J. R. (1996). Identity orientation and decisional strategies. *Personality and Individual Differences, 20,* 597–606.

Berzonsky, M. D., & Kuk, L. S. (2000). Identity status, identity processing style, and the transition to university. *Journal of Adolescent Research, 15,* 81–98.

Betancourt, H., & Lopez, S. R. (1993). The study of culture, ethnicity, and race in American psychology. *American Psychologist, 48,* 629–637.

Bettelheim, B. (1961). The problem of generations. In E. Erikson (Ed.), *The challenge of youth.* New York: Doubleday.

Betz, N. E., Harmon, L. W., & Borgen, F. H. (1996). The relationships of self-efficacy for the Holland themes to gender, occupational group membership, and vocational interests. *Journal of Counseling Psychology, 43,* 90–98.

Bieber, I. (1962). *Homosexuality: A psychoanalytic study.* New York: Basic Books.

Bird, G. W., & Kemerait, L. N. (1990). Stress among early adolescents in two-earner families. *Journal of Early Adolescence, 1,* 344–365.

Birndorf, S., Ryan, S., Auinger, P., & Aten, M. (2005). High self-esteem among adolescents: Longitudinal trends, sex differences, and protective factors. *Journal of Adolescent Health, 37,* 194–201.

Bjorklund, D. F. (1989). *Children's thinking.* Pacific Grove, CA: Brooks/Cole.

Blinn-Pike, L., Berger, T. J., & Hewett, J. (2004). Sexually abstinent adolescents: An 18-month follow-up, *Journal of Adolescent Research, 19,* 495–511.

Bloch, D. P. (1989). Using career information with dropouts and at-risk youth. *Career Development Quarterly, 38,* 160–171.

Block, J. H. (1978). Another look at sex differentiation in the socialization behaviors of mothers and fathers. In J. Sherman & F. Denmark (Eds.), *Psychology of women: Future directions of research.* New York: Psychological Dimensions.

Blumenthal, S. J., & Kupfer, D. J. (1988). Overview of early detection and treatment strategies for suicidal behavior in young people. *Journal of Youth and Adolescence, 17,* 1–23.

Blyth, D. A., & Leffert, N. (1995). Communities as contexts for adolescent development: An empirical analysis. *Journal of Adolescent Research, 10,* 64–87.

Bolognini, M., Plancherel, B., Bettschart, W., & Halfon, O. (1996). Self-esteem and mental health in early adolescence: Development and gender differences. *Journal of Adolescence, 19,* 233–245.

Bosma, H. A., Jackson, S. E., Zijsling, D. H., Zani, B., Cicognani, E., Xerri, M. L., Honess, T. M., & Charman, L. (1996). Who has the final say? Decisions on adolescent behavior within the family. *Journal of Adolescence, 19,* 277–291.

Bottvin, G. J., & Griffin, K. W. (2004). Life Skills Training: Empirical findings and future directions. *Journal of Primary Prevention, 25,* 211–232.

Bowker, A. (2004). Predicting friendship stability during early adolescence. *Journal of Early Adolescence, 24,* 85–112.

Bowlby, J. (1969). *Attachment and loss: Vol. 1. Attachment.* New York: Basic Books.

Bowlby, J. (1980). *Attachment and loss: Vol. 3. Loss.* New York: Basic Books.

Boyes, M. C., & Chandler, M. (1992). Cognitive development, epistemic doubt, and identity formation in adolescence. *Journal of Youth and Adolescence, 21,* 277–304.

Bracey, J. R., Bámaca, M. Y., & Umaña-Taylor, A. J. (2004). Examining ethnic identity and self-esteem among biracial and monoracial adolescents. *Journal of Youth and Adolescence, 33,* 123–132.

Bradley, L. A., Flannagan, D., & Fuhrman, R. (2001). Judgment biases and characteristics of friendships of Mexican American and Anglo-American girls and boys. *Journal of Early Adolescence, 21,* 405–424.

Braswell, J. S., Lutkus, A. D., Grigg, W. S., Santapau, S. L., Tay-Lim, B., & Johnson, M. (2001). *The nation's report card: Mathematics 2000* (NCES 2001517). Retrieved from the National Center for Educational Statistics Web site: http://nces.ed.gov/nationsreportcard/mathematics/results

Brendgen, M., Markiewicz, D., Doyle, A. B., & Bukowski, W. M. (2001). The relations between friendship quality, ranked-friendship preference, and adolescents' behavior with their friends. *Merrill-Palmer Quarterly, 47,* 395–415.

Brewster, A. B., & Bowen, G. L. (2004). Teacher support and the school engagement of Latino middle and high school students at risk of school failure. *Child and Adolescent Social Work Journal, 21,* 47–67.

Brice-Heath, S. (1982). Questioning at home and at school: A comparative study. In G. Spindler (Ed.), *The school achievement of minority children: New perspectives.* Hillsdale, NJ: Erlbaum.

Brody, G. H., Dorsey, S., Forehand, R., & Armistead, L. (2002). Unique and protective contributions of parenting and classroom processes to the adjustment of African American children living in single-parent families. *Child Development, 73,* 274–286.

Brody, G. H., Stoneman, Z., & McCoy, J. K. (1994). Forecasting sibling relationships in early adolescence from child temperaments and family processes in middle childhood. *Child Development, 65,* 771–784.

Bronfenbrenner, U. (1979a). Contexts of child rearing. *American Psychologist, 34,* 844–850.

Bronfenbrenner, U. (1979b). *The ecology of human development.* Cambridge, MA: Harvard University Press.

Bronfenbrenner, U. (1990). Discovering what families need. In D. Blankenhorn, S. Bayme, & J. B. Elshtian (Eds.), *Rebuilding the nest* (pp. 27–38). Milwaukee, WI: Family Service American.

Bronfenbrenner, U. (1994). Ecological models of human development. *International Encyclopedia of Education* (2nd ed., Vol. 3, pp. 1643–1647).

Brookman, R. R. (1988). Sexually transmitted diseases. In M. D. Levine & E. R. McArney (Eds.), *Early adolescent transitions.* Lexington, MA: D.C. Heath.

Brooks, J. (1999). *The process of parenting* (5th ed.). Mountain View, CA: Mayfield.

Brooks, L. (1990). Counseling special groups: Women and ethnic minorities. In D. Brown, L. Brooks, & Associates (Eds.), *Career choice and development.* San Francisco: Jossey-Bass.

Brooks-Gunn, J., & Ruble, D. N. (1982). The development of menstrual-related beliefs and behaviors during early adolescence. *Child Development, 53,* 1567–1577.

Brown, B. B., & Lohr, M. J. (1987). Peer group affiliation and adolescent self-esteem: An integration of ego-identity and symbolic-interaction theories. *Journal of Personality and Social Psychology, 52,* 47–55.

Brown, D. (1990). Summary, comparison, and critique of major theories. In D. Brown, L. Brooks, & Associates (Eds.), *Career choice and development.* San Francisco: Jossey-Bass.

Brown, L. M., & Gilligan, C. (1992). *Meeting at the crossroads: Women's psychology and girls' development.* Cambridge, MA: Harvard University Press.

Browne, K. D., & Hamilton-Giachritsis, C. (2005). The influence of violent media on children and adolescents: A public-health approach. *Lancet, 365,* 702–710.

Bruckner, H., & Bearman, P. (2005). After the promise: The STD consequences of adolescent virginity pledges. *Journal of Adolescent Health, 36,* 271–278.

Brunquell, D., Crichton, L., & Egeland, B. (1981). Maternal personality and attitude in disturbances of child rearing. *American Journal of Orthopsychiatry, 51,* 680–690.

Bryant, A. L., Schulenberg, J. E., O'Malley, P. M., Bachman, J. G., & Johnston, L. D. (2003). How academic achievement, attitudes, and behaviors relate to the course of substance use during adolescence: A 6-year, multiwave national longitudinal study. *Journal of Research on Adolescence, 13,* 361–397.

Bryk, A. S., & Raudenbush, S. W. (1988). Toward a more appropriate conceptualization of research on school effects: A three-level hierarchical linear model. *American Journal of Education, 97,* 65–108.

Buchanan, C. M., Maccoby, E. E., & Dornbusch, S. M. (1992). Adolescents and their families after divorce: Three residential arrangements compared. *Journal of Research on Adolescence, 2,* 261–291.

Buist, K. L., Dekovic, M., Meeus, W., & van Aken, M. A. G. (2002). Developmental patterns in adolescent attachment to mother, father and sibling. *Journal of Youth and Adolescence, 31,* 167–176.

Bukowski, W. M., Newcomb, A. F., & Hoza, B. (1987). Friendship conceptions among early adolescents: A longitudinal study of stability and change. *Journal of Early Adolescence, 7,* 143–152.

Bumpus, M. F., Crouter, A. C., & McHale, S. M. (2001). Parental autonomy granting during adolescence: Exploring gender differences in context. *Developmental Psychology, 37,* 163–173.

Bunge, S. A., Dudovic, N. M., Thomason, M. E., Vaidya, C. J., & Gabrieli, J. D. E. (2002). Immature frontal lobe contributions to cognitive control in children: Evidence from fMRI. *Neuron, 33,* 301–311.

Bunting, L., & McAuley, C. (2004a). Teenage pregnancy and motherhood: The contribution of support. *Child & Family Social Work, 9,* 207–215.

Bunting, L., & McAuley, C. (2004b). Research review: Teenage pregnancy and parenthood: The role of fathers. *Child and Family Social Work, 9,* 295–303.

Burns, A. M., & Dunlop, R. K. (2001). "Which basket are your eggs in?" Emotional investments from early adolescence to early adulthood among sons and daughters of divorced and nondivorced parents. *Journal of Family Studies, 7,* 56–71.

Buzwell, S., & Rosenthal, D. (1996). Constructing a sexual self: Adolescents' sexual self-perceptions and sexual risk-taking. *Journal of Research on Adolescence, 6,* 489–513.

Bybee, J., Glick, M., & Zigler, E. (1990). Differences across gender, grade level, and academic track in the content of the ideal self-image. *Sex Roles, 22,* 349–358.

Byrnes, J. P., & Takahira, S. (1993). Explaining gender differences on SAT-math items. *Developmental Psychology, 29,* 805–810.

Caldwell, M. S., Rudolph, K. D., Troop-Gordon, W., & Kim, D-Y. (2004). Reciprocal influences among relational self-views, social disengagement, and peer stress during early adolescence. *Child Development, 75,* 1140–1154.

Camarena, P. M., Sarigiani, P. A., & Petersen, A. C. (1990). Gender-specific pathways to intimacy in early adolescence. *Journal of Youth and Adolescence, 19,* 19–32.

Campbell, D. (1974). *The Strong-Campbell interest inventory.* Palo Alto, CA: Stanford University Press.

Campione, J. C., & Brown, A. L. (1978). Toward a theory of intelligence: Contributions from research with retarded children. *Intelligence, 2,* 279–304.

Capaldi, D. M., Stoolmiller, M., Clark, S., & Owen, L. D. (2002). Heterosexual risk behaviors in at-risk young men from early adolescence to young adulthood: Prevalence, prediction, and association with STD contraction. *Developmental Psychology, 38,* 394–406.

Carlo, G., Fabes, R. A., Laible, D., & Kupanoff, K. (1999). Early adolescence and prosocial/moral behavior. II: The role of social and contextual influences. *Journal of Early Adolescence, 19,* 133–147.

Carr, M., & Jessup, D. L. (1997). Gender differences in first-grade mathematics strategy use: Social and metacognitive influences. *Journal of Educational Psychology, 89,* 318–328.

Carnegie Council on Adolescent Development. (1989). Turning points: Preparing American youth for the 21st century. New York: Carnegie Foundation.

Carver, P. R., Egan, S. K., & Perry D. G. (2004). Children who question their heterosexuality. *Developmental Psychology, 40,* 43–53.

Casas, J. M., Wagenheim, B. R., Banchero, R., & Mendoza-Romero, J. (1994). Hispanic masculinity: Myth or psychological schema meriting clinical consideration? *Hispanic Journal of Behavioral Sciences, 16,* 315–331.

Casey, M. B. (2001). Spatial-mechanical reasoning skills versus mathematics self-confidence as mediators of gender differences on mathematics subtests using cross-national gender-based items. *Journal for Research in Mathematics Education, 32,* 28–57.

Catsambis, S., Mulkey, L. M., & Crain, R. L. (2001). For better or worse? A nationwide study of the social psychological effects of gender and ability grouping in mathematics. *Social Psychology of Education, 5,* 83–115.

Cavanagh, S. (2004). The sexual debut of girls in early adolescence: The intersection of race, pubertal timing, and friendship group characteristics. *Journal of Research on Adolescence, 14,* 285–312.

Centers for Disease Control. (1993). Condom use and sexual identity among men who have sex with men—Dallas, 1991. *Morbidity and Mortality Weekly Report, 42,* 7–17.

Centers for Disease Control. (1994). Guidelines for school health programs to prevent tobacco use and addiction. *Morbidity and Mortality Weekly Report, 43,* 1–18.

Centers for Disease Control. (2001). School-based tobacco use prevention programs. *MMWR Highlights, 50* (31). Available at http://www.cdc.gov/tobacco/research_data/youth/mmwr_oregon?factsheet.htm

Centers for Disease Control. (2004a). *Obesity still a major problem, new data show.* Available at http://www.cdc.gov/nchs/pressroom/04facts/obesity.htm

Centers for Disease Control. (2004b). *Improving the health of adolescents and young adults: A guide for states and communities.*

Centers for Disease Control. (2004c). *Fact sheet for public health personnel: Male latex condoms and sexually transmitted diseases.* Available at http://www.cdc.nchstp/od/latex.htm

Centers for Disease Control. (2005a). *Healthy youth! Physical activity.* Available at http://www.cdc.gov/HealthyYouth/PhysicalActivity/

Centers for Disease Control. (2005b). *Prevalence of overweight among children and adolescents: United States, 1999–2002.* Available at http://www.cdc.gov/nchs/products/pubs/pubd/hestats/overwght99.htm

Centers for Disease Control. (2005c). *Trends in reportable sexually transmitted diseases in the United States, 2004.* Available at http://www.cdc.gov/std/stats

Centers for Disease Control. (2005d). *Unintended and teen pregnancy prevention: Teen pregnancy.* Available at http://www.cdc.gov/reproductivehealth/UnintendedPregnancy/Teen.htm.

Centers for Disease Control. (2005e). National Center for Injury Prevention and Control. WISQARS [Web-based Injury Statistics Query and Reporting System]. Available at http://webappa.cdc.gov/sasweb/ncip/mortrate10_sy.html

Centers for Disease Control. (2006a). Racial/ethnic disparities in diagnoses of HIV/AIDS—33 states, 2001–2004. *Morbidity and Mortality Weekly Reports, 55,* 121–125.

Centers for Disease Control. (2006b). *Estimated numbers of cases and rates (per 100,000 population) of HIV/AIDS by race/ethnicity, age category, and sex, 2004.* Available at http://www.cdc.gov/hiv/topics/surveillance/resources/reports/2004report/table5b.htm

Centers for Disease Control and Prevention. (1999a). *National Vital Statistics Reports, 47*(19).

Centers for Disease Control and Prevention. (1999b). *Prevalence of sedentary leisure-time behavior among adults in the United States.* Retrieved October 4, 1999, from http://www.cdc.gov/nchswww/products/pubs/pubd/hestats/3and4/sedentary.htm

Centers for Disease Control and Prevention. (1999c). *Intimate partner violence fact sheet.* Retrieved January 7, 2000, from http://www.cdc.gov/ncipc/dvp/ipvfacts.htm

Centers for Disease Control and Prevention. (2001a, September). *Sexually transmitted disease surveillance, 2000.* Retrieved from http://www.cdc.gov/std/stats/TOC2000. htm

Centers for Disease Control and Prevention. (2001b). *Tracking the hidden epidemics: Trends in STDs in the United States 2000.* Retrieved from http://www.cdc.gov/nchstp/dstd/Stats_Trends/Trends2000.pdf

Centers for Disease Control and Prevention. (2002a). AIDS cases in adolescents and adults under age 25, by sex and exposure category, reported through December 2001, United States. Table 13. *HIV/AIDS surveillance report, 13*(2). Retrieved from http://www.cdc.gov/hiv/stats/ hasr1302.pdf

Centers for Disease Control and Prevention. (2002b, June 28). Youth risk behavior surveillance—United States, 2001 (No. SS-4). *Morbidity and Mortality Weekly Reports, 51.* Retrieved from http://www.cdc.gov/mmwr/PDF/SS/ SS5104.pdf

Centers for Disease Control and Prevention. (2004). Youth risk behavior surveillance—United States, 2003. *Morbidity and Mortality Weekly Reports, 53,* No. SS-2.

Chao, R. K. (1994). Beyond parental control and authoritarian parenting style: Understanding Chinese parenting through the cultural notion of training. *Child Development, 65,* 1111–1119.

Chassin, L., Flora, D. B., & King, K. M. (2004). Trajectories of alcohol and drug use and dependence from adolescence to adulthood: The effects of familial alcoholism and personality. *Journal of Abnormal Psychology, 113,* 483–498.

Chase-Lansdale, P. L., Wakschlag, L. S., & Brooks-Gunn, J. (1995). A psychological perspective on the development of caring in children and youth: The role of the family. *Journal of Adolescence, 18,* 515–556.

Cheek, D. B. (1974). Body composition, hormones, nutrition, and adolescent growth. In M. M. Grumbach, G. D. Grave, & F. E. Mayer (Eds.), *Control of the onset of puberty.* New York: Wiley.

Chen, E., Langer, D. A., Raphaelson, Y. E., & Matthews, K. A. (2004). Socioeconomic status and health in adolescents: The role of stress interpretations. *Child Development, 75,* 1039–1052.

Cheng, J. C. Y., Maffulli, N., Leung, S. S. S. F., Lee, W. T. K., Lau, J. T. F., & Chan, K. M. (1999). Axial and peripheral bone mineral acquisition: A 3-year longitudinal study in Chinese adolescents. *European Journal of Pediatrics, 156,* 506–512.

Cheng, T. L., Savageau, J. A., Sattler, A. L., & DeWitt, T. G. (1993). Confidentiality in health care: A survey of knowledge, perceptions, and attitudes among high school students. *JAMA: Journal of the American Medical Association, 268,* 1404.

Cheung, C. C., Thornton, J. E., Nurani, S. D., Clifton, D. K., & Steiner, R. A. (2001). A reassessment of leptin's role in triggering the onset of puberty in the rat and mouse. *Neuroendocrinology, 74,* 12–21.

Children's Defense Fund. (2005). *Students outreach programs.* Retrieved April 8, 2005, from http://www.childrensdefense.org/studentoutreach/shout.asp

Chiu, M. L., Feldman, S. S., & Rosenthal, D. A. (1992). The influence of immigration on parental behavior and adolescent distress in Chinese families residing in two Western nations. *Journal of Research on Adolescence, 2,* 205–239.

Chodorow, N. (1978). *The reproduction of mothering.* Los Angeles: University of California Press.

Chodorow, N. (2004). Psychoanalysis and women: A personal thirty-five-year retrospect. In J. A. Winer, W. W. Anderson & C. C. Kieffer (Eds.), *Psychoanalysis and women* (pp. 101–129). Hillsdale, NJ: Analytic Press.

Chomsky, N. (1957). *Syntactic structures.* The Hague: Mouton.

Cicchetti, D., & Lynch, M. (1995). Failures in the expectable environment and their impact on individual development: The case of child maltreatment. In D. Cicchetti & D. J. Cohen (Eds.), *Developmental psychopathology: Vol. 2. Risk, disorder, and adaptation* (pp. 32–71). New York: Wiley.

Cillessen, A. H. N., & Mayeux, L. (2004). From censure to reinforcement: Developmental changes in the association between aggression and social status. *Child Development, 75,* 147–163.

Civil Rights Project. (2005). *Confronting the graduation rate crisis in California.* Available at http://www.civilrightsproject.harvard.edu/research/dropouts/dropouts05.php

Claes, M. (1998). Adolescents' closeness with parents, siblings, and friends in three countries: Canada, Belgium, and Italy. *Journal of Youth and Adolescence, 27,* 165–184.

Clark, B. (1988). *Growing up gifted* (3rd ed.). New York: Macmillan.

Clasen, D. R., & Brown, B. B. (1985). The multidimensionality of peer pressure in adolescence. *Journal of Youth and Adolescence, 14,* 451–468.

Clayton, P. E., & Trueman, J. A. (2000). Leptin and puberty. *Archives of Disease in Children, 83,* 1–3.

Clayton, P. E., Gill, M. S., Hall, C. M., Tillmann, V., Whatmore, A. J., & Price, D. A. (1997). Serum leptin through childhood and adolescence. *Clinical Endocrinology, 46,* 727–733.

Cleary, T. J., & Zimmerman, B. J. (2004). Self-regulation empowerment program: A school-based program to enhance self-regulated and self-motivated cycles of student learning. *Psychology in the Schools, 41,* 537–550.

Cleveland, H. H., Wiebe, R. P., & Rowe, D. C. (2005). Sources of exposure to smoking and drinking friends among adolescents: A behavioral-genetic evaluation. *Journal of Genetic Psychology, 166,* 153–169.

Cobb, N. J., Ong, A. D., & Tate, J. (2001). Reason-based evaluations of wrongdoing in religious and moral narratives. *International Journal for the Psychology of Religion, 11,* 259–276.

Cohen, R. J., & Swerdlik, M. E. (1999). *Psychological testing and assessment* (4th ed.). Mountain View, CA: Mayfield.

Colarossi, L. G. (2001). Adolescent gender differences in social support: Structure, function and provider type. *Social Work Research, 25,* 233–241.

Colarossi, L. G., & Eccles, J. S. (2000). A prospective study of adolescents' peer support: Gender differences and the influence of parental relationships. *Journal of Youth and Adolescence, 29,* 661–678.

Cole, D. A., Martin, J. M., Peeke, L. A., Seroczynski, A. D., & Fier, J. (1999). Children's over- and underestimation of academic competence: A longitudinal study of gender differences, depression, and anxiety. *Child Development, 70,* 459–473.

Coleman, J. (1961). *The adolescent society.* Glencoe, IL: Free Press.

Coleman, P. (1993). Testing the school system: Dropouts, accountability, and social policy. *Curriculum Inquiry, 23,* 329–342.

Coles, Robert. (1970). *Erik Erikson: The growth of his work.* Boston: Little, Brown.

Coley, R. L., & Chase-Lansdale, P. L. (1998). Adolescent pregnancy and parenthood: Recent evidence and future directions. *American Psychologist, 53,* 152–166.

Colom, R., Escorial, S., & Rebollo, I. (2004). Sex differences on the Progressive Matrices are influenced by sex differences on spatial ability. *Personality and Individual Differences, 37,* 1289–1293.

Colom, R., Lluis-Font, J. M., & Andres-Pueyo, A. (2005). The generational intelligence gains are caused by decreasing variance in the lower half of the distribution: Supporting evidence for the nutrition hypothesis. *Intelligence, 33,* 83–91.

Comer, J. P. (1985). The Yale–New Haven Primary Prevention Project: A follow-up study. *Journal of the American Academy of Child Psychiatry, 24,* 154–160.

Comer, J. P. (1988). Educating poor minority children. *Scientific American, 259,* 42–48.

Comer, J. P., Haynes, N. M., Joyner, E. T., & Ben-Avie, M. (Eds.). (1996). *Rallying the whole village: The Comer process for reforming education.* New York: Teachers College Press.

Commons, M. L., & Richards, F. A. (1982). A general model of stage theory. In M. L. Commons, F. A. Richards, & S. Armon (Eds.), *Beyond formal operations: Late adolescent and adult cognitive development.* New York: Praeger.

Condry, J. C., & Ross, D. F. (1985). Sex and aggression: The influence of gender label on the perception of aggression in children. *Child Development, 56,* 225–233.

Connell, C. M., & Janevic, M. R. (2003). Health and human development. In I. B. Weiner (Ed.), *Handbook of psychology* (Vol. 6, pp. 579–600). Hoboken, NJ: Wiley.

Connell, J. P., Halpern-Felsher, B. L., Clifford, E., Crichlow, W., & Usinger, P. (1995). Hanging in there: Behavioral, psychological, and contextual factors affecting whether African American adolescents stay in high school. *Journal of Adolescent Research, 10,* 41–63.

Connolly, J., Craig, W., Goldberg, A., & Pepler, D. (2004). Mixed-gender groups, dating, and romantic relationships in early adolescence. *Journal of Research on Adolescence, 14,* 185–207.

Constantinople, A. (1973). Masculinity-femininity: An exception to a famous dictum? *Psychological Bulletin, 80,* 389–407.

Cooper, C. R., Grotevant, H. D., & Condon, S. M. (1983). Individuality and connectedness in the family as a context for adolescent identity formation and role-taking skill. In H. D. Grotevant & C. R. Cooper (Eds.), *Adolescent development in the family.* San Francisco: Jossey-Bass.

Corville-Smith, J., Ryan, B. A., Adams, G. R., & Delicandro, T. (1998). Distinguishing absentee students from regular attenders: The combined influence of personal, family, and school factors. *Journal of Youth and Adolescence, 27,* 626–641.

Costanzo, P. R. (1970). Conformity development as a function of self-blame. *Journal of Personality and Social Psychology, 14,* 366–374.

Costos, D., Ackerman, R., & Paradis, L. (2002). Recollections of menarche: Communication between mothers and daughters regarding menstruation. *Sex Roles, 46,* 49–59.

Cota-Robles, S., Neiss, M., & Rowe, D. C. (2002). The role of puberty in violent and nonviolent delinquency among Anglo American, Mexican American, and African American boys. *Journal of Adolescent Research, 17,* 364–376.

Cotgrove, A., Zirinsky, L., Black, D., &Weston, D. (1995). Secondary prevention of attempted suicide in adolescence. *Journal of Adolescence, 18,* 569–577.

Cottrell, L., Lli, X., Harris, C., D'Alessandri, D., Atkins, M., Richardson, B., & Stanton, B. (2003). Parent and adolescent perceptions of parental monitoring and adolescent risk involvement. *Parenting: Science and Practice, 3,* 179–195.

Courtney, M. L., & Cohen, R. (1996). Behavior segmentation by boys as a function of aggressiveness and prior information. *Child Development, 67,* 1034–1047.

Covington, M. V. (1983). Strategic thinking and the fear of failure. In S. F. Chipman, J. Segal, & R. Glaser (Eds.), *Thinking and learning skills: Current research and open questions* (Vol. 2). Hillsdale, NJ: Erlbaum.

Craig, W. M., Pepler, D., Connolly, J., & Henderson, K. (2001). Developmental context of peer harassment in early adolescence. In J. Juvonen & S. Graham (Eds.), *Peer harassment in school: The plight of the vulnerable and victimized* (pp. 242–261). New York: Guilford Press.

Cramer, P. (1998). Freshman to senior year: A follow-up of identity, narcissism, and defense mechanisms. *Journal of Research in Personality, 32,* 156–172.

Cramer, P. (2000). Development of identity: Gender makes a difference. *Journal of Research in Personality, 34,* 42–72.

Crawford, M., & Popp, D. (2003). Sexual double standards: A review and methodological critique of two decades of research. *Journal of Sex Research, 40,* 13–26.

Crockett, D. (2003). Critical issues children face in the 2000s. *School Psychology Quarterly, 18,* 446–453.

Crosnoe, R., & Elder, G. H., Jr. (2004). Family dynamics, supportive relationships, and educational resilience during adolescence. *Journal of Family Issues, 25,* 571–602.

Crosnoe, R., & Needham, B. (2004). Holism, contextual variability, and the study of friendships in adolescent development. *Child Development, 75,* 264–279.

Cross, W. E., Jr. (1980). Models of psychological nigrescence: A literature review. In R. L. Jones (Ed.), *Black psychology.* New York: Harper & Row.

Cross, W. E., Jr. (2005). Ethnicity, race, and identity. In T. S. Weisner (Ed.), *Discovering successful pathways in children's development: Mixed methods in the study of childhood and family life* (pp. 171–182). Chicago: University of Chicago Press.

Crouter, A. C., & Crowley, M. S. (1990). School-age children's time alone with fathers in single- and dual-earner families: Implications for the father–child relationship. *Journal of Early Adolescence, 10,* 296–312.

Crystal, D. S., & Stevenson, H. W. (1995). What is a bad kid? Answers of adolescents and their mothers in three cultures. *Journal of Research on Adolescence, 5,* 71–91.

Csikszentmihalyi, M. (1990). *Flow: The psychology of optimal experience.* New York: Harper & Row.

Csikszentmihalyi, M. (1997). *Finding flow.* New York: Basic Books.

D'Amico, E. J., & Fromme, K. (2002). Brief prevention for adolescent risk-taking behavior. *Addiction, 97,* 563–574.

de Anda, D., Baroni, S., Boskin, L., Buchwald, L., Morgan, J., Ow, J., Gold, J. S., & Weiss, R. (2000). Stress, stressors and coping among high school students. *Children and Youth Services Review, 22,* 441–463.

Darling, C. A., & Hicks, M. W. (1982). Parental influence on adolescent sexuality: Implications for parents as educators. *Journal of Youth and Adolescence, 11,* 231–245.

Darroch, J. E., Frost, J. J., Singh, S., et al. (2001). *Teenage sexual and reproductive behavior in developed countries: Can more progress be made?* New York: Alan Guttmacher Institute.

Davey, F. H., & Stoppard, J. M. (1993). Some factors affecting the occupational expectations of female adolescents. *Journal of Vocational Behavior, 43,* 235–250.

Davies, P. T., & Windle, M. (2001). Interparental discord and adolescent adjustment trajectories: The potentiating and protective role of intrapersonal attributes. *Child Development, 72,* 1163–1178.

Davis, S. F., Grover, C. A., Becker, A. H., & McGregor, L. N. (1992). Academic dishonesty: Prevalence, determinants, techniques, and punishments. *Teaching of Psychology, 19,* 16–20.

Davison, K. K., & Susman, E. J. (2001). Are hormone levels and cognitive ability related during early adolescence? *International Journal of Behavioral Development, 25,* 416–428.

Dees, W. L., Dissen, G. A., Hiney, J. K., Lara, F., & Ojeda, S. R. (2000). Alcohol injection inhibits the increased secretion of puberty-related hormones in the developing female rhesus monkey. *Endocrinology, 141,* 1325–1331.

Dees, W. L., Srivastava, V. K., & Hiney, J. K. (2001). Alcohol and female puberty: The role of intraovarian systems. *Alcohol Research and Health, 25,* 271–275.

Deutsch, M. (1993). Educating for a peaceful world. *American Psychologist, 48,* 510–517.

Diamond, L. M., & Lucas, S. (2004). Sexual-minority and heterosexual youths' peer relationships: Experiences, expectations, and implications for well-being. *Journal of Research on Adolescence, 14,* 313–340.

DiBlasio, F. A., & Benda, B. B. (1992). Gender differences in theories of adolescent sexual activity. *Sex Roles, 27,* 221–236.

Dick, D. M., Rose, R. J., Pulkkinen, L., & Kaprio, J. (2001). Measuring puberty and understanding its impact: A longitudinal study of adolescent twins. *Journal of Youth and Adolescence, 30,* 385–399.

DiClemente, R. J. (1998). Preventing sexually transmitted infections among adolescents: A clash of ideology and science. *Journal of the American Medical Association, 279,* 1574–1575.

Diener, M. L., & Lucas, R. E. (2004). Adults' desires for children's emotions across 48 countries: Associations with individual and national characteristics. *Journal of Cross-Cultural Psychology, 35,* 525–547.

A Different Side of the Game, Inc. (2005). *The Foundation Center: Youth in philanthropy.* Available at: http://youth.fdncenter.org/youth_stories_kiisha_v.html

Digest of Education Statistics. (1993). U.S. Department of Education. Washington, DC: U.S. Government Printing Office.

Digest of Education Statistics. (1996). U.S. Department of Education. Washington, DC: U.S. Government Printing Office.

Dillard, A. (1974). *Pilgrim at Tinker Creek.* New York: Harper's Magazine Press.

Dmitrieva, J., Chen, C., Greenberger, E., & Gil-Rivas, V. (2004). Family relationships and adolescent psychosocial outcomes: Converging findings from Eastern and Western cultures. *Journal of Research on Adolescence, 14,* 425–447.

Dodge, K. A. (1983). Behavioral antecedents of peer social status. *Child Development, 54,* 1386–1399.

Donahue, M. J., & Benson, P. L. (1995). Religion and the well-being of adolescents. *Journal of Social Issues, 51,* 145–160.

Donnay, D. A. C., & Borgen, F. H. (1996). Validity, structure, and content of the 1994 Strong Interest Inventory. *Journal of Counseling Psychology, 43,* 275–291.

Dornbusch, S. M., Carlsmith, L., Gross, R. T., Martin, J. A., Jenning, D., Rosenberg, A., & Duke, D. (1981). Sexual development, age, and dating: A comparison of biological and sociological influences upon the set of behaviors. *Child Development, 52,* 179–185.

Dornbusch, S. M., Ritter, P. L., Leiderman, P. H., Roberts, D. F., & Fraleigh, M. J. (1987). The relation of parenting style to adolescent school performance. *Child Development, 58,* 1244–1257.

Doueck, H. J., Ishisaka, A. H., & Greenaway, K. D. (1988). The role of normative development in adolescent abuse and neglect. *Family Relations, 37,* 135–139.

Douglas-Hall, A., & Koball, H. (2003). *Parental employment in low-income families.* National Center for Children in Poverty. Available at http://www.nccp.org/pub_pe104.html

Douvan, E., & Adelson, J. (1966). *The adolescent experience.* New York: Wiley.

Dovidio, J., & Gaertner, S. (1986). *Prejudice, discrimination, and racism.* Orlando, FL: Academic Press.

Dowdy, B. B., & Kliewer, W. (1998). Dating, parent–adolescent conflict, and behavioral autonomy. *Journal of Youth and Adolescence, 27,* 473–492.

Downey, G., Purdie, V., & Schaffer-Neitz, R. (1999). Anger transmission from mother to child: A comparison of mothers in chronic pain and well mothers. *Journal of Marriage and the Family, 61,* 62–73.

Drumm, P., & Jackson, D. W. (1996). Developmental changes in questioning strategies during adolescence. *Journal of Adolescent Research, 11,* 285–305.

Dryfoos, J., & Maquire, S. (2002). *Inside full-service community schools.* Thousand Oaks, CA: Corwin Press.

DuBois, D. L., Felner, R. D., Brand, S., Phillips, R. S. C., & Lease, A. M. (1996). Early adolescent self-esteem: A developmental-ecological framework and assessment strategy. *Journal of Research on Adolescence, 6,* 543–579.

DuBois, D. L., & Hirsch, B. J. (1990). School and neighborhood friendship patterns of Blacks and Whites in early adolescence. *Child Development, 61,* 524–536.

Dubow, E. F., Arnett, M., Smith, K., & Ippolito, M. R. (2001). Predictors of future expectations of inner-city children: A 9-month prospective study. *Journal of Early Adolescence, 21,* 5–28.

Ducharme, J., Doyle, A. B., & Markiewicz, D. (2002). Attachment security with mother and father: Associations with adolescents' reports of interpersonal behavior with parents and peers. *Journal of Social and Personal Relationships, 19,* 203–231.

Duckworth, A. L., & Seligman, M. E. P. (2005). Self-discipline outdoes IQ in predicting academic performance of adolescents. *Psychological Science, 16,* 939–944.

Dunkel, C. S. (2000). Possible selves as a mechanism for identity exploration. *Journal of Adolescence, 23,* 519–529.

Dunkel, C. S., & Anthis, K. S. (2001). The role of possible selves in identity formation: A short-term longitudinal study. *Journal of Adolescence, 24,* 765–776.

Dunlop, R., Burns, A., & Bermingham, S. (2001). Parent–child relations and adolescent self-image following divorce: A 10-year study. *Journal of Youth and Adolescence, 30,* 117–134.

Dunn, R., & Dunn, K. (1993). *Teaching secondary students through their individual learning styles: Practical approaches for grades 7–12.* Boston: Allyn & Bacon.

Dunphy, D. (1963). The social structure of urban adolescent peer groups. *Sociometry, 26,* 230–246.

Dusek, J. B., & McIntyre, J. G. (2003). Self-concept and self-esteem development. In G. R. Adams & M. D. Berzonsky (Eds.), *Blackwell handbook of adolescence* (pp. 291–309). Malden, MA: Blackwell.

Dweck, C. S. (1986). Motivational processes affecting learning. *American Psychologist, 41,* 1040–1048.

Dweck, C. S. (1989). Motivation. In A. Lesgold & R. Glaser (Eds.), *Foundations for a psychology of education.* Hillsdale, NJ: Erlbaum.

Dweck, C. S. (1999). *Self-theories: Their role in motivation, personality and development.* Philadelphia: Psychology Press.

Dweck, C. S. (2002). Beliefs that make smart people dumb. In R. J. Sternberg (Ed.), *Why smart people can be so stupid* (pp. 24–41). New Haven, CT: Yale University Press.

Dweck, C. S. (2002). Messages that motivate: How praise molds students' beliefs, motivation, and performance (in surprising ways). In J. Aronson (Ed.), *Improving academic achievement: Impact of psychological factors on education* (pp. 37–60).

Dweck, C. S., & Molden, D. C. (2005). Self-theories: Their impact on competence motivation and acquisition. In A. J. Elliot & C. S. Dweck (Eds.), *Handbook of competence and motivation* (pp. 122–140). New York: Guilford Press.

Dweck, C. S., & Reppucci, N. D. (1973). Learned helplessness and reinforcement responsibility in children. *Journal of Personality and Social Psychology, 25,* 109–116.

Dyk, P. H., & Adams, G. R. (1990). Identity and intimacy: An initial investigation of three theoretical models using cross-lag panel correlations. *Journal of Youth and Adolescence, 19,* 91–110.

Eaves, L., Silberg, J., Foley, D., Bulik, C., Maes, H., Erkanli, A., Angold, A., Costello, E. J., & Worthman, C. (2004). Genetic and environmental influences on the relative timing of pubertal change. *Twin Research, 7,* 471–481.

Eberly, M. B., & Montemayor, R. (1999). Adolescent affection and helpfulness toward parents: A 2-year follow-up. *Journal of Early Adolescence, 19,* 226–248.

Eccles, J. S. (2004). Schools, academic motivation, and stage-environment fit. In R. Lerner and L. Steinberg (Eds.), *Handbook of adolescent psychology.* New York: Wiley.

Eccles, J. S., & Barber, B. L. (1999). Student council, volunteering, basketball, or marching band: What kind of extracurricular involvement matters? *Journal of Adolescent Research, 14,* 10–43.

Eccles, J. S., Buchanan, C. M., Midgley, C., Fuligni, A. J., & Flanagan, C. (1991). Individuation reconsidered: Autonomy and control during early adolescence. *Journal of Social Issues, 47,* 53–68.

Egan, S. K., & Perry, D. G. (2001). Gender identity: A multidimensional analysis with implications for psychosocial adjustment. *Developmental Psychology, 37,* 451–463.

Egley, A., Jr. (2002). National youth gang survey trends from 1996 to 2000. *OJJDP Fact Sheet.* Available at http://www.ncjrs.gov/pdffiles1/ojjdp/fs200203.pdf

Eisenberg, J. (2004). To cheat or not to cheat: Effects of moral perspective and situational variables on students' attitudes. *Journal of Moral Education, 33,* 163–178.

Eisenberg, N., Zhou, Q., & Koller, S. (2001). Brazilian adolescents' prosocial moral judgment and behavior: Relations to sympathy, perspective taking, gender-role orientation, and demographic characteristics. *Child Development, 72,* 518–534.

Eisert, D. C., & Kahle, L. R. (1986). The development of social attributions: An integration of probability and logic. *Human Development, 29,* 61–81.

Elkind, D. (1961). The child's conception of his religious denomination: I. The Jewish child. *Journal of Genetic Psychology, 99,* 209–225.

Elkind, D. (1962). The child's conception of his religious denomination: II. The Catholic child. *Journal of Genetic Psychology, 101,* 185–193.

Elkind, D. (1963). The child's conception of his religious denomination: III. The Protestant child. *Journal of Genetic Psychology, 103,* 291–304.

Elkind, D. (1967). Egocentrism in adolescence. *Child Development, 38,* 1025–1034.

Elkind, D. (1978). *A sympathetic understanding of the child: Birth to sixteen* (2nd ed.). Boston: Allyn & Bacon.

Elkind, D. (1980). Strategic interactions in early adolescence. In J. Adelson (Ed.), *Handbook of adolescence.* New York: Wiley.

Elliott, B. A., & Larson, J. T. (2004). Adolescents in mid-sized and rural communities: Forgone care, perceived barriers, and risk factors. *Journal of Adolescent Health, 35,* 303–309.

Ellis, B. J. (2004). Timing of pubertal maturation in girls: An integrated life history approach. *Psychological Bulletin, 130*(6) 920–958.

Ellison, C. G., Echevarria, S., & Smith, B. (2005). Religion and abortion attitudes among U.S. Hispanics: Findings from the 1990 Latino National Political Survey. *Social Science Quarterly, 86,* 192–208.

Else-Quest, N. M., Hyde, J. S., & DeLamater, J. D. (2005). Context counts: Long-term sequelae of premarital intercourse or abstinence. *Journal of Sex Research, 42,* 102–112.

Emmons, R. A., & Paloutzian, R. F. (2003). The psychology of religion. *Annual Review of Psychology, 54,* 1–26.

Engels, R. C. M. E., Deković, M., & Meeus, W. (2002). Parenting practices, social skills and peer relationships in adolescence. *Social Behavior and Personality, 30,* 3–18.

Ennett, S. T., & Bauman, K. E. (1996). Adolescent social networks: School, demographic, and longitudinal considerations. *Journal of Adolescent Research, 11,* 194–215.

Enright, R. D., Santos, M. J., & Al-Mabuk, R. (1989). The adolescent as a forgiver. *Journal of Adolescence, 12,* 95–110.

Entwisle, D. R., & Alexander, K. L. (1990). Beginning school math competence: Minority and majority comparisons. *Child Development, 61,* 454–471.

Entwisle, D. R., Alexander, K. L., Olson, L. S., & Ross, K. (1999). Paid work in early adolescence: Developmental and ethnic patterns. *Journal of Early Adolescence, 19,* 363–388.

Epstein, J. (1990). What matters in the middle grades—Grade span or practices? *Phi Delta Kappan, 71,* 438–444.

Epstein, L. H. (1994). Ten-year outcome of behavioral family-based treatment for childhood obesity. *Health Psychology, 13,* 373–383.

Erikson, E. H. (1950). *Childhood and society.* New York: Norton.

Erikson, E. H. (1954). Problems of infancy and early childhood. In G. Murphy & A. J. Bachrach (Eds.), *An outline of abnormal psychology.* New York: Modern Library.

Erikson, E. H. (1956). The problem of ego identity. *Journal of the American Psychoanalytic Association, 4,* 56–121.

Erikson, E. H. (1959). Identity and the life cycle: Selected papers. *Psychological Issues Monograph, Series 1, No. 1.* New York: International Universities Press.

Erikson, E. H. (1963). *Childhood and society* (2nd ed.). New York: Norton.

Erikson, E. H. (1968). *Identity, youth and crisis.* New York: Norton.

Evans, G. W. (2004). The environment of childhood poverty. *American Psychologist, 59,* 77–92.

Evans, J. P., & Taylor, J. (1995). Understanding violence in contemporary and earlier gangs: An exploratory application of the theory of reasoned action. *Journal of Black Psychology, 21,* 71–81.

Fan, X. T., & Chen, M. (2001). Parental involvement and students' academic achievement: A meta-analysis. *Educational Psychology Review, 13,* 1–22.

Farber, E. (1987). The adolescent who runs. In B. S. Brown & A. R. Mills (Eds.), *Youth at high risk.* (DHHS Publication No. ADM 87–1537). Washington, DC: U.S. Government Printing Office.

Farver, J. A. M., Narang, S. K., & Bhadha, B. R. (2002). East meets West: Ethnic identity, acculturation, and conflict in Asian Indian families. *Journal of Family Psychology, 16,* 338–350.

Fauber, R., Forehand, R., Thomas, A. M., & Wierson, M. (1990). A mediational model of the impact of marital conflict on adolescent adjustment in intact and divorced families. *Child Development, 61,* 1112–1123.

Fechner, P. Y. (2003). The biology of puberty: New developments in sex differences. In C. Hayward (Ed.), *Gender differences at puberty* (pp. 17–28). New York: Cambridge University Press.

Feiring, C., & Lewis, M. (1991). The transition from middle childhood to early adolescence: Sex differences in the social network and perceived self-competence. *Sex Roles, 24,* 489–509.

Feiring, C., & Lewis, M. (1993). Do mothers know their teenagers' friends? Implications for individuation in early adolescence. *Journal of Youth and Adolescence, 22,* 337–354.

Feldman, C. F., Stone, A., & Renderer, B. (1990). Stage, transfer, and academic achievement in dialect-speaking Hawaiian adolescents. *Child Development, 61,* 472–484.

Feldman, S. S., Mont-Reynaud, R., & Rosenthal, D. A. (1992). When East moves West: The acculturation of values of Chinese adolescents in the U.S. and Australia. *Journal of Research on Adolescence, 2,* 147–173.

Feldman, S. S., & Rosenthal, D. A. (2000). The effect of communication characteristics on family members' perceptions of parents as sex educators. *Journal of Research on Adolescence, 10,* 119–150.

Felner, R. D., Brand, S., DuBois, D. L., Adam, A. M., Mulhall, P. F., & Evans, E. G. (1995). Socioeconomic disadvantage, proximal environmental experiences, and socioemotional and academic adjustment in early adolescence: Investigation of a mediated effects model. *Child Development, 66,* 774–792.

Fennema, E. (2000). *Gender and mathematics: What is known and what do I wish was known?* Prepared for the Fifth Annual Forum of the National Institute for Science Education, May 22–23, 2000, Detroit, MI. Retrieved from http://www.wcer.wisc.edu/nise/News_Activities/Forums/Fennemapaper.htm

Fennema, E., Carpenter, T. P., Jacobs, V. R., Franke, M. L., & Levi, L. W. (1998). A longitudinal study of gender differences in young children's mathematical thinking. *Educational Researcher, 27,* 6–11.

Field, A. E., Camargo, C. A., Taylor, C. B., Berkey, C. S., Frazier, L., & Gillman, M. W. (1999). Overweight, weight concerns, and bulimic behaviors among girls and boys. *Journal of the American Academy of Child and Adolescent Psychiatry, 38,* 754–760.

Field, A. E., Cheung, L., Wolf, A. M., Herzog, D. B., Gortmaker, S. L., & Colditz, G. A. (1999). Exposure to the mass media and weight concerns among girls. *Pediatrics, 103,* E36.

Finkenauer, C., Engels, R. C. M. E., & Meeus, W. (2002). Keeping secrets from parents: Advantages and disadvantages of secrecy in adolescence. *Journal of Youth and Adolescence, 31,* 123–136.

Fisk, W. R. (1985). Responses to "neutral" pronoun presentations and the development of sex-biased responding. *Developmental Psychology, 21,* 481–485.

Flavell, J. H. (1963). *The developmental psychology of Jean Piaget.* Princeton, NJ: Van Nostrand.

Flavell, J. H., Miller, P. H., & Miller, S. A. (1993). *Cognitive development* (3rd ed.). Englewood Cliffs, NJ: Prentice-Hall.

Fletcher, A. C., Darling, N. E., Steinberg, L., & Dornbusch, S. M. (1995). The company they keep: Relation of adolescents' adjustment and behavior to their friends' perceptions of authoritative parenting in the social network. *Developmental Psychology, 31,* 300–310.

Flynn, J. R. (1984). The mean IQ of Americans: Massive gains 1932 to 1978. *Psychological Bulletin, 95,* 29–51.

Fondacaro, M. R., Dunkle, M. E., & Pathak, M. K. (1998). Procedural justice in resolving family disputes: A psychological analysis of individual and family functioning in late adolescence. *Journal of Youth and Adolescence, 27,* 101–119.

Ford, M. E., Wentzel, K. R., Wood, D., Stevens, E., & Siesfeld, G. A. (1989). Processes associated with integrative social competence: Emotional and contextual influences on adolescent social responsibility. *Journal of Adolescent Research, 4,* 405–425.

The forgotten half. (1989, June 26). *U.S. News and World Report,* pp. 45–53.

Fouts, G., & Burggraf, K. (1999). Television situation comedies: Female body images and verbal reinforcements. *Sex Roles, 40,* 473–481.

Fowler, J. W. (1981). *Stages of faith: The psychology of human development and the quest for meaning.* San Francisco: Harper & Row.

Fowler, J. W. (2001). Faith development theory and the postmodern challenges. *International Journal for the Psychology of Religion, 11,* 159–172.

Fox, M. A., Connolly, B. A., & Snyder, T. D. (2005). *Youth indicators 2005: Trends in the well-being of American youth* (NCES 2005-050). U.S. Department of Education, National Center for Education Statistics. Washington, DC: U.S. Government Printing Office.

Frabutt, J. M., Walker, A. M., & MacKinnon-Lewis, C. (2002). Racial socialization messages and the quality of mother/child interactions in African American families. *Journal of Early Adolescence, 22,* 200–217.

Frank, N. C., & Kendall, S. J. (2001). Religion, risk prevention and health promotion in adolescents: A community-based approach. *Mental Health, Religion and Culture, 4,* 133–148.

Frankel, K. A. (1990). Girls' perceptions of peer relationship support and stress. *Journal of Early Adolescence, 10,* 69–88.

Franklin, A. J. (1985). The social context and socialization variables as factors in thinking and learning. In S. F. Chipman, J. W. Segal, & R. Glaser (Eds.), *Thinking and learning skills* (Vol. 2). Hillsdale, NJ: Erlbaum.

Fredricks, J. A., & Eccles, J. S. (2002). Children's competence and value beliefs from childhood through adolescence: Growth trajectories in two male-sex-typed domains. *Developmental Psychology, 38,* 519–533.

Freud, A. (1969). Adolescence as a developmental disturbance. In G. Caplan & S. Lebovici (Eds.), *Adolescence.* New York: Basic Books.

Freud, S. (1925a). The dissolution of the Oedipal complex. In J. Strachey (Ed.), *The standard edition of the complete psychological works of Sigmund Freud* (Vol. 19). London: Hogarth Press, 1961.

Freud, S. (1925b). Some psychical consequences of the anatomical distinction between the sexes. In J. Strachey (Ed.), *The standard edition of the complete psychological works of Sigmund Freud* (Vol. 19). London: Hogarth Press, 1961.

Freud, S. (1954). *Collected works, standard edition.* London: Hogarth Press.

Frey, C. U., & Rothlisberger, C. (1996). Social support in healthy adolescents. *Journal of Youth and Adolescence, 25,* 17–31.

Friman, P. C., Woods, D. W., Freeman, K. A., Gilman, R., Short, M., McGrath, A. M., & Handwerk, M. L. (2004). Relationships between tattling, likeability, and social classification: A preliminary investigation of adolescents in residential care. *Behavior Modification, 28,* 331–348.

Frisch, R. E. (1984). Body fat, puberty, and fertility. *Biological Reviews of the Cambridge Philosophical Society, 59,* 161–188.

Frisco, M. L., Muller, C., & Dodson, K. (2004). Participation in voluntary youth-serving associations and early adult voting behavior. *Social Science Quarterly, 85,* 660–676.

Frohman, L., Cameron, J., & Wise, P. (1999). Neuroendocrine systems: II. Growth, reproduction, and lactation. In M. J. Zigmond, F. E. Bloom, S. C. Landis, J. L. Roberts, & L. R. Squire (Eds.). *Fundamental neuroscience* (pp. 1151–1187). San Diego: Academic Press.

Fuligni, A. J., & Eccles, J. S. (1993). Perceived parent–child relationships and early adolescents' orientation toward peers. *Developmental Psychology, 29,* 622–632.

Fuligni, A. J., Yip, T., & Tseng, V. (2002). The impact of family obligation on the daily activities and psychological well-being of Chinese American adolescents. *Child Development, 73,* 302–314.

Furman, W., & Buhrmester, D. (1992). Age and sex differences in perceptions of networks of personal relationships. *Child Development, 63,* 103–115.

Furrow, J. L., King, P. E., & White, K. (2004). Religion and positive youth development: Identity, meaning, and prosocial concerns. *Applied Developmental Science, 8,* 17–26.

Furstenberg, F. F., Jr., Brooks-Gunn, J., & Morgan, S. P. (1987). *Adolescent mothers in later life.* New York: Cambridge University Press.

Gaddis, A., & Brooks-Gunn, J. (1985). The male experience of pubertal change. *Journal of Youth and Adolescence, 14,* 61–69.

Galambos, N. L., & Maggs, J. L. (1990). Putting mothers' work-related stress in perspective: Mothers and adolescents in dual-earner families. *Journal of Early Adolescence, 10,* 313–328.

Galambos, N. I., Sears, H. A., Almeida, D. M., & Kolaric, G. C. (1995). Parents' work overload and problem behavior in young adolescents. *Journal of Research on Adolescence, 5,* 201–223.

Gallagher, A. M., & De Lisi, R. (1994). Gender differences in Scholastic Aptitude Test: Mathematics problem solving among high-ability students. *Journal of Educational Psychology, 86,* 204–211.

Gallagher, A. M., De Lisi, R., Holst, P. C., McGillicuddy-De Lisi, A. V., Morely, M., & Cahalan, C. (2000). Gender differences in advanced mathematical problem solving. *Journal of Experimental Child Psychology, 75,* 165–190.

Garbarino, J. (1980). Some thoughts on school size and its effects on adolescent development. *Journal of Youth and Adolescence, 9,* 19–31.

Garbarino, J. (1999). *Lost boys.* New York: Free Press.

Garber, J., Robinson, N. S., & Valentiner, D. (1997). The relation between parenting and adolescent depression: Self-worth as a mediator. *Journal of Adolescent Research, 12,* 12–33.

Gardner, H. (1983). *Frames of mind.* New York: Basic Books.

Gardner, H. (1999). *Intelligence reframed: Multiple intelligences for the 21st century.* New York: Basic Books.

Gardner, H. (2006). *Multiple intelligences: New horizons in theory and practice.* New York: Basic Books.

Garland, A. F., & Zigler, E. (1993). Adolescent suicide prevention: Current research and social policy implications. *American Psychologist, 48,* 169–182.

Garlick, D. (2002). Understanding the nature of the general factor in intelligence: The role of individual differences in neural plasticity as an explanatory mechanism. *Psychological Review, 109,* 116–136.

Gateway to College. (2005). Available at http://www.gatewaytocollege.org/educators.htm

Gathercole, S. E., Pickering, S. J., Ambridge, B., & Wearing, H. (2004). The structure of working memory from 4 to 15 years of age. *Developmental Psychology, 40,* 177–190.

Gavin, L. A., & Furman, W. (1989). Age differences in adolescents' perceptions of their peer groups. *Developmental Psychology, 25,* 827–834.

Gavin, L. A., & Furman, W. (1996). Adolescent girls' relationships with mothers and best friends. *Child Development, 67,* 375–386.

Gazelle, H., & Rudolph, K. D. (2004). Moving toward and away from the world: Social approach and avoidance trajectories in anxious solitary youth. *Child Development, 75,* 829–849.

Ge, X., Brody, G. H., Conger, R. D., Simons, R. L., & Murry, V. M. (2002). Contextual amplification of pubertal transition effects on deviant peer affiliation and externalizing behavior among African American children. *Developmental Psychology, 38,* 42–54.

Ge, X., Conger, R. D., & Elder, G. H. (1996). Coming of age too early: Pubertal influences on girls' vulnerability to psychological distress. *Child Development, 67,* 3386–3400.

Ge, X., Conger, R. D., & Elder, G. H., Jr. (2001a). Pubertal transition, stressful life events, and the emergence of gender differences in adolescent depressive symptoms. *Developmental Psychology, 37,* 404–417.

Ge, X., Conger, R. D., & Elder, G. H., Jr. (2001b). The relation between puberty and psychological distress in adolescent boys. *Journal of Research on Adolescence, 11,* 49–70.

Ge, X., Conger, R. D., Lorenz, F. O., Elder, G. H., Montague, R. B., & Simons, R. L. (1992). Linking family economic hardship to adolescent distress. *Journal of Research on Adolescence, 2,* 351–378.

Ge, X., Natsuaki, M. N., & Conger, R. D. (2006). Trajectories of depressive symptoms and stressful life events among male and female adolescents in divorced and nondivorced families. *Development and Psychopathology, 18,* 253–273.

Gee, C. B., & Rhodes, J. E. (2003). Adolescent mothers' relationship with their children's biological fathers: Social support, social strain and relationship continuity. *Journal of Family Psychology, 17,* 370–383.

Geller, L. G. (1985). *Word play and language learning for children.* Urbana, IL: National Council of Teachers of English.

General Accounting Office. (2003). *Youth illicit drug use prevention: DARE long-term evaluations and federal efforts to identify effective programs.* Retrieved from http://www.gpoaccess.gov/gaoreports/index.html

Geuzaine, C., Debry, M., & Liesens, V. (2000). Separation from parents in late adolescence: The same for boys and girls? *Journal of Youth and Adolescence, 29,* 79–91.

Gibbs, J. T. (1989). Black American adolescents. In J. T. Gibbs, L. N. Huang, & Associates (Eds.), *Children of color.* San Francisco: Jossey-Bass.

Giles-Sims, J., & Crosbie-Burnett, M. (1989a). Stepfamily research: Implications for policy, clinical interventions, and further research. *Family Relations, 38,* 19–23.

Giles-Sims, J., & Crosbie-Burnett, M. (1989b). Adolescent power in stepfather families: A test of normative-resource theory. *Journal of Marriage and the Family, 51,* 1065–1078.

Gilliam, M. L., Warden, M. W., & Tapia, B. (2004). Young Latinas recall contraceptive use before and after pregnancy: A focus group study. *Journal of Pediatric Adolescent Gynecology, 17,* 279–287.

Gilligan, C. (1982). *In a different voice: Psychological theory and women's development.* Cambridge, MA: Harvard University Press.

Gilligan, C. (1986). Exit-voice dilemmas in adolescent development. In A. Foxley, M. S. McPherson, & G. O'Donnell (Eds.), *Development, democracy, and the art of trespassing: Essays in honor of Albert O. Hirschman.* Notre Dame, IN: University of Notre Dame Press.

Gilligan, C. (1988b). Exit-voice dilemmas in adolescent development. In C. Gilligan, J. V. Ward, J. M. Taylor, & B. Bardige (Eds.), *Mapping the moral domain.* Cambridge, MA: Harvard University Press.

Gilligan, C. (1989a). Preface: Teaching Shakespeare's sister. *Making connections: The relational worlds of adolescent girls at Emma Willard School.* Cambridge, MA: Harvard University Press.

Gilligan, C. (1989b). Prologue. In C. Gilligan, N. P. Lyons, & T. J. Hanmer (Eds.), *Making connections: The relational worlds of adolescent girls at Emma Willard School.* Cambridge, MA: Harvard University Press.

Gilligan, C. (1996). The centrality of relationships in psychological development: A puzzle, some evidence, and a theory. In G. G. Noam & K. W. Fischer (Eds.), *Development and vulnerability in close relationships* (pp. 237–261). Hillside, NJ: Erlbaum.

Gilligan, C. (2004). Recovering Psyche: Reflections on life-history and history. In J. A. Winer, W. W. Anderson, and C. C. Kieffer (Eds.), *Psychoanalysis and women* (pp. 131–147). Hillsdale, NJ: Analytic Press.

Gilligan, C., & Attanucci, J. (1988). Two moral orientations: Gender differences and similarities. *Merrill-Palmer Quarterly, 34,* 223–237.

Gilligan, C., Lyons, N. P., & Hanmer, T. J. (Eds.). (1989). *Making connections.* Troy, NY: Emma Willard School.

Ginsburg, H., & Opper, S. (1988). *Piaget's theory of intellectual development.* (3rd ed.). Englewood Cliffs, NJ: Prentice-Hall.

Ginzburg, E. (1972). Toward a theory of occupational choice: A restatement. *Vocational Guidance Quarterly, 20,* 169–176.

Ginzburg, E. (1990). Career development. In D. Brown, L. Brooks, & Associates (Eds.), *Career choice and development.* San Francisco: Jossey-Bass.

Goldsmith, H. H., Buss, A. H., Plomin, R., Rothbart, M. K., Thomas, A., Chess, S., Hinde, R. A., & McCall, R. B. (1987). Roundtable: What is temperament? Four approaches. *Child Development, 58,* 505–529.

Goldstein, A., Harrington, M., & Woodbury, R. (1999). The Columbine tapes: In final secret videos they recorded before the massacre, the killers reveal their hatred—and their lust for fame. *Time,* December 20, 1999, p. 40.

Goldstein, S. E., Davis-Kean, P. E., & Eccles, J. S. (2005). Parents, peers, and problem behavior: A longitudinal investigation of the impact of relationship perceptions and characteristics on the development of adolescent problem behavior. *Developmental Psychology, 41,* 401–413.

Goodwin, R. D., Pine, D. S., and Hoven, C. W. (2003). Asthma and panic attacks among youth in the community. *Journal of Asthma, 40,* 139–145.

Goossens, L. (2001). Global versus domain-specific statuses in identity research: A comparison of two self-report measures. *Journal of Adolescence, 24,* 681–699.

Gottfredson, G. D., Gottfredson, D. C., Payne, A. A., & Gottfredson, N. C. (2005). School climate predictors of school disorder: Results from a national study of delinquency prevention in schools. *Journal of Research in Crime and Delinquency, 42,* 412–444.

Gottfried, A. E., Gottfried, A. W., & Bathurst, K. (2002). Maternal and dual-earner employment status and parenting. In M. H. Bornstein (Ed.), *Handbook of parenting: Vol. 2. Biology and ecology of parenting* (2nd ed., pp. 207–229). Mahwah, NJ: Erlbaum.

Gowen, L. K., Feldman, S. S., Diaz, R., & Yisrael, D. S. (2004). A comparison of the sexual behaviors and attitudes of adolescent girls with older vs. similar-aged boyfriends. *Journal of Youth and Adolescence, 33,* 167–175.

Graber, J. A. (2003). Puberty in context. In C. Hayward (Ed.), *Gender differences at puberty* (pp. 307–325). New York: Cambridge University Press.

Graber, J. A., & Brooks-Gunn, J. (2002). Adolescent girls' sexual development. In G. M. Wingood & R. J. DiClemente (Eds.), *Handbook of women's sexual and reproductive health* (pp. 21–42). New York: Kluwer Academic/Plenum.

Graber, J. A., Lewinsohn, P. M., Seeley, J. R., & Brooks-Gunn, J. (1997). Is psychopathology associated with the timing of pubertal development? *Journal of the American Academy of Child and Adolescent Psychiatry, 36,* 1768–1776.

Grabber, J. A., Seeley, J. R., Brooks-Gunn, J., & Lewinsohn, P. M. (2004). Is pubertal timing associated with psychopathology in young adulthood? *Journal of the American Academy of Child and Adolescent Psychiatry, 43,* 718–726.

Grady, M. A., & Bloom, K. S. (2004). Pregnancy outcomes of adolescents enrolled in a centering pregnancy program. *Journal of Midwifery and Women's Health, 49,* 412–420.

Graham, S., & Juvonen, J. (2002). Ethnicity, peer harassment, and adjustment in middle school: An exploratory study. *Journal of Early Adolescence, 22,* 173–199.

Granillo, T., Jones-Rodriguez, G., & Carvajal, S. C. (2005). Prevalence of eating disorders in Latina adolescents: Associations with substance use and other correlates. *Journal of Adolescent Health, 36,* 214–220.

Grant, H., & Dweck, C. S. (2003). Clarifying achievement goals and their impact. *Journal of Personality and Social Psychology, 85,* 541–553.

Gray, N. J., Klein, J. D., Noyce, P. R., Sesselberg, T. S., & Cantrill, J. A. (2005). Health information-seeking behaviour in adolescence: The place of the Internet. *Social Science and Medicine, 60,* 1467–1478.

Greenough, W. T., Black, J. E., & Wallace, C. S. (1987). Experience and brain development. *Child Development, 58,* 539–559.

Gregory, A., & Weinstein, R. S. (2004). Connection and regulation at home and in school: Predicting growth in achievement for adolescents. *Journal of Adolescent Research, 19,* 405–427.

Greif, G. L., & DeMaris, A. (1990). Single fathers with custody. *Families in Society, 71,* 259–266.

Gross, B. (1990). Here dropouts drop in—and stay! *Phi Delta Kappan, 71,* 625–627.

Grotevant, H. D., & Cooper, C. R. (1986). Individuation in family relationships. *Human Development, 29,* 82–100.

Gunnoe, M. L., & Hetherington, E. M. (2004). Stepchildren's perceptions of noncustodial mothers and noncustodial fathers: Differences in socioemotional involvement and associations with adolescent adjustment problems. *Journal of Family Psychology, 18,* 555–563.

Haffner, D. W., & Wagoner, J. (1999). Vast majority of Americans support sexuality education. *SIECUS Report,* August/September.

Hains, A. A., & Szyjakowski, M. (1990). A cognitive stress-reduction intervention program for adolescents. *Journal of Counseling Psychology, 37,* 79–84.

Hall, C. S. (1999). *A primer of Freudian psychology.* New York: Meridian Books.

Hall, T. (2002). *Differentiated instruction.* Wakefield, MA: National Center on Acccessing the General Curriculum. Retrieved August 25, 2005, from http://www.cast.org/publications/ncac/ncac_diffinstruc.html

Hallinan, M. T., & Teixeira, R. A. (1987). Opportunities and constraints: Black-white differences in the formation of interracial friendships. *Child Development, 58,* 1358–1371.

Halpern, C. T., Udry, J. R., Campbell, B., & Suchindran, C. (1999). Effects of body fat on weight concerns, dating, and sexual activity: A longitudinal analysis of black and white adolescent girls. *Developmental Psychology, 35,* 721–736.

Halpern, C. J. T., Udry, J. R., Suchindran, C., & Campbell, B. (2000). Adolescent males' willingness to report masturbation. *Journal of Sex Research, 37,* 327–335.

Halpern, D. W., Joyner, K., Udry, J. R., & Suchindran, C. (2000). Smart teens don't have sex (or kiss much either). *Journal of Adolescent Health, 26,* 213–225.

Hamer, D. H., Hu, S., Magnuson, V.-L., Hu, N., & Pattatucci, A. M. L. (1993). A linkage between DNA markers on the X-chromosome and male sexual orientation. *Science, 261,* 321–326.

Hamm, J. (2000). Do birds of a feather flock together? The variable bases for African American, Asian American, and European American adolescents' selection of similar friends. *Developmental Psychology, 36,* 209–219.

Hardy, C. L., Bukowski, W. M., & Sippola, L. K. (2002). Stability and change in peer relationships during the transition to middle-level school. *Journal of Early Adolescence, 22,* 117–142.

Harris, D. R., and Sim, J. J. (2002). Who is multiracial? Assessing the complexity of lived race. *American Sociological Review, 67,* 614–627.

Hart, D., & Fegley, S. (1995). Prosocial behavior and caring in adolescence: Relations to self-understanding and social judgment. *Child Development, 66,* 1346–1359.

Hart, T. A., & Heimberg, R. G. (2001). Presenting problems among treatment-seeking gay, lesbian, and bisexual youth. *Journal of Clinical Psychology, 57,* 615–627.

Hartup, W. W. (1993). Adolescents and their friends. In B. Laursen (Ed.), *New directions for child development* (pp. 3–22). San Francisco: Jossey-Bass.

Harvey, O. J., & Rutherford, J. (1980). Status in the informal group. *Child Development, 31,* 377–385.

Hatcher, R., Hatcher, S., Berlin, M., Okla, K., & Richards, J. (1990). Psychological mindedness and abstract reasoning in late childhood and adolescence: An exploration using new instruments. *Journal of Youth and Adolescence, 19,* 307–326.

Hattie, J., Marsh, H. W., Neill, J. T., & Richards, G. E. (1997). Adventure education and Outward Bound: Out-of-class experiences that make a lasting difference. *Review of Educational Research, 67,* 43–87.

Hauser, S. T., Borman, E. H., Jacobson, A. M., Powers, S. I., & Noam, G. G. (1991). Understanding family contexts of adolescent coping: A study of parental ego development and adolescent coping strategies. *Journal of Early Adolescence, 11,* 96–124.

Hausmann, M., Slabbekoorn, D., Van Goozen, S. H. M., Cohen-Kettenis, P. T., & Guentuerkuen, O. (2000). Sex hormones affect spatial abilities during the menstrual cycle. *Behavioral Neuroscience, 114,* 1245–1250.

Havighurst, R. J. (1952). *Developmental tasks and education.* New York: Longman.

Havighurst, R. J. (1972). *Developmental tasks and education.* New York: David McKay.

Hayes, C. D. (Ed.). (1987). *Risking the future: Adolescent sexuality, pregnancy, and childbearing* (Vol. 1). Washington, DC: National Academy Press.

Haynie, D. L., Nansel, T., Eitel, P., Crump, A. D., Saylor, K., Yu, K., & Simons-Morton, B. (2001). Bullies, victims, and bully/victims: Distinct groups of at-risk youth. *Journal of Early Adolescence, 21,* 29–49.

Hays, S. P., Hays, C. E., & Mulhall, P. F. (2003). Community risk and protective factors and adolescent substance use. *Journal of Primary Prevention, 24,* 125–142.

Health Access Survey. (2003). *Minnesota's uninsured: Findings from the 2001 Health Access Survey.* Available at http://www.health.state.mn.us/divs/phsc/hep/yearissueb.cfm

Healthy Youth. (2005). Retrieved from http://www.cdc.gov/healthyyouth/injury/slides/slides14.htm

Heath, S. B. (1993). Inner city life through drama: Imagining the language classroom. *TESOL Quarterly, 27,* 177–192.

Heath, S. B. (1994). The project of learning from the inner-city youth perspective. In F. A. Villarruel & R. M. Lerner (Eds.), *Promoting community-based programs for socialization and learning: New directions for child development* (pp. 25–34). San Francisco: Jossey-Bass.

Heavenly Hats. (2005). *The Foundation Center: Youth in philanthropy* Available at http://youth.fdncenter.org/youth_stories_anthony_leanna.html.

Hedges, L. V., & Nowell, A. (1995). Sex differences in mental test scores, variability, and numbers of high-scoring individuals. *Science, 269,* 41–45.

Hedley, A. A., Ogden, C. L., Johnson, C. L., Carroll, M. D., Curtin, L. R., & Flegal, K. M. (2004). Prevalence of overweight and obesity among U.S. children, adolescents, and adults, 1999–2002. *JAMA: Journal of the American Medical Association, 291,* 2847–2850.

Helwig, C. C., Hildebrandt, C., & Turiel, E. (1995). Children's judgments about psychological harm in social context. *Child Development, 66,* 1680–1693.

Helwig, C. C., & Kim, S. (1999). Children's evaluations of decision-making procedures in peer, family, and school contexts. *Child Development, 70,* 502–512.

Hendry, L. B., Glendinning, A., & Shucksmith, J. (1996). Adolescent focal theories: Age-trends in developmental transitions. *Journal of Adolescence, 19,* 307–320.

Henggeler, S. W. (1989). Delinquency in adolescence Newbury Park, CA: Sage.

Henry, K. L., Slater, M. D., & Oetting, E. R. (2005). Alcohol use in early adolescence: the effect of changes in risk taking, perceived harm and friends' alcohol use. *Journal of Studies on Alcohol, 66,* 275–283.

Herbert, J., & Stipek, J. (2005). The emergence of gender differences in children's perceptions of their academic competence. *Journal of Applied Developmental Psychology, 26,* 276–295.

Herlihy, C. M., & Kemple, J. J. (2005). *The Talent Development middle school model: The 2002–2003 school year; an update to the December 2004 report.* Retrieved from http://www.mdrc.org

Herman, M. (2004). Forced to choose: Some determinants of racial identification in multiracial adolescents. *Child Development, 75,* 730–748.

Herrera, R. S., & DelCampo, R. L. (1995). Beyond the superwoman syndrome: Work satisfaction and family functioning among working-class, Mexican-American women. *Hispanic Journal of Behavioral Sciences, 17,* 49–60.

Hertel, B. R., & Donahue, M. J. (1995). Parental influences on God images among children: Testing Durkheim's metaphoric parallelism. *Journal for the Scientific Study of Religion, 34,* 186–199.

Hetherington, E. M. (1989). Coping with family transitions: Winners, losers, and survivors. *Child Development, 60,* 1–14.

Hetherington, E. M., Cox, M., & Cox, R. (1982). Effects of divorce on children and parents. In M. E. Lamb (Ed.), *Nontraditional families.* Hillsdale, NJ: Erlbaum.

Hetherington, E. M., Hagan, M. S., & Anderson, E. R. (1989). Marital transitions: A child's perspective. *American Psychologist, 44,* 303–312.

Hetherington, E. M., & Kelly, J. (2002). *For better or worse: Divorce reconsidered.* New York: Norton.

Hetherington, E. M., & Stanley-Hagan, M. (2002). Parenting in divorced and remarried families. In M. Bornstein (Ed.), *Handbook of parenting: Vol 3. Being and becoming a parent* (2nd ed.). Mahwah, NJ: Erlbaum.

Heyman, G. D., & Giles, J. W. (2004). Valence effects in reasoning about evaluative traits. *Merrill-Palmer Quarterly, 50,* 86–109.

Hill, N. E., Castellino, D. R., Lansford, J. E., Nowlin, P., Dodge, K. A., Bates, J. E., & Pettit, G. S. (2004). Parent academic involvement as related to school behavior, achievement, and aspirations: Demographic variations across adolescence. *Child Development, 75,* 1491–1509.

Hiller-Sturmhofel, S., & Bartke, A. (1998). The endocrine system: A review. *Alcohol Health and Research World, 22,* 153–164.

Hingson, R. W., Strunin, L., Berlin, B., & Heeren, T. (1990). Beliefs about AIDS, use of alcohol and drugs, and unprotected sex among Massachusetts adolescents. *American Journal of Public Health, 80,* 295–299.

Hodges, E. V. E., Finnegan, R. A., & Perry, D. G. (1999). Skewed autonomy-relatedness in preadolescents' conceptions of their relationships with mother, father, and best friend. *Developmental Psychology, 35,* 737–748.

Hoerster, K. D., Chrisler, J. C., & Rose, J. G. (2003). Attitudes toward and experience with menstruation in the U.S. and India. *Women & Health, 38,* 77–95.

Hof, P. R., Trapp, B. D., deVellis, J., Claudio, L., & Colman, D. R. (1999). The cellular components of nervous tissue. In M. J. Zigmond, F. E. Bloom, S. C. Landis, J. L. Roberts, & L. R. Squire (Eds.), *Fundamental neuroscience* (pp. 41–70). San Diego: Academic Press.

Hoffman, M. L. (1980). Moral development in adolescence. In J. Adelson (Ed.), *Handbook of adolescent psychology.* New York: Wiley.

Hoffman, M. L. (1988). Moral development. In M. H. Bornstein & M. E. Lamb (Eds.), *Developmental psychology: An advanced textbook.* Hillsdale, NJ: Erlbaum.

Hogan, R. (1980). The gifted adolescent. In J. Adelson (Ed.), *Handbook of adolescence.* New York: Wiley.

Hogan, R., Viernstein, M. C., McGinn, P. V., Daurio, S., & Bohannon, W. (1977). Verbal giftedness and sociopolitical intelligence. *Journal of Educational Psychology, 50,* 135–142.

Hogan, R., & Weiss, D. (1974). Personality correlates of superior academic achievement. *Journal of Counseling Psychology, 21,* 144–149.

Hoge, D. R., Johnson, B., & Luidens, D. A. (1995). Types of denominational switching among Protestant young adults. *Journal for the Scientific Study of Religion, 34,* 253–258.

Hogue, A., & Steinberg, L. (1995). Homophily of internalized distress in adolescent peer groups. *Developmental Psychology, 31,* 897–906.

Holland, J. L. (1961). Creative and academic performance among talented adolescents. *Journal of Educational Psychology, 52,* 136– 147.

Holland, J. L. (1985a). *Making vocational choices: A theory of vocational personalities and work environments* (2nd ed.). Englewood Cliffs, NJ: Prentice-Hall.

Holland, J. L. (1985b). *Manual for the Vocational Preference Inventory.* Odessa, FL: Psychological Assessment Resources.

Holland, J. L. (1987). Current status of Holland's theory of careers: Another perspective. *Career Development Quarterly, 36,* 24–30.

Hooper, C. J., Luciana, M., Conklin, H. M., & Yarger, R. S. (2004). Adolescents' performance on the Iowa Gambling Task: Implications for the development of decision making and ventromedial prefrontal cortex. *Developmental Psychology, 40,* 1148–1158.

Hopmeyer Gorman, A., Kim, J., & Schimmelbusch, A. (2002). The attributes adolescents associate with peer popularity and teacher preference. *Journal of School Psychology, 40,* 143–165.

Horney, K. (1937). *The neurotic personality of our time.* New York: Norton.

Horney, K. (1967). *Feminine psychology.* New York: Norton.

Horowitz, F. D., & O'Brien, M. (1986). Gifted and talented children. *American Psychologist, 41,* 1147–1152.

Howes, P., & Cicchetti, D. (1993). A family/relational perspective on maltreating families: Parallel processes across systems and social policy implications. In D. Cicchetti & S. L. Toth (Eds.), *Child abuse, child development, and social policy* (pp. 399–438). Norwood, NJ: Ablex.

Huebner, A. J., & Mancini, J. A. (2003). Shaping structured out-of-school time use among youth: The effects of self, family, and friend systems. *Journal of Youth and Adolescence, 32,* 453–463.

Huebner, A. J., Shettler,L., Matheson, J. L., Meszaros, P. S., Piercy, F. P., & Davis, S. D. (2005). Factors associated with former smokers among female adolescents in rural Virginia. *Addictive Behaviors, 30,* 167–173.

Huff, C. R. (1996). The criminal behavior of gang members and non-gang, at-risk youth. In C. R. Huff (Ed.), *Gangs in America* (2nd ed.). Thousand Oaks, CA: Sage.

Huff, C. R., & Trump, K. S. (1996). Youth violence and gangs: School safety initiatives in urban and suburban school districts. *Education and Urban Society, 28,* 492–503.

Humphrey, L. L. (1989). Observed family interactions among subtypes of eating disorders using structural analysis of social behavior. *Journal of Consulting and Clinical Psychology, 57,* 206–214.

Hur, Y., & Bouchard, T. J., Jr. (1995). Genetic influences on perceptions of childhood family environment: A reared apart twin study. *Child Development, 66,* 330–345.

Huston, A., McLoyd, V., & Garcia Coll, C. (1994). Children and poverty: Issues in contemporary research. *Child Development, 65,* 275–282.

Huttenlocher, P. R. (1990). Morphometric study of human cerebral cortex development. *Neuropsychologia, 28,* 517–527.

Hyde, J. S. (1984). Children's understanding of sexist language. *Developmental Psychology, 20,* 697–706.

Hyde, J. S. (1991). *Understanding human sexuality* (4th ed.). New York: McGraw-Hill.

Hyde, J. S., & Durik, A. M. (2005). Gender, competence, and motivation. In A. J. Elliott & C. S. Dweck (Eds.) *Handbook of competence and motivation* (pp. 375–391). New York: Guilford Press.

Hyde, J. S., & Kling, K. C. (2001). Women, motivation, and achievement. *Psychology of Women Quarterly, 25,* 364–378.

Imbimbo, P. V. (1995). Sex differences in the identity formation of college students from divorced families. *Journal of Youth and Adolescence, 24,* 745–761.

Inhelder, B., & Piaget, J. (1958). *The growth of logical thinking from childhood to adolescence.* New York: Basic Books.

Insel, P. M., & Roth, W. T. (2000). *Core concepts in health* (8th ed., 2000 Update). Mountain View, CA: Mayfield.

Irwin, C. E., Jr. (2004). Eating and physical activity during adolescence: Does it make a difference in adult health status? *Journal of Adolescent Health, 34,* 459–460.

Jackson, J. F. (1993). Human behavioral genetics, Scarr's theory, and her views on interventions: A critical review and commentary on their implications for African American children. *Child Development, 64,* 1318–1332.

Jacobson, K. C. (2000). Parental monitoring and adolescent adjustment: An ecological perspective. *Journal of Research on Adolescence, 10,* 65–97.

Jadack, R. A., Hyde, J. S., Moore, C. F., & Keller, M. L. (1995). Moral reasoning about sexually transmitted diseases. *Child Development, 66,* 167–177.

Jaffe, S., & Hyde, J. S. (2000). Gender difference in moral orientation: A meta-analysis. *Psychological Bulletin, 126,* 703–726.

Jarrett, R. L. (1995). Growing up poor: The family experiences of socially mobile youth in low-income African American neighborhoods. *Journal of Adolescent Research, 10,* 111–134.

Jensen, L. A., Arnett, J. J., Feldman, S. S., & Cauffman, E. (2002). It's wrong, but everybody does it: Academic dishonesty among high school and college students. *Contemporary Educational Psychology, 27,* 209–228.

Jensen, L. A., Arnett, J. J., Feldman, S. S., & Caaffman, E. (2004). The right to do wrong: Lying to parents among adolescents and emerging adults. *Journal of Youth and Adolescence, 33,* 101–112.

Jensen-Campbell, L. A., Adams, R., Perry, D. G., Workman, K. A., Furdella, J. Q., & Egan, S. K. (2002). Agreeableness, extraversion, and peer relations in early adolescence: Winning friends and deflecting aggression. *Journal of Research in Personality, 36,* 224–251.

Jodl, K. M., Michael, A., Malanchuk, O., Eccles, J. S., & Sameroff, A. (2001). Parents' roles in shaping early adolescents' occupational aspirations. *Child Development, 72,* 1247–1265.

Joebgen, A. M., & Richards, M. H. (1990). Maternal education and employment: Mediating maternal and adolescent emotional adjustment. *Journal of Early Adolescence, 10,* 329–343.

Johns, M., Schmader, T., & Martins, A. (2005). Knowing is half the battle: Teaching stereotype threat as a means of improving women's math performance. *Psychological Science, 16,* 175–179.

Johnson, B. M., Shulman, S., & Collins, W. A. (1991). Systematic patterns of parenting as reported by adolescents: Developmental differences and implications for psychosocial outcomes. *Journal of Adolescent Research, 6,* 235–252.

Johnson, M. K. (2002). Social origins, adolescent experiences, and work value trajectories during the transition to adulthood. *Social Forces, 80,* 1307–1341.

Johnston, L. D., O'Malley, P. M., Bachman, J. G., & Schulenberg, J. E. (2005). *Monitoring the Future national results on adolescent drug use: Overview of key findings, 2004.* Retrieved from http://www.monitoringthefuture.org

Johnston, L. D., O'Malley, P. M., & Bachman, J. G. (1989). *Drug use, drinking, and smoking: National survey results from high school, college, and young adult populations, 1975–1988* (DHHS Publication No. ADM 89–1638). Washington, DC: U.S. Government Printing Office.

Jones, M. C. (1965). Psychological correlates of somatic development. *Child Development, 36,* 899–911.

Jones, M. C., & Bayley, N. (1950). Psychological maturing among boys as related to behavior. *Journal of Educational Psychology, 41,* 129–148.

Jones, R. K., Darroch, J. E., & Singh, S. (2005). Religious differentials in the sexual and reproductive behaviors of young women in the United States. *Journal of Adolescent Health, 36,* 279–288.

Jones, S. D., Ehiri, J., & Anyanwu, E. (2004). Female genital mutilation in developing countries: An agenda for public health response. *European Journal of Obstetrics & Gynecology and Reproductive Biology, 116,* 144–151.

Jonson-Reid, M. (2002). After a child abuse report: Early adolescents and the child welfare system. *Journal of Early Adolescence, 22,* 24–48.

Josselson, R. L. (1980). Ego development in adolescence. In J. Adelson (Ed.), *Handbook of adolescent psychology.* New York: Wiley.

Josselson, R. L. (1982). Personality structure and identity status in women as viewed through early memories. *Journal of Youth and Adolescence, 11,* 293–299.

Josselson, R. L. (1987). *Finding herself: Pathways to identity development in women.* San Francisco: Jossey-Bass.

Josselson, R. L. (1988). The embedded self: I and thou revisited. In D. K. Lapsley & F. C. Power (Eds.), *Self, ego, and identity.* New York: Springer-Verlag.

Josselson, R. L. (1992). *The space between us.* San Francisco: Jossey-Bass.

Juan-Espinosa, M., Garcia, L., Colom, R., & Abad, F. J. (2000). Testing the age related differentiation hypothesis through the Wechsler's scales. *Personality and Individual Differences, 29,* 1069–1075.

Juvenile Justice Evaluation Center. (2004). *Disproportionate Minority Contact (DMC).* Retrieved from http://wwww.jrsa.org/jjec/programs/dmc/

Kalil, A., Ziol-Guest, K. M., & Coley, R. L. (2005). Perceptions of father involvement patterns in teenage-mother families: Predictors and links to mothers' psychological adjustment. *Family Relations: Interdisciplinary Journal of Applied Family Studies, 54,* 197–211.

Kandel, D. B. (1975). Stages in adolescent involvement in drug use. *Science, 190,* 912–914.

Kandel, D. B. (1978). Similarity in real-life adolescent friendship pairs. *Journal of Personality and Social Psychology, 36,* 306–312.

Kandel, D. B. (1996). The parental and peer contexts of adolescent deviance: An algebra of interpersonal influences. *Journal of Drug Issues, 26,* 289–315.

Kandel, D. B. (2002). Examining the gateway hypothesis. In D. B. Kandel (Ed.), *Stages and pathways of drug involvement: Examining the gateway hypothesis* (pp. 3–15). New York: Cambridge University Press.

Karofsky, P. S., Zeng, L., & Kosorok, M. R. (2001). Relationship between adolescent-parental communication and initiation of first intercourse by adolescents. *Journal of Adolescent Health, 28,* 41–45.

Kaufman, P., Alt, M. N., & Chapman, C. D. (2001). *Dropout rates in the United States: 2000* (NCES 2002-114). Washington, DC: U.S. Department of Education, National Center for Education Statistics.

Keefe, K., & Berndt, T. J. (1996). Relations of friendship quality to self-esteem in early adolescence. *Journal of Early Adolescence, 16,* 110–129.

Kegan, R. (1982). *The evolving self.* Cambridge, MA: Harvard University Press.

Kegan, R. (1994). *In over our heads.* Cambridge, MA: Harvard University Press.

Kelger, M. C., Oman, R. F., Vesely, S. K., McLeroy, K. R., Aspy, C. B., Rodine, S., & Marshall, L. (2005). Relationships among youth assets and neighborhood and community resources. *Health Education and Behavior, 32,* 380–397.

Keller, M., & Wood, P. (1989). Development of friendship reasoning: A study of interindividual differences in intraindividual change. *Developmental Psychology, 25,* 820–826.

Kennison, S. M., & Trofe, J. L. (2003). Comprehending pronouns: A role for word-specific gender stereotype information. *Journal of Psycholinguistic Research, 32,* 355–378.

Kenny, M. E., & Gallagher, L. A. (2002). Instrumental and social/relational correlates of perceived maternal and paternal attachment in adolescence. *Journal of Adolescence, 25,* 203–219.

Kerestes, M., Youniss, J., & Metz, E. (2004). Longitudinal patterns of religious perspective and civic integration. *Applied Developmental Science, 8,* 39–46.

Kerfoot, M., Harrington, R., & Dyer, E. (1995). Brief home-based intervention with young suicide attempters and their families. *Journal of Adolescence, 18,* 557–568.

Kernan, C. L., & Greenfield, P. M. (2005). Becoming a team: Individualism, collectivism, ethnicity, and group socialization in Los Angeles girls' basketball. *Ethos, 33,* 542–566.

Keselman, A. (2003). Supporting inquiry learning by promoting normative understanding of multivariable causality. *Journal of Research in Science Teaching, 40,* 898–921.

Kett, J. F. (1977). *Rites of passage.* New York: Basic Books.

Khanlou, N. (2004). Influences on adolescent self-esteem in multicultural Canadian secondary schools. *Public Health Nursing, 21,* 404–411.

Kilpatrick, D. G., Acierno, R., Saunders, B., Resnick, H. S., Best, C. L., & Schnurr, P. P. (2000). Risk factors for adolescent substance abuse and dependence: Data from a national sample. *Journal of Consulting and Clinical Psychology, 68,* 19–30.

King, P. E. & Furrow, J. L. (2004). Religion as a resource for positive youth development: Religion, social capital, and moral outcomes. *Developmental Psychology, 40,* 703–713.

Kingston, M. H. (1977). *The woman warrior.* New York: Vintage Books.

Kinsey, A. C., Pomeroy, W. B., & Martin, C. E. (1948). *Sexual behavior in the human male.* Philadelphia: Saunders.

Kinsey, A. C., Pomeroy, W. B., Martin, C. E., & Gebhard, P. H. (1953). *Sexual behavior in the human female.* Philadelphia: Saunders.

Kirby, D. (2002). Effective approaches to reducing adolescent unprotected sex, pregnancy, and childbearing. *The Journal of Sex Research, 39,* 51–57.

Kirby, D. B., Baumler, E., Coyle, K. K., Base-Engquist, K., Parcel, S. S., Harrist, R., & Banspach, S. W. (2004). The "Safer Choices" intervention: Its impact on the sexual behaviors of different subgroups of high school students. *Journal of Adolescent Health, 35,* 442–452.

Klebanov, P. K., & Brooks-Gunn, J. (1992). Impact of maternal attitudes, girls' adjustment, and cognitive skills upon academic performance in middle and high school. *Journal of Research on Adolescence, 2,* 81–102.

Klein, J. D. (2005). Adolescent pregnancy: Current trends and issues. *Pediatrics, 116,* 281–286.

Klein, M. W. (1995). *The American street gang.* New York: Oxford University Press.

Klein, S. S. (1985). *Handbook for achieving sex equity through education.* Baltimore, MD: Johns Hopkins University Press.

Kling, K. C., Hyde, J. S., Showers, C. J., & Buswell, B. N. (1999). Gender differences in self-esteem: A meta-analysis. *Psychological Bulletin, 125,* 470–500.

Klonsten, A. T., Shaalvik, E. M., & Espnes, G. A. (2004). Physical self-concept and sports: Do gender differences still exists? *Sex Roles, 50,* 119–127.

Knox, M., Funk, J., Elliott, R., & Bush, E. G. (2000). Gender differences in adolescents' possible selves. *Youth and Society, 31,* 287–309.

Kochman, T. (1987). The ethnic component in black language and culture. In M. J. Rotheram & J. S. Phinney (Eds.), *Children's ethnic socialization: Pluralism and development* (pp. 219–238). Beverly Hills, CA: Sage.

Koff, E., & Rierdan, J. (1995). Preparing girls for menstruation: Recommendations from adolescent girls. *Adolescence, 30,* 795–811.

Kohlberg, L. (1976). Moral stages and moralization: The cognitive developmental approach. In T. Lickona (Ed.), *Moral development and behavior.* New York: Holt, Rinehart & Winston.

Kohlberg, L. (1984). *The psychology of moral development.* New York: Harper & Row.

Kohlberg, L., & Kramer, R. (1969). Continuities and discontinuities in childhood and adult moral development. *Human Development, 12,* 93–120.

Kohut, S., Jr. (1988). *The middle school: A bridge between elementary and high schools* (2nd ed.). Washington, DC: National Education Association.

Koss, M. P., Dinero, T. E., Seibel, C. A., & Cox, S. L. (1988). Stranger and acquaintance rape: Are there differences in the victim's experience? *Psychology of Women Quarterly, 12,* 1–24.

Kratcoski, P. C., & Kratcoski, L. D. (1986). *Juvenile delinquency.* Englewood Cliffs, NJ: Prentice-Hall.

Krieger, N., & Fee, E. (1994). Social class: The missing link in U.S. health data. *International Journal of Health Services, 24,* 25–44.

Krishnakumar, A., & Black, M. M. (2003). Family processes within three-generation households and adolescent mothers' satisfaction with father involvement. *Journal of Family Psychology, 17,* 488–498.

Kroger, J. (1988). A longitudinal study of ego identity status interview domains. *Journal of Adolescence, 11,* 49–64.

Kroger, J. (1992). Intrapsychic dimensions of identity during late adolescence. In G. R. Adams, T. P. Gullotta, & R. Montemayor (Eds.), *Adolescent identity formation.* Newbury Park, CA: Sage.

Kroger, J. (1995). The differentiation of "firm" and "developmental" foreclosure identity statuses: A longitudinal study. *Journal of Adolescent Research, 10,* 317–337.

Kroger, J. (2000). Ego identity status research in the new millennium. *International Journal of Behavioral Development, 24,* 145–148.

Kroger, J. (2003). Identity development during adolescence. In G. R. Adams & M. D. Berzonsky (Eds.), *Blackwell Handbook of adolescence* (pp. 205–226). Malden, MA: Blackwell.

Krumboltz, J. D. (1991). *Career beliefs inventory.* Palo Alto, CA: Consulting Psychologists Press.

Kulin, H. E. (1991a). Puberty, hypothalamic-pituitary changes of. In R. M. Lerner, A. C. Petersen, & J. Brooks-Gunn (Eds.), *Encyclopedia of adolescence* (Vol. 2, pp. 900–907). New York: Garland.

Kulin, H. E. (1991b). Puberty, endocrine changes at. In R. M. Lerner, A. C. Petersen, & J. Brooks-Gunn (Eds.), *Encyclopedia of adolescence* (Vol. 2, pp. 897–899). New York: Garland.

Kuperminc, G. P., Blatt, S. J., Shahar, G., Henrich, C., & Leadbeater, B. J. (2004). Cultural equivalence and cultural variance in longitudinal associations of young adolescent self-definition and interpersonal relatedness to psychological and school adjustment. *Journal of Youth and Adolescence, 33,* 13–30.

Kurdek, L. A., & Fine, M. A. (1994). Family acceptance and family control as predictors of adjustment in young adolescents: Linear, curvilinear, or interactive effects? *Child Development, 65,* 1137–1146.

Kuttler, A. F., Parker, J. G., & La Greca, A. M. (2002). Developmental and gender differences in preadolescents' judgments of the veracity of gossip. *Merrill-Palmer Quarterly, 48,* 105–132.

Kwak, K. (2003). Adolescents and their parents: A review of intergenerational family relations for immigrant and non-immigrant families. *Human Development, 46,* 15–136.

Lacombe, A. C., & Gay, J. (1998). The role of gender in adolescent identity and intimacy decisions. *Journal of Youth and Adolescence, 27,* 795–802.

Ladd, K. L., McIntosh, D. N., & Spilka, B. (1998). Children's God concepts: Influences of denomination, age, and gender. *International Journal for the Psychology of Religion, 8,* 49–56.

LaFromboise, T. D., & Low, K. G. (1989). American Indian children and adolescents. In J. T. Gibbs, L. N. Huang, & Associates (Eds.), *Children of color.* San Francisco: Jossey-Bass.

Laird, R. D., Pettit, G. S., Bates, J. E., & Dodge, K. A. (2003). Parents' monitoring-relevant knowledge and adolescents' delinquent behavior: Evidence of correlated developmental changes and reciprocal influences. *Child Development, 74,* 752–768.

Lam, T. H., Stewart, S. M., Leung, G. M., Lee, P. W. H., Wong, J. P. S., & Ho, L. M. (2004). Depressive symptoms among Hong Kong adolescents: Relation to atypical sexual feelings and behaviors, gender dissatisfaction, pubertal timing, and family and peer relationships. *Archives of Sexual Behavior, 33,* 487–496.

Lambert, S. F., Brown, T. L., Phillips, C. M., & Ialongo, N. S. (2004). The relationship between perceptions of neighborhood characteristics and substance use among urban African American adolescents. *American Journal of Community Psychology, 34,* 205–218.

Lamborn, S. D., Dornbusch, S. M., & Steinberg, L. (1996). Ethnicity and community context as moderators of the relations between family decision making and adolescent adjustment. *Child Development, 67,* 283–301.

Landau, S., Lorch, E. P., & Milich, R. (1992). Visual attention to and comprehension of television in attention-deficit hyperactivity disordered and normal boys. *Child Development, 63,* 928–937.

Langer, L. M., Tubman, J. G., & Duncan, S. (1998). Anticipated mortality, HIV vulnerability, and psychological distress among adolescents and young adults at higher and lower risk for HIV infection. *Journal of Youth and Adolescence, 27,* 513–538.

Lapsley, D. K., FitzGerald, D. P., Rice, K. G., & Jackson, S. (1989). Separation-individuation and the "new look" at the imaginary audience and personal fable: A test of an integrative model. *Journal of Adolescent Research, 4,* 483–505.

Larson, R. W. (2000). Toward a psychology of positive youth development. *American Psychologist, 55,* 170–183.

Larson, R. W. (2002). Globalization, societal change, and new technologies: What they mean for the future of adolescence. *Journal of Research on Adolescence, 12,* 1–30.

Larson, R., & Richards, M. H. (1994). *Divergent realities.* New York: Basic Books.

Larson, R. W., & Almeida, D. M. (1999). Emotional transmission in the daily lives of families: A new paradigm for studying family process. *Journal of Marriage and the Family, 61,* 30–37.

Larson, R. W., & Gilman, S. (1999). Transmission of emotions in the daily interactions of single-mother families. *Journal of Marriage and the Family, 61,* 21–37.

Larson, R. W., & Richards, M. H. (1991). Boredom in the middle school years: Blaming schools versus blaming students. *American Journal of Education, 99,* 418–443.

Larson, R. W., Richards, M. H., Moneta, G., Holmbeck, G., & Duckett, E. (1996). Changes in adolescents' daily interactions with their families from ages 10 to 18: Disengagement and transformation. *Developmental Psychology, 32,* 744–754.

Larson, R. W. & Wilson, S. (2004). Adolescence across place and time: Globalization and the changing pathways to adulthood. In R. Lerner & L. Steinberg (Eds.), *Handbook of adolescent psychology.* New York: Wiley.

Lau, S., & Lau, W. (1996). Outlook on life: How adolescents and children view the life-style of parents, adults and self. *Journal of Adolescence, 19,* 293–296.

Laursen, B., Coy, K. C., & Collins, W. A. (1998). Reconsidering changes in parent–child conflict across adolescence: A meta-analysis. *Child Development, 69,* 817–832.

Laursen, B., Pulkkinen, L., & Adams, R. (2002). The antecedents and correlates of agreeableness in adulthood. *Developmental Psychology, 38,* 591–603.

Ledoux, S., Choquet, M., & Manfredi, R. (1993). Associated factors for self-reported binge eating among male and female adolescents. *Journal of Adolescence, 16,* 75–91.

Legters, N. E. (2000). Small learning communities meet school-to-work: Whole school restructuring for urban comprehensive high schools. In M. G. Sanders (Ed.), *Schooling students placed at risk: Research, policy, and practice in the education of poor and minority adolescents* (pp. 309–337). Mahwah, NJ: Erlbaum.

Lehr, S. T., DiIorio, C., Dudley, W. N., & Lipana, J. A. (2000). The relationship between parent–adolescent communication and safer sex behaviors in college students. *Journal of Family Nursing, 6,* 180–196.

Leland, N. L., & Barth, R. P. (1993). Characteristics of adolescents who have attempted to avoid HIV and who have communicated with parents about sex. *Journal of Adolescent Research, 8,* 58–76.

Lempers, J. D., & Clark-Lempers, D. S. (1992). Young, middle, and late adolescents' comparisons of the functional importance of five significant relationships. *Journal of Youth and Adolescence, 21,* 53–96.

Lempers, J. D., & Clark-Lempers, D. S. (1993). A functional comparison of same-sex and opposite-sex friendships during adolescence. *Journal of Adolescent Research, 8,* 89–108.

Lerner, R. M. (2002). *Concepts and theories of human development* (3rd ed.). Mahwah, NJ: Erlbaum.

Lerner, R. M., Anderson, P. M., Balsano, A. B., Dowling, E. M., & Bobek, D. L. (2003). Applied developmental science of positive human development. In R. M. Lerner, A. A. Easterbrooks, & J. Mistry (Eds.), *Handbook of psychology: Vol. 6. Developmental psychology* (pp. 535–558). Hoboken, NJ: Wiley.

Lerner, R.M., et al. (2005). Positive youth development, participation in community youth development programs, and community contributions of fifth grade adolescents: Findings from the first wave of the 4-H study of positive youth development. *Journal of Early Adolescence, 25,* 17–71.

Leslie, M. B., Stein, J. A., & Rotheram-Borus, M. J. (2002). Sex-specific predictors of suicidality among runaway youth. *Journal of Clinical Child and Adolescent Psychology, 31,* 27–40.

LeVay, S. (1991). A difference in hypothalamic structure between heterosexual and homosexual men. *Science, 253,* 1034–1037.

Leventhal, T., & Brooks-Gunn, J. (2000). The neighborhoods they live in: The effects of neighborhood residence on child and adolescent outcomes. *Psychological Bulletin, 126,* 309–337.

Lever, J. (1976). Sex differences in the games children play. *Social Problems, 23,* 478–487.

Lever, J. (1978). Sex differences in the complexity of children's play and games. *American Sociological Review, 43,* 471–483.

Levinson, D. J. (1978). *The seasons of a man's life.* New York: Ballantine Books.

Levitt, M. J., Guacci-Franco, N., & Levitt, J. L. (1993). Convoys of social support in childhood and early adolescence: Structure and function. *Developmental Psychology, 29,* 811–818.

Li, X., Sano, H., & Merwin, J. C. (1996). Perception and reasoning abilities among American, Japanese, and Chinese adolescents. *Journal of Adolescent Research, 11,* 173–193.

Liben, L. S., Bigler, R. S., & Krogh, H. R. (2002). Language at work: Children's gendered interpretations of occupational titles. *Child Development, 73,* 810–828.

Liben, L. S., Susman, E. J., Finkelstein, J. W., Chinchilli, V. M., Kunselman, S., Schwab, J., et al. (2002). The effects of sex steroids on spatial performance: A review and an experimental clinical investigation. *Developmental Psychology, 38,* 236–253.

Licht, B. G., Linden, T. A., Brown, D. A., & Sexton, M. A. (1984, August). *Sex differences in achievement orientation: An "A" student phenomenon?* Paper presented at the meeting of the American Psychological Association, Toronto, Canada.

Life Skills Training Program. Available at www.lifeskillstraining.com/program.cfm

Ling, P. M., & Glantz, S. A. (2002). Using tobacco-industry marketing research to design more effective tobacco-control campaigns. *Journal of the American Medical Association, 287,* 2983–2989.

Lips, H. M. (1997). *Sex and gender: An introduction* (3rd ed.). Mountain View, CA: Mayfield.

Lips, H. M. (2003). The gender pay gap: Concrete indicator of women's progress toward equality. *Analysis of Social Issues and Public Policy, 3,* 87–109.

Lips, H. M. (2005). *Sex and gender: An introduction* (5th ed.). New York: McGraw-Hill.

Lipsitz, J. (1984). *Successful schools for young adolescents.* New Brunswick, NJ: Transaction Books.

LoSciuto, L., Rajala, A. K., Townsend, T. N., & Taylor, A. S. (1996). An outcome evaluation of Across Ages: An intergenerational mentoring approach to drug prevention. *Journal of Adolescent Research, 11,* 116–129.

Lottes, L. L. (2002). Sexual health policies in other industrialized countries: Are there lessons for the United States? *Journal of Sex Research, 39,* 79–83.

Loukas, A., & Robinson, S. (2004). Examining the moderating role of perceived school climate in early adolescent adjustment. *Journal of Research on Adolescence, 14,* 209–233.

Lovelace, M. K. (2005). Meta-analysis of experimental research based on the Dunn and Dunn model. *Journal of Educational Research, 98,* 176–183.

Lovitt, T. C. (1989). *Introduction to learning disabilities.* Boston: Allyn & Bacon.

Lowry, R., Galuska, D. A., Fulton, J. E., Burgeson, C. R., & Kann, L. (2005). Weight management goals and use of exercise for weight control among U.S. high school students, 1991–2001. *Journal of Adolescent Health, 36,* 320–326.

Lucas, B. (1988). Family patterns and their relationship to obesity. In K. L. Clark, R. B. Parr, & W. P. Castelli (Eds.), *Evaluation and management of eating disorders.* Champaign, IL: Life Enhancement Publications.

Luna, B., Garver, K. E., Urban, T. A., Lazar, N. A., & Sweeney, J. A. (2004). Maturation of cognitive processes from late childhood to adulthood. *Child Development, 75,* 1357–1372.

Luzzo, D. A., Funk, D., & Strang, J. (1996). Attributional retraining increases career decision-making self-efficacy. *Career Development Quarterly, 44,* 378–386.

Luzzo, D. A., James, T., & Luna, M. (1996). Effects of attributional retraining on the career beliefs and career exploration behavior of college students. *Journal of Counseling Psychology, 43,* 415–422.

Luzzo, D. A., & Ward, B. E. (1995). The relative contributions of self-efficacy and locus of control to the prediction of vocational congruence. *Journal of Career Development, 21,* 307–317.

Lynn, R., & Irwing, P. (2004a). Sex differences on the advanced progressive matrices in college students. *Personality and Individual Differences, 37,* 219–223.

Lynn, R., & Irwing, P. (2004b). Sex differences on the progressive matrices: A meta-analysis. *Intelligence, 32,* 481–498.

Lyon, J. M., Henggeler, S., & Hall, J. A. (1992). The family relations, peer relations, and criminal activities of Caucasian and Hispanic-American gang members. *Journal of Abnormal Child Psychology, 20,* 439–449.

MacKay, A. P., Fingerhut, L. A., & Duran, C. R. (2000). *Adolescent Health Chartbook. Health, United States, 2000.* Hyattsville, MD: National Center for Health Statistics.

Mackey, K., Arnold, M. L., & Pratt, M. W. (2001). Adolescents' stories of decision making in more and less authoritative families: Representing the voices of parents in narrative. *Journal of Adolescent Research, 16,* 243–268.

MacKinnon, J. L., & Marcia, J. E. (2002). Concurring patterns of women's identity status styles, and understanding of children's development. *International Journal of Behavioral Development, 26,* 70–80.

Magarey, A. M., Boulton, T. J. C., Chatterton, B. E., Schultz, C., Nordin, B. E. C., & Cockington, R. A. (1999). Bone growth from 11 to 17 years: Relationship to growth, gender, and changes with pubertal status including timing of menarche. *Acta Paediatrica, 88,* 139–146.

Maguire, K., Pastore, A. L., & Flanagan, T. J. (1993). *Sourcebook of criminal justice statistics 1992.* U.S. Department of Justice, Bureau of Justice Statistics. Washington, DC: U.S. Government Printing Office.

Major, B., & Forcey, B. (1985). Social comparisons and pay evaluations: Preferences for same sex and same-job wage comparisons. *Journal of Experimental Social Psychology, 21,* 393–405.

Malecki, C. K., & Demaray, M. K. (2003). What type of support do they need? Investigating student adjustment as related to emotional, informational, appraisal, and instrumental support. *School Psychology Quarterly, 18,* 231–252.

Malinowski, B. (1925). Magic, science, and religion. In J. Needham (Ed.), *Science, religion and reality* (pp. 18–94). New York: Macmillan.

Mann, L., Harmoni, R., & Power, C. (1989). Adolescent decision-making: The development of competence. *Journal of Adolescence, 12,* 265–278.

Marcia, J. E. (1966). Development and validation of ego identity status. *Journal of Personality and Social Psychology, 3,* 551–558.

Marcia, J. E. (1976). Identity six years after: A follow-up study. *Journal of Youth and Adolescence, 5,* 145–150.

Marcia, J. E. (1980). Identity in adolescence. In J. Adelson (Ed.), *Handbook of adolescent psychology.* New York: Wiley.

Marcia, J. E. (1988). Common processes underlying ego identity, cognitive/moral development, and individuation. In D. K. Lapsley & F. C. Power (Eds.), *Self, ego and identity: Integrative approaches.* New York: Springer-Verlag.

Marcia, J. E. (2002). Adolescence, identity, and the Bernardone family. *Identity, 2,* 199–209.

Marcia, J. E., Waterman, A. S., Matteson, D. R., Archer, S. L., & Orlofsky, J. L. (1993). *Ego identity: A handbook for psychosocial research.* New York: Springer-Verlag.

Margolin, L., Miller, M., & Moran, P. B. (1989). When a kiss is not just a kiss: Relating violations of consent in kissing to rape myth acceptance. *Sex Roles, 20,* 231–243.

Markey, C. N., Tinsley, B. J., Ericksen, E. J., Ozer, D. J., & Markey, P. M. (2002). Preadolescents' perceptions of females' body size and shape: Evolutionary and social learning perspectives. *Journal of Youth and Adolescence, 31,* 137–146.

Markstrom, C. A. (1999). Religious involvement and adolescent psychosocial development. *Journal of Adolescence, 22,* 205–221.

Markstrom-Adams, C., Hofstra, G., & Dougher, K. (1994). The ego-virtue of fidelity: A case for the study of religion and identity formation in adolescence. *Journal of Youth and Adolescence, 23,* 453–469.

Markstrom-Adams, C., & Smith, M. (1996). Identity formation and religious orientation among high school students from the United States and Canada. *Journal of Adolescence, 19,* 247–261.

Marsh, H. W. (1992). Extracurricular activities: Beneficial extension of the traditional curriculum or subversion of academic goals? *Journal of Educational Psychology, 84,* 553–562.

Marsiglia, F. F., Miles, B. W., Dustman, P., & Sills, S. (2002). Ties that protect: An ecological perspective on Latino/a urban pre-adolescent drug use. *Journal of Ethnic and Cultural Diversity in Social Work, 11,* 191–220.

Martorano, S. C. (1977). A developmental analysis of performance on Piaget's formal operations tasks. *Developmental Psychology, 13,* 666–672.

Masters, W. H., Johnson, V. E., & Kolodny, R. C. (1988). *Human sexuality* (3rd ed.). Boston: Little, Brown.

Matkovic, V., Ilich, J. Z., Skugor, M., Badenhop, N. E., Goel, P., Clairmont, A., et al. (1997). Leptin is inversely related to age at menarche in human females. *Journal of Clinical Endocrinology and Metabolism, 82,* 3239–3245.

Maynard, R. A., Trenhold, C., Devaney, B., Johnson, A., Clark, M. A., Homrighausen, J., & Kalay, E. (2005). *First-year impacts of four Title V, Section 510 abstinence education programs.* Retrieved from http://aspe.hhs.gov/hsp/05/abstinence/

Maynard, R. C. (1990, August 5). An example of how Afro-American parents socialize children. *Oakland Tribune.*

Mayr, E. (1982). *Growth of biological thought: Diversity, evolution, and inheritance.* Cambridge, MA: Harvard University Press.

Mazor, A., & Enright, R. D. (1988). The development of the individuation process from a social-cognitive perspective. *Journal of Adolescence, 11,* 29–47.

McComb, C. (2003). *Teens and social service: Who volunteers?* The Gallup Organization. Retrieved from http://poll.gallup.com/content/default.aspx?CI=8500

McCullough, M. E., Emmons, R. A., & Tsang, J. (2002). The grateful disposition: A conceptual and empirical topography. *Journal of Personality and Social Psychology, 82,* 112–127.

McCullough, M. E., Kilpatrick, S. D., Emmons, R. A., & Larson, D. B. (2001). Is gratitude a moral affect? *Psychological Bulletin, 127,* 249–266.

McDonald, P., Colwell, B., & Backinger, C. L. (2003). Better practices for youth tobacco cessation: Evidence of review panel. *American Journal of Health Behavior, 27* (Suppl. 2), S144–S158.

McElhaney, K. B., & Allen, J. P. (2001). Autonomy and adolescent social functioning: The moderating effect of risk. *Child Development, 72,* 220–235.

McFarlane, A. H., Bellissimo, A., Norman, G. R., & Lange, P. (1994). Adolescent depression in a school-based community sample: Preliminary findings on contributing social factors. *Journal of Youth and Adolescence, 23,* 601–620.

McGue, M., Sharma, A., & Benson, P. (1996). The effect of common rearing on adolescent adjustment: Evidence from a U.S. adoption cohort. *Developmental Psychology, 32,* 604–613.

McKinney, J. P., & McKinney, K. G. (1999). Prayer in the lives of late adolescents. *Journal of Adolescence, 22,* 279–290.

McLanahan, S. S., Astone, N. M., & Marks, N. (1988, June). *The role of mother-only families in reproducing poverty.* Paper presented at the Conference on Poverty and Children, Lawrence, KS.

McLanahan, S. S., & Booth, K. (1989). Mother-only families: Problems, prospects, and politics. *Journal of Marriage and the Family, 51,* 557–580.

McLoyd, V. C. (1998). Socioeconomic disadvantage and child development. *American Psychologist, 53,* 185–204.

McNelles, L. R., & Connolly, J. A. (1999). Intimacy between adolescent friends: Age and gender differences in intimate affect and intimate behaviors. *Journal of Research on Adolescence, 9,* 143–159.

McVey, G. L., Pepler, D., Davis, R., Flett, G. L., & Abdolell, M. (2002). Risk and protective factors associated with disordered eating during early adolescence. *Journal of Early Adolescence, 22,* 75–95.

Mechanic, D., & Hansell, S. (1989). Divorce, family conflict, and adolescents' well-being. *Journal of Health and Social Behavior, 30,* 105–116.

Meeus, W., & Dekovic, M. (1995). Identity development, parental and peer support in adolescence: Results of a national Dutch survey. *Adolescence, 30,* 931–944.

Meeus, W., Iedema, J., Maassen, G., & Engels, R. (2005). Separation-individuation revisited: On the interplay of parent–adolescent relations, identity and emotional adjustment in adolescence. *Journal of Adolescence, 28,* 89–106.

Meichenbaum, D. H. (1985). *Stress inoculation training.* New York: Pergamon.

Meschke, L. L., Bartholomae, S., & Zentall, S. R. (2002). Adolescent sexuality and parent–adolescent processes: Promoting healthy teen choices. *Journal of Adolescent Health, 31,* 264–279.

Meschke, L. L., Zweig, J. M., Barber, B. L., & Eccles, J. S. (2000). Demographic, biological, psychological, and social predictors of the timing of first intercourse. *Journal of Research on Adolescence, 10,* 315–338.

Michael, A., & Eccles, J. S. (2003). When coming of age means coming undone: Links between puberty and psychosocial adjustment among European American and African American girls. In C. Hayward (Ed.), *Gender differences at puberty* (pp. 277–303). New York: Cambridge University Press.

Michel, A. (1986). *Down with stereotypes? Eliminating sexism from children's literature and school textbooks.* Washington, DC: UNESCO.

Midgley, C., Arunkumar, R., & Urdan, T. C. (1996). "If I don't do well tomorrow, there's a reason": Predictors of adolescents' use of academic self-handicapping strategies. *Journal of Educational Psychology, 88,* 423–434.

Miller, B. C., & Fox, G. L. (1987). Theories of adolescent heterosexual behavior. *Adolescent Research, 2,* 269–282.

Miller, C. T., & Downey, K. T. (1999). A meta-analysis of heavyweight and self-esteem. *Personality and Social Psychology Review, 3,* 68–84.

Miller, G. A., Galanter, E., & Pribram, K. H. (1960). *Plans and the structure of behavior.* New York: Holt, Rinehart & Winston.

Miller, J. (Ed.). (1973). *Psychoanalysis and women.* New York: Brunner/Mazel.

Miller, J. (1976). *Toward a new psychology of women.* Boston: Beacon Press.

Miller, J. G., & Bersoff, D. M. (1989). When do American children and adults reason in social conventional terms? *Developmental Psychology, 24,* 366–375.

Miller, K. E. (1990). Adolescents' same-sex and opposite-sex peer relations: Sex differences in popularity, perceived social competence, and social cognitive skills. *Journal of Adolescent Research, 5,* 222–241.

Miller, R. L. (1989). Desegregation experiences of minority students: Adolescent coping strategies in five Connecticut high schools. *Journal of Adolescent Research, 4,* 173–189.

Miller-Johnson, S., Costanzo, P. R., Coie, J. D., Rose, M. R., Browne, D. C., & Johnson, C. (2003). Peer social structure and risk-taking behaviors among African American early adolescents. *Journal of Youth and Adolescence, 32,* 375–384.

Minuchin, S., Rosman, B., & Baker, L. (1978). *Psychosomatic families: Anorexia nervosa in context.* Cambridge, MA: Harvard University Press.

Mischel, W., & Mischel, H. N. (1976). A cognitive social-learning approach to morality and self-regulation. In T. Lickona (Ed.), *Moral development and behavior: Theory, research, and social issues.* New York: Holt, Rinehart & Winston.

Mitchell, L. K., & Krumboltz, J. D. (1987). The effects of cognitive restructuring and decision-making training on career indecision. *Journal of Counseling and Development, 66,* 171–174.

Mitchell, L. K., & Krumboltz, J. D. (1990). Social learning approach to career decision making: Krumboltz's theory. In D. Brown, L. Brooks, & Associates (Eds.), *Career choice and development.* San Francisco: Jossey-Bass.

Miville, M. L., Koonce, D., Darlington, P., & Whitlock, B. (2000). Exploring the relationships between racial/cultural identity and ego identity among African Americans and Mexican Americans. *Journal of Multicultural Counseling and Development, 28,* 208–224.

Mizell, M. H. (1999). *Thirty and counting.* Available at http://mlted.ah.siue.edu/pds/modules/exceptionallms/thirtyactivity.htm

Moffitt, T. E. (1997). Adolescent-limited and life-course-persistent offending: A complementary pair of developmental theories. In T. P. Thornberry (Ed.), *Developmental theories of crime and delinquency* (pp. 11–54). New Brunswick, NJ: Transaction Books.

Molina, B. S. G., & Chassin, L. (1996). The parent–adolescent relationship at puberty: Hispanic ethnicity and parent alcoholism as moderators. *Developmental Psychology, 32,* 675–686.

Money, J. (1988). Commentary: Current status of sex research. *Journal of Psychology and Human Sexuality, 1,* 5–16.

Montemayor, R., & Van Komer, R. (1985). The development of sex differences in friendship patterns and peer group structure during adolescence. *Journal of Early Adolescence, 5,* 285–294.

Montgomery, M. J. (2005). Psychosocial intimacy and identity: From early adolescence to emerging adulthood. *Journal of Adolescent Research, 20,* 346–374.

Moore, K. A., & Glei, D. (1995). Taking the plunge: An examination of positive youth development. *Journal of Adolescent Research, 10,* 15–40.

Moore, S., & Cartwright, C. (2005). Adolescents' and young adults' expectations of parental responsibilities in stepfamilies. *Journal of Divorce and Remarriage, 43,* 109–127.

Mortimer, J. T., Finch, M. D., Ryu, S., Shanahan, M. J., & Call, K. T. (1996). The effects of work intensity on adolescent mental health, achievement, and behavioral adjustment: New evidence from a prospective study. *Child Development, 67,* 1243–1261.

Mortimer, J. T., Finch, M., Shanahan, M., & Ryu, S. (1992). Work experience, mental health, and behavioral adjustment in adolescence. *Journal of Research on Adolescence, 2,* 25–57.

Mounts, N. S. (2001). Young adolescents' perceptions of parental management of peer relationships. *Journal of Early Adolescence, 21,* 92–122.

Mounts, N. S., & Steinberg, L. (1995). An ecological analysis of peer influence on adolescent grade point average and drug use. *Developmental Psychology, 31,* 915–922.

Mukherjee, P., Miller, J. H., Shimony, J. S., Philip, J., Nehra, D., Snyder, A. Z., et. al. (2002). Diffusion tensor MR imaging of gray and white matter development during normal human brain maturation. *American Journal of Neuroradiology, 23,* 1445–1456.

Mulholland, A. M., & Mintz, L. B. (2001). Prevalence of eating disorders among African American women. *Journal of Counseling Psychology, 48,* 111–116.

Müller, U., Overton, W. F., & Reene, K. (2001). Development of conditional reasoning: A longitudinal study. *Journal of Cognition and Development, 2,* 27–49.

Mullet, E., & Girard, M. (2000). Developmental and cognitive points of view on forgiveness. In M. E. McCullough, K. I. Pargament, & C. E. Thoresen (Eds.), *Forgiveness: Theory, research, and practice* (pp. 111–132). New York: Guilford Press.

Mullis, R. L. & Chapman, P. (2000). Age, gender, and self-esteem differences in adolescent coping styles. *Journal of Social Psychology, 140,* 539–541.

Munroe, R. (1955). *Schools of psychoanalytic thought.* New York: Dryden Press.

Munson, M. L., & Sutton, P. D. (2005). Births, marriages, divorces, and deaths: Provisional data for 2004. *National Vital Statistics Reports,* vol *53* no 21. Hyattsville, MD: National Center for Health Statistics.

Muntner, P., He, J., Cutler, J. A., Wildman, R. P., & Whelton, P. K. (2004). Trends in blood pressure among children and adolescents. *JAMA: Journal of the American Medical Association, 291,* 2107–2113.

Murdock, T. B., Miller, A., & Kohlhardt, J. (2004). Effects of classroom context variables on high school students' judgments of the acceptability and likelihood of cheating. *Journal of Education Psychology, 96,* 765–777.

Muuss, R. E. (1975). Adolescent development and the secular trend. In R. E. Muuss (Ed.), *Adolescent behavior and society: A book of readings.* New York: Random House.

Muuss, R. E. (1990). *Adolescent behavior and society* (4th ed.). New York: Random House.

Nadeem, E., Whaley, S. E., & Anthony, S. (2006). Characterizing low-income Latina adolescent mothers: Living arrangements, psychological adjustment, and use of services. *Journal of Adolescent Health, 38,* 68–71.

Nansel, T. R., Overpeck, M., Pilla, R. S., Ruan, W. J., Simons-Morton, B., & Scheidt, P. (2001). Bullying behaviors among U.S. youth: Prevalence and association with psychosocial adjustment. *Journal of the American Medical Association, 285,* 2094–2100.

National Assembly of Health and Human Service Organizations. (1999). *Runaway and homeless youth.* Retrieved January 6, 2000, from http://www.nassembly.org/html/runhome.html

National Center for Children in Poverty. (2003). *Low-income children in the United States.* Available at http://www.nccp.org/pub_cpf04.html

National Center for Education Statistics. (1995). *The condition of education, 1995.* Washington, DC: U.S. Department of Education.

National Center for Education Statistics. (2003). *Condition of education 2003.* Washington, DC: U.S. Department of Education.

National Center for Health Statistics. (2004). *Health, United States, 2004 with chartbook on trends in the health of Americans.* Hyattsville, MD: U.S. Department of Education.

National Clearinghouse on Child Abuse and Neglect Information. (2005). Washington, DC: U.S. Department of Health and Human Services. Available at http://nccanch.acf.hhs.gov/topics/prevention

National Institute of Allergy and Infectious Diseases. (2005). *HIV infection in adolescents and young adults in the U.S.* Available at http://www.niaid.nih.gov/factsheets/hisadolescent.htm

National Runaway Switchboard. (2004). http://www.nrscrisisline.org

National School Safety Center. (1998). *Total school-associated violent death count: July 1992 to Present.* Updated June 18, 1998. Retrieved from http://www.nccsl.org

Needle, R. H., Su, S. S., & Doherty, W. J. (1990). Divorce, remarriage, and adolescent substance use: A prospective longitudinal study. *Journal of Marriage and the Family, 52,* 157–169.

Neisser, U. (1967). *Cognitive psychology.* New York: Appleton-Century-Crofts.

Neisser, U. (1976). *Cognition and reality.* San Francisco: Freeman.

Neisser, U., Boodoo, G., Bouchard, T. J., Jr., Boykin, A. W., Brody, N., Ceci, S. J., et al. (1996). Intelligence: Knowns and unknowns. *American Psychologist, 51,* 77–101.

Nelson, L. J., and Barry, C. M. (2005). Distinguishing features of emerging adulthood: The role of self-classification as an adult. *Journal of Adolescent Research, 20,* 242–262.

Nelson, M. R. (1988). Issues of access to knowledge: Dropping out of school. In L. N. Tanner (Ed.), *Critical issues in curriculum, 87th yearbook of the National Society for the Study of Education.* Chicago: University of Chicago Press.

Newman, B. M., & Newman, P. R. (2001). Group identity and alienation: Giving the We its due. *Journal of Youth and Adolescence, 30,* 515–538.

Newman, D. L. (2005). Ego development and ethnic identity formation in rural American Indian adolescents. *Child Development, 76,* 734–746.

Newman, J. (1985). Adolescents: Why they can be so obnoxious. *Adolescence, 20,* 635–645.

Nitz, K., Ketterlinus, R. D., & Brandt, L. J. (1995). The role of stress, social support, and family environment in adolescent mothers' parenting. *Journal of Adolescent Research, 10,* 358–382.

Nolin, M. J., & Petersen, K. K. (1992). Gender differences in parent–child communication about sexuality. *Journal of Adolescent Research, 7,* 59–79.

Noom, M. J., Dekovic, M., & Meeus, W. (2001). Conceptual analysis and measurement of adolescent autonomy. *Journal of Youth and Adolescence, 30,* 577–595.

Norton, E. M., Durlak, J. A., & Richards, M. H. (1989). Peer knowledge of and reactions to adolescent suicide. *Journal of Youth and Adolescence, 18,* 427–437.

Nosek, B. A., Banaji, M. R., & Greenwald, A. G. (2002). Math = male, me = female, therefore math ≠ me. *Journal of Personality and Social Psychology, 83,* 44–49.

Nucci, L., Camino, C., & Sapiro, C. M. (1996). Social class effects on northeastern Brazilian children's conceptions of areas of personal choice and social regulation. *Child Development, 67,* 1223–1242.

Nye, B., Hedges, L. V., & Konstantopoulos, S. (2001). The long-term effects of small classes in early grades: Lasting benefits in mathematics achievement at grade 9. *Journal of Experimental Education, 69,* 245–257.

O'Brien, S. F., & Bierman, K. L. (1988). Conceptions and perceived influence of peer groups: Interviews with preadolescents and adolescents. *Child Development, 59,* 1360–1365.

O'Donnell, L., Stueve, A., O'Donnell, C., Duran, R., San Doval, A., Wilson, R. F., et al. (2002). Long-term reductions in sexual initiation and sexual activity among urban middle schoolers in the Reach for Health service learning program. *Journal of Adolescent Health, 31,* 93–100.

O'Donnell, L., Stueve, A., San Doval, A., Duran, R., Haber, D., Atnafou, R., et al. (1999). The effectiveness of the Reach for Health community youth service learning program in reducing early and unprotected sex among urban middle school students. *American Journal of Public Health, 89,* 176–181.

Offer, D., Ostrov, E., & Howard, K. I. (1981). *The adolescent.* New York: Basic Books.

Office of Juvenile Justice and Delinquency Prevention. (2002). *Statistical briefing book.* Retrieved from http://ojjdp.ncirs.org/ojstatbb/corrections/qa08203.asp?qaDate=20021030

Office of National Drug Control Policy. (2005). *Media campaign: New report shows that teens who receive anti-drug messages are less likely to use drugs.* Available at http://www.mediacampaign.org/newsroom/press05/072905.html

Office of the Surgeon General. (2001). *The Surgeon General's call to action to promote sexual health and responsible sexual behavior.* Rockville, MD: Author.

Ogbu, J. U. (1981). Black education: A cultural-ecological perspective. In H. P. McAdoo (Ed.), *Black families.* Beverly Hills: Sage.

Ogbu, J. U. (1992). Understanding cultural diversity and learning. *Educational Researcher, 21,* 5–14.

Okun, M. A., & Sasfy, J. H. (1977). Adolescence, the self-image and formal operations. *Adolescence, 12,* 373–379.

Olweus, D. (1978). *Aggression in the schools: Bullies and whipping boys.* Washington, DC: Hemisphere Press (Wiley).

Olweus, D. (1993). *Bullying at school: What we know and what we can do*. Cambridge, MA: Blackwell.

Olweus, D. (1999). Norway. In P. K. Smith, Y. Morita, J. Junger-Tas, D. Olweus, R. Catalano, & P. Slee (Eds.), *The nature of school bullying: A cross-national perspective* (pp. 28–48). New York: Routledge.

Olweus, D. (2001). Peer harassment: A critical analysis and some important issues. In J. Juvonen & S. Graham (Eds.), *Peer harassment in school: The plight of the vulnerable and victimized* (pp. 3–20). New York: Guilford Press.

Oman, R. F., Vesely, S., Aspy, C. B., McLeroy, K. R., Rodine, S., & Marshall, L. (2004). The potential protective effect of youth assets on adolescent alcohol and drug use. *American Journal of Public Health, 94,* 1425–1430.

Orlofsky, J., & Frank, M. (1986). Personality structure as viewed through early memories and identity status in college men and women. *Journal of Personality and Social Psychology, 5,* 580–586.

Orlofsky, J., Marcia, J. E., & Lesser, I. M. (1973). Ego identity status and the intimacy versus isolation crisis of young adulthood. *Journal of Youth and Adolescence, 27,* 211–219.

Osherson, D. N., & Markman, E. M. (1975). Language and the ability to evaluate contradictions and tautologies. *Cognition, 3,* 213–226.

Osipow, S. H. (1983). *Theories of career development* (3rd ed.). Englewood Cliffs, NJ: Prentice-Hall.

Owings, J., & Stocking, C. (1985). *High school and beyond: Characteristics of high school students who identify themselves as handicapped.* Washington, DC: National Center for Education Statistics, U.S. Department of Education.

Oxford, M. L., Gilchrist, L. D., Lohr, M. J., Gillmore, M. R., Morrison, D. M., & Spieker, S. J. (2005). Life course heterogeneity in the transition from adolescence to adulthood among adolescent mothers. *Journal of Research on Adolescence, 15,* 479–504.

Ozawa, M. N. (2004). Social welfare spending on family benefits in the United States and Sweden: A comparative study. *Family Relations, 53,* 301–309.

Ozer, E. J., & Weinstein, R. S. (2004). Urban adolescents' exposure to community violence: The role of support, school safety, and social constraints in a school-based sample of boys and girls. *Journal of Clinical Child and Adolescent Psychology, 33,* 463–476.

Pakaslahti, L., Karjalainen, A., & Keltikangas-Jarvinen, L. (2002). Relationships between adolescent prosocial problem-solving strategies, prosocial behaviour, and social acceptance. (2002). *International Journal of Behavioral Development, 26,* 137–144.

Palinscar, A. S., & Brown, A. L. (1984). Reciprocal teaching of comprehension-monitoring activities. *Cognition and Instruction, 1,* 117–175.

Panel on High-Risk Youth. Commission on Behavioral and Social Sciences and Education, National Research Council. (1993). *Losing generations: Adolescents in high-risk settings.* Washington, DC: National Academy Press.

Papini, D. R., Farmer, F. L., Clark, S. M., & Snell, W. E., Jr. (1988). An evaluation of adolescent patterns of sexual self-disclosure to parents and friends. *Journal of Adolescent Research, 3,* 387–401.

Papini, D. R., Snell, W. E., Belk, S. S., & Clark, S. (1988, April). *Developmental correlates of women's and men's sexual self-disclosures.* Paper presented at the meeting of the Southwestern Psychological Association, Tulsa, OK.

Parker, J. G., & Gottman, J. M. (1989). Social and emotional development in a relational context. In T. J. Berndt & G. W. Ladd (Eds.), *Peer relationships in child development.* New York: Wiley.

Parker, S., Nichter, M., Nichter, N., Vuckovic, N., Sims, C., & Ritenbaugh, C. (1995). Body image and weight concern among Afro American and White adolescent females: Differences that make a difference. *Human Organization, 54,* 103–115.

Pasley, B. K., & Ihenger-Tallman, M. (1989). Boundary ambiguity in remarriage: Does ambiguity differentiate degree of marital adjustment and integration? *Family Relations, 38,* 46–52.

Paterson, J. E., Field, J., & Pryor, J. (1994). Adolescents' perceptions of their attachment relationships with their mothers, fathers, and friends. *Journal of Youth and Adolescence, 23,* 579–600.

Patrikakou, E. N. (1996). Investigating the academic achievement of adolescents with learning disabilities: A structural modeling approach. *Journal of Educational Psychology, 88,* 435–450.

Patterson, S. J., Sochting, I., & Marcia, J. E. (1992). The inner space and beyond: Women and identity. In G. R. Adams, T. P. Gullotta, & R. Montemayor (Eds.), *Adolescent identity formation.* Newbury Park, CA: Sage.

Paus, T., Zijdenbos, A., Worsley, K., Collins, D. L., Blumenthal, J., Giedd, J. N., Rapoport, J. L., & Evans, A. C. (1999). Structural maturation of neural pathways in children and adolescents: In vivo study. *Science, 283,* 1908–1911.

Pearl, R., Bryan, T., & Herzog, A. (1990). Resisting or acquiescing to peer pressure to engage in misconduct: Adolescents' expectations of probable consequences. *Journal of Youth and Adolescence, 19,* 43–55.

Pellegrini, A. D., & Long, J. D. (2002). A longitudinal study of bullying, dominance, and victimization during the transition from primary school through secondary school. *British Journal of Developmental Psychology, 20,* 259–280.

Perkins, D. N. (1987). Knowledge as design: Teaching thinking through content. In J. B. Baron & R. J. Sternberg (Eds.), *Teaching thinking skills: Theory and practice.* New York: Freeman.

Perry, C. L., Komro, K. A., Veblen-Mortenson, S., Bosma, L. M., Farbakhsh, K., Munson, K. A., Stigler, M. H., & Lytle, L. A. (2003). A randomized controlled trial of the middle and junior high school D.A.R.E. and D.A.R.E. Plus programs. *Archives of Pediatrics and Adolescent Medicine, 157,* 178–184.

Perry, W. G. (1970). *Forms of intellectual and ethical development in the college years.* San Francisco: Holt, Rinehart & Winston.

Petersen, A. C., Compas, B. E., Brooks-Gunn, J., Stemmler, M., Ey, S., & Grant, K. (1993). Depression in adolescence. *American Psychologist, 48,* 155–168.

Pettit, G. S., Bates, J. E., Dodge, K. A., & Meece, D. W. (1999). The impact of after-school peer contact on early adolescent externalizing problems is moderated by parental monitoring, perceived neighborhood safety, and prior adjustment. *Child Development, 70,* 768–778.

Pew Internet and American Life Project. (2001). Available at http://www.pewinternet.org

Phelps, L., Johnston, S. S., Jimenez, D. P., Wilczenski, F. L., Andrea, R. K., & Healy, R. W. (1993). Figure preference, body dissatisfaction, and body distortion in adolescence. *Journal of Adolescent Research, 8,* 297–310.

Phelps, S. B., & Jarvis, P. A. (1994). Coping in adolescence: Empirical evidence for a theoretically based approach to assessing coping. *Journal of Youth and Adolescence, 23,* 359–371.

Philliber, S., Kaye, J., & Herrling, S. (2001). *The national evaluation of the Children's Aid Society Carrera-Model Program to prevent teen pregnancy.* Retrieved from the Children's Aid Society Web site: http://www.childrensaidsociety.org/media/general/cas-full_12-site_report1.pdf

Phinney, J. (1989). Stages of ethnic identity development in minority group adolescents. *Journal of Early Adolescence, 9,* 34–49.

Phinney, J. (1990). Ethnic identity in adolescents and adults: Review of research. *Psychological Bulletin, 108,* 499–514.

Phinney, J. (1993). A three-stage model of ethnic identity development. In M. Bernal & G. Knight (Eds.), *Ethnic identity: Formation and transmission among Hispanics and other minorities* (pp. 61–79). Albany: State University of New York Press.

Phinney, J. (1996). When we talk about American ethnic groups, what do we mean? *American Psychologist, 51,* 918–927.

Phinney, J. S. (2005). Ethnic identity in late modern times: A response to Rattansi and Phoenix. *Identity, 5,* 187–194.

Phinney, J. S., Baumann, K., & Blanton, S. (2001). Life goals and attributions for expected outcomes among adolescents from five ethnic groups. *Hispanic Journal of Behavioral Sciences, 23,* 363–377.

Phinney, J. S., Cantu, C. L., & Kurtz, D. A. (1997). Ethnic and American identity as predictors of self-esteem among African-American, Latino, and White adolescents. *Journal of Youth and Adolescence, 26,* 165–185.

Phinney, J. S., & Cobb, N. J. (1996). Reasoning about intergroup relations among Hispanic and Euro-American adolescents. *Journal of Adolescent Research, 11,* 306–324.

Phinney, J. S., & Devich-Navarro, M. (1997). Variations in bicultural identification among African American and Mexican American adolescents. *Journal of Research on Adolescence, 7,* 3–32.

Phinney, J. S., Ferguson, D. L., & Tate, J. D. (1997). Intergroup attitudes among ethnic adolescents: A causal model. *Child Development, 68,* 955–969.

Phinney, J. S., & Haas, K. (2003). The process of coping among ethnic minority first-generation college freshmen: A narrative approach. *Journal of Social Psychology, 143,* 707–726.

Phinney, J. S., Kim-Jo, T., Osorio, S., & Vilhjalmsdottir, P. (2005). Autonomy and relatedness in adolescent–parent disagreements: Ethnic and developmental factors. *Journal of Adolescent Research, 20,* 8–39.

Phinney, J., & Kohatsu, E. (1997). Ethnic and racial identity and mental health. In J. Schulenberg, J. Maggs, & K. Hurrelmann (Eds.), *Health risks and developmental transitions during adolescence.* New York: Cambridge University Press.

Phinney, J. S., Ong, A., & Madden, T. (2000). Cultural values and intergenerational value discrepancies in immigrant and non-immigrant families. *Child Development, 71,* 528–539.

Phinney, J., & Rosenthal, D. A. (1992). Ethnic identity in adolescence: Process, context, and outcome. In G. Adams, R. Montemayor, & T. Gulotta (Eds.), *Advances in adolescent development* (Vol. 4). Newbury Park, CA: Sage.

Phinney, J. S., & Rotheram, M. J. (1987). Children's ethnic socialization: Themes and implications. In M. J. Rotheram & J. S. Phinney (Eds.), *Children's ethnic socialization: Pluralism and development.* Beverly Hills: Sage.

Phinney, J., & Tarver, S. (1988). Ethnic identity search and commitment in black and white eighth graders. *Journal of Early Adolescence, 8,* 265–277.

Piaget, J. (1952a). *The child's conception of number.* New York: Humanities Press.

Piaget, J. (1952b). *The origins of intelligence in children.* New York: International Universities Press.

Piaget, J. (1954). *The construction of reality in the child.* New York: Basic Books.

Piaget, J. (1965). *The moral judgment of the child.* New York: Free Press.

Piaget, J. (1971). *Biology and knowledge.* Chicago: University of Chicago Press.

Pikas, A. (2002). New developments of the Shared Concern Model. *School Psychology International, 23,* 307–326.

Pinquart, M., & Silbereisen, R. K. (2002). Changes in adolescents' and mothers' autonomy and connectedness in conflict discussions: An observational study. *Journal of Adolescence, 25,* 509–522.

Pinquart, M., Silbereisen, R. K., & Wiesner, M. (2004). Changes in discrepancies between desired and present states of developmental tasks in adolescence: A 4-process model. *Journal of Youth and Adolescence, 33,* 467–477.

Place, D. M. (1975). The dating experience for adolescent girls. *Adolescence, 10,* 157–174.

Plomin, R., & Daniels, D. (1987). Why are children in the same family so different from one another? *Behavioral and Brain Sciences, 10,* 1–60.

Plomin, R., Reiss, D., Hetherington, E. M., & Howe, G. W. (1994). Nature and nurture: Genetic contributions to measures of the family environment. *Developmental Psychology, 30,* 32–43.

Polivy, J., & Herman, C. P. (2002). Causes of eating disorders. *Annual Review of Psychology, 53,* 187–213.

Pollack, S., & Gilligan, C. (1982). Images of violence in Thematic Apperception Test stories. *Journal of Personality and Social Psychology, 42,* 159–167.

Poole, M. E., & Evans, G. T. (1988). Adolescents' self-perceptions of competence in life skill areas. *Journal of Youth and Adolescence, 18,* 147–173.

Postman, N. (1982). *The disappearance of childhood.* New York: Delacorte.

Powell, G. J. (1985). Self-concepts among Afro-American students in racially isolated minority schools: Some regional differences. *Journal of the American Academy of Child Psychiatry, 24,* 142–149.

Powers, S. I., Hauser, S. T., Schwartz, J. M., Noam, G. G., & Jacobson, A. M. (1983). Adolescent ego development and family interaction: A structural-developmental perspective. In H. D. Grotevant & C. R. Cooper (Eds.), *Adolescent development in the family.* San Francisco: Jossey-Bass.

Pratt, M. W., Arnold, M. L., Pratt, A. T., & Diessner, R. (1999). Predicting adolescent moral reasoning from family climate: A longitudinal study. *Journal of Early Adolescence, 19,* 148–175.

Pratt, M. W., Hunsberger, B., Pancer, S. M., & Alisat, S. (2003). A longitudinal analysis of personal values socialization: Correlates of a moral self-ideal in late adolescence. *Social Development, 12,* 563–585.

Pratt, M. W., Norris, J. E., van de Hoef, S., & Arnold, M. L. (2001). Stories of hope: Parental optimism in narratives about adolescent children. *Journal of Social and Personal Relationships, 18,* 603–623.

Project Toward No Drug Abuse. Available at http://modelprograms.samhas.gov/pdfs/FactSheets/ProjectTND.pdf

Pulkkinen, L., & Kokko, K. (2000). Identity development in adulthood: A longitudinal study. *Journal of Research in Personality, 34,* 445–470.

Purcell, P., & Stewart, L. (1990). Dick and Jane in 1989. *Sex Roles, 22,* 177–185.

Putallaz, M. (1983). Predicting children's sociometric status from their behavior. *Child Development, 54,* 1417–1426.

Quatman, T., Sokolik, E., & Smith, K. (2000). Adolescent perception of peer success: A gendered perspective over time. *Sex Roles, 43,* 61–84.

Quatman, T., & Watson, C. M. (2001). Gender differences in adolescent self-esteem: An exploration of domains. *Journal of Genetic Psychology, 162,* 93–117.

Quinlivan, J. A., Box, H., & Evans, S. F. (2003). Postnatal home visits in teenage mothers: A randomised controlled trial. *The Lancet, 361,* 893–900.

Quinlivan, J. A., Luehr, B., & Evans, S. F. (2004). Teenage mothers' predictions of their support levels before and actual support levels after having a child. *Journal of Pediatric Adolescent Gynecology, 17,* 273–278.

Raja, S. N., McGee, R., & Stanton, W. R. (1992). Perceived attachments to parents and peers and psychological well-being in adolescence. *Journal of Youth and Adolescence, 21,* 471–485.

Rakic, P. (1995). Corticogenesis in human and nonhuman primates. In M. S. Gazzaniga (Ed.), *The cognitive neurosciences* (pp. 127–145). Cambridge, MA: MIT Press.

Ramirez, O. (1989). Mexican American children and adolescents. In J. T. Gibbs, L. N. Huang, & Associates (Eds.), *Children of color.* San Francisco: Jossey-Bass.

Raudenbush, S. W., Rowan, B., & Cheong, Y. F. (1993). Higher order instructional goals in secondary schools: Class, teacher, and school influences. *American Educational Research Journal, 30,* 523–553.

Reese, H. W., & Overton, W. F. (1970). Models of development and theories of development. In L. R. Goulet & P. B. Baltes (Eds.), *Life-span developmental psychology: Research and theory.* New York: Academic Press.

Regan, P. C., & Berscheid, E. (1995). Gender differences in beliefs about the causes of male and female sexual desire. *Personal Relationships, 2,* 345–358.

Regnerus, M. D., & Elder, G. H., Jr. (2003). Staying on track in school: Religious influences in high- and low-risk settings. *Journal for the Scientific Study of Religion, 42,* 633–649.

Reid, M., Landesman, S., Treder, R., & Jaccard, J. (1989). "My family and friends": Six- to twelve-year-old children's perceptions of social support. *Child Development, 60,* 896–910.

Rembeck, G. I., & Gunnarsson, R. K. (2004). Improving pre- and post-menarcheal 12-year-old girls' attitudes toward menstruation. *Health Care for Women International, 25,* 680–698.

Renk, K., & Creasey, G. (2003). The relationship of gender, gender identity and coping strategies in late adolescence, *Journal of Adolescence, 26,* 159–168.

Repetti, R. L. (1994). Short-term and long-term processes linking job stressors to father–child interaction. *Social Development, 3,* 1–15.

Repetti, R. L., Taylor, S. E., & Seeman, T. E. (2002). Risky families: Family social environments and the mental and physical health of offspring. *Psychological Bulletin, 128,* 330–366.

Resnick, M., Harris, L., & Blum, R. (1993). The impact of caring and connectedness on adolescent health and well-being. *Journal of Pediatrics and Child Health, 29,* (Suppl. 1), 3–9.

Restak, R. (1984, November). Master clock of the brain and body. *Science Digest,* pp. 54–104.

Reyes, O., & Jason, L. A. (1993). Pilot study examining factors associated with academic success for Hispanic high school students. *Journal of Youth and Adolescence, 22,* 57–71.

Reynolds, A. J., Ou, S., & Topitzes, J. W. (2004). Paths of effects of early childhood intervention on educational attainment and delinquency: A confirmatory analysis of the Chicago Child–Parent Centers. *Child Development, 75,* 1299–1328.

Reynolds, A. J., & Temple, J. A. (1998). Extended early childhood intervention and school achievement: Age thirteen findings from the Chicago Longitudinal Study. *Child Development, 69,* 231–246.

Reynolds, A. J., Temple, J. A., Robertson, D. L., & Mann, E. A. (2001). Long-term effects of an early childhood intervention on educational achievement and juvenile arrest: A 15-year follow-up of low-income children in public schools. *Journal of the American Medical Association, 285,* 2339–2346.

Rice, K. G., & Mulkeen, P. (1995). Relationships with parents and peers: A longitudinal study of adolescent intimacy. *Journal of Adolescent Research, 10,* 338–357.

Richards, M. H., Miller, B. V., O'Donnell, P. C., Wasserman, M. S., & Colder, C. (2004). Parental monitoring mediates the effects of age and sex on problem behaviors among African American urban young adolescents. *Journal of Youth and Adolescence, 33,* 221–233.

Rideout, V. (2001). *Generation Rx.com: How young people use the Internet for health information.* Menlo Park, CA: Kaiser Family Foundation.

Riegel, K. F. (1973). *Dialectic operations: The final period of cognitive development.* Princeton, NJ: Educational Testing Service.

Rigby, K. (2001). Health consequences of bullying and its prevention in schools. In J. Juvonen & S. Graham (Eds.), *Peer harassment in school: The plight of the vulnerable and victimized* (pp. 310–331). New York: Guilford Press.

Rogoff, B. (1990). *Apprenticeship in thinking: Cognitive development in social context.* New York: Oxford University Press.

Rogoff, B. (2003). *The cultural nature of human development.* New York: Oxford University Press.

Rogoff, B., Baker-Sennett, J., Lacasa, P., & Goldsmith, D. (1995). Development through participation in sociocultural activity. *New Directions for Child Development, 67,* 45–65.

Roisman, G. I. Masten, J. S., Coatsworth, J. D., and Tellegen, A. (2004). Salient and emerging developmental tasks in the transition to adulthood. *Child Development, 75,* 123–133.

Romero, A. J. (2005). Low-income neighborhood barriers and resources for adolescents' physical activity. *Journal of Adolescent Health, 36,* 253–259.

Ronde, K., Pizacani, B., Stark, M., Pietrukowicz, M., Mosbaek, C., Romoli, C., Kohn, M., & Moore, J. (2001). Effectiveness of school-based programs as a component of a statewide tobacco control initiative—Oregon, 1999–2000. *Morbidity and Mortality Weekly Report, 50,* 663–666.

Rose, A. J., & Asher, S. R. (2004). Children's strategies and goals in response to help-giving and help-seeking tasks within a friendship. *Child Development, 75,* 749–763.

Rose, A., Koo, H. P., Bhaskar, B., Anderson, K., White, G., & Jenkins, R. R. (2005). The influence of primary caregivers on the sexual behavior of early adolescents. *Journal of adolescent Health, 37,* 135–144.

Rose, A. J., Swenson, L. P., & Waller, E. M. (2004). Overt and relational aggression and perceived popularity: Developmental differences in concurrent and prospective relations. *Developmental Psychology, 40,* 378–387.

Rosenblum, G. D., & Lewis, M. (1999). The relations among body image, physical attractiveness, and body mass in adolescence. *Child Development, 70,* 50–64.

Rosenthal, D. A., & Feldman, S. S. (1992). The nature and stability of ethnic identity in Chinese youth: Effects of length of residence in two cultural contexts. *Journal of Cross-Cultural Psychology, 23,* 213–227.

Rosenthal, D. A., & Feldman, S. S. (1999). The importance of importance: Adolescents' perceptions of parental communication about sexuality. *Journal of Adolescence, 22,* 835–852.

Rosenthal, D. A., & Hrynevich, C. (1985). Ethnicity and ethnic identity: A comparative study of Greek-, Italian-, and Anglo-Australian adolescents. *International Journal of Psychology, 20,* 723–742.

Rosenthal, D. A., Senserrick, T., & Feldman, S. S. (2001). A typology approach to describing parents as communicators about sexuality. *Archives of Sexual Behavior, 30,* 463–482.

Rostosky, S. S., Wilcox, B. L., Wright, M. L. C., & Randall, B. A. (2004). The impact of religiosity on adolescent sexual behavior: A review of the evidence. *Journal of Adolescent Research, 19,* 677–697.

Roth, M. A., & Parker, J. G. (2001). Affective and behavioral responses to friends who neglect their friends for dating partners: Influences of gender, jealousy and perspective. *Journal of Adolescence, 24,* 281–296.

Roth, P. (1969). *Portnoy's complaint.* New York: Random House.

Rotheram, M. J., & Phinney, J. S. (1983). *Intercultural attitudes and behaviors of children.* Paper presented at the meeting of the Society for Intercultural Evaluation, Training and Research, San Germignano, Italy.

Rotheram, M. J., & Phinney, J. S. (1987). Ethnic behavior patterns as an aspect of identity. In J. Phinney & M. Rotheram (Eds.), *Children's ethnic socialization: Pluralism and development.* Beverly Hills: Sage.

Rotheram-Borus, M. J., & Phinney, J. S. (1990). Patterns of social expectations among black and Mexican-American children. *Child Development, 61,* 542–556.

Rotheram-Borus, M., Rosario, M., Van Rossem, R., Reid, H., & Gillis, R. (1995). Prevalence, course, and predictors of multiple problem behaviors among gay and bisexual male adolescents. *Developmental Psychology, 31,* 75–85.

Rotheram-Borus, M. J., Song, J., Gwadz, M., Lee, M., Van Rossem, R., & Koopman, C. (2003). Reductions in HIV risk among runaway youth. *Prevention Science, 4,* 173–187.

Rowley, A. A., Roesch, S. C., Jurica, B. J., & Vaughn, A. A. (2005). Developing and validating a stress appraisal measure for minority adolescents. *Journal of Adolescence, 28,* 547–557.

Royle, R., Barrett, M., & Buchanan-Barrow, E. (1998, July). *"Religion is the opiate of the masses" (Marx, 1876): An investigation of the salience of religion for children.* Paper presented at the XVth Biennial Meeting of the International Society for the Study of Behavioural Development, Berne, Switzerland.

Rubin, K. H., Dwyer, K. M., Booth-LaForce, C., Kim, A. H., Burgess, K. B., Rose-Krasnor, L. (2004). Attachment, friendship, and psychosocial functioning in early adolescence. *Journal of Early Adolescence, 24,* 326–356.

Ruble, D. N., & Brooks-Gunn, J. (1982). The experience of menarche. *Child Development, 53,* 1557–1566.

Ruck, M. D., Peterson-Badali, M., & Day, D. M. (2002). Adolescents' and mothers' understanding of children's rights in the home. *Journal of Research on Adolescence, 12,* 373–398.

Rudder, T. (2002). *Teen volunteerism: A model for America.* The Gallup Organization. Available at http://www.gallup.com/poll/content/default.aspx?ci=5695

Russell, S. T., & Joyner, K. (2001). Adolescent sexual orientation and suicide risk: Evidence from a national study. *American Journal of Public Health, 91,* 1276–1283.

Russo, R. G. (2006). The extent of public education nondiscrimination policy protections for lesbian, gay, bisexual, and transgender students: A national study. *Urban Education, 41,* 115–150.

Ryan, J. M., Tracey, T. J. G., & Rounds, J. (1996). Generalizability of Holland's structure of vocational interests across ethnicity, gender, and socioeconomic status. *Journal of Counseling Psychology, 43,* 330–337.

Ryan, K. E., & Ryan, A. M. (2005). Psychological processes underlying stereotype threat and standardized math test performance. *Educational Psychologist, 40,* 53–63.

Salmivalli, C. (2001). Group view on victimization: Empirical findings and their implications. In J. Juvonen & S. Graham (Eds.), *Peer harassment in school: The plight of the vulnerable and victimized* (pp. 398–419). New York: Guilford Press.

Sanders, G., Sjodin, M., & de Chastelaine, M. (2002). On the elusive nature of sex differences in cognition: Hormonal influences contributing to within-sex variation. *Archives of Sexual Behavior, 31,* 145–152.

Santelli, J. S., Nystrom, R. J., Brindis, C., Juszczak, L., Klein, J. D., Bearss, N., Kaplan, D. W., Hudson, M., & Schlitt, J. (2003). Reproductive health in school-based health centers: Findings from the 1998–99 census of school-based health centers. *Journal of Adolescent Health, 32,* 443–451.

Satter, E. (1988). Should the obese child diet? In K. Clark, R. Parr, & W. Castelli (Eds.), *Evaluation and management of eating disorders.* Champaign, IL: Life Enhancement Publications.

Scaramella, L. V., Conger, R. D., Spoth, R., & Simons, R. L. (2002). Evaluation of a social contextual model of delinquency: A cross-study replication. *Child Development, 73,* 175–195.

Scarr, S. (1992). Developmental theories for the 1990s: Development and individual differences. *Child Development, 63,* 1–19.

Scarr, S. (1993). Biological and cultural diversity: The legacy of Darwin for development. *Child Development, 64,* 1333–1353.

Schaie, K. W. (1965). A general model for the study of development problems. *Psychological Bulletin, 64,* 92–107.

Schiedel, D. G., & Marcia, J. E. (1985). Ego identity, intimacy, sex role orientation, and gender. *Developmental Psychology, 21,* 149–160.

Schonert-Reichl, K. A. (1999). Relations of peer acceptance, friendship adjustment, and social behavior to moral reasoning during early adolescence. *Journal of Early Adolescence, 19,* 249–279.

Schoon, I., Parsons, S., & Sacker, A. (2004). Socioeconomic adversity, educational resilience, and subsequent levels of adult adaptation. *Journal of Adolescent Research, 19,* 383–404.

Schreiber, J. B. (2002). Institutional and student factors and their influence on advanced mathematics achievement. *Journal of Educational Research, 95,* 247–255.

Schultz, P. W., Gouveia, V. V., Cameron, L. D., Tankha, G., Schmuck, P., & Franek, M. (2005). Values and their relationship to environmental concern and conservation behavior. *Journal of Cross-Cultural Psychology, 36,* 457–475.

Schwartz, S. J., & Montgomery, M. J. (2002). Similarities or differences in identity development? The impact of acculturation and gender on identity process and outcome. *Journal of Youth and Adolescence, 31,* 359–372.

Schwartz, S. J., Mullis, R. L., Waterman, A. S., & Dunham, R. M. (2000). Ego identity status, identity style, and personal expressiveness: An empirical investigation of three convergent constructs. *Journal of Adolescent Research, 15,* 504–521.

Schwartzberg, N. S., & Dytell, R. S. (1996). Dual-earner families: The importance of work stress and family stress for psychological well-being. *Journal of Occupational Health Psychology, 1,* 211–223.

Schweder, R. A., Mahapatra, M., & Miller, J. (1987). Culture and development. In J. Kagan (Ed.), *The emergence of moral concepts in young children.* Chicago: University of Chicago Press.

Sedikides, C., Gaertner, L., Vevea, J. L. (2005). Pancultural self-enhancement reloaded: A meta-analytic reply to Heine (2005). *Journal of Personality and Social Psychology, 89,* 539–551.

Seginer, R. (1998). Adolescents' perceptions of relationships with older siblings in the context of other close relationships. *Journal of Research on Adolescence, 8,* 287–308.

Seiber, J. E. (1980). A social learning approach to morality. In M. Windmiller, N. Lambert, & E. Turiel (Eds.), *Moral development and socialization.* Boston: Allyn & Bacon.

Seligman, M. E. P., & Csikszentmihalyi, M. (2000). Positive psychology: An introduction. *American Psychologist, 55,* 5–14.

Selman, R. L. (1980). *The growth of interpersonal understanding.* New York: Academic Press.

Selye, H. (1982). Stress: Eustress, distress, and human perspectives. In S. B. Day (Ed.), *Life stress* (Vol. 3). New York: Van Nostrand Reinhold.

Sessa, F. M., & Steinberg, L. (1991). Family structure and the development of autonomy during adolescence. *Journal of Early Adolescence, 11,* 38–55.

Shafii, M., Carrigan, S., Whittinghill, J. R., & Derrick, A. (1985). Psychological autopsy of completed suicide in children and adolescents. *American Journal of Psychiatry, 142,* 1061–1064.

Shalitin, S., & Phillip, M. (2003). The role of obesity and leptin in the pubertal process and pubertal growth—a review. *International Journal of Obesity and Related Metabolic Disorders, 27,* 869–874.

Shedler, J., & Block, J. (1990). Adolescent drug use and psychological health: A longitudinal inquiry. *American Psychologist, 45,* 612–630.

Sheley, J. F., Zhang, J., Brody, C. J., & Wright, J. D. (1995). Gang organization, gang criminal activity, and individual gang members' criminal behavior. *Social Science Quarterly, 76,* 53–69.

Shifflett-Simpson, K., & Cummings, E. M. (1996). Mixed message resolution and children's responses to interadult conflict. *Child Development, 67,* 437–448.

Sickmond, M. (2004). Juveniles in corrections. *National Report Series Bulletin.* Retrieved from Office of Juvenile Justice and Delinquency Prevention, U.S. Department of Justice Web site: http://www.ojp.usdoj.gov/ojjdp

SIECUS. (2001). *Toward a sexually healthy America.* Washington, DC. Author.

Siegler, R. S., & Alibali, M. W. (2004). *Children's thinking* (4th ed.). Upper Saddle River, NJ: Prentice-Hall.

Siewert, E. A., Stallings, M. C., & Hewitt, J. K. (2003). Genetic and environmental analysis of behavioral risk factors for adolescent drug use in a community twin sample. *Twin Research, 6,* 490–496.

Silverberg, S. B., & Steinberg, L. (1990). Psychological well-being of parents with early adolescent children. *Developmental Psychology, 26,* 658–666.

Silverman, I. W. (2003). Gender differences in resistance to temptation: Theories and evidence. *Developmental Review, 23,* 219–259.

Silverstein, B., Perdue, L., Peterson, B., & Kelly, E. (1986). The role of the mass media in promoting a thin standard of bodily attractiveness for women. *Sex Roles, 14,* 519–532.

Simmons, R. G., & Blyth, D. A. (1987). *Moving into adolescence.* New York: Aldine de Gruyter.

Simpson, G. E., & Yinger, J. M. (1985). *Racial and cultural minorities* (5th ed.). New York: Plenum Press.

Sionean, C., DiClemente, R. J., Wingood, G. M., Crosby, R., Cobb, B. K., Harrington, K., et al. (2002). Psychosocial and behavioral correlates of refusing unwanted sex among African-American adolescent females. *Journal of Adolescent Health, 30,* 55–63.

Skal, P., Ireland, M., & Borowsky, I. W. (2003). Smoking among American adolescents: A risk and protective factor analysis. *Journal of Community Health, 28,* 79–97.

Skinner, B. F. (1938). *The behavior of organisms: An experimental analysis.* New York: Appleton-Century-Crofts.

Skinner, B. F. (1953). *Science and human behavior.* New York: Macmillan.

Skinner, B. F. (1961). *Cumulative record* (rev. ed.). New York: Appleton-Century-Crofts.

Skoe, E. E., Cumberland, A., Eisenberg, N., Hansen, K., & Perry, J. (2002a). The influences of sex and gender-role identity on moral cognition and prosocial personality traits. *Sex Roles, 46,* 295–309.

Skoe, E. E., Eisenberg, N., & Cumberland, A. (2002b). The role of reported emotion in real-life and hypothetical moral dilemmas. *Personality and Social Psychology Bulletin, 28,* 962–973.

Slaughter-Defoe, D. T., Nakagawa, K., Takanishi, R., & Johnson, D. J. (1990). Toward cultural/ecological perspectives on schooling and achievement in African- and Asian-American children. *Child Development, 61,* 363–383.

Slavin, R. E. (1985). Cooperative learning: Applying contact theory in desegregated schools. *Journal of Social Issues, 41,* 45–62.

Slavin, R. E., Hurley, E. A., & Chamberlin, A. (2003). Cooperative learning and achievement: Theory and research. In W. M. Reynolds & G. E. Miller (Eds.) *Handbook of psychology* (Vol. 7, pp. 177–198). New York: Wiley.

Slicker, E. K. (1998). Relationship of parenting style to behavioral adjustment in graduating high school seniors. *Journal of Youth and Adolescence, 27,* 345–372.

Sloan, J., Kellermann, A., Reay, D., Ferris, J., Koepsell, T., Rivara, F., Rice, C., Gray, L., & LoGerfo, J. (1988). Handgun regulation, crime, assaults, and homicides. *New England Journal of Medicine, 319,* 1256–1262.

Smetana, J. (1988). Concepts of self and social convention: Adolescents' and parents' reasoning about hypothetical and actual family conflicts. In M. R. Gunnar (Ed.), *21st Minnesota Symposium on Child Psychology.* Hillsdale, NJ: Erlbaum.

Smetana, J. G. (2000). Middle-class African American adolescents' and parents' conceptions of parental authority and parenting practices: A longitudinal investigation. *Child Development, 71,* 1672–1686.

Smetana, J. G., & Asquith, P. (1994). Adolescents' and parents' conceptions of parental authority and personal autonomy. *Child Development, 65,* 1147–1162.

Smetana, J. G., & Berent, R. (1993). Adolescents' and mothers' evaluations of justifications for disputes. *Journal of Adolescent Research, 8,* 252–273.

Smetana, J. G., Braeges, J. L., & Yau, J. (1991). Doing what you say and saying what you do: Reasoning about adolescent–parent conflict in interviews and interactions. *Journal of Adolescent Research, 6,* 276–295.

Smetana, J. G., Campione-Barr, N., & Daddis, C. (2004). Longitudinal development of family decision making: Defining healthy behavioral autonomy for middle-class African American adolescents. *Child Development, 75,* 1418–1434.

Smith, A. (2000). The inter-ethnic friendships of adolescent students: A Canadian study. *International Journal of Intercultural Relations, 24,* 247–258.

Smith, C., Denton, M. L., Faris, R., & Regnerus, M. (2002). Mapping American adolescent religious participation. *Journal for the Scientific Study of Religion, 41,* 597–612.

Smith, M. K. (2000, 2004). *"Full-service schooling," the encyclopedia of informal education.* Retrieved from http://www.infed.org/schooling/f-serv.htm. Last update: January 30, 2005.

Smith, T. E. (1990). Parental separation and the academic self-concepts of adolescents: An effort to solve the puzzle of separation effects. *Journal of Marriage and the Family, 52,* 107–118.

Smokowski, P. R., Mann, E. A., Reynolds, A. J., & Fraser, M. W. (2004). Childhood risk and protective factors and late adolescent adjustment in inner-city minority youth. *Children and Youth Services Review, 26,* 63–91.

Snarey, J. R. (1985). Cross-cultural universality of social-moral development: A critical review of Kohlbergian research. *Psychological Bulletin, 97,* 202–232.

Snow, R. E. (1986). Individual differences and the design of educational programs. *American Psychologist, 41,* 1029–1039.

Snowden, C. T., & Ziegler, T. E. (2000). Reproductive hormones. In J. T. Cacioppo, L. G. Tassinary, & G. Berntson (Eds.), *Handbook of psychophysiology* (2nd ed., pp. 368–396). New York: Cambridge University Press.

Snyder, H. N. (2004). Juvenile arrests 2002. *Juvenile Justice Bulletin.* Retrieved from Office of Juvenile Justice and Delinquency Prevention, U.S. Department of Justice Web site: http://www.ojp.usdoj.gov/ojjdp

Snyder, T. C., & Hoffman, C. M. (2002). *Digest of education statistics, 2001* (NCES 2002-130). Washington, DC: U.S. Department of Education, National Center for Education Statistics.

Snyder, T. D., & Tan, A. G. (2005). *Digest of Education Statistics.* Department of Education, National Center for Education Statistics. Available at http://nces.ed.gov/programs/digest/d04

Sokolov, E. M. (1963). Higher nervous functions: The orienting reflex. *Annual Review of Physiology, 25,* 545–580.

Solomon, G. (1990). Using technology to reach at-risk students. *Electronic Learning, 9,* 14–15.

Sommer, K., Whitman, T. L., Borkowski, J. G., Schellenbach, C., Maxwell, S., & Keogh, D. (1993). Cognitive readiness and adolescent parenting. *Developmental Psychology, 29,* 389–398.

Sorkhabi, N. (2005). Applicability of Baumrind's parent typology to collective cultures: Analysis of cultural explanations of parent socialization effects. *International Journal of Behavioral Development, 29,* 552–563.

Sourcebook of Criminal Justice Statistics 2003. Retrieved from http://www.albany.edu/sourcebook/pdf/t345.pdf

Sowell, E. R., Thompson, P. M., Tessner, K. D., & Toga, A. W. (2001). Mapping continued brain growth and gray matter density reduction in dorsal frontal cortex: Inverse relationships during postadolescent brain maturation. *Journal of Neuroscience, 21,* 8819–8829.

Sowell, T. (1978). Race and IQ reconsidered. In T. Sowell (Ed.), *American ethnic groups.* The Urban Institute.

Spence, S. H. (2003). Social skills training with children and young people: Theory, evidence and practice. *Child and Adolescent Mental Health, 8,* 84–96.

Spencer, M. B. (1985). Racial variations in achievement prediction: The school as a conduit for macrostructural cultural tension. In H. McAdoo & J. McAdoo (Eds.), *Black children: Social, educational, and parental environments.* Beverly Hills, CA: Sage.

Spiel, C., Glück, J., & Gössler, H. (2001). Stability and change of unidimensionality: The sample case of deductive reasoning. *Journal of Adolescent Research, 16,* 150–168.

Spinazzola, J., Wilson, H.W., & Stocking, V. B. (2002). Dimensions of silencing and resistance in adolescent girls: Development of a narrative method for research and prevention. In L. H. Collins, M. R. Dunlap, & J. C. Chrisler (Eds.), *Charting a new course for feminist psychology* (pp. 111–138). Westport, CT: Praeger/Greenwood.

Spires, H. A., Gallini, J., & Riggsbee, J. (1992). Effects of schema-based and text structure-based cues on expository prose comprehension in fourth graders. *Journal of Experimental Education, 60,* 307–320.

Spreen, O. (1988). *Learning disabled children growing up.* New York: Oxford University Press.

Sroufe, L. A. (1989). Relationships, self and individual adaptation. In A. J. Sameroff & R. N. Emde (Eds.), *Relationship disturbances in early childhood: A developmental approach* (pp. 70–94). New York: Basic Books.

Stams, G.-J., Juffer, F., & van Jzendoorn, M. H. (2002). Maternal sensitivity, infant attachment, and temperament in early childhood predict adjustment in middle childhood: The case of adopted children and their biologically unrelated parents. *Developmental Psychology, 38,* 806–821.

Starkman, N., & Rajani, N. (2002). The case for comprehensive sex education. *AIDS Patient Care and STDs, 16,* 313–318.

Steele, C. M. (1992). Race and the schooling of Black Americans. *The Atlantic Monthly, 269,* pp. 68–78.

Steele, C. M., & Aronson, J. (1995). Stereotype threat and the intellectual test performance of African Americans. *Journal of Personality and Social Psychology, 5,* 797–811.

Steele, J., James, J. B., & Barnett, R. C. (2002). Learning in a man's world: Examining the perceptions of undergraduate women in male-dominated academic areas. *Psychology of Women Quarterly, 26,* 46–50.

Stein, J. A., & Newcomb, M. D. (1999). Adult outcomes of adolescent conventional and agentic orientations: A 20-year longitudinal study. *Journal of Early Adolescence, 19,* 39–65.

Stein, J. H., & Reiser, L. W. (1994). A study of white middle-class adolescent boys' responses to "semenarche" (the first ejaculation). *Journal of Youth and Adolescence, 23,* 373–384.

Steinberg, L. (1987). The impact of puberty on family relations: Effects of pubertal status and pubertal timing. *Developmental Psychology, 23,* 451–460.

Steinberg, L. (2001). We know some things: Parent–adolescent relationships in retrospect and prospect. *Journal of Research on Adolescence, 11,* 1–19.

Steinberg, L., with Brown, B. B., & Dornbusch, S. M. (1996). *Beyond the classroom.* New York: Simon & Schuster.

Steinberg, L., Fegley, S., & Dornbusch, S. (1993). Negative impact of part-time work on adolescent adjustment: Evidence from a longitudinal study. *Developmental Psychology, 29,* 171–180.

Steinberg, L., Lamborn, S. D., Darling, N., Mounts, N. S., & Dornbusch, S. M. (1994). Over-time changes in adjustment and competence among adolescents from authoritative, authoritarian, indulgent, and neglectful families. *Child Development, 65,* 754–770.

Sternberg, R. J. (1981). Intelligence and nonentrenchment. *Journal of Educational Psychology, 73,* 1–16.

Sternberg, R. J. (1984). Mechanisms of cognitive development: A componential approach. In R. J. Sternberg (Ed.), *Mechanisms of cognitive development.* New York: Freeman.

Sternberg, R. J. (1985). *Beyond I.Q.: A triarchic theory of human intelligence.* New York: Cambridge University Press.

Sternberg, R. J., & Rifkin, B. (1979). The development of analogical reasoning processes. *Journal of Experimental Child Psychology, 27,* 195–232.

Stevens-Long, J., & Commons, M. L. (1992). *Adult life: Developmental processes* (4th ed.). Mountain View, CA: Mayfield.

Stevenson, H. C., McNeil, J. D., Herrero-Taylor, T., & Davis, G. Y. (2005). Influence of perceived neighborhood diversity and racism experience on the racial socialization of Black youth. *Journal of Black Psychology, 31,* 273–290.

Stevenson, H. W., Chen, C., & Uttal, D. H. (1990). Beliefs and achievement: A study of black, white, and Hispanic children. *Child Development, 61,* 508–523.

Stice, E. (2002). Risk and maintenance factors for eating pathology: A meta-analytic review. *Psychological Bulletin, 128,* 825–848.

Stice, E., Killen, J. D., Hayward, C., & Taylor, C. B. (1998). Age of onset for binge eating and purging during late adolescence: A 4-year survival analysis. *Journal of Abnormal Psychology, 107,* 671–675.

Strauss, L. T., Herndon, J., Chang, J., Parker, W. Y., Bowens, S. V., & Berg, C. J. (2005). Abortion surveillance—United States, 2002. *Morbidity and Mortality Weekly Reports, 54,* 1–31.

Strong, B., & DeVault, C. (2001). *Human sexuality* (4th ed.). New York: McGraw-Hill.

Subkoviak, M. J., Enright, R. D., Wu, C., Gassin, E. A., Freedman, S., Olson, L. M., & Sarinopoulos, I. (1995). Measuring interpersonal forgiveness in late adolescence and middle adulthood. *Journal of Adolescence, 18,* 641–655.

Subrahmanyam, K., & Greenfield, P. M. (2004). Constructing sexuality and identity in an Internet teen chatroom. *Journal of Applied Developmental Psychology, 25,* 651–666.

Sue, S. (1991). Ethnicity and culture in psychological research and practice. In J. Goodchilds (Ed.), *Psychological perspectives on human diversity in America* (pp. 51–85). Washington, DC: American Psychological Association.

Sukhodolsky, D. G., Kassinove, H., & Gorman, B. S. (2004). Cognitive-behavioral therapy for anger in children and adolescents: A meta-analysis. *Aggression and Violent Behavior, 9,* 247–269.

Summers-Effler, E. (2004). Little girls in women's bodies: Social interaction and the strategizing of early breast development. *Sex Roles, 51,* 29–44.

Sun, Y. (2001). Family environment and adolescents' well-being before and after parents' marital disruption: A longitudinal analysis. *Journal of Marriage and the Family, 63,* 697–713.

Sundet, J. M., Barlaug, D. G., & Torjussen, T. M. (2004). The end of the Flynn effect? A study of secular trends in mean intelligence test scores of Norwegian conscripts during half a century. *Intelligence, 32,* 349–362.

Super, D. E. (1981). A developmental theory: Implementing a self concept. In D. H. Montross & C. J. Shinkman (Eds.), *Career development in the 1980s: Theory and practice.* Springfield, IL: Thomas.

Super, D. E. (1990). A life-span, life-space approach to career development. In D. Brown, L. Brooks, & Associates (Eds.), *Career choice and development* (2nd ed., pp. 197–261). San Francisco: Jossey-Bass.

Surgeon General's Report. (1988). *The health consequences of smoking: Nicotine addiction.* U.S. Department of Health and Human Services. Washington, DC: U.S. Government Printing Office.

Susman, E. J., Dorn, L. D., & Schiefelbein, V. L. (2003). Puberty, sexuality, and health. In I. B. Weiner (Ed.), *Handbook of psychology* (Vol. 6, pp. 295–324). Hoboken, NJ: Wiley.

Suzuki, L. K., & Calzo, J. P.(2004). The search for peer advice in cyberspace: An examination of online teen bulletin boards about health and sexuality. *Applied Developmental Psychology, 25,* 685–698.

Swarr, A. E., & Richards, M. H. (1996). Longitudinal effects of adolescent girls' pubertal development, perceptions of pubertal timing, and parental relations on eating problems. *Developmental Psychology, 32,* 636–646.

Switzer, J. Y. (1990). The impact of generic word choices: An empirical investigation of age- and sex-related differences. *Sex Roles, 22,* 69–82.

Tanner, J. M. (1968). Earlier maturation in man. *Scientific American, 218,* 21–27.

Tanner, J. M. (1972). Sequence, tempo and individual variation in growth and development of boys and girls aged twelve to sixteen. In J. Kagan & R. Coles (Eds.), *Twelve to sixteen: Early adolescence.* New York: Norton.

Tanner, J. M. (1991). Menarche, secular trend in age of. In R. M. Lerner, A. C. Petersen, & J. Brooks-Gunn (Eds.), *Encyclopedia of adolescence* (Vol. 2, pp. 637–641). New York: Garland.

Tavris, C., & Wade, C. (1984). *The longest war: Sex differences in perspective* (2nd ed.). San Diego, CA: Harcourt Brace Jovanovich.

Taylor, R. D. (1996). Adolescents' perceptions of kinship support and family management practices: Association with adolescent adjustment in African American families. *Developmental Psychology, 32,* 687–695.

Teddlie, C., Kirby, P. C., & Stringfield, S. (1989). Effective vs. ineffective schools: Observable differences in the classroom. *American Journal of Education, 97,* 221–236.

Teen Research Unlimited. (2001). *Teens spend $155 billion in 2000.* Retrieved from: http://www.teenresearch.com/Prview.cfm?edit_id=75

Teitelman, A. M. (2004). Adolescent girls' perspectives of family interactions related to menarche and sexual health. *Qualitative Health Research, 14,* 1292–1308.

Tenenbaum, H. R., & Leaper, C. (2003). Parent-child conversations about science: The socialization of gender inequities? *Developmental Psychology, 39,* 34–47.

ter Bogt, T., Raaijmakers, Q., & van Wel, F. (2005). Socialization and development of the work ethic among adolescents and young adults. *Journal of Vocational Behavior, 66,* 420–437.

Terman, L. M. (1925). *Genetic studies of genius: Vol. 1. Mental and physical traits of a thousand gifted children.* Stanford, CA: Stanford University Press.

Thomas, J. J., & Daubman, K. A. (2001). The relationship between friendship quality and self-esteem in adolescent girls and boys. *Sex Roles, 45,* 53–65.

Thompson, S. H., Corwin, S. J., Rogan, T. J., & Sargent, R. G. (1999). Body-size beliefs and weight concerns among mothers and their adolescent children. *Journal of Child and Family Studies, 7,* 91–108.

Thornberry, T. P., Krohn, M. D., Lizotte, A. J., & Chard-Wierschem, D. (1993). The role of juvenile gangs in facilitating delinquent behavior. *Journal of Research in Crime and Delinquency, 30,* 55–87.

Thornton, M. C., Chatters, L. M., Taylor, R. J., & Allen, W. R. (1990). Sociodemographic and environmental correlates of racial socialization by black parents. *Child Development, 61,* 401–409.

Tidwell, R. (1988). Dropouts speak out: Qualitative data on early school departures. *Adolescence, 23,* 939–954.

Tittle, C. K. (1986). Gender research and education. *American Psychologist, 41,* 1161–1168.

Tobias, A. L. (1988). Bulimia: An overview. In K. Clark, R. Parr, & W. Castelli (Eds.), *Evaluation and management of eating disorders.* Champaign, IL: Life Enhancement Publications.

Toch, T. (1993). Violence in schools. *U.S. News and World Report, 115,* 31–37.

Tolson, J. M., & Urberg, K. A. (1993). Similarity between adolescent best friends. *Journal of Adolescent Research, 8,* 274–288.

Toossi, M. (2004). Labor force projections to 2012: The graying of the U.S. workforce. *Monthly Labor Review, 127,* 37–57. Available at http://www.bls.gov/opub/ted/

Toubia, N. (1994). Female circumcision as a public health issue. *New England Journal of Medicine, 331,* 712–716.

Towey, K., & Fleming, M. (2005). *Healthy youth 2010: Supporting the 21 critical adolescent objectives.* Available at http://www.ama-assn.org/ama/pub/category/1943.html

Trautman, P. D., & Rotheram, M. J. (1986). Reported in Trautman, P. D. (1989). Specific treatment modalities for adolescent suicide attempters. In *Report of the Secretary's Task Force* (Vol. 3.) Washington, DC: U.S. Government Printing Office.

Treboux, D., & Busch-Rossnagel, N. A. (1990). Social network influences on adolescent sexual attitudes and behaviors. *Journal of Adolescent Research, 5,* 175–189.

Triandis, H. C. (1988). Collectivism vs. individualism: A reconceptualization of a basic concept in cross-cultural psychology. In G. Verma & C. Bagley (Eds.), *Cross-cultural studies of personality, attitudes and cognition* (pp. 60–95). London: MacMillan.

Troiano, R. P., & Flegal, K. M. (1998). Overweight children and adolescents: Description, epidemiology, and demographics. *Pediatrics, 101,* 497–504.

Troth, A., & Peterson, C. C. (2000). Factors predicting safe-sex talk and condom use in early sexual relationships. *Health Communication, 12,* 195–218.

Tschann, J. M., & Adler, N. E. (1997). Sexual self-acceptance, communication with partner, and contraceptive use among adolescent females: A longitudinal study. *Journal of Research on Adolescence, 7,* 413–430.

Tschirgi, J. E. (1980). Sensible reasoning: A hypothesis about hypotheses. *Child Development, 51,* 1–10.

Tucker, C. J., Updegraff, K. A., McHale, S. M., & Crouter, A. C. (1999). Older siblings as socializers of younger siblings' empathy. *Journal of Early Adolescence, 19,* 176–198.

Turiel, E. (1983). *The development of social knowledge: Morality and convention.* Cambridge, England: Cambridge University Press.

Turnage, B. F. (2004). African American mother–daughter relationships mediating daughters' self-esteem. *Child and Adolescent Social Work Journal, 21,* 155–173.

Turner, H. A., & Kopiec, K. (2006). Exposure to interparental conflict and psychological disorder among young adults. *Journal of Family Issues, 27,* 131–158.

Twenge, J. M., & Crocker, J. (2002). Race and self-esteem: Meta-analyses comparing Whites, Blacks, Hispanics, Asians, and American Indians and Comment on Gray-Little and Hafdahl (2000). *Psychological Bulletin, 128,* 371–408.

Umaña-Taylor, A. J., Diversi, M., & Fine, M. A. (2002). Ethnic identity and self-esteem of Latino adolescents: Distinctions among the Latino populations. *Journal of Adolescent Research, 17,* 303–327.

Underwood, J., & Szabo, A. (2003). Academic offenses and e-learning: Individual propensities in cheating. *British Journal of Educational Technology, 34,* 467–477.

Urban Institute. (2005). *Education in the age of accountability.* Available at http:/www.urban.org/content/IssuesInFocus/EducationintheAgeofAccountability/Education.htm

Urberg, K. A. (1992). Locus of peer influence: Social crowd and best friend. *Journal of Youth and Adolescence, 21,* 439–450.

Urberg, K. A., Degirmencioglu, S. M., Tolson, J. M., & Halliday-Scher, K. (1995). The structure of adolescent peer networks. *Developmental Psychology, 31,* 540–547.

U.S. Bureau of the Census. Baugher, E., & Lamison-White, L. (1996a). *Current population reports, Series P60-194, Poverty in the United States: 1995.* Washington, DC: U.S. Government Printing Office.

U.S. Bureau of the Census. Day, J. C. (1996b). *Current population reports, Series P25–1130, Population projections of the United States by age, sex, race, and Hispanic origin: 1995 to 2050.* Washington, DC: U.S. Government Printing Office.

U.S. Bureau of the Census. (1998a). *Current population reports, Series P25, Marital status and living arrangements: March 1998 (update).* Washington, DC: U.S. Government Printing Office.

U.S. Bureau of the Census. (1998b). *Current population reports, Series P20–500.* Washington, DC: U.S. Government Printing Office.

U.S. Bureau of the Census. (1999a). Retrieved January 4, 2000, from http://www.census/gov/population/socdemo/school/report98/tab0.1txt

U.S. Bureau of the Census. (1999b). *Current population reports, Series P60, Consumer income.* Washington, DC: U.S. Government Printing Office.

U.S. Bureau of the Census. (2000, January 13). *Projections of the total resident population by 5-year age groups, and sex with special age categories: Middle series, 2075 to 2100* (NP-T3-H). Retrieved from http://www.census.gov/population/projections/nation/summary/np-t3-h.txt

U.S. Bureau of the Census. (2001a). *Statistical abstract of the United States* (121st ed.). Retrieved from http://www.census.gov/prod/2002pubs/01 statab/stat-ab01.html

U.S. Bureau of the Census. (2001b). *Population by age, sex, race, and Hispanic or Latino origin for the United States: 2000* (PHC-T-9). Table 1. Retrieved from http://www.census.gov/population/cen2000/phc-t9/tab01.pdf

U.S. Bureau of the Census. (2002, May 3). From birth to seventeen: The living arrangements of children, 2000. In *The population profile of the United States: 2000 (Internet release)*(pt. 2). Retrieved from http://www.census.gov/ population /pop-profile /2000/chap06.pdf

U.S. Bureau of the Census. (2004). *U.S. interim projections by age, sex, race, and Hispanic origin.* Available at http://www.census.gov/ipc/ www/usinterimproj/

U.S. Bureau of the Census. (2005). *Poverty thresholds 2004.* U.S. Department of Health and Human Services. The 2004 Health and Human Services Policy Guidelines. Available at http://aspe.hhs.gov/ poverty/04poverty.shtml

U.S. Bureau of Labor Statistics. (2002). *Occupational outlook handbook, 2002–2003 edition.* Retrieved from http://www.bls.gov/oco/ oco2003.htm

U.S. Bureau of Labor Statistics. (2005a). *Employment projections.* Retrieved from http://www.bls.gov/emp/emptab4.htm

U.S. Bureau of Labor Statistics. (2005b). *Occupational outlook handbook, 2004 edition.* Retrieved from http://www.bls.gov/oco/

U.S. Bureau of Labor Statistics. (2005c). Differences in earnings by age and sex in 2004. *Monthly Labor Review.* Available at http://www.bls .gov/opub/ted/

U.S. Census Bureau (2005). America's families and living arrangements: 2004. Retrieved from http://www.census/gov/population/ www/socdemo/hh-fam/cps2004.html

U.S. Department of Education. (1988). *Ninth annual report to Congress on the implementation of the Education of the Handicapped Act.* Washington, DC: OSERS.

U.S. Department of Education. (1996). *Digest of educational statistics 1996, NCES 96-133.* Washington, DC: U.S. Government Printing Office.

U.S. Department of Education, National Center for Education Statistics. (1998). *The condition of education, 1998: Indicator 37: Homework and television viewing.* Retrieved from http://nces.ed.gov/ pubs98/condition98/c9837a01. html

U.S. Department of Health and Human Services, Children's Bureau. (1998). *Child Maltreatment 1996: Reports from the States to the National Child Abuse and Neglect Data System.* Washington, DC: U.S. Government Printing Office.

U.S. Department of Health and Human Services, Office of the Assistant Secretary for Planning and Evaluation. (2002a, May 2). Population, family, and neighborhood. In *Trends in the well-being of America's children & youth, 2001* (sect. 1). Retrieved from http://aspe.hhs .gov/hsp/ 01trends/contents.htm#PF

U.S. Department of Health and Human Services, Office of the Assistant Secretary for Planning and Evaluation. (2002b, May 2). Economic security. In *Trends in the well-being of America's children & youth, 2001* (sect. 2). Retrieved from http://aspe.hhs.gov/hsp/01trends/ contents. htm #ES

U.S. Department of Health and Human Services, Office of the Assistant Secretary for Planning and Evaluation. (2002c, May 2). Social development and behavioral health. In *Trends in the well-being of America's children & youth, 2001* (sect. 4). Retrieved from http:// aspe.hhs. gov/hsp/01trends/contents.htm#SD

U.S. Department of Health and Human Services, Office of the Assistant Secretary for Planning and Evaluation. (2005). *Suicide warning signs.* Available at http://www.mentalhealth.samhsa.gov/ publications/allpubs/walletcard/

U.S. Department of Health and Human Services, Office of the Assistant Secretary for Planning and Evaluation. (2006). *The 2006 HHS poverty guidelines.* Available at http://aspe.hhs.gov/poverty/ 06poverty.shtml

U.S. Department of Justice, Bureau of Justice Statistics. (1995). *School crime supplement to the national crime victimization survey, Spring.* Washington, DC: Bureau of Justice Statistics.

U.S. Department of Labor. (2000). *Report on the youth labor force.* Retrieved from http://www.bls.gov/opub/rylf/rylfhome.htm

van Manen, T. G., Prins, P. J. M., & Emmelkamp, P. M. G. (2004). Reducing aggressive behavior in boys with a social cognitive group treatment: Results of a randomized controlled trial. *Journal of the American Academy of Child and Adolescent Psychiatry, 43,* 1478–1487.

van Wel, F., Linssen, H., & Abma, R. (2000). The parental bond and the well-being of adolescents and young adults. *Journal of Youth and Adolescence, 29,* 307–318.

Vazsonyi, A. T., Hibbert, J. R., & Snyder, J. B. (2003). Exotic enterprise no more? Adolescent reports of family and parenting processes from youth in four countries. *Journal of Research on Adolescence, 13,* 129–160.

Ventura, S. J., Mathews, T. J., & Curtin, S. C. (2000). Declines in teenage birth rates, 1991–98: Update of national and state trends. *National Vital Statistics Reports, 47,* 1–9.

Verma, S. & Saraswathi, T. S. (2002). Adolescents in India: Street urchins or Silicon Valley millionaires? In B. B. Brown, R, Larson, & T. S. Saraswathi (Eds.), *The World's Youth: Adolescence in Eight Regions of the Globe* (pp. 105–140). New York: Cambridge University Press.

Vicary, J. R., Klingaman, L. R., & Harkness, W. L. (1995). Risk factors associated with date rape and sexual assault of adolescent girls. *Journal of Adolescence, 18,* 289–306.

Vigil, J. D. (1988). *Barrio gangs.* Austin: University of Texas Press.

Vosniadou, S., & Brewer, W. F. (1992). Mental models of the earth: A study of conceptual change in childhood. *Cognitive Psychology, 24,* 535–585.

Vowell, P. R. & Chen, J. (2004). Predicting academic misconduct: A comparative test of four sociological explanations. *Sociological Inquiry, 74,* 226–249.

Voyer, D. (1996). The relation between mathematical achievement and gender differences in spatial abilities: A suppression effect. *Journal of Educational Psychology, 88,* 563–571.

Vuchinich, S., Angelelli, J., & Gatherum, A. (1996). Context and development in family problem solving with preadolescent children. *Child Development, 67,* 1276–1288.

Vygotsky, L. (1978). *Mind in society.* Cambridge, MA: Harvard University Press.

Wadden, T. A., Brownell, K. D., & Foster, G. D. (2002). Obesity: Responding to the global epidemic. *Journal of Consulting and Clinical Psychology, 70,* 510–525.

Wadsworth, M. E., Gudmundsen, G. R., Raviv, T., Ahlkvist, J. A., McIntosh, D. N., Kline, G. H., Rea, J., & Burwell, R. A. (2004). Coping with terrorism: Age and gender differences in effortful and involuntary responses to September 11th. *Applied Developmental Science, 8,* 143–157.

Wagner, B. M., Cohen, P., & Brook, J. S. (1996). Parent/adolescent relationships: Moderators of the effects of stressful life events. *Journal of Adolescent Research, 11,* 347–374.

Wagner, R. K., & Sternberg, R. J. (1986). Tacit knowledge and intelligence in the everyday world. In R. J. Sternberg & R. K. Wagner (Eds.), *Practical intelligence: Nature and origins of competence in the everyday world.* New York: Cambridge University Press.

Wainright, J. L., Russell, S. T., & Patterson, C. J. (2004). Psychosocial adjustment, school outcomes, and romantic relationships of adolescents with same-sex parents. *Child Development, 75,* 1886–1898.

Waizenhofer, R. N., Buchanan, C. M., & Jackson-Newsom, J. (2004). Mothers' and fathers' knowledge of adolescents' daily activities: Its sources and its links with adolescent adjustment. *Journal of Family Psychology, 18,* 348–360.

Waldinger, R. J., Diguer, L., Guastella, F., Lefebvre, R., Allen, J. P., Luborsky, L., & Hauser, S. T. (2002). The same old song: Stability and change in relationship schemas from adolescence to young adulthood. *Journal of Youth and Adolescence, 31,* 17–29.

Wallerstein, J. S. (2004). The unexpected legacy of divorce: Report of a 25-year study. *Psychoanalytic Psychology, 21,* 353–370.

Wallerstein, J. S., Lewis, J. M., & Blakeslee, S. (2000). *The unexpected legacy of divorce: A 25-year landmark study.* New York: Hyperion.

Walters, J. M., & Gardner, H. (1986). The theory of multiple intelligences: Some issues and answers. In R. J. Sternberg & R. K. Wagner

(Eds.), *Practical intelligence: Nature and origins of competence in the everyday world.* New York: Cambridge University Press.
Wapner, M. L. (1980). Personal communication.
Wapner, M. L. (1990). Personal communication.
Ward, L. M. (2002). Does television exposure affect emerging adults' attitudes and assumptions about sexual relationships? Correlational and experimental confirmation. *Journal of Youth and Adolescence, 31,* 1–15.
Ward, S. L., & Overton, W. F. (1990). Semantic familiarity, relevance, and the development of deductive reasoning. *Developmental Psychology, 26,* 488–493.
Warren, M. P. (1983). Physical and biological aspects of puberty. In J. Brooks-Gunn & A. C. Petersen (Eds.), *Girls at puberty: Biological and psychosocial perspectives.* New York: Plenum Press.
Wason, P. C., & Johnson-Laird, P. N. (1972). *Psychology of reasoning: Structure and content.* Cambridge, MA: Harvard University Press.
Waters, A. (2005a). Slow food, slow schools: Transforming education through a school lunch program. Available at http://www.edibleschoolyard.org/homepage.html
Waters, A. (2005b). On making school lunch an academic subject. (Personal communication.)
Webster, C. (1994). Effects of Hispanic ethnic identification on marital roles in the purchase decision process. *Journal of Consumer Research, 21,* 319–331.
Wechsler, D. (1981). *WAIS-R Manual: Wechsler Adult Intelligence Scale—Revised.* San Antonio, TX: Psychological Corporation.
Weimann, E. (2002). Gender-related differences in elite gymnasts: The female athlete triad. *Journal of Applied Physiology, 92,* 2146–2152.
Weiner, I. B. (1980). Psychopathology in adolescence. In J. Adelson (Ed.), *Handbook of adolescent psychology.* New York: Wiley.
Wentzel, K. R. (2002). Are effective teachers like good parents? Teaching styles and student adjustment in early adolescence. *Child Development, 73,* 287–301.
Werner, E. (1989, April). Children of the garden island. *Scientific American,* pp. 106–111.
Werner, E. (1989). High-risk children in young adulthood: A longitudinal study from birth to 32 years. *American Journal of Orthopsychiatry, 59,* 72–81.
Werner, E., & Smith, R. (1982). *Vulnerable but invincible: A longitudinal study of resilient children and youth.* New York: McGraw-Hill.
Werner, E., & Smith, R. (1992). *Overcoming the odds: High-risk children from birth to adulthood.* Ithaca, NY: Cornell University Press.
Whitbeck, L. B., Yoder, K. A., Hoyt, D. R., & Conger, R. D. (1999). Early adolescent sexual activity: A developmental study. *Journal of Marriage and the Family, 61,* 934–946.
White, F. A., & Matawie, K. M. (2004). Parental morality and family processes as predictors of adolescent morality. *Journal of Child & Family Studies, 13,* 219–233.
White, K. L., Speisman, J. C., & Costos, D. (1983). Young adults and their parents: Individuation to mutuality. In H. D. Grotevant & C. R. Cooper (Eds.), *Adolescent development in the family.* San Francisco: Jossey-Bass.
Whitehorn, J., Ayonrinde, O., & Maingay, S. (2002). Female genital mutilation: Cultural and psychological implications. *Sexual and Relationship Therapy, 17,* 161–170.
Wicherts, J. M., Dolan, C. V., Hessen, D. J., Oosterveld, P., van Baal, G. C. M., Boomsma, D. I., & Span, M. M. (2004). Are intelligence tests measurement invariant over time? Investigating the nature of the Flynn effect. *Intelligence, 32,* 509–537.
Williams, J. M., & Currie, C. (2002). Self-esteem and physical development in early adolescence: Pubertal timing and body image. *Journal of Early Adolescence, 20,* 129–149.
Williams, J. M., & White, K. A. (1983). Adolescent status systems for males and females at three age levels. *Adolescence, 18,* 381–389.
Wilson, W. J. (1996). *When work disappears: The world of the new urban poor.* New York: Knopf.
Wintre, M. G., Hicks, R., McVey, G., & Fox, J. (1988). Age and sex differences in choice of consultant for various types of problems. *Child Development, 59,* 1046–1055.
Wirth, L. (1945). The problem of minority groups. In R. Linton (Ed.), *The science of man in the world crisis.* New York: Columbia University Press.
Women on Words and Images. (1975). *Dick and Jane as victims: Sex stereotyping in children's readers* (Expanded ed.). Princeton, NJ: Author.
Woody, J. D., Russel, R., D'Souza, H. J., & Woody, J. K. (2000). Adolescent non-coital sexual activity: Comparisons of virgins and non-virgins. *Journal of Sex Education and Therapy, 25,* 261–268.
Wright, L. S., Frost, C. J., & Wisecarver, S. J. (1993). Church attendance, meaningfulness of religion, and depressive symptomatology among adolescents. *Journal of Youth and Adolescence, 22,* 559–568.
Wyche, K., Obolensky, N., & Glood, E. (1990). American Indian, Black American, and Hispanic American youth. In M. J. Rotheram-Borus, J. Bradley, & N. Obolensky (Eds.), *Planning to live: Evaluating and treating suicidal teens in community settings* (pp. 355–389). Tulsa: University of Oklahoma Press.
Xie, H., Cairns, R. B., & Cairns, B. D. (2002). The development of social aggression and physical aggression: A narrative analysis of interpersonal conflicts. *Aggressive Behavior, 28,* 341–355.
Xiong, Z. B., Eliason, P. A., Detzner, D. S., & Cleveland, M. J. (2005). Southeast Asian immigrants' perceptions of good adolescents and good parents. *Journal of Psychology, 139,* 159–175.
Yasui, M., Dorham, C. L., & Dishion, T. J. (2004). Ethnic identity and psychological adjustment: A validity analysis for European American and African American adolescents. *Journal of Adolescent Research, 19,* 807–825.
Yau, J., & Smetana, J. G. (1993). Chinese-American adolescents' reasoning about cultural conflicts. *Journal of Adolescent Research, 8,* 419–438.
Yau, J., & Smetana, J. G. (1996). Adolescent–parent conflict among Chinese adolescents in Hong Kong. *Child Development, 67,* 1262–1275.
Yeung, D. Y. L., Tang, C. S., & Lee, A. (2005). Psychosocial and cultural factors influencing expectations of menarche: A study on Chinese premenarcheal teenage girls. *Journal of Adolescent Research, 20,* 118–135.
Ying, Y. (1994). Chinese American adults' relationship with their parents. *International Journal of Social Psychology, 40,* 35–45.
Yoder, J. D., & Kahn, A. S. (1993). Working toward an inclusive psychology of women. *American Psychologist, 48,* 846–850.
Youniss, J. (1980). *Parents and peers in social development.* Chicago: University of Chicago Press.
Youniss, J., McLellan, J. A., Su, Y., & Yates, M. (1999). The role of community service in identity development: Normative, unconventional, and deviant orientations. *Journal of Adolescent Research, 14,* 248–261.
Youniss, J., McLellan, J. A., & Yates, M. (1999). Religion, community service, and identity in American youth. *Journal of Adolescence, 22,* 243–253.
Youniss, J., & Smollar, J. (1989). Adolescents' interpersonal relationships in social context. In T. J. Berndt & G. W. Ladd (Eds.), *Peer relationships in child development.* New York: Wiley.
Youth Indicators. (2005). *Trends in the well-being of American youth.* U.S. Department of Education, National Center for Education Statistics. Washington, DC: U.S. Government Printing Office.
Youth Service California. (2005). *Why youth service matters.* Available at http://www.yscal.org/ysmatters/stats.html
Zaider, T. I., Johnson, J. G., & Cockell, S. J. (2000). Psychiatric comorbidity associated with eating disorder symptomatology among adolescents in the community. *International Journal of Eating Disorders, 28,* 58–67.

Zeldin, S., & Price, L. A. (1995). Creating supportive communities for adolescent development: Challenges to scholars. *Journal of Adolescent Research, 10,* 6–14.

Zimmerman, B. J. (2000). Attaining self-regulation: A social-cognitive perspective. In M. Boekaerts, P. Pintrich, & M. Seidner (Eds.), *Self-regulation: Theory, research, and applications* (pp. 13–39). Orlando, FL: Academic Press.

Zimmerman, B. J., Bandura, A., & Martinez-Pons, M. (1992). Self-motivation for academic attainment: The role of self-efficacy beliefs and personal goal-setting. *American Educational Research Journal, 29,* 663–676.

Zimmerman, P., & Becker-Stoll, F. (2002). Stability of attachment representations during adolescence: The influence of ego-identity status. *Journal of Adolescence, 25,* 107–124.

Credits

PHOTO CREDITS

Chapter 1

p. 2: © SW Productions/Getty Images; p. 6: © Mary Kate Denny/PhotoEdit; p. 21: © Elizabeth Crews; p. 23: © Ryan McVay/Getty Images; p. 25: © Tony Freeman/PhotoEdit; p. 26: © Brand X Pictures/PunchStock; p. 27: © Michelle Bridwell/PhotoEdit

Chapter 2

p. 30: © Sven Martson/The Image Works; p. 33: © Royalty-Free/CORBIS; p. 34: © Joel Gordon; p. 39: © Ken Heyman/Woodfin Camp; p. 40: © Steve Mason/Getty Images; p. 41: © AP/Wide World Photos; p. 43: © Bettmann/CORBIS; p. 46 top: © Bettmann/CORBIS; p. 46 bottom: © Bettmann/CORBIS; p. 47: © Comstock/PictureQuest; p. 50: © Rachel Chodorow-Reich; p. 52: Courtesy of Carol Gilligan, photographer Jerry Bauer; p. 57: © Sam Forencich

Chapter 3

p. 62: © David Young-Wolff/PhotoEdit; p. 70: © Spencer Grant/PhotoEdit; p. 72: © BananaStock/JupiterImages; p. 75: © Ryan McVay/Getty Images; p. 81: © Creatas/PunchStock; p. 82: © PhotoDisc/Getty Images; p. 86: © Image Source/JupiterImages; p. 89: © Steve Mason/Getty Images; p. 91: © David Madison 2006

Chapter 4

p. 98: © Photodisc/Getty Images; p. 101: © Medio Images; p. 103: © Michael Newman/PhotoEdit; p. 107: © Skjold Photographs; p. 108: © Suzanne Arms/Jeroboam; p. 110: © Ellen Sinisi/The Image Works; p. 114: © Myrleen Ferguson Cate/PhotoEdit; p. 115: © Creatas/PunchStock; p. 116: © Michelle Bridwell/PhotoEdit; p. 117: © David Young-Wolff/PhotoEdit; p. 119: © Paul Conklin/PhotoEdit; p. 122: © Frank Simonetti/Index Stock; p. 123: © Myrleen Ferguson Cate/PhotoEdit; p. 124: © BananaStock/PunchStock; p. 126: © Sven Martson/The Image Works; p. 127: © Photodisc/Punch Stock

Chapter 5

p. 130: © Joan Lifton/Actuality; p. 132: © Amanda Clement/Getty Images; p. 134: © BananaStock/PunchStock; p. 140: © Brand X Pictures/Alamy; p. 142: © Fannie Pryce/The Image Works; p. 143: © Robert Eckert/Index Stock; p. 144: © Comstock; p. 145: © David Simson/Stock Boston; p. 150: © David Young-Wolff/PhotoEdit; p. 152: © BananaStock/PunchStock; p. 155: © Tony Freeman/PhotoEdit; p. 156: © Jim Corwin/Stock Boston; p. 160: © Joel Gordon; p. 163: © Steve Moore/Index Stock; p. 166: © Joel Gordon; p. 167: © Donna Binder

Chapter 6

p. 170: © Bob Daemmrich/Stock Boston; p. 180: © Syracuse Newspapers/Gary Walts/The Image Works; p. 184: © Joan Lifton/Actuality; p. 188: © The McGraw-Hill Companies, Inc./Jill Braaten, photographer; p. 191: Courtesy of the Children's Defense Fund; p. 194: © The McGraw-Hill Companies, Inc./Jill Braaten, photographer; p. 203: © image100 Ltd

Chapter 7

p. 208: © BananaStock/PunchStock; p. 213: © David Young-Wolff/PhotoEdit; p. 214: © Elizabeth Crews; p. 217: © BananaStock/PunchStock; p. 220: © Elizabeth Crews/The Image Works; p. 222: © Bob Daemmrich/Stock Boston; p. 225: © BananaStock/PunchStock; p. 229: © Jonathan Nourok/PhotoEdit; p. 231: © Bob Daemmrich/Stock Boston; p. 234: © BananaStock/PunchStock; p. 236: © Roberto Soncin Gerometta

Chapter 8

p. 242: © Getty Images; p. 244: © BananaStock/JupiterImages; p. 248: © SW Productions/Getty Images; p. 249: © David Young-Wolff/PhotoEdit; p. 250: © Michael Newman/PhotoEdit; p. 252: © CORBIS; p. 253: © Bill

Bachmann/Stock Boston; p. 254: © Leland Bobbe/Taxi/Getty Images; p. 257: © David Young-Wolff/PhotoEdit; p. 258: © A. Ramey/PhotoEdit; p. 261: © Digital Vision; p. 262: © Tom Carter/PhotoEdit; p. 265: © Digital Vision; p. 268: © Joel Gordon; p. 269: © Joel Gordon

Chapter 9

p. 274: © BananaStock/JupiterImages; p. 277: © Will Hart/PhotoEdit; p. 278: © Creatas/PunchStock; p. 279: © Mary Kate Denny/PhotoEdit; p. 280: © Bob Daemmrich/The Image Works; p. 282: © Mark Richard/PhotoEdit; p. 292: © Creatas/PunchStock; p. 294: © Jonathan Nourok/PhotoEdit; p. 297: © The McGraw-Hill Companies, Inc./Gary He, photographer; p. 298: © David Young-Wolff/Stone/Getty Images; p. 299: © Elizabeth Crews; p. 305: © Syracuse Newspapers/C. W. McKeen/The Image Works

Chapter 10

p. 318: © BananaStock/JupiterImages; p. 327: © image100 Ltd; p. 330: © Joel Gordon; p. 333: © image100 Ltd; p. 334: © James Prigoff and Henry Chalfant; p. 337: © Digital Vision; p. 339: © Mary Kate Denny/PhotoEdit; p. 341: © Steve Smith/Getty Images; p. 345: © Royalty-Free/CORBIS; p. 348: © Mark Richard/PhotoEdit; p. 349: © Jeff Greenberg/PhotoEdit; p. 352: © Nancy Richmond/The Image Works

Chapter 11

p. 356: © Comstock/PictureQuest; p. 360: © Banana Stock/JupiterImages; p. 363: © Skjold Photographs; p. 365: © Bradley D. Lanphere/Stock Boston; p. 372: Courtesy of Nancy Cobb; p. 377: © Digital Vision/PunchStock; p. 380: © The McGraw-Hill Companies, Inc./Jill Braaten, photographer; p. 385: © Brand X Pictures/PunchStock

Chapter 12

p. 390: © Digital Vision; p. 393: © The McGraw-Hill Companies, Inc./Jill Braaten, photographer; p. 399: © Robert Yager/Stone/Getty Images; p. 403: © A. Ramey/PhotoEdit; p. 404: © Doug Menuez/Getty Images; p. 408: © BananaStock/PunchStock; p. 413: © Owen Franken/Stock Boston; p. 414: © BananaStock/PunchStock; p. 418: © Mary Steinbacher/PhotoEdit; p. 422: © Manchan/Getty Images

Chapter 13

p. 426: © Creatas Images/JupiterImages; p. 428: © Robert Brenner/PhotoEdit; p. 431: © Mary Kate Denny/PhotoEdit; p. 435: © Comstock Images; p. 437: © Ryan McVay/Getty Images; p. 441: © Bonnie Kamin/Photo Edit

Chapter 14

p. 446: © Brian Bailey/Stone/Getty Images; p. 450: © David Buffington/Getty Images; p. 457: © Royalty-Free/CORBIS; p. 458: © Bradley D. Lanphere/Stock Boston

TEXT AND LINE ART CREDITS

Chapter 1

p. 24 Adapted from R. C. Maynard, "An Example of How Afro-American Parents Socialize Children," *Oakland Tribune,* August 5, 1990. Used with permission. **Figure 1.6,** p. 17 From *Child Development in the Social Context* by C. B. Kopp and J. B. Krakow, p. 648, 1982. Reprinted by permission of Pearson Education.

Chapter 2

pp. 50–52 Reprinted by permission of the publisher from Carol Gilligan, *In a Different Voice: Psychological Theory and Women's Development,* pp. 35–37. Cambridge, Mass: Harvard University Press. Copyright © 1982 Harvard University Press.

Chapter 3

Figure 3.5, p. 73 Adapted from D. B. Cheek, "Body Composition, hormones, nutrition, and adolescent growth" in M. M. Grumbach, G. D. Grave, F. E. Mayers, (eds.), *Control of the Onset of Puberty,* John Wiley & Sons, 1974. Used with permission of the publisher. **Figures 3.6, 3.7,** p. 74 From P. M. Insel & W. T. Roth, *Core Concepts in Health,* 8th Edition, 2000 Update. Copyright © The McGraw-Hill Companies. Reprinted with permission from The McGraw-Hill Companies. **Figure 3.8,** p. 78: Adapted from J. M. Tanner, "Earlier Maturation in Man, *Scientific American,* Vol. 218, 26, 1968. Reprinted with permission. **Figure 3.9,** p. 80 Adapted from R. Larson and M. H. Richards, *Divergent Realities.* Copyright © 1994 by Reed Larson and Maryse Richards. Reprinted by permission of Basic Books, a member of Perseus Books, L.L.C. **Table 3.1,** p. 85 From L. K. Suzuki and J. P. Calzo, "The Search for Peer Advice in Cyberspace: An Examination of Online Teen Bulletin Boards About Health and Sexuality," *Applied Developmental Psychology, 25,* 685–698, 2004. Reprinted with permission from Elsevier. **Table 3.2,** p. 87 Reproduced by permission of the Society for Applied Anthropology from S. Parker, M. Nichter,

M. Nichter, N. Vuckovic, C. Sims & C. Ritenbaugh, *Body Image and Weight Concerns among Afro-American and White Adolescent Females: Differences that Make a Difference,* 1995, *Human Organization,* Vol. 54, No. 2, p. 106.

Chapter 4

Figure 4.1, p. 102 From B. Inhelder and J. Piaget, *The Growth of Logical Thinking from Childhood to Adolescence.* Copyright © 1958 Basic Books. Reprinted by permission of Basic Books, a member of Perseus Books, L.L.C. **Figure 4.2,** p. 102 S. C. Martorano, "A Developmental Analysis of Performance on Piaget's Formal Operations Tasks," *Developmental Psychology,* Vol. 13, pp. 666–672. Copyright © 1977 American Psychological Association. Reprinted with permission. **Figure 4.4,** p. 109 Adapted from P. C. Wason and P. N. Johnson-Laird, *Psychology of Reasoning: Structure and Content,* Harvard University Press, 1972. Reprinted with permission from B. T. Batsford Ltd. **Figure 4.5,** p. 111 From Ronald J. Cohen and Mark E. Swerdlik, *Psychological Testing and Assessment: An Introduction to Tests and Measurement,* 4th Edition, 1999. Reprinted with permission from The McGraw-Hill Companies.

Chapter 5

p. 136 From J. Brooks, *The Process of Parenting,* 5th Edition. Copyright © 1999 Mayfield Publishing Company. Reprinted with permission from The McGraw-Hill Companies. p. 138 Adapted from C. R. Cooper, H. D. Grotevant, & S. M. Condon, "Individuality and Connectedness in the Family as a Context for Adolescent Identity Formation and Role-Taking Skill" in H. D. Grotevant & C. R. Cooper (Eds.) *Adolescent Development in the Family,* Jossey-Bass. Reprinted with permission of John Wiley & Sons, Inc. p. 139 From J. Brooks, *The Process of Parenting,* 5th Edition. Copyright © 1999 Mayfield Publishing Company. Reprinted with permission from The McGraw-Hill Companies. pp. 140–141 From Erikson, E. H. *Identity, Youth and Crisis,* W. W. Norton, pp. 130–131. Reprinted with permission from W. W. Norton & Company. **Figure 5.2,** p. 157 D. L. DuBois, R. D. Felner, S. Brand, R. S. C. Phillips, & A. M. Lease, "Early adolescent self-esteem: A developmental-ecological framework and assessment strategy," *Journal of Research on Adolescence, 6,* 543–579, 1996. Reprinted with permission from Lawrence Erlbaum Associates. **Table 5.3,** p. 165 Adapted from R. Josselson, *The Space Between Us,* Jossey Bass, 1992. Reprinted with permission from John Wiley & Sons.

Chapter 6

Figure 6.1, p. 176 Adapted from T. Alfieri, D. N. Ruble, & E. T. Higgins, "Gender Stereotypes During Adolescence: Developmental Changes and the Transition to Junior High School," *Developmental Psychology, 32,* 1129–1137, 1996. Reprinted with permission of the American Psychological Association. **Table 6.1,** p. 177 Adapted from S. Buzwell & D. Rosenthal. (1996). Constructing a Sexual Self: Adolescents' Sexual Self-Perceptions and Sexual Risk-Taking. *Journal of Research on Adolescence, 6,* 489–513. Used with permission from Lawrence Erlbaum Associates. p. 183 Adapted from W. H. Masters, V. E. Johnson, & R. C. Kolodny, *Human Sexuality,* Third Edition, Allyn and Bacon, 1998. Copyright © 1998 by Pearson Education. Reprinted by permission of the publisher. **Figure 6.3,** p. 186 Adapted from A. C. Kinsey, W. B. Pomeroy, & C. E. Martin, *Sexual Behavior in the Human Male,* W. B. Saunders, 1948. Reprinted by permission of The Kinsey Institute for Research in Sex, Gender, and Reproduction, Inc. **Figure 6.4,** p. 193 Adapted from R. Schwartz. (1992). *AIDS Medical Guide.* San Francisco AIDS Foundation and Centers for Disease Control. (1991). *HIV Infection and AIDS: Are You at Risk?* Reprinted with permission of the San Francisco AIDS Foundation.

Chapter 7

Table 7.1, p. 215 J. G. Smetana & R. Berent, "Adolescents' and mothers' evaluations of justifications for disputes," *Journal of Adolescent Research,* 1993, Volume 8, pp. 252–273. Copyright © 1993 Sage Publications. Reprinted with permission. **Table 7.2,** p. 216 J. G. Smetana & P. Asquith, "Adolescents' and parents' conceptions of parental authority and personal autonomy," *Child Development,* 1994, Vol. 65, pp. 1147–1162. Copyright © 1994 Society for Research in Child Development. Reprinted with permission of Blackwell Publishing. **Table 7.3,** p. 219 Adapted from D. Baumrind, "The influence of parenting style on adolescent competence and substance use," *Journal of Early Adolescence,* 1991, Vol. 11, pp. 56–95. Copyright © 1991 Sage Publications. Reprinted by permission of Sage Publications. p. 230 Adapted from J. Brooks, *The Process of Parenting,* Fifth Edition, 1999, Mountain View, CA. Mayfield. Reprinted with permission of The McGraw-Hill Companies.

Chapter 8

Figure 8.1, p. 267 P. R. Costanzo, 1970, "Conformity Development as a Function of Self-Blame," *Journal of Personality and Social Psychology,* 1970, 14, 366–374, figure 1, p. 370. Reprinted with permission of The American Psychological Association.

Chapter 9

p. 281 D. N. Perkins, "Knowledge as Design: Teaching thinking through content" in J. B. Baron & R. J. Sternberg (Eds.), *Teaching thinking skills: Theory and Practice,* W. H. Freeman, 1987. Reprinted with permission. **Figure 9.2,** p. 290 Adapted from D. Olweus, "Peer Harassment: A Critical Analysis and Some Important Issues," in J. Juvonen & S. Graham (Eds.), *Peer Harassment in School: The Plight of the Vulnerable and Victimized,* 2001, pp. 3–20. Figure I.1. Reprinted with permission of The Guilford Press. **Figure 9.3,** p. 300 Organization for Economic Cooperation and Development (OECD). (2004). *Learning for Tomorrow's World: First Results from the OECD Programme for International Student Assessment (PISA) 2003.* Reprinted with permission. **Figure 9.4,** p. 301 Organization for Economic Cooperation and Development (OECD). (2004). *Learning for Tomorrow's World: First Results from the OECD Programme for International Student Assessment (PISA) 2003.* Reprinted with permission.

Chapter 10

Figure 10.4, p. 324 From J. T. Mortimer, M. D. Finch, S. Ryu, M. J. Shanahan & K. T. Call, 1996, "The Effects of Work Intensity on Adolescent Mental Health, Achievement, and Behavioral Adjustment: New Evidence from a Prospective Study," *Child Development,* 67, 1243–1261. Reprinted with permission. **In More Depth,** p. 342 Reprinted from L. K. Mitchell & J. D. Krumboltz, 1987, "The Effects of Cognitive Restructuring and Decision-Making Training on Career Indecisions," *Journal of Counseling and Development,* 66, 171–174. ACA. Reprinted with permission. No further reproduction authorized without written permission from the American Counseling Association. **Figure 10.8,** p. 350 From A. J. Franklin, 1985, "The Social Context and Socialization Variables as Factors in Thinking and Learning," in S. F. Chipman, J. W. Segall & R. Glaser (Eds.), *Thinking and Learning Skills,* Volume 2. Reprinted with permission of Lawrence Erlbaum Associates, Inc.

Chapter 11

Figure 11.3, p. 366 M. E. Ford, K. R. Wentzel, D. Wood, E. Stevens, G. A. Siesfeld. (1989). Processes associated with integrative social competence: Emotional and contextual influences on adolescent social responsibility. *Journal of Adolescent Research, 4,* 405–425. Reprinted by permission of Sage Publications, Inc.

Chapter 12

Table 12.2, p. 401 J. P. Evans & J. Taylor, (1995), Understanding violence in contemporary and earlier gangs: An exploratory application of the theory of reasoned action. *Journal of Black Psychology, 21,* 71–81. Reprinted with permission from Sage Publications. **Table 12.3,** p. 402 J. P. Evans & J. Taylor, (1995), Understanding violence in contemporary and earlier gangs: An exploratory application of the theory of reasoned action. *Journal of Black Psychology, 21,* 71–81. Reprinted with permission from Sage Publications. **In More Depth,** p. 407 Adapted from *Diagnostic and Statistics Manual of Mental Disorders,* 4th ed. © 1994 American Psychiatric Association. **Figure 12.4,** p. 420 Adapted from S. J. Blumenthal & D. J. Kupfer, "Overview of early detection and treatment strategies for suicidal behavior in young people," *Journal of Youth and Adolescence,* Vol. 17, pp. 1–23, 1988. Copyright © 1988 Plenum Publishing. Reprinted with permission.

Chapter 14

Figure 14.1, p. 456 Adapted from J. Stevens-Long & M. Commons, 1992. *Adult life: Developmental processes,* 4th ed. Mountain View, CA: Mayfield. Reproduced with permission from The McGraw-Hill Companies. **Figure 14.2,** p. 457 Adapted from J. Stevens-Long & M. Commons, 1992. *Adult life: Developmental processes,* 4th ed. Mountain View, CA: Mayfield. Reproduced with permission from The McGraw-Hill Companies. **Figure 14.3,** p. 459 Adapted from J. Stevens-Long & M. Commons, 1992. *Adult life: Developmental processes,* 4th ed. Mountain View, CA: Mayfield. Reproduced with permission from The McGraw-Hill Companies.

Author Index

Subject Index